Using SmartWare® II

Andrew N. Schwartz

CORPORATION
LEADING COMPUTER KNOWLEDGE

Using SmartWare® II

Copyright © 1989 by Que® Corporation.

All rights reserved. Printed in the United States of America. No part of this book may be used or reproduced in any form or by any means, or stored in a database or retrieval system, without prior written permission of the publisher except in the case of brief quotations embodied in critical articles and reviews. Making copies of any part of this book for any purpose other than your own personal use is a violation of United States copyright laws. For information, address Que Corporation, 11711 N. College Ave., Carmel, IN 46032.

Library of Congress Catalog No.: 89-62474

ISBN 0-88022-405-3

This book is sold *as is*, without warranty of any kind, either express or implied, respecting the contents of this book, including but not limited to implied warranties for the book's quality, performance, merchantability, or fitness for any particular purpose. Neither Que Corporation nor its dealers or distributors shall be liable to the purchaser or any other person or entity with respect to any liability, loss, or damage caused or alleged to be caused directly or indirectly by this book.

92 91 90   8 7 6 5 4 3 2

Interpretation of the printing code: the rightmost double-digit number is the year of the book's printing; the rightmost single-digit number, the number of the book's printing. For example, a printing code of 89-1 shows that the first printing of the book occurred in 1989.

Using SmartWare II is based on SmartWare Version 1.01.

DEDICATION

To my brothers,
Steve and Charles

Publishing Director
  Lloyd J. Short

Acquisitions Editor
  Karen A. Bluestein

Product Director
  David Maguiness

Production Editor
  Jo Anna W. Arnott

Editors
  Sara Allaei
  Mary Arthur
  Jeannine Freudenberger
  Jay McNaught
  Gregory Robertson
  Daniel Schnake
  Janet Thrush

Technical Editor
  Rudolf E. Wolf

Indexer
  Sherry Massey

Editorial Assistant
  Renee Ackermann

Book Design and Production

  Dan Armstrong
  Bill Basham
  Brad Chinn
  Don Clemons
  Sally Copenhaver
  Tom Emrick
  Dennis Hager
  Harmon
  Betty
  Jodi

  David Kline
  Larry Lynch
  Lori A. Lyons
  Jennifer Matthews
  Cindy L. Phipps
  Joe Ramon
  Dennis Sheehan
  Louise Shinault
  Bruce Steed
  Mary Beth Wakefield
  Jenny Watson

Composed in Times Roman by Que Corporation.

About the Author

Andrew N. Schwartz

Andrew N. Schwartz received his B.A. from Amherst College and his M.B.A. from the Amos Tuck School of Business Administration at Dartmouth College. He is president of his own computer consulting and development company in St. Louis, Missouri. The firm specializes in database management and information analysis applications. Previously, he was a consulting manager for Tymshare, Inc., a computer services company.

The author is president of the St. Louis Users' Group for the IBM PC and a member of the Independent Computer Consultants Association.

The author of *Using Smart* and *Smart Tips, Tricks and Traps*, published by Que Corporation, Mr. Schwartz has written several articles for *PC Magazine* and is a frequent contributor to *SmarTimes* and computer publications in the St. Louis area. He is on the faculty of the University of Missouri, and lectures regularly on Smart, SmartWare II and other software topics.

CONTENTS AT A GLANCE

Introduction 1

Part I Using the SmartWare II Database

Chapter 1	Using the Database Module 11
Chapter 2	Setting Up Your Database 21
Chapter 3	Entering, Deleting, and Viewing Data............. 57
Chapter 4	Locating, Selecting, and Arranging Data 73
Chapter 5	Working with Multiple Files..................... 105
Chapter 6	Printing Database Data and Creating Reports 117
Chapter 7	Interfacing Files and Integrating 143

Part II Using the SmartWare II Spreadsheet

Chapter 8	Using the Spreadsheet Module.................. 163
Chapter 9	Formatting Spreadsheet Cells 181
Chapter 10	Manipulating Data........................... 213
Chapter 11	Operating the Spreadsheet..................... 233
Chapter 12	Protecting and Viewing Worksheets............... 255
Chapter 13	Spreadsheet Graphics......................... 265
Chapter 14	Printing Worksheet Data and Creating Reports...... 285
Chapter 15	Integrating the Spreadsheet with Other Modules 299

Part III Using the SmartWare II Word Processor

Chapter 16	Using the Word Processor Module 307
Chapter 17	Manipulating Text 333
Chapter 18	Formatting Text 355
Chapter 19	Using the Spellchecker and Thesaurus 387
Chapter 20	Generating a Table of Contents 399
Chapter 21	Printing and Merging Text 417
Chapter 22	Integrating the Word Processor with Other Modules 429

Part IV Using SmartWare II Communications

| Chapter 23 | Using the Communications Module............... 441 |

Part V Using SmartWare II Project Processing

Chapter 24   Project Processing 471

Part VI Using SmartWare II Functions

Chapter 25   Date, Time, and Text Functions 539
Chapter 26   Business and Mathematical Functions 567
Chapter 27   Module Specific and Special Functions........... 593
Chapter 28   Tools: Commands Common To All Modules 621

Appendix A   Quick Keys 653
Appendix B   File Extensions................................ 665
Appendix C   Command Comparison: Smart 3.10 versus
             SmartWare II 669
Appendix D   Converting from Smart 3.10.................... 719
Appendix E   Collation Sort Sequence versus
             ASCII Sort Sequence........................... 727
Index 731

TABLE OF CONTENTS

Introduction 1
   What Is SmartWare II? 1
   Who Should Use this Book? 2
   Getting Started with SmartWare II 3
      Installing SmartWare II 3
      Configuring SmartWare II 3
      Beginning a SmartWare II Session 3
   Common Features of the SmartWare II Modules 5
      Command Execution 5
      Quick Keys 6
      Windows 6
      Pop-up Menus 6
   What's in This Book 7

I Using the SmartWare II Database

1 Using the Database Module 11
   New Features of the SmartWare II Database 12
   Understanding Database Concepts 13
   Understanding Fixed-Length and
      Variable-Length Records 15
   Using Key Fields 16
   Understanding Data Types 16
      Alphanumeric 16
      Numeric 17
      Date 17
      Time 17
      Counter 17
      Inverted 17
   Working with the SmartWare II Database 17
      Identifying Fields 18
      Moving the Cursor 19
   Chapter Summary 20

2 Setting Up Your Database 21
   Creating the Database 21
      Creating a View 22
      Creating a File 23
      Creating Fields 24

	Designing Your Database	30
	Adding Notes to a View	30
	Adding a Box to a View	30
	Adding a Menu for a Field	31
	Creating a Bar Menu	31
	Creating a Pop-Up Menu	32
	Calculated Fields	33
	Field Rules	34
	Creating a Table	35
	Attaching a Data File or a Field	41
	Editing a View	42
	Editing Field Declarations	42
	Rearranging the View	43
	Deleting a Declaration	43
	Setting Input Order	44
	Duplicating a File	45
	Duplicating a Field	46
	Painting New Colors	46
	Modifying a File	46
	Setting Database Preferences	46
	Working with Data Files and Views	48
	Loading Views	48
	Activating Views	50
	Unloading Views	50
	Saving Files	52
	Getting Information about a View	52
	Renumbering the Count Field	54
	Repairing Damages	54
	Changing Passwords	55
	Attaching a Password to a File	55
	Removing a Password from a File	55
	Attaching a Password to a View	55
	Removing a Password from a View	56
	Chapter Summary	56
3	**Entering, Deleting, and Viewing Data**	**57**
	Entering Data	57
	Updating Data	60
	Deleting Records	62
	Marking Records	63
	Removing Records	64
	Viewing Data	64
	Browsing Your Data	65

	Doing Windows....................................	67
	Splitting the Screen.............................	67
	Closing Windows...............................	69
	Full-Screen Viewing of a Window................	69
	Linking Two Windows...........................	69
	Using the Data Goto Command.........................	70
	Chapter Summary.....................................	72
4	**Locating, Selecting, and Arranging Data**...........	**73**
	Selecting Records with the Data Find Command..........	73
	Selecting Field Names.................................	74
	Using Logical Operators in a Search....................	74
	Entering your Search Criterion..........................	75
	Selecting Data Find Options............................	75
	Optimized Data Find..................................	77
	Using the Data Query Command.......................	78
	Performing an Immediate Query.................	79
	QBE (Query By Example).......................	80
	Query View Expressions........................	84
	Summary Statistics............................	86
	Data Replacement.............................	88
	Query Optimization...................................	90
	Saving a Query Definition..............................	91
	Running a Saved Query Definition......................	91
	Modifying a Query Definition..........................	92
	Erasing a Query Definition.............................	92
	Selecting Records Manually............................	92
	Arranging Data.......................................	93
	Using File Keys................................	93
	Adding a Key.............................	94
	Deleting Keys............................	96
	Fixing Keys..............................	96
	Sorting a View..	96
	Creating a Sort Definition......................	97
	Performing the Sort............................	98
	Changing a Sort Definition.....................	99
	Immediate Sorting.............................	99
	Deleting a Sort Definition......................	100
	Changing the Order of a View..........................	100
	Arranging a View.....................................	101
	Changing to Original View Order.......................	101
	Changing to Key Order................................	101
	Changing to Index Order..............................	102
	Chapter Summary.....................................	102

xi

5 Working with Multiple Files 105

Relating Two Views 105
    Defining Relationships 106
    Executing the Relate Command 108
    Modifying the Relation Definition 109
    Erasing a Relation Definition 109
Transacting Views 110
    Creating a Transaction Definition 110
    Executing a Transaction 114
    Changing a Transaction Definition 114
    Erasing a Transaction Definition 114
Copying Data from One File to Another 114
Chapter Summary 116

6 Printing Database Data and Creating Reports 117

Printing from a View 117
Printing the Current Record 120
Creating Formal Reports 121
Creating a Form Report 126
Form Item Definitions 127
Printing Labels 128
Moving, Removing, and Editing Form Declarations .. 130
Choosing Fonts 130
Creating a Table Report 132
    Specifying Table Columns 132
    Selecting Fields for a Report 133
    Selecting Calculations for a Report 134
    Selecting Text for a Report 135
    Moving, Removing, and Editing Table Items 135
Using Column Fonts 135
Using Breakpoints 135
    Specifying Breakpoint Options 136
    Editing Breakpoint Specifications 138
    Removing a Breakpoint 138
    Choosing Breakpoint Fonts 138
Specifying Grand Totals 139
Defining a Table Report Title 139
Choosing Table Fonts 140
Printing the Report 140
Modifying a Report 141
Deleting a Report 141
Chapter Summary 141

7 Interfacing Files and Integrating 143

Importing Files 143
    ASCII Files 144
    Fixed-Format Files 144
    Smart Files 145
    Using the File Import Command 145
    Importing a Fixed-Format File 146
Converting a Smart Version 3.10 File 146
Converting a dBASE File 147
Exporting Files 147
Summarized Records 148
    Creating a Cross-Tab Definition 149
        Column Definitions 150
        Row Definitions 150
        Options 150
    Cross-Tab Commands 151
    Creating a Column Summary Definition 152
    Entering Match Equations 152
    Running a Cross-Tab Definition 156
    Changing a Cross-Tab Definition 157
    Erasing a Cross-Tab Definition 157
Integrating the Smartware II Modules 157
    Sending Data to the Communications Module 157
    Sending Data to the Spreadsheet Module 158
    Sending Data to the Word Processor Module 159
    Sending Summarized Data 159
Chapter Summary 160

II Using the SmartWare II Spreadsheet

8 Using the Spreadsheet Module 163

New Features of the SmartWare II Spreadsheet 164
Using SmartWare II Rows and Columns 166
Spreadsheet Size 167
Entering Data in the Enter Mode 168
    Using Numeric and Text Operators 168
    Using Relative and Absolute Cell References 170
    Entering Dates 171
    Entering Text 172
    Entering Time 172
Taking Precautions 172

Working with Spreadsheet Files	172
Loading a Worksheet	173
Activating a Worksheet	175
Saving a Worksheet to a Disk File	175
Clearing a Worksheet from Memory	176
Setting Preferences	177
Chapter Summary	178

9 Formatting Spreadsheet Cells ... 181

Setting the Layout Default Formats for New Worksheets	182
Setting the Recalculation Order	182
Setting the Default Value Format Options	182
Numeric Format	183
Currency Format	184
General Format	184
Date Format	184
Time Format	185
Scientific Notation Format (E-Notation)	186
Percent Format	186
Bar Notation	186
Setting the Default Text Format Options	187
Sizing the Columns and Rows	187
Setting Print Definitions	188
Changing Default Formats	189
Formatting New Values and Text	189
Formatting Numeric Values	189
Numeric Entries	190
Currency Entries	192
General Entries	192
Date Entries	192
Time Entries	193
Scientific Notation (E-Notation)	194
Percent Entries	194
Bar Notation	195
Justifying Text Entries	195
Reformatting Existing Values and Text	195
Changing Value Formats	196
Numeric Entries	196
Currency Entries	197
General Entries	198
Date Entries	198
Time Entries	199

Scientific Notation (E-Notation)	199
Percent Entries	200
Bar Notation	200
Resetting Cell Formats	200
Viewing Worksheet Formulas and Maps	200
Viewing Worksheet Formulas	201
Displaying a Worksheet Map	202
Redisplaying Worksheet Values	203
Changing Justification	203
Changing Column Width and Row Height	204
Selecting Type Fonts	205
Choosing a Font for New Entries	206
Choosing a Font for Existing Entries	209
Editing or Attaching Fonts to Your Worksheet	209
Editing the Fonts of New Worksheets	210
Editing the Fonts of Existing Worksheets	210
Removing Fonts	211
Altering Row and Column Number Displays	211
Chapter Summary	212

10 Manipulating Data 213

Using the Edit Copy Command	215
Copying Cells in a Row	216
Copying Cells to the Right	217
Copying Cells to Other Areas	220
Using the Edit Value-Copy Command	221
Using the Edit Move Command	222
Moving Columns	222
Moving Rows	223
Moving Blocks	223
Using the Edit Insert Command	226
Inserting Columns	226
Inserting Rows	227
Inserting Blocks	227
Using the Edit Delete Command	228
Deleting Columns	228
Deleting Rows	229
Deleting Blocks	229
Using the Edit Blank Command	230
Clearing Columns	230
Clearing Rows	231
Clearing Blocks	231
Clearing the Worksheet	231

	Editing a Worksheet Cell	231
	Chapter Summary	232
11	**Operating the Spreadsheet**	**233**
	Establishing Order in Columns and Rows	233
	Naming a Block of Cells	235
	Defining a Named Block	236
	Printing Block Names	236
	Editing a Named Block Definition	236
	Removing a Name	237
	Using the Sheet Goto Command	237
	Searching Through Your Worksheet	239
	Auditing your Worksheet	241
	Retaining Title Rows or Columns	243
	Recalculating the Worksheet	244
	Filling your Worksheet Automatically	246
	Using the Matrix Commands	248
	Transposing Columns and Rows	248
	Performing Matrix Parallel Operations	249
	Performing Matrix Multiplication	250
	Computing Linear Regression	251
	Using Additional Sheet Matrix Options	252
	Combining Files	253
	Chapter Summary	254
12	**Protecting and Viewing Worksheets**	**255**
	Protecting Worksheets	255
	Locking the Worksheet	255
	Temporarily Unlocking Worksheet Cells	256
	Preventing Changes and Hiding Formulas	257
	Unlocking the Worksheet	257
	Using Worksheet Passwords	258
	Attaching a Password to a Worksheet	258
	Removing a Password from a Worksheet	259
	Hiding Portions of your Worksheet	259
	Using Windows	260
	Creating a Window	260
	Removing a Window	261
	Filling the Screen with One Window	262
	Scrolling Two Windows Simultaneously	262
	Removing Links between Windows	263
	Chapter Summary	263

13 Spreadsheet Graphics ... 265
New Features in SmartWare II Spreadsheet Graphics ... 265
The Graphics Command ... 266
- Defining a Graph ... 267
  - Creating a Bar/Line Graph ... 267
  - Creating a Pie Graph ... 274
  - Creating a Layer Graph ... 276
  - Creating an X-Y Graph ... 277
  - Creating a Text Graph ... 279
  - Combining Graphs ... 280
- Using the Graphics Generate Command ... 281
  - Displaying the Graph ... 282
  - Printing Your Graph ... 282
  - Generating Metafiles ... 282
- Chapter Summary ... 283

14 Printing Worksheet Data and Creating Reports ... 285
Printing Your Worksheet ... 285
Selecting Print Options ... 288
Printing Formulas ... 289
Printing a Worksheet Map ... 290
Printing Formal Reports ... 292
- Defining a Report ... 292
- Printing a Report ... 296
- Establishing Default Options ... 297
- Printing a Page Layout Description ... 297
- Erasing a Report Definition ... 297
Chapter Summary ... 297

15 Integrating the Spreadsheet with Other Modules ... 299
Importing External Files into the Worksheet ... 299
Exporting Worksheet Data to Different Files ... 300
Sending Worksheet Data to Other Application Modules ... 301
- Sending Data to the Communications Module ... 301
- Sending Data to the Database ... 302
- Sending Data to the Word Processor ... 303
Chapter Summary ... 303

III Using the SmartWare II Word Processor

16 Using the Word Processor Module 307

New Features in SmartWare II Word Processor 307
Using the Word Processor 309
    Entering New Text 310
    Moving the Cursor 311
    Switching to Command Mode 312
    Specifying a Range 312
        Marking Blocks 312
        Marking Columns 314
    Effects of Commands 314
    Setting Defaults 315
        Setting Pagination Defaults 315
        Character Insertion Mode. 315
        Default Paragraph Format 316
        Special Character Display 317
        Document Auto-Save 317
        Dictionary Preferences 318
        Miscellaneous Items 318
Working with Files 319
    Loading Documents. 319
    Unloading Documents 321
    Saving Files 321
    Renaming Documents 322
    Appending Documents 323
    Protecting Your Files 323
        Locking a Document 324
        Unlocking a Document 325
Working with Multiple Columns 325
    Defining Equal-Width Columns 325
    Defining Variable-Width Columns. 326
    Entering Multiple Column Text 326
    Terminating a Multiple Column Area 328
    Editing a Multiple Column Area 328
    Adding a Column 328
    Adding an Entry 329
    Changing the Column Widths 329
    Deleting an MCA Column 330
    Deleting Linked Column Entities. 331
    Moving Columns or Entities 331
    Deleting a Multiple-Column Area 331
Chapter Summary 332

| 17 | **Manipulating Text** | 333 |

- Moving Text 333
  - Using Block Marking 334
  - Using Column Marking 335
- Copying Text 337
  - Using Block Marking 337
  - Using Column Marking 339
- Inserting Text 339
- Deleting Text 340
  - Using Block Marking 340
  - Using Column Marking 341
- Recovering Deleted Text 341
- Using Windows 342
  - Creating Windows 342
  - Removing Windows 344
- Searching for Text 345
- Replacing Text 347
- Moving in the Document 349
  - Changing Windows 350
  - Changing Documents 350
  - Moving to a Marker 351
  - Moving to a Location 351
  - Using Location Specifications in Combination 352
- Using Markers 353
  - Setting a Marker 353
  - Finding a Marker 354
  - Removing a Marker 354
- Chapter Summary 354

| 18 | **Formatting Text** | 355 |

- Using Rulers 356
  - Editing the Current Ruler 357
    - Changing Margins 358
    - Changing Characters Per Inch 358
    - Changing Indentation 359
    - Changing Normal Tabs 359
    - Changing Decimal Tabs 359
    - Changing Incremental Tabs 360
    - Clearing Tabs 360
    - Changing Justification 360
    - Changing Spacing 361
  - Naming the Ruler Format 361
  - Saving the Ruler 362
  - Editing the Default Ruler 362

Editing Named Rulers	363
Copying Rulers	364
Copying the Current Ruler	364
Copying the Default Ruler	365
Copying a Named Ruler	365
Changing the Ruler of Multiple Paragraphs	365
Deleting a Ruler	367
Deleting the Current Ruler	367
Deleting a Named Ruler	367
Using Formatting Features	367
Using Indent Tabs	367
Using Page Breaks	368
Automatic Pagination	368
Manual Pagination	369
Using Keep Areas	369
Using Widow and Orphan Settings	370
Using Document Sections	371
Creating a Section	371
Removing a Section	371
Moving a Section	371
Using Hidden Text	372
Hiding Text	372
Unhiding Text	373
Using Fonts	374
Creating a Font	375
Selecting a Font	377
Changing a Font	378
Editing a Font	378
Removing a Font	378
Using Bold and Underscore	379
Creating and Using Footnotes	379
Inserting a Footnote	379
Modifying a Footnote	381
Deleting a Footnote	381
Moving a Footnote	381
Changing Between Document and Text Modes	382
Displaying and Hiding Special Characters	383
Rearranging Lines of Text	384
Sorting NonMCA Document Areas	384
Sorting Multiple Column Areas	385
Chapter Summary	386

19	**Using the Spellchecker and Thesaurus**	**387**
	The Smart Spellchecker	387
	Operating the Smart Spellchecker	388
	Setting Spellcheck Preferences	389
	Correcting Misspellings	390
	Correcting Other Errors	392
	Creating Dictionary Files	392
	Observing Counts	393
	Creating Custom Dictionaries	394
	Hyphenation	394
	Special Spellchecker Parameters	395
	The Smart Thesaurus	396
	Chapter Summary	398
20	**Generating a Table of Contents and Index**	**399**
	Table of Contents	399
	Selecting Table of Contents Options	400
	Adding Table of Contents References	402
	Generating a Table of Contents	403
	Removing a Table of Contents Marker	404
	Indexing your Document	404
	Selecting Index Options	404
	Adding an Index Marker	407
	Editing your Index Entry	411
	Deleting an Index Reference	412
	Generating an Index	412
	Paragraph Numbering	412
	Selecting Paragraph Number Options	413
	Inserting Paragraph Numbers	414
	Removing Paragraph Numbers	414
	Moving and Copying Paragraphs with Numbers	415
	Chapter Summary	415
21	**Printing and Merging Text**	**417**
	Setting Default Print Options	417
	Using Headings and Footings	418
	Printing Dates	420
	Printing Page Numbers	420
	Printing Page Format	421
	Printing Footnotes	421
	Setting Section Options	421
	Printing your Document	422

	Printing in Enhanced Mode.	424
	Merging Text	425
	Merging Data from a File.	425
	Merging Data from the Screen.	427
	Chapter Summary.	428
22	**Integrating the Word Processor with Other Modules**	**429**
	Reading Files into Text.	429
	Writing Text to a File	430
	Using Block Marking	430
	Using Column Marking	432
	Sending Text to Other Application Modules.	432
	Sending Data to the Data Manager	433
	Sending Data to the Spreadsheet	434
	Sending Data to the Communications Module	434
	Importing Graphics into Text	435
	Inserting a Graph.	436
	Displaying a Graph.	436
	Removing a Graph from your Document	437
	Chapter Summary.	438

IV Using SmartWare II Communications

23	**Using the Communications Module**	**441**
	New Features of SmartWare II Communications	441
	SmartWare II Communications.	441
	Understanding the Status Screen	442
	Setting the Communications Parameters	444
	Creating and Using Terminal Settings	444
	Loading the Definition.	449
	Changing the Current Settings.	450
	Changing Duplex Settings	450
	Dialing a Remote Computer.	451
	Handling Data.	452
	Receiving Data.	452
	Sending Data.	453
	Estimating the Transfer Time	454
	Capturing to the Screen	455
	Capturing to the Buffer.	455
	Capturing to a File	456
	Capturing to the Printer	456
	Filtering Characters	456

Communications Project Processing 457
    The Lata Get Command......................... 457
    The Data Match Command 458
    The Data Output Command 458
Customizing the Communications Module................. 459
    Keyboard Definition 459
    File Format Definition 461
    Modem Definition.............................. 462
    Communications Preferences 464
Integrating with other Smart Modules 466
Chapter Summary...................................... 467

V   Using SmartWare II Project Processing

24   Project Processing... 471

Project File Operations 471
    Creating and Editing a Project File 472
        Remember Start Command 472
        Remember Finish Command 473
    Editing a Project File 473
    Running a Project File 475
    Using Other Project File Tools 475
        Compile................................... 475
        Trace 476
        Remember Tools Print 478
    Using Project File Commands 478
    Using Project File Structure 479
Declaring a Program Main Section....................... 479
Functions.. 480
    Using a Function as a Procedure 480
    Using a Function as a Command................... 480
    Using a Function as a Function 481
Variables.. 481
    Local 482
    Global...................................... 483
    Public 483
    External 484
    Variable Dimensions........................... 484
        Arrays 484
        Redimensioning an Array 484

Display Commands	485
Beep	485
Sound	485
Message	486
Wait	486
Locate	487
Repaint	487
Control Commands	488
Execute	488
Transfer	488
Keys	489
Screenon and Screenoff	489
Until and Waitfor	489
Handling Macro Keys	490
Key Execution Timing	490
Other Keys Terms	491
Reply	491
Command Level Control	492
The Suspend Command	492
Remember Execute Command	493
The Exit Command	493
The Stop Command	494
The Quit Command	494
Execution Order Commands	494
The Jump Command	495
The Label Command	495
Operating System Commands	495
The Tools OS Command	496
The Osexit Command	496
Peripheral Commands	497
Printer Commands	497
The Lprint and Lprintraw Commands	497
The Open-Printer and Close-Printer Commands	497
File Commands	498
The Fopen Command	498
The Fclose Command	499
The Fread Command	500
The Fwrite Command	500
The Fseek Command	501
The Fposition Command	501
Memory Access Commands	502
The Peek and Poke Commands	502
The Smartpeek and Smartpoke commands	502

Assignment Statements	503
The Let Command	503
The Pack and Unpack Commands	503
Keyboard Assignment Statements	504
The Screen Shortinput Command	504
The Screen Input Command	504
Input Screens	506
Screen Commands	506
Screen Clear	507
The Screen Menu Command	507
The Screen Shortmenu Command	509
The Screen Prompt Command	510
The Screen Print Command	511
Screen Save and Restore	512
The Screen Scroll Command	513
Command Line Substitution	514
Avoiding Limitations	515
The Clear Command	515
The Lock and Unlock Statements	516
Logical Decision Commands	517
The IF Statement	517
The WHILE Command	519
The Case Command	520
The FOR Command	521
Project File Execution Control	522
The Autohelp Command	522
The Single-step Command	522
The Quiet Command	523
The Debug Statement	523
Comments	524
Czbreak	524
Application Module Specific Commands	524
Database Commands	524
Entering and Updating Records	525
Data Enter Blank	525
Data Update Only-One	525
The Let Command	525
The Lock-Record Command	526
The Cancel-Record Command	526
Record Deletion	527
Special Data Goto Commands	527
Line	527
Field Calculation	528

Spreadsheet 528
   Cursor Location 528
   Sheet Goto Commands............................ 528
   Cursor Command 529
Data Entry 529
   Cursor 529
   Assignment 530
   Locked Cells 530
Word Processor 531
   Commands that Mark Text 531
   Editing Rulers.................................. 532
   Toggle Commands 533
Communications 533
   The Data Match Command 533
   The Data Get Command 533
   The Data Output Command....................... 534
   The Empty Command 534
   The Break-Key Command 534
Project Processing Error Handling 534
   The Cerror Function 534
   The Lerror Function 535
   The Error Command 535
   The Errormessage Command 535
   On Error....................................... 535
Chapter Summary.................................... 536

VI   Using SmartWare II Functions

25   Date, Time, and Text Functions 539

The SmartWare II Operators........................... 539
   Numeric Operators 539
   Text Operators.................................. 540
   Relational Operators 540
   Logical Operators 541
Functions... 542
   Date Functions.................................. 542
   Time Functions 548
   Text Functions.................................. 553

26 Business and Mathematical Functions 567
Business Functions................................. 567
Numeric Functions................................. 575
Random Functions 578
Statistical Functions................................ 580
Logical Functions................................... 583
Transcendental Functions............................ 589
Trigonometric Functions 589
Input Functions.................................... 590

27 Module Specific and Special Functions 593
Spreadsheet Functions 593
Statistical Database Functions........................ 600
Word Processor Functions........................... 605
Database Functions 607
Project Processing Functions......................... 612

28 Tools: Commands Common to All Modules 621
Directory Commands 622
    Display Option................................. 622
    Making A New Subdirectory 624
    Changing to a New Directory 624
    Removing a Directory............................ 625
Tools File Command................................ 626
    Copying a File.................................. 626
    Erase Option 629
    Renaming Files 629
    Printing Files................................... 630
Preferences 631
    Global Preferences............................... 631
        Autohelp 632
        Beeper 632
        Display of File Names for File Prompting........... 632
        Automatic File Backup 632
        Quiet Execution of Project Files.................. 632
        Single-step Execution of Project Files 633
        Time Format................................ 633
        Date Style 633
        Currency Symbol 633
        Currency Symbol Location 634
        Decimal Separator 634
        Thousands Separator.......................... 634

	Division by Zero	634
	Paging File Path	634
	Default Data Path	634
	Running Project Files Automatically	634
	Hardware Preferences	635
	Text Screen	636
	Graphics Screen	636
	Printer	636
	Time Out (seconds)	637
	Port	637
	Paper Width and Length	637
	Paper Feed	637
	Plotter	637
	Plotter Paper Size	638
	Pen Speed	638
	Plotter Pen Width	638
	SmartWare II Pen Colors	638
	Communications	638
	Computer/Keyboard	638
	Network	638
	Macro Keys	639
	Creating a Macro	639
	Editing A Macro	640
	Clearing Macros	641
	Viewing Macros	642
	Saving Macros	642
	Loading Macros	643
	Erasing Saved Macros	643
	Creating New Fonts	643
	Editing Text Files	646
	Using the Calculator	649
	Chapter Summary	651
A	**Quick Keys**	**653**
	System-Wide Quick Keys	653
	Spreadsheet Quick Keys	654
	Word Processor Quick Keys	657
	Database Quick Keys	661
	Communications Quick Keys	662
B	**File Extensions**	**665**

C	**Command Comparison: Smart 3.10 versus SmartWare II**	**669**
	The Communications Module	669
	The Database Module	675
	The Main Menu	688
	Project Processing	690
	The Spreadsheet Module	694
	The Word Processor Module	707
D	**Converting from Smart 3.10**	**719**
	Converting the Database	720
	Other Database Files	722
	Converting the Spreadsheet	722
	Converting the Word Processor	722
	Custom Dictionaries	723
	Converting the Communications Module	724
	Converting Project Files	724
	Summary	725
E	**Collation Sort Sequence versus ASCII Sort Sequence**	**727**
	Index	**731**

PREFACE

Just as *Using Smart* was intended to be a practical, business-oriented book, *Using SmartWare II* maintains a similar concept. This book is based on actual usage of SmartWare II with my clients in solving everyday business problems. All of the examples in this book are drawn from real business situations, many of which you may be likely to encounter in your own work.

In this book, you will find the instructions necessary for operating SmartWare II, some pointers for using it quickly and effortlessly, and some suggestions on avoiding pitfalls. I have written it as if I were sitting next to you, guiding you along the way as you learn to use the software.

Use this book to learn how to develop your initial applications. As your applications grow and mature, refer to the book again to further your understanding of SmartWare II. The Index will help you put your finger on specific topics quickly.

If you are converting from the Smart 3.10 version, I have included several items in this book to help you. Appendix C has a chart that compares the Smart 3.10 commands with those of SmartWare II; if you know the old command, this chart will help you find the equivalent new command. Appendix D covers conversion tips and techniques. Throughout the book, you will find references to major differences from previous Smart versions. I include these either to alert you to an expanded capability or to warn you of a possible obstacle.

SmartWare II is even more powerful and comprehensive than previous versions of Smart. This book will help you navigate through the many features and commands so that you can make full use of all the SmartWare II capabilities.

ACKNOWLEDGMENTS

The following employees of Informix Software have been extremely helpful in answering questions and providing an understanding of the inner workings of the SmartWare II product.

Diana Sexton
Rick Vreeland
Karl Rose
Dennis Kelleher
Eric Entzeroth
Amy Livingood-Rogers
Dustan Jackson
Kevin Mayfield
Alan Simmons
Sam Belcher
Louise Bergeron
Holly Reith

I would like to extend thanks to Jim Heffernan for his boundless enthusiasm and encouragement.

Pegg Kennedy, formerly of Que Corporation, deserves particular mention. Without her faith, honesty, and positive attitude, I would never have made it through the first two books, and thus would not have been able to write this one.

My clients deserve appreciation for not only their suggestions and ideas, but also their patience during the development of this book.

Especially, I'd like to thank my wife, Debbie, for her understanding and confidence while I was writing *Using SmartWare II*. Thanks, Deb.

TRADEMARK ACKNOWLEDGMENTS

Que Corporation has made every reasonable effort to supply trademark information about company names, products, and services mentioned in this book. Trademarks indicated below were derived from various sources. Que Corporation cannot attest to the accuracy of this information.

1-2-3 is a registered trademark of Lotus Development Corporation.

CompuServe Information Service is a registered trademark of CompuServe Incorporated and H&R Block, Inc.

Dow Jones News/Retrieval is a registered service mark of Dow Jones & Company, Inc.

SmartWare is a registered trademark of Informix Software, Inc.

CONVENTIONS USED IN THIS BOOK

The conventions used in this book have been established to help you learn to use the program quickly and easily. As much as possible, the conventions correspond with those used in the SmartWare II documentation.

Material that you are to type is in *italic*. Messages that appear on-screen are in a `special typeface`. Menu options and commands are in upper- and lowercase.

Introduction

Welcome to *Using SmartWare II*. The SmartWare II system is an integrated software product containing today's most needed business applications:

Database
Spreadsheet
Word Processor
Communications

Other stand-alone packages on the market today allow the importing and exporting of data to and from other programs, but the process is usually both time-consuming and cumbersome. With SmartWare II, the data flows smoothly, and one application can span several modules.

What Is SmartWare II?

SmartWare II is a complete revision of the original Smart software, which accounts for its new name. This book is based on Version 1.01 of SmartWare II, released in August, 1989. Throughout the book, you will see references and comparisons to the most recent Smart release, 3.10.

The SmartWare II system consists of four application modules (Database, Spreadsheet, Word Processor, and Communications), the Project Processing Language, and the functions and standards necessary to form the several parts into an integrated whole.

Unlike other integrated programs that have smaller modules "shoehorned" into a dominant one, SmartWare II's modules are powerful enough to stand alone. Each module, in fact, can be purchased separately. If you need at least two modules, however, it makes sense to buy the entire system. Each module is capable of standing alone as a full featured product, but the real beauty of the system lies in the integration of the modules—their capability of sharing data.

Who Should Use This Book?

If you are upgrading from Smart to SmartWare II, you will find this book to be a valuable guide to the differences and benefits of SmartWare II. Whenever possible, I have pointed out important dissimilarities so that you can take advantage of them—or avoid some pitfalls. Be sure to read Appendix D, which discusses conversion techniques.

If you are using SmartWare II for the first time, you will find this book to be an invaluable aid. *Using SmartWare II* provides many examples, explanations, tips, and cautionary notes that cannot be covered in the software manuals. In each section, a single model is used to demonstrate the operation of every command in constructing and running an application. In the Spreadsheet section, for example, a financial model for a sample company is built from the ground up and then integrated with spreadsheets from other divisions within the same corporation.

Efficient ways of working with SmartWare II, as well as inefficient methods to avoid, are highlighted in this book. A product with the depth of SmartWare II sometimes has quirks or undocumented features; these also are noted. Having this book at your elbow as you build your applications can save you many hours of frustration.

If you are already familiar with SmartWare II, you also can make use of this book. You will learn ways to improve your application designs for more efficient processing. When I showed drafts of this book to some of my clients, I got the reaction, "So that's how that works!"

If you are running just one or two of the modules, you already know how frustrating it can be to learn the product on your own. Let *Using SmartWare II* help you explore the other modules. I wrote this book as though I were standing over your shoulder, showing you how to accomplish what you want to do.

If you have not worked with the Project Processing language yet, be sure to read Chapter 24. Many readers said that I should have included more information on the programming language in the *Using Smart* book. This topic has been greatly expanded and enhanced in *Using SmartWare II*.

If you are considering purchasing SmartWare II, you can use this book to determine whether SmartWare II is the product for you. If you find that it is, this book will give you a head start on the development of your applications.

Do you still need the manuals? Yes, absolutely. This book is not intended to take their place. Many setup, configuration, and other one-time instructions that cannot be covered here are found in the manuals. The manuals also include reference tables and error messages not covered in *Using SmartWare II*.

What you will find in this book are clear explanations of the commands and features, complete with examples and cross references. The chapters are designed so that related commands are grouped together, and the entire book is thoroughly indexed so you can find subjects quickly and easily.

Getting Started with SmartWare II

Beginning your work with SmartWare II can be divided into separate operations:

1. Installing the program on your hard disk.
2. Setting module preferences.
3. Beginning a SmartWare II session.

Installing SmartWare II

Fortunately, the installation program guides you through each step of selecting the hardware and options you will need. You should create a separate subdirectory on your hard disk to store the SmartWare II system files. The following command creates a subdirectory that you can use:

    md\SmartII

Insert disk 1 in the floppy disk drive and make that drive current. If you have the disk in the A drive, type *A:* and press Enter to make it current. Now type:

    Install C

Press Enter if this is correct. (If you are installing on a disk other than the C drive, you should substitute the appropriate letter.) The Install program will guide you through the remainder of the installation.

Configuring SmartWare II

The final phase of the installation program allows you to establish the initial configurations for your system. After you begin a SmartWare II session, you can use the Tools Preferences Global and Tools Preferences Hardware commands to make any changes. Both of these commands are covered in Chapter 28. Each module also has a menu of preference settings; these are covered individually in the module sections of this book.

Beginning a SmartWare II Session

SmartWare II is easier to use if you add the system sub-directory to your Path statement in the Autoexec.Bat file. An example of a Path statement is as follows:

    path C:\;C:\DOS;C:\smartII

4 Using SmartWare II

If you have not specified a default data path, you should change to the subdirectory containing your data. The simplest way to begin a SmartWare II session is to type *Smart* and press Enter. The Main Menu is displayed.

Select the module you want to run by pressing the initial letter of the module, or move the cursor highlight block and press Enter. After you are comfortable with the SmartWare II system, you may want to initiate an application module directly, without going through the Main Menu. If you add one of the following letters after the Smart command, you can begin the desired module directly:

C	Communications
D	Database
S	Spreadsheet
W	Word Processor

You can select several other options when you enter the SmartWare II system. (Any module identifying letter must be entered before an option switch.) The option switches are explained in the following list:

Option	Explanation
-p	Execute a project file after entering Smart. For example, `Smart -pinvoice`.
-r	Reserve an amount of memory (in kilobytes) for use with the DOS access mode. If you temporarily exit to the operating system, using the Ctrl-O Quick key, use of this option can guarantee sufficient memory for execution of a program. For example, `Smart -r48`.
-a	Execute a command upon entering Smart. For example, `Smart -afile load custom-view "person.vw"`.
-n	Don't use the installed 8087 or 80287 coprocessor chip. For example, `Smart -n`.
-d	Specify the default data path. This command overrides the path in Tools Preferences Global. For example, `Smart -d\mydata`.
-f	Ignore the network driver in the Hardware Preferences. For example, `Smart -f`.
-s	Specify the subdirectory containing the SmartWare II system. Use this if the subdirectory is not in the path. For example, `Smart -s\SmartII`.
-e	Ignore expanded memory. For example, `Smart -e`.
-x	Use expanded memory, suppress disk paging. For example, `Smart -x`.
-y	Use expanded memory but don't go beyond normal memory. For example, `Smart -y`.

The last three options affect the usage of the Expanded Memory capabilities available with any of the supported Expanded Memory boards. If you have one of these boards, the Smart system uses memory up to the maximum to work with even larger spreadsheets or documents. Unless you have specific reasons for doing so, you should not have to use these last three options.

You can use any of the options in conjunction with each other. If you use the same set of options repeatedly, you may want to create a batch file to store them and make it easier to begin a SmartWare II session.

Common Features of the SmartWare II Modules

Certain features are common throughout the SmartWare II system. Once you have learned these features in one module, you can use them in the others, as well.

Command Execution

The commands in SmartWare II have a tree structure; each selection leads to another branch in the tree. The menu level of each module offers the primary commands.

One way to begin the execution of a command is to move the cursor highlight block to the command you want and press Enter. A faster way to execute a command or to select an option is to type the initial letter of the command. In the Database, for example, press the letter *P* to begin execution of the Print command. You see the following options:

    Current-Record View Report

Press *C* if you want to print information from the current record of the view in the current window. Next, you see the following options:

    List Page View

If you want to print data from just the current page, press *P* to select the Page option.

During the process of executing a command, you sometimes are prompted for a file name. Frequently, you have the choice of selecting from among a set of existing files or entering a new name. In these instances, a pop-up menu of the existing files is displayed. You can move the cursor to the name of the file and press Enter, or you can type the file name instead.

If you select the wrong option to a command, press Esc to return to the previous prompting level. If you want to return to the menu level without pressing Esc multiple times, press the Alt-Z key combination.

Quick Keys

Although selecting commands and options from the menus is fast, many commands have Quick keys. These shortcut Quick keys are built into the SmartWare II system and consist of either a function key (F1 through F10) or a key combination using the Control key (Ctrl) or the Alternate key (Alt). Similar commands in each module usually have the same Quick key; for example, the File Load Quick key is Alt-L in every module. Some exceptions exist, however. See Appendix A for a list of all the Quick keys.

The F1 Quick key provides context-sensitive Help at any time. In most cases, the Help screen will relate to exactly the command or procedure you are executing. This feature works even from one of the command option selections or an option menu. Once you have initiated Help, you can use function keys to search for related topics or to display help on different topics. Press Esc to return to what you were doing.

The F10 key is used throughout the SmartWare II system to indicate that you have finished with your work and want to save the menu or definition. If you are defining a report, building a project file, entering data, or defining a query, use the F10 key to save your work and return to the previous command level. If you want to exit without saving, press Esc.

Windows

Windows are common throughout the SmartWare II system. Initially, only one window is displayed. Use the Window Split command to create other windows to divide the current window either vertically or horizontally. If the window is too small, use the Window Zoom command to have it fill the monitor screen temporarily. The maximum number of windows varies from module to module.

Pop-up Menus

In most cases, when you are prompted to select a file or definition item, you are presented with a pop-up menu. You can respond to it in several ways. The easiest way is to use the cursor-control keys to move the arrow to the desired selection and then press Enter. You also can type the name of the selection in response to the prompt on the command line. If you want to load a file from another subdirectory, for example, you can enter the path and the name of the file:

\mydata\vendor

You also can use the F5 function key to select a new subdirectory and display the files, allowing you to choose from a pop-up menu.

You control the display of file names in the pop-up menu with file extensions. Each file extension in the SmartWare II system has a special meaning. For example, .DOC files are Word Processor document files and .WS files are Spreadsheet worksheets. Refer to Appendix B for a complete list of the file extensions used in SmartWare II.

What's in This Book

Using SmartWare II consists of 28 chapters organized into six major parts. At the end of the book, you will find five appendixes containing more information.

Part I, "Using the SmartWare II Database," discusses the Database in detail. Seven chapters guide you through setting up your database, entering, viewing, and manipulating your data, working with multiple file, printing reports, and integrating the Database with other modules.

Part II, "Using the SmartWare II Spreadsheet," explains how the Spreadsheet works, and leads you through the set-up process. You learn how to format spreadsheet cells, manipulate data, protect your spreadsheets, use graphics, print reports, and integrate the Spreadsheet with other modules.

Part III, "Using the SmartWare II Word Processor," covers word processing in detail. Seven chapters discuss formatting and manipulating text, using the spell checker and thesaurus, generating a table of contents and index, printing and merging text, as well as integrating this module with the others.

Part IV, "Using SmartWare II Communications," discusses everything you need to know about this module. You will learn about setting parameters, dialing a remote computer, capturing data, communications project processing, customizing the Communications module, and integrating it with the other modules.

Part V, "Using Project Processing," covers yet another way to execute SmartWare II commands. This section discusses how to create and edit a project file. You will learn how to use project file commands and functions, and perform error checking.

Part VI, "Using Functions," details the many functions available in SmartWare II. You will learn about date, time, and text functions; business and mathematical functions; and the functions that are specific to the various modules. This part of the book discusses the SmartWare II operators (numeric, text, relational, and logical), trigonometric and statistical functions, and many others.

8 Using SmartWare II

Part I

Using the SmartWare II Database

Includes

Using the Database Module
Setting Up Your Database
Entering, Deleting, and Viewing Data
Locating, Selecting, and Arranging Data
Working with Multiple Files
Printing Database Data and Creating Reports
Integrating the Database with Other Modules

Using the Database Module

The SmartWare II Database is designed for easy, efficient storage and reporting of detailed data. Depending on the amount of disk space available, one data file can store information about 2 billion employees or inventory items!

In the SmartWare II Database, data storage is independent of the reporting procedures, enabling you to create reports that vary widely in both form and content. Data entry can be customized for different users of an application, allowing for several levels of responsibility and security. As data is entered, it can be checked for validity or used to calculate new data items.

You sometimes may have difficulty in deciding whether to use the Database or the Spreadsheet for an application. If your applications include large lists of items that you are updating constantly, if much of the data is alphabetic, or if you need several different reporting formats, you probably need to use the Database. On the other hand, if your application is small, is primarily numeric, and involves modeling and what-if analysis, you might be better off using the SmartWare II Spreadsheet module.

Both databases and spreadsheets have advantages, but each program has its place in the right application. This section of *Using SmartWare II* presents concepts of the SmartWare II Database, and it presents methods for making the Database work for you.

New Features of the SmartWare II Database

Of all the SmartWare modules, the one that has changed the most from previous versions of Smart is the Database. Following is a list of the important new features of the SmartWare II Database module.

1. The size limitations of the Database have increased. Depending on disk space, you now can have a file with 2 billion records. Each record can have as many as 31,000 characters, with 1,000 fields per file. The largest alphanumeric field can be 31,000 characters; the display width for a numeric field can be 255 characters.

2. Keys are updated automatically, using a new key file structure. On a network, a file used by multiple workstations does not interfere with key maintenance. You can specify that key fields be unique.

3. A custom view (comparable to a custom screen in previous versions of Smart) can reference multiple files simultaneously. Using keys and linkages, file relationships can be maintained dynamically, for display, verification, and reporting purposes. As many as 127 files can be referenced in a view. A view is not limited to the size of your monitor screen; the view can be 32,000 lines long and 255 columns wide. You can change views and edit them as needed.

4. As many as 255 files can be open simultaneously, both in single-user mode and on networks.

5. You can change file structures after they have been defined, even if the files contain data.

6. You can define your own alpha field masks; the special field types SSN and PHONE are not offered in this version of SmartWare. A mask can provide dashes or parentheses, and the mask also can require that entered data fall into specified ranges, that the data be specific characters, upper- or lowercase, or that it completely fill the field.

7. View fields can have rules assigned to them, which perform error checking, input order branching, or even color changes. Input order branching allows the field prompting order to change, depending on the contents of a specific field. As many as 2,000 rules can be assigned to each field.

8. Two types of data entry menus are available, one which is similar to a SmartWare II pop-up menu, and the other which is similar to a bar type menu for shorter lists. In either case, to enter data, move the cursor and press enter.

9. The standard view is similar to the Browse On view in previous Smart versions. Updating records on the standard view is similar to changing cells in a spreadsheet; you move the cursor from record to record, and from field to field.

10. The Query facility has been changed to add a Query By Example capability for easy record selection. The full query editor has been retained for more complex situations. The view is automatically ordered by the newly created index at the successful completion of the query. You also can use a query to create a new file.

11. A new Cross-Tab feature replaces the Write Summarized command. You can specify conditions for each field. Nine types of summary operations can be performed.

12. Reporting is easier now that you can reference multiple files in a single view; you don't have to use the Relate command as often as before to pull data together from various files for reporting purposes. You can print a report with the totals, omitting the details. Different printer fonts can be used in the report. Report definitions are independent of a specific view, and the definitions reference fields and items by name, rather than by number. In a combination report, the form can be split between the top and bottom of the page, enabling you to have headings and footings. You can reprint the form if the table overflows onto successive pages. You can specify calculations at break points and in table headings.

13. Transactions can have multiple driven views for a single driver view. The audit report provides expanded information about the match and reports both the previous and new field values.

14. The FETCHFIELD function enables you to reference a field of a previous record. There are several FILE and TABLE functions that allow you to perform statistical operations on an entire file or on a table in a view. The TABLELOOKUP and FILELOOKUP functions work similarly to the VLOOKUP function of the Spreadsheet.

Understanding Database Concepts

Reviewing a few basic database concepts will help you to understand the Smart-Ware II Database module.

- Database. A database consists of one or more data files of related information.

- File. Information in a database is stored in *files*, in much the same way that data in your office is stored in file cabinets. A file cabinet drawer, for example, is used to store your company's personnel records. You

- Record. If you think of a file cabinet in database terms, the file drawer is a data file, and each piece of paper in the drawer is a *record* in that file. The record contains information related to one subject; a group of records makes up a data file. In SmartWare II, a file can have as many as 2 billion records.

- Field. A record in a file can store different pieces of information about an employee, such as first name, last name, city, state, phone number, department, and so forth. On a personnel form, these items of information might be entered on separate lines or portions of lines. In a database, these individual lines are called *fields*. Each record in a data file will probably have several fields. Each record in the SmartWare II Database can have as many as 1,000 fields.

- View. A *view* is a definition that you create to look at or work with one or more attached files. Every data file has its own standard view, showing all fields in a row and column fashion (see fig. 1.1). A custom view may show some (or all) fields of a file, may impose entry or update restrictions and rules, and may provide for default or field calculations. You can include notes and other helpful information in a view. An example of a custom view is shown in figure 1.2.

Fig. 1.1.

An example of a standard view.

```
┌ Window 1 ─────────────────────────────────────────────────────┐
│SSN         FIRST      LAST         AG S DEPT EMPDATE  WAGE     PCT │
│345-98-7593 Rosanna    Ronaldo      52 M ACCT 10/01/1959  $878.75 5.3│
│498-48-3988 Debbie     Linden       29 F MFGR 06/20/1975 $1,483.79 4.5│
│239-87-0076 Michael    Davis        61 M SALE 05/25/1969  $734.56 8.7│
│200-23-0300 Julius     Karenski     41 M MKTG 08/28/1971 $1,028.33 1.6│
│087-63-5490 Jeff       Harris       34 M ACCT 07/01/1970  $629.23 9.2│
│598-44-5922 LeAnne     Markus       48 F SALE 10/30/1965  $887.49 6.5│
│876-33-8989 Marilyn    Lester       55 F MKTG 09/05/1975 $1,516.26 4.3│
│987-65-7653 David      Marzetti     47 M ACCT 10/30/1985  $901.45 1.2│
│387-59-8374 Charles    Steffans     25 M DATA 10/15/1981  $654.34 5.8│
│498-34-5998 Paula      Bernstein    30 F SALE 06/15/1975 $1,804.56 6.7│
│776-39-8763 Alfred     Adelson      68 M ACCT 07/23/1945  $956.43 7.8│
│345-54-2287 Ellen      Aliakbari    35 F MFGR 08/15/1972  $997.66 4.3│
│198-03-3024 Howard E.  Peters       18 M MKTG 10/01/1985 $1,544.00 0.0│
│                                                                │
└────────────────────────────────────────────────────────────────┘
Menu: Data File Order Print Tools Window Help Remember Quit
View: person3.vws    Window:1                    Rec:1  ( 1 )
Browse Cross-Tabs Delete Enter Find Goto Query Relate Send Transact Utilities
```

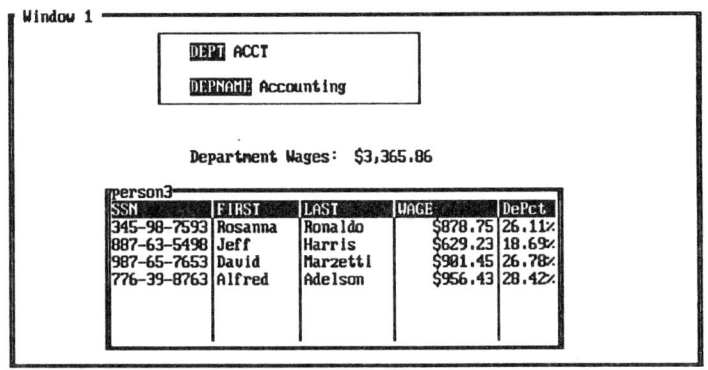

Fig. 1.2.

An example of a custom view.

Understanding Fixed-Length and Variable-Length Records

When you look at any form, such as an employment application, each field usually has the same amount of space in every record. Although some people have longer last names than others, the form generally has space for the longest probable name. The field size for BIRTHDATE certainly does not need to vary from individual to individual. If one record's fields are the same size as the corresponding fields for the next record, these fields are called fixed-length fields.

What do you do if the amount of data you want to store varies greatly from record to record? What if, for example, your employment application form asks applicants to write a paragraph telling why they are applying for the job. Some applicants will write their life histories; others will simply state that they need the money. How do you accommodate these different-sized answers?

One method of dealing with this problem is to define a fixed-length field that is as long as the longest answer you expect to receive. This solution certainly works, although you will probably waste a great deal of space.

The SmartWare II Database provides the capability of defining a file as variable-length, rather than fixed-length. In the variable-length configuration, an alphabetic field is only as long as the data contained in it. When you create a file, you have the choice of defining it as either fixed-length or variable-length. Although variable-length files save space, they generally take longer to read and write than fixed-length files.

Whatever the format, fixed or variable, a SmartWare Database has a maximum record length of 31,000 characters, or bytes, per record. You usually can think of a byte as equivalent to a letter, such as *A* or *B*. SmartWare II stores numbers in an internal 8-byte format.

Using Key Fields

As you enter data into your database, each record is stored in a sequential fashion, immediately after the previously entered record. This method is acceptable if you always want to look at data in this order, but usually you want to look at your data in other orders. You may want your file of employees listed in alphabetical order by last name, and not in the order in which they were hired.

Although the SmartWare II Database can sort your data into any order based on the contents of one or more fields, you may decide that the order of one field is always important. In your employee database, for example, you may want to be able to switch rapidly to look at the list in alphabetical order. To accomplish this quick switch in the SmartWare II Database, you define one or more *key fields*. By defining a key field, you establish a list that is always maintained in order by the contents of that field. Although you don't see the list, it exists in a separate file; you use the Order Change Key command to display and work with your file in the order of the key field.

In previous versions of Smart, you needed to indicate that you wanted your key list to be updated to keep it current when you added a new record or changed an existing one. In SmartWare II, the key updating process is automatic.

Understanding Data Types

Your databases can have six types of fields, each with a different use. These six field types are alphanumeric, numeric, date, time, counter, and inverted.

Alphanumeric

Alphanumeric fields (often called alpha fields) can contain any characters, letters, numbers, or special symbols. Alpha fields are used for names, addresses, product descriptions, codes, and sometimes numbers. With the field-masking capabilities available in view definitions, you can set up an alpha field to store Social Security numbers, phone numbers, product codes, and so on, each with dashes or other punctuation in the correct locations. With masking, you can specify that the entries into an alpha field that you are using for Social Security numbers, for example, be all numeric.

Numeric

Numeric data fields can contain numbers with or without decimal places. Typically, you declare a numeric field to store a value to use in a calculation, such as a pay rate, a price, or a quantity. In figures 1.1 and 1.2, the WAGE field is numeric.

Date

The SmartWare II Database stores dates in special numeric fields as a sequential number calculated from the beginning date of January 1, 1900. In figure 1.1, EMPDATE is a date field. In SmartWare II, you have the option to display four-digit years, rather than two-digit years. The default display is the one you selected as Date2 in the Tools Preferences Global menu, but you can specify a different display format if you want.

Time

Like the date field, time is stored in a numeric format, representing a fraction of a day. For example, .25 means 6 a.m. The default display, either the 12- or 24-hour clock format, is taken from the Tools Preferences Global menu, unless you specify otherwise.

Counter

Counter is a special numeric field that increments automatically each time you enter a new record.

Inverted

An inverted field is a special alpha field that allows you to enter multiple words and then sort on the last word. You might use this feature for storing employee names, including the first name, middle initial, and last name. If an inverted field is a key, the last word (last name, in this example) is used as the primary sort. The maximum size of an inverted field is 100 bytes.

Working with the SmartWare II Database

As you work with the SmartWare II Database, you are frequently called upon to select fields. Methods of indentifying fields and controlling cursor and record locations are covered here.

Identifying Fields

When using the SmartWare II Database, you often are prompted to specify the field (or fields) to which a command applies. You may need to do so for the Order Sort command, a calculation, the Print Report command, or any other command that calls for field identification. You can identify fields in several ways.

When prompted to select a field, as in figure 1.3, you can move the highlight cursor block to the desired field and press F6. The name of the field is inserted on the command line, followed by a semicolon.

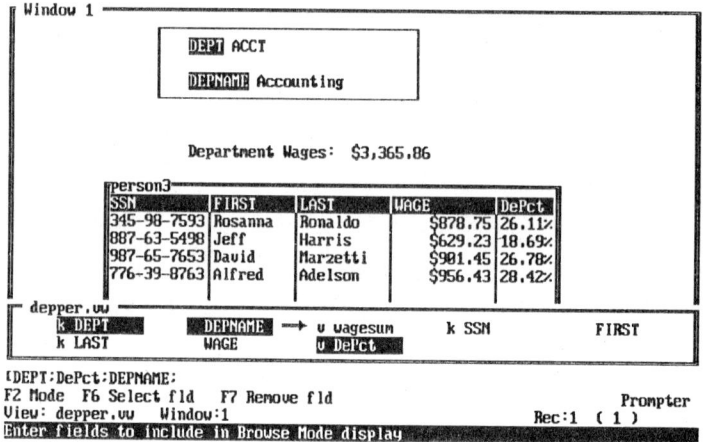

Fig. 1.3.

Selecting fields using the highlight block.

You can type the names of the field and the semicolons on the command line without moving the cursor. If you use this method, you may want to switch the mode from Prompter to Editor, so that you can edit the list as you build it. If you type the names, the field in the pop-up window is highlighted when you press the semicolon.

If you want to specify a range of adjacent fields, use the vertical bar (|) to separate the beginning field from the last field, as in figure 1.4. Note that if you used the F6 key to select the field, the semicolon must be removed before typing the vertical bar.

In figure 1.4, the first four fields were selected by specifying *dept|ssn;*. When the you press the semicolon after the field at the end of the range, all fields in the range are highlighted. You can continue to specify individual fields on the same line, separating them by semicolons, or you can specify additional ranges, using the vertical bar between the fields beginning and ending the range.

In SmartWare II you must use field names. You no longer can use field numbers or abbreviations for the field names.

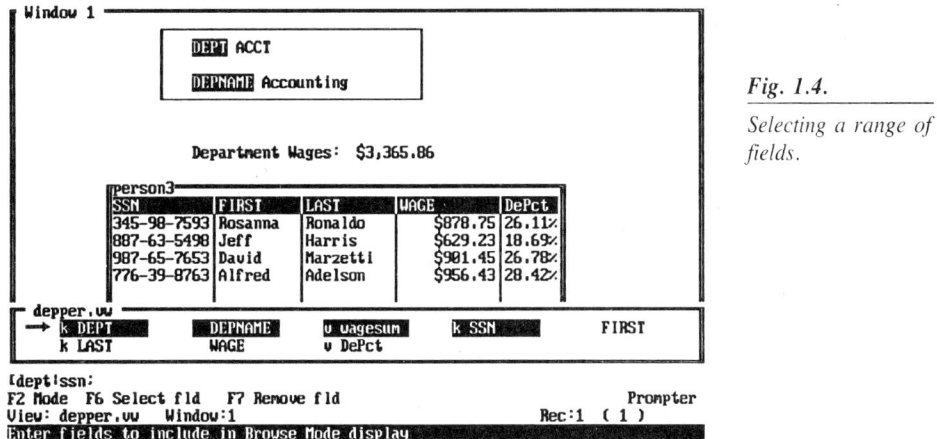

Fig. 1.4.

Selecting a range of fields.

Moving the Cursor

Mastery of the cursor-control keys can make using the SmartWare II Database easy, quick, and enjoyable. The Num Lock key is used to control the functions of the numeric keypad. Num Lock is a toggle; you press Num Lock once to use the number functions of the numeric keypad, and you press it again to use the cursor-control functions.

Used alone, the arrow keys generally move the cursor one space (the left- and right-arrow keys) or one line (the up- and down-arrow keys). The movement is nondestructive; if you are in the Update mode, for instance, you do not destroy the contents of a field by moving the cursor over the contents. In Data Browse mode, the right- and left-arrow keys shift one field at a time, enabling you to view any fields off the edge of your monitor screen. If you want to move the cursor the width of your screen, use the Ctrl-right-arrow or Ctrl-left-arrow keys.

The Ctrl-Home and Ctrl-End key combinations move the cursor to the beginning and end of a file, respectively. The page movement keys, PgUp and PgDn, move through the file or from one screen to another. If you are in Browse mode, PgUp moves up through your file by the number of lines displayed on the screen. If you are in the Data Enter mode and you have a multiple page view, PgUp moves up to the preceding page of that view, and PgDn moves in the opposite direction.

In addition to the cursor-control keys, you can use two function keys. The F5 key accesses the previous record of a database, and the F6 key goes to the next record. You can use these function keys in addition to the up- and down-arrow keys, both in and out of the Browse mode. If you are not in the Browse mode, however, you can use the F5 and F6 keys to access only the previous or next records.

Chapter Summary

This chapter reviewed basic concepts of databases in general, and of the SmartWare II Database in particular. A knowledge of the structure of database files and of the types of data they contain is important for a solid understanding of the ways in which you will be able to create files.

Setting Up Your Database

A database, as explained in Chapter 1, is a collection of related records that you treat as a group. Each record, in turn, consists of a number of data items stored in fields, which also are treated as a group. For example, a file of personnel information may contain one record for each employee, and each record may store information such as Last Name, First Name, Address, and so on. If you have a file of invoice information, you can use one record for each invoice, and the fields can include Invoice Number, Date, Customer Number, and Amount.

This chapter explains how to create views and databases, and how to set them up to your liking.

Creating the Database

If you used previous versions of Smart, you remember that you created a file before you created any custom screens. In SmartWare II, if you want to create a database, you must do so in the process of creating a custom view. When the database is created, a standard view is also created. The standard view displays all fields of the file in the Browse mode.

As you create your custom view, you may make it as plain or fancy as you want. Even though you are creating a new database, you may decide to attach additional files to the custom view and assign special rules and display format options. However, if you are just beginning to use SmartWare II, you may decide to create a straightforward custom view to go with the database; you can always create a fancy, sophisticated view later.

Creating a View

No matter what kind of data items your file will contain, take a few minutes to write down as many fields as you can think of that you might want to include in your database. You can save some time and frustration if you define all your fields at the outset. Later in this chapter, you will learn how to modify a file structure.

Issue the File Create command to begin the process of creating a new view and a database file; the Quick key is Alt-C. You are prompted:

> Enter a new view name:

Notice that even though you want to create a new database, you are prompted for a view name. In order to create a database, you must create a custom view through which you can manage or see the data. A standard view is also created each time you create a database. Although the standard view will have the same name as the database, the custom view may have a different name. The file extension of a custom view is VW; a standard view is VWS. The extensions are automatically assigned during the process of creating files and views. (For a complete list of SmartWare file extensions, refer to Appendix B.)

A view name can have a maximum of eight characters and must follow the DOS file-naming conventions. You should select a name that is easy to recognize because you will use the name frequently in your application.

You must select a custom view name that is not already in use. If you try to use the name of an existing view, the error will not be detected until after the next few prompts, when the following error message will be displayed:

> View screen already exists

Press Esc to return to the menu level. After you enter a new name for the view, you are prompted:

> New Similar

If you are creating a brand new custom view, select New. If the view is similar to an existing custom view, select Similar, and you are prompted:

> Custom-View Standard-View

Select whether the view is similar to an existing custom or standard view. In either case, a pop-up window displays the names of the existing custom or standard views.

Whether your view is new or similar, you are prompted:

> No-Password Password

If you want to restrict access to the view, select Password. Remember, for your data to be truly secure, you also must give a password to the data files you create.

Chapter 2: Setting Up Your Database

View passwords may be a maximum of 16 characters in length and may include spaces and special characters. Passwords are case sensitive; *PASSWORD* is not the same as *password*, so be careful. Keep an eye on your Caps Lock key, because the password you type is not displayed on the screen. You are prompted to repeat the password for verification and to make sure that you know what you typed. But do not forget your password; you cannot recover files if you do not remember your password.

Now you are ready to begin the definition of your new view. The View/Data-file Definition screen is displayed (see fig. 2.1):

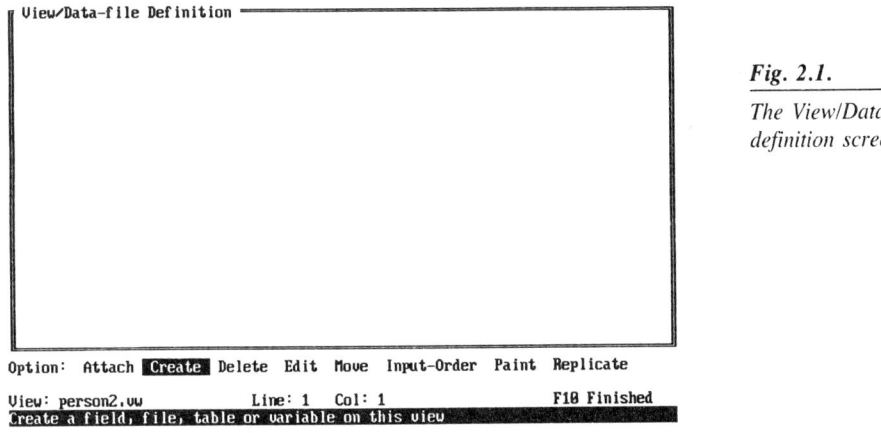

Fig. 2.1.

The View/Data-file definition screen.

The View/Data-file Definition mode has eight commands. Begin by selecting the command to create a file.

Creating a File

Select Create if you want to create a file. This command has eight options, as shown in figure 2.2.

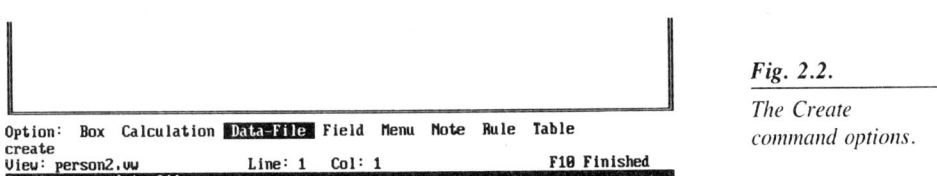

Fig. 2.2.

The Create command options.

Select Data-File if you want to create a new database. You are prompted:

    Enter a new filename:

A database name can have a maximum of eight characters and must follow the DOS file-naming conventions. You should select a name that is easy to recognize, because you will use the name frequently in your application.

After typing the name of the new database, you are prompted:

    Fixed-Length Variable-Length

Remember that in a fixed-length file, the alpha fields in each record are the same length as the corresponding fields of every other record. Valid reasons exist for selecting either fixed-length or variable-length record formats; refer to Chapter 1 for a complete discussion of these reasons and their implications. After selecting fixed or variable, the next prompt is:

    No-Password Password

If you want to restrict access to the file, select Password. Remember, for your data to be truly secure, you also must give passwords to the views you create, as mentioned previously in this chapter. Database passwords may be a maximum of 16 characters in length and may include spaces and special characters. Passwords are case sensitive, so be careful. You are prompted to repeat the password for verification and to make sure that you know what you typed. But do not forget your password; you cannot recover a file if you do not remember what your password is.

Once you have finished password entry, the database has been created. Simple, wasn't it? But wait, you have not created any fields for this database. Field creation is the next step.

Creating Fields

If you are creating a "fancy" custom view, the cursor position is significant, because it determines the location of the field you are about to create. If you are creating a plain custom view, you can simply position the fields down the left side of the view, similar to standard screens of previous Smart versions. If you want something that looks better, move the cursor to where you want the field to be located.

To create a field, select the Create command again, and this time choose the Field option; you are prompted:

    Enter a Field Name:

Type the name of the field you want to create; field names may be a maximum of 20 characters, and may include spaces and some special characters. Do not include a period or the left or right square brackets in a field name, however.

After you have entered the name for the new field, you are prompted:

```
Data-File View Project-Processing
```

The field may exist in the data file, may be purely a field that is calculated in the view, or may be a project-processing variable. Select Data-File if the field is to exist in the database. A screen similar to the one shown in figure 2.3 is displayed.

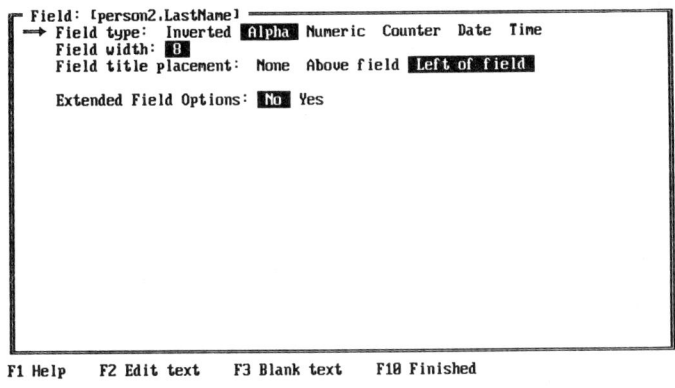

Fig. 2.3.

The initial field definition screen.

Initially, you must make the following three decisions about each field you declare.

1. Field type. Six field types are available. They are

    Inverted
    Alpha
    Numeric
    Counter
    Date
    Time

    Refer to Chapter 1 for a complete discussion of these field types. Move the highlight block to the choice you want on this menu.

2. Field width. This option tells the program the number of characters you want to display. The default is 8; you should change the width as needed. The storage widths of alpha and inverted fields are equal to your initial field width selection. Numeric, counter, date, and time fields are physically stored as 8 bytes in the data file, but the view display width may vary. Later in this chapter, you will see how to edit the display width of any field or the file width of alpha or inverted fields.

3. Field title placement. The title may be positioned to the left of the field or above it; if you include a note in the view to indicate the field name or title, you should select None to omit the title.

In figure 2.4 you see the specifications of a field to store a Last Name; the width is set at 15. When you select the extended field options, the screen changes to the screen shown.

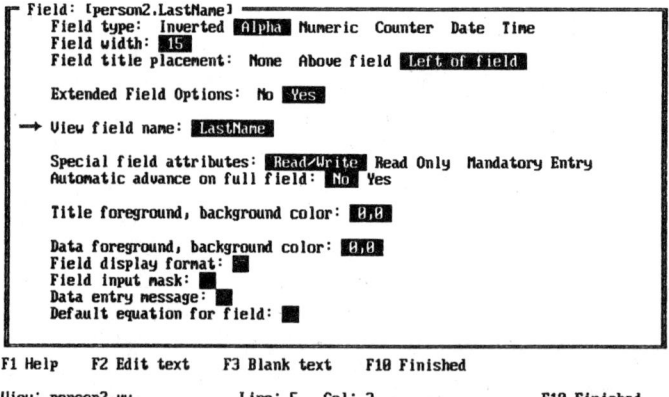

Fig. 2.4.

The Field Declaration options.

You can choose from among several options to enhance the functionality of the field.

1. View field name. You can change the name of the field as it appears in the custom view and in view field references; the name of the field in the actual database and the standard view remain unchanged.

2. Special field attributes. If the entry of data into this field is optional, select Read/Write; if you want only to read the field and not be able to change it, select Read Only. If you must enter the field, select Mandatory Entry.

3. Automatic advance on full field. If you want the cursor to go automatically to the next field if the current field is filled during data entry or update, select Yes.

4. Title foreground, background color. 0,0
   Data foreground, background color. 0,0

   You can select the foreground and background colors of both the data and the title. Press F6 to display the available choices.

5. Field display format. Display formats have four categories. They should be entered in the order listed, without spaces between them.

Chapter 2: Setting Up Your Database **27**

a. **Degrees of precision.** This selection represents the number of decimal places for a numeric field. The number must be between 0 and 15. If you do not specify, the system uses the default from the Tools Preferences Database menu covered later in this chapter.

b. **Alignment.** Use the letters L, R, or M to specify justification of Left, Right or Middle (centered). The default justification is left. This selection applies to both numeric and alphabetic field types.

c. **Type.** If you want a numeric field to be displayed in a special manner, either with a dollar sign, percent sign, or commas, or in a special or date format, you may specify a set of type characters:

$ Dollar sign
%   Percent
E   Scientific E-Notation
H   Histogram
,   Commas separating thousands
Dn Date format, where n = 1, 2, or 3 for each of the date types.
Tn Time format, where n = 1 (12-hour format) or 2 (24-hour format)
D   Custom Date displays. You can use the following reserved designations for portions of a custom date display:

    dd   Numeric day (e.g. 24)
    day   Day of the week (e.g. Saturday)
    mm   Numeric Month (e.g. 05)
    Mon   Text month, three-character abbreviation (e.g. Aug)
    Month Text month, no abbreviation (e.g. August)
    yy   Numeric year, two digit (e.g. 89)
    yyyy   Numeric year, four digit (e.g. 1989)

If you specify a custom date display, the number in the field is interpreted as a sequential number that begins with January 1, 1900. The display appears as a date represented by the number. For example, the format:

    Dmon dd, yyyy

displays the number 23912 as:

    Jun 20, 1965

You can use the special date formats for both numeric and date field types. **Note:** You do not need to know the sequential numbers used in displaying dates; the program takes care of that.

d. Additional options. Several other options are available for numeric fields only.

F Fill with asterisks (*)
Z Blank if zero
P Negative number surrounded by parentheses
C Negative number with "cr" (credit)
B Negative number with "cr" and positive with "db" (debit)

As an example, 2r$, displays a right-justified number with two decimals preceded by a dollar sign. A comma will separate the thousands.

6. Field input mask. An input mask may be used with either an alpha or an inverted field either to limit the characters you may insert into the field or to provide additional editing or interpretive marks. The following special symbols are used to create edit masks:

A Alphabetic character (not alphanumeric)
X Alphanumeric character, special characters allowed
Numeric character only (0-9)
N Letter or number only, no special characters
L Force the entry to lower case
U Force the entry to upper case
[] Specify a list of allowable characters
{} Specify an optional condition
- Specify a range of allowable characters
! Negate a character or a range
* Repeat a specification
\ Literal character symbol

The use of edit masks can help you ensure that your data is as accurate as possible. Some examples of the use of edit masks are as follows:

###-###-#### SSN. Note that the # symbol signifies a numeric; the dashes are used as interpretive characters.

(###) ###-#### PHONE. This mask is equivalent to the phone number field in previous versions of Smart.

[MF] Only the letters M or F are allowable; uppercase only, single character.

[MFmf]U Allows M or F in either upper- or lowercase, but changes the entry to uppercase.

[A-D]Allows the range A through D

[A-D][1-3] The first character must be from A to D; the second character must be from 1 to 3.

#####AAA The first five characters must be numeric and the next three must be alphabetic.

*4au Four mandatory characters, alphabetic, convert to uppercase.

*4{au} A maximum of four characters, alphabetic, convert to uppercase.

 [C-I!E] Letters C through I except E

7. Data entry message. You can enter a message to appear on the second command line during data entry or update. The message can provide a long explanation of the field, or may give allowable codes. The maximum length of the message is 100 characters.

8. Default equation for field. You can enter an equation to be evaluated when the cursor is positioned in the field. In data entry or if the field is blank in update, the result of the equation is inserted into the field. You can manually override the default.

Press F10 to complete the field declaration; you are returned to the view declaration command. The screen showing the completed definition of all our example fields is shown in figure 2.5.

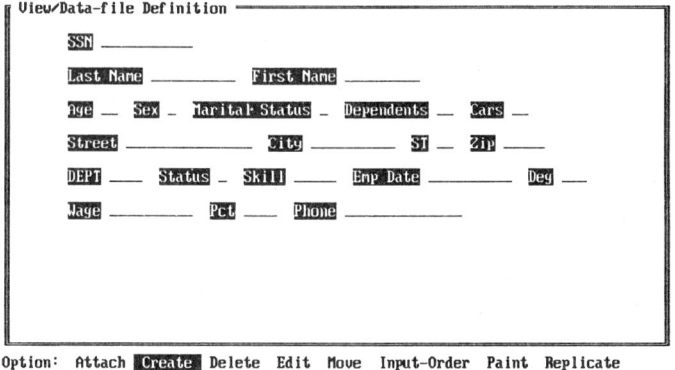

Fig. 2.5.

Completed field definitions.

Don't worry if the field is in the wrong location or if you change your mind about the declaration. You can move the field (or whole blocks of fields), and you can edit the field either during file creation or by executing File Modify from the menu level.

Designing Your Database

In addition to inserting fields on your view, you can add notes to provide information or instructions and boxes or lines to make the view easier to use. There are two types of menus you can attach to a field to make data entry easier and more accurate. You can create rules to improve accuracy, highlight special dates, or vary the input order. And you can add a table of data from a linked file.

Adding Notes to a View

Text information in the view is called a Note. A note may contain instructions, code interpretations, or explanations. To add a note to the view, position your cursor in the upper left corner of the area in which you want the note and execute the Create Note command (see fig. 2.6.) You can specify an optional color, if you want. Type the message and press F10 to complete the note.

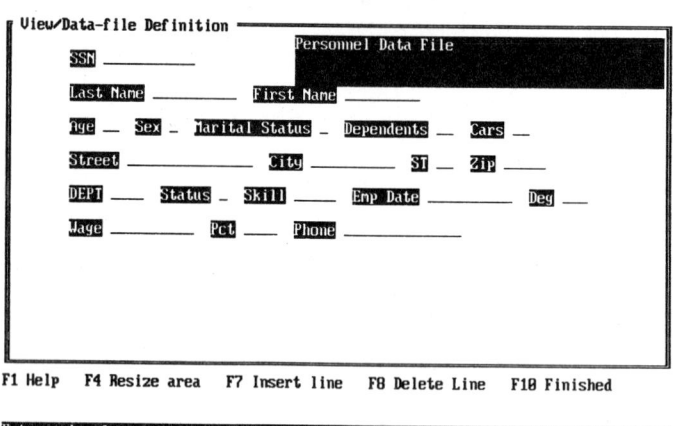

Fig. 2.6.
Adding a view note.

In the note definition area, press Enter to advance the cursor to successive lines; text does not wrap automatically to the next line. Use the function keys to change the size of the area (F4), to insert a blank line (F7), or delete (F8) an existing line.

Adding a Box to a View

You may outline certain areas of a view with either a double- or a single-line box. Position the cursor at the upper left corner of the box area and execute the Create Box command. You are prompted:

```
Double Single
```

You also are prompted for an optional foreground color; press Enter to accept the default color. Next, move the cursor to the lower right corner of the box area and press Enter (see fig. 2.7).

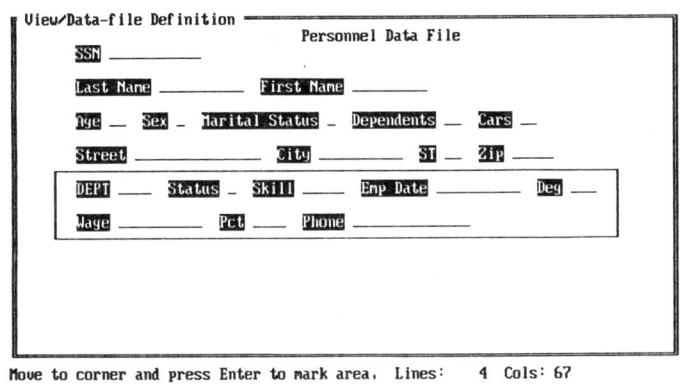

Fig. 2.7.

Adding a box to a view.

To draw a horizontal line, do not move the cursor down when creating a box; simply move the cursor to the right. Drawing a box through a field or a note will not cause an error, because the box will skip around a previously created item.

Adding a Menu for a Field

If a field has a limited set of possible entries, you can create one of two types of menus to use when entering the data, instead of typing the entry. These are bar menus and pop-up menus.

Creating a Bar Menu

Use the bar menu if the choices can be limited to a total of 500 characters and you have enough space on the view to display the bar without overlaying another field. When you execute the Create Menu command, you are prompted to select a field. Move the cursor and press Enter or F6. You then see the following options:

    Bar Popup

Select Bar for a bar menu. The unoccupied space to the right and below the designated field is highlighted; if needed, you can resize the space with the F4 key. Next, type the possible choices in the area, separated by spaces (see fig. 2.8). Press the F10 function key to complete the menu creation.

Fig. 2.8.

A bar menu.

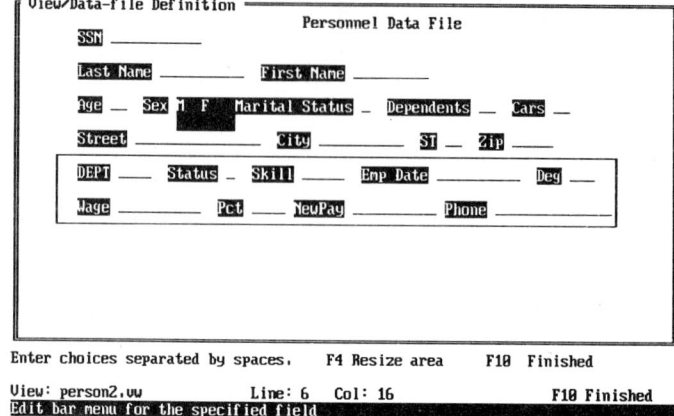

When you enter or update a record containing a bar menu, use the space bar to move the highlight block from one menu choice to the next; you do not make the field entries by typing them.

Creating a Pop-Up Menu

If the menu is longer than 500 characters, or you do not have enough space in the view to position a bar menu, you can create a pop-up menu. Select the Popup option to begin creating it; a pop-up menu editor is displayed. Type your menu selections, separated by semicolons. Press F10 to save the menu. Figure 2.9 shows the entry of the percentages in the example; figure 2.10 shows the use of the pop-up menu during data entry.

Fig. 2.9.

The pop-up menu editor.

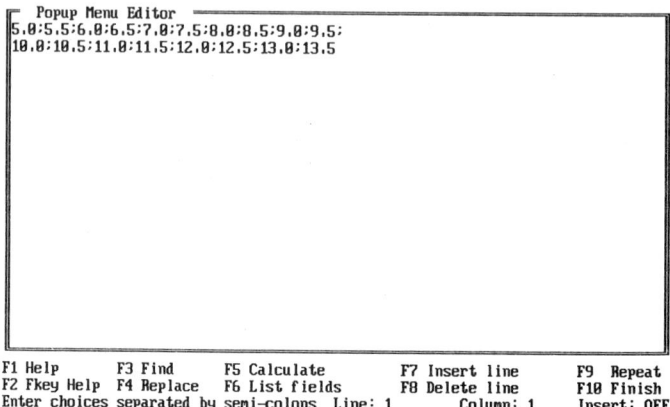

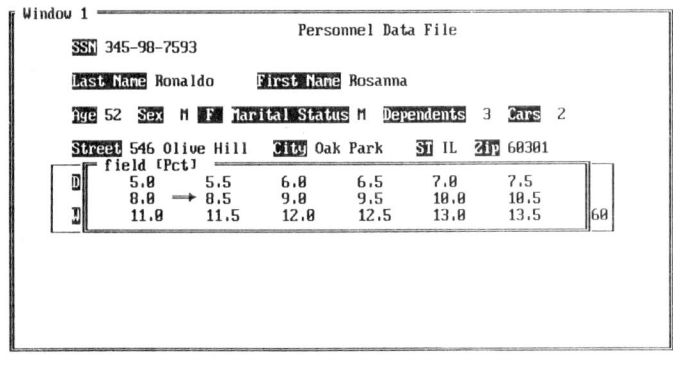

Fig. 2.10.

Using a pop-up menu editor.

Using a menu for data entry not only improves accuracy and uniformity, but also may save keyboard time. You can have as many as 64 items in a pop-up menu, none of which may exceed the size of the field.

Calculated Fields

If a field is to be calculated from other fields, execute the Create Calculation command. If you already have positioned the cursor on the field to be calculated, simply press Enter when the field list is displayed. If not, move the cursor or type the name of the field and press Enter. You see these options:

    Immediate Wait Manual

During data entry or update, if the calculation is to take place as soon as the cursor enters the field, select Immediate; the cursor automatically advances to the following field. If you select Wait, you must press Enter to perform the calculation and exit the field. Manual calculation requires you to press Alt-F5, which displays the value and also allows you to change it. (In previous versions of Smart, changing the value of a calculated field was impossible.)

When the calculation editor is displayed, type the formula. Press the F6 key to display field names to help you create the formula. For example, you can create a view field called NewPay with the following formula:

    [wage] * (1 + [pct]/100)

The formula calculates the new salary, as increased by the [pct] field.

If the formula for a calculated field uses existing fields in the record, the input order is vital. For the formula to be calculated correctly, the fields in the formula must have been entered already.

Field Rules

You can declare field rules to take the following actions:

1. Check the validity of entered data and display an error message
2. Change the field color
3. Jump to another field

To create a rule, execute the Create Rule command; select the field and press Enter. A menu similar to the one shown in figure 2.11 is displayed.

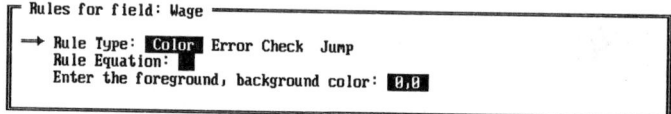

Fig. 2.11.

The rule declaration menu.

On the first line of the menu, select the type of rule you want to create, either Color, Error Check, or Jump. In figure 2.12, the color of the Wage field is changed if the wage is greater than 1,000. Note that any valid equation is allowable in the formula; the formula may reference any field in the view or a project-processing variable, or may use any SmartWare II function. The formulas may be a maximum of 100 characters.

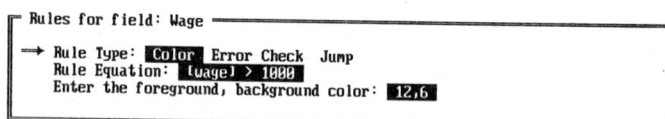

Fig. 2.12.

Using the color rule.

In figure 2.13, a rule is established to require that employee age be between 18 and 70. The error message is entered on the third line of the rule definition menu. Note that the error condition occurs if the rule is violated. If you have an error rule, data entry cannot continue until the error condition is corrected. The message can be as long as 100 characters.

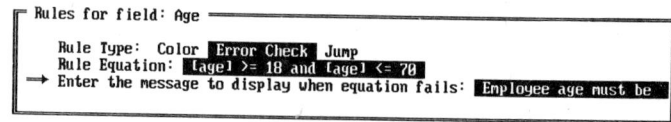

Fig. 2.13.

Using the error check rule.

A useful formula for validating an entry in a key field of another file is one similar to the following:

   iserr(filelookup([dept.dept],[dept.depname],[])) <> 1

In this example, an error will result if an invalid department code is entered. In figure 2.14, a rule is established to change the prompting order based on a rule.

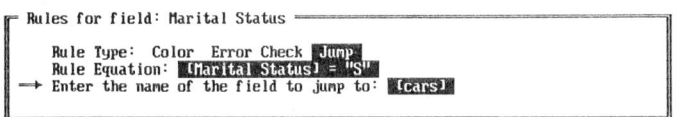

Fig. 2.14.

Using the jump rule.

In this example, prompting jumps to the [cars] field if the [Marital Status] field contains an S.

If the rules formulas use existing fields in the record, the input order is important. For the formulas to be calculated correctly, the fields in the formulas must have been entered already.

Creating a Table

A table in a view is a box displaying records from another file linked to the *main* or *driver* file of the view. This capability to perform a dynamic link between two or more files is one of the outstanding features of the SmartWare II Database module.

To illustrate the use of a table, continue to use the example of the personnel system. Up to this point, you have been creating a view in which each employee has one record. Now, to show the use of the table feature, you will create a view that has one main record for each department. The table box will display information about each employee in the department.

Figure 2.15 displays the department code and department name fields.

To define a table, position the cursor in the upper left corner of the area for the table and execute the Create Table command. You see this prompt:

   Enter a new table name:

Enter the name for the table. You can use the file name from which the data is to be displayed, or any name of your choice; the name is for reference purposes only. Now you are prompted to move the cursor down to the bottom line of the table and press Enter. This movement defines the height of the table; the fields you attach to the table will define the width. A table must have no fewer than 4 nor more than 19 lines. The table options menu shown in figure 2.16 is displayed.

Fig. 2.15.

The department view declarations.

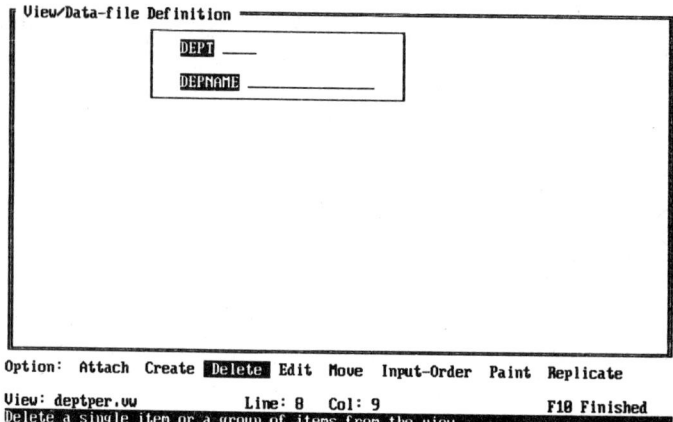

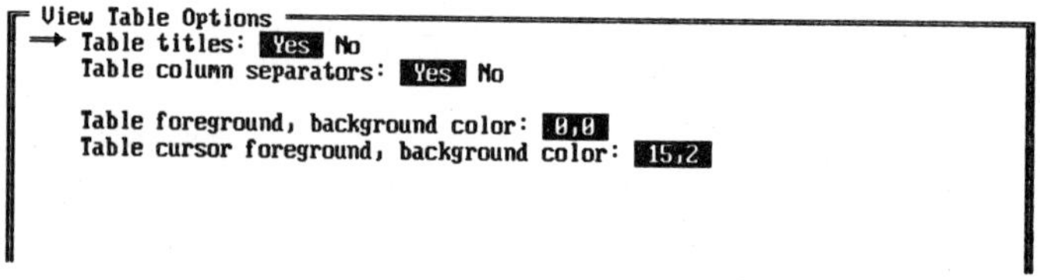

Fig. 2.16.

The View Table Options menu.

Table titles display the field names at the top of each column of the table. Column separators use a single vertical line to delineate each field. You also can change the foreground and background colors of the table cursor and the table itself. Figure 2.17 shows the table after it has been defined, but before any fields have been attached to it. Note that the table name is included in the table border.

Fig. 2.17.

A table definition.

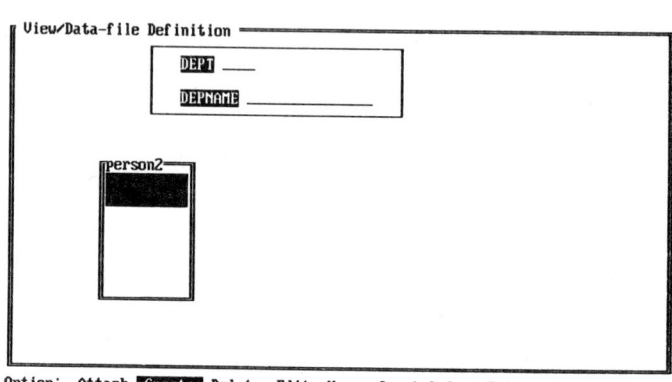

Note that the table definition process is in effect as long as the following notation appears at the bottom right of the status line:

    F10 Exit Table

Any commands you issue now will affect the table; when you press F10, the table definition will be complete and you return to the option list for the main view area.

You are not ready yet to complete the table definition process, however. You need to attach the data file that will be linked to the driver database, DEPT. To attach a data file, issue the command Attach Data-File. Select an existing database from those listed in the pop-up window. (Actually, you are selecting the standard view of a database.) When you press Enter, the database is attached, but you don't see any visible indication.

The attachment of the data file for the table is a necessary step in preparation for the attachment of the fields you want to display in the table area. To begin field selection, issue the Attach Field command. A list of the fields from the newly attached data file is displayed in a pop-up window, as in figure 2.18.

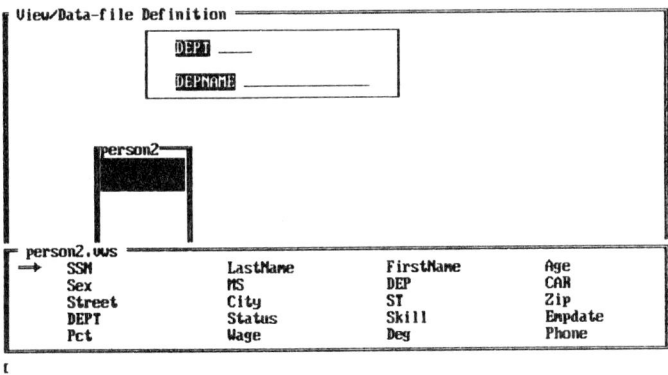

Fig. 2.18.

A list of fields displayed with Table Field Attachment.

Notice that the field names are the names used in the original definition of the file in the earlier part of this chapter, not the view names used in the definition of the custom view. This usage occurs because you are attaching the standard view of the data file, not any of its custom views.

When the field list is displayed, select one to include in the table area. Figure 2.19 shows the appearance of the table area after one field has been attached. Although you might expect to be able to attach several fields at one time, you must select them individually.

Fig. 2.19.

A table with attached field.

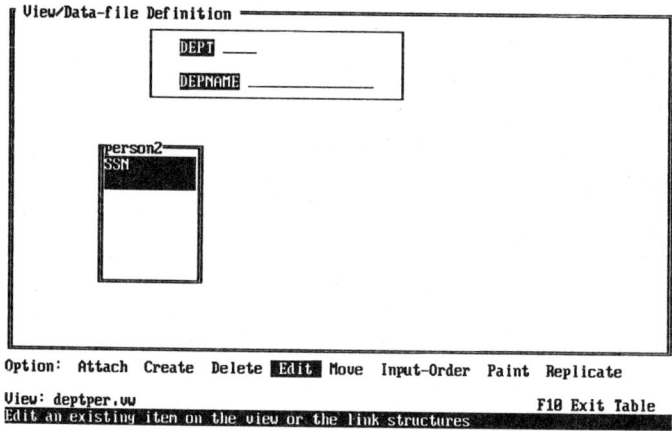

As each field is attached, the table area expands to the right. The table can contain fields from only one data file; if you have already attached several data files to the view, use the F3 or F4 keys to select the view from which to attach the fields.

As you attach fields to a table, each new one is added to the right. If you want a different order, you can move the cursor before you attach the next field, because new fields are always inserted to the right of the highlighted column. After the attachment of several fields, you may notice that the table area does not expand automatically for new fields; use the Edit Table command to enlarge the area.

Figure 2.20 shows the completed table with four fields attached. Not all fields from the database have to be attached, nor do you need to attach the link field(s). (Actually, the attachment of the link field(s) would be a waste of space, because they will be the same for each record of the table.)

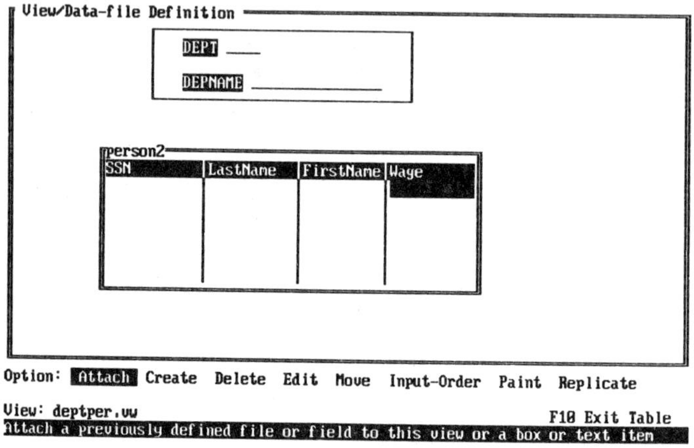

Fig. 2.20.

Completed table definition.

Before pressing F10 to exit the table definition process, you need to establish the linkage between the data file in the table and the main driver view. Execute the Edit Links command to define this relationship. Figure 2.21 shows the link definition menu.

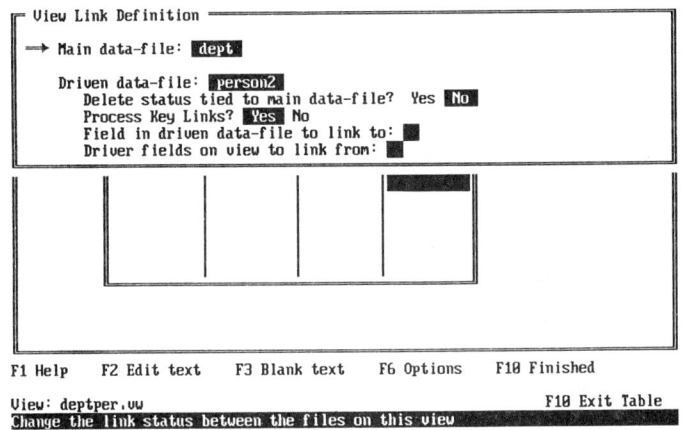

Fig. 2.21.

The Link Definition menu.

The names of the main data file and the driven (table) data file are already filled in for you. The other entries are as follows:

1. `Delete status tied to main data-file?` If you answer *Yes* to this item, deleting the record in the main data file (using the Data Delete Record command) causes the linked records in the table to be deleted and disappear from the table.

2. `Process Key Links?` Normally, you should answer *Yes* to this item. Answering *No* would be a temporary step to allow you to make some changes to the files to allow the links to work.

3. `Field in driven data-file to link to.` Press F6 to display the names of the fields in the table file; select the field(s) to be used as the link between the two files.

4. `Driver fields on view to link from.` Press F6 to display the names of the fields in the main file; select the field(s) to be used as the link between the two files.

Figure 2.22 shows the complete linkage menu. Press F10 to complete the editing of the data file links.

Fig. 2.22.

Completed data file links.

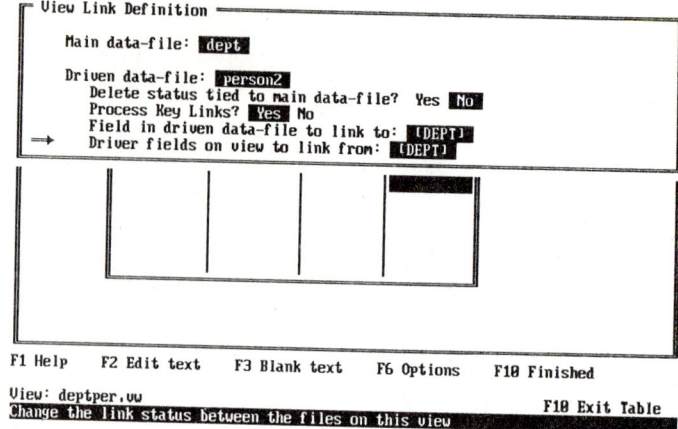

Linkage between the two files does not have to be limited to just one field. If, for example, the main file contains both department ([dept]) and building ([bldg]) fields, you can establish a link based on the multiple key [dept;bldg]. In this example, the table file must have a key in which the department code is the major key and building is the minor key.

Don't worry if you forget to establish file linkages before you exit from the Table definition process; you will receive an error, and the linkage menu will be displayed automatically for you. If you have finished defining the table, press F10 to return to the main view definition level.

If the view creation is complete, press F10 to return to the main menu level. If your driven database does not have a key for the link field, you are prompted to create one, as in figure 2.23.

Fig. 2.23.

Adding a key for the Driven Table.

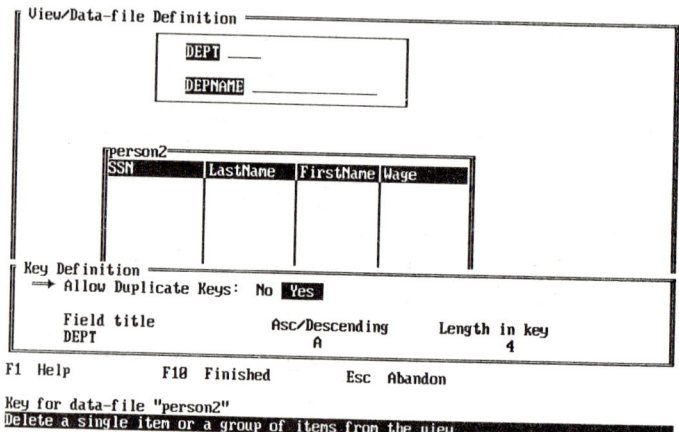

For a complete discussion of key fields, refer to Chapter 4 on arranging data.

Figure 2.24 shows the completed custom view. Note that the records in the table area represent employees working in the accounting department.

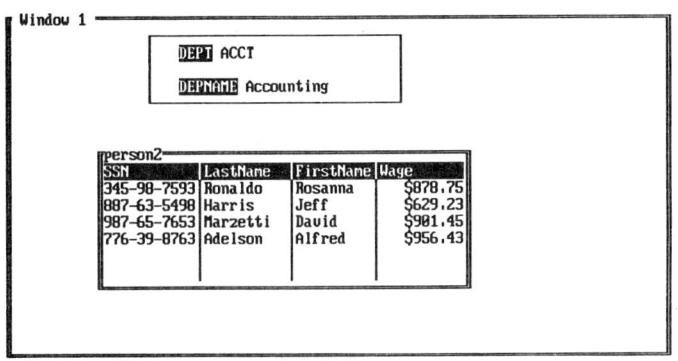

Fig. 2.24.

A completed custom view with table.

If you press the F6 to go to the next record, the next department is displayed, along with the table showing the employees in the department.

If you are still creating your view, several other commands are important.

Attaching a Data File or a Field

As you learned in the creation of the table, if you want to reference fields from an existing data file, you must first attach the file. This fact holds true whether or not the data file is in a table. When you issue the Attach command, you are prompted:

    Data-File Field

When you select Data-File, a pop-up menu displays the names of existing databases in the current subdirectory. Select the one you want to attach and press Enter. (The pop-up window actually displays the names of the standard views; you cannot attach a custom view.) There is no further action to be taken, nor is there any indication that the attachment has taken place.

Once you have attached a file, you can attach a field. Execute the Attach command again, and this time, select the Field option. A pop-up window displays the names of the fields in one of the attached files. Use the F3 or F4 function keys to change the display to show fields from other attached files. If you select a field with a name duplicated in two or more attached files, you are prompted:

    Duplicate field name. Enter a new view field name:

Enter a new name to be used in the view; this name represents the field you have attached. For uniqueness, fields in a view must not have the same names, although the actual name of a field in one attached data file can be the same as a field in another.

Editing a View

Before you complete the creation of your view, you can edit any of your declarations. Select the Edit command, and you are prompted with the option list shown in figure 2.25.

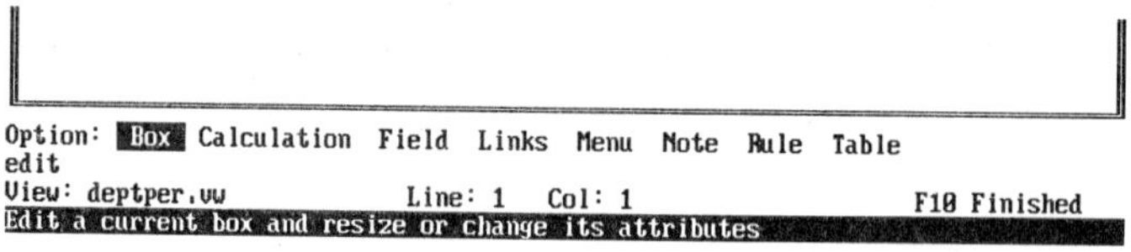

Fig. 2.25.

The File Creation Edit options.

```
Option: Box Calculation Field Links Menu Note Rule Table
edit
View: deptper.vw           Line: 1   Col: 1              F10 Finished
Edit a current box and resize or change its attributes
```

The editing of the declarations is similar to their initial creation, with the exception of fields.

Editing Field Declarations

If you change your mind about a field declaration, you can edit the field by selecting Edit and then Field. When you edit a field, you can actually alter the field's display width. For an alpha or inverted field, the display width may be shorter than the database field width, and thus you can conserve the view display area. You will not be able to see the entire field all at the same time, however, because the field scrolls horizontally as you enter data into it.

In figure 2.26, you are prompted to move the cursor to resize the field's display width. If the field is alpha, you can move the cursor down to create a multiple-line input field.

If the field is alpha or inverted, the display width does not have to be the same as the real database field; you can change one without changing the other. If the field is numeric, the display width and the actual width must be the same.

```
┌─View/Data-file Definition ────────────────────┐
│            ┌──────────────┐                    │
│            │ DEPT  ___    │                    │
│            │ DEPNAME -_____-│                │
│            └──────────────┘                    │
│                                                │
│   ┌person2─────────────────────────┐           │
│   │ SSN     │LastName│FirstName│Wage│          │
│   │         │        │         │    │          │
│   │         │        │         │    │          │
│   │         │        │         │    │          │
│   └─────────┴────────┴─────────┴────┘          │
└────────────────────────────────────────────────┘
Move to corner and press Enter to mark area.  Lines:   1  Cols: 15
Use arrow keys to resize the field's screen display width
View: deptper.vw          Line: 4   Col: 43              F10 Finished
Enter name of field to edit
```

Fig. 2.26.

Editing a field.

Rearranging the View

Once fields and other items have been declared, you can move them around for better appearance or usability. Select Move from the command list, and you are prompted:

    Block Item

If you want to move a whole block of items, move your cursor to the upper left corner of the block and then select Block. You are prompted to move the cursor to the lower right corner to define the block; press Enter to complete the block definition. Move the cursor to the new location and press Enter again.

If you want to move just one item, select Item. You are prompted:

    Box Field Note Table

To move a field, select Field; a pop-up window displays the field names. Select the field to move and press Enter. You then move the cursor to the new area and press Enter. If you move a Table, you also are prompted with the names of the existing tables. To move a Box or a Note, you must position the cursor on the appropriate item; if the cursor is not on the item, the command will have no effect.

Deleting a Declaration

If you want to delete one or more declarations, select the Delete command. You are prompted:

    Block Item

If you select Item, you are prompted with the following list of options:

    Box Calculation Data-File Field Menu Note Rule Table

This list is the same list of items in the option list for the Create command.

If you have several items to delete, position your cursor in the upper left corner of the area and execute Delete Block. You are prompted to move the cursor to the lower right corner of the block. When you press Enter, all declarations in the block are deleted. If no items exist in the block, you receive the error message:

    No items selected

Be careful, because if you are deleting a field, you are prompted:

    Delete fields from data-file also? (y/n)

If you answer *Y* to this question, not only will you delete the field from the view, but also from the real database. Answer *N* if you want to remove the field from only the view. When deleting a block, the boundaries of the block do not have to completely surround the items to delete; if the block border touches the item, it will be deleted.

Setting Input Order

In a custom view, you have absolute control over the prompting order of the fields. The initial order will be that in which you attached or created the fields. It is particularly important to enter factors of a calculation prior to the calculated field itself.

Although the natural prompting order is left-to-right, top-to-bottom, you may find circumstances in which you want a different order. To set the prompting order of your view, select the Input-Order command. You see a display similar to that in figure 2.27.

The fields of the view are displayed with numbers to indicate the fields' current prompting order. The following function keys can be used to change the order:

    F3   Go to the Previous field
    F4   Go to the Next field
    F6   Increment all fields by 1
    Alt-R   Set natural order (left-to-right, top-to-bottom)
    Alt-O   Reset to the original order

You can type a new order number for a field, or you can increment all fields by 1 if you press the F6. Press Alt-R to set the natural top-to-bottom order. Press F10 when you have finished.

```
┌ View/Data-file Definition ─────────────────────────────┐
│                    Personnel Data File                  │
│                                                         │
│      SSN 1 _____                                       │
│      Last Name 2_____  First Name 3_____          │
│      Age 4_ Sex 5_ Marital Status 6 Dependents 7_ Cars 8_│
│      Street 9_____ City 10_____ St 11 Zip 12__   │
│      DEPT 13_ Status 1 Skill 15__ Emp Date 16_____ Dep 17_│
│      Wage 18_____ Pct 19_ NeuPay 20_____ Phone 21____ │
│                                                         │
└─────────────────────────────────────────────────────────┘

F3 Prev fld   F4 Next fld   F6 Inc flds   Alt-A Auto row   Alt-O Original order
This fields order: 1
View: person2.vw              Line: 4  Col: 12                   F10 Finished
Change the input order of the view fields for data entry
```

Fig. 2.27.

Setting the input order.

Duplicating a File

If you want to create a copy of a database, make sure that the original database is not loaded. (This method is contrary to the rules of previous Smart versions.) Begin by executing the File Create command from the menu level. However, instead of creating a New view, select the Similar option. You are asked whether the view is to be a copy of a custom view or a standard view. A pop-up window displays the names of the existing views, and you are prompted:

    Enter the view name:

Select the name of the view you want to copy and press Enter. After selecting a password option, the custom view is displayed, and the file creation/modify command list is presented. From the command list, select Replicate. You are prompted:

    Data-File Field

To duplicate a database, select the Data-File option. A pop-up menu displays the names of the data files attached to the original view. Select the name of the file to duplicate and press Enter. You are then prompted:

    Enter a new data-file name:

Type the name of the new data file you want to create and press Enter. After you select either fixed- or variable-length and a password option, the previous data file is detached, and a new one is created and automatically attached to your new view. At the completion of the process, you will have a view similar to the original and a database structure identical to the original you selected—without the data, however. The structure of the new database will be in place, but no records will be in the file.

Duplicating a Field

If you have several similar fields, making a copy of the definition of one of them is often easier than creating a new definition from scratch. First, position the cursor where you want the new field. Then select the Replicate command and the Field option. A pop-up menu displays the names of the fields in the view. After you select the field to copy, you are prompted:

    Enter a new field name:

Type the name of the new field and press Enter. The new field may be one of the following:

    Data-File View Project-Processing

Even if the original field is a Data-File field, the copy may be one of the other types. The new field will be inserted into the view at the indicated location. If you want to make any changes to the declaration, use the Edit command.

Painting New Colors

If you select the Paint command, you can change the colors of any of the following items:

    Border Cursor Data Graphics Titles Window-Area

If you have always accepted the default colors, such as for a field or a box, you can change the colors with the Paint command. If you have chosen your own specific colors in the declarations, however, you cannot change them with this command; you must modify the file to change the colors of those items.

Modifying a File

Even after you have created a database or a custom view, you can change either of them with the File Modify command. (This capability is a major change from previous Smart versions.) When you select File Modify, the same commands are available as offered by the File Create command.

If you change a database, however, be careful if you change field lengths. If you shorten a field, you run the risk of truncating some of the data. If you make a field larger, you will not automatically lengthen the display of the field in all the custom views from which the field is referenced.

Setting Database Preferences

To establish the default preferences for the SmartWare II Database, execute the Tools Preferences Database command. The menu is shown in figure 2.28.

Chapter 2: Setting Up Your Database **47**

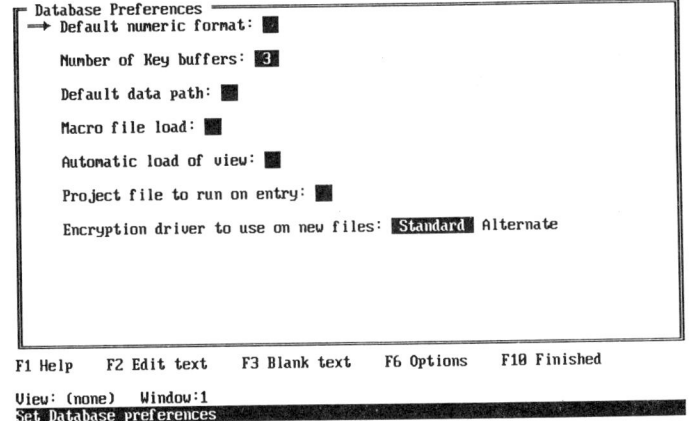

Fig. 2.28.

The Tools Preferences Database.

The items on the preferences menu are as follows:

Default numeric format. If you do not specify a format for a numeric field when you create a view, the format entered here is used. One typical format, for instance, may be numbers with two decimal places, right justified, with commas and a currency symbol: *2r$,.*

Number of Key buffers. The key buffers consume about 3,000 bytes of memory each; they are used to speed the operation of commands that use keys. Unless you have an unusually key intensive application, leave the number of buffers at three.

Default data path. If you want your Database files stored in a specific subdirectory, enter the full path name of the subdirectory here. Otherwise, the default data path is determined by the subdirectory from which you begin the Database session. Alternately, you can override the default path with the -d entry switch.

Don't forget that during a SmartWare II session, you can change the data path by using the Tools Directory New-Directory command.

Macro file load. To automatically load a macro definition file at the beginning of a Database session, enter the name of the macro file here. You should specify the full path of the macro file if you ever enter the Database from different subdirectories.

Automatic load of view. To automatically load a view, enter the name of the view here. You should specify the full path of the view if you ever enter the Database from different subdirectories. If you do not specify a file extension, the default is .VW, a custom view. To load a standard view, you must supply the view name and extension .VWS.

Project file to run on entry. If you want to run a project file automatically when you begin the Database, enter the name of the project file here.

Encryption driver to use on new files. You should select Standard unless your company has an alternate driver to be used. Contact Informix if you have your own encryption driver.

Press F10 to save the changes you have made in the Tools Preferences Database menu.

Working with Data Files and Views

When you begin a SmartWare II Database session, you have a blank slate because you have neither loaded any files to work with nor indicated what you want to do. To work with files or views, you must first provide the names of the views to be used in processing.

The Database can accommodate files containing thousands of records, but your computer's internal memory cannot hold that many records. This disparity is one of the big differences between the Database and the Spreadsheet modules.

The Spreadsheet loads the contents of all columns and rows into random access memory (RAM) and will page to disk and expanded memory but still cannot handle files as large as those handled by the Database.

The Database reads groups of records from the disk into an internal buffer (an area of memory set aside for data), thus handling huge files in small increments.

As you move through your file reading and writing records, SmartWare II empties and refills the buffer as needed to make room for additional records. Some records you have entered or updated may therefore be written to your disk, and some may still reside in the buffer area in RAM. If your computer loses power, you lose only those changes in the buffer, not those already written to disk.

Loading Views

The purpose of the File Load command is to open and prepare a view and its associated files for processing and to display the view in the current window. The Quick key is Alt-L. The File Load command options are as follows:

Custom-View Standard-View

A standard view displays the fields of just one file in the browsed mode. If you select Standard-View, a pop-up window displays the names of the standard views in the current subdirectory.

A custom view usually displays selected fields from one or more attached files, but does not necessarily display all fields. (Actually, you can create a custom view that is not attached to any database at all.) If you select Custom-View, a pop-up window displays the names of the custom views in the current subdirectory (see fig. 2.29). The prompt is as follows:

    Enter the custom view name:

If the view you want to load is displayed, move the cursor and press Enter. Alternately, you can type the name of the view and then press Enter.

```
┌─ File Listing ──────────────────────────────────────────┐
│ → cars       depper      dept        dept2      deptper │
│   deptsex    empdepst    inventry    parthist   perdep  │
│   person2    person5     person6     person8    state   │
│   ven1                                                  │
└─────────────────────────────────────────────────────────┘
Enter the custom view name:
F4 Look for a file  F5 Display directories
Path:                                         424  9-09-89  9:09
Enter name of the custom view to load
```

Fig. 2.29.

Loading a custom view.

If necessary, precede the view name with the drive letter and path designation. For example, you might enter:

    C:\bill\invoice

to load the view called Invoice that is in the \bill subdirectory. You also can look for a view with the F4 key or change subdirectories with the F5 key.

When you load a view, all files attached to the view are opened simultaneously.

If the view has been protected with a password, you are prompted to enter the password as follows:

    Enter password:
    Enter the password for view (pathname\viewname)

The password does not print as you type it; press Enter when you have finished. If you have typed the password incorrectly, the following error message appears:

    Wrong password

Press any key to clear the error and then enter the password again. After three attempts, if you still have not entered the correct password, a final error message is displayed:

    Invalid password

The File Load command is then aborted and you are returned to the menu level. If you have assigned a password to a view, for absolute security you must also assign a password to the attached files. If someone wants to read your data, they can load the standard view and look at the file if it does not have a password.

When the view is loaded, the first record for the main file—in physical, not logical order—is displayed in the current window. If you want to work with your file in a different order, use the Order Change command. Refer to Chapter 4 for more information.

Notice that the initial order of the records in the main file is physical, rather than logical. If there are other files attached to the view, their records are referenced in a key sequence to link with the driver file of the view.

Thus in figure 2.24 the first record in the department file will be for the Accounting Department; this is the driver file of the view. In the table, however, the employee records are scattered throughout the Person2 file.

Although you cannot load the same view twice, you can load different views to which the same data file is attached. What if a view is already loaded in the current window when you load a different view? The old view, which remains active, is removed from the current window; the newly loaded view becomes current in the window. (To verify that the old view is still active, you can use the File Display-Active command to display a list of all active views and files.) You can display the original view by using the Data Goto View command or the F4 Quick key.

Be careful when you return to the old view, however. In previous versions of Smart, the file reverted to sequential order once it was removed from a window. In SmartWare II, a file retains its order even in the background when not displayed in a window.

Activating Views

If you want to make a view active but do not want to displace the view in the current window, use the File Activate command. This command is identical to the File Load command except that the view is not displayed in a window. When you want to display the view, use the Data Goto View command or the F4 function key.

If there is no view in the current window, the File Activate command operates like the file Load command, displaying the first physical driver record.

If you are beginning to execute an application that involves many password-protected views, it is useful to activate all of them at the outset so that you dispense with password entry. You can then use the Data Goto View command to access the different views.

Unloading Views

When you finish working with a view, you should unload it. Unloading is not absolutely necessary, but because each active file consumes a portion of available

RAM, failure to unload may result in slower processing or memory shortages. The Quick key is Alt-U.

When you execute the File Unload command, you are given the choice of unloading All or a View (see fig. 2.30).

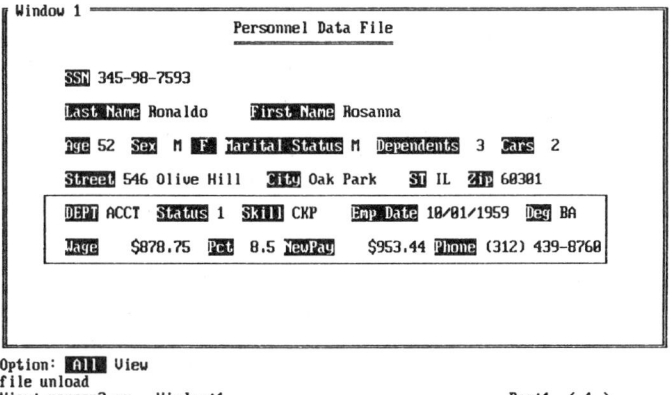

Fig. 2.30.

The File Unload command options.

If you select All, every active view is unloaded. Any records in the internal buffers are written to the databases, and the database files and views are closed. Windows are not automatically closed, however; you must use the Window Close command to reduce the number of windows. Typically, you use the File Unload All command if you are finished with one application and are ready to begin another. If you use F10 and Quit to exit the Smart Database altogether, all views are unloaded automatically.

If you select the File Unload View command, the pop-up menu displays the names of the open views. To select the view you want to unload, use the cursor keys to move the arrow, and then press Enter (see fig. 2.31). You can type the name of the view. Notice that the file extensions are included in the display to distinguish between standard views (.VWS) and custom views (.VW). Refer to Appendix B for a complete list of file extensions.

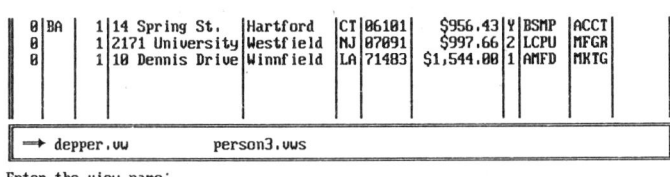

Fig. 2.31.

Prompting for views to unload.

Any active view can be unloaded, whether or not the view is in the current window. If you unload the current view, the window is left blank; use the Data Goto File (or the F4 function key) to display one of the other active files in the window.

Saving Files

The Smart Database periodically writes to disk as you enter new records or update existing ones. But several records in the internal buffer may not have been written to disk yet. To ensure that these records are written out and that your file is safely stored on disk, use the File Save command. If you have been entering new records and will be away from your computer for a few minutes, you should use the File Save command to write the new records to the disk.

The Quick key for the File Save command is Alt-S; it has no options. Be aware, however, that only the files attached to the view in the current window are saved when you use this command. If you want to save other files, they must be attached to the view in the current window for the File Save command to have any effect.

Getting Information about a View

The Data Utilities Information command displays useful information about the current view and attached files. Figures 2.32 and 2.33 show a portion of the information about the sample personnel file used throughout the Database section of this book. The Quick key for the Data Utilities Information command is Alt-F.

Fig. 2.32.

Data utilities information.

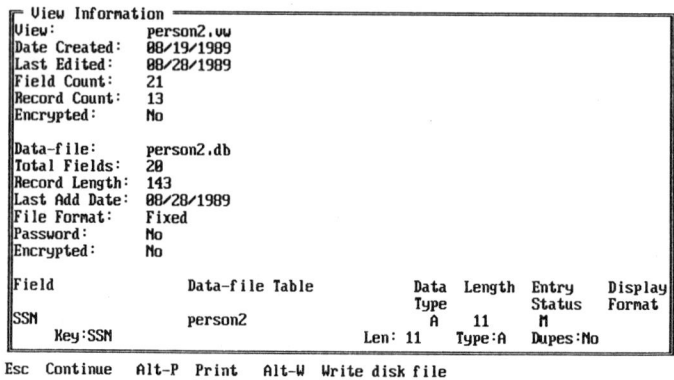

Chapter 2: Setting Up Your Database

```
┌─ View Information ─────────────────────────────────────────────────────┐
│Field              Data-file Table         Data   Length  Entry   Display│
│                                           Type           Status  Format │
│SSN                person2                  A      11      M             │
│     Key:SSN                            Len: 11   Type:A  Dupes:No       │
│                                                                         │
│Last Name          person2                  A      10      M             │
│     Key:Last Name                      Len: 10   Type:A  Dupes:Yes      │
│          First Name                    Len:  9   Type:A  Dupes:Yes      │
│                                                                         │
│First Name         person2                  A       9     R/W            │
│Age                person2                  N       8     R/W      r0    │
│Sex                person2                  A       1      M             │
│Marital Status     person2                  A       1     R/W            │
│Dependents         person2                  N       8     R/W      r0    │
│Cars               person2                  N       8     R/W      r0    │
│Street             person2                  A      15     R/W            │
│City               person2                  A      10     R/W            │
│ST                 person2                  A       2     R/W            │
│Zip                person2                  A       5     R/W            │
└─────────────────────────────────────────────────────────────────────────┘
 Esc Continue   Alt-P  Print    Alt-W  Write disk file

 File: dbinfo.txt                    Line: 34      Column: 1     Insert: ON
 Browse Cross-Tabs Delete Enter Find Goto Query Relate Send Transact Utilities
```

Fig. 2.33.

Data utilities information.

The following information about the view is shown at the top of figure 2.32:

1. Name of the view
2. Date created
3. Date last edited
4. Count of the number of fields in the view
5. Count of the number of records
6. Encryption status

Next follows information about each the files attached to the view:

1. Name of the data-file
2. Linkage to the main file, if appropriate
3. Count of the number of fields in the file
4. Record length of the file
5. Date data last added
6. File format (Fixed/Variable)
7. Password status (Yes/No)
8. Encryption Status (Yes/No)

In figure 2.33, you see information about each field in the view:

1. Field name
2. Data file of the field
3. Table name in which the field is displayed
4. Data type
5. Field length (not display width)
6. Entry status
7. Display format
8. Input mask

If a field is the major sort of a key, this is indicated, and the minor keys are listed. Duplicate key status is also shown.

If a field is calculated, the calculation formula is listed on the line below the field.

You can print the entire Information display by pressing the Alt-P key combination; Alt-W writes the information to a file of your choice. Press Esc or F10 to return to the menu.

Be aware that if you have selected fields in the Browse mode, only those fields will be listed in the Data Utilities Information Display.

Renumbering the Count Field

The Data Utilities Change-Count command renumbers the count field for a file or sets the value for the next record entered. When you select this option, you are prompted:

    Enter the new count:

Enter the number of the new count value. You are prompted:

    Next Renumber

Select Next to assign the value you have entered to the count field of the next record entered; current records are left unchanged. Select Renumber to renumber all records, beginning with the first physical record in the file. You are prompted for the name of the file to which to assign the new count.

Repairing Damages

If a data file becomes damaged or if the standard view is accidentally erased or damaged, you can use the Data Utilities File-Fix command.

If the damage to the file is not too severe, you can use the Data-File option to repair a database. A pop-up menu prompts you to enter the name of the file. If the file is variable length, the PIX file is rebuilt and any unused space is eliminated from the data file. The PIX file keeps track of the length of each record in a variable length file and other vital information. If this PIX file is damaged, you should use the Data Utilities File-Fix command to reconstruct it. Any keys are also rebuilt automatically.

Select the View option of the Data Utilities File-Fix command to rebuild the standard view for a file. The database itself has enough information contained in it to perform this reconstruction. Custom views are not affected by this command.

Changing Passwords

When you initially create a view or a data file, you have the opportunity of assigning a password at that time. Later, you can use the File Password command to add, change or remove a password for either the current view or data file. When you execute the command, you are prompted:

    Data-File View

If you select Data-File, you are prompted to Attach or Remove a password.

Attaching a Password to a File

If you select Attach, a pop-up window prompts you for the name of the data file to which to attach the password. The only choices are the data files attached to the current view. When you have selected the data file, you are prompted:

    No-Encryption Encryption

In order to load a passworded data file, you must know the password. Encryption provides yet another degree of protection. If you select encryption, you are warned:

    Warning: File will be rewritten. Continue? (y/n)

The entire file must be written into the encrypted format. In case anything should go wrong, you should have a backup of this file. Finally, you are prompted:

    Enter new password:

Passwords may be as long as 16 characters. Remember that passwords are case sensitive; *password* is not the same as *PASSWORD*. After typing the password, you are prompted to type it again for verification.

Removing a Password from a File

Execute the File Password Data-File Remove command to delete a password from a file attached to the current view. A pop-up window prompts you for the name of the data file. If the file is encrypted, you are cautioned that it will be rewritten in an unencrypted format. Once you decide to proceed, you are prompted to enter the data file password.

Attaching a Password to a View

Execute the File Password View Attach command to add or change a password for a view. You are prompted for the new password, and again for verification.

Passwords on views are automatically encrypted. When you load a view to which a passworded data file is attached, you are prompted for only the password of the view, because the passwords of the data files are contained in the view definition.

When you create a new data file and assign a password at the time of creation, both the data file and the standard view will have the same password. Later, you may use the File Password View Attach command if you want to change the password of the view.

Removing a Password from a View

To remove a password from a view, execute the File Password View Remove command. You are prompted to enter the password for the view.

Chapter Summary

The File Create and File Modify command are of primary importance if you are building your own application. Both standard and custom views can be protected by passwords to provide security for sensitive applications. You can build databases and views from scratch or you can duplicate them from originals.

A standard view displays all the fields of the file in the Browse mode. You cannot apply any special rules, edit masks, or display formats to the fields in a standard view. A custom view, however, can contain fields from multiple files simultaneously, and enables you to change the display format, create an edit mask, and permit messages to be displayed for each field during data entry.

This chapter introduced the commands you use to make a view active, to deactivate a view, and to ensure the safe storage of your data on disk.

Entering, Deleting, and Viewing Data

This chapter discusses entering data from the keyboard. You learn how to enter data into both custom and standard views and how to update the views. This chapter introduces the Data Delete and the Data Utilities Purge commands, which you can use to prevent the processing of database records or to remove records from the database.

Although some applications rely heavily on manipulation of views and printed reports, many other applications are more screen oriented. In such applications, seeing the view on-screen is most important. This chapter discusses the primary ways of seeing views, switching between them, and looking at different portions of your views.

Entering Data

To enter new records into your database, you use the Data Enter command; the Quick key is Alt-E. When you execute the command, you see an input representation of the view in the current window. Figure 3.1 shows an example of a data-entry screen using a custom view.

Note that the optional data-entry message is displayed on the command line. In this example, Social Security Number is the data-entry message. Both this special entry message and the prompting order were established during the creation of the view. Figure 3.2 shows a data-entry form using a standard view.

Fig. 3.1.

Custom view data-entry screen.

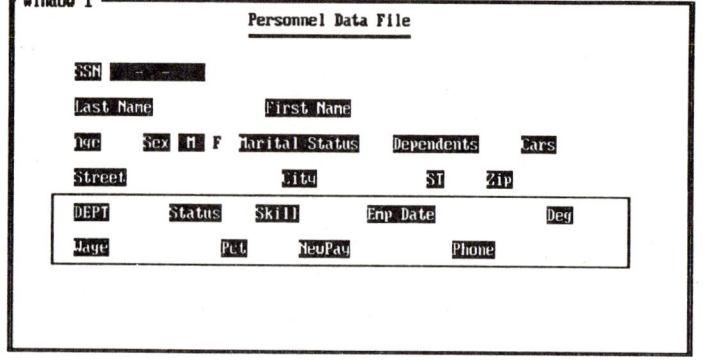

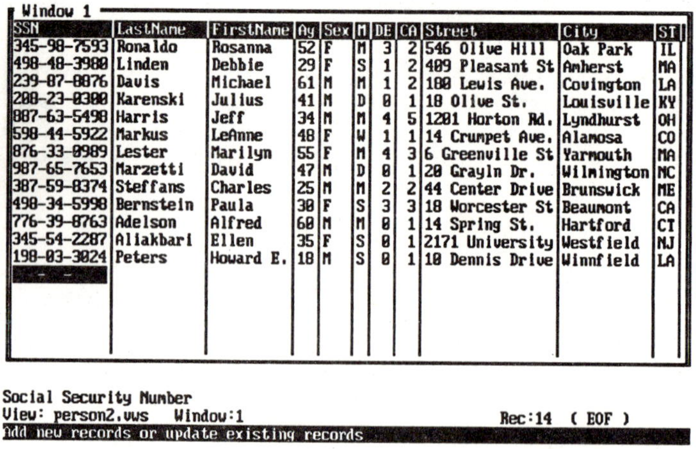

Fig. 3.2.

A standard view data-entry screen.

When using a custom view, you see just one record at a time. With the standard view, data entry is comparable to the spreadsheet module, allowing you to see both previous and successive entries. In either case, you can use the following function keys:

- F1 Help
- F2 Enter the system date
- F3 Return to the previous field
- F4 Advance to the next field
- F5 Return to the previous record
- F6 Advance to the next record. Use this key if you do not need to enter data into remaining fields of the record
- F7 Reformat a multiple line alpha field

Chapter 3: Entering, Deleting, and Viewing Data

F8   Delete the field contents, regardless of cursor position in the field
F9   Repeat the field contents from the last record accessed; this may or may not be the previous record in the file
F10   Enter the value and advance to next field
Esc   Return to the command menu

When entering data, you can press either Enter to advance to the next field or F10. When you create a view, you can elect to advance automatically when the field is full. If you have established mandatory fields, you cannot bypass them.

Date entries can be made in the MM/DD/YY format; the current century is assumed. If you want to enter the current system date, press the F2 key. Use the Alt-F2 key to enter the current time into a time field. When entering numerics, only numbers, the decimal point, and a minus sign can be used; do not try to enter a dollar sign or a comma. Both the decimal point and the decimal digits can be omitted if the decimals are zero.

When you have completed entering your new records, press Esc to return to the command level. If you press Esc in the middle of a record, you are prompted:

```
Save current changes to record? (y/n)
```

Press *N* if you want to discard the field entries for the current record; otherwise, press *Y* to retain them. Records you entered previously in the same session are not affected.

If your view has key fields, the keys are updated automatically when you return to the command level. In previous Smart versions, you were prompted to update the keys; this additional step has become unnecessary with SmartWare II.

Some additional keyboard keys are worth noting. The Insert mode status is important if you need to change a field's contents. The status of the Ins key is not displayed, but if the Insert mode is on, a letter you type in the middle of a field slides the other characters to the right. If the Insert mode is off, a new letter overlays the character at the current cursor position.

Use the F7 key to reformat a multiple-line alphanumeric field. When possible, the F7 key breaks the entry between words, similar to word wrapping in the Word Processor. The effect is cosmetic, however. Other commands and operations on the field, such as reporting, are not affected one way or the other.

There is a built-in calculator you can use while in the Data Entry mode. If you are about to enter a field for which you need to reach for your venerable calculator, press Alt-T instead. The Field Text Editor screen is displayed, enabling you to enter your formula or calculation. Any literals, fields, or SmartWare functions are available. Press F5 to perform the calculation and display the results on the status line. If you are satisfied with the result, erase the formula, using the F8 key for a single-line formula or Alt-F2 for a multiple-line formula. Use Ctrl-C to insert the result on the first line of the editor, and use F10 to return to the Data Entry mode and automatically insert the results of the formula calculation into the field. (In previous versions of Smart, the Alt-K invoked the calculator to perform this task.)

If you have created a manually calculated field, press Alt-F5 to display the calculation results when the cursor is on the field. You can override the results if desired.

A word of caution: Although it is possible to enter a double quotation mark into an alpha field, it is not recommended. Quotation marks are used to delineate alpha fields when records are exported to external files in either the ASCII or Smart formats. An extra quotation mark in the middle of one of these fields will surely confuse things.

Remember that when you create a view, certain fields can be designated as *read-only* or as *mandatory*. Because a read-only field is bypassed, it is probably of little value in a view used for initial data entry. If you make a field mandatory, you are required to enter data into the field. If you neglect to enter data into a mandatory field, you receive the following error message:

    Mandatory entry. Please enter something into field [field]

If you have specified an error rule, your own error message is displayed. An example of an error message for the AGE field is as follows:

    Employee age must be between 18 and 70.

A field with a character-specific input mask accepts only the characters in the mask. If the mask is used to delineate portions of the input, such as the hyphens in the SSN field, the masking characters are automatically skipped during entry.

Updating Data

Changing the contents of an existing record is identical to adding a new record. Instead of executing the Data Enter command (or Alt-E) to display a blank record, find the record you want to change and press the Esc key to initiate the Data Update mode. Figure 3.3 shows a custom-view record in a the process of being updated.

You use the same function keys in the Data Update mode as you use in the Data Entry mode. Figure 3.4 shows the update process in a standard view.

Note that when you update a file using the standard view, you can move from record to record, just as you can move the cursor from row to row in the Spreadsheet; accessing the same field in multiple records can be quite easy when you use a standard view.

When using either a custom view or the standard view, pay attention to the status of your Ins key, particularly because the status is not shown on-screen. If the Insert mode is on, a letter you type in the middle of a field pushes the other characters to the right. If the Insert mode is off, a new letter overlays the character at the current cursor position.

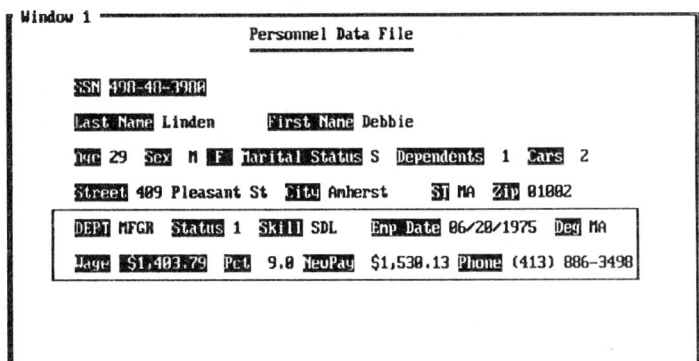

Fig. 3.3.

Updating a record in a custom view.

Window 1

SSN	LastName	FirstName	Ag	Sex	M	DE	CA	Street	City	ST
198-03-3024	Peters	Howard E.	18	M	S	0	1	10 Dennis Drive	Winnfield	LA
208-23-0300	Karenski	Julius	41	M	D	0	1	10 Olive St.	Louisville	KY
239-07-0076	Davis	Michael	61	M	M	1	2	100 Lewis Ave.	Covington	LA
345-54-2287	Aliakbari	Ellen	35	F	S	0	1	2171 University	Westfield	NJ
345-98-7593	Ronaldo	Rosanna	52	F	M	3	2	546 Olive Hill	Oak Park	IL
387-59-0374	Steffans	Charles	25	M	M	2	2	44 Center Drive	Brunswick	ME
498-34-5998	Bernstein	Paula	30	F	S	3	3	10 Worcester St	Beaumont	CA
498-48-3988	Linden	Debbie	29	F	S	1	2	409 Pleasant St	Amherst	MA
598-44-5922	Markus	LeAnne	40	F	W	1	1	14 Crumpet Ave.	Alamosa	CO
776-39-0763	Adelson	Alfred	60	M	M	0	1	14 Spring St.	Hartford	CT
876-33-0989	Lester	Marilyn	55	F	M	4	3	6 Greenville St	Yarmouth	MA
887-63-5498	Harris	Jeff	34	M	M	4	5	1201 Horton Rd.	Lyndhurst	OH
987-65-7653	Marzetti	David	47	M	D	0	1	20 Grayln Dr.	Wilmington	NC

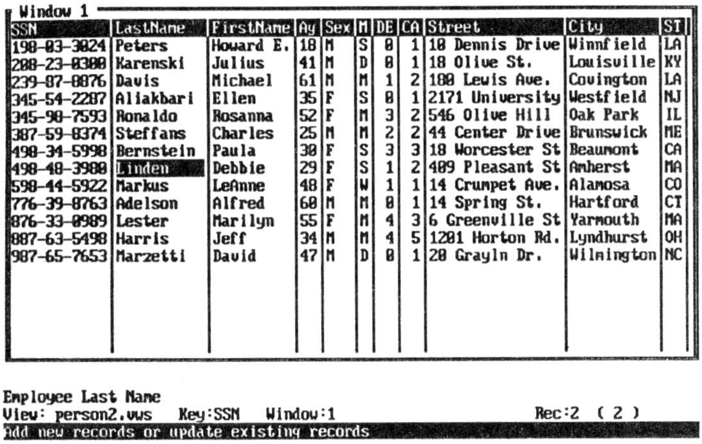

Fig. 3.4.

Updating a record in a standard view.

When using the Data Enter command, you are always adding records to the physical end of the file. When you update a view, you can work in any established order. The order can be based on a key or on an index from either the Data Query or Order Sort commands; records can also be updated in the order in which they were entered. Change the order of your file to make updating as quick and easy as possible.

The Data Entry mode is actually a special form of updating. When in the Data Update mode, if you advance from record to record until you get to the end of your file, you will be in the Data Entry mode. In either case, press Esc to return to the Command mode.

If your view contains a table, as in figure 3.5, you can still use the F3 and F4 keys to move the cursor from field to field.

Fig. 3.5.

Updating a view with embedded table.

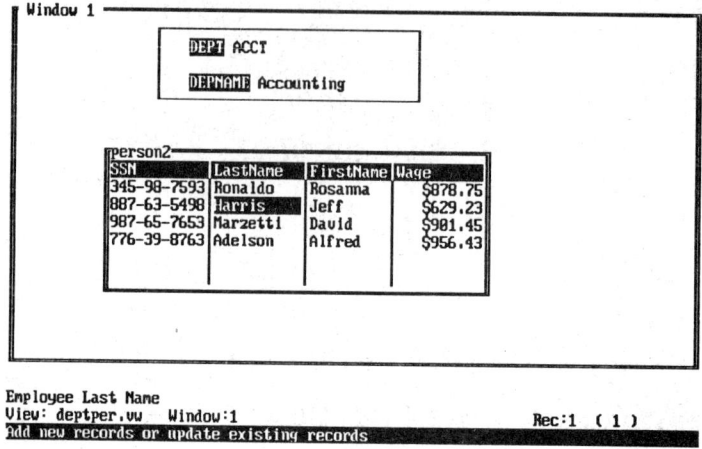

Press the F4 or Enter to move into the table area; use the F3 key to move the cursor from the first column of any table row back into the main view area. If there is a main area field beyond the table, the F4 key moves the cursor from the last column of any table row to that field. Another way to exit the table is to press F10. If you move the cursor down past the last row of any column, you invoke the Data Entry mode for the table.

In the Data Update mode, you can remove a row from the table by pressing Ctrl-F8. The record is actually marked for deletion in the data file but disappears from the view table.

Deleting Records

At some time, you may no longer carry a particular product, or an employee may have left the company. In such a case, you want to delete the inactive records from the file. By purging deleted records, you will not only save disk space, but you also may find that your application runs faster.

Deleting records is a two-step process in the SmartWare II Database. First, you mark main view area records for deletion with Data Delete Record command (or Replace Delete in a Query). Next, you use the Data Utilities Purge command to remove deleted records from the file and make additional disk space available. In the SmartWare II Database, deleting a record flags it for deletion but does not remove it from the file. Therefore, you can undelete records, if necessary, before you perform a purge. If a record is deleted, it is noted at the right of the status line.

Marking Records

The Data Delete command has two options:

    Record Table-Record

If the view is a single file view, or if the cursor is in the main file area, when you select Record, the current record is marked for deletion. In figure 3.6, the word DEL at the right of the status line indicates that the record has been marked for deletion.

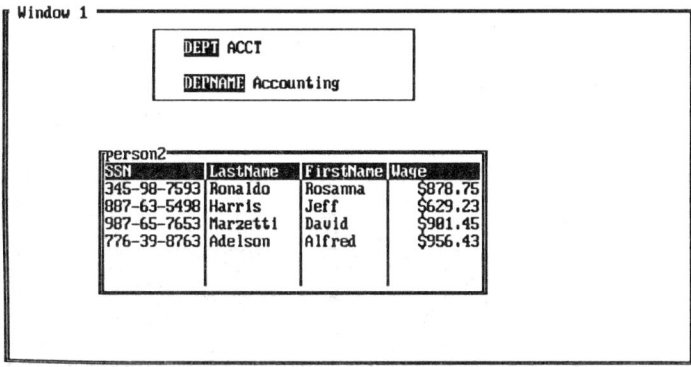

Fig. 3.6.

A record marked for deletion.

The Quick key for the Data Delete Record command is Alt-D. The command is a toggle; execute it once and the record is marked for deletion. If you execute the command again, the record is activated. Although most Database commands do not process deleted records, some of them do. The Print Current-Record and Print View commands print deleted records, but Print Report does not. The Data Query command can be used not only to isolate deleted records, but also to activate them selectively if needed.

If your view contains multiple linked files, you may remember a question in the Edit Links subcommand when you created the view. The question was whether the delete status option should be set to Yes. If you did set it to Yes, deleting the main view record deletes all the records in the view table at one time. When they are deleted, the view table records disappear, although they still exist in the table data file. Execute the Data Delete Record command again to reverse the effects of deleting not only the main view record but also the table records. If the delete status option in the linkage is set to No, deleting the main record has no effect on the delete status or the visibility of the table records.

If you want to delete only certain records within the table area, you first must move the cursor to the table. Use the Data Goto Table command to select the table and move the cursor. Once in the table area, move the cursor to the record you want to delete and execute the Data Delete Table-Record command. The table record is marked for deletion and disappears from the table.

The Data Delete Table-Record command is not a toggle. Because the record disappears from the table, there is no way to move the cursor to it. If you accidentally delete the wrong record, load a view in which the file is primary (or the standard view) and undelete the record with the Data Delete Record command.

Removing Records

The Data Delete commands mark records for deletion without removing them from database. If you want to eliminate the records, use the Data Utilities Purge command. Before you can use this command, you must be sure to unload all views to which the file is attached. (Execute the File Display-Active command to see which files are active.)

Because a file that you purge is rewritten, you should back up or make a copy of the file before beginning the process, in case anything goes wrong with your computer or the power goes off. Your regular backup copy may be sufficient, or you can use the Tools File Copy command to copy the database.

When you execute the Data Utilities Purge command, a pop-up menu displays the names of the databases in the current subdirectory. The names of active files are displayed, too, so if you select one that is still loaded, you will receive the following error message:

    Data-file must be unloaded before executing this command

If the message appears and you have selected the correct file, unload all views to which the file is attached and execute the Data Utilities Purge command again. You are prompted as follows:

    Do you have a backup of this file? (y/n)

If you are comfortable with the degree of backup you have, answer *Y* to purge the deleted records.

In SmartWare II, the key file is automatically rebuilt during the Data Utilities Purge command. In previous versions of Smart, you needed to reorganize the keys following a Utilities Purge command.

Viewing Data

When you load a view, it is opened in the current window and you see the first physical record of the main/driver file of the view. The main portion of a view shows you one record at a time from the main/driver file; a table within a view can show you multiple records from other files, which are driven by the driver file simultaneously. To view other main records, you use the F6 key to view the next record and the F5 key to view the preceding record. Pressing Ctrl-Home moves to the first record of a view; Ctrl-End moves to the last record.

Views containing many fields or much text may occupy more than one page. You can use the PgDn key to display the next page of the same record and PgUp the display the preceding page. A view also can extend horizontally beyond the limits of your monitor screen; use the left- and right-arrow keys to see the complete view.

Browsing Your Data

Often, you will want to see several records at one time. If you are looking for the record of a particular individual or customer, for example, you may want to view an entire page of records. You can view several records in a row and column mode by using the Data Browse command.

In Browse mode, the entire window is filled with as many records and fields as the window will hold (see fig. 3.7).

```
┌ Window 1 ─────────────────────────────────────────────────────────┐
│SSN        │Last Name │First Nam│Ag│Sex│M│De│Ca│Street          │City     │
│345-98-7593│Ronaldo   │Rosanna  │52│F  │M│3 │2 │546 Olive Hill  │Oak Park │
│498-48-3988│Linden    │Debbie   │29│F  │S│1 │2 │489 Pleasant St │Amherst  │
│239-87-0876│Davis     │Michael  │61│M  │M│1 │2 │188 Lewis Ave.  │Covington│
│288-23-0300│Karenski  │Julius   │41│M  │D│0 │1 │18 Olive St.    │Louisville│
│887-63-5498│Harris    │Jeff     │34│M  │M│4 │5 │1281 Horton Rd. │Lyndhurst│
│598-44-5922│Markus    │LeAnne   │48│F  │W│1 │1 │14 Crumpet Ave. │Alamosa  │
│876-33-0989│Lester    │Marilyn  │55│F  │M│4 │3 │6 Greenville St │Yarmouth │
│987-65-7653│Marzetti  │David    │47│M  │D│0 │1 │28 Grayln Dr.   │Wilmington│
│387-59-8374│Steffans  │Charles  │25│M  │M│2 │2 │44 Center Drive │Brunswick│
│498-34-5998│Bernstein │Paula    │30│F  │S│3 │3 │18 Worcester St │Beaumont │
│776-39-8763│Adelson   │Alfred   │60│M  │M│0 │1 │14 Spring St.   │Hartford │
│345-54-2287│Aliakbari │Ellen    │35│F  │S│0 │1 │2171 University │Westfield│
│198-03-3024│Peters    │Howard E.│18│M  │S│0 │1 │18 Dennis Drive │Winnfield│
│                                                                            │
└────────────────────────────────────────────────────────────────────────────┘
Menu: Data File Order Print Tools Window Help Remember Quit
View: person2.vv   Window:1                        Rec:1 ( 1 )
Browse Cross-Tabs Delete Enter Find Goto Query Relate Send Transact Utilities
```

Fig. 3.7.

Information displayed in the Browse mode.

The column headings are the field names, some of which are truncated because the fields are shorter than their names. For example, although the name of the fourth field is AGE, only AG shows because the field is two digits wide. Fields that use a bar menu for data entry will show more of the field name.

When you invoke Browse mode, the status line does not change. The highlight block points to the current record; the same record remains current as in the Normal mode. You can move the highlight block to the preceding record by pressing

F5 or the up-arrow key, or to the following record by pressing F6 or the down-arrow key.

To display your records in the Browse mode, execute the Data Browse command. The options for this command are as follows:

    All Fields Off

To display all fields, select All; the Quick key for this option is Alt-B. The Quick key is a toggle; press it again, and it turns off the Browse mode, the equivalent of Data Browse Off.

If you want to view only certain fields in the Browse mode, select the Fields option. You are prompted to select the fields you want to view and work with. You can select the fields in any order. Be aware, however, than once you have selected fields to Browse, other fields will not be available for many commands. If, for example, you have not selected the AGE field in the Data Browse command, you cannot Query or Sort on this field—a change from earlier Smart versions. In this case, you should perform the Data Query or Order Sort command before you execute the Data Browse command.

The Browse mode can be useful for selecting records that need further processing. To change an employee record, for example, you move the arrow to the employee's name and then press Esc to update the record. At the conclusion of the update process, the screen remains in the Browse mode.

The PgUp and PgDn keys work differently in Browse mode than they do in Normal mode. Use the PgUp key to scroll up one window page and the PgDn key to scroll down one window page. If you are at the top of a view, PgUp moves the pointer to the first record of that view.

The Home and End keys move the pointer to the first and last records displayed on-screen. Ctrl-Home and Ctrl-End move to the first and last records in the view respectively.

Sometimes a view contains more fields than can be viewed at one time on-screen. In such cases, you can use the right-arrow to scroll one field to the right and the left-arrow to scroll one field to the left. To scroll one full screen to the right or left, use the Ctrl-right-arrow or Ctrl-left-arrow key combinations. In previous versions of Smart, using the Control key with either the right or left arrow key would shift the screen one character at a time.

Only custom views can be placed into the Browse mode; standard views, by definition, are always in the Browse, row and column mode. The Browse mode of a custom screen can appear very similar to a standard view. In figure 3.8, the upper window is a browsed custom view and the lower window is the corresponding standard view.

Chapter 3: Entering, Deleting, and Viewing Data **67**

```
┌ Window 1 ─────────────────────────────────────────────────────────┐
│SSN         │Last Name │First Nam│Ag│Sex│M│De│Ca│Street          │City      │
│345-98-7593│Ronaldo   │Rosanna  │52│F  │M │3 │2 │546 Olive Hill  │Oak Park  │
│498-48-3980│Linden    │Debbie   │29│F  │S │1 │2 │409 Pleasant St│Amherst   │
│239-87-8876│Davis     │Michael  │61│M  │M │1 │2 │100 Lewis Ave. │Covington │
│288-23-0300│Karenski  │Julius   │41│M  │D │0 │1 │18 Olive St.   │Louisville│
│887-63-5498│Harris    │Jeff     │34│M  │M │4 │5 │1201 Horton Rd.│Lyndhurst │
│598-44-5922│Markus    │LeAnne   │48│F  │W │1 │1 │14 Crumpet Ave.│Alamosa   │
┌ Window 2 ─────────────────────────────────────────────────────────┐
│SSN         │LastName  │FirstName│Ag│Sex│M│DE│CA│Street          │City      │ST│
│345-98-7593│Ronaldo   │Rosanna  │52│F  │M │3 │2 │546 Olive Hill  │Oak Park  │IL│
│498-48-3980│Linden    │Debbie   │29│F  │S │1 │2 │409 Pleasant St│Amherst   │MA│
│239-87-8876│Davis     │Michael  │61│M  │M │1 │2 │100 Lewis Ave. │Covington │LA│
│288-23-0300│Karenski  │Julius   │41│M  │D │0 │1 │18 Olive St.   │Louisville│KY│
│887-63-5498│Harris    │Jeff     │34│M  │M │4 │5 │1201 Horton Rd.│Lyndhurst │OH│
│598-44-5922│Markus    │LeAnne   │48│F  │W │1 │1 │14 Crumpet Ave.│Alamosa   │CO│
│876-33-0989│Lester    │Marilyn  │55│F  │M │4 │3 │6 Greenville St│Yarmouth  │MA│
│987-65-7653│Marzetti  │David    │47│M  │D │0 │1 │20 Grayln Dr.  │Wilmington│NC│
│387-59-8374│Steffans  │Charles  │25│M  │M │2 │2 │44 Center Drive│Brunswick │ME│

Menu: Data File Order Print Tools Window Help Remember Quit
View: person2.vws   Window:2                        Rec:1 ( 1 )
Browse Cross-Tabs Delete Enter Find Goto Query Relate Send Transact Utilities
```

Fig. 3.8.

Browsed view versus standard view.

In the Browse mode, the column headings of the custom view are the view names, which may vary from the database field names. Note that in figure 3.8, the second column is labeled Last Name for the custom view but LastName for the standard view. The differences between the two types of views become even more apparent when you update or enter new records. A custom view reverts to the non-Browse mode temporarily when you maintain your data; a standard view lets you update or add new data while maintaining the row and column appearance.

Doing Windows

The SmartWare II Database can display multiple windows simultaneously, as seen in figure 3.8. This powerful feature is used to display several views concurrently, link them by a common field, or display different portions of one view or file. If you need to see more data than a small window can display, you can zoom the current window at any time so that it fills the monitor screen.

Splitting the Screen

The Window Split command is used to create additional windows on your monitor screen. The options are as follows:

    Horizontal Vertical

There are two Quick keys for the Window Split command: Alt-H splits the screen horizontally, and Alt-V splits it vertically.

When you select either option, move the cursor to the upper left corner of the location you have chosen for the new window and press Enter. You are prompted:

    Position the dividing line; then press Enter

If you select Vertical, move the cursor to the right; if you select Horizontal, move the cursor down. A minimum amount of space is required; if you do not provide enough space, you will receive the error message:

    Window too small

The result of a horizontal split is shown in figure 3.9. The current window is bordered by a double line (all windows other than the current one are bordered by a single line). The window number is displayed in the upper left corner of the window border, and both the window number and view name are shown on the status line; all status-line information refers to the current window.

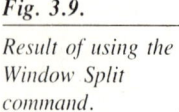

Fig. 3.9.

Result of using the Window Split command.

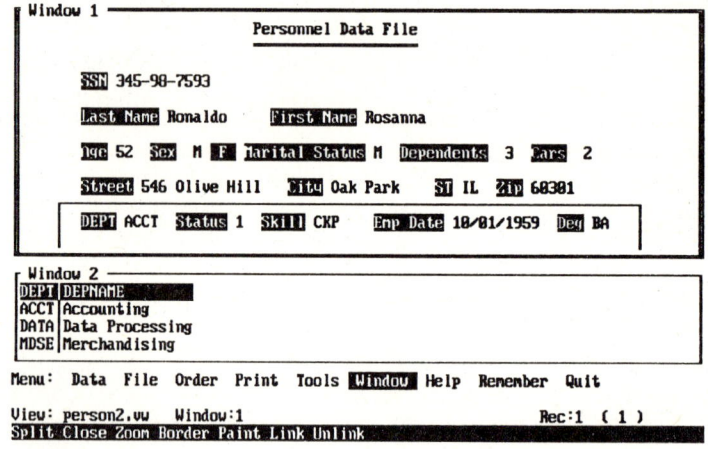

In figure 3.9, the current window number is 1. If you go to the other window, the current window number will be 2.

A new window initially displays the same view as the window from which it was created. Usually, however, you want to have a different view in the new window. To display a different view, you can either go to the window and use the File Load command to load another view or use the Data Goto View command to display an active view.

In the example shown in figure 3.9, the DEPT view has been loaded into window 2. The Browse mode has been initiated. You can invoke the Browse mode in one window without affecting any other window.

You can display as many as 25 windows on a standard monitor screen. If you have a screen or screen driver that can display more than the standard 25 lines by 80 columns, or if you turn off the window borders, you can display even more windows. The more windows you have, however, the less you can see. In many cases, multiple windows are convenient; in other cases, they are mandatory for using certain commands.

Closing Windows

You remove windows with the Window Close command; the Quick key is Alt-W. When you execute the Window Close command, the current window disappears and an adjacent window expands to fill the available screen space. If only one window is active, you cannot close it. Even when you close a window, the view it contained remains active; it is not automatically unloaded. Unlike earlier versions of Smart, however, a view that is not in a window retains its order.

Full-Screen Viewing of a Window

To create a full-screen display of a window, select the Window Zoom command. The Quick F7 key toggles the Zoom display; the Window Zoom command has no options.

Although most commands can be executed while a window is zoomed, you cannot split or close a window in this mode. To execute one of these commands, you must use the Window Zoom command again to return to the multiple-window display.

Linking Two Windows

The Window Link command is used to join two views that share a common field. The linking fields in both views must be of the same data type, and the link field in the link-to view must be a key. Both views in figure 3.10 contain a department code field. The Window Link command can be used to display automatically the record on the top line in window 2, which has a department code field matching that of the current record in window 1.

Although it is necessary for the link-to view to have as a key the field to be used in the linkage, it is not necessary to order the link-to view by the key. (This is a departure from the requirements of earlier Smart versions.) The link-to view can be in either key or physical order. You cannot have the view ordered by an index, or you will receive the following error message when you attempt to execute the link:

```
Cannot process external link; view is in index order
```

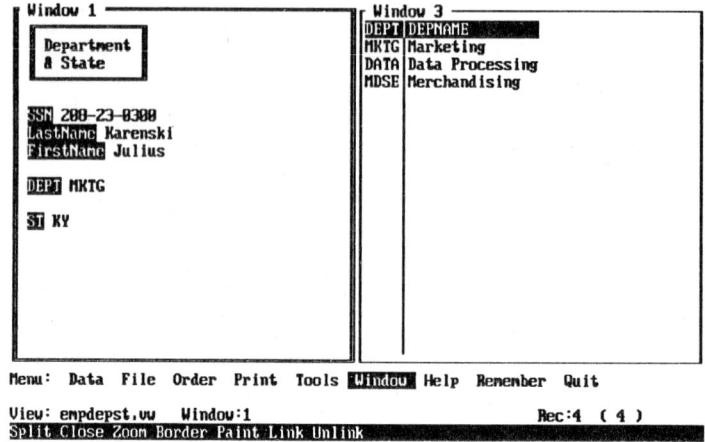

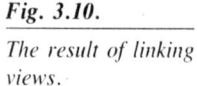

Fig. 3.10.
The result of linking views.

To link two views, make sure that the link-from view is in your current window. When you execute the Window Link command, you are prompted to identify the link-from field. Next, a pop-up window displays the names of the loaded views, and you are prompted to identify the link-to view. Finally, you are prompted to select the link-to field in the link-to view.

Once the link is established, as you change from record to record in the link-from view, the matching record in the link-to view is displayed as the top line in the window. Unlike previous versions of Smart, there is no pointer to identify the matching record. If no match for the link-from field exists, the program beeps.

Unfortunately, only one link can be active from a view at one time. However, you can chain a link from one view to another. View 1 may be linked to view 2, view 2 may be linked to view 3, and so on. Intervening views do not have to be visible in windows for a linkage chain to work.

To remove a linkage, use the Window Unlink command. Your current view must be the link view for the linkage to be broken.

Using the Data Goto Command

The Data Goto command has several functions; the Quick key is F4. The options to the commands are:

    Page Record Table View Window

The first three options are used to view different portions of the current view. The other options allow you to switch views or windows.

When you choose Page, you are asked whether you want to view the next or the preceding page of the current view. This is the same as using the PgDn or PgUp keys.

When you choose Record, you are prompted:

    Next Previous Record-Number

You can go to the next or preceding logical record in your view. These options have the same effect as the F6 and F5 function keys.

If you select Record-Number, you are asked to supply a record number. If the view is ordered by an index, you enter a logical record number. If the view is in physical order or is ordered by a key, the record number is physical.

In earlier versions of Smart, you could respond to the Record-Number option with either $+n$ to move the cursor forward n number of records or $-n$ to move back n number of records. The exact equivalent is not available in the SmartWare II Database. The Quick keys Alt-F5 and Alt-F6 to skip records are no longer available.

Although entering a $+3$, for example, does not create an error message, the cursor simply goes to record number 3; the plus sign is ignored. If you want to skip three records, however, you can respond *record* $+3$ at the prompt for the record number. Typing *record* -3 moves you back three records. Remember, however, that if the view is in either physical or key order, record numbers are physical, rather than logical. Only if the view is ordered by an index are record numbers logical.

If the view has a table and you want to be able to look at additional records in the table beyond those shown, select the Table option. You are prompted to identify the name of the table. Once you have accessed the table, use the cursor-control keys to go from record to record.

Use the Data Goto View command to return to the main portion of the view.

To display a different view in the current window, select the View option. The view you want to display must be active at the time you execute the command; if it is not active, use the File Load command.

When you execute the Data Goto View command, a pop-up window displays the names of the active views. Select the view you want to display in the current window and press Enter. The view retains its order even when it is in the background, and the view is not automatically in sequential or physical order. (This is a change from earlier Smart versions.)

To change your current window, select the Window option and enter the number of the window you want. Instead of this command, you can use the Quick keys Alt-F8 to go to the next sequentially numbered window or Alt-F7 to go to the preceding window. If only two windows are open, you can use either key to toggle between them. Note that the current window has a double-line border and that the current window number is displayed in the status line.

Chapter Summary

So that you can work easily with your data, the SmartWare II Database provides several useful ways for creating custom and standard views, entering data, and then viewing your data. Using either a standard view or a custom view, you can display all the fields for one record simultaneously.

You use the Browse mode when you want to view several records at the same time. In the Browse mode, you can specify the fields you want to see and can arrange them in the order that is best for you. Remember, however, that the fields you do not select are not available for use in other commands while in the Browse mode.

Using the SmartWare II windowing capabilities, you can display multiple views simultaneously; you also can link views, relating one to another.

Locating, Selecting, and Arranging Data

You know that when you are looking for the record of a specific employee in your personnel file, you can use the Data Browse command to display a full screen of records at one time. You can advance manually through the view until you find the record you want. If employees are listed in alphabetical order by last name, finding a specific person is certainly easier. But what if the file contains several thousand records? Suppose that the search pattern is complex, and you are trying to find records of employees earning less than $875, for example. The Data Find command provides the solution.

Selecting Records with the Data Find Command

You use the Data Find command to search through your file and display a record that meets specified conditions, or criteria. You can search for records containing values that are equal to the criterion you specify, records containing values that are greater than or less than your criterion, or records that simply contain the search value somewhere in the designated field. You can search the whole file, search forward from the current record, or even search backward through the file. There are options for handling upper- and lowercase differences and whole-word conditions.

Although some of the options work on only alphanumeric fields, the Data Find command operates on all types of data fields. The Quick key is F3.

The Data Find command is used to search for one record at a time. For example, you may search for a record so that you can view it or change the contents. If you want to find all the records meeting certain conditions, use the Data Query command covered later in this chapter. You also should use the Data Query if the search condition is more complicated than you can specify in the Data Find command.

Selecting Field Names

When you execute the Data Find command, a pop-up menu of field names is displayed. Use the cursor-control keys to move to the desired search field. You can press F6 to select the correct field, or simply press Enter; you also can type the field name on the prompt line. Most of the time you will probably select only one field to search. You can search multiple fields simultaneously; in such a case, you would find the record in which any of the fields match your search criterion. In figure 4.1, the Wage field has been selected. Unless you are performing a special binary search, you can select either a data file field or a view field.

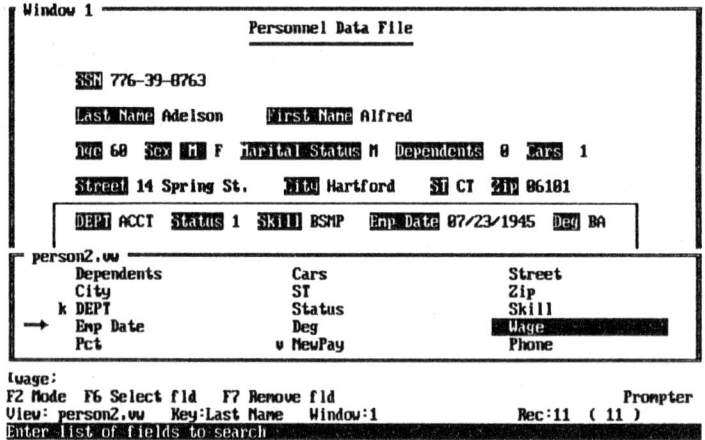

Fig. 4.1.

Data file field selection.

Using Logical Operators in a Search

When you have selected a field, you are shown a menu of logical operators you can use to match your search value against the file contents (see fig. 4.2).

You should select the Equal option to search for field contents that match exactly the text or value you supply in the search criterion. If you are looking for the record of a particular employee, for example, use the Equal option to match the employee's last name or Social Security number.

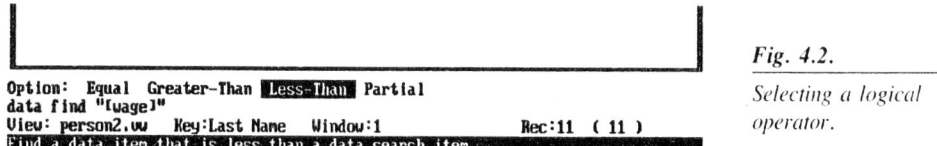

Fig. 4.2.
Selecting a logical operator.

Select Greater-Than or Less-Than if you are searching for a record with a field value that is either greater than or less than the value you supply. (Although you will usually use these options with numeric data, they work with alpha and inverted fields, too.)

Use the Partial option if you are searching for a word or a string of characters that is somewhere in an alpha or an inverted field. The Partial option would find *Green* in the address *6 Greenville St.*

Entering your Search Criterion

After you select a logical search operator, you are prompted to enter your search criterion:

    Enter the data search item:

Type the value or string of characters for which you are searching (see fig. 4.3.) If the field is alpha, do not use quotation marks, even if there is a space in the middle of the string; only if there is a trailing space after the word do you need beginning and ending quotation marks.

Fig. 4.3.
Entering the data search item.

Selecting Data Find Options

After you enter the search item, or criterion, you are prompted to enter additional option specifications (see fig. 4.4). Press the initial letter of each option you want to use; options can be used in combination and can be entered in any order. Press Enter after you have indicated the options that you want to use.

```
Enter Options:
data find "[wage]" less-than "675" options
B Backward  F Forward  G Global  I Ignore case  W Whole words only
Enter search option
```

Fig. 4.4.

Data Find options.

The Backward option searches from the current record to the beginning of the view. The Global option always searches the whole view from the beginning, regardless of the current record position. If you specify Forward, or if you do not enter a directional option at all, the search will begin with the current record and go to the end of the view. The search of the view is based on the logical order.

The Ignore Case option disregards the case of both the field contents and the search criterion. Thus you do not have to remember whether you entered names or other alphabetic data in upper- or lowercase.

The Whole Words Only option finds records in which the search string is an entire word—that is, a word with either a blank or a field terminator at both ends. (This option should be used with the Partial operator only.) If an employee lives on Green street, for example, you can search for the whole word and find *Green* without finding *Greenville*.

After you have entered the search options, the program begins looking through the file to find the first record that meets your search criterion. If a record is found, it is displayed, and you see the message shown in figure 4.5.

```
Window 1
                         Personnel Data File

    SSN 887-63-5498

    Last Name Harris        First Name Jeff

    Age 34  Sex  MI  F  Marital Status M  Dependents  4  Cars  5

    Street 1281 Horton Rd.  City Lyndhurst   ST OH  Zip 44124

    DEPT ACCT  Status 1  Skill KPR     Emp Date 07/01/1970  Deg BA

    Wage     $629.23  Pct  9.2  NewPay     $687.12 Phone (614) 776-3398

Data found in [Wage].  Continue search?  (y/n)

View: person2.vw   Window:1                              Rec:5  ( 5 )
Enter search option
```

Fig. 4.5.

A record is found.

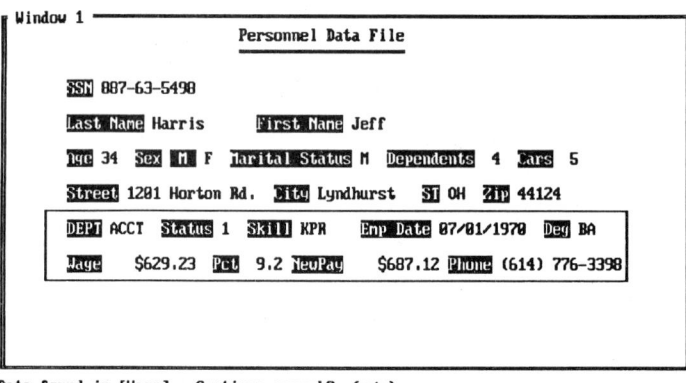

If this is not the record you want, press Y to continue the search (don't press Enter). If another record meets the criterion, it is displayed, and you are prompted again. If no more records satisfy the search, you see the following message:

```
No more occurrences of data, press any key
```

When you press a key, the current record becomes the last record that met the search criteria. If no records met the criteria, you see the message:

```
End of search without finding data, press any key
```

After you press a key, the current record remains the same as when you invoked the Data Find command.

If the search is successful and you find the record you want, press N in response to the prompt; the record is displayed and you are returned to the menu. You can execute any command, such as an update. If you want to continue to search your data file, the Alt-R Quick key repeats the most recent Data Find command. (If you selected the Global search option and stopped at the first find, use the Alt-R Quick key to return to the same record.)

Optimized Data Find

The Data Find command searches the file record by record, beginning at the position you specify. Each record is matched to the search criterion. This search method can be compared to thumbing through a stack of index cards, looking for the record of an employee with a specific Social Security number. Under a set of exact conditions, however, you can perform an optimized binary search, the fastest search mode possible. The specific conditions are as follows:

1. The field on which you want to search must be the major field of a key. These major key fields are marked with a lowercase *k* in pop-up field menus. Unlike previous versions of Smart, the view does not have to be ordered by the key field, however.

2. The search must apply to just a single field.

3. You must use the Equal search operator.

4. You cannot use the Ignore Case option; use the Global option. (You can omit the Global option if the view is ordered by the key field.)

If you have a large file or if you need to find records quickly, the optimized binary search is better than the sequential search technique. If you need to locate inventory quantities quickly, for instance, you can search for the part-number field of your inventory view in just a few seconds, even if thousands of part numbers are contained in your database. If you performed the search without this binary search technique, it might take 15 to 20 minutes, depending on the amount of data in the file and the type of hardware you have.

If the program finds an exact match, the first matching record is displayed, and you are asked whether you want to continue the search. If an exact match is not found, the system stops at the record containing the next highest value beyond the search item, and the following message is displayed:

```
Data not found; displaying closest match, press any key
```

Frequently you can save time by entering an abbreviation for a name, rather than typing the full name in a search. You can use the search string *Kar* to locate the record containing the last name *Karenski*. However, unlike previous versions of Smart, you must pay attention to capitalization if you use this technique. Because key fields are organized in the ASCII sequence, all lowercase letters are sorted after the uppercase letters. Thus if your search string is *kar* rather than *Kar,* all the uppercase entries will be bypassed. You cannot specify Ignore Case if you want to use the optimized, binary-search method.

Using the Data Query Command

No command in the SmartWare II Database is more powerful, yet more misunderstood, than the Data Query command. You can use Data Query to create an index that enables you to work with just a portion of your data file. The rules for creating the index may be simple or extremely complex. You can enter the rules through the QBE (Query by Example) selection procedure, or for the maximum degree of flexibility, the view expression facility. You can select records at either the high or low end of field values—the five top sales representatives in the company, for example.

The Data Query command can provide summary values and statistics about the data in your file, such as the number of customers or total sales volume for a particular territory. You also can use the Data Query command to perform calculations and to change values in database fields—each sales representative over quota receives a 5 percent raise, for example.

The primary function of the Data Query command is to create an index of the records that meet your search criteria. Suppose, for example, that your current database task involves only those employees who live in Massachusetts. You would use the Data Query command (or the Alt-Q Quick key) to select the appropriate employees, create the index, and then order the file by the index. In SmartWare II, a successful selection query automatically orders the file by the index it creates; in previous versions of Smart, ordering was a separate step.

Search criteria can be straightforward, or they can also be complex, involving multiple fields that contain alphanumeric, numeric, date, and other types of data. The QBE facility, introduced with SmartWare II, provides a quick and easy way to perform a record selection. Alternative forms of the QBE offer compound selection criteria.

When you perform a Query, the file is not automatically returned to physical order. This feature of the Data Query command can be a great advantage when you perform multiple, successive record selections. If, for example, your first query limits records to those individuals living in Massachusetts, your next query would begin with that selection. If the next query limits the order to records of individuals who are married, you end up with married Massachusetts residents. As you will see, however, you can apply both of these conditions at once instead of using successive queries.

Note that both the selection of records and the order of their presentation are maintained from query to query. If you have started the file, the order in which the records are presented by the index will be carried through to the next index when you execute a Data Query.

As long as you don't change your data file, an index can be used repeatedly. For instance, if you have a file of products, you can create indexes of products for a particular category, style, or price class. But if you add a new product or change the price class of an existing product, you must re-create the indexes. An index, unlike a key, is not updated automatically. Therefore, indexes should be considered temporary files to be written over or deleted when the base file is changed.

The second most common use of the Data Query command does not create an index at all. Rather, the Data Query command can change the contents of your file, using any calculation or function available in the SmartWare II Database. You can perform the calculation for all records in the file or in the current order. Alternatively, during the query itself, you can specify the conditions under which the calculation and data replacement is to be performed. But because the results of the calculation go directly into the data file, this point can be perilous as well as powerful. If you are unsure about the outcome of a complex query of this type, make a backup copy of the file before proceeding.

Finally, the Data Query command can provide summary values and statistics about the file, using the statistical database (SDb) functions. These functions include FILECOUNT, FILESUM, FILEAVERAGE, and others. (For a complete list of these functions, refer to Chapter 27.)

The Data Query command has five options:

    Create   Execute   Modify   Now   Remove

Once you have created (and modified, if necessary) a query definition, select the Execute option to save and perform the query. But if you want to perform the query immediately, without naming the definition, select the Now option.

Performing an Immediate Query

If you have a query that you are not going to use repeatedly and that is relatively straightforward, use the Data Query Now command. Because you cannot name your query definition when using the Data Query Now command, it is perfect for those interactive, one-time uses.

The Data Query Now command displays the Query Editor screen, showing the fields of the current view, omitting the data (see fig. 4.6).

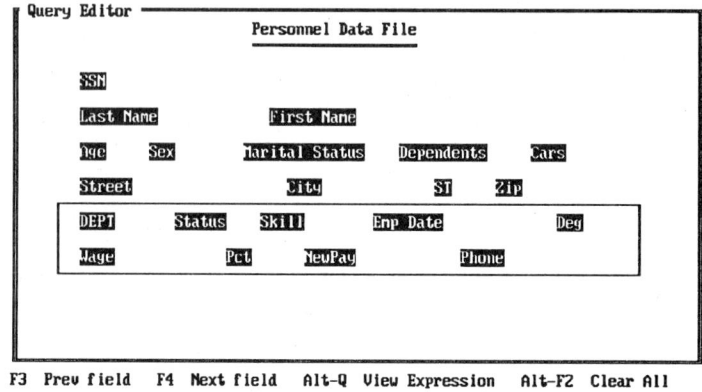

Fig. 4.6.

The Query Editor screen.

If the view is in Browse mode, the Query editor display also is browsed.

When performing a Query Now, you can use either the QBE method, or you can create a View Expression. View Expressions, equivalent to Query definitions in previous versions of Smart, can be more comprehensive and complex than QBE specifications.

QBE (Query By Example)

In the easiest QBE selection specification, simply move the cursor to the field you want to use as the basis for the Query and enter the value you are trying to find. For example, if you want to find all the employees in the accounting department, move the cursor to the DEPT field and enter *ACCT*. The effect is to select all records in which the DEPT field is equal to *ACCT* (see fig. 4.7).

Use the Enter or F4 key to advance to the next field and the F3 key to access the previous field. Once you have entered the search criterion, press the F10 key to execute the query. At the successful completion of the query, the Query Summary is displayed (see fig. 4.8).

The Query Summary shows the number of records searched, the number of records matching the search criteria, and the name of the index created. (When performing Data Query Now, the index QNOW is automatically created; if you are using

Chapter 4: Locating, Selecting, and Arranging D

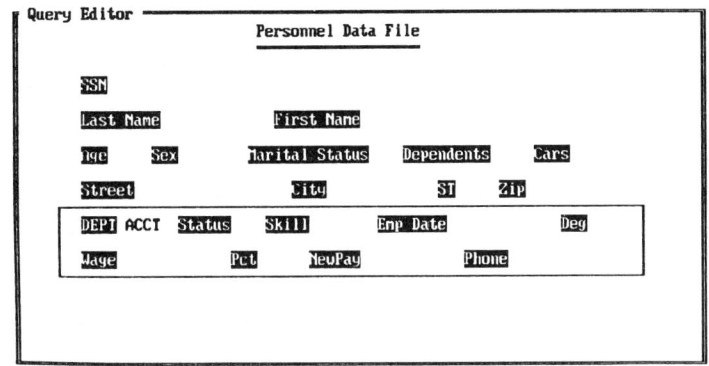

Fig. 4.7.

Query By Example, Field Equality.

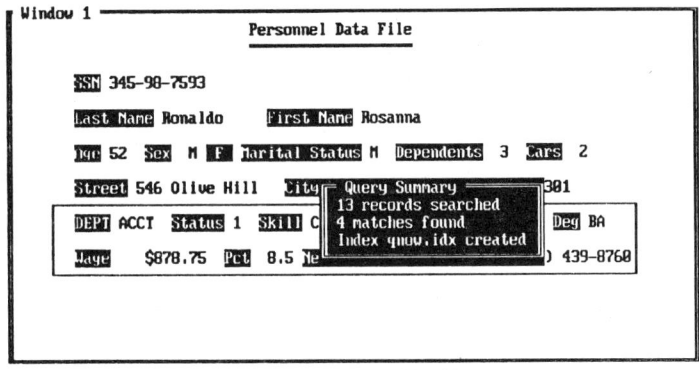

Fig. 4.8.

The Query Summary screen.

QNOW, then QNOW1 will be created.) When you press F10 or Esc, the view orders by the index. Only the records satisfying your search criteria are shown. If you print an employee list at this time, for example, only the employees working in the accounting department would print.

You can perform a compound query using the QBE just as easily. Figure 4.9 shows a query for the male employees in the accounting department.

When you select Query Now again, the previous query specification is maintained. In this example, you only need to add the M selection criterion in the SEX field; the prior query specification still contained *ACCT* for the department. To start fresh, use the Alt-F2 key to clear the previous query definition.

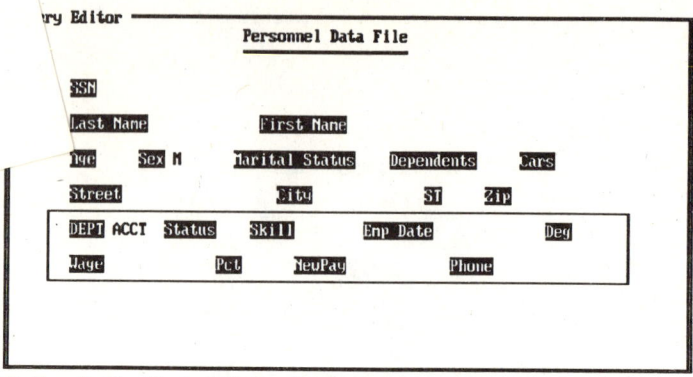

When search criteria for two fields are specified individually, as in this example, a record must meet both criteria simultaneously to be accepted. Thus, employees must be both male (M) and work in the accounting department (ACCT) to pass the test. QBE specifications employ the *and* logical operator unless you specify otherwise.

You can enter compound expressions into single fields in the QBE screen. For example, if you want all employees in either ACCT or SALE, the entry should be as follows:

    ACCT or SALE

Notice that you must use the *or* logical connector in the field. Although in English we might ask for "all employees in accounting and sales," in SmartWare II, employees cannot work in both simultaneously; at least not in our sample database.

You can enter QBE expressions that are longer than the display width of the field: the expressions simply extend past the display area. If you want to view the complete entry after completing the expression, press F3 to return to the field. Your expression will appear on the second command line. Notice that you usually do not have to enclose literals in quotation marks, even though they are alphas. Quotation marks are only necessary with ambiguous entries or when you have leading or trailing blanks.

So far, all of our entries in the QBE fields have specified equality. That is, we have searched for DEPT equal to ACCT, DEPT equal to SALE, and SEX equal to M. You also can specify other relationships if you enter the appropriate symbols:

=	Equal (this is the default)
= =	Equal, regardless of case
!	Contains the string of characters somewhere in the alpha field
!!	The alpha field omits the string

>	Greater than
<	Less than
>=	Greater than or equal (or xxx..)
<=	Less than or equal (or ..xxx)
<>	Not equal

Thus, if you want to search for employees with a wage equal to or greater than 1000, you would enter the following in the WAGE field:

```
>= 1000
```

Using the "double-dot" notation, you can enter the same criterion this way:

```
1000..
```

This double-dot notation is particularly useful for selecting a range. The following entry selects a range of 1000 to 1500, inclusive:

```
1000..1500
```

This method is easier than writing the more complicated expression:

```
>= 1000 and <= 1500
```

Date ranges are easily entered using the double-dot format:

```
7/1/70..12/1/75
```

In previous versions of Smart (using the view expression), this type of date range selection required using the DAYS function to convert the dates to a sequential number from the beginning of the 20th century. Stick to QBE when you can.

As I mentioned earlier, an implied *and* condition always exists between fields in the QBE. You can override this default by entering part of the expression in the QBE format and part in the full expression format. Thus, if you want all Massachusetts employees *or* all accounting employees, enter the following expression in the state (ST) field:

```
MA or [dept] = "ACCT"
```

You should note that the full expression formats have different requirements.

You can use an asterisk (*) or a question mark (?) as wild cards to search for a portion of a string in an alpha field:

```
M*
```

In the department field, this will search for all department codes beginning with the letter M. The asterisk can stand for any number of characters. The question mark stands for an individual character.

```
?A??
```

This expression searches for all department codes with the letter A as the second character, followed by two more characters. These wild cards are valid for alpha strings, date, and time searches.

"*/15/*"

This expression searches for date fields specifying the 15th of any month. (You must use quotation marks with date and time wild card searches if the first character is an asterisk.)

The high and low search criteria select records based on field relationships between records. If you enter *high 5* into the WAGE field, the query selects those records with the five highest wages.

Query View Expressions

If your query expression is too complex for the QBE method, or if you need additional workspace, you can use the Query View Expression. To invoke the View Expression editor, press Alt-Q in the Query Editor (see fig. 4.10).

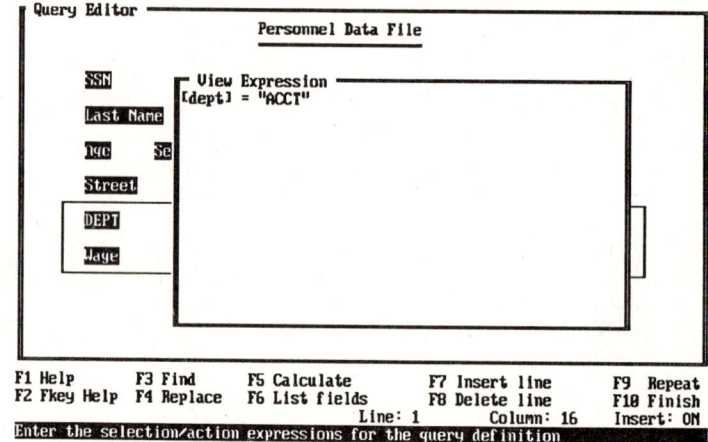

Fig. 4.10.

The Query View Expression Editor screen.

An expression to search for the employees in the accounting department has been entered into the view editor. (Rules for using this editor are similar to those of the Tools Text-Editor.) Query View Expressions differ from QBE expressions in the following ways:

- You must specify the field name in square brackets; use the F6 key to display field names for you.

- The relational operator is required, even if it is an equal sign.

- Alpha strings must be enclosed by quotation marks.

Once you have typed the Query View Expression, press F10 to save the expression. The word View appears on the status line of the Query editor to indicate that a view expression is in effect. Press F10 again to begin the execution of the query.

If a view is in effect when you select the Data Query Now again, the view expression displays automatically. If you do not want to use a view expression, press the F10 to return to the QBE editor and press Alt-F2 to clear the view expression.

In addition to embedding fixed values (such as ACCT) in a Query View Expression, you can include project variables as follows:

    [age] > $age

Under the control of a project file, a value can be assigned to the variable $age. That value substitutes for the variable wherever it appears in the query definition. Thus, without manual intervention, you can use one definition repeatedly under varying conditions.

Functions can be used in query definitions. A range of dates in the Query View Expression format looks like the following:

    days([emp date]) >= days("7/1/70") and
    days([emp date]) <= days("12/1/75")

The days function yields the number of days between the specified date and 12/31/1899. Refer to Chapter 25 for more information about date and time functions.

Be careful when you save the query definition; the system checks only the syntax of your definition, not the contents. Thus, you could type a field name in error, but if the construction of the statement is correct, you would not get an error message until you used the definition.

You may want to use the Query View Expression editor if an *or* condition exists between fields as follows:

    [st] = "MA" or [dept] = "ACCT"

Compare this statement to the QBE equivalent shown previously. Note that the field name, the equal sign, and the quotation marks have been added for the state (ST) field. The remainder of the expression remains the same.

Sometimes the use of parentheses is important for proper evaluation of an expression; the portions of the expression inside the parentheses are evaluated first. Consider the expression in figure 4.11, which searches for two kinds of records:

1. Employees who live in Massachusetts
2. Married employees who work in the accounting department

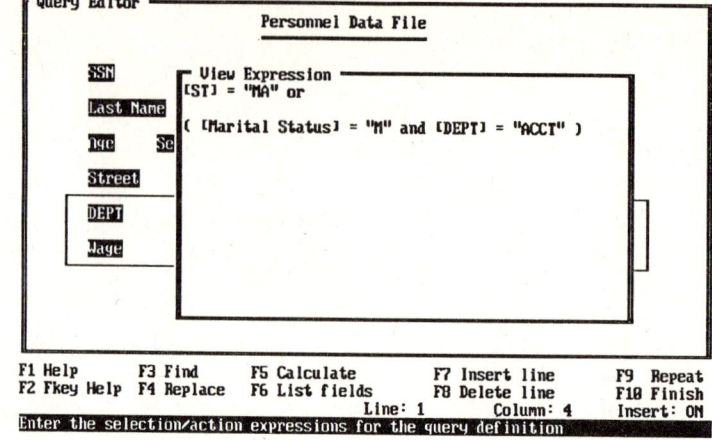

Fig. 4.11.

A compound search criterion with parentheses.

The first criterion selects employees if they live in MA, no matter what their marital status or department. Similarly, the second criterion does not care what state the employee lives in—just that the employee must be married and must work in accounting.

Summary Statistics

In addition to selecting records based on logical criteria, the Data Query command can display summary file statistics. However, as extensive as the capabilities of the query view expressions are, they cannot provide you these quick summary statistics; only the QBE editor provides quick summary statistics. The functions available are the statistical database functions (called SDb functions):

FILEAVERAGE	Average of a field
FILECOUNT	Count of the records
FILEMAX	Maximum of a field
FILEMIN	Minimum of a field
FILESTD	Population standard deviation
FILESTDEV	Sample standard deviation
FILESUM	Sum of a field
FILESUMSQ	Sum of squares of a field
FILEVAR	Variance of a field

Figure 4.12 shows the QBE editor; the query calls for the sum of the wages. Just the name of the function, filesum, is entered into the Wage field.

Chapter 4: Locating, Selecting, and Arranging Data **87**

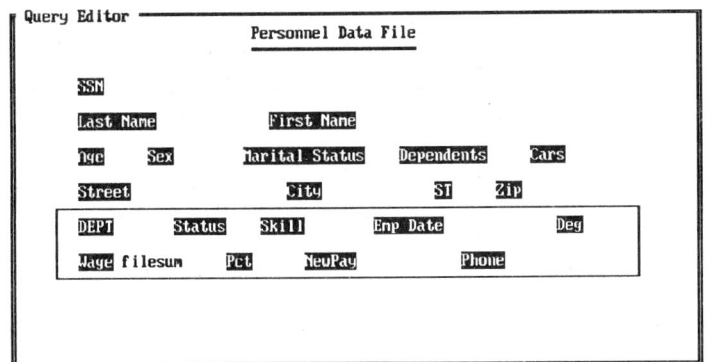

Fig. 4.12.

The QBE editor.

The Query Summary command displays the calculated value (see fig. 4.13).

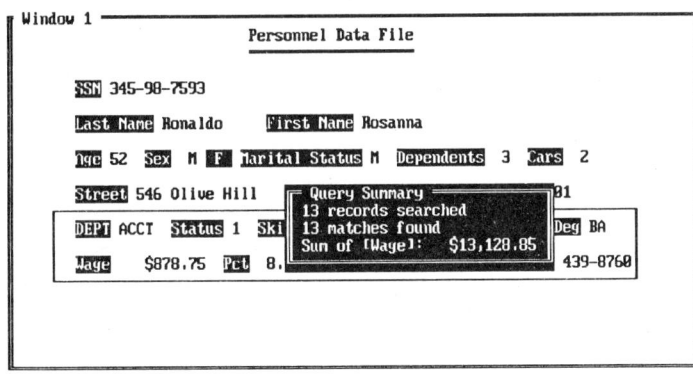

Fig. 4.13.

The Query Summary statistics screen.

If you use the QBE to display file statistics, an index is not created and the order of the view is not changed. Queries that display file statistics operate in the current order of the view. Press Esc or F10 to return to the menu.

You can include selection criteria with the request to display file statistics. The query in figure 4.14 asks for the wage average of the employees in the accounting department.

Fig. 4.14.

QBE Summary statistics with summary selection.

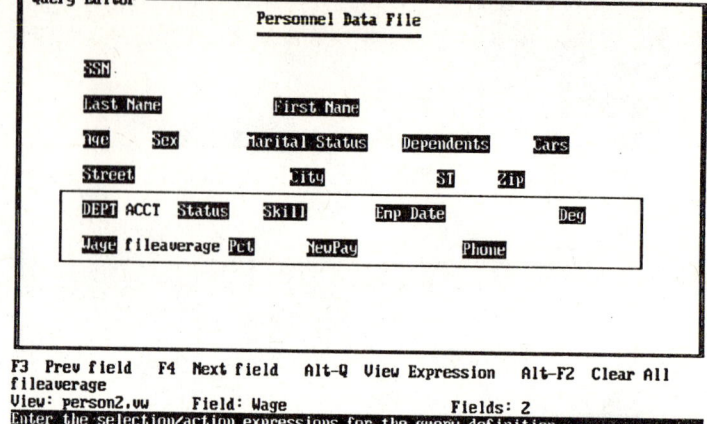

If you need to screen on the same field you are requesting a summary for, enter the criterion first, followed by a comma and the name of the function:

   1000..,fileaverage

This request calls for an average of the wages over $1,000.

The Data Query command does not automatically ignore deleted records. When using a command that processes deleted records in addition to active ones, such as the Print View command, you may want to make the command skip over deleted records. The view expression in figure 4.15 selects only active records in which the wage is greater that 800.

Fig. 4.15.

Skipping deleted records.

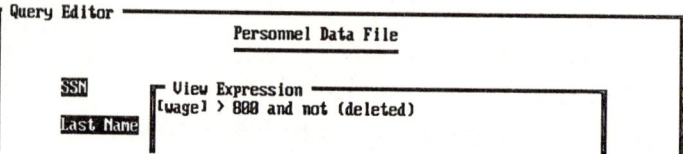

You also can use the not (deleted) criterion in a QBE definition; no equivalent (active) criterion exists.

Data Replacement

The third use of the Data Query command replaces data in your file; you can use either the QBE or Query View Expression editors. The replacement data can be made through all the records of the current order of the view or can be based on selection criteria in the replacing query. In figure 4.16, for individuals in Massachusetts and in the manufacturing department, Wage is replaced by NewPay, and Pct is set at zero.

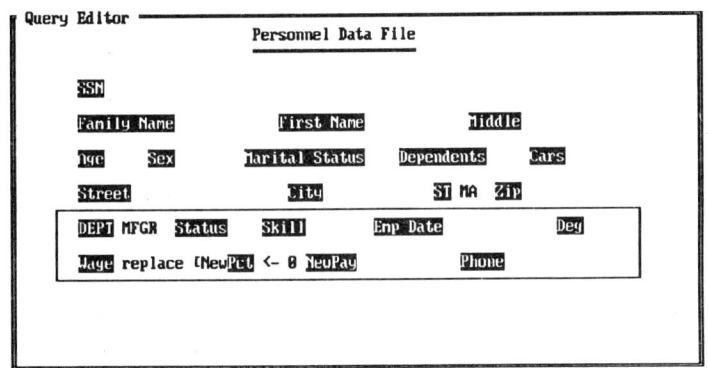

Fig. 4.16.

QBE replacement.

You can use either the word *replace* to indicate the action, as in the Wage field, or a simulated arrow made up of the less-than sign and a dash (<—), as in the Pct field. Note that you can replace multiple fields at one time. The equivalent Query View Expression is shown in figure 4.17.

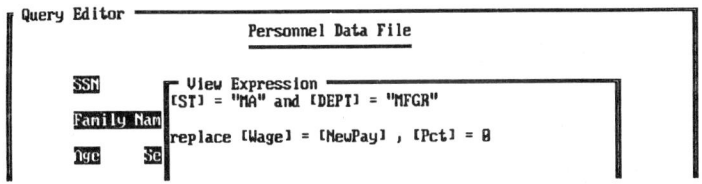

Fig. 4.17.

Query View Expression replacement.

When making multiple replacements with a Query View Expression, you enter the word *replace* once, and separate the replacement expressions with commas. After execution, the Query Summary displays the number of matched records and the number of replacements performed.

You also can replace activate and replace delete. These replacements are not toggle actions, as with the Data Delete Record command. If you replace the delete status of a deleted record, it remains deleted.

Query Optimization

In a query, if you are looking for a field equal to a specified value, and the field is the major sort of a key, the Data Query command uses the key file to perform an optimized search. Under the proper conditions, a Query selection takes a few seconds, as opposed to several minutes. The following conditions are necessary for an optimized search:

- The view must have a key.

- The view must be in either physical order or in order by a key; it cannot be ordered by an index. If the view is ordered by a key, it need not be the key of the search field. For example, if you are searching for a Social Security number, the view can be ordered by the key of Last Name.

- The query definition must search for a value equal to the major sort of the key. If you have a combination key of DEPT and Location, for example, the optimized search works only if you search for a DEPT, not a Location.

- Although you can search for only a single value, you can include search criteria for other fields. Thus, you can search for only one Last Name at a time. But you can qualify that Last Name search with other criteria. If you search for a key field of Last Name equal to Harris, for example, you can also include the search for DEPT equal to ACCT. The addition of the DEPT field does not prohibit the optimized search, it just further qualifies the result.

- If you are using a view expression instead of a QBE search, the key search criterion must be last in a sequence of criteria. The special operator where must be used instead of the and operator as follows:

[DEPT] = "ACCT" and [age] > 40 where [Last Name] = "Harris"

The where operator must always precede the key search phrase, even if no other search criteria exist, as follows:

where [Last Name] = "Harris"

QBE searches have nothing like the required where that is needed for an optimized search.

The optimized search feature of the Data Query command is similar to using a key field in the Data Find command.

Saving a Query Definition

When you perform a Data Query Now command, the query definition is stored temporarily in a file called QNOW.DFQ. Although you can use this definition to execute the same query over again, it is overwritten the next time you perform a Query Now command.

To save a query definition under a name of your own choice, use the Data Query Create command. When you execute this command, you are prompted to enter the name of a new query definition. (Make sure that you do not have a query definition with the same name, or you will receive an error.) Once you have typed a new name, you are prompted:

```
New   Similar
```

If you are creating a new query, select New, or select Similar to make a variation of an existing definition. If you select Similar, a pop-up window displays the names of the query definitions in your current subdirectory.

From this point, the process of creating a named query definition is the same as making the definition for a Query Now. You can use both the QBE and Query View Expressions. When you have completed the definition, press F10 to save it and return to the menu level.

Running a Saved Query Definition

Once you have created a Data Query definition, you can use it by selecting the Data Query Execute command. A pop-up window displays the names of the query definitions; select the one you want to run and press Enter. You are prompted:

```
Index   Data-File
```

If you select Index, a pop-up window displays the names of your existing index files. You can reuse an index file (if you are not currently using it), or you can supply the name for a new index. The numbers of the records that meet your conditions are written to the index file during the execution of the query. When completed, your view is automatically ordered by the index.

Instead of creating an index, you can elect to create a new data file containing the actual records that meet the query conditions. When you select Data-File, you are prompted for the name of the new data file. After entering the name, a pop-up window prompts you to select the fields you want to have in the new file. Select the fields to write to the new database and press Enter.

At the conclusion of the query, the new file is automatically loaded using the standard view. A query summary window pops up to tell you the number of records searched and found. Remember that you have created a new data file and now you have a copy of some of the records and fields from the original view. Any fields from the view that were view fields or project variables are now database fields in the new file. Calculated fields are transformed into data file fields.

Modifying a Query Definition

You can change a Query Definition if you select the Data Query Modify command. You are prompted to select the name of the definition to change.

Erasing a Query Definition

To erase a Query definition, use the Data Query Remove command. When you select the name, you are prompted:

```
Are you sure? (y/n)
```

If you answer *Y*, the definition is erased from the disk.

Selecting Records Manually

If you want to select records manually and create an index, select the Order Manual command. You are prompted for the name of an index. If you use a new index, you select the records you want. If, however, you use an index previously created for this view, the records in the index are automatically highlighted. However, make sure that the index was not created for a different view, or you will receive the following error message:

```
Index file does not match main data-file
```

Press any key to abort the Order Manual command. By selecting an existing index for the view, you can use the Order Manual command to change manually an index created through the Data Query or Order Sort commands.

The records of the view display in the Browse mode as in figure 4.18.

The current record is indicated by the highlight block in the first field. Move the cursor to a record you want to select and press F7; press it again to deselect a record. When you have selected all the records you need, press the F10 to order the view by the index.

When you use the Order Manual command, the view displays in physical order for the record selection, even if the view is ordered by an index; you do not have to execute the Order Change Physical command first. Even if you are changing an index created by the Order Sort command, the records of the view are displayed in physical order. However, if the view was ordered by a key, it is displayed in the key order for the record selection.

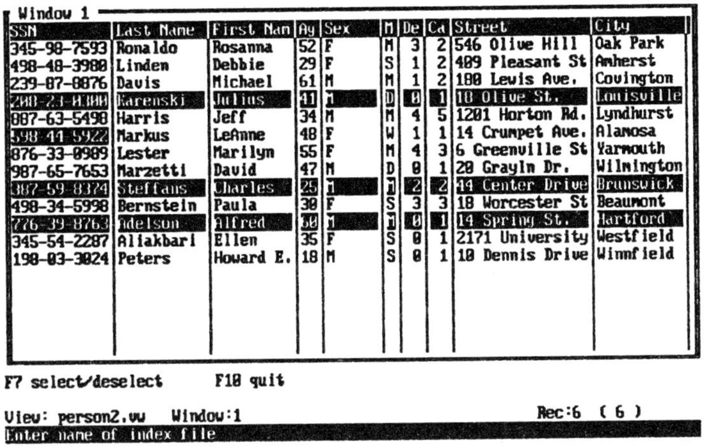

Fig. 4.18.

Order Manual record selection.

Arranging Data

The order in which data is entered in your file is probably not the order in which you intend to view it. Instead of viewing your list of employees in the order they were hired, you may want to arrange the records by last names, for example, or by department code. You can put the records in sequence according to the contents in virtually any field or combination of fields in the file. You use the Order commands to view your data in various arrangements.

In previous Smart versions, when you created a file, you were prompted to create a key field. In SmartWare II, you add key fields after the file is created. This chapter explains how to add and use key files and what their advantages are.

You don't need a key field to view your data in a sequence other than that of the physical record order. You can sort the view at any time and use the resulting index to work with the view in the new sequence.

Using File Keys

When you designate a key field or a group of key fields, you indicate that the system is to maintain a permanent reference file to keep track of each record in the order determined by the contents of the key field(s). If you set up as a key field the SSN field in a personnel file, for example, the SmartWare II database maintains a list of the record numbers in Social Security number order in a special KEY file.

When you change to the key order, this list is used to display the records in the Social Security number sequence. When you order your database by a key, the data is not actually sorted, but is only displayed in the order of the key; as a result, the process is instantaneous, and takes no longer for a large file than for a small one.

In previous versions of Smart, when you finished data entry or update, you were prompted to update the key fields. In SmartWare II, a different key-maintenance method is used that reduces the time to update the keys. For users of SmartWare II on a network, keys are updated automatically, even when multiple users have the file open simultaneously.

The Quick key Alt-G issues the Order Key command. The prompts are as follows:

    Add   Delete   Rebuild

To add a key to your file, consisting of one or more fields, select the Add option.

Adding a Key

As the name implies, the Order Key Add command is used to add a key to an existing file. Any data file field can be used as a key field, although usually key fields contain discrete values or text, such as department codes, last names, or Social Security numbers, rather than continuous values such as wages, ages, or numbers of dependents.

When you select the Add option to the Order Key command, a pop-up window displays the names of the view fields. In figure 4.19, the last and first names are selected, creating a compound key field.

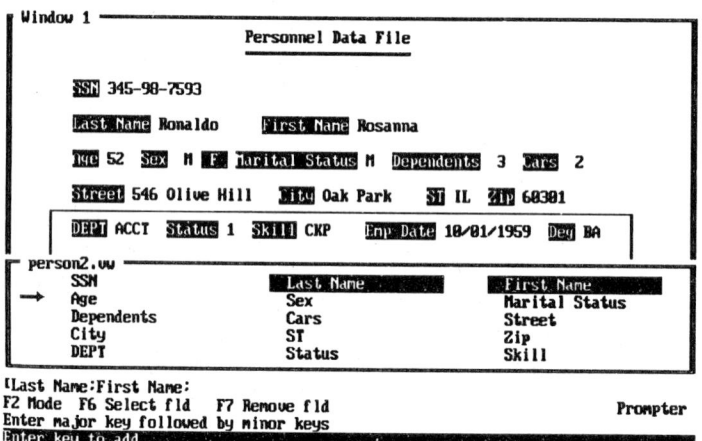

Fig. 4.19.

Selecting fields to create a key.

The first field you select is the major key field, followed by the minor key fields. In this example, when you order the file by the last name key field, not only will the last names be in order, but if there are any employees with identical last names, the records will be sorted in order by first name. After you add a key, a lowercase k is displayed next to the major key field in any pop-up menu of fields.

After you have selected the field or fields to constitute the key, a screen similar to figure 4.20 is displayed.

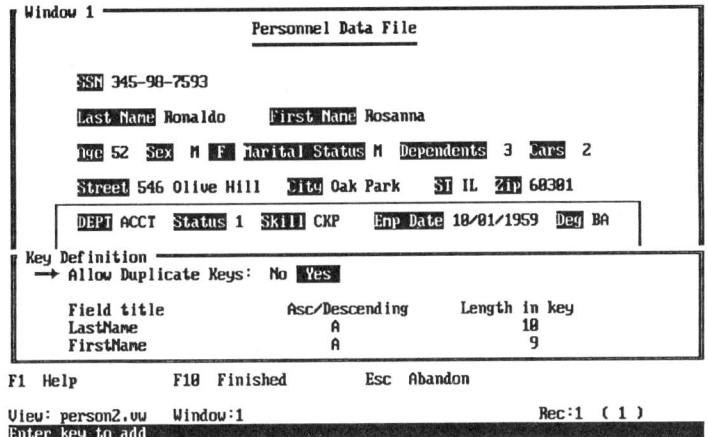

Fig. 4.20.

Key definition options.

If you want to prevent multiple records in your file from having identical keys, select the No option to the duplicate key question. Because, in our example, it can happen that you have two employees with both the same last and first names, you should leave the selection at *Yes*. However, if you designate SSN as a key, you should select *No* to prevent the accidental entry of duplicate Social Security numbers. (This feature is a welcome addition to SmartWare II.)

The default sorting order is always ascending (A), and the default key length is the full length of the field. If you want to arrange your key entries in descending sequence, move the cursor to the field and press *D*. A descending sequence is particularly useful if you want to see the most recent record first in a date field.

Be aware, however, that in the SmartWare II Database, the ASCII sorting sequence is used for key maintenance, rather than the collation sequence used throughout the rest of the SmartWare II system. In an ascending ASCII sequence, all uppercase letters appear before lowercase letters; in the collation sequence, both upper- and lowercase A come before either upper- or lowercase B. Refer to Appendix E for a comparison of the two sorting sequences.

The field lengths appear in the third column of the menu in figure 4.20. Usually, the default field length is appropriate for the key field length; occasionally, however, you may want to use just a portion of the field as the actual key. Do so only if the key field is very long and you are sure you can get the desired sort sequence by using just a portion of the field as the key. You may be able to save a small amount of key-maintenance processing time. Be careful if you take this approach, however, and be aware of the contents of the field. For example, if you shorten a last name key to six characters, you cannot guarantee that Andersen will appear before Anderson.

To change the length of the key field, use the right-arrow key to move the cursor to the third column, and use the up- or down-arrow keys to point to the proper field. Type the new value you want to use as the key length.

The SmartWare II database has a maximum limit of 100 characters per key field, and 500 characters for all keys. You can have as many as 15 keys for a view, and each key can be made up of a maximum of 16 fields.

Press F10 to complete the process of adding a key. The program will sort the keys and return to the menu level. Your view is automatically ordered by the key you have just created. (In previous versions of Smart, you had to execute the Order command separately to use the newly created key.)

You can add a key for only data file fields; you cannot add a key for a field that exists only in the view. Because a data file field can be attached to several views, adding a key for a data file field in one view automatically adds it for the same field in other views.

Deleting Keys

To delete a key, execute the Order Key command and select the Delete option. A pop-up menu displays the names of the fields in the view. Point to the key field to delete and press Enter.

If the key is in use, even if being used by another active view not in a window, you will receive the following error message:

```
Key field is in use. Cannot delete the key.
```

Change the view to physical order or unload the active view that references the key, and execute the command again to delete the key.

Fixing Keys

If, for some reason, the key file is deleted or becomes damaged, you can repair it by executing the Order Key Rebuild command. All keys for the main file of the view will be reconstructed.

Sorting a View

Sorting a view is similar to using a key to arrange records. There are some significant differences, however. Some commands require not only that the file be in a specific order, but also that the order be established by a key field. The Window Link command, for example, requires a key field in the link-to view. When you order a file by a key, all the records are available and in the order specified by the key field.

You use the Order Sort command to sort a view and create an index. An index contains a list of record numbers, similar to a key file.

Unlike a key file, however, the list is not automatically updated when data in the file is added or changed. An index is static; once you change a field on which the sort was based or add a record, you must sort the view to re-create the index.

The Order Sort command can be used on a subset of the records of a view. If you have used the Data Query command to select certain records, based on selection criteria, you can sort just those records into the order you need. In this case, you cannot use a key, because a key addresses all records of a view. (The Data Query command is discussed in this chapter.)

The Quick key for the Order Sort command is Alt-J; there are five options:

    Create Execute Modify Now Remove

You can select the options by pressing the initial letter or by moving the highlight block and pressing Enter.

Creating a Sort Definition

Select the Create option to construct a sort definition. As with other commands that create a definition, the definition is stored in a file for later use. When you execute the command, you are prompted to enter a new name for a sort definition. (Do not use an existing name; an error will result later.)

A pop-up window displays the names of the fields of the view. In figure 4.21, the DEPT and Wage fields are both selected, thus creating a compound sort definition.

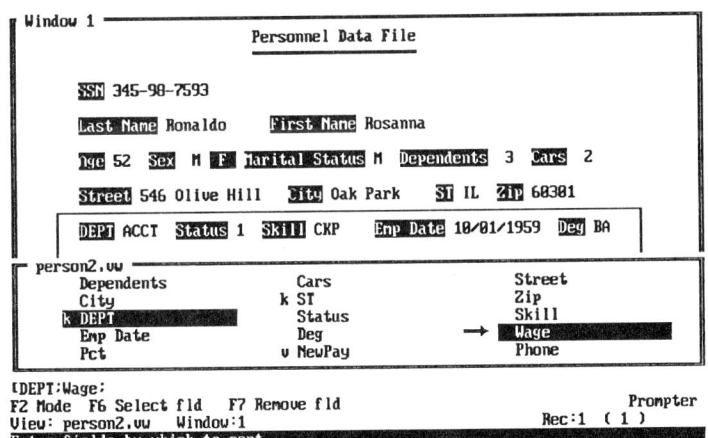

Fig. 4.21.

Selecting fields to create a sort definition.

The first field you select is the major sort field, followed in order by the minor sort fields. You can select either data file fields or view fields. After you have selected the field or fields to make up the sort, you see a screen similar to the one in figure 4.22.

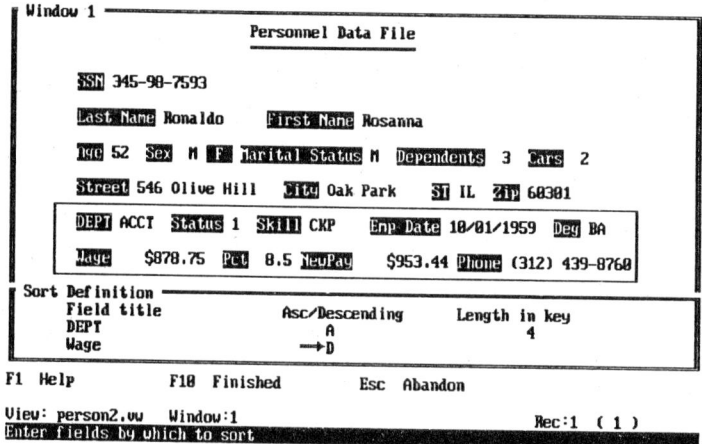

Fig. 4.22.

Sort definition options.

The default sorting order is always ascending, and the default length is the full length of alpha fields. If you want to arrange your sort fields in descending sequence, move the cursor to the field and press *D*. A descending sequence is particularly useful if you want to see the most recent record in a date field. In figure 4.22, the sorting order is descending wage in department code. When using the Order Sort command, the collation sorting sequence is used; remember that keys use the ASCII sort sequence. Refer to Appendix E for a comparison of the two sorting sequences.

For alpha fields, the field lengths appear in the third column of the Options menu. Usually, the default field length is appropriate for the sort field length; occasionally, however, you may want to use just a portion of the field. Do so only if the field is very long and you are sure you can get the desired sort sequence by using a portion of the field. You can be able to save a small amount of sorting time. Be careful if you take this approach, however, and be aware of the contents of the field. Press the F10 to complete the sort definition.

Performing the Sort

Once you have created a sort definition, you sort the view by using the Order Sort Execute command. A pop-up menu displays the names of the existing sort definitions; select the one you want and press Enter. You are prompted:

    Enter a new sort index filename:

A pop-up menu displays the names of existing index files; you can select one to use, or you can type the name of a new index. If an existing index is not being used and it is outdated, you can select it, and it will be overwritten. Remember that an index is static, and that once you have added new records to your file or have changed the contents of fields on which a prior sort was based, the index is outdated.

After selecting an index file, the view is sorted and is automatically ordered by the index. (In previous versions of Smart, you needed to perform an additional step to display the data file by the index.)

You should keep in mind several points about the sorting process. The Order Sort command operates in the current order of the view. If you have ordered your view so that only 10 percent of the records are in use, Smart sorts only those records. In such a case, it is probably faster to execute a Data Query command first to limit the number of records, and then to execute the Order Sort command so that fewer records need to be sorted.

Sort definitions are independent of the view for which they were created, because they store the field names. As long as a view contains the fields identified in the sort definition, the definition can be used. If the view is lacking one or more fields from the definition, you receive one or both of the following error messages:

```
Invalid field entered
Invalid number of keys in sort definition file
```

You can sort a view using a view field, rather than being restricted to using only data file fields, as you are when you add a key.

Changing a Sort Definition

SmartWare II enables you to change a sort definition. Execute the command Order Sort Modify and select the name of the definition you want to change. You can make changes to the field selections and the mix of ascending or descending sort sequences. Press F10 to save the changes.

Immediate Sorting

If you want to perform a one-time sort and you don't want to store the definition, execute the Order Sort Now command. With one major exception, using this command provides the same result as using a sort definition. The exception is that a sort definition permits a mix of ascending and descending orders if you specify a multiple-field sort. The Order Sort Now command, however, requires that all fields be sorted in either ascending or descending order.

Smart uses the collation table sorting techniques to ensure that upper- and lowercase words are sorted together. In a conventional ascending sort by ASCII values, however, all words in uppercase letters come before all words in lowercase.

You are prompted for the name of an index and for the fields to use in the sort. Next you are prompted:

    Ascending   Descending

Once you respond, the view is sorted, the index is created, and the view is automatically ordered by the index.

Deleting a Sort Definition

You can erase sort definitions with the Order Sort Remove command. A pop-up menu displays the names of the sort definition files in the current subdirectory.

Changing the Order of a View

SmartWare II database files are created in physical order; each new record is appended to the file immediately following the preceding record. Each time a view is loaded, the default sequence is physical order.

In several chapters of this book, the physical order of a view is compared to the logical order. You use the Order Change command to change the logical order of a view so that you can view or process the records in a sorted or selected order. You also use the Order Change command to reset the view to the physical order.

The logical order of a view can refer to two different conditions. In the first condition, the view is arranged by the contents of one or more fields. For example, you can sort your view by ZIP code for a mailing list, or you can use an existing key to arrange it by Social Security number. In the second condition, you can use the Data Query command to select a subset of the total number of records, based on a logical criterion. An example of this usage might be "all the records for individuals living in Ohio, Maine, and Kansas." A view can be both a subset and in sorted order simultaneously.

When you order a view, you do not physically rearrange the records on the disk. Whether you use a key field or a specifically created index, you use the Order Change command to select the way a view is displayed or made available for processing. You can order a view quickly because the sorting to create or maintain the index or key has already been done.

Arranging a View

As you have already seen, the process of creating a key or executing a sort not only creates the list of records, but also orders the view by the resulting key or index file.

You use the Order Change command to apply an existing key or index to the view manually. In both cases, the key or index will have already been created.

When you execute the Order Change command, you are prompted:

    Key   Index   Physical

You can select the options by pressing the initial letter or by moving the highlight block and pressing Enter.

Changing to Original View Order

The Order Change Physical command changes the order of the view to the original physical order and makes all the records available for viewing or processing. Use this command to reset the order of the view after it has been changed by either of the other two options. When you originally load a view, it is in physical order. (In previous versions of Smart, when you used the Goto command to display an active file in the current window, the file automatically was in sequential order; this is no longer true in SmartWare II, because a view can remain ordered by a key or an index even when it is in the background.)

Changing to Key Order

To set the order of the view by any of the key fields, use the Order Change Key command. A pop-up menu of field names appears, and you select the appropriate field from the menu (see fig. 4.23).

Use the cursor keys to point to the key field and press Enter. You also can type the field name on the prompt line. Notice that the key fields are preceded by the lowercase letter *k*. After the view has been ordered by a key field, all records in the view are available in the key order; the order is reflected on the status line.

```
┌─ person2.vw ──────────────────────────────────────────────┐
│ → k SSN            Last Name            First Name        │
│     Age            Sex                  Marital Status    │
│     Dependents     Cars                 Street            │
│     City           ST                   Zip               │
│   k DEPT           Status               Skill             │
└───────────────────────────────────────────────────────────┘
```

Fig. 4.23.

Selecting key order.

Only the major-sort key, of course, shows up in the pop-up menu. To see the list of minor keys that can be beneath the major key, use the Data Utilities Information command.

Changing to Index Order

You use the Order Sort and Data Query commands to create temporary index files. These files, just like the keys, are lists of record numbers in the order in which the records are to be displayed and processed. Unlike keys, however, index files are not automatically updated when you add records to a file or change field values. Index files must be re-created as needed.

When you execute the Order Change Index command, a pop-up menu displays the names of the index files in the current subdirectory (see fig. 4.24).

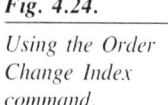

Fig. 4.24.

Using the Order Change Index command.

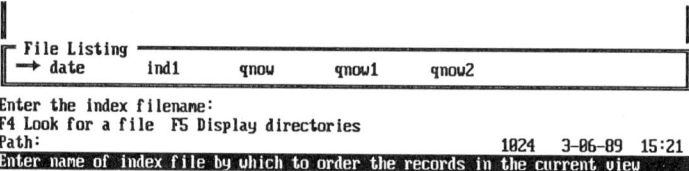

The Order Sort command creates an index that is used to arrange the view in order by the contents of one or more fields. These fields are usually not key fields. Thus, even though ZIP is not a key field, you can sort the view by the ZIP field. The Order Sort command automatically orders the view by the index. Even after you change the order of the view at a later time, or even unload the view, however, the index file remains. Use the Order Change Index command to apply a previously created index to the view.

The Data Query command creates an index of selected records based on a set of criteria that you supply. Similarly, this command automatically orders the view by the created index. You can return to the subset of records selected by a previous Data Query by using the Order Change Index command.

If you need to process a sorted subset of your data file, you should execute the Data Query first, to limit the number of records, and then perform the Order Sort. By limiting the number or records to sort, you can save processing time.

Chapter Summary

The capability to arrange your data in a logical way is vital to the management of databases. The capability to display and process records in an order other than the one in which they are entered is one of the hallmarks of a database system.

You can use the Data Find command to search your file in logical order to locate records that satisfy your search criteria. Although you can perform an accurate search, the SmartWare II Database can perform the task faster and more accurately, especially if the file is very large. For rapid access, you can initiate an extremely fast binary search under certain exact conditions.

To make the most of your mastery of the SmartWare II Database, you should have a solid understanding of the Data Query command. Its capabilities can be invaluable in selecting the appropriate records for use in reports or transactions. Once a set of records is selected, it can be used repeatedly in multiple commands. You must perform the screening operations over again only if you add new records or change existing records that match the screening criteria.

In the Data Query command, you can specify selection criteria with multiple conditions, or you can decide to perform several passes through the data, screening further and further each time you query. The Query By Example definition process provides an easy way to enter the criteria for most queries; use a query View Expression for more complex definitions.

Also, the Data Query command can perform calculations on either the entire file or selected records. You can designate one or more destination fields. Use the Data Query command to display summary statistics about your view, using the SDb Table functions.

Finally, the Data Query command can create a new database. The records in the database will meet the criteria of the query definition; you have the option to select the desired fields.

Working with Multiple Files

Most of the examples in this book have involved only one view at a time. This chapter explains how to use multiple view commands in the SmartWare II Database.

The Database module offers several ways of handling multiple views, each of which is discussed in this chapter. You can choose the method that best fits your needs. If you need to create a new file from two existing views, you can use the Data Relate command. (Frequently, however, you can create a new, multiple-file view to substitute for relating two existing views.) If you need to move data or to post activity from one view to another, you use the Data Transact command. If you have created a new file that is similar to one that already exists, you can use the Data Utilities Append command to transfer data from one to the other.

Relating Two Views

The Window Link command is an example of joining two views. Each view remains a separate entity with its own structure and data, even though the files share a common field. Similarly, you can create views that allow you to view and work with fields from multiple files simultaneously. Sometimes you need to have data from several views stored in one physical file, however. In these cases, use the Data Relate command; the Quick key is Alt-N. The Data Relate command creates a new database and a standard view; the field names may be the same as in the originating views, but you have the opportunity to change them in the relation definition.

The Data Relate command can define four different types of relationships between two views. The most common relation is one for creating a new file containing all

105

records from the two views that match on a common field or group of fields. For example, you may want to create a file that uses data from the personnel file and the names of the departments from the department file. (The DEPT field of the personnel file contains abbreviations for the department names.) This relation is called an *Intersect* relation. The four relation types are summarized as follows:

1. The Intersect relation creates new records only when the linking fields match in both views.

2. The Not-Intersect relation creates new records only when no match is found between the two views. For example, you may want to create a file of all employees not assigned to an existing department and all the departments that have no employees.

3. The Subtract relation can be used to create records from one view that do not match records in the other view. You may, for example, want to create records for departments without employees.

4. The Union relation option creates records for all conditions, regardless of whether the linking fields match. This relation is the sum of the results from the Intersect and Not-Intersect options.

Defining Relationships

Unlike some of the commands discussed up to this point, the Data Relate command has so many options that you must create a definition before you can use the command. After you have created the definition, the definition may be used to execute the relation on a repetitive basis. The definition may be edited if needed.

Before you begin creating the definition, make sure that both source views are loaded. The views do not have to appear in windows, but they both must be loaded. The view called *View 2* in the definition must have a *key*, which is used as the link between the two views.

When you select the Data Relate command, you see the following options on-screen:

    Create Execute Modify Remove

When you select the Create option to establish a new relation definition, you are prompted to type the definition name. The names of the existing definitions are not shown, so make sure that you do not use one that already exists. If you do, you receive an error and must start over.

When you have entered a new relation name, the Relate definition screen is displayed (see fig. 5.1).

```
┌─ Relate definition (depper) ──────────────────────┐
│ → View 1 : ■                                      │
│       Link field(s) : ■                           │
│     View 2 : ■                                    │
│       Link field(s) : ■                           │
│     Relate type : Intersect Not-Intersect Subtract Union │
│     New Database : ■                              │
│     New Database Fields : ■                       │
└───────────────────────────────────────────────────┘
```

Fig. 5.1.

The Relate Definition menu.

Enter the name of View 1 on the first line; use the F6 key to display a pop-up menu of view names.

Enter the name(s) of View 1 link field(s) on line 2 of the relate definition. Again, you can use the F6 key to display a pop-up menu of field names to help you with the entry.

On the third line, enter the name of View 2 for the relation. Remember, View 2 must have the link field(s) declared as a key. (In previous versions of Smart, File 1 was required to have the link field as a key.)

If the link field(s) for View 2 (line 4) are not keys, you see the following error message:

    View 2 field is not a key field

You may enter multiple link fields if the key has been declared with minor fields. The link fields are not required to have the same names in View 1 as in View 2.

On the fifth line of the definition, select from the following relate types:

    Intersect Not-Intersect Subtract Union

On the sixth line, enter the name of the file to be created when you execute the relation. Although this output file may exist when you create the definition, it must not exist when you execute the relation. (Use the Tools File Erase command to erase both the database file and the standard view file prior to executing the relation, if the relation has been run previously.)

Note that in SmartWare II, both the relate type and the name of the output file are embedded in the relate definition. In previous versions of Smart, these entries were provided at the time you executed the relation.

On the last line of the definition, enter the names of the data fields you want to write to the new database. Use the F6 key to display a pop-up menu of field names. Use either the F3 or F4 key to display the fields from the other view during this field selection process. (Don't select either of the link fields as database fields; the link fields from View 2 will be carried forward automatically.) Figure 5.2 shows a completed relate definition.

When you press F10, a list of the fields selected in the relation definition is displayed in the lower portion of the screen (see fig. 5.3).

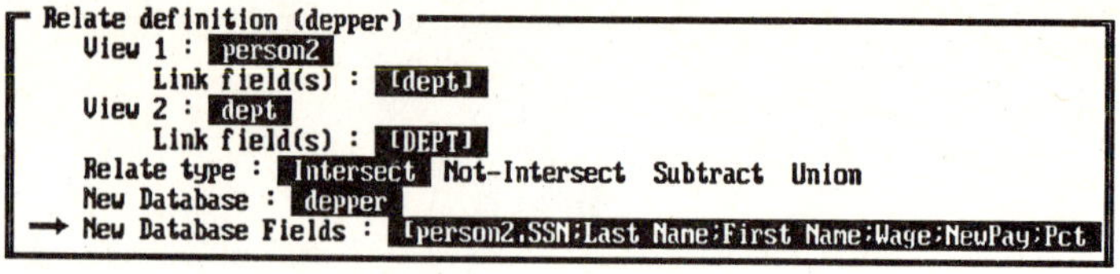

Fig. 5.2.

The completed relate definition.

Fig. 5.3.

The relation field name selection.

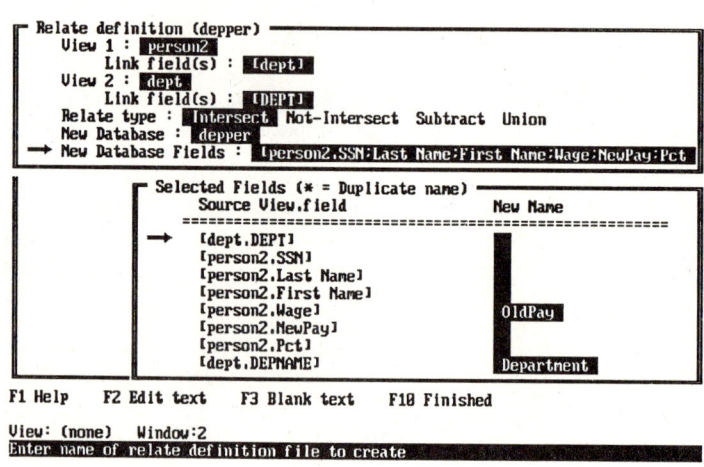

If there are any field names duplicated in Views 1 and 2, you must provide a different name for one of them; duplicate names are marked with an asterisk. You also may provide any other field name changes as desired. Note that view and project processing fields from the source views are written as actual database fields in the destination file. Calculated fields are carried forward as actual values, not as calculation formulas. Press F10 to complete the relate definition.

Executing the Relate Command

After the relation has been defined, you may create the new database by selecting the Data Relate Execute command. A pop-up menu displays the names of the existing relation definitions. Remember, both source views must be loaded at the time you execute the command, but they do not have to be in windows.

The output file must not exist when you execute the relation. Use the Tools File Erase command to erase both the database file and the standard view file prior to executing the relation if you have run the relation previously. (Refer to Appendix B for a complete list of file extensions.)

View 1 may be in any order: key, physical, or index. The view you specified as View 2 must have the link field(s) as a key, but it does not need to be ordered by that key. The view must not be ordered by an index, however, or the following error message results:

```
Cannot process external link; view is in index order
```

If you see this message, change the order of the view either to key or to physical and execute the command again. (If View 1 also has the link field as a key, processing speed is improved, but using the link field as a key is not necessary for the successful operation of the command.)

Note that in SmartWare II, both the relate type and the name of the output file are contained in the relate definition. In prior versions of Smart, these selections were provided at execution time.

After execution of the Data Relate Execute command, the output file is automatically loaded into the current window, using the standard screen. Any display formats or input masks are not carried forward into the new view. Figure 5.4 shows the file resulting from the relation example.

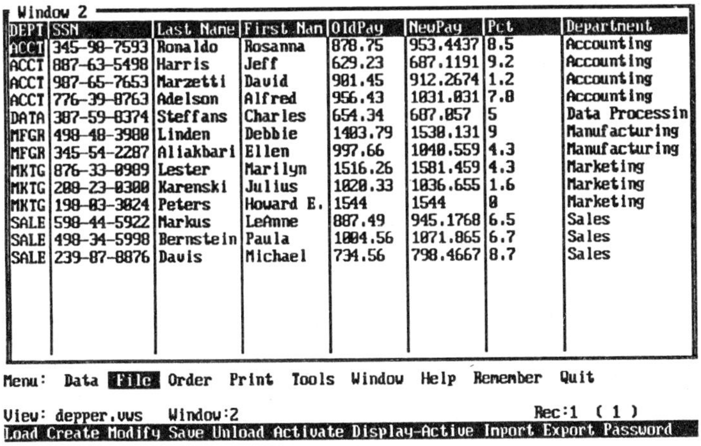
Window 2

DEPT	SSN	Last Name	First Nam	OldPay	NewPay	Pct	Department
ACCT	345-98-7593	Ronaldo	Rosanna	878.75	953.4437	8.5	Accounting
ACCT	887-63-5498	Harris	Jeff	629.23	687.1191	9.2	Accounting
ACCT	987-65-7653	Marzetti	David	901.45	912.2674	1.2	Accounting
ACCT	776-39-8763	Adelson	Alfred	956.43	1031.031	7.8	Accounting
DATA	387-59-8374	Steffans	Charles	654.34	687.057	5	Data Processin
MFGR	498-48-3980	Linden	Debbie	1403.79	1530.131	9	Manufacturing
MFGR	345-54-2287	Aliakbari	Ellen	997.66	1040.559	4.3	Manufacturing
MKTG	876-33-0989	Lester	Marilyn	1516.26	1581.459	4.3	Marketing
MKTG	208-23-0300	Karenski	Julius	1020.33	1036.655	1.6	Marketing
MKTG	198-03-3024	Peters	Howard E.	1544	1544	0	Marketing
SALE	598-44-5922	Markus	LeAnne	887.49	945.1768	6.5	Sales
SALE	498-34-5998	Bernstein	Paula	1004.56	1071.865	6.7	Sales
SALE	239-87-8876	Davis	Michael	734.56	798.4667	8.7	Sales

Menu: Data File Order Print Tools Window Help Remember Quit

View: depper.vws Window:2 Rec:1 (1)

Load Create Modify Save Unload Activate Display-Active Import Export Password

Fig. 5.4.

A new file created by the Data Relate command.

Modifying the Relation Definition

To change the relation definition, execute the Data Relate Modify command. The source views must be loaded if you intend to continue using them in the relate. The process of modifying the definition is similar to the process of creating it.

Erasing a Relation Definition

If you no longer need a relation definition, use the Data Relate Remove command. A pop-up menu displays the names of the existing relation definitions; select the one to erase and press Enter.

Remember, because SmartWare II has the capability of referencing fields from multiple files in a view, you may not need to use the Data Relate command as often as you may have in previous versions of Smart. A multiple-file view may frequently replace the Intersect option of the Data Relate command. For example, a view containing the department name from the DEPT file and all the data from the Person2 file could be used instead of the output file from the Data Relate command.

Transacting Views

The Data Transact command is used to post data from one view to another. Typically, you have a *master,* or *driven,* view and a *transaction,* or *driver,* view. You might post daily or weekly transactions from a transaction view to reflect activity during the period. For example, the master view can be inventory data, and the transaction view can contain individual sales records, showing the item number and the quantity sold (or returned). At the end of the day or week, the Data Transact command is used to subtract the quantity sold from the inventory view in a *batch* mode. (If you have designed your system so that the inventory is debited immediately from the master file as each sale is made, you do not need the Data Transact command to update the on-hand inventory file.)

Like the Data Relate command, the Data Transact command is used with two files that share one or more linking fields. These fields must be of the same type, but they need not have the same names.

The driver view contains the records that cause the transaction to take place, but fields in the driver view can be either the source or the destination of the transaction. In the same transaction, the driver can contain both source and destination fields. (In previous Smart versions, the driver file could be either the source or the destination, but not both simultaneously.) In our sales transaction example, the view of sales records is the driver file because you want the master file to be updated for each sale.

The Quick key for the Data Transact command is Alt-T; when you execute the command, you see these options:

    Create Execute Modify Remove

Select the Create option to develop the transaction definition.

Creating a Transaction Definition

Before beginning to create the transaction definition, make sure that both views are loaded. The link field of the driven view must be a key. Figure 5.5 shows the views used in this example. The view in window 1 contains the Inventory file, which contains one record for each inventory item. The important fields are the item number and the quantity on hand. The view in window 2 contains one record for each sale, with the item number and the quantity sold. A third field, which is blank initially, is reserved for the backorder quantity.

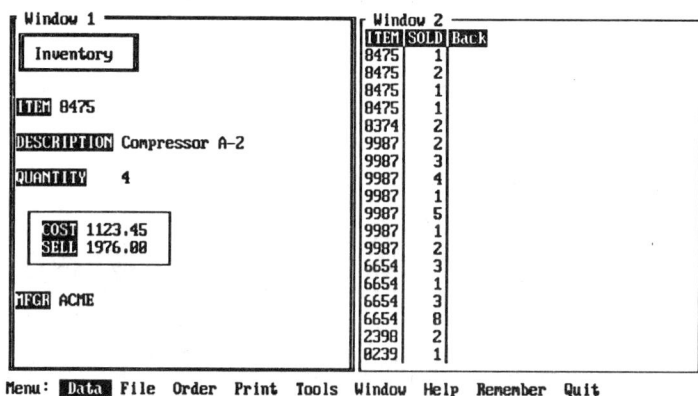

Fig. 5.5.

Transaction sample files.

When you execute the Data Transact Create command, you are prompted to enter a new transaction definition name. The names of the existing definitions are not displayed, so make sure that you enter a new name; if you enter the name of an existing definition, you see this error message:

    Error creating definition file

You can save yourself one step if the driver view is current when you create the definition, because the name of the driver file is filled in for you automatically. Figure 5.6 shows the initial Transaction Definition menu.

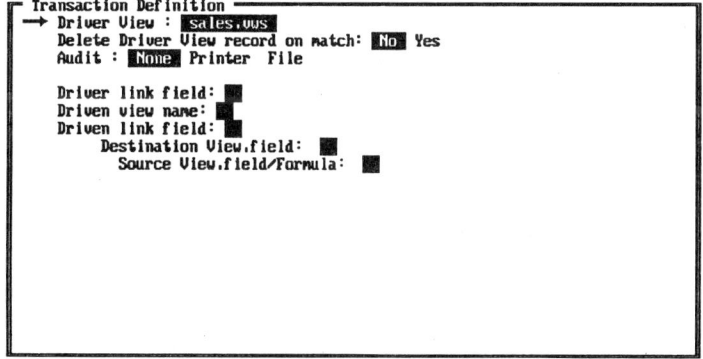

Fig. 5.6.

The Transaction Definition menu.

To create the transaction definition, you must complete the following items on the menu:

- Driver View. If your driver view was in the current window when you executed the Data Transact Create command, this response is filled in for you. If not, press F6 to display a pop-up menu of active views and select the view to be the driver. Remember, the transaction activity takes place for each active record in the driver view.

- Delete Driver View record on match? Since the Data Transact command does not process deleted records, you can avoid accidentally processing the same driver records twice if you select Yes. The records are not automatically purged from the file, but are simply marked for deletion.

- Audit: None Printer File. An audit report can be written either to the printer or to a disk file during the processing of the transaction. An audit report shows the following information:

  - The transaction definition name and date and time of execution
  - The view names
  - The record numbers processed
  - The value of the link fields
  - Destination fields, and their original and final values

  If you choose to write the audit report to a file, the default file extension is .AUD. (When you execute the transaction, the audit file must not exist, or you get an error message. This is a change from previous Smart versions.)

- Driver link field. Enter the name of the field from the driver file to be used as the link to the driven file. Use the F6 key to display a menu of field names. You can enter multiple fields if corresponding multiple link fields are entered for the driven view.

  When you enter the name of a driver link field, an input block for an additional driver link field is automatically created; multiple driver links are possible in a transaction.

- Driven view name. Use the F6 key to display a menu of the active views.

- Driven link field. Enter the name of the field from the driven file to be used as the link to the driver file. Use the F6 key to display a menu of field names. You can enter multiple fields if corresponding multiple link fields have been entered for the driver view. The link fields for the driven view must be a major key and its minor keys.

- Destination, View field. Use the F6 key to display a menu of the names of the fields. The destination field may be in either the driver view or the driven view. Use the F3 or F4 keys to display the fields from the alternate views.

  When you enter the name of a destination field, an input block for an additional destination field is automatically created; multiple destinations are possible in a single transaction. In the same transaction, you can specify destination fields in both the driven and driver files; this capability is new with SmartWare II. Additional destination fields can be inserted manually with the F7 key.

- Source View, field/Formula. Enter the formula to be executed when the transaction takes place. You can use the F6 key to display a menu of field names, and the F3 or F4 keys to alternate between views. You can use the F5 key to bring up the full screen editor for creating complex expressions. Any mathematical expressions or Smart functions are valid in transaction formulas.

  The capability to enter a formula in a transaction is a significant enhancement in SmartWare II. In previous versions of Smart, you could only add, subtract or move the source field to the destination.

Figure 5.7 shows the completed transaction definition for the current example.

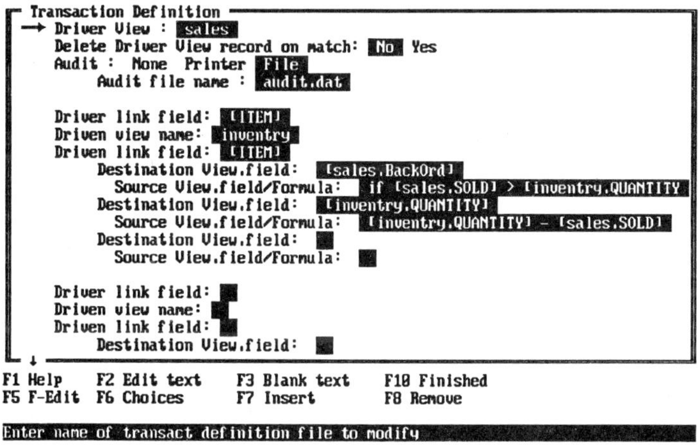

Fig. 5.7.

The completed transaction definition.

Notice that the first destination is the backorder (BackOrd) field in the sales file. Figure 5.8 shows the formula as it appears in the full-screen formula editor.

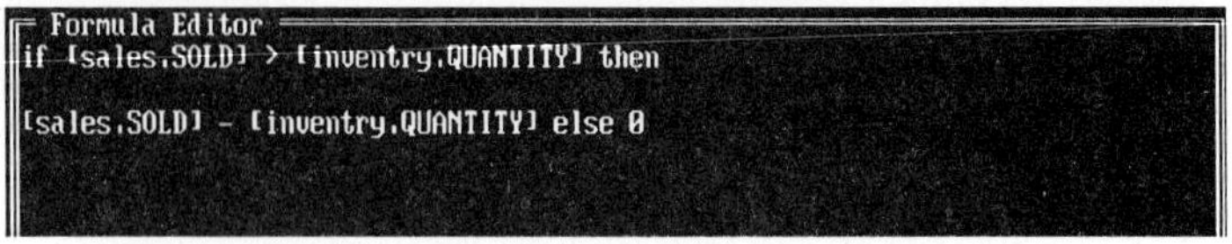

Fig. 5.8.

The backorder transaction formula.

```
Formula Editor
if [sales.SOLD] > [inventry.QUANTITY] then
[sales.SOLD] - [inventry.QUANTITY] else 0
```

The second destination is the Quantity field in the Inventory view. Notice that the formula specifies that the quantity sold is to be subtracted from the quantity on hand and then inserted into the field for the quantity on hand.

When you have completed the transaction definition, press the F10 key to save it.

Executing a Transaction

After you have defined the transaction, select the Data Transact Execute command. You must have both views loaded, and the link field of the driven view must be a key. The driven view does not need to be ordered by the key, but it must not be ordered by an index. Remember, if you have specified the audit report to be written to a file, you must make sure that the file does not exist when you execute the transaction. (This requirement is a change from previous versions of Smart.)

Changing a Transaction Definition

To change the definition of a transaction, execute the Data Transact Modify command. A pop-up menu displays the names of the existing transaction definitions; select the one you want to change and press Enter. Make sure that both views are loaded when you modify the definition.

Erasing a Transaction Definition

If you no longer need a transaction definition, use the Data Transact Remove command. A pop-up menu displays the names of the existing transaction definitions; select the one to erase and press Enter.

Copying Data from One File to Another

If you want to copy data from one view to another, make sure that you have both the source and destination views loaded; the destination view should be in your current window. When you execute the Data Utilities Append command, a pop-up menu displays the names of the active files, and you see this prompt:

    Enter the source data-file name:

Select the source file and press Enter. A menu similar to the one shown in figure 5.9 is used to specify both the source and destination fields.

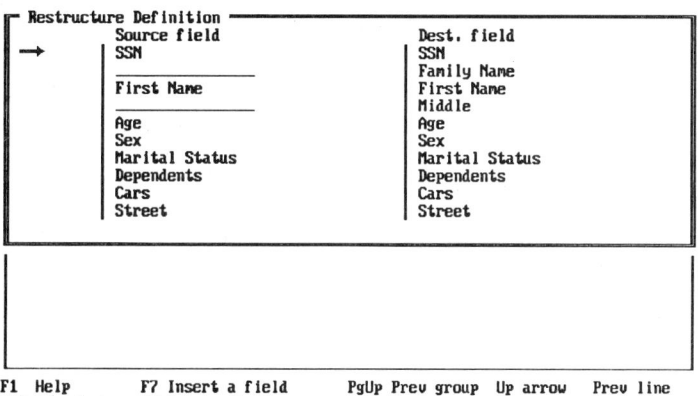

Fig. 5.9.

The Data Utilities Append field selection.

Note that where possible, fields from the source file have been matched to those in the destination file by their names. If the spelling of a field name is different, you may specify the source field manually. Move the cursor to the empty source field line and press F7. A pop-up menu enables you to specify the source field for the destination. When you select a source field, its name is inserted on the definition screen.

If there is no appropriate source field for a destination, leave the entry blank. You can fill in missing fields later with a manual update, or a Data Transact or Query. Although field names are compared between the source and destination, the data types are not checked. Moving the contents of an alphanumeric field to a numeric field results in a zero value. Moving the contents of a numeric field to an alphanumeric field causes the numeric value to be stored as alphanumeric text; this is one way to change numeric data to alphanumeric.

Press F10 to complete the definition and proceed to append the records from the source file to the destination.

The source view may be ordered by an index if you want only the selected records to be appended to the destination view. The Data Utilities Append command replaces both the Utilities Restructure and Utilities Concatenate commands from previous versions of Smart. Both the source and destination views must be single data-file views.

Chapter Summary

The SmartWare II Database uses key fields to relate records in files between which data is to be shared. The Data Relate command is used to select fields from two views resulting in a third file.

The Data Transact command is used to post data in either direction between a transactions file and a master file by matching key fields and executing a formula to replace a destination field. Batch-oriented applications can be developed with this command. A complete audit trail can be printed or stored in a disk file.

Use the Data Utilities Append command to copy records from one file to another. Matching field names are automatically recognized, or you may manually specify the fields to copy.

Printing Database Data and Creating Reports

In most computer applications, you must be able to produce reports from your views. If you are the only one using the system, you may only need screen displays or simple reports. But if other people or companies see data from your system, you also will need formal reports.

The SmartWare II Database can produce both quick reports in a standard format, with few "bells and whistles," and formal reports in a wide variety of formats you design. The Print View and Print Current-Record commands produce reports rapidly and easily. The Print Report command produces formal reports in many different formats.

Printing from a View

To print several records from the view in the current window, use the Print View command. (Alt-P is the Quick key for just the Print command.) The Print View command is used for quick reporting from a view when you don't need a fancy format. When you execute the Print View command, you are prompted:

    List   Report

If you want the fields printed in columns with one record per line, select the Report option. (Don't confuse this option with the Print Report command, discussed later in this chapter.) A pop-up menu prompts you to select the names of the fields to print. Enter the fields in the order (left to right) that you want them to appear on the report. When you have completed the field selection, you see the following prompt:

    Screen   Printer

117

This command does not have the option of directing the output to a disk file; use the Print Report command if you want to save the output.

If output is directed to the screen, you can control the scrolling speed by pressing a number between 1 and 10 (1 is the slowest, and 10, represented by 0, is the fastest). The default scrolling rate is 5. To make the scrolling pause, press any key; press a key again to resume scrolling.

If you direct output to the printer, be sure that your paper is positioned with the print head at the top of a page; a form feed is issued after the printing finishes.

Field names are used as column headings; the column width equals either the display width or the field name, whichever is greater. (When you create a view, if your field names are smaller than the fields themselves, you can save space by using the Print View Report command instead of the Report option.) The screen and printer displays automatically wrap around; fields that don't fit on the first line are printed on the next line. The result can be difficult to read. The printer width for this command is governed by the settings in the Tools Preferences Hardware.

The Print View Report command chosen from the view in figure 6.1 gives the output shown in figure 6.2.

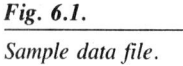

Fig. 6.1.

Sample data file.

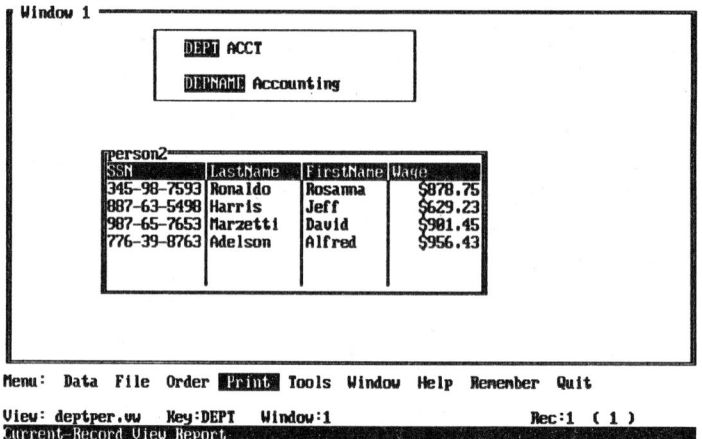

Note that the records from the table are single-spaced and that the fields from the main view area are printed only once, with a blank line between the main view records.

To cancel output to either the screen or the printer, press Ctrl-Z. On the screen, the print procedure is canceled immediately, and you are prompted to press a key to continue. On the printer, you are prompted:

```
Output to device paused - continue? (y/n)
```

DEPT	DEPNAME	SSN	LastName	FirstName	Wage
ACCT	Accounting	345-98-7593	Ronaldo	Rosanna	$878.75
		887-63-5498	Harris	Jeff	$629.23
		987-65-7653	Marzetti	David	$901.45
		776-39-8763	Adelson	Alfred	$956.43
DATA	Data Processing	387-59-8374	Steffans	Charles	$654.34
MDSE	Merchandising				
MFGR	Manufacturing	498-48-3980	Linden	Debbie	$1,403.79
		345-54-2287	Aliakbari	Ellen	$997.66
MKTG	Marketing	876-33-0989	Lester	Marilyn	$1,516.26
		208-23-0300	Karenski	Julius	$1,020.33
		198-03-3024	Peters	Howard E.	$1,544.00
SALE	Sales	598-44-5922	Markus	LeAnne	$887.49
		498-34-5998	Bernstein	Paula	$1,004.56
		239-87-8876	Davis	Michael	$734.56

Fig. 6.2.

Result of the Print View Report command.

Press *N* to cancel or *Y* to continue printing. This feature enables you to pause the printer without having to reprint the whole report—handy when you need to change or adjust the paper.

If you have to print many fields or if the fields are long, you may want to use the List option instead of the Report option. The List option prints the fields one below each other, as shown in figure 6.3.

Note that the physical number of the main data file record is printed, as well as the active flag (either *Y* or *N*). If the flag is N, the record is not active and is thus deleted. All records (including deleted records) are printed in physical, key, or index order.

If you don't want to print deleted records, use the Data Query command to create an index that does not contain deleted records. The Print View command begins printing at the first record in the logical sequence and continues through the last record. The current record remains unchanged at the completion of the command. If you print fields from both the main data file and a table in the List format, the table fields are indented.

Fig. 6.3.

Output from the Print View List command.

```
Record #: 1   Act: Y
DEPT: ACCT
DEPNAME: Accounting
    SSN: 345-98-7593
    LastName: Ronaldo
    FirstName: Rosanna
    Wage: $878.75

    SSN: 887-63-5498
    LastName: Harris
    FirstName: Jeff
    Wage: $629.23

    SSN: 987-65-7653
    LastName: Marzetti
    FirstName: David
    Wage: $901.45

    SSN: 776-39-8763
    LastName: Adelson
    FirstName: Alfred
    Wage: $956.43

Record #: 5   Act: N
DEPT: DATA
DEPNAME: Data Processing
    SSN: 387-59-8374
    LastName: Steffans
    FirstName: Charles
    Wage: $654.34

Record #: 6   Act: Y
DEPT: MDSE
DEPNAME: Merchandising

Record #: 2   Act: Y
DEPT: MFGR
DEPNAME: Manufacturing
    SSN: 498-48-3980
    LastName: Linden
    FirstName: Debbie
    Wage: $1,403.79

    SSN: 345-54-2287
    LastName: Aliakbari
    FirstName: Ellen
    Wage: $997.66
```

Printing the Current Record

The Print Current-Record command prints information from just the current record. When you execute the command, you are prompted:

List   Page   View

If you select the List option, all fields are immediately printed in the format shown in figure 6.3. You are not prompted for field names.

If you select the Page option, you are prompted whether you want All or Data. Selecting All will print everything on the screen: the text, any boxes or lines, and the data itself. Figure 6.4 shows output from the All option. Choosing Data prints only the actual data itself, without any boxes, lines, notes, or field names.

```
DEPT ACCT
DEPNAME Accounting
```

SSN	LastName	FirstName	Wage
345-98-7593	Ronaldo	Rosanna	$878.75
887-63-5498	Harris	Jeff	$629.23
987-65-7653	Marzetti	David	$901.45
776-39-8763	Adelson	Alfred	$956.43

Fig. 6.4.

The Print Current-Record Page All command.

Although the Page option prints just the current page of the current record, the View option prints all pages of the current record. The same prompts—All and Data—are available.

Creating Formal Reports

As you have seen, the Print Current-Record and Print View commands are quick and easy to use; their disadvantages are inflexible formatting and printing deleted records. The Print Report command overcomes these drawbacks, producing formal, elaborate reports—but defining a formal report is more complex.

When using the Print Report facility, you can produce two basic types of reports: tables and forms. Report Tables are similar to the output produced by the Print View Report command—you can print as many as four detail lines on the report for each record from the file, and data fields are aligned in columns. You can supply your own column headers (different from just the field names), specify the column spacing, designate report headers and footings, and control column breakpoints. Also, you can include calculations in areas other than the body of the report: the headings, footings, and breakpoints. Lastly, wide alpha fields in Report tables can wrap around in a shorter column than the field itself.

Report Forms are the other basic type of report. In a Report Form, a record's individual fields can be positioned on a page (like preprinted forms). Each record of the view is represented by one page of the report instead of a detail line.

Using the Print Report command, you can define reports that combine these two report types by splitting the page into a combination report with one form part and one table part. Data in the two parts of a combination report comes from different areas of a single view, typically the main area and a table. To print an invoice, for example, you could make the top portion of the report a form, with data coming from the main view area, and print the invoice line items in table format at the bottom of the report, with data coming from the view table. (In previous versions of Smart, a combination report drew data from two different files linked by a common field.)

Figure 6.5 shows the view used as an example in the presentation of the formal reporting in the SmartWare II Database. Figure 6.6 shows a sample report.

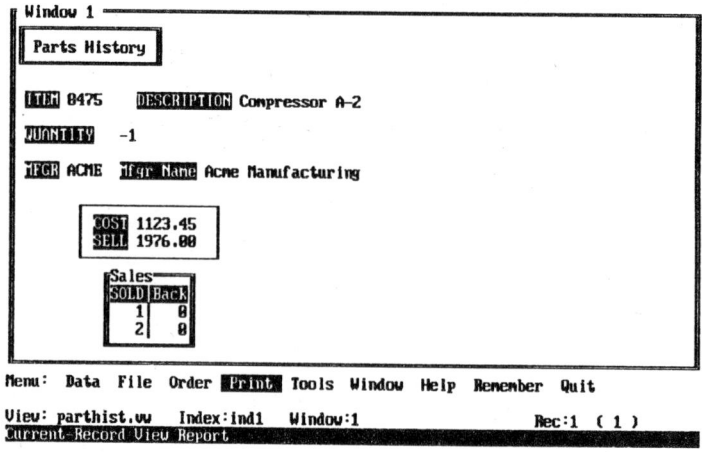

Fig. 6.5.
Sample files for a formal report.

Fig. 6.6.
Sample combination report.

ABERDEEN SALES CORPORATION
Item Sales by Manufacturer

Manufacturer Code: ACME   09/08/1989
              Name: Acme Manufacturing

Mfgr	Item Number	Description	Quantity On Hand	Cost	Sales Price	Qty. Sold	Margin Dollars	Qty. BkOrd
ACME	8475	Compressor A-2	-1	1123.45	1976.00	1	852.55	0
						2	1,705.10	0
						1	852.55	0
						1	852.55	1
		Total for Compressor A-2:				5	4,262.75	1
	9987	Cap	80	10.23	20.75	2	21.04	0
						3	31.56	0
						4	42.08	0
						1	10.52	0
						5	52.60	0
						1	10.52	0
						2	21.04	0
		Total for Cap:				18	189.36	0

4,452.11

Although the report in figure 6.6 is not complicated, it illustrates important features of the Print Report command. The data in the top portion (the form) comes from the a file that contains manufacturer codes and names. This file is attached to the main area of the view.

The data in the bottom portion of the report (the table) comes from the other fields in the main area of the view and the view table. The main file of this view has one record for each item in inventory, with item number, description, manufacturer code, quantity on hand, cost, and selling price. The individual sales records from the sales file are shown in the table of the view, including the quantity sold and backorders. Although this report has only one view, three files are attached to it. (Up to 127 files can be attached to a view.)

As you can see, one page is devoted to each manufacturer. The name of the manufacturer is printed in the heading, along with report titles and a date. The table portion of the report prints selected data fields for each item produced by the manufacturer and data for each sales record. Note the customized column headings and totals of three columns containing amounts and dollars. The following explains how to construct and execute this report.

For best results, make sure that you have selected the correct printer before beginning your report definition; different printers have different physical boundaries. When you execute the Print Report command, you are prompted:

```
Create   Execute   Modify   Remove
```

When you select Create to begin the construction of a new report definition, you are prompted to enter the name. Make sure that the name is new, because if you enter an existing name, you will receive an error. The existing report definition names are not displayed. After a name is entered, this prompt will appear:

```
New   Similar
```

If the report is new and different, select New. If the report is a variation of an existing report, select Similar. For new reports, you see the prompt as shown in figure 6.7.

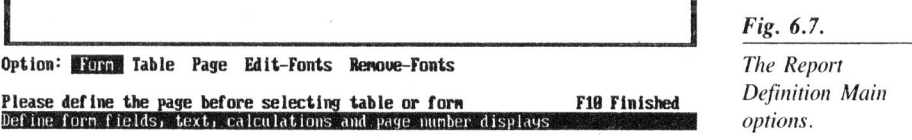

Fig. 6.7.
The Report Definition Main options.

Note that you must define the page before you can begin defining either the form or the table. The page definition for this report is shown in figures 6.8, 6.9, and 6.10.

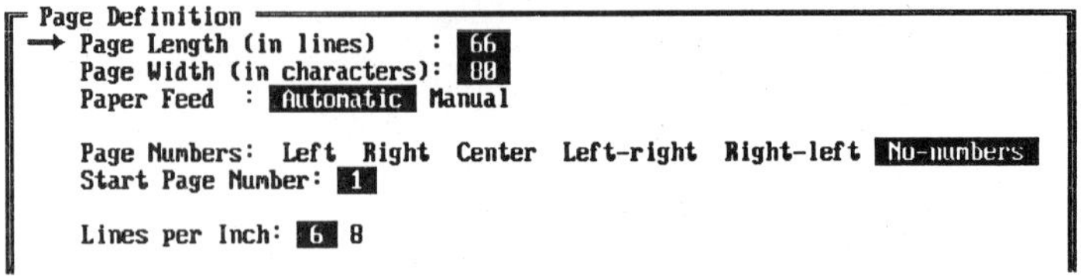

Fig. 6.8.

Report Page Definition—Page 1.

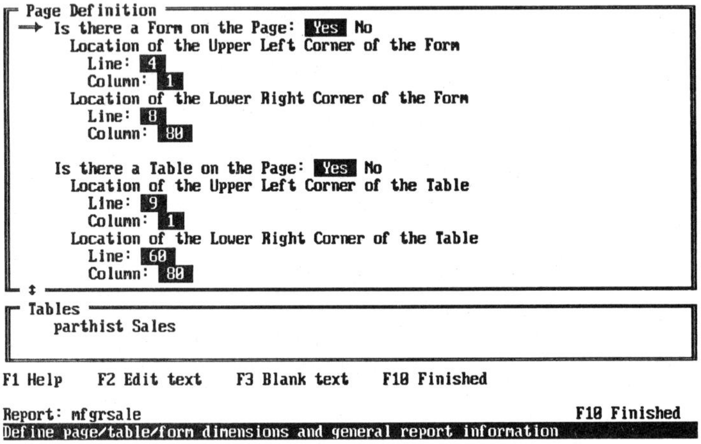

```
┌─ Page Definition ──────────────────────────────────────────────┐
│ → Page Length (in lines)       : 66                            │
│   Page Width (in characters):    80                            │
│   Paper Feed    : Automatic  Manual                            │
│                                                                │
│   Page Numbers: Left  Right  Center  Left-right  Right-left  No-numbers │
│   Start Page Number: 1                                         │
│                                                                │
│   Lines per Inch: 6  8                                         │
└────────────────────────────────────────────────────────────────┘
```

Fig. 6.9.

Report Page Definition—Page 2.

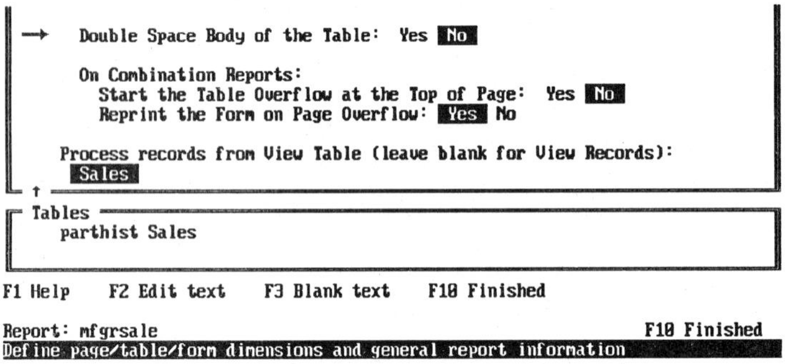

```
┌─ Page Definition ──────────────────────────────────────────────┐
│ → Is there a Form on the Page: Yes  No                         │
│   Location of the Upper Left Corner of the Form                │
│     Line:   4                                                  │
│     Column: 1                                                  │
│   Location of the Lower Right Corner of the Form               │
│     Line:   8                                                  │
│     Column: 80                                                 │
│                                                                │
│   Is there a Table on the Page: Yes  No                        │
│   Location of the Upper Left Corner of the Table               │
│     Line:   9                                                  │
│     Column: 1                                                  │
│   Location of the Lower Right Corner of the Table              │
│     Line:   60                                                 │
│     Column: 80                                                 │
├─ Tables ───────────────────────────────────────────────────────┤
│     parthist  Sales                                            │
└────────────────────────────────────────────────────────────────┘
 F1 Help    F2 Edit text    F3 Blank text    F10 Finished
 Report: mfgrsale                                     F10 Finished
 Define page/table/form dimensions and general report information
```

Fig. 6.10.

Report Page Definition—Page 3.

```
│ →  Double Space Body of the Table: Yes  No                     │
│                                                                │
│    On Combination Reports:                                     │
│      Start the Table Overflow at the Top of Page: Yes  No      │
│      Reprint the Form on Page Overflow: Yes  No                │
│                                                                │
│    Process records from View Table (leave blank for View Records): │
│      Sales                                                     │
├─ Tables ───────────────────────────────────────────────────────┤
│     parthist  Sales                                            │
└────────────────────────────────────────────────────────────────┘
 F1 Help    F2 Edit text    F3 Blank text    F10 Finished
 Report: mfgrsale                                     F10 Finished
 Define page/table/form dimensions and general report information
```

The following is a discussion of the selection items on the Report Page Definition menu:

Page Length. This is the physical length of the page in lines. The default is 66, based on 6 lines per inch and 11 inch paper. Even if you have a laser printer that can print only 60 lines on the page, the page length must always reflect the physical paper size. If you elect to print the report at 8 lines per vertical inch, change this setting to 88 for 11 inch paper.

Page Width. The default width is 80 characters if your default font is spaced at 10 characters per inch. Report spacing is based on Font 0 for your printer.

Paper Feed. Select Automatic or Manual.

Page Numbers. Select the location for printing page numbers in the table portion of a report. The page numbers will always be printed at the bottom of the page, but you have a choice of horizontal location.

Start Page Number. The default is 1. You can enter a different starting page number.

Lines per Inch. Select either 6 or 8. If you change to 8 lines per inch, however, be sure to change the page length from 66 to 88 for 11 inch paper.

Is there a Form on the Page? If you select *Yes*, the following prompts appear:

```
Location of the Upper Left Corner of the Form
     Line:
     Column:
Location of the Lower Right Corner of the Form
     Line:
     Column:
```

Enter the boundaries for the form part of a report definition. Don't exceed the boundaries of the page or overlap the form boundaries with the table boundaries. The lower line must not exceed the last line capable of being printed; for example, many laser printers cannot print beyond line 60.

Is there a Table on the Page? If you answer *Yes*, the following prompts appear:

```
Location of the Upper Left Corner of the Table
     Line:
     Column:
Location of the Lower Right Corner of the Table
     Line:
     Column:
```

Again, you should enter the boundaries of the table part of your report definition. Make sure that you do not exceed the boundaries of the page or overlap the form boundaries with the table boundaries.

Double Space Body of the Table? Answer *Yes* or *No*.

Start the Table Overflow at the Top of Page? For a combination report, you must answer this item and the next.

With enough records, the table part overflows to successive pages. You can print at the top of successive pages or below the form area. If you are using preprinted forms, you will probably answer *No* to this question, because the table data would obliterate the preprinting. If you are printing on plain paper, the usual answer is *Yes*.

Reprint the Form on Page Overflow? If the table overflows onto successive pages and it prints below the form area, you can reprint the form on successive pages. (This feature is new to SmartWare II.)

Process records from View Table. If your current view has a table and you want to print records from it, enter the name of the table here. If you do not want to print from the table, leave this item blank. The box at the bottom of the screen displays the names of all tables in the current view.

Press F10 to save the Page menu settings. Now you can proceed to define the Form or the Table part of your report, or both, if you are creating a combination report.

Creating a Form Report

When you select Form from the main option list, the form definition screen is displayed. The completed definition screen is shown in figure 6.11.

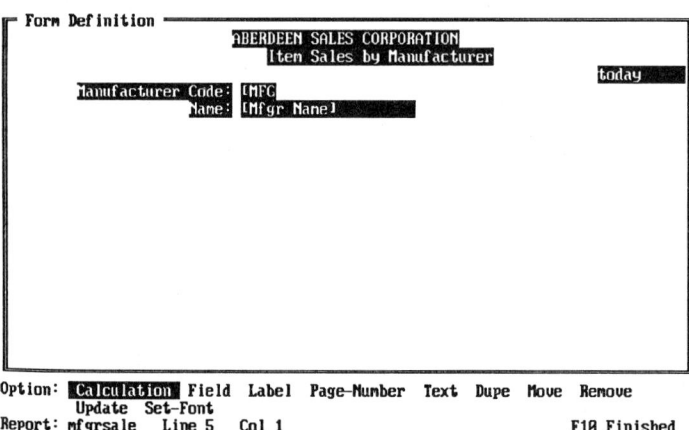

Fig. 6.11.

A completed form.

The form options fall into three categories: item definitions and editing, item positioning, and font selection.

Form Item Definitions

You can define five different types of items in a form definition:

```
Calculation   Field   Label   Page-Number   Text
```

To define a calculation, move the cursor to the upper left corner of the calculation location and select the Calculation option. You are prompted to move the cursor to the lower right corner of the area and press Enter. Next, enter the equation on the status line; press F6 to display the names of the fields from the view if you need help in remembering them. When you have completed the formula, the option menu is displayed (see fig. 6.12).

```
┌─ Calculated Options ─────────────────────────────────┐
│     Flag the Display on Overflow:  Yes  No           │
│     Justify: Left  Center  Right                     │
│ →   Display:  General  Formatted  Date  Time  Histogram │
│     Precision: 0                                     │
│     Special Formatting: None  Dollars  Percent  E-Notation │
│     Negative Formatting: Minus  Parenthesis  Credit  Debit │
│     Use Commas: Yes  No                              │
│     Check Protection: Yes  No                        │
│     Blank when Value is Zero: Yes  No                │
└──────────────────────────────────────────────────────┘
F1 Help    F2 Edit text    F3 Blank text    F10 Finished
```

Fig. 6.12.

The Calculated Field Option menu.

Set the options for the calculated field to establish the format:

Flag the Display on Overflow? If you answer *Yes* and the contents of the calculation exceeds the defined area, an error message displays when the report executes.

Justify. Select Left, Center, or Right.

For numeric calculations, select one of the following display options:

```
General   Formatted   Date   Time   Histogram
```

If you select a formatted display, select the following choices:

Precision
Special Formatting
Negative Formatting
Comma usage
Check Protection
Blank when Value is Zero

If you select the Date format, you are prompted to select from among date formats 1, 2, or 3. The selection of the time format prompts for either the 12- or 24-hour formats.

Press F10 to complete the definition of a form calculation.

To position a field in the form area, move the cursor to the upper left location and select the Field option. A pop-up menu prompts you for field names. Select the field you want and press Enter.

Initially, a solid line the width of the field is drawn on the screen; if the field is the width you want and in the location you want, simply press Enter. If you want the field shorter than the display width, move the cursor to the left. If you want to start the field in a different location, move the cursor to the new starting location and press F2 to drop the anchor. Move the cursor to the lower right corner, and press Enter when the field is wide enough. The formatting options in calculations also appear here.

Setting up a page number in the form is similar to setting up a field. Once you have defined the area, the options include not only justification and overflow flagging, but you are prompted for a page numbering control string. The following is the default:

    page *

In this string, the actual page number will begin at the location of the asterisk. If you use this string, make sure to define a field that is wide enough. Six characters is sufficient if the number of pages does not exceed nine. You can supply your own page number control string if you want.

To insert text in the form, position the cursor in the upper left corner of the text area and select the Text option. The screen will display the largest box possible that does not interfere with any other declaration. Don't worry about the box being too large; it automatically resizes to fit the text you enter. You can reposition the upper left corner of the box with the F2 key.

After you define the size of the text area, press Enter. The text area is highlighted, and you can type the text. Notice that you can enter text on multiple lines of the area; the editing characteristics are identical to the Tools Text. You can select right, left, or centered justification. If you select centered justification, the text displayed in the form definition will not show centered, but it will print centered on the report.

Printing Labels

The Label option is used primarily for mailing labels, but you could also use it in the *bill to* or *ship to* area of an invoice. You can specify several fields in one area, with one list of fields per line. Use semicolons between the field names; you can specify a maximum of 15 fields per line.

To select a label, position the cursor at the upper left corner of the label area and select the Label option. Move the cursor to the lower right corner and press Enter. Press the F6 key to display a pop-up menu of field names; select one or more fields and press Enter. Do this for all lines of your labels and press F10 when you have finished.

Besides the justification and overflow flag options, you also have the following option:

    Obtain the Next Record Before processing the Label?

This option is significant if you have two or more labels across the page. Depending on your printer's characteristics, the label printing process may be faster if you can handle label stock that is 2-up or 3-up. For the first label on the left, the answer to this prompt should be *No*; answer *Yes* for subsequent labels to the right. Use the Dupe option to simplify copying your label area information; then use the Update option to change the answer to this prompt from *No* to *Yes*. On a dot-matrix printer you should define only one set of labels across the page, not all the way down the page. Set the page length to match the height of one label. On a laser printer, the whole page must be defined. Figure 6.13 shows a sample label declaration.

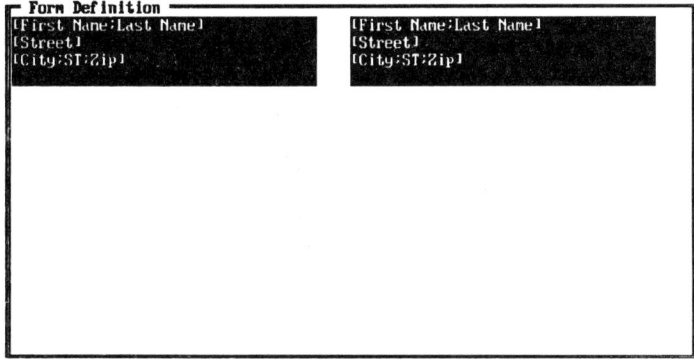

Fig. 6.13.

Label declaration.

The Label option has two advantages for printing mailing labels: neatness and versatility. If a particular line contains no data, the blank line is suppressed and successive lines are moved up. Blanks from individual fields on a line are trimmed, leaving only one blank between fields. The versatility comes from the Label option's capability to print labels 2-up or 3-up from different records.

Labels have some disadvantages, however. Fields cannot be formatted differently from the way they appear in the view. Also, you cannot insert text in a label, such as a comma after the city in an address.

Moving, Removing, and Editing Form Declarations

Several options on the form definitions screen help you change the content or placement of the form declarations. The Move command moves a declaration or a block of declarations to a new location. Position the cursor at the upper left corner of the block and select the Move command; then move the cursor to the lower right and press Enter. Now move the block to the new location and press Enter. Note that everything in the block moves simultaneously; you do not have to move one field at a time.

The Remove command deletes declarations from the form. Position the cursor on the item to remove and select the Remove command. No double-check exists to protect you; the declaration vanishes immediately.

The Update command changes the contents of an item. If it is a text area, you can insert and delete any of the text entry. If it is a field area, you can change the display options. If the item is a calculation, you can both edit the formula and change the display options.

To copy a declaration, use the Dupe command. Position the cursor on the item and select the command, then move the cursor to the upper left corner of the new area and press Enter. The item duplicates immediately. Use the Update command if you want to change the options of the copy.

Choosing Fonts

You can print your report in different fonts, depending on the capabilities of your printer. If you select the Set-Font option, you are prompted:

    Default   Change

To establish the font of new form items you are about to enter, select Default; to change the font of an individual item or a block of existing item, select Change. If the cursor is positioned on an item, only the font of that item changes. If you want to change the font of a whole block, position the cursor at the upper left corner of the block and then select the Change option.

When you set the default for new items, a pop-up menu displays the fonts that already exist for the report, and you are prompted to enter the font number to use. If you want a font that is not listed, press the F6 key to define a new font, and a menu similar to figure 6.14 is displayed:

Chapter 6: Printing Database Data and Creating Reports

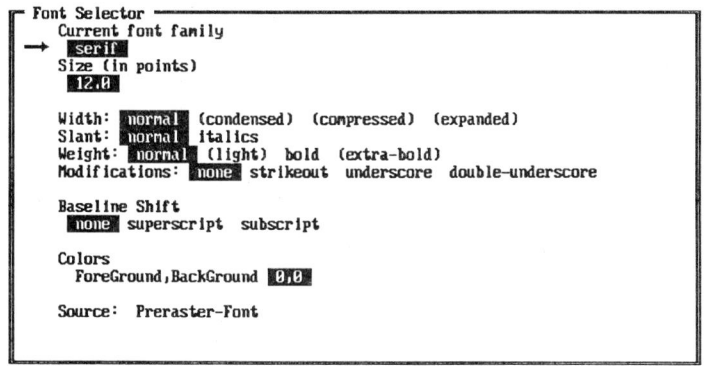

Fig. 6.14.

The Font Definition menu.

Enter a number and press the F6 key to assign the number to the font. If you do not enter a number, the next sequential font number is used. On the font definition menu, you have the following choices:

Current font family. Press F6 to display a menu of available choices of type styles.

Size (in points). Type the size you would like to have. You also can press F6 to display a menu of available prerasterized font sizes for the selected family. The F6 option is not displayed if no prerasterized font sizes are available.

Width. Move the highlight block to select normal, condensed, compressed, or expanded. Do not select any widths in parenthesis, because they are not available for the font family.

Slant. Select normal or italics.

Weight. Select normal, light, bold, or extra-bold. Don't select any weights in parentheses, because they are not available for the font family.

Modifications. Select none, strikeout, underscore, or double-underscore.

Baseline Shift. Select none, superscript, or subscript.

Colors. On an appropriate printer, you can select both ForeGround and BackGround colors. Press F6 to help you with your selection.

Press F10 when you complete the font definition menu. Note that when the cursor is positioned on an item in the form, the font number shows on the status line.

You can set the default font for new form items by selecting the Default option. Selecting a font or defining a new one is similar to the Change option. If you select large fonts, you may need to provide additional spacing either horizontally or vertically to allow for complete printing and to prevent overlap.

Do not select any font modification choices in parentheses since these selections are not available for the current font family and size. If you do make one of these selections, the system will use as close a font as possible.

When you complete the definition of the report form, press F10 to return to the main option list of the report definition process.

Note that in figure 6.6, the heading is centered; but in figure 6.11, the heading is offset. Text in proportional fonts is not centered automatically for you; in order to achieve centering, you must manually position proportional items.

Creating a Table Report

To define a table report or a table part of a combination report, select the Table option from the main option list of the Print Report Create command. The following are primary options in the table definition:

    Columns Breakpoints Grand-Totals Titles Set-Font

You should set up the columns of the report first.

Specifying Table Columns

Like the form specification, the table columns specification contains information items (Fields, Calculations, or Text) and operations (see fig. 6.15).

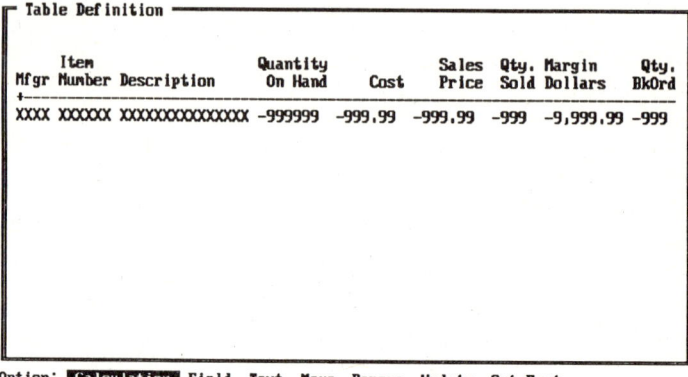

Fig. 6.15.

Selecting options from the Table Definition menu.

Selecting Fields for a Report

Any field can be selected for printing in the report. To enter a field, position the cursor and select the Field option. A pop-up menu displays the list of available fields. You can select a field with the cursor control keys or type the field name on the prompt line. Press Enter, and a secondary menu shows the options for the field display. Figure 6.16 shows the options for an alpha field; figure 6.17 shows the additional options for a numeric field.

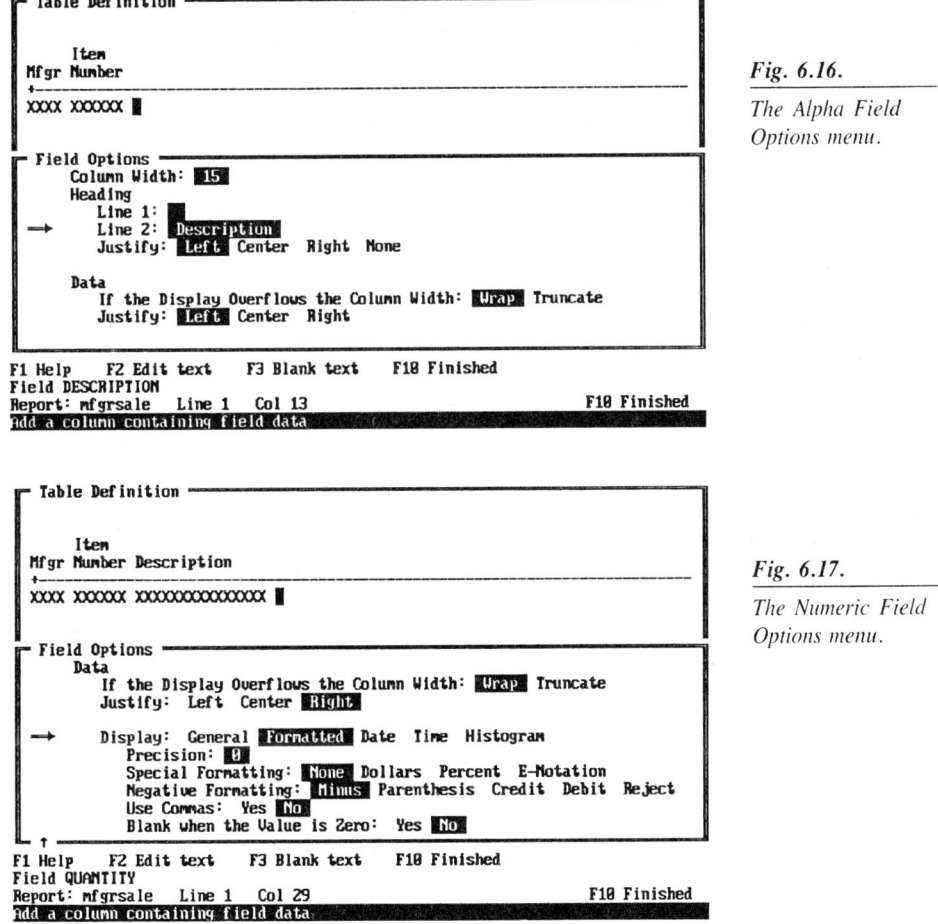

Fig. 6.16.

The Alpha Field Options menu.

Fig. 6.17.

The Numeric Field Options menu.

Compare the many field options listed under the Print Report command with the lack of options in the Print Current-Record and Print View commands. You can specify a column width; the default is either the field size or the width of the field name, whichever is longer. If the name is longer than the field, you can shorten the column width and select heading lines that fit in the new width.

Keeping the column width in mind, you can select heading lines as needed. Two lines of headings can be selected. Options for justifying the headings are Left, Right, Center, and None. The selection None allows you to position the heading by entering leading blank characters. If the field is alpha and the column width is shorter than the field width, when you choose the Truncate option, the field contents are chopped off at the end of the column. If you select the Wrap option, the field contents are printed on multiple lines in the column, with breaks between words when possible.

If the field is numeric, you have additional display options:

General   Formatted   Date   Time   Histogram

For a formatted display, select the following choices:

Precision
Special Formatting
Negative Formatting
Comma usage
Blank when Value is Zero

If you select the Date format, you are prompted to select from among date formats 1, 2, or 3. The selection of the time format prompts for either the 12- or 24-hour formats.

Press F10 to complete the entry of a field. Notice that alpha fields are marked with an X and numeric fields are marked with a 9; degrees of decimal precision are noted by the display of the decimal point. The minus sign is there to remind you to leave enough space for negative values.

Selecting Calculations for a Report

When you select the Calculated option, you are prompted to enter the calculation on the command line, as shown in figure 6.18. Calculations can contain any valid field name, constant, or function. The calculation can be performed on numeric, alphanumeric, date, or time data. The options are the same as those for the selection of a field.

A calculation formula can be up to 255 characters long; the formula will scroll to the right as you type.

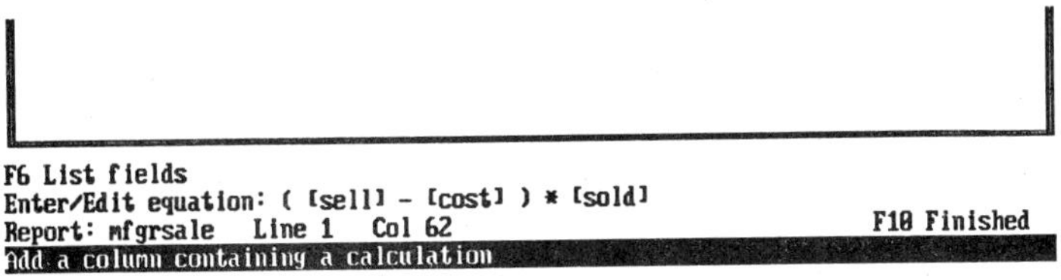

```
F6 List fields
Enter/Edit equation: ( [sell] - [cost] ) * [sold]
Report: mfgrsale   Line 1   Col 62                    F10 Finished
Add a column containing a calculation
```

Fig. 6.18.

Entering a table calculation.

Selecting Text for a Report

You can enter a maximum of 255 characters of text or "literals" in the body of the table. The options are the same as for text fields.

Moving, Removing, and Editing Table Items

Just as in the creation of a form, you can modify the definition or placement of the table items.

If you select Update from the menu to edit fields, you can change the options; if you use Update to edit calculations or text, you can change the options and either the formula or the text. To move a field, position the cursor anywhere in the field and select the Move option from the menu. Then position the cursor where you want the leftmost character of the field to appear and press Enter. (If a field is already located there, that field and any others to the right will be moved right automatically.)

To remove a field, position the cursor on the field and select the Remove option. No double-check exists with the Remove option command, so be careful.

Using Column Fonts

With the Set-Font option, you can establish the font for an individual column item or for new items you are going to declare. Select the Default option to choose a font for new columns; select the Change option to alter the font for an existing item. If the contents of the column is left justified, you can select either a proportional or monospaced font; if the column is right justified, the font must be monospaced.

Using Breakpoints

After all your columns are specified, define your breakpoints. By defining breakpoint options, you specify the action to be taken when the contents of a field (typically a sort field) in the current record are different from the contents of the same field in the previous record. For best results, the sequence of the breakpoint fields should match the start sequence of the view.

You can specify any or all of five output lines for the breakpoint. The results line can consist of a blank line, a single- or double-underscore, the results themselves, or none of these.

Specifying Breakpoint Options

Refer to the sample report in figure 6.6; note that the total margin dollars for the 11 records of the ACME manufacturer (at the bottom of the page) are followed by a single underscore, the total, and then a double underscore. Compare this output to the specifications shown in figure 6.19 for the breakpoint output lines.

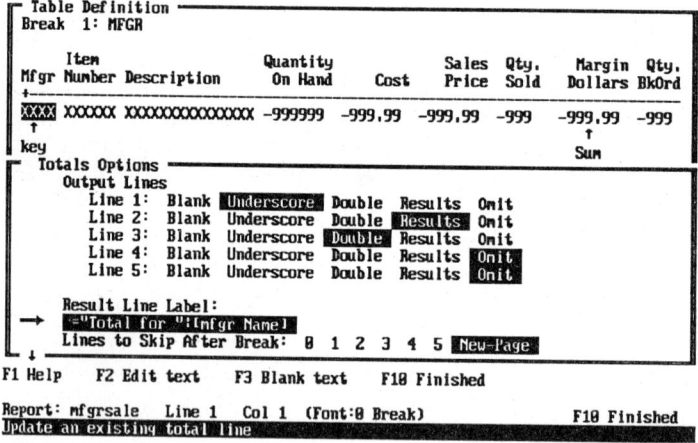

Fig. 6.19.

The Breakpoint Totals Options menu—Page 1.

The result on the report is labeled with the name of the manufacturer. You can label the result with either a literal or you can specify a calculation. If you use a calculation, the first character must be an equal (=) sign, followed by the calculation itself. (This feature is new with SmartWare II.) Note that I choose to skip to a new page after the break, so that each manufacturer begins on a new page.

The remaining Totals options are shown in figure 6.20. By suppressing the printing of duplicate field entries, break fields print only once for each breakpoint. In this example, the manufacturer code prints only once in the table part of each page. If a manufacturer has enough records to carry onto a second page, the code is reprinted at the top.

You can print a count of the records in the break group. If you have several types of summarizations to print at the breakpoint, you can have the calculation labeled for easier identification. Even if only one detail record exists in the break group, you may still want to print a summary—select *Yes* to choose this option.

Chapter 6: Printing Database Data and Creating Reports

You can specify the exact line and column location of the breakpoint results, in case areas are specified at the bottom of a page for totals, such as on an invoice.

Press F10 to save the options. Now you can specify the type of summarization to be printed at the breakpoint. The choices are shown in figure 6.21.

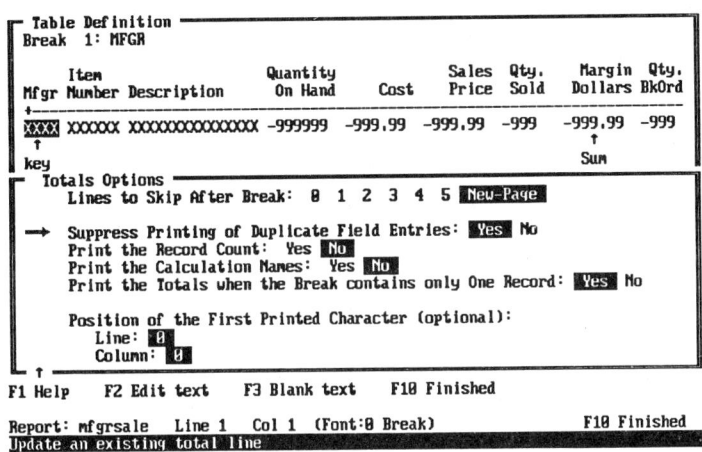

Fig. 6.20.

The Breakpoint Totals Options menu—Page 2.

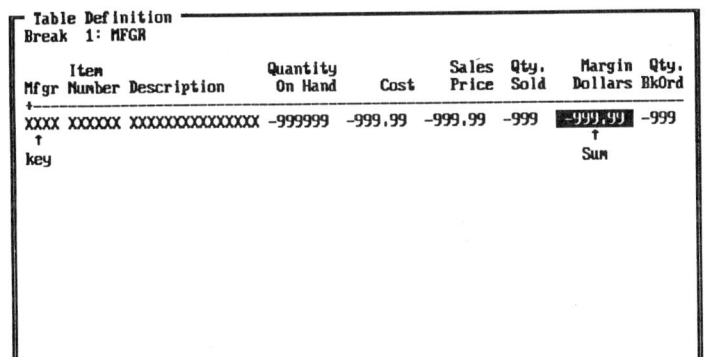

Fig. 6.21.

The Breakpoint summarization options.

Move the highlight block to point to the field to use as the source of the result and then indicate the type of operation by pressing the appropriate key:

    A   Average
    C   Count
    D   Standard-Deviation
    M   Maximum

N	Minimum
Q	Sum-Squares
R	Remove
S	Sum
V	Variance

In figure 6.21, the Margin Dollars field is the source of the summarization. Although just the Sum calculation is specified in this example, you can specify multiple summarization types for a field. Before you save the breakpoint specifications, you can individually remove any of the breakpoint types you have assigned for any fields.

Even after all breakpoints are defined, you can add an additional breakpoint by selecting the Add option. You can add a breakpoint as a final break or insert a new breakpoint logically between existing breaks. If you want to insert a breakpoint before an existing break field, use the F3 or F4 key to select the breakpoint and then press Enter.

Editing Breakpoint Specifications

You can edit the specifications for your breakpoints by selecting the Update option. Use the F3 and F4 key to select the breakpoint to edit; press Enter to complete the selection. You can press Enter again to retain the same breakpoint key. To replace the breakpoint key with a different field, use the cursor keys or the F6 key. You can change any of the breakpoint specifications, including the addition or removal of source fields or summarization types.

Removing a Breakpoint

To delete a breakpoint, select the Remove option. Use the F3 and F4 key to select a breakpoint key and press Enter.

Choosing Breakpoint Fonts

You can print breakpoint lines with individually selected fonts. When you select the Set-Font option, you are prompted:

    Default   Change

To set the font for new breakpoints you are about to define, select Default. To alter the font for an existing breakpoint, select Change. Use the F3 and F4 key to select the breakpoint for which you want to change the font and press Enter. From this point, font selection proceeds as in the form or table definitions.

Specifying Grand Totals

The Grand-Totals option specifies results at the end of a report. The option specifications are similar to those of Breakpoints, including multiple summarization types.

Defining a Table Report Title

You have defined the contents of a report; you may also need a heading and, possibly, a footing to identify and explain your report. Form reports and combination reports probably don't need headings, because text is usually specified in the body of the report. On the other hand, table reports often have headings. Select the Titles option to define a table report title.

Figure 6.22 shows that you can specify up to three lines of headings at the top and three lines of footings at the bottom of every page.

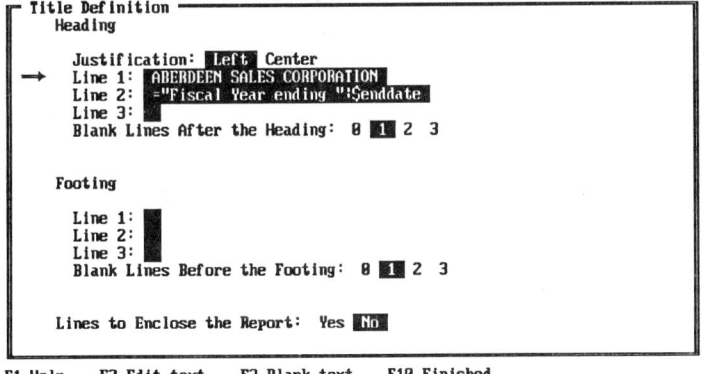

Fig. 6.22.

The table report titles.

Use the highlight block to center or left justify the headings. The following codes can also be included in headings or footings:

%L   Left Justified
%C   Centered
%R   Right Justified
%P   Page number
%D   System date
%T   System time
%F   Current view

These codes are similar to those used in the headings of Word Processor documents. The codes can be entered in either upper- or lowercase. You can include a calculation on a heading or footing line; the first character of the line must be an equal sign, followed by any valid Smart calculation. You can use any field or function; in figure 6.22 a project processing variable provides date variability in the heading.

If specified, horizontal lines enclose the report below the heading and above the footing. Press F10 to conclude the title definition process.

Choosing Table Fonts

From the main option list for the Table, if you select the Set-Font option, you are prompted:

    Default Column-Headings Heading-Titles Footing-Titles

By selecting Default, you can establish the font for any new Table items. If you select Column-Headings, you can set the font for the column headings. You also can set the fonts of the heading or footing titles.

The main option list of the Print Report Create command has two font-related choices:

    Edit-Fonts Remove-Fonts

Once you assign fonts throughout your report, you may find that you do not like the way they appear. If Font 3 should be 12 points rather than 14 points, for example, do not change every item that has Font 3 assigned to it. Instead, use the Edit-Fonts option to change the font itself.

Use the Remove-Fonts option to get rid of any unused fonts for this report; unused fonts are marked with an asterisk (*). Removing unused fonts frees additional computer memory.

Printing the Report

After creating your report definition, use the Print Report Execute command to print the report. When you execute the command, a pop-up menu of available report definitions is displayed. Once you have selected the report, you are prompted:

    Disk Printer Screen

If you choose Disk, you are prompted for an output file name. Type a standard DOS file name; the default extension will be .PRT if you do not supply one. If the file already exists, you are asked if you want to continue; answer *Y* to overwrite the file. The disk file is generated in ASCII format, regardless of your current printer or font selections.

Four additional prompts exist for printing:

Detail or Totals-Only. By selecting Totals-Only, you can create a summary report that omits the details. Only the breakpoint lines are printed.

Start page. Physical page on which to begin printing. Press Enter for a default of page 1.

End page. Page on which to end printing. If you press Enter, the default is the last page of the report.

Number of copies. The default is 1.

If you send the report to the screen, you can control the scrolling rate by pressing a number from 1 to 10 (1 is slowest and 10 is fastest; 0 represents 10 for this purpose). Press any key to pause the report; any other key will resume the display.

Regardless of the report destination, use the Ctrl-Z to cancel printing. If you are sending to the printer or a disk file, you can cancel or resume the printing.

Modifying a Report

Use the Print Report Modify command to change an existing report definition. A pop-up menu displays the names of the existing reports.

Deleting a Report

If you have a report definition you no longer need, use the Print Report Remove command to delete it. Be careful: the report definition is erased immediately.

Chapter Summary

The Print Current-Record and Print View commands are used for quick and easy reports that do not require special formats or options. The Print Report command is used for formal reports with exacting requirements, including calculations, breakpoints and fonts. The Print Report command options are extensive; by mastering them, you can produce outstanding printed output.

Integrating the Database with Other Modules

Many Database applications are entirely self-contained; there is no need to interface with files outside the module. In a self-contained system, you use the Data Enter command to add new data to your files and views; any output is in the form of reports from the Print command.

However, if you need to read data from an external file and store it in your database, or if you need to write data to another system, the information in this chapter is important. The process of reading data from an external DOS file is called *importing*; the process of writing data to a DOS file is called *exporting*. You can import data from five different types of files, including Smart Version 3.10 databases. You can export data to six different file types. In addition to the File Import and File Export commands, you can use the Data Send command to transfer data from the Database to one of the other SmartWare II modules.

Using the Data Send command to transfer data directly to another module is a major feature of an integrated system like SmartWare II. If you purchase four separate software packages to perform database management, word processing, spreadsheet, and communications, passing data from one package to another takes time and effort. You need to write out the data, exit the software, run a conversion routine (if one exists), initiate the next program, and, finally, read in the data. The SmartWare II system, however, automatically handles formatting the data and transferring it to the new module.

Importing Files

The File Import command is used to read data from one of five types of external files for storage in the data file in the current window. As each record is read from the external file, a new record is created in the internal data file. An external file can derive from another program (such as BASIC), another complete system (such as dBASE), or it can be downloaded from your company's mainframe computer. The File Import command—another way to get data—converts data from a Smart Version 3.10 data file to SmartWare II format. (Refer to Appendix D for a discussion of conversion techniques.)

ASCII Files

In a broad sense, an ASCII file is one that you can look at in a text editor (such as the Tools Text-Editor) or that you can type at the DOS operating system level and view on your screen without seeing an array of bizarre characters and "smiling faces." With the SmartWare II Database, you can import three types of ASCII files.

The first file type is actually called *ASCII*; this type of file is comma delimited. Commas separate the fields (see fig. 7.1) and double quotation marks enclose the alpha fields. When you import an ASCII file, each line will create a record in your database.

Fig. 7.1.

A sample ASCII file.

```
"345-98-7593","Ronaldo",52,878.75,"(312) 439-8760","10/01/1959"
"498-48-3980","Linden",29,1403.79,"(413) 886-3498","06/28/1975"
"239-87-8876","Davis",61,734.56,"(318) 997-6621","05/25/1969"
"288-23-8300","Karenski",41,1020.33,"(606) 779-5080","08/28/1971"
"887-63-5490","Harris",34,629.23,"(614) 776-3398","07/01/1970"
"598-44-5922","Markus",48,887.49,"(303) 797-5939","10/30/1965"
"876-33-0989","Lester",55,1516.26,"(617) 873-0979","09/05/1975"
"987-65-7653","Marzetti",47,901.45,"(704) 472-0042","10/30/1985"
"387-59-8374","Steffans",25,654.34,"(207) 878-4000","10/15/1981"
"498-34-5998","Bernstein",30,1004.56,"(916) 475-4228","06/15/1975"
"776-39-8763","Adelson",60,956.43,"(203) 739-3095","07/23/1945"
"345-54-2287","Aliakbari",35,997.66,"(201) 727-9242","08/15/1972"
"198-03-3024","Peters",18,1544,"(318) 729-5060","10/01/1985"
```

Fixed-Format Files

Each field in a fixed-format file has the same length in every record (see fig. 7.2). If the data does not fill the field entirely, blank spaces fill the remainder. No delimiters separate the fields, and each line matches one record in a data file. Because delimiters don't exist, the lengths of the fields in the external file must match the lengths of the corresponding fields in the Smartware II Database. If the fields lengths do not match, data is read incorrectly.

```
345-98-7593Ronaldo     52   878.75(312) 439-8760 10/01/1959
498-48-3980Linden      29  1403.79(413) 886-3498 06/20/1975
239-87-8876Davis       61   734.56(318) 997-6621 05/25/1969
208-23-0300Karenski    41  1020.33(606) 779-5088 08/20/1971
887-63-5498Harris      34   629.23(614) 776-3398 07/01/1970
598-44-5922Markus      48   887.49(303) 797-5939 10/30/1965
876-33-0989Lester      55  1516.26(617) 873-0979 09/05/1975
987-65-7653Marzetti    47   901.45(704) 472-0042 10/30/1985
387-59-8374Steffans    25   654.34(207) 878-4880 10/15/1981
498-34-5998Bernstein   30  1004.56(916) 475-4228 06/15/1975
776-39-8763Adelson     60   956.43(203) 739-3095 07/23/1945
345-54-2287Aliakbari   35   997.66(201) 727-9242 08/15/1972
198-03-3024Peters      18  1544.00(318) 729-5060 10/01/1985
```

Fig. 7.2.

A sample fixed-format file.

Smart Files

Similar to ASCII files, Smart files are capable of transferring from one module to another (see fig. 7.3). Text fields are still enclosed in double quotation marks, but fields are delimited by spaces (not commas). Note that the field names are listed on the first line of the file. (Do not confuse an external format Smartware II file with an internal Smart data file from Version 3.10.)

```
"SSN" "Last Name" "Age" "Wage" "Phone" "Emp Date"
"345-98-7593" "Ronaldo" 52 878.75 "(312) 439-8760" "10/01/1959"
"498-48-3980" "Linden" 29 1403.79 "(413) 886-3498" "06/20/1975"
"239-87-8876" "Davis" 61 734.56 "(318) 997-6621" "05/25/1969"
"208-23-0300" "Karenski" 41 1020.33 "(606) 779-5088" "08/20/1971"
"887-63-5498" "Harris" 34 629.23 "(614) 776-3398" "07/01/1970"
"598-44-5922" "Markus" 48 887.49 "(303) 797-5939" "10/30/1965"
"876-33-0989" "Lester" 55 1516.26 "(617) 873-0979" "09/05/1975"
"987-65-7653" "Marzetti" 47 901.45 "(704) 472-0042" "10/30/1985"
"387-59-8374" "Steffans" 25 654.34 "(207) 878-4880" "10/15/1981"
"498-34-5998" "Bernstein" 30 1004.56 "(916) 475-4228" "06/15/1975"
"776-39-8763" "Adelson" 60 956.43 "(203) 739-3095" "07/23/1945"
"345-54-2287" "Aliakbari" 35 997.66 "(201) 727-9242" "08/15/1972"
"198-03-3024" "Peters" 18 1544 "(318) 729-5060" "10/01/1985"
```

Fig. 7.3.

A sample Smart file.

Using the File Import Command

When you execute the File Import command, you are prompted as follows:

    ASCII Dbase Fixed Smart 310-Smart

Select the type of file you want to import. If you are importing an ASCII or Smart format file, make sure that the current window contains either the standard view of the destination file or a custom view of the data file. (You cannot import data into a view with two data files attached.) When you select either of these file types, you are prompted:

    Enter the filename:

Type the full name of the external file, including the extension, and press Enter. A pop-up window displays the names of the fields in the view. By using the F6 key or typing the field names, select the data file fields in the order in which they occur in the external file. The external file does not have to contain data for all fields in the database; just select the names of the fields that exist. If there is a field in the external file that you do not want to read, type a zero and a semicolon (*0;*) to skip the field. Any leftover fields at the end of the external file record are skipped automatically.

After you identify the fields, Smartware II imports the data and displays the number of records on the command line. The database keys are automatically updated.

Importing a Fixed-Format File

Reading a fixed-format file is different from an ASCII or Smart format file. Because no delimiters exist between the fields in a fixed-format file, the field sizes define the beginning and end of the data to be read into each database field. If the field is an alpha field, the field size in the external file must match the actual database field size, regardless of the width displayed in the view. If the view is standard, the storage width and display width will be identical.

If the field is numeric, the width of the field in the external file must match the display width of the field in the view. Even though all numeric database fields are stored as 8 bytes, the external file must match the display width. The length of the external record must exactly match the sum of the lengths of the individual fields.

Because external field delimiters are not present, you must read all of the fields in the fixed-format file; you cannot skip any, as you can when reading an ASCII or Smart format file. The technique of entering *0;* to skip a field will not work because you cannot indicate the length of the field to skip.

Converting a Smart Version 3.10 file

The 310-Smart option converts a database from the Smart Version 3.10 format to the SmartWare II format. Because this option is a conversion process, you create a new destination file instead of reading the database into an existing file. When you select this option, you are prompted:

    Enter the filename:

A pop-up window displays the names of the database (DB) files in the current subdirectory. (Keeping separate subdirectories for Version 3.10 files and Smart-Ware II files is often helpful.) If the source file is displayed, select the name or type the name of the database to convert, including the subdirectory path. Next, you are prompted:

    Enter the new name for the data-file:

Type the name for the new SmartWare II data file to be created. If the 3.10 database is in the current subdirectory, you must supply a different name. As the file converts, the program displays the record count on the first command line and the following messages on the second line:

```
Importing 310 records
Converting 310 keys
```

At the completion of the conversion, the standard view for the data file is displayed in the current window. Refer to Appendix D for additional suggestions for converting Smart Version 3.10 to SmartWare II.

Converting a dBASE File

Converting a dBASE database to SmartWare II format is similar to converting a Smart 3.10 database. When you select the Dbase option, a pop-up menu displays the dBASE file names in the current subdirectory. (dBASE databases have extension .DBF.) When you select the name, the program proceeds without further prompts. Because you are not prompted for a new data file name, the resulting SmartWare II database will have the same name as the dBASE file; make sure that no conflict exists before you begin the command.

Exporting Files

Just as you can import data from an external file, you can write data to an external file. When you execute the File Export command, you are prompted:

```
ASCII Dif M-Sylk Smart Text 3-Dbase
```

Examples of the ASCII and Smart files are shown in figures 7.1 and 7.3. The text format is shown in figure 7.4.

SSN	Last Name	Age	Wage	Phone	Emp Date
345-98-7593	Ronaldo	52	$878.75	(312) 439-8760	10/01/1959
498-48-3980	Linden	29	$1,403.79	(413) 886-3498	06/28/1975
239-87-0876	Davis	61	$734.56	(318) 997-6621	05/25/1969
208-23-0300	Karenski	41	$1,020.33	(606) 779-5080	08/28/1971
887-63-5498	Harris	34	$629.23	(614) 776-3398	07/01/1970
598-44-5922	Markus	48	$887.49	(303) 797-5939	10/30/1965
876-33-0989	Lester	55	$1,516.26	(617) 873-8979	09/05/1975
987-65-7653	Marzetti	47	$901.45	(704) 472-0042	10/30/1985
387-59-8374	Steffans	25	$654.34	(207) 878-4880	10/15/1981
498-34-5998	Bernstein	30	$1,004.56	(916) 475-4220	06/15/1975
776-39-8763	Adelson	60	$956.43	(203) 739-3095	07/23/1945
345-54-2287	Aliakbari	35	$997.66	(201) 727-9242	08/15/1972
198-03-3024	Peters	18	$1,544.00	(318) 729-5060	10/01/1985

Fig. 7.4.

A sample text export file.

Note that the format in figure 7.4 is fixed. The fixed-format is indicated by the lack of special delimiters between the fields and quotation marks around the alpha fields. At least one space exists between each field, and alpha fields may also contain spaces. The header record lists the complete name of each field, so if a field name is longer than the field width, the name determines the output width. Note that numeric fields retain their display formats; the WAGE field in figure 7.4 contains a dollar sign and a comma.

For all options other than 3-Dbase, you are prompted as follows:

    Row-Format Column-Format

Select Row-Format if you want each database record to create a record in the external file. If you select Column-Format, every field from the database will create an external record. Figure 7.1 shows an ASCII file written in Row-Format; figure 7.5 shows four records of the same file written in Column-Format. Note that in column format, the field name is shown as the first field.

Fig. 7.5.

A sample ASCII file in column format.

```
"SSN","345-98-7593","498-48-3988","239-87-8876","288-23-8388"
"Last Name","Ronaldo","Linden","Davis","Karenski"
"Age",52,29,61,41
"Wage",878.75,1483.79,734.56,1828.33
"Phone","(312) 439-8768","(413) 886-3498","(318) 997-6621","(686) 779-5888"
"Emp Date","10/01/1959","06/20/1975","05/25/1969","08/20/1971"
```

The Dif and M-Sylk formats are special interface protocols used by certain spreadsheet programs; you may need to write your file in one of these two formats if you are exporting data to a spreadsheet other than SmartWare II. The 3-Dbase option exports data to the dBASE III format. With this option, the file is limited to 128 fields and a maximum alpha field size of 254 characters.

After selecting the fields, you are prompted for the name of the file to write. Make sure that the file does not already exist, or you will receive an error. A Dif file has an automatic extension of .DIF; a 3-Dbase file has extension .DBF. The other formats do not have an extension unless you supply one.

Summarized Records

The Data Cross-Tab command summarizes numerical fields in a database. (If you have used previous versions of Smart, you will find that this command is an expansion of the Write Summarized command.) Eight different summary types are available, similar to the types of summaries offered in Report Table breakpoints. The capabilities of Data Cross-Tabs include the following:

- You can specify logical record selection formulas for both rows and columns, enabling you to define exactly the parameters of the cross tabulation.

- The same database record can be counted more than once in the same tabulation, enabling you to perform several steps in one pass of the file.

- The output from the Data Cross-Tab can be either an external file in the Smart format or a new database.

- The external Smart format file can be read into the Spreadsheet module for further computation and printing, or you can print directly from the new database. (Don't forget that the Print Report command can omit the printing of the details of a report, thus enabling you to perform summarized reporting.)

Creating a Cross-Tab Definition

When you execute the Data Cross-Tab command, you are prompted:

    Create Execute Modify Remove

When you select the Create option to define a Cross-Tab, you are prompted to enter the definition name. Type the name of a new definition and press Enter. Make sure that you use a new name, or you will receive the following error message:

    Definition file already exists

When you supply a new definition name, the Cross-Tab definition screen in figure 7.6 is shown.

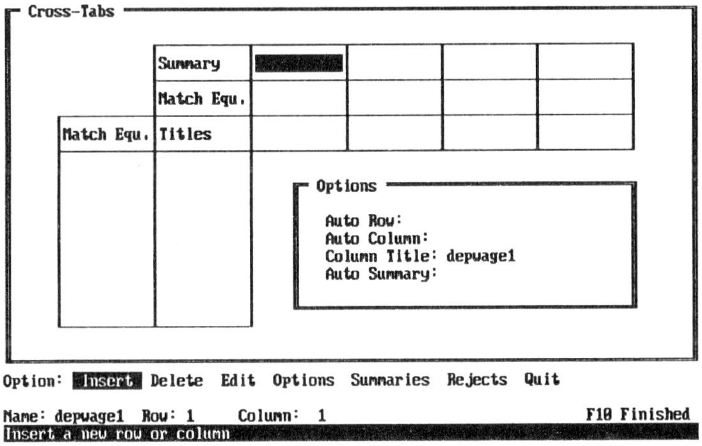

Fig. 7.6.

A Cross-Tab definition.

The definition screen is divided into three primary areas: column definitions across the top, row definitions down the left side, and options in the middle.

Column Definitions

You may create as many as three types of column specifications:

Summary. The types of summary definitions and the fields they operate upon will be entered into this area. Sum[wage], Avg[newpay], and Count are typical summary definitions. To create a summary definition, select the Summaries option.

Match Equ. Record selection criteria are entered into these boxes. The selection formulas determine how records are included in the summary definition calculation for the column. A different set of selection criteria can be entered for each row. The possibilities include criteria like the following:

[wage] > 1000
[sex] = "F"
[age] > 35 and [st] = "MA"

Select the Edit option to enter the formulas into the Match Equation boxes.

Titles Titles creates the first row of the external Smart file or the field names of the resulting database. Use the Edit option to create the titles.

Row Definitions

You may create as many as two types of row specifications:

Match Equ. Record selection criteria are entered into these boxes. The selection formulas determine how records are included in the summary definition calculation for the row. A different set of selection criteria can be entered for each row. Use the Edit option to enter the formulas into the Match Equation boxes.

An individual database record is available for a cell calculation if the database passes the selection criteria for both the row and the column. If selection criteria are not exclusive, the same record may be available in more than one cell.

Titles Titles creates the first column of the external Smart file or the first field of the resulting database. Use the Edit option to create titles.

Options

The Data Cross-Tab options include automatic row and column generation. You may also provide a title for column 1 of the output file.

Auto Row Rather than specifying a selection formula for each unique occurrence of a field as a row match equation, you can select the Auto Row option so that each unique instance of the selected field will appear on a separate row. (This is equivalent to the Match Unique option of the Write Summarized command in previous Smart versions.) When you select Auto Row, the row titles will consist of the field contents. Column summary definitions, matching equations, and titles can be created as desired with the Options Row-Automatic option.

Auto Column Just as you can set up the automatic generation of rows, you can do the same with columns. If you use the Auto Column feature, the row summary definition is entered as the Auto Summary in the options box. The Options Column-Automatic option is used to define automatic column generation.

Column Title Column Title creates the first text item on the first row of the external Smart file or the name of the first field of the resulting database. If you import the Smart file into the spreadsheet, this title will be in row 1, column 1.

Cross-Tab Commands

You can use either the Command mode or the Expert mode; the Esc key toggles between them. The Command mode has the following commands:

- *Insert*. Use this command to insert a new column or a new row before the current cursor position.

- *Delete*. Delete the row or column at the current cursor position.

- *Edit*. Edit or create the match equations or the titles.

- *Options*. Establish the Row-Automatic, Column-Automatic, or Title options.

- *Summaries*. Establish the summary definitions for the columns.

- *Rejects*. Create an "all other" matching equation for either columns or rows. If you use this option, any records not matching the selection criteria of any of the specific formulas will be accumulated into this row or column.

- *Quit*. Select this option to exit the Cross-Tab definition without saving your work. (You cannot use the Esc, because this key toggles between the Command mode and the Expert mode.) When you execute this command, if you have made changes, you are prompted:

    Abandon changes? (y/n)

To return to the menu level of the Database without saving your Cross-Tab definition, answer *Y*; respond with an *N* if you do not want to abort the definition. If you want to save your definition and return to the Database menu level, you must press the F10 key.

Use the cursor-control keys to move the highlight block from cell to cell as you construct your Cross-Tab definition.

Creating a Column Summary Definition

To create a Column Summary definition, position the highlight block in the summary cell for the desired column and select the Summaries option. The summary definition types are listed on the command lines, as shown in figure 7.7.

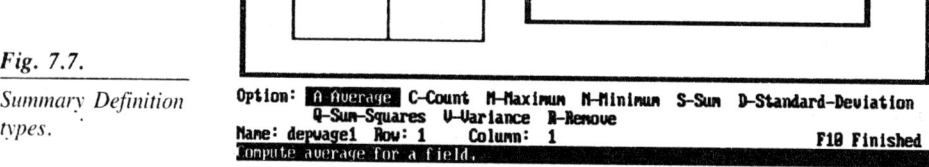

Fig. 7.7.
Summary Definition types.

Select the type of summary you want by the unique identifying letter. The nine different choices are the following:

A	Average of the field.
C	Count of the number of records.
M	Maximum value of the field.
N	Minimum value of the field.
S	Sum of the field.
D	Standard Deviation.
Q	Sum of the Squares.
V	Variance.
R	Remove the existing summary definition.

You are prompted for a field name in a pop-up window. Because the summarization process is mathematical, you must select only numerical fields unless you are simply counting records. When you press Enter, the summarization type and field are entered into the summary cell.

Entering Match Equations

To create a match equation, position the cursor on the appropriate Match Equ. column or row cell and select the Edit option. Enter the equation on the command line, using the F6 key to display the names of the fields in the current view. The following are typical equations:

   [wage] > 1000
   [sex] = ''F''
   [age] > 35 and [st] = ''MA''
   ([age] > 35 and [st] = ''MA'') or ([dept] = ''ACCT'' and [sex] = ''F'')

Formulas can be as simple or as complex as needed. The maximum formula length is 255 characters.

Formulas do not have to be exclusive. If the same record is accepted by several formulas, it can be processed more than once. If a record does not meet any of the criteria, it will not be counted at all. Consider the following two formulas:

[wage] < 1000
[wage] > 1000

These formulas omit records with [wage] fields that are exactly equal to 1000. Be careful.

In the body of the Cross-Tab matrix, a record is used in the summary calculation if it meets the matching equations for both the row and column of the cell.

Figure 7.8 shows the definition for the calculation of the sum of the wages by department. Figure 7.9 shows the resulting Smart format external file.

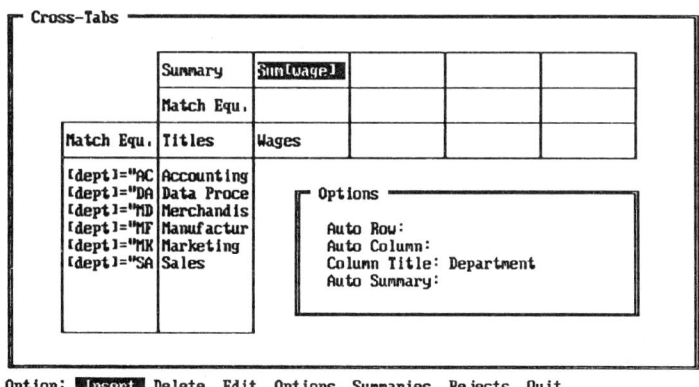

Fig. 7.8.

Cross-Tab wage sum by department definition.

"Department" "Wages"
"Accounting" 3365.86
"Data Processing" 654.34
"Merchandising" 0
"Manufacturing" 2401.45
"Marketing" 4080.59
"Sales" 2626.61

Fig. 7.9.

Cross-Tab wage sum by department result.

The definition in figure 7.10 shows additional column definitions. In previous versions of Smart, these definitions were called Row Summaries. The resulting file is shown in figure 7.11.

Fig. 7.10.

Cross-Tab multiple column definition.

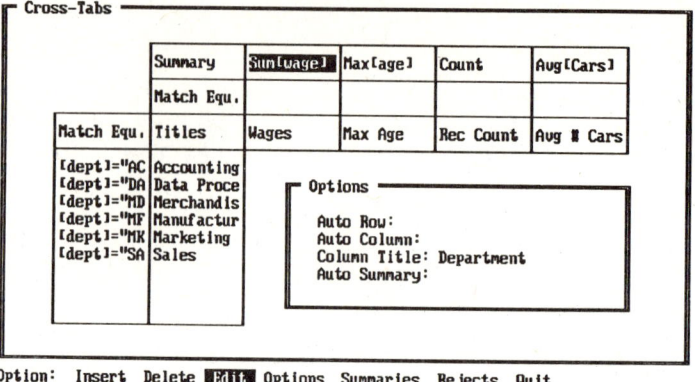

Fig. 7.11.

Cross-Tab multiple column result.

```
"Department" "Wages" "Max Age" "Rec Count" "Avg # Cars"
"Accounting" 3365.86 60 4 2.25
"Data Processing" 654.34 25 1 2
"Merchandising" 0 0 0 0
"Manufacturing" 2401.45 35 2 1.5
"Marketing" 4080.59 55 3 1.66666666666667
"Sales" 2626.61 61 3 2
```

The definition in figure 7.12 shows the use of the Column Automatic option. Notice that the Auto Column option is established as the field [sex] and that the summary definition is Sum[wage]. In previous versions of Smart, this type of definition was called Column/Row. Figure 7.13 shows the results.

Fig. 7.12.

Cross-Tab automatic column definition.

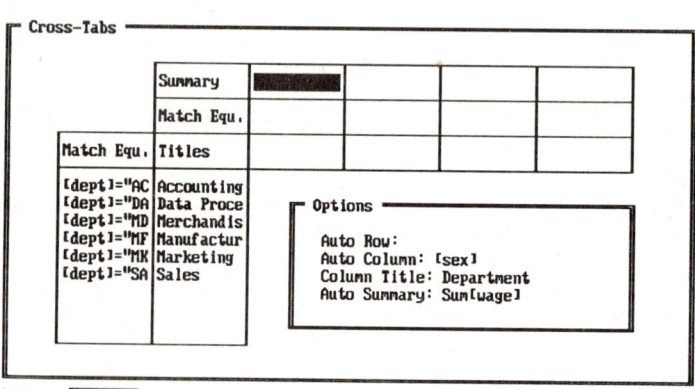

```
"Department" "F" "M"
"Accounting" 878.75 2487.11
"Data Processing" 0 654.34
"Merchandising" 0 0
"Manufacturing" 2401.45 0
"Marketing" 1516.26 2564.33
"Sales" 1892.85 734.56
```

Fig. 7.13.

Cross-Tab automatic column result.

Individual column summaries can be combined with automatic column generation. If we had left the Sum[wage] definition in column 1 (see fig. 7.8) and added the Auto Column definition by [sex] as in figure 7.12, the total wages for each department would also have been generated.

The three examples have specifically designated the departments by row. Also, you can use the Row-Automatic option to generate the rows automatically, similar to the automatic generation of the columns.

None of these examples use the formula criteria that can explicitly specify the records that are eligible for each cell. In figure 7.14, column 1 specifies the following formula:

   [age] < 40 and [sex] = "M"

In the Expert mode, the full formula is shown on the command line. In column 2, the Rejects option selects all other records. Figure 7.15 shows the results of the definition in figure 7.14.

```
┌─ Cross-Tabs ─────────────────────────────────────────┐
│           │Summary   │Sum[wage]│Sum[wage] │   │   │
│           │Match Equ.│[age]<40 │Rejects   │   │   │
│ Match Equ.│Titles    │Pay-M40  │Pay-Others│   │   │
│[dept]="AC"│Accounting│                              │
│[dept]="DA"│Data Proce│ ┌─ Options ──────────────┐   │
│[dept]="MD"│Merchandis│ │                        │   │
│[dept]="MF"│Manufactur│ │ Auto Row:              │   │
│[dept]="MK"│Marketing │ │ Auto Column:           │   │
│[dept]="SA"│Sales     │ │ Column Title: Department│  │
│           │          │ │ Auto Summary:          │   │
│           │          │ └────────────────────────┘   │
└──────────────────────────────────────────────────────┘
F2 - Edit    F6 - List Fields     Esc - Command Mode    F10 - Finished
[age] < 40 and [sex] = "M"
Name: depwage4   Row: 2    Column: 1                   F10 Finished
Edit the row or column information
```

Fig. 7.14.

Cross-Tab using matching equation definition.

```
"Department" "Pay-M40" "Pay-Others"
"Accounting" 629.23 2736.63
"Data Processing" 654.34 0
"Merchandising" 0 0
"Manufacturing" 0 2401.45
"Marketing" 1544 2536.59
"Sales" 0 2626.61
```

Fig. 7.15.

Cross-Tab using matching equation result.

Finally, figure 7.16 shows a definition for counting records (employees) by age groups in the rows, and combinations of sex and marital status in the columns. For example, the equation for column 1 is as follows:

    [sex] = "F" and [marital status] = "S"

You can see the formula for the second row on the command line in figure 7.16. Figure 7.17 shows the results.

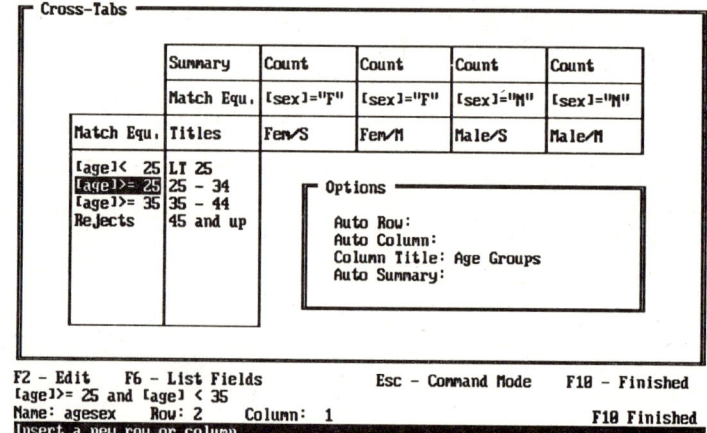

Fig. 7.16.

Cross-Tab using row and column equation-definition.

Fig. 7.17.

Cross-Tab using row and column equation-result.

You can have as many as 1,000 row equations and 1,000 column equations in one Cross-Tab definition.

Running a Cross-Tab Definition

Once you create a Cross-Tab definition, select the Data Cross-Tab Execute command to perform the summarization. A pop-up menu prompts you to select the definition. Once you choose the definition, you are prompted:

    Smart Data-File

To create an external file in the Smart format, select the Smart option; you are prompted to enter a file name. Make sure that the file does not already exist, or you will receive an error. A file extension is not automatically provided.

If you want to create a database, select the Data-File option. You are prompted for the name of a new database. You receive an error message if the data file already exists. When the data file is created, the standard screen automatically loads into the current window.

Changing a Cross-Tab Definition

To alter a Cross-Tab definition, execute the Data Cross-Tab Modify command. From the pop-up window, select the name of the definition to modify and press Enter. Then use the same commands to make the modifications that you used when you originally created the definition. Press F10 to save the definition.

Erasing a Cross-Tab Definition

If you no longer need a Cross-Tab definition, select the Remove option to the Data Cross-Tab command. Select the name of the definition to erase it from the disk.

Integrating the Smartware II Modules

As you have learned, the File Export command creates an external file in one of several formats; after creating the file, you can continue to work in the Database. A file in the Smart format can be used for transferring data from one SmartWare II module to another.

The Data Send command combines the individual steps of exporting a Smart file, quitting to another module, and then reading the file just written.

Although the Data Send command options are similar to the File Export command, there are some differences. When you execute the command, you are prompted:

    Communications Spreadsheet Wordprocessor

Select the Smartware II module to send data to.

Sending Data to the Communications Module

If you select the Communications option to the Data Send command, you see the following prompt:

    Data Text

With either option, a file is written to the disk, having the name of the view and the .IFF extension. IFF files are only temporary; they are automatically erased when you Quit from the Communications module.

When you transmit a text file and select the Default option in the Communications module, the current IFF file is sent. The Data option sends IFF files in Smart format; the Text option sends in the Text format (see figure 7.4). After you select the format, you are prompted to indicate the file orientation:

    Row-Format Column-Format

Select Row-Format if you want each database record to create a record. If you select Column-Format, every field from the database will create an external record.

Next, you are prompted for the fields to send; a pop-up menu displays the field names in the current view. The final prompt is the following:

    Enter a project file name, if needed:

If you want to execute a project file in the Communications module after the data is sent, type the file name here. This feature is valuable when you develop complex applications that involve several modules. If you do not want to start a project file in the new module, simply press Enter. The data is sent immediately to the Communications module.

Sending Data to the Spreadsheet module

When you send data to the Spreadsheet module, you are immediately prompted:

    Row-Format Column-Format

Select Row-Format to create one spreadsheet row for each database record, or Column-Format to create one spreadsheet row for each field and one column for each record. Next, you are prompted for the fields to send; a pop-up menu displays the names of the fields in the current view.

The final prompt is the following:

    Enter a project file name, if needed:

If you want to execute a project file in the Spreadsheet module after the data is sent, type the file name here. If you do not want to start a project file in the new module, simply press Enter. The data is sent immediately to the Spreadsheet module.

As the data is sent, a temporary file is written to the disk with the name of the view and extension .IFF. Once the Spreadsheet module is initiated, the data is automatically imported from the file. The new spreadsheet is assigned the name of the view from which the data was sent. Upon successful completion of the Data Send command, the IFF file is erased from the disk.

Sending Data to the Word Processor Module

As with the Communications option, if you select the Wordprocessor option of the Data Send command, you are prompted:

    Data Text

In either case, a temporary file is written to the disk with the name of the view and extension .IFF. Select the Data option if you want to go directly into print merge operations. (When you execute the Print Merge File command in the Word Processor module and select the Default file, the current IFF file is used.) The Data option writes IFF files in the Smart format. Note, however, that numeric fields are sent as alpha fields, including any display formatting of commas or dollar signs.

Select the Text option if you want the data loaded automatically into the text area of a new document. (The IFF file looks like it has been exported in the Text format.) If you select the Text format, you are prompted to indicate the file orientation:

    Row-Format Column-Format

Select Row-Format if you want each database record to create a line in the document. If you select Column-Format, every field from the database will create a line.

Next, you are prompted for the fields to send; a pop-up menu displays the names of the fields in the current view. The final prompt is the following:

    Enter a project file name, if needed:

If you want to execute a project file in the Word Processor module after the data is sent, type the file name here. If you do not want to start a project file in the new module, simply press Enter. The data is sent immediately to the Word Processor module. If you send the data as Text, it is read into the workspace of a new, unnamed document and the IFF file is erased. If you send the data as Data, the IFF file is not erased immediately. When you select the [default] file in a Print Merge command, the current IFF file is used as the source of the data. When you Quit from the Wordprocessor, the IFF file is erased.

Sending Summarized Data

Previous versions of the Smart Database offered the option to send summarized data to the other modules. To send summarized data from the SmartWare II Database, use the Data Cross-Tab command to write a file in the Smart format. If you need a fixed-format file, you can create a new database with the Data Cross-Tab command and then send the data to another module.

Chapter Summary

Each module of the Smartware II system has enough features to stand on its own; if you want a complete data manager system and don't care about word processing or spreadsheet capabilities, you could select the SmartWare II Database. However, the full strength of the integrated SmartWare II system becomes apparent when you use several modules and share data among them. The File Import and File Export commands permit you to read and write data in various formats, including the special Smart format. The Data Send command (available in every module) is used to pass data automatically from one module to another and to transfer control immediately to the destination module.

The Data Cross-Tab command can be used for both analysis of numerical data and summarization. You can define complete logical selection criteria for both the rows and columns of the output matrix. Eight different types of summary definitions are available. The result of the Data Cross-Tab command can be either an external file in the Smart format or a new SmartWare II database.

Part II

Using the SmartWare II Spreadsheet

Includes

Using the Spreadsheet Module

Formatting Spreadsheet Cells

Manipulating Data

Operating the Spreadsheet

Protecting and Viewing Spreadsheets

Using Spreadsheet Graphics

Printing Spreadsheet Data and Creating Reports

Integrating the Spreadsheet with Other Modules

Using the Spreadsheet Module

Around the office, you probably have worked with a manual spreadsheet—a piece of paper divided into rows and columns. You write numbers and other information into the spaces, called *cells*, where the rows and columns intersect. The SmartWare II Spreadsheet application is a computer representation of a manual spreadsheet. On the computer, you enter some of the entries from the keyboard; that is, the values are not derived from any other values on the sheet. The entries can be numeric values, such as numbers of employees, dollars, or percentages. Other input entries on the worksheet can include date and time values or text items, such as department names.

Not all the entries on a worksheet are input items; some are calculated from other entries. You can, for example, calculate a total at the bottom of a column of values. Sometimes you may even have totals of totals. To prepare such a spreadsheet with pencil and paper, you have to get out your calculator, do the calculations, and then write in the answers.

Preparing a large manual spreadsheet may not be so bad if you have to do it only once. But the ineffectiveness of the paper spreadsheet quickly becomes apparent when someone asks you, "What would the totals look like if you changed these three values?" and "Can you get me the answers before the meeting in 10 minutes?"

An electronic spreadsheet such as the SmartWare II Spreadsheet is really just a computerized form of the pencil-and-paper version. You still must enter the input values (for example, you must use your judgment to estimate the budget for the accounting department), but you don't have to perform the calculations. To have the computer perform the calculations for you, you write formulas in the cells that will contain the computed values. Then, when you enter the input values, the computer automatically performs the calculations.

You also can use the results of calculations as input for other calculations. You can appreciate the efficiency of an electronic spreadsheet when you have to change a few values, because you don't have to go back and perform all the calculations again—the computer does them for you. (This assumes, of course, that you have constructed the formulas correctly!)

Certain features of the SmartWare II Spreadsheet simplify the construction of your worksheet. If you have a set of input and calculation cells in a column for the month of January, for example, you can use the Edit Copy command to create similar columns for the rest of the months and for the yearly totals. If you need more space in the middle of the worksheet, you can use the Edit Insert command to add a row or a column. The remainder of the worksheet is then adjusted to accommodate the added rows or columns. In addition, if you want to rearrange your worksheet to make it more presentable or easier to work with, you can move portions of the sheet to other areas.

Some commands in the Spreadsheet are used to control the formatting and display of spreadsheet data. You use the Layout Justify command to control the positions of text within cells, or the Layout Format command to change the number of decimal places displayed or the format in which dates are displayed.

You also can use the Graph command to create and print graphs from the data in your worksheet. Several different formats are possible, including bar graphs, line graphs, hi-lo, and pie graphs. A full range of legend, title, color, pattern, and size options are available. The graphing capabilities of the Spreadsheet are competitive with those of many software packages that have been developed *just* to create graphs.

This chapter introduces you to the basic concepts of the SmartWare II Spreadsheet. You learn how to construct a spreadsheet and move around in it. You also learn about formulas and data entry. Finally, you learn how to load, save, and unload a spreadsheet.

First, however, the next section previews features that are new with the SmartWare II Spreadsheet.

New Features of the SmartWare II Spreadsheet

The new command list is probably the biggest change with SmartWare II. Most of the actual operations of the Spreadsheet have not changed from earlier versions, but they are executed with a different command sequence. Appendix C provides a translation table.

Worksheets recalculate only as needed; when you make changes to the spreadsheet, it does not automatically recalculate unaffected cells. You do not have to wait until

Chapter 8: Using the Spreadsheet Module **165**

recalculation is completed before executing the next command. In many cases, recalculation can continue in the background while you continue to work.

You can format spreadsheet cells before you enter any data into them. Smart's memory-saving feature of conserving the space of unused cells did not permit you to preformat cells in previous versions. With SmartWare II, you can preformat cells using the Layout Format command without wasting the space of truly empty cells.

Some new features enable you to audit the construction and usage of your worksheet. Using the Sheet Audit command, you can highlight cells that cause circular references, that are a *child* or *parent* to the current cell, or that are used in formulas. You also can audit specific types of formulas, such as formulas using external references.

As an additional audit tool, you can print a coded *map* of your spreadsheet that shows the different types of entries in each cell. The symbols representing formulas, text, and values within the map are set from the Tools Preferences Spreadsheet menu. You can print this map in the normal or a sideways orientation.

In fact, you can print not only the map but also the entire worksheet in a sideways orientation if you have too much data to fit on your paper. (Previously, you had to purchase a separate utility program to print a spreadsheet sideways.) When printing, you can select from a variety of fonts, and if your printer has the capability, you can define your own fonts from a set of available typefaces. To accommodate large fonts, you can vary the print height of individual rows.

A new set of file combination commands enables you to add, subtract, or copy partial or entire worksheets. You do not need to load the source worksheet before executing the command.

Many changes have been made to the graphing features:

- Text and composite graphs are supported, as are dual y-axis plots in linear or log scales.

- You can store these graphs in an industry-standard, hardware independent Metafile format and then include them in the body of SmartWare II Word Processor text or share them with many other graphics software products.

- Spreadsheet Graphics also support multiple fonts in various slants and weights; you can specify the height of the characters in point sizes. Many of the fonts are proportionally spaced.

A number of minor features have been added to SmartWare II:

- You can hide individual cells or blocks of cells as well as columns.

- You can export data in the ASCII format.

- Several more Lotus 1-2-3 compatibility features have been added.
- More spreadsheet control has been added in project processing.
- A quick-execute feature enables you to execute a command quickly and immediately return to the data entry mode.
- The Find command (now called Sheet Find) can be restricted to a block of cells; you can search for empty or highlighted cells, as well as errors, text or values.

Using SmartWare II Rows and Columns

Like a paper spreadsheet, a worksheet in the SmartWare II Spreadsheet module consists of columns and rows. Figure 8.1 shows an empty worksheet screen. Notice that the columns and rows have identifying numbers.

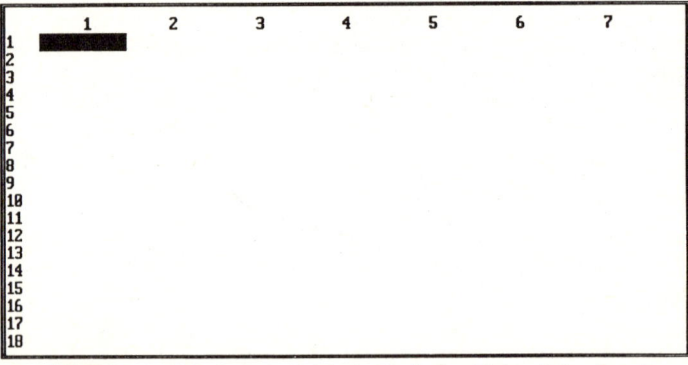

Fig. 8.1.

An empty spreadsheet screen.

You can see columns 1 through 7 and rows 1 through 18. You can view only a portion of your worksheet at any time; the rest of it is still "out there," however. By moving the cursor, you can view the other sections of the worksheet. (Changing the column width enables you to view a larger or smaller number of columns on the screen. Some of the SmartWare II screen drivers enable you to view additional rows as well as columns.)

Each cell has an *address* that is determined by the row and column numbers. For example, the cell in row 1, column 1, has the address *r1c1*. The status line at the bottom of the screen shows the location of the cursor on the worksheet, along with the name of the worksheet, the font in the current cell, and the font that you have specified for new input items. A count of the number of formulas remaining to be recalculated also appears as the calculations take place.

Spreadsheet Size

The SmartWare II Spreadsheet has a maximum of 9,999 rows and 999 columns, but you probably will not use all of them in one worksheet. You can produce such a large worksheet because the SmartWare II Spreadsheet ignores blank cells. If you don't make an entry in a cell or preformat it, then that cell is not stored in the disk file, nor does it take up space in RAM when you use the worksheet. Because spreadsheets can have many blank cells, the effective size of the sheet you can create is much larger than it would be if the blank cells consumed memory space.

The Spreadsheet has both an Enter mode and a Command mode. You use Esc to toggle between the two modes. When the spreadsheet is in the Enter mode, the word Enter: appears on the command line. In the Command mode, you see a list of the various commands below the status line (see fig. 8.1).

A new feature of SmartWare II enables you to execute a single command from the Enter mode without having to toggle between the two modes. While in the Enter mode, you simply press a slash (/) to display the Command mode menu. After the command you select is completed, you are returned immediately to the Enter mode. (Make sure you press the forward slash, not the back slash (\); the back slash is used to enter repeating text in a cell.)

The spreadsheet cursor is a highlighted block that fills the cell. In figure 8.1, cell r1c1 is highlighted. You can use the cursor keys to move the cursor to another cell. The following cursor movement keys also can be used:

Keystroke	*Moves cursor to*
Home	Top cell, current column, current screen
End	Bottom cell, current column, current screen
Tab	Right cell, current row, current screen
Shift-Tab	Left cell, current row, current screen
PgUp	Up one window (18 rows), current column
PgDn	Down one window (18 rows), current column
Ctrl-Right	Right one window, current row
Ctrl-Left	Left one window, current row
Ctrl-Home	Row 1, column 1 of worksheet
Ctrl-End	Last row used, column 1 of worksheet

In addition to the cursor keys, the Sheet Goto command is used to move the cursor to a specified cell in the current worksheet or to another worksheet in either the same window or a different window. When you use Sheet Goto, you specify the cell by the row and column designation or by a name you have defined.

Entering Data in the Enter Mode

To enter a number into a cell in the Enter mode, you make sure that the cursor is on the correct cell and then type the number. As soon as you type the first digit of the value, the prompt on the command line changes to

    Enter value:

The number you type is displayed on-screen after this prompt. When you press Enter or use the arrow keys to move the highlight block, the number appears in the cell. (The cell can store numbers of up to 15 significant digits.) When you enter the number, the second line of the command area indicates that the cell contains a value and displays the cell value.

Sometimes the first digit you type is not a number; valid initial characters for a numeric value include the minus sign (−) for a negative number and the decimal point (.). If you enter the dollar sign ($) in front of a number, it is displayed in front of the value in the cell. The presence of this formatting character does not prevent the use of the cell value in calculations.

Not all cells contain values; you also enter formulas in the cells of a spreadsheet. For example, a cell that stores the sum of a column of values is based on a formula. You can enter formulas in two ways. If you type an equal sign (=) after the Enter prompt, the prompt changes to

    Enter formula:

You can then enter a formula containing up to 240 characters. If your formula is longer than 240 characters, press Alt-F instead of the equal sign. This keystroke takes you to the large formula editor, which enables you to construct a formula as long as 1,000 characters. To enter a formula, you can type the equal sign (=) or press Alt-F from either the Command or the Enter mode.

Using Numeric and Text Operators

Formulas can contain any of the usual arithmetic and algebraic operators, as well as two special text operators:

Numeric Operators

    +   Addition
    −   Subtraction
    *   Multiplication
    /   Division
    ^   Exponentiation

Text Operators

    &   Concatenate with a separating space
    | Concatenate without a separating space

In addition to these operators, formulas can contain any of the SmartWare II functions. (See Chapter 26, "Using SmartWare II's Mathematical Functions," for more information on SmartWare II functions.) Perhaps the simplest formula you could write would be

    1 + 2

This formula would work, of course, even though there would not be much point to entering it. But if the numbers were in separate cells, using a formula may be worth the trouble. For instance, suppose that the 1 is in row 1 column 2 (r1c2) and the 2 is in row 2 column 2 (r2c2), and you want the sum to appear below the values. The formula in row 3 column 2 (r3c2) would read

    r1c2 + r2c2

The result of the formula is recalculated manually if you change the contents of cell r1c2 or r2c2 and then press F5 to recalculate the worksheet. The "Setting Preferences" section at the end of this chapter explains how to change from manual to automatic recalculation and discusses why you may prefer one method over the other.

If you want to add the values in 75 rows rather than just the two in our previous example, you don't have to type the individual addresses for each cell in the column; you simply use the SUM function, one of the most frequently used functions in the Spreadsheet. The following formula sums the values in rows 1 through 75 of column 5:

    SUM(r1:75c5)

Notice that the colon (:) is used to designate "through." The colon also can be used to designate consecutive columns. For example, the formula

    SUM(r1:75c5:10)

calculates the sum of a *block* (several consecutive rows and columns); the block extends from row 1 through row 75 and from column 5 through column 10.

When entering a formula, you can type the column numbers, or you can have SmartWare II enter them for you as you move the cursor. To have SmartWare II enter the previous formula, perform the following steps:

1. Using the cursor keys, move the cursor to the cell where you want to enter the formula.

2. Press the equal sign (=). The command line displays the prompt `Enter formula:`.

3. Type

   sum(

   The beginning of your formula appears on the command line following the prompt.

4. Move the cursor to r1c5 and press F2 to mark the beginning of the block.

5. Move the cursor to r75c10; note that as you move the cursor, the formula on the command line changes to reflect the current cursor position.

6. Type).

7. Press Enter, and the formula is complete.

When you press F2 (step 4), you in effect "drop an anchor" to designate the beginning of the cell block (or *range*). Pressing the close parenthesis key when the formula has been completed at row 75 column 10 marks the end of the block. By using this method to have the program enter the cell addresses, you avoid having to find the cells and write down the addresses before you enter the formula.

Formulas can include any of the numeric, date, time, text, business, statistical, or logical functions as well as IF statements. Figure 8.2 shows an example of a formula with multiple IF statements.

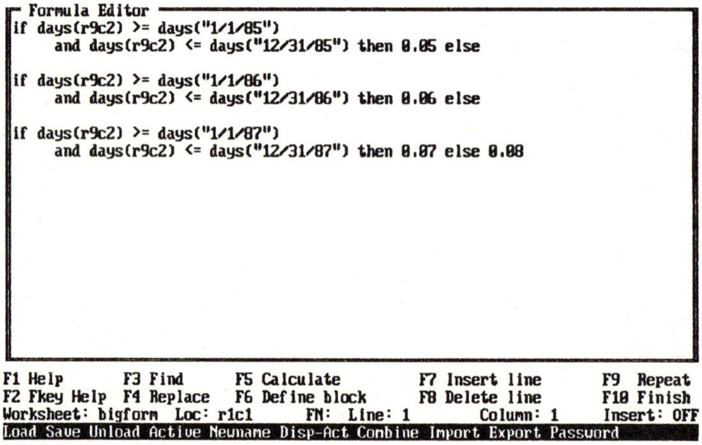

Fig. 8.2.

A complex formula on the editor screen.

```
┌─ Formula Editor ─────────────────────────────────────────────┐
│ if days(r9c2) >= days("1/1/85")                              │
│       and days(r9c2) <= days("12/31/85") then 0.05 else      │
│                                                              │
│ if days(r9c2) >= days("1/1/86")                              │
│       and days(r9c2) <= days("12/31/86") then 0.06 else      │
│                                                              │
│ if days(r9c2) >= days("1/1/87")                              │
│       and days(r9c2) <= days("12/31/87") then 0.07 else 0.08 │
│                                                              │
│                                                              │
│                                                              │
│                                                              │
│                                                              │
│                                                              │
│                                                              │
│ F1 Help       F3 Find      F5 Calculate      F7 Insert line       F9 Repeat │
│ F2 Fkey Help  F4 Replace   F6 Define block   F8 Delete line       F10 Finish│
│ Worksheet: bigform  Loc: r1c1        FN:  Line: 1      Column: 1  Insert: OFF│
└─ Load Save Unload Active Newname Disp-Act Combine Import Export Password ───┘
```

Using Relative and Absolute Cell References

The cell references in the formula in figure 8.2 are known as *relative addresses*. If you copy the formula

   r1c1 + r2c1

from cell r3c1 to r3c2, the copied formula in r3c2 is adjusted to read as follows:

r1c2 + r2c2

This capability of copying formulas on a relative basis is one of the sensational features of a computer spreadsheet. The formula in this example reads, in effect, "Add the value that is two cells above the current cell to the value that is one cell above the current cell, and place the answer in the current cell."

If your calculations are the same from column to column, you often can use the Edit Copy command with relative addressing. Sometimes, however, you want to specify that the source data *must* come from a certain row, column, or cell, no matter what cell contains the formula. A copy of the formula still needs to reference the row, column, or cell that you designated in the original formula. Referencing cells in this way is called *absolute addressing*. Examples of absolute addresses are

   r[11]c[5]   Always row 11; always column 5
   r[11]c5   Always row 11; column is relative
   r11c[5]   Row is relative; always column 5

Notice that square brackets are used to signify absolute row or column numbers. In formula entry, if you select cells by moving the cursor so that the cell addresses are entered for you, you can press F3 to change from relative addressing, the default setting, to absolute addressing.

Entering Dates

Before entering a date in a worksheet cell, you need to decide which date format you want to use.

In the Tools Preferences Global menu, the date style selection determines the order of the month, day, and year. You should select the order in which you would like to use and view the months (MM), days (DD), and years (YY). The following examples are based on the default numeric date order of month, day, and year (MMDDYY).

If you select the DATE1 format, the date is displayed as 12-Jan-90 or 12-January-90. If you specify *yyyy* for the year, the four-digit year is used. The DATE2 format can show the date as 01/12/90, 01-12-90, or 01/12/1990. When you begin to enter a date, first press @ to select DATE1 or # for DATE2. Then enter the date in one of these two formats:

   mm/dd/yy
   mm-dd-yy

The value that is stored in the cell is actually the number of days since December 31, 1899. The system just displays the cell contents in the form of the date style you have selected.

Entering Text

You can enter text directly if the initial character is a letter. If the first character is not a letter, precede the entry with a double quotation mark ("). Text entries can include up to 240 characters.

Entering Time

You can enter time values in the 12- or 24-hour format. Precede the entry with a colon (:) for the 12-hour format or a semicolon (;) for the 24-hour format, and then enter the time as HH:MM:SS (hours, minutes, and seconds) or just HH:MM. If you are using the 12-hour convention, add A or P after the entry. In SmartWare II, time is actually stored as a number representing a fraction of the full 24-hour day; using the special entry symbols displays the number in the desired time formats.

Taking Precautions

When you are building or editing your worksheet, it is entirely *RAM resident*; in other words, a complete copy of the worksheet is stored in the computer's memory. This can be both an advantage and a disadvantage.

With your worksheet resident in RAM, you can make changes without affecting the copy on disk. The Spreadsheet is therefore an excellent vehicle for performing "what if" analyses. You can try many different scenarios and never change the original disk copy. When you save the worksheet, however, the original is overwritten if you save the worksheet under the original name. If you want to preserve the original version on disk, provide a new worksheet name at the prompt.

On the other hand, if a power outage occurs while you are working, you are at a serious disadvantage. Because the disk contains no record of the work you have performed since the last time you saved the worksheet, you lose any changes you have made. If you make a considerable number of changes, be sure to use the File Save command periodically.

Working With Spreadsheet Files

The procedures for loading, saving, and unloading spreadsheet files are similar to the methods you use in the other SmartWare II modules. You may already be familiar with the commands File Load, File Activate, File Save, and File Unload.

Loading a Worksheet

When you first enter the Spreadsheet, a blank window is displayed and the system is in the Enter mode. If you want to load an existing worksheet, you need to switch to the Command mode, or you can use the Quick key Alt-L. (You can specify a specific worksheet to be loaded automatically for you; refer to the Tools Preferences Spreadsheet menu.) To use the File Load command, press Esc to switch to the Command mode (see fig. 8.3). When you load a worksheet, it is read from the disk and displayed in the current window.

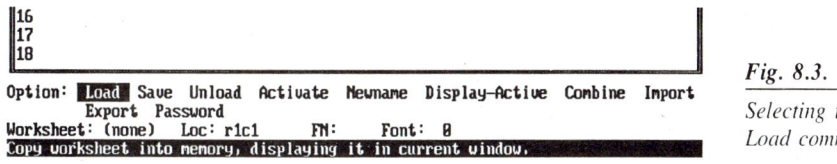

Fig. 8.3.

Selecting the File Load command.

When you select the Load option from the File command, a pop-up window appears with the names of all the worksheet files in the current default subdirectory (see fig. 8.4).

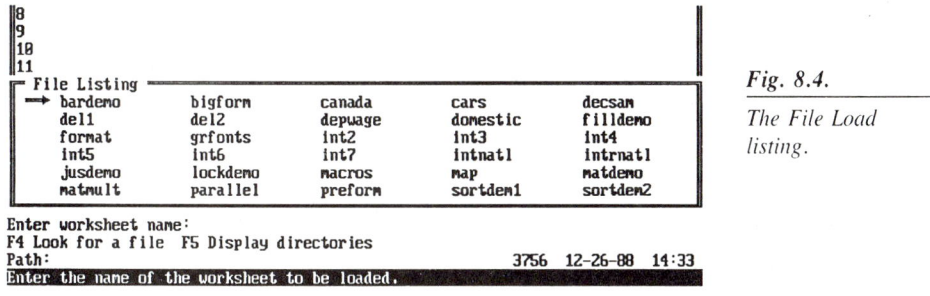

Fig. 8.4.

The File Load listing.

To select a worksheet, use the cursor keys to move the arrow to the desired worksheet and press Enter, or type the name of the worksheet at the following prompt:

    Enter worksheet name:

The size, date, and time of the worksheet at the cursor are displayed on the status line. If you want to load a file that is not in the current subdirectory or need to locate a file in another subdirectory, you can use the function keys F4 (look for a file) or F5 (display directories). If you know part of the name of the file but forget its location, press the F4 key. The following prompt is displayed:

    Enter the file specification

You should enter the criteria in the same way you search for file names when using the Tools Directory Display command. The asterisk and question mark "wild cards" are valid.

For example, if you are looking for a worksheet that begins with the letter *D* but you forget the subdirectory location, enter the following file specification:

   c:\d*.ws

The specified directory (in this example, the root) and all subordinate subdirectories are searched for files that match the selection criteria. Each subdirectory is searched in turn, and if a matching file is found, the following message is displayed:

   File was found in <*directory name**filename*> Continue Searching (y/n)

Press *Y* to continue the search. Press *N* to halt the search and display a pop-up window containing names of files to load. Move the cursor to the file you want and press Enter. Rather than selecting a file, you can press F5 twice to display all the worksheets in the subdirectory.

If you want to display all the worksheets in the subdirectory, press F5 twice, and then press *Y* if you want to continue the search. Otherwise, press *N* to halt the search and display a pop-up window enabling you to load the file.

If you don't press *N* to stop the search, the following message is displayed when the list of available files is exhausted:

   End of search, press any key

The original pop-up window of files from the current subdirectory continues to be displayed.

When you execute the File Load command, if you know the subdirectory but forget the name of the file, press F5. A pop-up window displays the following symbols:

Display	*Meaning*
\	Root Directory of current disk
..	Subdirectory immediately parent to the current subdirectory

The names of any subdirectories subordinate to the current subdirectory also are displayed. Move the cursor to the entry in the pop-up window and press Enter. The names of the subdirectories subordinate to the selected subdirectory are displayed. Move the cursor to the desired subdirectory and press Enter.

To display the names of all the subdirectories subordinate to the root directory, for example, select the root directory symbol (\) by pressing Enter after you press F5. Then select the subdirectory you want by pressing Enter.

To display a pop-up window with the names of the worksheets in the selected subdirectory, press F5 again. If the file you want to load is displayed, move the cursor to the name of the file and press Enter.

If the name of the file you are looking for is not displayed, you can display the subdirectory names again by pressing F5 once more. Thus, you can use F5 to toggle between the display of the file names and the subdirectory names. Press F7 to change the displayed directory.

Once you have selected a file to load, if you have attached a password to your worksheet, the `Enter password:` prompt appears on-screen. You must type the password and press Enter. Remember that passwords are sensitive to case; *PASSWORD* is not the same as *password*. You have three chances to type the correct password before the load command is aborted.

When loading a worksheet, if you enter the name of a worksheet that does not exist, the following prompt is displayed:

`Create new worksheet? (y/n)`

Answer *Y* to create the new worksheet. The current window is cleared, but the previous worksheet remains active.

Activating a Worksheet

The File Activate command is used in much the same way as the File Load command. The main difference is that when you use the File Activate command, the activated worksheet is not displayed. You can display the newly activated file later using the Sheet Goto command, but the current worksheet remains in place. You can use the File Display-Active command to display a list of all loaded or activated worksheets.

If you activate a worksheet without loading one previously into the current window, the activated worksheet is still not displayed. This is in contrast to the operation of the File Load and File Activate commands in the SmartWare II Database module. In the Database, if you activate a file without loading one previously, the File Activate command is treated as a File Load command, and the file is displayed in the current window.

Saving a Worksheet to a Disk File

You use the File Save command (or the Quick key Alt-S) to write the current worksheet to a disk file while retaining it in the window. Because SmartWare II worksheets are RAM resident, using the File Save command frequently is a good habit to acquire. You can protect yourself against losing a substantial amount of work in the event of a power outage or a hardware malfunction.

When you initiate the File Save command, you are prompted,

    Enter worksheet name:

If you want to save the file under the current name, just press Enter. If a previous version of the worksheet file already exists on disk, that version is replaced by the current worksheet. If such a file does not exist, the file is created. (If you have requested automatic file backup in Global Preferences, the previous version becomes the BWS file.)

You may want to save the file under a new name, however. If you are examining various scenarios for a budget, for example, you may want to save each scenario under a different name. In such a case, type a new name in response to the prompt and press Enter. If you already have a file on disk with that name, you are prompted,

    Worksheet already exists. Continue? (y/n)

Press *Y* to overwrite the existing disk file; if you press *N*, you are prompted to enter an alternate name.

If your worksheet has not yet been named, you must enter a name before you can save the file.

Clearing a Worksheet from Memory

Use the File Unload command (or the Quick key Alt-U) to clear a worksheet from memory in order to make room for other worksheets.

If only one worksheet is active and it is in the current window, the File Unload command requires no further action. If you have modified but not saved the worksheet since the last change, you are prompted,

    Worksheet has been modified. Save before unloading? (y/n)

If you press *N*, the window is cleared, and the changes you made since the last File Save are lost. If you type *Y*, the worksheet is saved to the disk under the current name and cleared from RAM. If you want to keep both the original disk version and a copy of the one you have modified, you must save the worksheet under a different name.

If more than one worksheet is active when you select File Unload, you are prompted,

    Enter worksheet name:

You must type the name of the worksheet you want to unload; no pop-up menu displays the names of the active worksheets. If you have forgotten which are loaded, you can use the File Display-Active command to display them on your screen. (If you just press Enter, the currently displayed worksheet is unloaded.) When you supply the name of an active worksheet and press Enter, an unmodified worksheet is removed from RAM immediately. As mentioned previously, if the file has been modified, you are asked whether you want to save it before unloading.

When the worksheet in the current window is unloaded, the window is cleared and the name is changed to *none*. You have one other option when you use the File Unload command. In response to the prompt for a worksheet name, you can type *ALL* to clear all worksheets from memory.

You must be careful when you use the File Unload All command; *you are not prompted to save individual files before they are unloaded.* You are cautioned, however, with the following prompt:

    Unload all files without saving? (y/n)

If some of your worksheets have been modified and you have not saved each one individually, the changes are lost when you select File Unload All and answer *Y* to this prompt. (This option works differently from the Database, in which File Unload All automatically saves all files.

If you answer *N* to this prompt, the command is aborted. You can use the File Save command or the File Unload command to specify individual files and make sure the changes are saved. (Use the File Display-Active command to display the names and modification status of the active files.)

You terminate a SmartWare II Spreadsheet session by pressing F10 and then Quit. If you have worksheets loaded that have been modified but not saved, you are prompted for each one individually:

    Save modified worksheet *[name]*? (y/n)

The name of the worksheet appears in place of *[name]* in this prompt. Answer *Y* to save the worksheet or *N* to discard any changes you have made. After you have selected Quit, you cannot press Esc to remain in the Spreadsheet module; you must leave the module.

Setting Preferences

Before you create your first spreadsheet, you should set the Spreadsheet preferences. Figure 8.5 shows the Spreadsheet Preferences screen, which is accessed with the Tools Preferences command.

First, set the default Recalculation mode to Automatic or Manual. If it is set to manual, you must press F5 to recalculate your worksheets. If you want to make several entries in a spreadsheet before recalculating, recalculating manually is

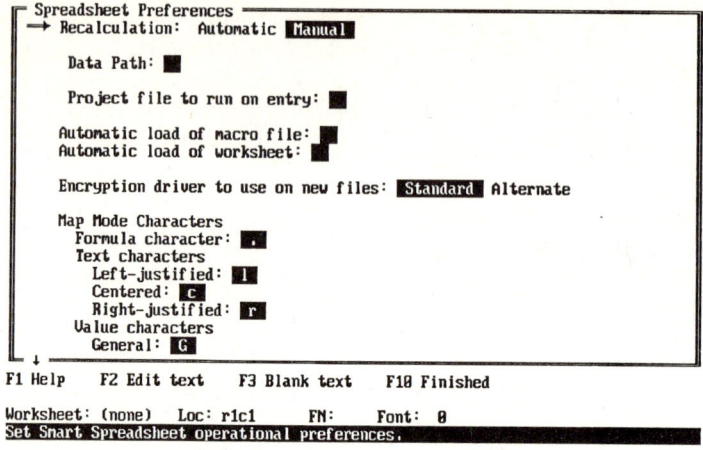

Fig. 8.5.

The Spreadsheet Preferences screen.

probably faster. No matter what default setting you specify, you can change the Calculation mode for an individual worksheet with the Sheet Calc-Mode command.

Set a default data path for your spreadsheet files if they are usually located in just one subdirectory. If you leave this entry blank, the initial data subdirectory is the "home" directory from which you initiated the SmartWare II session. You can change the current directory during a work session with the Tools Directory New-Directory command.

If you always want to run a specific project file when you begin a Spreadsheet session, enter the name of the project file, preceded by the full path.

If a macro file is to be automatically loaded, enter the full path and name of the file. Similarly, if a worksheet is always to be loaded, enter the path and name. A worksheet with a password is always saved in an encrypted (scrambled) format on disk. Select the Standard encryption driver to be used when you assign passwords to your worksheets. If you or your company has an alternate driver you want to use, contact Informix for installation instructions.

The remainder of the Spreadsheet preferences are map mode character specifications; Chapter 14 explains how to establish map symbols and display spreadsheet maps.

Chapter Summary

The SmartWare II Spreadsheet is a powerful tool for creating, maintaining, and using electronic spreadsheets. A solid understanding of the basic concepts will lead you to a full appreciation of the power and flexibility of the different commands.

Chapter 8: Using the Spreadsheet Module

This chapter has explained the four commands used to handle files in the SmartWare II Spreadsheet module: File Load, File Activate, File Save, and File Unload. Before you can use a worksheet, it must be loaded or activated. To retain a copy of the worksheet on your disk, use the File Save command. You use the File Unload command to clear a worksheet from RAM in order to make way for other worksheets.

Now that you know how to load your worksheets, the following chapter, "Formatting Spreadsheet Cells," describes some of the commands you use to construct a worksheet. Also included in this section on the SmartWare II Spreadsheet module are explanations of the commands you need to build, change, and use spreadsheets within the SmartWare II system.

Formatting Spreadsheet Cells

The formatting commands in the SmartWare II Spreadsheet module are used to alter the appearance of the worksheet on the screen and in printed reports. These commands control column width, justification of text and values, decimal display, font selection, and text attributes such as boldface and underscoring.

The menu settings you select through the Layout Worksheet-Options New-Sheet command control the default format for new worksheets. After you have begun to create a new worksheet, you can change the format of data you are about to enter by using a similar menu displayed through the Layout Worksheet-Options Current-Sheet command, or you may use the Layout Default commands. You use some formatting commands to establish the format of text or data you have not yet entered, and you use other commands to alter the format of text or values that you have already entered. With SmartWare II, you can preformat cells that do not contain entries even though you have not entered any data into them. With the exception of preformatted cells, SmartWare II allocates memory space only to cells that contain text, values, or formulas. To SmartWare II, empty cells do not exist, although they appear on-screen and can be addressed by formulas. A cell exists only after you make an entry into it or preformat it.

The format of a cell remains associated with that cell when you save the worksheet to disk, so it is still in effect the next time you load the worksheet. However, some commands do erase the formats. For example, the Edit Blank and Edit Delete commands erase any formats associated with cells. When you blank a cell, it no longer exists and therefore cannot have a format unless you preformat it again. When you delete a block of cells, other rows, columns, or cells, which have their own formats, assume the locations of the deleted area.

You have to change formats only if you need to depart from the defaults you have established for your current worksheet or for all new worksheets. If you want two decimal places for values on every worksheet you create, you can set this default in the Layout Worksheet-Options New-Sheet menu, and you never have to change it again. You can establish similar options for each individual existing worksheet.

Before learning how to set the defaults or change the format for a worksheet you have already started, you need to learn how to set the default formats for any new worksheet you create.

Setting the Layout Default Formats for New Worksheets

Execute the Layout Worksheet-Options New-Sheet command to set the defaults for new spreadsheets. If you establish the default conditions you require most often, you avoid having to make numerous individual changes to worksheets after you have begun creating them.

Setting the Recalculation Order

The possible recalculation order selections are

```
Natural Row Column
```

Normally, you use the Natural order, which recalculates worksheet formulas in the order they are needed. In a hierarchy of formulas, the formulas that are calculated from entries are recalculated first, any formulas that depend on the results of the first level of formulas are calculated next, and so on.

If you want to ignore the Natural recalculation order, you can recalculate your worksheet by Row or by Column. Selecting Row causes the formulas to be recalculated left to right within each row, one row at a time, beginning at row one. If you select Column, the formulas are recalculated top to bottom within each column, one column at a time, beginning at column one.

After you have started to construct your worksheet, you use the Sheet Calc-Mode Calc-Order command to change the order of calculation.

Setting the Default Value Format Options

By moving the highlight block with the space bar or the cursor movement keys, you can make default format selections for both value and text entries and formulas. To indicate how you want new numeric value entries displayed, move the highlight block to one of the eight format options.

Numeric Format

Select the Numeric format if you want your entries formatted as decimal numbers without a currency symbol. Figure 9.1 shows the numeric value format options.

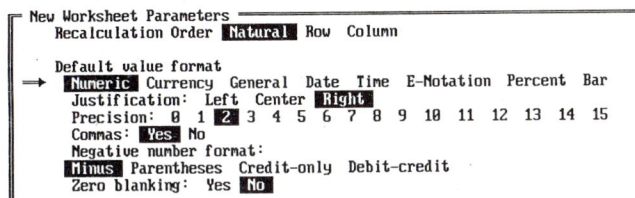

Fig. 9.1.

New-Sheet Numeric value format options.

Justification options control the placement of cell contents when the number of characters is less than the width of the cell. Normally, you select Right justification for values so that the decimals are aligned.

The Precision option refers to the number of decimal places. You can choose to display as many as 15 decimal positions in cells containing numeric values. The value displayed is automatically rounded to the number of decimals you have selected. Be aware, however, that regardless of the number of decimal places you choose to have displayed, the Spreadsheet always uses the real values in the cell in formulas. Thus, the total that is calculated and displayed in the Spreadsheet may differ from the total of the values displayed in the cells.

If you insert commas, the thousands separator character is positioned after every third digit to the left of the decimal point. (You select the actual character—a comma, period, or blank—from the Tools Preferences Global menu.)

You have four options for displaying negative numbers; your selection affects the display of negative numbers as follows:

Selection	Effect
Minus	Negative numbers are shown with a leading minus sign: −334.80
Parentheses	Negative numbers are enclosed in parentheses: (25.34)
Credit-only	Negative numbers are displayed with cr to the right: 225.00cr
Debit-credit	Negative numbers are displayed with cr to the right: 225.00cr, and positive numbers are displayed with db to the right: 447.50db

If you want to suppress the display of zero values and zero formula results, select Yes for the Zero Blanking option.

Currency Format

The options for the currency format are the same as for the numeric format. When you select Currency, however, all value entries are preceded by the currency symbol. The currency symbol choice and location is selected from the Tools Preferences Global menu.

Regardless of the default value format, if you precede a value with a dollar sign ($) when entering it into your worksheet, the format of the cell is established as currency.

General Format

If you are not overly concerned about the format of numeric entries in your worksheet, you can select the General format (see fig. 9.2), which has only the Justification option.

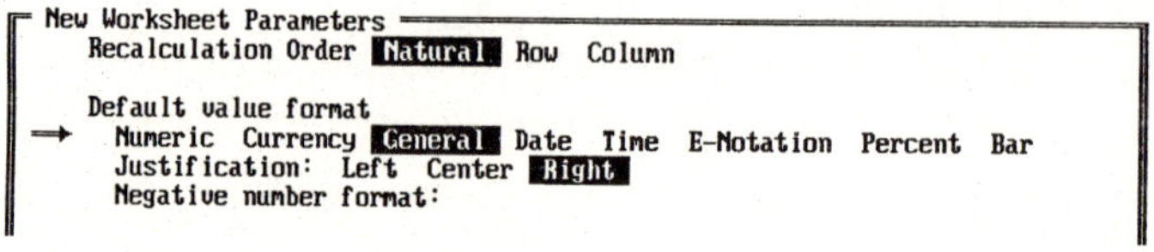

Fig. 9.2.

New-Sheet General value format options.

```
┌─ New Worksheet Parameters ─────────────────────────────────────────┐
│     Recalculation Order  Natural  Row  Column                       │
│                                                                     │
│     Default value format                                            │
│  →    Numeric  Currency  General  Date  Time  E-Notation  Percent  Bar │
│       Justification:  Left  Center  Right                           │
│       Negative number format:                                       │
└─────────────────────────────────────────────────────────────────────┘
```

The General format uses the following formatting conditions:

1. No commas are displayed.

2. Negative numbers are shown with a leading minus sign.

3. Zero values are displayed.

4. As many digits to the right of the decimal as necessary are displayed, up to 14. Trailing zeros to the right of the decimal are not displayed. Because your values may have different numbers of decimal digits, the decimal points may not align.

5. Any numbers that exceed 14 significant digits to the left of the decimal or are too large for the cell size are displayed in scientific E− notation.

Date Format

You use the Date option to display new numeric entries in one of the three date formats (see fig. 9.3). Each date format has a different layout; you should select a layout for each format in the Tools Preferences Global menu.

```
┌ New Worksheet Parameters ─────────────────────────┐
│    Recalculation Order  Natural  Row  Column      │
│                                                   │
│    Default value format                           │
│ →    Numeric  Currency  General  Date  Time  E-Notation  Percent  Bar │
│      Justification:  Left  Center  Right          │
│      Negative number format:                      │
│      Date type:  Date-1  Date-2  Date-3           │
└───────────────────────────────────────────────────┘
```

Fig. 9.3.

New-Sheet Date value format options.

A typical configuration for date displays is as follows:

Format	Typical Display
Date-1	26 Dec 88
Date-2	12/26/88
Date-3	Dec 1988

You can choose the actual configuration to assign; in SmartWare II you have the capability of defining date formats with four-digit years. Refer to Chapter 25 for further information about the use of date fields within SmartWare II.

The Spreadsheet actually stores dates as the number of days since the beginning of the 20th century. For example, 12,345 represents 10/19/33. Because you will probably not enter a date in this format, you can indicate a date entry by preceding the entry with @ for the Date-1 display or # for the Date-2 display. You can then enter the date in a more natural format, such as *10/19/33*. If you use these formatting symbols, you do not have to use the Layout Default Values Date command.

Time Format

If you want to display your numeric entries in the Time format, the decimal portion of a value you enter is interpreted as a fraction of a day and is displayed as a time value that shows hours, minutes, and seconds. Figure 9.4 shows the options you have for setting the Time format.

In the 12-hour format, follow the time entry with an *A* for a.m. or *P* for p.m.

The following are examples of the fractional representation of time entries:

Entry	Time Display
.25	06:00:00A
.75	06:00:00P
1.75	06:00:00P
.6	14:24:00 (24-hour format)
.6	02:24:00P (12-hour format)

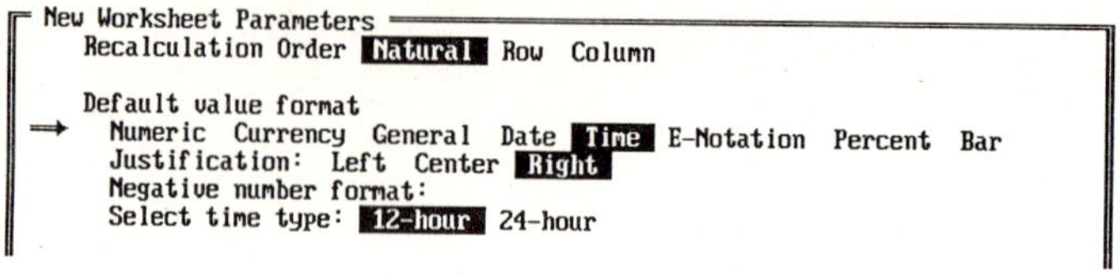

Fig. 9.4.

New-Sheet Time value format options.

```
┌─ New Worksheet Parameters ──────────────────────────────┐
│    Recalculation Order  Natural  Row  Column            │
│    Default value format                                 │
│ →    Numeric  Currency  General  Date  Time  E-Notation  Percent  Bar │
│      Justification:  Left  Center  Right               │
│      Negative number format:                            │
│      Select time type:  12-hour  24-hour                │
└─────────────────────────────────────────────────────────┘
```

Note that in SmartWare II, a time value is stored as a number, and the decimal portion of the number is used to present a time format display. In previous Smart versions, time entries were stored as special versions of text.

Scientific Notation Format (E-Notation)

Scientific notation is used to display values that are extremely small or extremely large. The following examples illustrate the results of specifying scientific notation when a precision of 11 is selected:

Value	*Display*
9976621.413	9.97662141300E+06
−302.4754228	−3.02475422800E+02

You can choose to display as many as 15 decimal positions in cells containing numeric values. The value displayed is rounded to the number of decimal places you have selected. Be aware, however, that regardless of the number of decimal places you choose to display, the Spreadsheet formulas always use the real values in the cell.

Percent Format

The options for percent entries are identical to those for numeric entries (see fig. 9.1). When you select Percent, however, as opposed to Numeric, all value entries are displayed as percents and followed by the percent sign. If you specify two decimal places, for example, an entry of *.345* is displayed as 34.50%. The underlying value, however, is stored as a decimal number, not as a percent.

Bar Notation

You can display an elementary bar graph with the Bar option. A plus sign (+) is displayed for each unit of positive value, and a minus sign (−) for each unit of negative value (see fig. 9.5). A period (.) represents a zero value. If the number of characters of the bar exceeds the column width, the cell is filled with asterisks (*). (Refer to the section in this chapter on the use of the Layout Cell-Size Width command to correct this problem.) If the underlying value of a bar cell contains decimals, the bar graph reflects only the integer portion of the value.

Chapter 9: Formatting Spreadsheet Cells

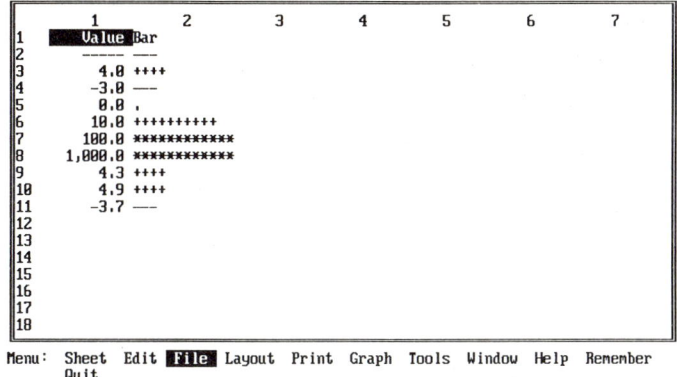

Fig. 9.5.

Effect of Layout Default Values Bar command.

Setting the Default Text Format Options

To set the default text format options, you must select one of the following options (see fig. 9.6):

    Left Center Right

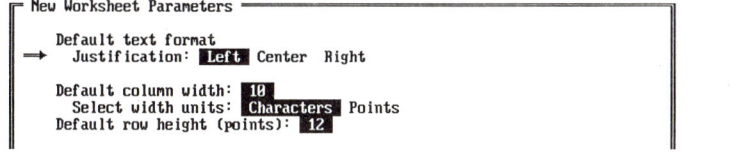

Fig. 9.6.

New-Sheet text format, column, and row sizing options.

The option you select determines the justification of newly entered text. As with values, existing entries are not affected. Typically, text entries are left-justified.

Sizing the Columns and Rows

Figure 9.6 also shows the options for sizing the columns and rows. You can set the column width in characters or points. If you select Characters, you must select a width from 0 to 74.

If you select Points as the horizontal unit of measure, a standard of 7 points per inch is used. After you have begun to construct your worksheet, use the Layout Cell-Size Width command to change the widths of individual columns or the Layout Set-Measure command to switch between character and point measurement.

You also can set the default row height to provide better spacing when you print your worksheet with large fonts. Enter a number between 1 and 300. Row height is measured in points; at 72 points per vertical inch, you can achieve a maximum row height of slightly more than 4 inches. You will not observe any difference on your screen, however; the setting takes effect only when you print your worksheet in the Enhanced mode.

Setting Print Definitions

You set the print options for new worksheets in the Worksheet Print Definition portion of the New-Sheet menu (see fig. 9.7).

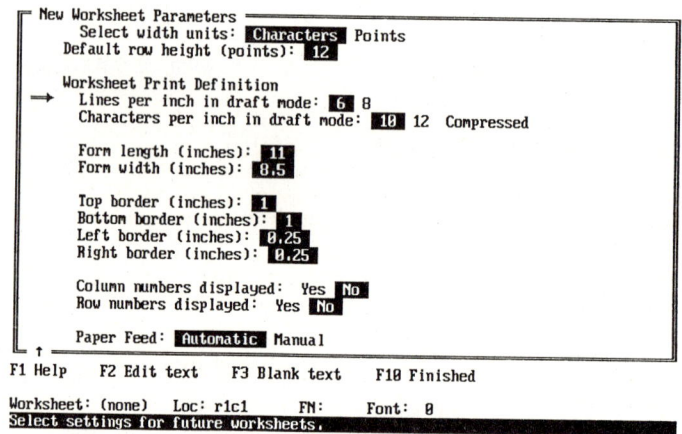

Fig. 9.7.

New-Sheet Print Definition options.

You can set the lines per inch, for the Draft mode only, to 6 or 8. In the Enhanced mode, the number of lines you can print on a page is governed by the row heights. Similarly, you set the number of characters per horizontal inch in the Draft mode to 10, 12, or compressed. If you are using a proportional font and printing in the Enhanced mode, these settings do not apply.

The form length and width must be set in inches. If needed, you can set top, bottom, left, and right borders (margins) in inches.

SmartWare II has the capability of printing the row and column numbers with a worksheet. Select Yes to display the row or column numbers. These settings do not affect your screen display. To alter the screen display of row or column numbers, use the Window Numbers command.

If you must manually feed paper into your printer and you want it to stop while you do so, change the paper feed setting to Manual; otherwise, it should be set on Automatic. Even if your printer uses cut sheets, the setting should be Automatic if the sheets feed automatically.

Changing Default Formats

After you have begun to construct your worksheet, you use the menu provided by the Layout Worksheet-Options Current-Sheet command to set the defaults for the current worksheet or to change the defaults while you are working on it. The menu is similar to the New-Sheet menu, with two exceptions:

1. You cannot reset the recalculation mode from this menu. You must use the Sheet Calc-Mode Calc-Order command to reset the recalculation mode for an existing worksheet.

2. You must use the Layout Cell-Size command to change column widths and row heights as well as the unit of measure.

Making a change to the Current-Sheet menu is equivalent to making the similar selection using the Layout Default command, discussed next in this chapter. You may find it easier to use this menu approach rather than stepping through the options of the Layout Default command. Changes you make to the Current-Sheet menu are saved with the worksheet, so they are still in effect the next time you work with it.

Formatting New Values and Text

You use the Layout Default command to set the default formats for text or values you are about to enter. To set the default values for new entries, you can use either the Layout Default command or the Layout Worksheet-Options Current-Sheet command. (Remember, you have the choice of setting formats before you make new entries or changing the formats later.)

The formatting options for text and values apply to both literal entries and the results of formulas in the worksheet cells. The default formats are valid for the duration of the session with the current worksheet or until you change the default settings. Other worksheets active at the same time can have different default formats regardless of the windows in which they are displayed.

When you use the Layout Default command to change the default format for text you are about to enter, you do not affect the format of any existing cells; they retain the format you selected at the time you entered the data. Even if you change the values in existing cells, they retain their original formats. You use the Layout Format command to change the format of existing cells.

Formatting Numeric Values

To set the default format for numeric values and formulas you are about to enter, use the Layout Default Values command. Figure 9.8 shows the eight options to this command.

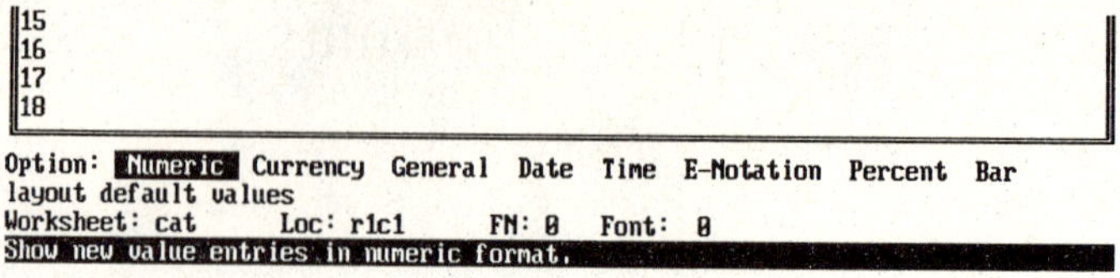

Fig. 9.8.
Layout Default Values options.

```
     15
     16
     17
     18
Option: Numeric  Currency  General  Date  Time  E-Notation  Percent  Bar
layout default values
Worksheet: cat       Loc: r1c1       FM: 0     Font: 0
Show new value entries in numeric format.
```

Numeric Entries

Select the Numeric option when you are planning to enter a number. After you select this option, you are prompted to select one of the following options:

        Commas Nocommas

The Commas option places a thousands separator after every third digit to the left of the decimal point. (Your actual selection of a comma, a period, or a blank as the thousands separator is made in the Tools Preferences Global menu.)

Next, you are given four options for displaying negative numbers; your selection affects the display of negative numbers as follows:

Selection	Effect
Minus	Negative numbers are shown with a leading minus sign: −334.80
Parentheses	Negative numbers are enclosed in parentheses: (25.34)
Credit-only	Negative numbers are displayed with cr to the right: 225.00cr
Debit-credit	Negative numbers are displayed with cr to the right: 225.00cr, and positive numbers are displayed with db to the right: 447.50db

After the selection of the display of negative numbers, the next prompt asks you to select the display of zero values:

        Show-All Zero-Blank

If you want all values to be displayed whether or not they are zeros, select the Show-All option. If you want zero values to be suppressed, select Zero-Blank. Your selection here affects the display only; any calculations that use the zero values are unaffected. If a value rounds to zero because of the number of decimal positions displayed, it is blanked.

The next prompt provides three options for justification:

        Left Center Right

These options control the placement of cell contents when the number of characters is less than the width of the cell. Normally, you select Right justification for values in order to align the decimals.

Chapter 9: Formatting Spreadsheet Cells 191

The final prompt is

    Enter decimal positions (0-15):

You can choose to display as many as 15 decimal positions (digits to the right of the decimal point) in cells containing numeric values. The value displayed is rounded to the number of decimal places you have selected. Be aware, however, that regardless of the number of decimal places you choose to have displayed, the Spreadsheet always uses the real values in the cell in formulas, as figure 9.9 illustrates.

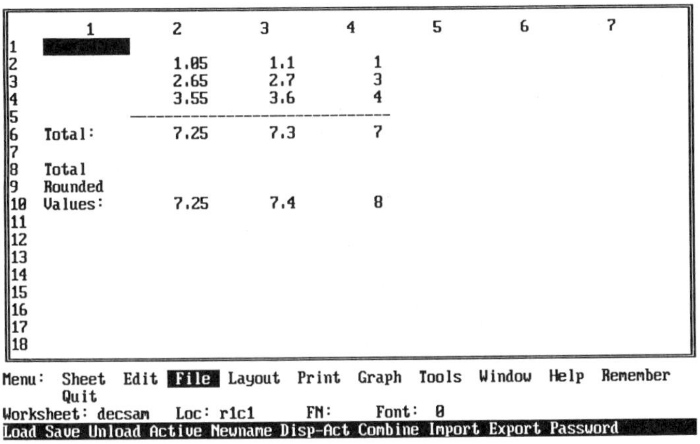

Fig. 9.9.

Rounding decimal numbers.

The numbers in cells r2c2, r3c2, and r4c2 of figure 9.9 were entered with two decimal places. The correct total of these values is displayed in r6c2. Columns 3 and 4 contain the same numbers as column 1; the only difference is that the cells are formatted to display only one decimal place in column 3 and no decimals in column 4. Notice that both the individual numbers and the totals have been rounded. Column 4 seems to show that 1 + 3 + 4 = 7. Some users may be upset by this.

To circumvent this problem, you can calculate the total as the sum of the rounded numbers, as shown in row 10. The formula used to calculate r10c3 is round(r2C3,1) + round(r3C3,1) + round(r4C3,1). The rounded answer is not the actual sum of the underlying values, but the worksheet has a more accurate appearance.

Currency Entries

The options for currency entries are identical to those for numeric entries. You must make choices about the following characteristics:

1. Commas or Nocommas
2. Display of negative numbers
3. Display of zero values
4. Justification
5. Number of decimal positions

When you select Currency, however, as opposed to Numeric, all value entries are preceded by the currency symbol. Make your selection for the currency symbol in the Tools Preferences Global menu.

General Entries

If you are not overly concerned about the format of the numeric entries in your worksheet, you can use the General format. Selecting the General option provides only one choice:

    Left Center Right

These options control the placement of cell contents when the number of characters is less than the width of the cell. Normally, you select Right justification for values, so that the decimals align, but justification may have no bearing here. The characteristics of the General format are as follows:

1. No commas are displayed.
2. Negative numbers are shown with a leading minus sign.
3. Zero values are displayed.
4. As many digits to the right of the decimal as necessary are displayed, up to 14. Trailing zeros to the right of the decimal are not displayed. Because your values may have different numbers of decimal digits, the decimal points may not align.
5. Any numbers that exceed 14 significant digits to the left of the decimal or are too large for the cell size are displayed in scientific notation.

Date Entries

The Date option is used to display new numeric entries in any of the three date formats. Each date format has a different layout; you should select a layout for each format in the Tools Preferences Global menu.

A typical configuration for date displays is as follows:

Format	Typical Display
Date-1	26 Dec 88
Date-2	12/26/88
Date-3	Dec 1988

You can choose the actual configuration to assign; in SmartWare II you have the capability of defining date formats with four-digit years. Refer to Chapter 25 for further information about the use of date fields within SmartWare II.

When you select the Date option, you are prompted:

    1 2 3

Select one of the date formats. The final prompt is for justification of the entries:

    Left Center Right

These options control the placement of cell contents when the number of characters is less than the width of the cell.

Time Entries

If you select the Time option, the decimal portion of a value you enter is interpreted as a fraction of a day and is displayed as a time value that shows hours, minutes and seconds.

When you select the Time option, you are prompted:

    12 24

If you want to represent time entries in the 12-hour clock format, select 12. Select 24 to display the time in the 24-hour format. In the 12-hour format, the time entry is followed by an A for a.m. or a P for p.m.

To enter a time in the format HH:MM or HH:MM:SS, precede the entry with a colon (:) for a 12-hour entry or a semicolon (;) for a 24-hour entry. If entering a 12-hour time, follow the entry with an *A* or a *P* to indicate a.m. or p.m. If you use these special formatting symbols, you do not have to use the Layout Default Values Time command. The final prompt enables you to select justification.

The following are examples of the fractional representation of time entries:

Entry	Time Display
.25	06:00:00A
.75	06:00:00P
1.75	06:00:00P
.6	14:24:00 (24-hour format)
.6	02:24:00P (12-hour format)

Note that in SmartWare II, a time value is stored as a number, and the decimal portion of the number is used to present a time format display. In previous Smart versions, time entries were stored as special versions of text.

Scientific Notation (E-Notation)

Scientific notation is used to display values that are extremely small or extremely large. The following examples illustrate the results of specifying scientific notation when a precision of 11 is selected:

Value	Display
9976621.413	9.97662141300E+06
−302.4754228	−3.02475422800E+02

When you select the E-notation option, the first prompt is

    Show-All Zero-Blank

If you want to display all values whether or not they are zeros, select the Show-All option. If you want to suppress the zero values, select Zero-Blank. Your selection here affects only the display; any calculations that use the zero values are unaffected. The next prompt deals with justification.

The final prompt is

    Enter decimal positions (0-15):

You can choose to display as many as 15 decimal positions in cells containing numeric values. The value displayed is rounded to the number of decimal places you have selected. Be aware, however, that regardless of the number of decimal places you choose to display, the Spreadsheet formulas always use the real values in the cell.

Percent Entries

The options for percent entries are identical to those for numeric entries. When you select Percent, however, as opposed to Numeric, all value entries are displayed as percents and followed by the percent sign. If you specify two decimal places, for example, an entry of .345 is displayed as 34.50%. The underlying value, however, is stored as a decimal number, not as a percent.

Bar Notation

You can display an elementary bar graph with the Bar option. A plus sign (+) is displayed for each unit of positive value, and a minus sign (−) for each unit of negative value. A period (.) represents a zero value. If the number of characters of the bar exceeds the column width, the cell is filled with asterisks (*). (Refer to the section in this chapter on the use of the Layout Cell-Size Width command to correct this problem.) If the underlying value of a bar cell contains decimals, the bar graph reflects only the integer portion of the value.

Justifying Text Entries

When you use the Layout Default Text command, you have only one selection to make. The prompt is

```
Left Center Right
```

These options control the placement of cell contents when the number of characters is less than the width of the cell. The option you select determines the justification of newly entered text. As with values, existing entries are not affected. Typically, text entries are left-justified.

Reformatting Existing Values and Text

Earlier, this chapter presented the Layout Default commands that are used to establish the formatting characteristics of values or text that you have not yet entered. This section covers the Layout Format commands, which you use to change the format of existing values or text. The Quick key to begin the selection of the options for these commands is Alt-Q.

In the SmartWare II Spreadsheet, you can preformat blank cells. In previous versions, preformatting was not possible because blank cells were not saved with the worksheet. When you format blank cells, a default, hidden value is stored with each cell, enabling the format to be saved. The capability of preformatting blank cells can save time, no matter whether the data is to be entered by you or by someone who does not know how to set the Layout Defaults. Whether you are formatting existing cells or preformatting blank cells, the initial prompt for the Layout Format command is

```
Block Columns Rows All Formula-Display
```

Although you still can move the cursor after this menu is displayed, you may find this command easier to use if you position the cursor on the starting location before you select the Layout Format command. (If you are going to select All, you don't have to worry about the position of the cursor because the entire worksheet is reformatted.) The Block option is used to specify a block of cells to be reformatted; you must select this option if you are preformatting blank cells. If the cursor is not already there, move the cursor to the upper left corner of the block and press F2 to mark the beginning of the block. Then move to the lower right corner of the block and press Enter to complete the block definition. You can define a block that consists of several rows and columns, just a portion of a row or a column, or even just a single cell.

When you select Rows or Columns, you are prompted for the number of rows or columns you want to reformat, beginning with the current location. You can type the number of rows or columns, or you can move the cursor so that the number is entered for you. Move the cursor down if you have specified Rows or to the right if you have selected Columns. Notice that the rows or columns are highlighted as you move the cursor.

After you have designated the range to be reformatted, the prompt in figure 9.10 is displayed.

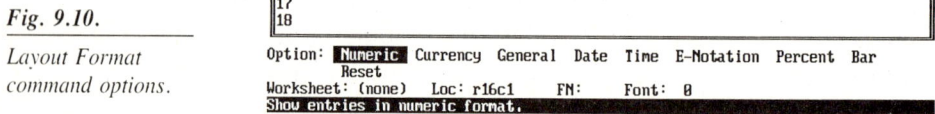

Fig. 9.10.

Layout Format command options.

Changing Value Formats

The Layout Format options are similar to those of the Layout Default Values command.

Numeric Entries

Select the Numeric option to change numeric entries. After you select this option, you are prompted to select one of the following options:

   Commas Nocommas

The Commas option places a thousands separator after every third digit to the left of the decimal point. (Your actual selection of a comma, a period, or a blank as the thousands separator is made in the Tools Preferences Global menu.)

Next, you are given four options for displaying negative numbers; your selection affects the display of negative numbers as follows:

Selection	Effect
Minus	Negative numbers are shown with a leading minus sign: −334.80
Parentheses	Negative numbers are enclosed in parentheses: (25.34)
Credit-only	Negative numbers are displayed with cr to the right: 225.00cr
Debit-credit	Negative numbers are displayed with cr to the right: 225.00cr, and positive numbers are displayed with db to the right: 447.50db

After the selection of the display of negative numbers, the next prompt asks you to select the display of zero values:

    Show-All Zero-Blank

If you want all values to be displayed whether or not they are zeros, select the Show-All option. If you want zero values to be suppressed, select Zero-Blank. Your selection here affects the display only; any calculations that use the zero values are unaffected.

The final prompt is

    Enter decimal positions (0-15):

You can choose to display as many as 15 decimal positions (digits to the right of the decimal point) in cells containing numeric values. The value displayed is rounded to the number of decimal places you have selected. Be aware, however, that regardless of the number of decimal places you choose to have displayed, the Spreadsheet always uses the real values in the cell in formulas.

Note that you are not given a prompt for justification; to change the justification of existing cells, use the Layout Justify command, covered later in this chapter.

Currency Entries

The options for currency entries are identical to those for numeric entries. You must make choices about the following characteristics:

1. Commas or Nocommas
2. Display of negative numbers
3. Display of zero values
4. Justification
5. Number of decimal positions

When you select Currency, however, as opposed to Numeric, all value entries are preceded by the currency symbol. Make your selection for the currency symbol on the Tools Preferences Global menu.

General Entries

If you are not overly concerned about the format of the numeric entries in your worksheet, you can use the General format. The characteristics of the General format are as follows:

1. No commas are displayed.
2. Negative numbers are shown with a leading minus sign.
3. Zero values are displayed.
4. As many digits to the right of the decimal as necessary are displayed, up to 14. Trailing zeros to the right of the decimal are not displayed. Because your values may have different numbers of decimal digits, the decimal points may not align.
5. Any numbers that exceed 14 significant digits to the left of the decimal or are too large for the cell size are displayed in scientific notation.

When you select the General option, there are no additional prompts.

Date Entries

The Date option is used to display new numeric entries in any of the three date formats. Each date format has a different layout; you should select a layout for each format in the Tools Preferences Global menu.

A typical configuration for date displays is as follows:

Format	Typical Display
Date-1	26 Dec 88
Date-2	12/26/88
Date-3	Dec 1988

You can choose the actual configuration to assign; in SmartWare II, you have the capability of defining date formats with four-digit years. Refer to Chapter 25 for further information about using date fields in SmartWare II.

When you select the Date option, you are prompted:

1 2 3

The Spreadsheet actually stores dates as the number of days since the beginning of the 20th century. For example, 12,345 represents 10/19/33. Because you will probably not enter a date in this format, you can indicate a date entry by preceding the entry with @ for the Date-1 display or # for the Date-2 display. The date selections are used to display these sequential numbers in a more usable format. To show a number in the Date-3 format, you must use the Layout Format command to change the display.

Time Entries

If you select the Time option, the decimal portion of a value you enter is interpreted as a fraction of a day and is displayed as a time value that shows hours, minutes, and seconds.

When you select the Time option, you are prompted:

    12 24

If you want to represent time entries in the 12-hour clock format, select 12. Select 24 to display the time in the 24-hour format. In the 12-hour format, the time entry is followed by an A for a.m. or a P for p.m.

Note that in SmartWare II, a time value is stored as a number, and the decimal portion of the number is used to present a time format display. In previous Smart versions, time entries were stored as special versions of text.

Scientific Notation (E-Notation)

Scientific notation is used to display values that are extremely small or extremely large. The following examples illustrate the results of specifying scientific notation when a precision of 11 is selected:

Value	*Display*
9976621.413	9.97662141300E+06
−302.4754228	−3.02475422800E+02

When you select the E-notation option, the first prompt is

    Show-All Zero-Blank

If you want to display all values whether or not they are zeros, select the Show-All option. If you want to suppress the zero values, select Zero-Blank. Your selection here affects only the display; any calculations that use the zero values are unaffected.

The final prompt is

    Enter decimal positions (0-15):

You can choose to display as many as 15 decimal positions in cells containing numeric values. The value displayed is rounded to the number of decimal places you have selected. Be aware, however, that regardless of the number of decimal places you choose to display, the Spreadsheet formulas always use the real values in the cell.

Percent Entries

The options to reformat percent cells are identical to those for numeric cells. You must make choices about the following characteristics:

1. Commas or Nocommas
2. Display of Negative numbers
3. Display of zero values
4. Number of decimal positions

When you select Percent, however, as opposed to Numeric, all value entries are displayed as percents and followed by the percent sign. If you specify two decimal places, for example, an entry of *.345* is displayed as 34.50%. The underlying value, however, is stored as a decimal number, not as a percent.

Bar Notation

You can display an elementary bar graph with the Bar option. A plus sign (+) is displayed for each unit of positive value, and a minus sign (−) for each unit of negative value. A period (.) represents a zero value. If the number of characters of the bar exceeds the column width, the cell is filled with asterisks (*). (Refer to the section in this chapter on the use of the Layout Cell-Size Width command to correct this problem.) If the underlying value of a bar cell contains decimals, the bar graph reflects only the integer portion of the value. Refer to figure 9.5 for an example of the use of the bar notation.

Resetting Cell Formats

If you execute the Layout Format command and select the Reset option, you can restore a designated area to the default format for the worksheet (see fig. 9.10). The default format is governed by your choices in the Layout Worksheet-Options Current-Sheet menu.

Viewing Worksheet Formulas and Maps

Use the Layout Format Formula-Display command to display the text or a map of the formulas in your worksheet. When you execute the command, your options are

    Map Text Values

Move the highlight block to the option you want and press Enter, or press the initial letter of the option on your keyboard.

Viewing Worksheet Formulas

If you select Text, the actual formulas of individual cells, not the results of the formulas, are displayed on the screen. (In this command, text means the text of the formulas, not to a data type in your worksheet.) Figure 9.11 shows a sample worksheet; figure 9.12 displays the formulas in the same worksheet.

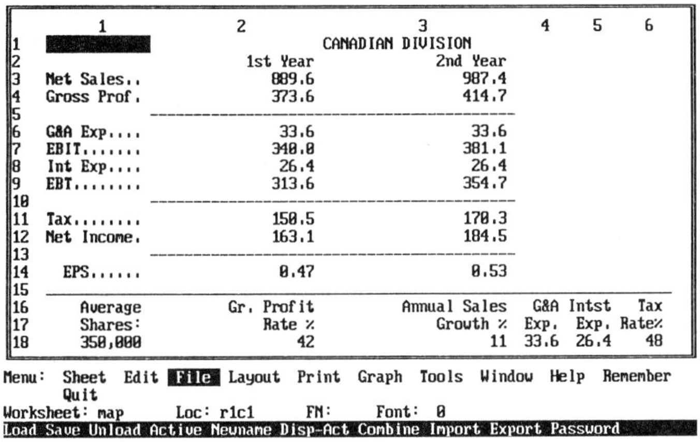

```
        1                 2               3            4     5     6
1                               CANADIAN DIVISION
2                          1st Year               2nd Year
3   Net Sales..              889.6                   987.4
4   Gross Prof.              373.6                   414.7
5                ----------------------------------------------
6   G&A Exp....               33.6                    33.6
7   EBIT.......              340.0                   381.1
8   Int Exp....               26.4                    26.4
9   EBT........              313.6                   354.7
10               ----------------------------------------------
11  Tax........              150.5                   170.3
12  Net Income.              163.1                   184.5
13               ----------------------------------------------
14    EPS......               0.47                    0.53
15  ----------------------------------------------------------------
16      Average           Gr. Profit         Annual Sales  G&A  Intst   Tax
17      Shares:             Rate %             Growth %   Exp.  Exp.  Rate%
18      350,000                 42                   11   33.6  26.4     40
Menu: Sheet  Edit  File  Layout  Print  Graph  Tools  Window  Help  Remember
      Quit
Worksheet: map       Loc: r1c1      FN:       Font: 0
Load Save Unload Active Newname Disp-Act Combine Import Export Password
```

Fig. 9.11.

Sample worksheet.

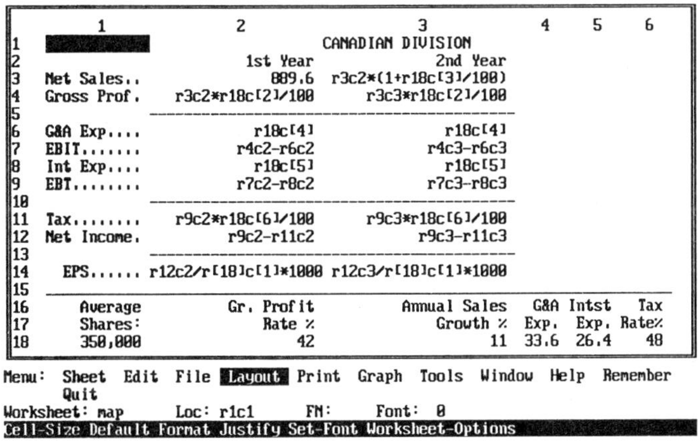

```
        1                 2               3            4     5     6
1                               CANADIAN DIVISION
2                          1st Year               2nd Year
3   Net Sales..              889.6   r3c2*(1+r18c[3]/100)
4   Gross Prof.      r3c2*r18c[2]/100       r3c3*r18c[2]/100
5                ----------------------------------------------
6   G&A Exp....            r18c[4]                 r18c[4]
7   EBIT.......          r4c2-r6c2               r4c3-r6c3
8   Int Exp....            r18c[5]                 r18c[5]
9   EBT........          r7c2-r8c2               r7c3-r8c3
10               ----------------------------------------------
11  Tax........      r9c2*r18c[6]/100       r9c3*r18c[6]/100
12  Net Income.         r9c2-r11c2              r9c3-r11c3
13               ----------------------------------------------
14    EPS...... r12c2/r[18]c[1]*1000 r12c3/r[18]c[1]*1000
15  ----------------------------------------------------------------
16      Average           Gr. Profit         Annual Sales  G&A  Intst   Tax
17      Shares:             Rate %             Growth %   Exp.  Exp.  Rate%
18      350,000                 42                   11   33.6  26.4     40
Menu: Sheet  Edit  File  Layout  Print  Graph  Tools  Window  Help  Remember
      Quit
Worksheet: map       Loc: r1c1      FN:       Font: 0
Cell-Size Default Format Justify Set-Font Worksheet-Options
```

Fig. 9.12.

Formulas displayed in sample worksheet in fig. 9.11.

If the characters in your formulas do not fit within the column widths, as much as possible is shown. You may want to temporarily widen necessary columns. (Use the Layout Cell-Size Width command.) The display of the formulas is saved with the worksheet if you don't change it back to values.

If you want to print the worksheet formulas, use the Print Formulas Worksheet command.

Displaying a Worksheet Map

If you select the Map option, a symbolic display of the location and type of worksheet entries is displayed on your screen. In a worksheet map, each worksheet cell is represented by two map cells. The contents of the cells are governed by your selections in the Tools Preferences Spreadsheet menu. Figure 9.13 shows the portion of the Tools Preferences Spreadsheet menu from which you select the map symbols.

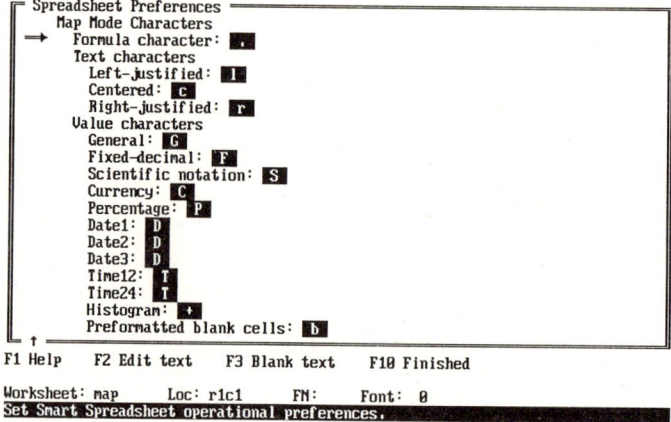

Fig. 9.13.

Tools Preferences Spreadsheet menu Map Mode Characters.

Figure 9.14 shows a map of the worksheet from figure 9.11. If you compare the symbol selection in figure 9.13 to the map, you can see that a period indicates that the cell contains a formula. Text entries are noted by their justification symbols, and value entries are represented by the appropriate symbolic value reference character.

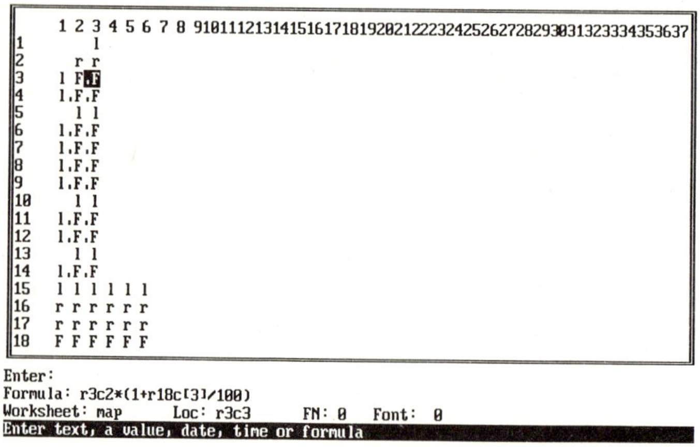

Fig. 9.14.

Layout Format Formula Display Map.

If you want to print the worksheet map, use the Print Map command.

Redisplaying Worksheet Values

To cancel the display of your worksheet in the Formula Display mode, issue the Layout Format Formula-Display Values command. The results of the formulas are again displayed.

Changing Justification

To change the justification of existing text, values, or formulas within a specified range, use the Layout Justify command. (The justification of newly entered text or values is established with the Layout Default command.) When you execute the command, you are prompted:

    Left Center Right

Selecting Left positions the cell contents at the left edge of the cell. Selecting Right positions the contents at the right. Center causes the contents to be centered in the cell. Figure 9.15 shows some examples.

```
         1              2              3         4    5
   <----------><----------><---------->
1
2  Left           Center          Right
3  ----           ------          -----
4  10.33          10.33           10.33
5  02 May 43      02 May 43       02 May 43
6  $19.95         $19.95          $19.95
7  +++++          +++++           +++++
8  33.45%         33.45%          33.45%
9  -44.40         -44.40          -44.40
10
11
```

Fig. 9.15.

Examples of justification.

In the financial model shown in figure 9.16, month names have been entered in row 2; they are right-justified. Left-justified row names have been entered in column 1. The titles of the assumption variables have been entered in rows 16 and 17; they are left-justified, except for the Average Shares: title, which is right-justified.

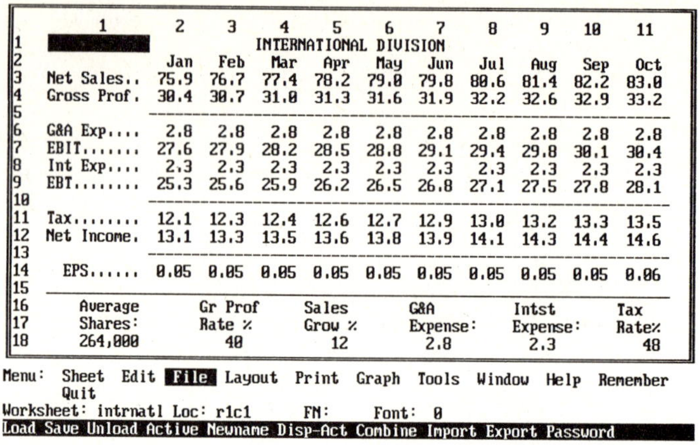

Fig. 9.16.

Financial model with right- and left-justification.

```
            1          2     3     4     5     6     7     8     9     10    11
                             INTERNATIONAL DIVISION
1
2                          Jan   Feb   Mar   Apr   May   Jun   Jul   Aug   Sep   Oct
3          Net Sales..   75.9  76.7  77.4  78.2  79.0  79.8  80.6  81.4  82.2  83.0
4          Gross Prof.   30.4  30.7  31.0  31.3  31.6  31.9  32.2  32.6  32.9  33.2
5          ─────────────────────────────────────────────────────────────────────────
6          G&A Exp....    2.8   2.8   2.8   2.8   2.8   2.8   2.8   2.8   2.8   2.8
7          EBIT.......   27.6  27.9  28.2  28.5  28.8  29.1  29.4  29.8  30.1  30.4
8          Int Exp....    2.3   2.3   2.3   2.3   2.3   2.3   2.3   2.3   2.3   2.3
9          EBT........   25.3  25.6  25.9  26.2  26.5  26.8  27.1  27.5  27.8  28.1
10         ─────────────────────────────────────────────────────────────────────────
11         Tax........   12.1  12.3  12.4  12.6  12.7  12.9  13.0  13.2  13.3  13.5
12         Net Income.   13.1  13.3  13.5  13.6  13.8  13.9  14.1  14.3  14.4  14.6
13         ─────────────────────────────────────────────────────────────────────────
14         EPS........   0.05  0.05  0.05  0.05  0.05  0.05  0.05  0.05  0.05  0.06
15
16            Average         Gr Prof       Sales          G&A          Intst          Tax
17            Shares:         Rate %        Grow %       Expense:      Expense:       Rate%
18            264,000           40            12           2.8           2.3            40

Menu:   Sheet  Edit  File  Layout  Print  Graph  Tools  Window  Help  Remember
        Quit
Worksheet: intrnatl  Loc: r1c1        FN:        Font: 0
Load Save Unload Active Newname Disp-Act Combine Import Export Password
```

Changing Column Width and Row Height

You use the Layout Cell-Size Width command to change the width of one or more columns of your worksheet. In SmartWare II, you can not only format blank cells in a block, but also change the width of blank columns. The width settings are saved with the worksheet.

Columns may vary in width from 0 to 80 characters. (You must turn off the display of the window border and the row numbers or use an expanded screen driver to display a column wider than 74 characters.) If you want to hide a column in the middle of your worksheet or display additional columns on the screen, set the width to 0. The default column width is established in the Layout Worksheet-Options New-Sheets menu.

Begin by positioning the cursor on the first column to be changed, and then execute the Layout Cell-Size command. The first prompt is

    Width Set-Measure Height

If you select Width, you are prompted:

    Enter width:

(The width of the current column is displayed at the prompt.)

Enter a number between 0 and 80. If you enter a number outside this range, you will get an error message, but not until after you specify the columns.

Your next prompt is

    Columns All

If you select All, every column in the worksheet is set to the width you have entered. If you select Columns, you are prompted:

    Enter number of columns:

You then enter the number of columns whose width you want to change. You can type a number or use the cursor to indicate the extent of the group of columns. Press Enter to complete the command. If you press Enter without typing a number, only the current column is changed.

Changing the width of a column does not change the contents of any cell in that column. If the column is not wide enough to show the cell contents, the cell is filled with asterisks (*) to alert you of this condition.

You can set column widths in characters or points. Before selecting the width, you may want to change the horizontal unit of measure from characters to points. SmartWare II uses a measure of 7 points per horizontal inch.

You also can change the height of individual rows to provide better spacing when you print your worksheet. If you select a large font, you will need additional spacing. To change the height of one or more rows, execute the Layout Cell-Size command and select the Height option. You are prompted:

    Enter height:

(The height of the current row is displayed at the prompt.) Enter a number between 1 and 300. Row height is measured in points; at 72 per vertical inch, you can achieve a maximum row height of a little over 4 inches. You will not observe any difference on your screen, however, because this setting takes effect only when you print your worksheet in the Enhanced mode.

The last prompt is

    Rows All

If you select All, every row in the worksheet is set to the height you have entered. If you select Rows, you are prompted:

    Enter number of rows:

You then enter the number of rows whose height you want to change. You can type a number or use the cursor to indicate the extent of the group of rows. Press Enter to complete the command. If you press Enter without typing a number, only the current row is changed.

Selecting Type Fonts

You use the Layout Set-Font command to select a printer font for new entries or to change the font of existing entries. When you execute this command, the prompt is

    Select Change Edit Remove

Choose Select when you want to set a new font for entries you have not yet made; use Change when you want to alter the font of existing entries. You can use the Edit option to add or change a font that is attached to the current worksheet or to add fonts to new worksheets you create. Select Remove to make unavailable any unused fonts from the current or future worksheets.

Choosing a Font for New Entries

To select a font for new entries, issue the Layout Set-Font Select command (the Quick key is F6). A menu of fonts similar to figure 9.17 is displayed.

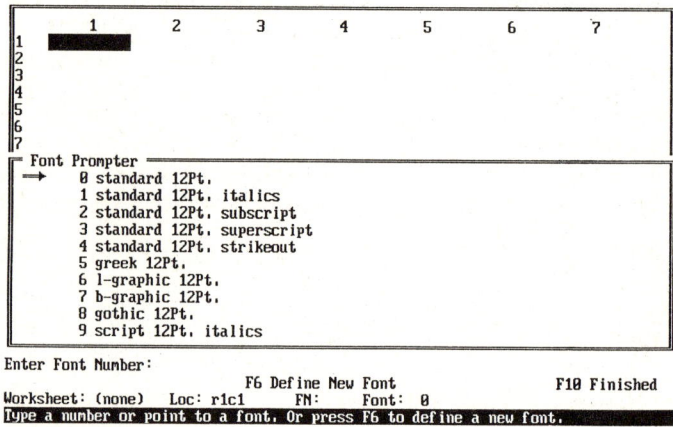

Fig. 9.17.

The Font Selection menu.

Depending on your printer, you may have as many as 63 different internal, or prerasterized, fonts available from which to choose. Notice that in the Spreadsheet module, as compared to the Wordprocessor module, each variation of a typeface, whether the variation is italics, bold, underscore, or bold and underscore, is a separate font number. Use your cursor key or the PgDn and PgUp keys to scan down the list.

In addition to the standard font 0, many printers have other resident fonts, such as italics, letter quality, or even script. Because you identify your printer by manufacturer and model number when you install the system, the list of resident fonts is available to the SmartWare II system. Whenever possible, resident fonts are used so that your computer doesn't have to construct each letter dot by dot. Resident fonts can be printed in the Spreadsheet's Draft mode.

The SmartWare II system offers several fonts in addition to your printer's resident fonts. You can print these nonresident fonts on your graphics printer because they are drawn by the computer, dot by dot. This process of drawing the individual dots of a letter is called *rasterization*. In rasterization, a typeface is used as the template to generate a specific font. In typesetting terms, a font represents not only the shape of the letter, but also its size, slant, and weight.

In SmartWare II, three types of fonts are available:

Type of Font	*Description*
Internal	An internal font is built into your printer. Its shape and size are stored in the printer's read-only memory (ROM). You can print internal fonts in the Draft mode. (Although cartridge fonts are stored in the printer, they can be printed in only the Enhance mode.)
Prerasterized	Prerasterized fonts come with SmartWare II; you also can construct them with the Tools New-Font command. The font description exists in a file in your computer. Because the description must be copied down to your computer when you print your worksheet, prerasterized fonts take longer to print than internal fonts. You must use the Enhanced mode of printing when using prerasterized fonts.
Filled Area	A filled-area font is similar to a prerasterized font, except that the complete font description doesn't already exist in a computer file; only the typeface template exists. When you print with a filled-area font, your computer must construct a temporary rasterized description of each letter. Obviously, this process takes longer than using an existing font description. You must use the Enhanced printing mode when using filled-area fonts. If you plan to use the same filled-area font repeatedly, you may want to rasterize it using the Tools New-Font command.

Some of the fonts shown in figure 9.17 are internal fonts, and some are prerasterized fonts, depending on the printer you are using. If you want to select one of these fonts, move the cursor to the desired font and press Enter.

If you want to select a font that is not on the menu, move the cursor to the font that most closely approximates the one you want and press F6 to define a new font. The New Font Definition menu, shown in figure 9.18, is displayed.

If the current font family is not the one you want, press F6 again to display a list of available font family choices. (A font family is sometimes called a *typeface*.) Figure 9.19 shows a list of font families available in the SmartWare II system.

The list of typefaces in figure 9.19 are those for which SmartWare II has the outlines and that can be drawn on your printer in various sizes and weights. Move the cursor to the typeface you want to use and press Enter.

The bottom line of the screen displays the source of the font you have selected (see fig. 9.18). If you are defining a new font, the source is Filled-Area-Font; if the font is already prerasterized, the source is Preraster-Font. If the font is not available and cannot be drawn exactly, the source is called a Dummy-Font. Try to use prerasterized fonts when you can; they print faster.

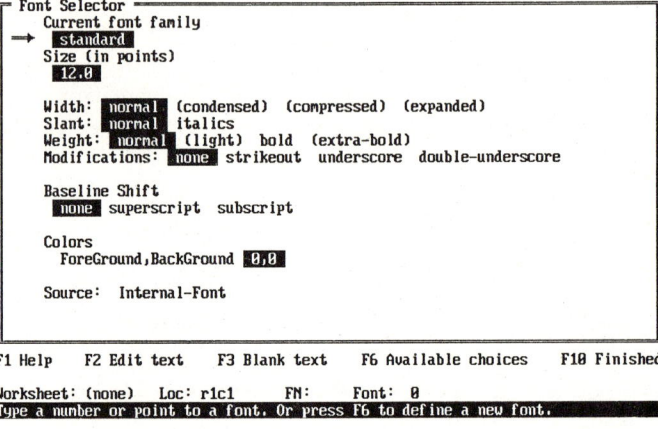

Fig. 9.18.

The New Font Definition menu.

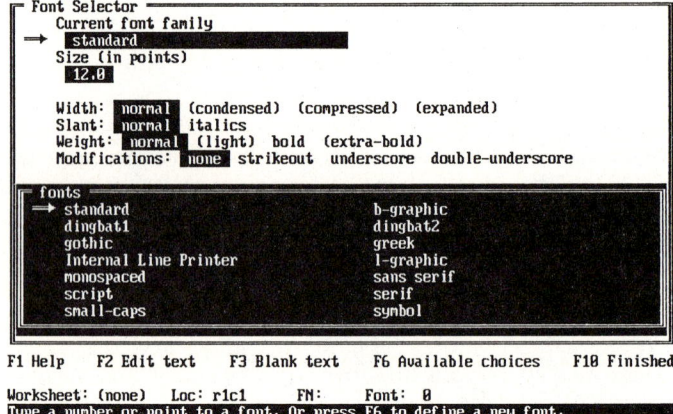

Fig. 9.19.

Available font families.

To select a size, you can type the size (in points) or press F6 to display a pop-up window of any existing prerasterized sizes for the selected typeface.

Move the highlight block to select your choices for the following options:

    Width
    Slant
    Weight
    Modifications
    Baseline Shift

Parentheses surrounding a selection indicate that it is not available and is a dummy font; the closest available font will be used.

If you have a color printer, you may select foreground and background colors; press F6 for a list of available choices and a color selection template.

Press F10 to save your new font design and return to the spreadsheet. The new font number assigned by the system is shown on the status line following `Font:`. (The number after `FN:` indicates the font of the contents of the current cell.)

If you simply want to alter the underscore or bold attributes of your current font, you can use the Quick key Ctrl-B to toggle the bold feature or Ctrl-U to toggle the underscore.

Remember that you use these Quick keys when selecting a font, not when changing the font of an existing cell or group of cells. If you have not specified the new font already in your spreadsheet, it is automatically assigned a number and attached to the spreadsheet.

Choosing a Font for Existing Entries

To change the font of existing entries, use the Layout Set-Font Change command. You are prompted:

```
Block Columns Rows All
```

If you select Columns or Rows, you should position your cursor before issuing the command or before responding to the previous prompt. You are then prompted for the number of rows or columns. Type the number, or use your cursor to have the system enter the number of rows or columns.

If you select Block, move the cursor to the top left of the range and press F2 to mark the beginning of the block; then move to the lower portion of the range and press Enter.

If you select All, you are given no additional prompts. After you have indicated the range of the font change, the menus and selection options are the same as for the font selection (see figs. 9.17 and 9.18). Remember that changing the font of existing cells in your worksheet does not affect the selected font. Any new entries are added to the worksheet in the font you selected with the Layout Set-Font Select command.

Editing or Attaching Fonts to Your Worksheet

You can use the Layout Set-Font command to edit or attach fonts to new worksheets or to the current worksheet.

Editing the Fonts of New Worksheets

Use the Layout Set-Font Edit New-Sheet command to attach new fonts to new worksheets you create. When you execute this command, you are prompted:

Enter Font Number (New Number for New Font):

A pop-up menu similar to figure 9.17 displays the numbers and names of the existing set of fonts. If you want to change the definition of one of the existing fonts, type its number and press Enter. If you want to add a new font, type a new number; they do not have to be sequential. The highest number you may use is 63.

A menu similar to figure 9.18 is displayed. If you are editing an existing font, the font characteristics are displayed on the menu. If you are creating a new font, the font at which the cursor was pointing is used as the template for the menu.

In either case, make the changes you want, and press F10 to save them. Now, any new documents you create will have the new (or edited) font attached. Existing worksheets, however, are not changed.

Editing the Fonts of Existing Worksheets

You can use the Layout Set-Font Edit Current-Sheet command for two purposes: to attach to your document at one time all the fonts you plan to use, or, having entered cells in various fonts, to edit the fonts without having to go back and change the font in each cell.

When you execute this command, you are prompted:

Enter Font Number (New Number for New Font):

A pop-up menu similar to figure 9.17 displays the numbers and names of the existing set of fonts. If you want to change the definition of one of the existing fonts, type its number and press Enter. If you want to add a new font, type a new number; they do not have to be sequential. The highest number you may use is 63.

A menu similar to figure 9.18 is displayed. If you are editing an existing font, the font characteristics are displayed on the menu. If you are creating a new font, the font at which the cursor was pointing is used as the template for the menu.

In either case, make the changes you want and press F10 to save them. If you have changed an existing font, it is automatically changed throughout your worksheet wherever the font is specified. For example, if you originally selected an italics font for emphasis, and now want to change it to standard bold, you can edit the italics font without having to search through your worksheet and change the font number of each affected cell.

Removing Fonts

When you execute the Layout Set-Font Remove command, you are prompted:

Current-Sheet New-Sheet

If you want to remove unused fonts from the current worksheet, select Current-Sheet. If you want to stop the attachment of a certain font to new worksheets, select New-Sheet.

With either selection, a pop-up window displays a list of the attached fonts (see fig. 9.20).

```
 ?
┌─ Font Prompter (Remove Fonts) ─────────────────┐
│  →   0 standard 12Pt.                          │
│   *  1 standard 12Pt. italics                  │
│      2 standard 12Pt. subscript                │
│   *  3 standard 12Pt. superscript              │
│      4 standard 12Pt. strikeout                │
│   *  5 greek 12Pt.                             │
│      6 l-graphic 12Pt.                         │
│   *  7 b-graphic 12Pt.                         │
│      8 gothic 12Pt.                            │
│   *  9 script 12Pt. italics                    │
│                                                │
└────────────────────────────────────────────────┘
Enter Font Number(s):
(* = Unused Font)         F6 Mark for Delete    F8 Mark All    F10 Finished
Worksheet: fonts    Loc: r6c1      FN:       Font: 10
Enter number or press F6 to mark font for deletion.
```

Fig. 9.20.

Font removal.

An asterisk (*) marks a font that is not used. To remove a font, move the cursor to the line with the font description and press F6. The line is highlighted. You may then move the cursor to a different line and mark that font for deletion, again by pressing F6. If you mistakenly mark the wrong font, just press F6 again to unmark it. If you prefer, you can type the numbers of the fonts you want to remove on the command line, separating them with spaces.

Pressing F8 marks all unused fonts for deletion. Note that you cannot delete a font that is in use; pressing F6 has no effect.

When you have marked the fonts you want to remove, press F10 to complete the command and return to the command level. To abort the command without deleting any fonts, press Esc.

Altering Row and Column Number Displays

Normally, a worksheet displays the row and column numbers in the window. If you want to turn off this display to improve the appearance of the screen or to gain additional row or column space, use the Window Numbers Row or the Window Numbers Column command.

These commands are toggles; each execution of the command turns the numbers on or off.

Your choice of row or column number displays applies to a worksheet within a window. The display in another window, even if it is in the same worksheet, is unaffected. Figure 9.21 shows the same worksheet displayed with and without row and column numbers. Note that the window number in the upper left corner is not shown when the row and column numbers are hidden.

Fig. 9.21.

Deleting row and column numbers.

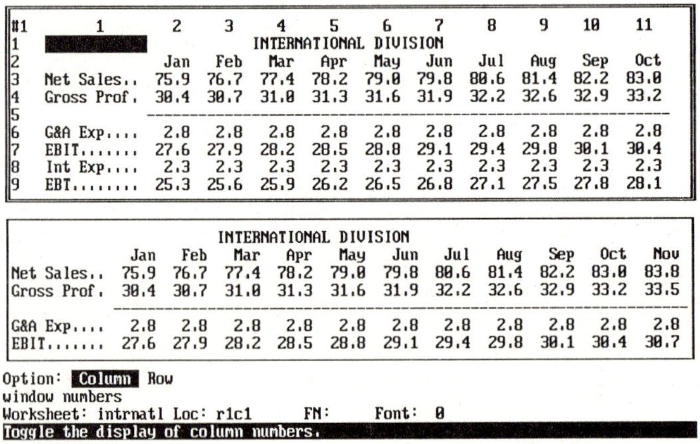

Your decision to display or hide row or column numbers has no effect on printing. Printing row and column numbers is governed by the following settings in the Worksheet Preferences menu offered in the command Layout Worksheet-Options Current-Sheet:

    Column numbers displayed: Yes No
    Row numbers displayed: Yes No

A similar menu is offered for new sheets you create.

Chapter Summary

Controlling the display of data in your worksheet can greatly enhance its appearance and usefulness, whether the worksheet is displayed on paper or on the screen. This chapter has covered the formatting commands you use to specify and alter the appearance of the cells in your worksheet. You can select formats before or after you enter the data into a cell or a group of cells. Whatever format is selected, the real value within the cell is unchanged.

10

Manipulating Data

This chapter discusses the commands you use for copying and moving data, text, and formulas, and the commands for deleting and inserting portions of worksheets. The concepts of relative and absolute addressing, also discussed in this chapter, are particularly important when you use the Edit Copy and Edit Move commands.

This chapter presents a model that illustrates the use of the data manipulation commands. Figure 10.1 shows one worksheet from this model, the final product. This chapter develops the model step by step, illustrating the necessary commands. In this way, you learn the use of the commands and the process of developing the model.

	1	2	3	4	5	6	7	8	9	10	11
1				INTERNATIONAL DIVISION							
2		Jan	Feb	Mar	Apr	May	Jun	Jul	Aug	Sep	Oct
3	Net Sales..	75.9	76.7	77.4	78.2	79.0	79.8	80.6	81.4	82.2	83.0
4	Gross Prof.	30.4	30.7	31.0	31.3	31.6	31.9	32.2	32.6	32.9	33.2
5											
6	G&A Exp....	2.8	2.8	2.8	2.8	2.8	2.8	2.8	2.8	2.8	2.8
7	EBIT.......	27.6	27.9	28.2	28.5	28.8	29.1	29.4	29.8	30.1	30.4
8	Int Exp....	2.3	2.3	2.3	2.3	2.3	2.3	2.3	2.3	2.3	2.3
9	EBT........	25.3	25.6	25.9	26.2	26.5	26.8	27.1	27.5	27.8	28.1
10											
11	Tax........	12.1	12.3	12.4	12.6	12.7	12.9	13.0	13.2	13.3	13.5
12	Net Income.	13.1	13.3	13.5	13.6	13.8	13.9	14.1	14.3	14.4	14.6
13											
14	EPS.......	0.05	0.05	0.05	0.05	0.05	0.05	0.05	0.05	0.05	0.06
15											
16	Average		Gr Prof		Sales		G&A		Intst		Tax
17	Shares:		Rate %		Grow %		Expense:		Expense:		Rate%
18	264,000		40		12		2.8		2.3		40

```
Menu:  Sheet  Edit  File  Layout  Print  Graph  Tools  Window  Help  Remember
       Quit
Worksheet: intrnatl Loc: r1c1        FM:      Font: 0
Load Save Unload Active Newname Disp-Act Combine Import Export Password
```

Fig. 10.1.

The completed spreadsheet model.

Part II: Using the SmartWare II Spreadsheet

The model was designed so that a user can change any of the assumptions at the bottom of the screen and observe the change in the financial figures in the worksheet. The current assumptions are as follows:

Average number of shares: 264,000
Gross profit percent: 40
Annual sales growth: 12
G&A expense per year: 2.8 (000)
Interest expense per year: 2.3 (000)
Tax rate: 48%

When the user of this model moves the cursor to any of the assumption-value cells on row 18 and makes a change, the entire worksheet is recalculated. Let's see how the model was built.

Figure 10.2 shows the beginnings of the model. Column 1 shows the values and the calculations for January; column 2 shows (for illustrative purposes) the formulas used in the calculated cells in column 1.

Fig. 10.2.

Values and formulas for the January calculations.

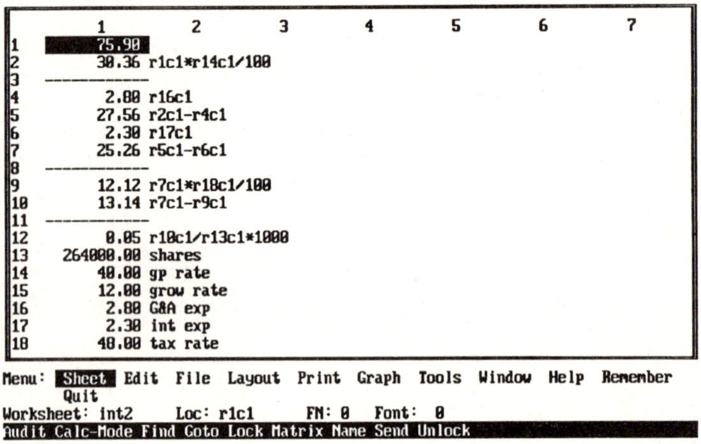

```
          1         2         3    4    5    6    7
1      75.90
2      30.36  r1c1*r14c1/100
3     ------
4       2.00  r16c1
5      27.56  r2c1-r4c1
6       2.30  r17c1
7      25.26  r5c1-r6c1
8     ------
9      12.12  r7c1*r18c1/100
10     13.14  r7c1-r9c1
11    ------
12      0.05  r10c1/r13c1*1000
13  264000.00 shares
14     40.00  gp rate
15     12.00  grow rate
16      2.00  G&A exp
17      2.30  int exp
18     40.00  tax rate

Menu: Sheet  Edit  File  Layout  Print  Graph  Tools  Window  Help  Remember
      Quit
Worksheet: int2   Loc: r1c1    FN: 0    Font: 0
Audit Calc-Mode Find Goto Lock Matrix Name Send Unlock
```

The following list explains the cell contents in column 1.

Row	Explanation
1	*Net Sales.* Input. To be calculated from annual growth rate (row 15) for February through December.
2	*Gross profit.* Calculated from the net sales multiplied by gross profit percentage (assumption in row 14 divided by 100).
4	*General and administrative (G&A) expense.* One of the assumption variables (row 16).

5   *Earnings before interest (EBIT)*. Gross profit minus G&A expense.

6   *Interest expense*. Assumption variable (row 17).

7   *Earnings before taxes (EBT)*. EBIT minus interest expense.

9   *Tax*. EBT multiplied by the tax rate percent (row 18 divided by 100).

10   *Net Income*. EBT minus tax.

12   *Earnings per share*. Net income divided by the number of shares (row 13) expressed in thousands.

This model works well for January. If you change any of the assumptions in rows 13 through 18, the calculations for January also change. If you have issued the Sheet Calc-Mode Automatic command, the recalculation takes place automatically. If the mode is set to Manual, you must press the F5 function key to perform the calculation.

The formulas in this simple model can be calculated through ordinary arithmetic. Notice that the rates in the assumptions in rows 14 through 18 are expressed as percentages rather than decimal fractions. When the rates are used in formulas, they must be divided by 100.

Using the Edit Copy Command

To expand the model to cover an entire year, you must first copy the January formulas for February through December. One problem exists, however. Normally, when you copy a formula, the system recognizes that the cell addresses are *relative* and makes the appropriate adjustments. When you copy cell r5c1 to cell r5c2, for example, the copy of the formula becomes r2c2 − r4c2. The references to column 1 have become references to column 2.

The assumptions in rows 13 through 18, however, belong only in column 1; you don't want to repeat them in columns 2 through 12. Therefore, any references to the assumptions must be *absolute* rather than relative. If a formula in column 10 needs to use one of the assumptions, for example, the formula should refer to column 1 instead of column 10.

In preparation for use of the Edit Copy command, the formulas in rows 2, 4, 6, 9, and 12 have been changed so that the assumption variables in rows 13 through 18 are referenced by absolute addresses (see fig. 10.3). The square brackets enclosing the row and column numbers indicate absolute addresses.

Fig. 10.3.

Absolute addresses.

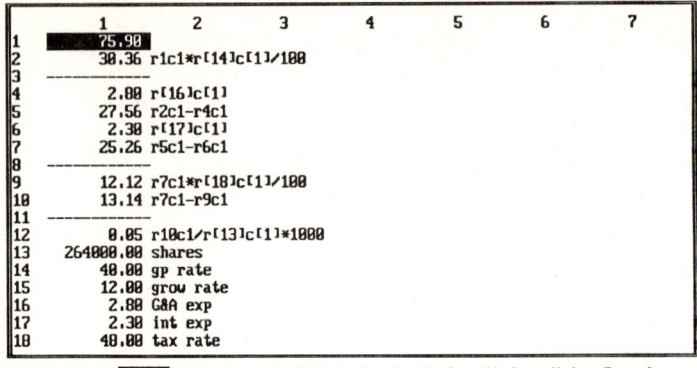

The Quick key for the Edit Copy command is Alt-C. This command is used to copy one or more cells on a worksheet to a new area. If you copy cells containing text or values, the data is copied directly. If you copy formulas containing addresses, relative addresses are changed to reflect the position of the new cell; absolute addresses remain unchanged.

The Edit Copy command has three options:

    Down Right From

Edit Copy Down makes a copy of all or part of a row. Edit Copy Right copies all or part of a column, and Edit Copy From copies a block of cells. Use the **Down** and **Right** options if you want to copy to areas adjacent to the source row or column. Use the **From** option to copy to a nonadjacent area of the worksheet.

Copying Cells in a Row

Before executing the Edit Copy Down command, position the cursor on the leftmost cell of the row you want to copy. This command has two options:

    Row Single-Cell

If you specify Row, you are prompted:

    Enter length of row:

The length of row refers to the number of columns you want to copy in the current row. Type the number and press Enter, or move the cursor to the right and have the system enter the number for you. As you move the cursor, the value to the

Chapter 10: Manipulating Data **217**

right of the prompt increases. Press Enter when you have reached the desired location. You are prompted:

    Enter number of copies:

The answer to this prompt determines how many copies are made. Note that when you use the Edit Copy command, the copied data overlays any existing data; additional rows are not inserted for you to make room for the copied data. If you need to insert rows to accept the data, use the Edit Insert command.

Using the Edit Copy Down Single-Cell command is equivalent to using the command Edit Copy Down Row and specifying a length of 1. Use this command sequence for copying just one cell.

Copying Cells to the Right

The Edit Copy Right command is similar to Edit Copy Down. You place the cursor on the cell at the top of the portion of the column to be copied and then execute the command.

When you select Edit Copy Right Column, you are prompted for the length of the column (number of rows) you want to copy. You can type the number, or you can move the cursor to the last row you want to copy and press Enter; the system then enters the number of rows for you.

You are then prompted as follows:

    Enter number of copies:

Your answer tells SmartWare II how many new columns to duplicate. The command Edit Copy Right Single-Cell is equivalent to Edit Copy Right Column with a length of 1, but using Edit Copy Right Single-Cell saves a few keystrokes.

To copy the values and formulas from column 1 (January) to columns 2 through 12 for the example worksheet, use the following steps.

1. Place the cursor on r2c1 and select Edit Copy Right.

2. Select the Column option.

3. In response to the prompt, move the cursor down to row 12 (see fig. 10.4). You don't want to copy the assumption variables.

4. Press Enter.

5. In response to the prompt for the number of copies, type *11*, because you need eleven more months for the model. Press Enter.

218 Part II: Using the SmartWare II Spreadsheet

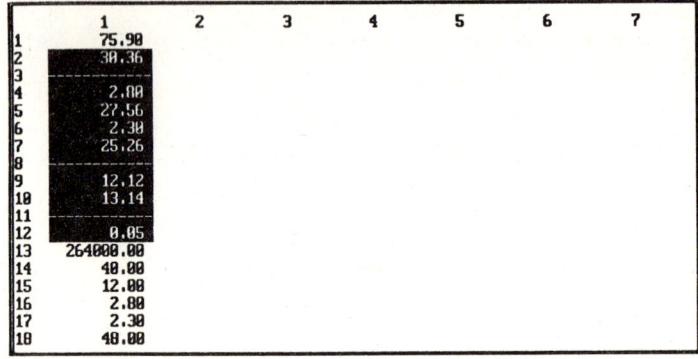

Fig. 10.4.

Using the Edit Copy Right Column command.

Figure 10.5 shows the almost finished product. The model is not quite finished, because you still need to take care of row 1 (Sales), the placement of the assumption variables, and the headings.

Fig. 10.5.

The almost completed model.

An annual growth rate is supplied as an assumption variable in row 15 of the model (cell r15c1). To apply this assumption to the sales row, you need to enter a formula in r1c2. In figure 10.6, the formula has been entered and the calculation has been performed. You can see the formula on the second command line at the bottom of the screen. (In the Enter mode, the formula at the cursor cell is displayed on the command line. If you are developing a worksheet in which you don't want other people to see the formulas, use the Sheet Lock Protect command, which is discussed in Chapter 12.)

	1	2	3	4	5	6	7
1	75.90	76.66					
2	30.36	30.66	0.00	0.00	0.00	0.00	0.00
3							
4	2.00	2.00	2.00	2.00	2.00	2.00	2.00
5	27.56	27.06	-2.00	-2.00	-2.00	-2.00	-2.00
6	2.30	2.30	2.30	2.30	2.30	2.30	2.30
7	25.26	25.56	-5.10	-5.10	-5.10	-5.10	-5.10
8							
9	12.12	12.27	-2.45	-2.45	-2.45	-2.45	-2.45
10	13.14	13.29	-2.65	-2.65	-2.65	-2.65	-2.65
11							
12	0.05	0.05	-0.01	-0.01	-0.01	-0.01	-0.01
13	264000.00						
14	40.00						
15	12.00						
16	2.00						
17	2.30						
18	40.00						

Enter:
Formula: r1c1*(1+r[15]c[1]/12/100)
Worksheet: Int4   Loc: r1c2   FN: 0   Font: 0
Enter a string, value, date, time or formula

Fig. 10.6.

Formula entered in row 1, column 2.

Notice that the formula in r1c2 refers to the value in r1c1, which is the net sales for January; the formula multiplies that value by 1 plus the monthly growth rate. The monthly growth rate is calculated from the yearly growth-rate percentage, located in cell r15c1. The formula in r1c2 refers to this yearly growth-rate assumption through an absolute reference, *r[15]c[1]*. This value is divided by 12 to produce a monthly percentage, and the percentage is divided by 100 to convert it to a decimal.

You need to carry this logic (of referencing the previous cell in the row) across to the remaining 10 columns of the model so that you can calculate figures for the next 10 months. To do this, execute Edit Copy Right Single-Cell, specify 10 copies at the prompt (see fig. 10.7), and press Enter.

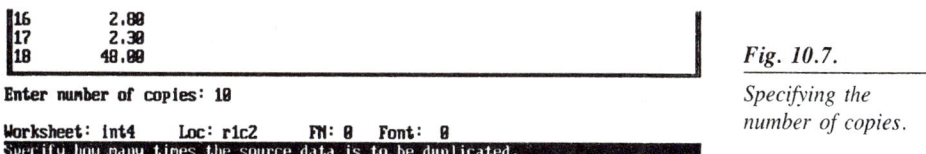

Fig. 10.7.

Specifying the number of copies.

Figure 10.8 shows the completed model after the formula in r1c2 has been copied.

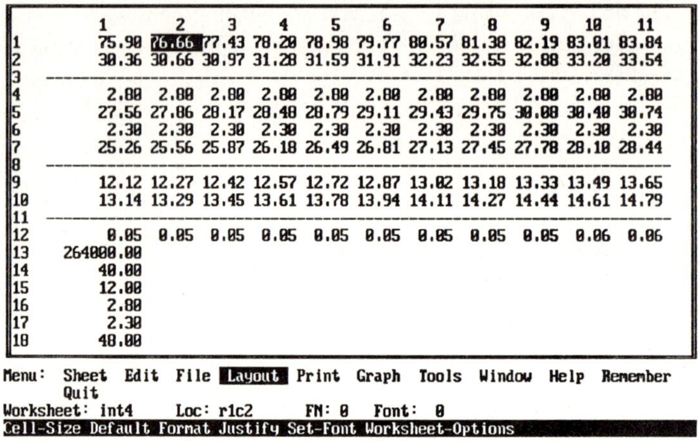

Fig. 10.8.

The completed model.

```
      1      2      3      4      5      6      7      8      9      10     11
1    75.90  76.66  77.43  78.20  78.98  79.77  80.57  81.38  82.19  83.01  83.84
2    30.36  30.66  30.97  31.28  31.59  31.91  32.23  32.55  32.88  33.20  33.54
3    ------------------------------------------------------------------------
4     2.00   2.00   2.00   2.00   2.00   2.00   2.00   2.00   2.00   2.00   2.00
5    27.56  27.86  28.17  28.48  28.79  29.11  29.43  29.75  30.08  30.40  30.74
6     2.30   2.30   2.30   2.30   2.30   2.30   2.30   2.30   2.30   2.30   2.30
7    25.26  25.56  25.87  26.18  26.49  26.81  27.13  27.45  27.78  28.10  28.44
8    ------------------------------------------------------------------------
9           12.12  12.27  12.42  12.57  12.72  12.87  13.02  13.18  13.33  13.49  13.65
10          13.14  13.29  13.45  13.61  13.78  13.94  14.11  14.27  14.44  14.61  14.79
11   ------------------------------------------------------------------------
12    0.05   0.05   0.05   0.05   0.05   0.05   0.05   0.05   0.05   0.06   0.06
13  264000.00
14    40.00
15    12.00
16     2.00
17     2.30
18    40.00
```

```
Menu:     Sheet  Edit  File  Layout  Print  Graph  Tools  Window  Help  Remember
          Quit
Worksheet: int4      Loc: r1c2       FN: 0     Font: 0
Cell-Size Default Format Justify Set-Font Worksheet-Options
```

Copying Cells to Other Areas

The Edit Copy Down and Right commands copy only to areas that are adjacent to the source row or column. These commands cannot copy both rows and columns at the same time, nor can they copy from one worksheet to another. To perform these tasks, use the Edit Copy From command.

When you execute the Edit Copy From command, you are prompted:

    Enter name or block reference for source:

The following help line appears below the prompt:

    F2 Drop anchor   F3 Absolute/Relative   F4 List of Block Names

If you have not already done so, position the cursor on the upper left cell of the block you want to copy and press F2 to mark the beginning of the block. Move the cursor to the lower right cell of the block and press Enter to finish defining the source block.

Next, you see the following prompt:

    Enter name or block reference for destination:

Your answer to this prompt designates the upper left corner of the destination block. You can move the cursor to the upper left cell of the block, or you can type the cell address or name. If you have defined named blocks within your worksheet, you can press F4 to display them when prompted for the source or the destination block. Use the Sheet Name Define command to assign a name to a block of cells in your worksheet.

To change from relative to absolute addressing, press F3. Addresses entered by the system are initially relative addresses. When you press F3 the first time, both the row and column designations are changed to absolute, with the numbers enclosed in square brackets. If you press F3 again, only the row is marked absolute. Press F3 again, and just the column is absolute. If you press F3 one more time, the entire block reference is returned to relative for both rows and columns.

You can copy a range from one active worksheet to another by prefacing the cell address or name with the name of the destination worksheet. To copy a block to cell r5c10 in a worksheet named BUDGET85, for example, you enter

budget85.r5c10

If the destination worksheet has a range named TABLE1, you enter

budget85.table1

You can specify a source block from a different worksheet in a similar manner, but if you use cell addresses to designate a range, you must provide the entire range of rows and columns of the source block rather than just the address of the upper left cell. Use colons to indicate the row and column ranges as follows:

budget85.r5:10c12:17

If you have a formula that references cells in another worksheet, the Edit Copy command adjusts those relative addresses in the same way it adjusts them in the current worksheet.

Using the Edit Value-Copy Command

The Edit Value-Copy command operates in the same way as the Edit Copy command. However, instead of copying formulas, it copies the results of the formulas and converts these results to values. Use the Edit Value-Copy command when you want the destination cells to have values identical to the displayed formula results in the source cells.

The Edit Value-Copy command is useful in retaining the results of various what-if scenarios. For instance, you run the model and Value-Copy the results; then you change the assumptions, run the model again, and compare the new results to those of the previous run. Remember that, because the cells copied with the Edit Value-Copy command are now *values*, they do not change when you alter the values of the cells used in the original formulas. The Edit Value-Copy command is similar to the File Combine Copy command, which is discussed in Chapter 11.

Using the Edit Move Command

The Quick key for the Edit Move command is Alt-M. This command is used to change the location of cell contents within a worksheet. As you construct a worksheet, you often need to rearrange the contents to make the worksheet easier to use.

Moving values or text should certainly be no problem for a good text editor or word processing program. Smartware II's Edit Move command is valuable because it goes beyond simply moving data: it adjusts cell references in formulas each time cells are moved. Formulas in cells within the moved range that reference other cells in the range are adjusted to reflect the new cell locations, as are cells outside the range that contain formulas referencing cells in the moved range. Because Smartware II adjusts these cell references, the calculated values of the formulas in the worksheet do not change when you use Edit Move.

When you move a block consisting of one or more partial rows or columns, the source cells overwrite the cells in the destination range; ideally, you should overwrite only blank cells. But be careful with this command; any formatting options that apply to the source range also are moved. (Refer to Chapter 9 for more information on formatting cells.) After the move is complete, the cells in the source range become blank, and their formatting is removed. However, if you move entire rows or columns, the source data does not overlay the destination; rather, it is inserted into the worksheet, pushing the data in the destination range out of the way. No blank row or column remains in the source data's original location.

The Edit Move command options are

    Block Columns Rows

These options are explained in the following sections.

Moving Columns

Before executing the Edit Move Columns command, position the cursor on the leftmost column to be moved. When you select the command, the first prompt is

    Enter number of columns:

You can type the number of columns to be moved (including the current column) or move the cursor to the right edge of the group of columns so that the system determines the number of columns. Press Enter. (If you press Enter without typing a value, the default value is 1.)

The next prompt is

    Enter column number of destination:

At this prompt you enter the number of the column where the first column you are moving is to be placed, or you can use the cursor to enter the number for you. If you want the range to begin with column 26, for example, you enter 26. The total number of columns in your worksheet remains unchanged after the move; no blank columns are created, and columns around the destination range are shifted to the right to make room. You do not overwrite any data when you use the Edit Move Columns command. (This is not true when use the Edit Move Block command, however.)

Moving Rows

The Edit Move Rows command is similar to the Edit Move Columns command. Position the cursor on the uppermost row you want to move and select the command. The first prompt is

    Enter number of rows:

Enter the number, or move the cursor to have the system determine the number of rows. Then press Enter. (If you press Enter without entering a value, the default value is 1.)

The next prompt is

    Enter row number of destination:

You then enter the number of the row where you want to place the first row of the range you are moving. You also can move the cursor so that the system enters the destination row for you. Press Enter to complete the command.

With this command, you do not create any blank rows, nor do you overwrite data in any of the existing rows. The rows around the destination range are shifted to accommodate the moved rows. If you do want to create blank rows, use the Edit Insert command.

Moving Blocks

The results of the Edit Move Block command can be quite different from those of the other two forms of the Move command, so you must be careful when using this command. The Edit Move Block command *does* overwrite any existing data or formulas in the destination range, and the cells in the source range are left blank at the completion of the command. The total number of rows and columns remains unchanged.

The first prompt of the Edit Move Block command is

    Enter name or block reference for source:

If you haven't already done so, move your cursor to the cell in the upper left corner of the source range, and press F2 to drop the anchor. Then move the cursor to the lower right cell, and press Enter to complete the range definition for the source.

The second prompt is similar to the first:

   Enter name or block reference for destination:

To answer this prompt, type the cell address of the upper left corner of the destination range or move the cursor; then press Enter.

To construct the financial model used in this chapter, the assumption variables must be moved from rows 14 through 18 to row 13 (see fig. 10.8). You use the Edit Move Block command to move this data.

In the following sequence, r14c1 is moved to r13c2. Figure 10.9 shows the beginning of the execution of the command. The cursor has been placed on r14c1, the Edit Move Block command has been executed, and the following prompt is displayed:

   Enter name or block reference for source:

Fig. 10.9.

Defining the source range for Edit Move Block.

```
                 1     2     3     4     5     6     7     8     9    10    11
              75.90 76.66 77.43 78.20 78.98 79.77 80.57 81.38 82.19 83.01 83.04
              30.36 30.66 30.97 31.28 31.59 31.91 32.23 32.55 32.88 33.20 33.54
           3  ─────────────────────────────────────────────────────────────────
           4   2.00  2.00  2.00  2.00  2.00  2.00  2.00  2.00  2.00  2.00  2.00
           5  27.56 27.86 28.17 28.48 28.79 29.11 29.43 29.75 30.08 30.40 30.74
           6   2.30  2.30  2.30  2.30  2.30  2.30  2.30  2.30  2.30  2.30  2.30
           7  25.26 25.56 25.87 26.18 26.49 26.81 27.13 27.45 27.78 28.10 28.44
           8  ─────────────────────────────────────────────────────────────────
           9  12.12 12.27 12.42 12.57 12.72 12.87 13.02 13.18 13.33 13.49 13.65
          10  13.14 13.29 13.45 13.61 13.78 13.94 14.11 14.27 14.44 14.61 14.79
          11  ─────────────────────────────────────────────────────────────────
          12   0.05  0.05  0.05  0.05  0.05  0.05  0.05  0.05  0.05  0.06  0.06
          13  264000.00
          14     40.00
          15     12.00
          16      2.00
          17      2.30
          18     40.00
Enter name or block reference for source:
F2 Drop anchor   F3 Absolute/Relative   F4 List of Block Names
Worksheet: int4      Loc: r14c1      FM: 0   Font: 0
Specify the block to be moved.
```

If the block contained more than one cell, you would press F2 to drop the anchor, move the cursor to the bottom right of the range, and press Enter. Because this block contains only one cell, you can just press Enter to define the source range.

In figure 10.10, the cursor has been moved to r13c2 to establish the destination range. Notice that the address r13c2 appears on the command line. Press Enter to complete the move.

```
         1     2     3     4     5     6     7     8     9    10    11
 1     75.90 76.66 77.43 78.20 78.98 79.77 80.57 81.38 82.19 83.01 83.84
 2     30.36 30.66 30.97 31.28 31.59 31.91 32.23 32.55 32.88 33.20 33.54
 3     ---------------------------------------------------------------
 4      2.00  2.00  2.00  2.00  2.00  2.00  2.00  2.00  2.00  2.00  2.00
 5     27.56 27.86 28.17 28.48 28.79 29.11 29.43 29.75 30.08 30.40 30.74
 6      2.30  2.30  2.30  2.30  2.30  2.30  2.30  2.30  2.30  2.30  2.30
 7     25.26 25.56 25.87 26.18 26.49 26.81 27.13 27.45 27.78 28.10 28.44
 8     ---------------------------------------------------------------
 9     12.12 12.27 12.42 12.57 12.72 12.87 13.02 13.18 13.33 13.49 13.65
10     13.14 13.29 13.45 13.61 13.78 13.94 14.11 14.27 14.44 14.61 14.79
11     ---------------------------------------------------------------
12      0.05  0.05  0.05  0.05  0.05  0.05  0.05  0.05  0.05  0.06  0.06
13    264000.00
14     40.00
15     12.00
16      2.00
17      2.30
18     40.00

Enter name or block reference for destination: r13c2
F2 Drop anchor  F3 Absolute/Relative  F4 List of Block Names
Worksheet: int4     Loc: r13c2     FN:       Font: 0
Specify the destination of the moved data.
```

Fig. 10.10.

Defining the destination range for Edit Move Block.

Figure 10.11 shows the worksheet after the Edit Move Block command has been completed. The cursor has been placed on r2c1 and the Enter mode has been invoked so that the formula appears on the command line. Note that the formula has been adjusted to reference the new position of the gross profit rate of 40 percent, which has just been moved to r13c2. None of the calculation results have changed as a result of the move.

```
         1     2     3     4     5     6     7     8     9    10    11
 1     75.90 76.66 77.43 78.20 78.98 79.77 80.57 81.38 82.19 83.01 83.84
 2     30.36 30.66 30.97 31.28 31.59 31.91 32.23 32.55 32.88 33.20 33.54
 3     ---------------------------------------------------------------
 4      2.00  2.00  2.00  2.00  2.00  2.00  2.00  2.00  2.00  2.00  2.00
 5     27.56 27.86 28.17 28.48 28.79 29.11 29.43 29.75 30.08 30.40 30.74
 6      2.30  2.30  2.30  2.30  2.30  2.30  2.30  2.30  2.30  2.30  2.30
 7     25.26 25.56 25.87 26.18 26.49 26.81 27.13 27.45 27.78 28.10 28.44
 8     ---------------------------------------------------------------
 9     12.12 12.27 12.42 12.57 12.72 12.87 13.02 13.18 13.33 13.49 13.65
10     13.14 13.29 13.45 13.61 13.78 13.94 14.11 14.27 14.44 14.61 14.79
11     ---------------------------------------------------------------
12      0.05  0.05  0.05  0.05  0.05  0.05  0.05  0.05  0.05  0.06  0.06
13    264000.00 40.00
14
15     12.00
16      2.00
17      2.30
18     40.00

Enter:
Formula: r1c1*r[13]c[2]/100
Worksheet: int4     Loc: r2c1     FN: 0     Font: 0
Enter a string, value, date, time or formula
```

Fig. 10.11.

The model after the Edit Move command has been completed.

The process of moving the remainder of the assumption variables to row 13 is similar. Cell r15c1 is moved to r13c5, cell r16c1 to r13c7, cell r17c1 to r13c9, and r18c1 to r13c11. The following section shows you how to insert blank lines so the assumption variables can be identified.

Using the Edit Insert Command

You use the Edit Insert command to add blank rows, columns, or blocks to your worksheet (see fig. 10.12). When you insert new blank ranges, the formulas in the shifted cells are adjusted to reflect the new cell numbers. The Quick key for the Edit Insert command is Alt-I.

Fig. 10.12.

Selecting the Edit Insert command.

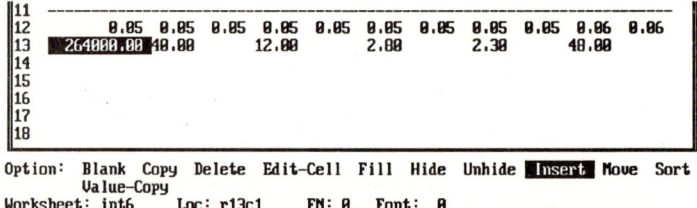

The Edit Insert command has three options:

    Block Columns Rows

In the following sections, you will become familiar with these options as we finish creating the financial model.

Inserting Columns

If you compare figure 10.11 with figure 10.1, you can see that you need to insert two rows above row 1 to make room for the titles, and one column before column 1 to make room for the row labels.

To insert columns in the worksheet, move your cursor to the column *before* which you want to insert the new columns and execute the Edit Insert Columns command. You are prompted:

    Enter number of columns:

You can respond with a number, or you can move the cursor to the right so that the system enters the number for you. Then press Enter. (If you don't type a value, the default number is 1.)

In response to the command, the designated column and the columns to its right are shifted to the right, and the formulas in the cells are adjusted. The cursor remains on the original column. Any format settings are shifted along with the data and formulas, and the new columns assume the default format settings.

Inserting Rows

To insert rows in the worksheet, move the cursor to the row *above* which you want to insert the new rows. When you select the Edit Insert Rows command, the following prompt appears:

```
Enter number of rows:
```

Type the number of rows you want to insert, or move the cursor so that the system enters the number. Then press Enter. (Again, if you don't enter a number, the value defaults to 1.)

When the command is executed, the rows are shifted down and the formulas in the cells are adjusted. The cursor remains on the original row. Format settings are shifted along with the affected rows.

Figure 10.13 shows the model after the new rows and columns have been inserted. Titles still need to be added, and some formatting remains to be done.

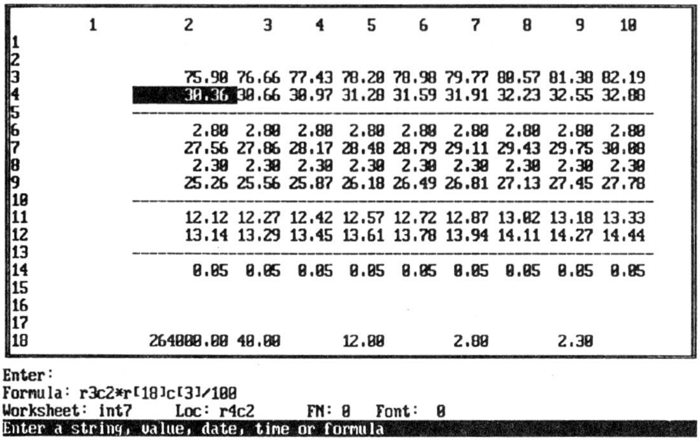

	1	2	3	4	5	6	7	8	9	10
1										
2										
3		75.90	76.66	77.43	78.20	78.98	79.77	80.57	81.38	82.19
4		30.36	30.66	30.97	31.28	31.59	31.91	32.23	32.55	32.88
5		-------	-------	-------	-------	-------	-------	-------	-------	-------
6		2.80	2.80	2.80	2.80	2.80	2.80	2.80	2.80	2.80
7		27.56	27.86	28.17	28.48	28.79	29.11	29.43	29.75	30.08
8		2.30	2.30	2.30	2.30	2.30	2.30	2.30	2.30	2.30
9		25.26	25.56	25.87	26.18	26.49	26.81	27.13	27.45	27.78
10		-------	-------	-------	-------	-------	-------	-------	-------	-------
11		12.12	12.27	12.42	12.57	12.72	12.87	13.02	13.18	13.33
12		13.14	13.29	13.45	13.61	13.78	13.94	14.11	14.27	14.44
13		-------	-------	-------	-------	-------	-------	-------	-------	-------
14		0.05	0.05	0.05	0.05	0.05	0.05	0.05	0.05	0.05
15										
16										
17										
18		264000.00	40.00		12.00		2.00		2.30	

```
Enter:
Formula: r3c2*r[18]c[3]/100
Worksheet: int7     Loc: r4c2     FN: 0   Font: 0
Enter a string, value, date, time or formula
```

Fig. 10.13.

The model after rows and columns have been inserted.

Inserting Blocks

The Edit Insert Block command enables you to define a range to be inserted in the body of a worksheet. You define the range by using the F2 key to drop the anchor at the upper left corner, entering the address, or pointing with the cursor to the bottom right corner of the range, and then pressing Enter.

Inserting a block causes data and formulas on the same rows as the specified range to be shifted to the right, opening up a "hole" in your worksheet. Be careful not to insert a block in the middle of a table, such as the one in our example model, because the columns will be moved out of alignment. If you accidentally insert a block where you do not want it, use the Edit Delete command to close up the hole.

Using the Edit Delete Command

The Quick key for the Edit Delete command is Alt-D. You use this command to erase columns, rows, or blocks from your worksheet. The remainder of the worksheet is shifted to close the gaps, and formulas are adjusted to reflect new cell addresses. Be careful: unless you save the worksheet before you begin deleting, you cannot recover the deleted material.

The Edit Delete command differs in an important way from the Edit Blank command, discussed later in this chapter. The Edit Delete command removes the designated range and closes the intervening spaces; columns are moved to the left, and rows are moved up. The Edit Blank command, however, clears out the data or text in the range, but the rest of the worksheet does not shift positions. Both commands, however, erase the text and data.

The options for the Edit Delete command are

    Block Columns Rows

The sections that follow show how to use these options and explain the differences between Edit Delete and Edit Blank.

Deleting Columns

To delete columns, position the cursor on the column you want to delete, or on the leftmost column of a range of columns, and issue the command. You are prompted:

    Enter number of columns:

You can type a number or move the cursor to the right to have the system determine the number of columns to delete. Then press Enter. (If you don't enter a number, the value defaults to 1, indicating only the current column.)

The designated columns are then deleted. The remaining columns to the right are shifted left, and formulas are adjusted. If any formulas in columns to the right of the selected range reference cells in the deleted range, the formulas are adjusted to refer to cells to the left of the deleted range. You may not get an error message, but the formula results may be wrong.

Deleting Rows

To delete rows from the worksheet, move the cursor to the first row you want to delete and issue the Edit Delete Rows command. The prompt is

```
Enter number of rows:
```

Type the number of rows you want to delete, or move the cursor to have the system enter the number. Press Enter. If you do not enter a number, the value defaults to 1. The rows you have specified are deleted, the rows below them are shifted upward, and formulas are adjusted. Take the same care when deleting rows as when deleting columns; you can have the same problems with formula references to cells in the deleted areas.

Deleting Blocks

When you issue the Edit Delete Block command, you are prompted:

```
Enter name or block reference:
```

Move the cursor to the upper left cell of the block to be deleted, and press F2 to drop the anchor. Then move the cursor to the lower right cell of the block and press Enter to complete the range designation. Instead of using the cursor, you can type the range address (for example, *r5:12c7:11*); you also can enter the name of a range if a name as been assigned to the block you want to delete.

When you have executed the command, the designated range is deleted, and cells on the same rows to the right of the deleted range are shifted to the left to fill the gap. Figure 10.14 illustrates the effect of deleting a block. The block in the window on the left is about to be deleted; the corresponding block in the window on the right has already been deleted.

#1	1	2	3	4	5
1	r1c1	r1c2	r1c3	r1c4	r1c5
2	r2c1	r2c2	r2c3	r2c4	r2c5
3	r3c1	r3c2	r3c3	r3c4	r3c5
4	r4c1	r4c2	r4c3	r4c4	r4c5
5	r5c1	r5c2	r5c3	r5c4	r5c5
6	r6c1	r6c2	r6c3	r6c4	r6c5
7	r7c1	r7c2	r7c3	r7c4	r7c5
8	r8c1	r8c2	r8c3	r8c4	r8c5
9	r9c1	r9c2	r9c3	r9c4	r9c5
10	r10c1	r10c2	r10c3	r10c4	r10c5
11	r11c1	r11c2	r11c3	r11c4	r11c5
12	r12c1	r12c2	r12c3	r12c4	r12c5
13	r13c1	r13c2	r13c3	r13c4	r13c5
14	r14c1	r14c2	r14c3	r14c4	r14c5
15	r15c1	r15c2	r15c3	r15c4	r15c5
16	r16c1	r16c2	r16c3	r16c4	r16c5
17	r17c1	r17c2	r17c3	r17c4	r17c5
18	r18c1	r18c2	r18c3	r18c4	r18c5

#2	1	2	3	4
1	r1c1	r1c2	r1c3	r1c4
2	r2c1	r2c2	r2c3	r2c4
3	r3c1	r3c2	r3c3	r3c4
4	r4c1	r4c2	r4c3	r4c4
5	r5c1	r5c2	r5c3	r5c4
6	r6c1	r6c4	r6c5	r6c6
7	r7c1	r7c4	r7c5	r7c6
8	r8c1	r8c4	r8c5	r8c6
9	r9c1	r9c4	r9c5	r9c6
10	r10c1	r10c4	r10c5	r10c6
11	r11c1	r11c2	r11c3	r11c4
12	r12c1	r12c2	r12c3	r12c4
13	r13c1	r13c2	r13c3	r13c4
14	r14c1	r14c2	r14c3	r14c4
15	r15c1	r15c2	r15c3	r15c4
16	r16c1	r16c2	r16c3	r16c4
17	r17c1	r17c2	r17c3	r17c4
18	r18c1	r18c2	r18c3	r18c4

```
Enter name or block reference: r6:10c2:3
F2 Drop anchor  F3 Absolute/Relative  F4 List of Block Names
Worksheet: del2     Loc: r10c3     FN: 0   Font: 0
Specify the block to be deleted.
```

Fig. 10.14.

The effect of the Delete Block command.

Notice that in rows 6 through 10, the cells to the right of the block have shifted to the left because the cells in those rows in columns 2 and 3 have been deleted. By examining the cell entries, you can see that the entry originally in r6c4 is now in cell r6c2, the entry originally in r6c5 is now in r6c3, and so on.

Using the Edit Blank Command

You use the Edit Blank command to erase values, text, and formulas from designated rows or columns or a specified block. In addition, you can use Edit Blank All to erase the entire worksheet in the current window. The Quick key is Alt-B.

Be sure that you understand the difference between Edit Blank and Edit Delete. The Edit Blank command removes the data and formulas from the cells, but the deleted range remains in place; no other cells are shifted. The Edit Delete command, as you have seen, not only erases the data and formulas, but also closes up the worksheet, removing the deleted block, rows, or columns.

If you have locked cells in the block, rows, or columns you want to blank, the system refuses to execute the command. (See Chapter 12 for information about locking and unlocking cells.) The following message appears on the command line:

```
Block contains [nr] locked cells, beginning at [address]
```

In this message, the number of locked cells in the designated range appears in place of *[nr]*, and the cell address of the first locked cell appears in place of *[address]*. The four Edit Blank options are as follows:

```
Block  Columns  Rows  All
```

Using the Edit Blank command is similar to using the Edit Delete command.

Clearing Columns

To execute Edit Blank Columns, position your cursor on the first column you want to blank and issue the command. The prompt is

```
Enter number of columns:
```

You can type the number of columns or move the cursor to the right so that the system designates the number for you. Press Enter to complete the command.

The blanked columns remain in place, but they contain no data. The current sheet default formatting applies.

Clearing Rows

To execute Edit Blank Rows, position your cursor on the first row you want to blank and issue the command. The prompt is

    Enter number of rows:

You can type the number of rows or move the cursor down so that the system designates the number for you. Press Enter to complete the command.

The blanked rows remain in place, but they contain no data. Cell formatting reverts to the default for the worksheet.

Clearing Blocks

When you execute the Edit Blank Block command, you are prompted:

    Enter name or block reference:

If you have not already done so, move your cursor to the upper left corner of the block to be blanked and press F2 to drop the anchor. Then move the cursor to the lower right corner of the block and press Enter to complete the block definition. The cells in the defined range are blanked out, their contents removed. No cells in the rest of the worksheet are shifted, although formula results may change if the formulas reference cells in the blanked range. A blank cell is evaluated as a zero if used in a formula.

Clearing the Worksheet

To blank an entire worksheet, use the Edit Blank All command. Be careful when you use this command, however; SmartWare II provides no warning prompt to verify that you really want to blank the whole worksheet.

Editing a Worksheet Cell

If you already have text, values, or a formula in a worksheet cell, you edit the cell with the Edit Edit-Cell command; the Quick key is Alt-E.

Short formulas (up to 240 characters) are displayed on the command line for editing. However, if the formula is long (maximum 1,000 characters), the full screen formula editor is invoked.

In the short formula editor, the cursor is positioned on the first character of the formula or text. You use the cursor keys to move the cursor within the editing workspace. Use Ins to toggle between overlay and insert modes. (The status of Ins is not shown with the short formula editor. In the full screen formula editor, the status of Ins is shown at the right of the status line.) You can use the full screen formula editor with a short formula by using the Quick key Alt-F.

After you have made the necessary changes to your formula, values, or text entries, press Enter to complete the editing process. Even if your calculation mode is set to Manual, the cell is recalculated after editing.

Chapter Summary

Developing a worksheet is usually a step-by-step process. First, you develop the kernel of the worksheet that contains the most important elements; then you expand the model to encompass the full range you want to cover. This chapter has discussed the commands you use to copy and move cells within your worksheet. In addition, you can use the Edit Insert and Edit Delete commands to increase or decrease the size of the worksheet.

11

Operating the Spreadsheet

After you construct a spreadsheet, a number of commands are available to make working with the spreadsheet easy and fast. You use the Edit Sort command, for example, to rearrange a block of columns or rows according to the contents of the cells.

This chapter also covers the naming of blocks of cells. In previous chapters, blocks of cells usually have been referenced with the colon notation to indicate a range. For example, *r1:5c10:17* indicates the block that extends from rows 1 to 5 through columns 10 to 17. You can use the Sheet Name command to simplify the reference to a block of cells in your worksheet.

In addition, you can use the Sheet Find command to search for specific values, text, or calculation errors. You also can use this command to search for empty cells that you have previously formatted.

Finally, this chapter describes the different methods of initiating calculations.

Establishing Order in Columns and Rows

You use the Edit Sort command to rearrange cells within a block according to the contents of designated rows or columns in that block. You can specify ascending or descending order, or you can mix sequences within the same command.

When you select the Edit Sort command, you are prompted:

    Enter name or block reference:

You can type the block address in row and column notation (*r3:7c5:10*, for example). An easier way is to move the cursor to the upper left corner of the block, press F2 to mark the beginning of the block, and then move the cursor to the lower right corner. The block is highlighted as you go; you press Enter to complete the block definition. You also can supply the name of a block, as discussed later in this chapter. Press F4 to display a list of block names.

After you have defined the block, you are prompted:

> Ascending Descending

Select the order that applies to the majority of rows or columns that you designate as the sort criteria, as explained next. Even though you specify Ascending or Descending order, you can override the selection on an individual row or column basis.

After you choose the desired order, you are prompted to select a sort key in a column or row:

> Column Row

If you select Column, you are prompted:

> Enter column number(s) of sort key:

By selecting Column, you indicate that the block is to be sorted according to the contents of cells in one or more columns of the block; the rows within the block are to be rearranged according to that sort key. You can enter the numbers of the columns, or you can move the cursor so that the numbers are entered for you.

You can specify as many as 15 separate columns as sort keys for the block. Each key can be sorted in ascending or descending order. For instance, if you specify Ascending order in response to the prompt, you can override this default by typing a *d* after the column number. The following example is the response you would enter to sort by column 7 ascending, 10 descending, and 8 ascending:

> 7 10d 8

If you specify Descending order as the default for the sort, you must enter an *a* to override that default for a specific column.

Press Enter when you have finished typing the sort column numbers. (If you press Enter without typing a column number, the current column is selected as the default.)

If you want to sort the block of data according to the contents of cells in one or more rows of the block, select a Row sort. You are prompted:

> Enter row number(s) of sort key:

When you select Row, the columns within the block are sorted according to the rows you specify as the keys. As with the column specification, you can designate multiple rows as sort keys. You also can override the default order by entering *a* (for ascending) or *d* (for descending) after the row number.

Press Enter when you have finished typing the sort row numbers. (If you press Enter without typing a row number, the current row is selected as the default.)

If the sorted cells contain formulas, the formulas are adjusted relative to the new cell locations. Sorting is performed in *collation* sequence; alphabetic characters are grouped together regardless of whether they are upper- or lowercase. In this sequence, both *ACCT* and *acct* occur before *DATA* in the sort order. In a sort based on pure ASCII values, *DATA* occurs before *acct*—and, for that matter, before *dATA*—because all uppercase letters have lower ASCII values than do lowercase letters. (ASCII is an acronym for American Standard Code for Information Interchange.)

Figure 11.1 shows a set of data sorted in two different sequences.

```
#1       1           2         3      #2       1           2         3
1   DEPT          WAGE                1   DEPT          WAGE
2                                     2
3   DATA           654.34             3   ACCT         3,365.86
4   MFGR         2,401.45             4   DATA           654.34
5   SALE         2,626.61             5   MFGR         2,401.45
6   ACCT         3,365.86             6   MKTG         4,080.59
7   MKTG         4,080.59             7   SALE         2,626.61
8                                     8
9                                     9
10  Sort [block]                      10  Sort [block]
11  Ascending                         11  Ascending
12  Using                             12  Using
13  Column 2                          13  Column 1
14                                    14
15                                    15
16  ██████                            16
17                                    17
18                                    18

Menu:   Sheet  Edit  File  Layout  Print  Graph  Tools  Window  Help  Remember
        Quit
Worksheet: sortdem1 Loc: r16c1     FN:        Font:   0
Blank Copy Delete Edit-Cell Fill Hide Unhide Insert Move Sort ValueCopy
```

Fig. 11.1.

Sorting the same set of data in two ways.

Naming a Block of Cells

You can use the Sheet Name command to assign a name to a block of cells. You then can use this name wherever you are prompted for a name or block reference. You also can use a block name with the Sheet Goto command to move your cursor from one location to another in the worksheet.

Block names are particularly useful if you are consolidating several worksheets into one. Although a formula enables you to reference specific cells in another worksheet, the references are not dynamic. If you move the referenced cells in the source file, the formulas in the destination file do not automatically readjust for the new location. But if the reference is to a *name* in the source file, the system can resolve the formula correctly no matter where the referenced cells are moved.

Names are stored as an integral part of the worksheet file. There is no separate command to save names, nor are they saved in a separate file. To retain block names, however, you must save your worksheet to disk even if you have not changed any data.

Defining a Named Block

To assign a name to a block, select the Define option. You are prompted:

    Enter new name:

The name can be as long as 15 characters, and it can contain numbers or letters, but it must not begin with a number. Names are not case sensitive, so it does not matter whether you enter them in upper- or lowercase letters. After you have typed the name, press Enter. SmartWare II then prompts you,

    Enter definition for this name:

At this prompt you define the block. You can enter the address in row and column notation; for example, *r3:7c5:10*. An easier way is to move the cursor to the upper left cell of the block, press F2 to drop the anchor, and then move the cursor to the lower right corner of the block. The block is highlighted as you go. Press Enter to complete definition of the block.

Printing Block Names

You use the Sheet Name Print command to print a list of block names. Figure 11.2 shows the output of this command. Note that the block names are printed in alphabetical order.

Fig. 11.2.

An example of output from the Sheet Name Print command.

```
User names for worksheet domestic
apr                          r2:14c5
aug                          r2:14c9
dec                          r2:14c13
dom                          r1:19c1:13
feb                          r2:14c3
jan                          r2:14c2
jul                          r2:14c8
jun                          r2:14c7
mar                          r2:14c4
may                          r2:14c6
nov                          r2:14c12
oct                          r2:14c11
sep                          r2:14c10
```

Editing a Named Block Definition

Instead of printing a list of the range names, you may simply want to use the Sheet Name Edit command to display a list of the range names on your screen. The primary function of the Sheet Name Edit command, however, is to edit named block definitions. When you select this command, a list of names and block definitions is displayed (see fig. 11.3).

```
            1      2    3    4    5    6    7    8    9   10   11
                        DOMESTIC DIVISION
1
2                     Jan  Feb  Mar  Apr  May  Jun  Jul  Aug  Sep  Oct
3         Net Sales.. 80.6 81.3 82.1 82.8 83.6 84.4 85.1 85.9 86.7 87.5
4         Gross Prof. 33.9 34.2 34.5 34.8 35.1 35.4 35.8 36.1 36.4 36.7
5         ------------------------------------------------------------
6         G&A Exp....  2.2  2.2  2.2  2.2  2.2  2.2  2.2  2.2  2.2  2.2
  User-names editor
     → apr                       r2:14c5
       aug                       r2:14c9
       dec                       r2:14c13
       dom                       r1:19c1:13
       feb                       r2:14c3
       jan                       r2:14c2
       jul                       r2:14c8
       jun                       r2:14c7
       mar                       r2:14c4
       may                       r2:14c6
       nov                       r2:14c12

 F1 Help    F2 Edit text    F3 Blank text    F10 Finished
 Worksheet: domestic Loc: r2c6    FN: 32  Font:  0
 Assign a name to a cell or block of cells.
```

Fig. 11.3.

Displaying a list of names and blocks.

Use the up- or down-arrow keys to select the name of the definition you want to edit. (You are editing the definition, not the name itself.) You can use the cursor keys to move around the definition as you edit it. Pressing Ins toggles between the Insert and Overwrite modes; the cursor changes to indicate the Insert status. You press the Ins key to change the Insert status. An underscore cursor indicates that the Insert mode is on; a block cursor indicates that it is off.

Removing a Name

To remove a name from the list, execute the command Sheet Name Undefine. You are prompted:

    Enter name:

Note that no pop-up menu appears to remind you of the names. If you need to see a list, use the Sheet Name Edit or Print command before selecting Sheet Name Undefine.

Using the Sheet Goto Command

The Quick key for the Sheet Goto command is F4. You use this multipurpose command to change windows, bring up a different worksheet in the current window, or move the cursor to a specified physical location, cell, or named block within the current window. You also can use the Sheet Goto command to move the cursor quickly, skipping blank cells.

When you select this command, you are prompted to select one of the following options:

Cell Sheet Window Other

If you want to move the cursor to a specific cell or named block, select Cell. You are prompted:

Enter name or cell reference:

Type the address of a cell or the name of a block. The cursor is moved to the cell or to the upper left corner of the block, and the worksheet is repositioned so that the cursor is in the upper left corner of the window.

If you have established window titles (see "Retaining Title Rows or Columns" later in this chapter), you can use the Sheet Goto Cell command to position your cursor within the titles area temporarily. Although your screen will present a dual display of the titles area, which may be confusing, using this feature to access the titles area of your worksheet is frequently preferable to dropping the titles and having to fix them again.

If you want to display a different worksheet in your current window, select the Sheet option. A pop-up window displays the names of the currently active worksheets. Move the cursor to the name of the worksheet you want to display in the current window and press Enter. If you have entered data into a new worksheet but have not yet assigned a name to it, it is identified as (none) in the list.

You can combine the effect of these two options by selecting the Cell option and typing a response that includes the name of a loaded worksheet and a cell or block address in one of the following formats:

DOMESTIC.r5c6

CANADA.shares

Note that the name of the worksheet is separated from the cell address by a period.

To go to another window, select the Window option. You are prompted:

Enter window number:

Type the number of the window in response to the prompt, and the cursor is repositioned in the specified window. The cursor position in the original window is retained while you are in a different window so that, when you return to the original window, the cursor is positioned where it was when you left.

You can use the Alt-F7 and Alt-F8 Quick keys to move the cursor to the previous or next numbered window. If your current window is 1, for example, Alt-F8 advances you to window 2; if you press Alt-F8 again, you advance to window 3. (If you have only two windows open, you return to window 1. In this case, Alt-F7 and Alt-F8 have the same effect.) In previous versions of the Smart Spreadsheet, you could not go to another window while the window was Zoomed. Now, with SmartWare II, you can go to another window while in the Zoomed or the Unzoomed mode.

If you want to move the cursor, skipping blank cells in your worksheet, or find the last filled cell before a blank cell, select the Other option. When you select this option, you are prompted:

    Press a direction key:

When you press one of the cursor arrow keys, the cursor is moved according to the following rules:

Current Cell	Next Cell	Cursor Stops On
Filled	Filled	Cell before the next blank cell
Filled	Blank	Next filled cell
Blank	Either	Next filled cell

When using the Sheet Goto Other command, any preformatted blank cells are considered to be filled, not blank.

Searching Through Your Worksheet

You use the Sheet Find command to search for a cell with specific contents (text or value); the Quick key is F3. You also can search for preformatted, empty cells or cells with calculation errors. Similarly, you can find a cell that has been highlighted by using the Sheet Audit command, discussed later in this chapter.

The search order of the Sheet Find command is always left to right and top to bottom within your worksheet, beginning at the cursor location. Because you cannot search backward through your worksheet, you should begin the process by placing the cursor in the upper left corner of the worksheet; use the Ctrl-Home key combination to move the cursor to row 1 column 1. If you have fixed window titles, the Sheet Find command stops at the cell closest to the target.

The Quick key Alt-R repeats the previous Sheet Find command. If you have not executed any other intervening commands, you also can use F9 to repeat the command. When you execute the Sheet Find command, you are prompted:

    Block All

If you want to confine your search to a block of cells, select Block. You are then prompted:

    Enter name or block reference:

You can type the block address in row and column notation (*r3:7c5:10*, for example). An easier way, of course, is to move the cursor to the upper left corner of the block and press F2 to drop the anchor; then move the cursor to the lower right corner and press Enter to complete the block definition. The block is highlighted as you go. You also can supply the name of a block, as discussed previously in this chapter.

If you want to search the entire worksheet, select All. In either case, you are prompted:

```
Calc-Error Empty Highlight Text Value
```

To find a calculation error, select the Calc-Error option. If any calculation errors exist in your worksheet, the cursor stops on the first one to the right and below your starting location. Only primary calculation errors are located; any calculation errors that result from an error in another cell (Error 7) are skipped. (A complete list of the SmartWare II System Formula Errors is in Appendix A of the *Formula Reference* manual.) If no calculation errors are found, you receive the following message:

```
No error found below current cell
```

To make sure that no calculation errors exist, you may want to reposition the cursor at r1c1 and press Alt-R to execute the find command again from the upper left corner of your worksheet. If an error is found, an explanation is displayed on the second command line. Press the F9 to continue the search, or press any other key to halt.

To find the first empty, preformatted cell, select the Empty option. The cursor stops on the first cell that has been formatted but that does not yet contain data. Note that this option does not find cells that have not been formatted, and thus are entirely blank.

If you have highlighted an area of your worksheet using the Sheet Audit command, you can display the first highlighted cell by selecting the Highlight option. (The Sheet Audit command is covered in the next section.)

To find a cell containing a specific text string, select the Text option. You are prompted:

```
Enter text:
```

Type the text string that you want to find. Because the search is not case sensitive, you do not have to worry about upper- or lowercase entries. The text you search for may be in the middle of a word; you do not have the option to search for whole word matches. If the text can be found in the current window without shifting the view of the worksheet, the cursor is moved and the view is unchanged.

To find a cell with a certain value, select the Value option. The prompt is

```
Enter value:
```

You can search for entered values and values that result from formulas; be aware, however, that the command searches for a match with the underlying value, not necessarily the number displayed. You may not be able to find a number that is displayed as a rounded number or as a date or time.

Auditing your Worksheet

A new feature introduced with SmartWare II is the Sheet Audit command, which enables you to highlight selected cells in your worksheet according to specific conditions. When you execute the Sheet Audit command, you are prompted with the following options:

Option	Function
Circular	Highlights all cells containing circular references.
Empty	Highlights all cells that have been formatted but that do not yet have data.
Formulas	Highlights your selection of six different types of formulas:

- *Blanks*—formulas that reference blank, unformatted cells.

- *Empty*—formulas that reference formatted cells containing no data.

- *Unused*—formulas not used in other worksheet formulas. Typically, these formulas are the results of a model. (In figure 11.4, the formulas in row 14 (EPS) would be highlighted.)

- *Xternal*—formulas that reference external worksheets.

- *Child*—cells that are used by the formula at the current cursor position. If any of the parents of the current cell change, the value of the current formula changes as well. The parents of the current cell may be values, text, or other formulas. Note that when you use this option, the position of the cursor is important.

Figure 11.4 illustrates the use of the Sheet Audit Formulas Child command. Note that the cursor is located on r14c3 (Earnings per Share) and that r12c3 (Net Income) and r18c1 (Average Shares) have been highlighted. You can observe from the formula on the command line that EPS is a function of Net Income and number of shares.

- *Parent*—cells that contain formulas referring to the current cell. If the contents of the current cell changes, the values of the highlighted cells also change. Note that when you use this option, the position of the cursor is significant.

Fig. 11.4.

Result of the Sheet Audit Formulas Child command.

```
               1      2     3     4     5     6     7     8     9    10    11
     1                          CANADIAN DIVISION
     2                Jan   Feb   Mar   Apr   May   Jun   Jul   Aug   Sep   Oct
     3   Net Sales.. 70.6  71.2  71.9  72.6  73.2  73.9  74.6  75.3  75.9  76.6
     4   Gross Prof. 29.7  29.9  30.2  30.5  30.8  31.0  31.3  31.6  31.9  32.2
     5   ─────────────────────────────────────────────────────────────────────
     6   G&A Exp....  2.8   2.8   2.8   2.8   2.8   2.8   2.8   2.8   2.8   2.8
     7   EBIT....... 26.9  27.1  27.4  27.7  28.0  28.2  28.5  28.8  29.1  29.4
     8   Int Exp....  2.2   2.2   2.2   2.2   2.2   2.2   2.2   2.2   2.2   2.2
     9   EBT........ 24.7  24.9  25.2  25.5  25.8  26.0  26.3  26.6  26.9  27.2
    10   ─────────────────────────────────────────────────────────────────────
    11   Tax........ 11.8  12.0  12.1  12.2  12.4  12.5  12.6  12.8  12.9  13.1
    12   Net Income. 12.8  13.0  13.1  13.2  13.4  13.5  13.7  13.8  14.0  14.1
    13   ─────────────────────────────────────────────────────────────────────
    14   EPS....... 0.04  0.04  0.04  0.04  0.04  0.04  0.04  0.04  0.04  0.04
    15
    16     Average       Gr Prof      Sales        G&A          Intst        Tax
    17     Shares:       Rate %       Grow %       Expense:     Expense:     Rate%
    18     350,000         42           11            2.8          2.2         40

Enter:
Formula: r12c3/r[18]c[1]*1000
Worksheet: canada    Loc: r14c3    FN: 0    Font: 0
Enter a string, value, date, time or formula
```

Figure 11.5 illustrates the use of the Sheet Audit Formulas Parent command. The cursor is located on r18c1 (Average Shares). The Sheet Audit command has highlighted the formulas in row 14, all of which reference the current cell.

Fig. 11.5.

Result of the Sheet Audit Formulas Parent command.

```
               1      2     3     4     5     6     7     8     9    10    11
     1                          CANADIAN DIVISION
     2                Jan   Feb   Mar   Apr   May   Jun   Jul   Aug   Sep   Oct
     3   Net Sales.. 70.6  71.2  71.9  72.6  73.2  73.9  74.6  75.3  75.9  76.6
     4   Gross Prof. 29.7  29.9  30.2  30.5  30.8  31.0  31.3  31.6  31.9  32.2
     5   ─────────────────────────────────────────────────────────────────────
     6   G&A Exp....  2.8   2.8   2.8   2.8   2.8   2.8   2.8   2.8   2.8   2.8
     7   EBIT....... 26.9  27.1  27.4  27.7  28.0  28.2  28.5  28.8  29.1  29.4
     8   Int Exp....  2.2   2.2   2.2   2.2   2.2   2.2   2.2   2.2   2.2   2.2
     9   EBT........ 24.7  24.9  25.2  25.5  25.8  26.0  26.3  26.6  26.9  27.2
    10   ─────────────────────────────────────────────────────────────────────
    11   Tax........ 11.8  12.0  12.1  12.2  12.4  12.5  12.6  12.8  12.9  13.1
    12   Net Income. 12.8  13.0  13.1  13.2  13.4  13.5  13.7  13.8  14.0  14.1
    13   ─────────────────────────────────────────────────────────────────────
    14   EPS....... 0.04  0.04  0.04  0.04  0.04  0.04  0.04  0.04  0.04  0.04
    15
    16     Average       Gr Prof      Sales        G&A          Intst        Tax
    17     Shares:       Rate %       Grow %       Expense:     Expense:     Rate%
    18     350,000         42           11            2.8          2.2         40

Enter:
Value: 350000
Worksheet: canada    Loc: r18c1    FN: 0    Font: 0
Enter a string, value, date, time or formula
```

Restore   Removes the highlight from any selected cells.

Unused   Highlights cells that are not referenced by formulas in your worksheet. The options are

                     All Text Values

Checking for unused values in your worksheet is very important because you may have intended to include a value in a formula and then overlooked it. Typically, only text headers are not used in formulas.

You can use the Sheet Audit command to track down logic errors in your worksheet and to prevent potential problems. You also may want to use the Layout Format Formula-Display and Print commands to help you document and debug your worksheets. Both commands have options that enable you to look at your worksheet in both the Map and Formula formats.

Retaining Title Rows or Columns

As you move through your worksheet, you may want to keep certain title rows or columns on the screen so that you can more easily determine what you are viewing. If your column headings are in rows 1 through 3, for example, you may want to fix these rows on the screen so that you still know what the columns contain when you scroll down to row 99.

You use the Window Titles command to fix a number of rows or columns (or both) so that they remain in place as you move through your worksheet; the Quick key is Alt-T. You can fix only the columns at the left of the worksheet and the rows at the top.

After you have established window titles, you can use the Sheet Goto Cell command to position your cursor within the titles area temporarily. Although your screen will present a dual display of the titles area, which may be confusing, using this feature to access the titles area of your worksheet is preferable to dropping the titles and having to fix them again. This feature is new to SmartWare II.

Titles are retained even after you save and unload a worksheet or go to a different sheet in the same window. Before using the Window Titles command, press Ctrl-Home to position your cursor on row 1, column 1; then select the Window Titles command. The options are

    Fix Drop

If you select Fix, you are prompted:

    Columns Rows

If you want to fix the display of one or more columns, select the Columns option. You are then prompted:

    Enter number of columns:

You can type a number, or you can move the cursor so that the system enters the number of columns for you. Press Enter when you have finished. (The number defaults to 1 if you just press Enter at the prompt.) The cursor moves to the first column outside the fixed area, and the columns you have fixed now remain in place on your screen as you move right and left to view different portions of your worksheet. Note that the Ctrl-Home key combination now moves the cursor to the upper left corner of the non-fixed area of your worksheet.

If you want to fix the position of one or more rows, select the Rows option. You are prompted:

    Enter number of rows:

Again, you can type a number or move the cursor so that the system enters the number of rows for you. Press Enter when you have finished. (The number defaults to 1 if you just press Enter at the prompt.) The cursor moves to the first row outside the fixed area, and the rows you have fixed now remain in place on your screen as you move up and down, viewing different portions of your worksheet.

To remove the title settings, choose the Drop option of the Window Titles command; this option simultaneously removes the row and the column titles.

Recalculating the Worksheet

You have the choice of automatically recalculating your worksheet after every change, or recalculating only when you want to. You also can select an iterative recalculation mode for certain modeling situations. The most appropriate method varies according to the types of changes you are making. In addition to selecting the timing of recalculation, you also can select the order in which recalculations are to be performed.

While you are building your worksheet, you probably don't want it to be recalculated automatically; recalculation takes time, and incomplete worksheet sections can display irrelevant data and annoying error messages. Even after a worksheet is built, you may want the system to wait until you finish entering several numbers before it recalculates. On the other hand, if you are modeling a worksheet and changing variables as you go, you may want the convenience of automatic recalculation.

In SmartWare II, when you change a cell in a worksheet and recalculation is performed, only the affected cells are recomputed. If the altered cell is the parent of formulas in other cells, only those formulas are recalculated. Of course, if these formulas are themselves parents of other formulas, the recalculation must continue until the chain is exhausted. To force a total recalculation of your entire worksheet, press the Shift-F5 key.

The Sheet Calc-Mode command is used to establish or determine the current recalculation mode. Your selection remains in effect for the duration of the session with the current worksheet or until you change the setting. The default setting for new worksheets is established in the Spreadsheet Preferences menu displayed when you execute the Tools Preferences Spreadsheet command.

When you execute the Sheet Calc-Mode command, you are prompted to select one of five options:

```
Automatic Manual Display Calc-Order Iterate
```

Usually, you select Automatic or Manual. To show the current setting, select the Display option; if the current setting is Manual, for example, the following display appears on the command line:

```
Recalculation mode: Manual Order: Natural, press any key
```

When the current setting is Manual, you must press the F5 key to recalculate your spreadsheet. The word CALC is displayed on the status line if values have been entered or changed and the worksheet has not been recalculated (see fig. 11.6).

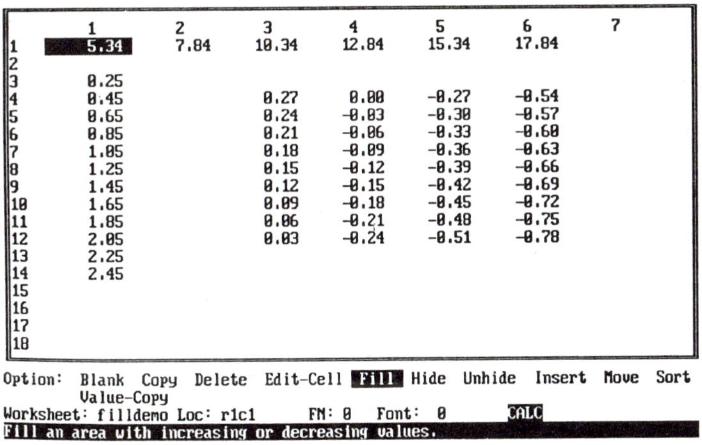

Fig. 11.6.

Examples of the Edit Fill command.

If the recalculation mode is set to Automatic, recalculation is performed each time you enter a new value; you do not have to press the F5 key to recalculate the worksheet. If you edit an individual cell, the recalculation of that cell is performed automatically at the completion of the edit process, even if your recalculation mode is set to Manual.

If you select the Iterate option, the calculation of the spreadsheet continues until specified conditions are met; the options are

```
Count Remove Test
```

If you select Count, you are prompted for the number of iterations to be performed. You can specify the Count option in the Automatic or Manual mode; the worksheet is automatically recalculated according to the number you have specified. To disable the Count option, set the value to zero or select the Remove option.

Selecting the Test option causes recalculation to continue until a test value is achieved or a maximum number of calculations is performed. When you select Test, you are prompted:

> Enter name or block reference:

You respond with the name or block reference of the cell containing the formula being calculated.

Next, you are prompted to

> Enter delta value:

Recalculation continues until the change in the value of the formulas in the test cell gets below the delta value. The next prompt is

> Enter maximum number of iterations:

If you do not enter a number, the default is zero. Do not set the number too high because you cannot halt processing during iterative recalculation. Note that the recalculation mode and iteration specifications are saved with the worksheet.

Iterative calculation is useful when your spreadsheet contains circular references, which are indicated by the key word CIRC on the status line. A circular reference does not necessarily indicate an error; you may find that using a "cut and try" approach is a legitimate modeling technique. The automatic iteration capability of the Sheet Calc-Mode command simplifies this approach.

You use the Remove option to cancel the use of the iteration feature of the Sheet Calc-Mode command.

Filling your Worksheet Automatically

You can use the Edit Fill command to generate new data values and enter them in designated cells on a worksheet. You can generate only numeric data (values) with this command; you cannot generate text.

Position the cursor at the starting location before you begin the Edit Fill command. The initial options are

> Block Columns Rows

If you select Columns or Rows, move the cursor to the leftmost column or the uppermost row of the area you want to fill.

When you select Columns, you are prompted:

> Enter number of columns:

Enter the number of columns for the range or move the cursor to the right to have the system enter the number for you. Press Enter when the number is correct. If you press Enter without typing a number, the value defaults to 1.

When you select Rows, you are prompted:

    Enter number of rows:

You then enter the number of rows for the range or move the cursor down to have the system enter the number for you. Press Enter when the number is correct. Again, if you press Enter without typing a number, the value defaults to 1.

If you select Block, you are prompted:

    Enter name or block reference:

You can type the block address in row and column notation (*r3:7c5:10*, for example). An easier method is to move the cursor to the upper left corner of the block and press F2 to drop the anchor; then move the cursor to the lower right corner and press Enter to complete the block definition. The block is highlighted as you go. You also can supply the name of a block, as discussed previously in this chapter.

After you have designated the range to fill, the next prompt is

    Enter start value:

Your answer should be the value that is to be entered in the first cell of the range—either the leftmost column, the uppermost row, or the upper left corner of the block. The number can be an integer or a decimal value.

The final prompt is

    Enter increment:

The increment is the amount to be added (or subtracted, if the number is negative) from cell to cell. The first cell contains the starting value, the next cell is the sum of the starting value and the increment, and so on.

Figure 11.6 illustrates examples of the Edit Fill command. In row 1, the starting value is 5.34 and the increment is 2.5. In cell r3c1, the starting value is .25 and the increment is 0.2.

The block in r4:12c3:6 is filled with values beginning with rows in a column before proceeding to the next column. (If you need to fill the columns within a row before proceeding to next row, use the Sheet Matrix Transpose command, which is discussed in the next section.)

If you reset the default format for new values using the Layout Default Values command, the numbers you enter with the Edit Fill command conform to the format you have selected. Alternately, the numbers you enter using the Edit Fill command can be reformatted later using the Layout Format command.

Using the Matrix Commands

The powerful Sheet Matrix commands have many uses in scientific and statistical applications, but you also may find them useful in business applications. Figure 11.7 shows the Sheet Matrix option list. This section describes only those commands that have the most applicability in the business environment.

Fig. 11.7.

The Sheet Matrix option list.

```
17
18
Option:  Aux  Diagonal  Invert  Multiply  M-Solve  Parallel  Regression  Sweep
         Transpose  Upper
Worksheet: matdemo  Loc: r10c6    FN: 0    Font: 0
Transpose a matrix.
```

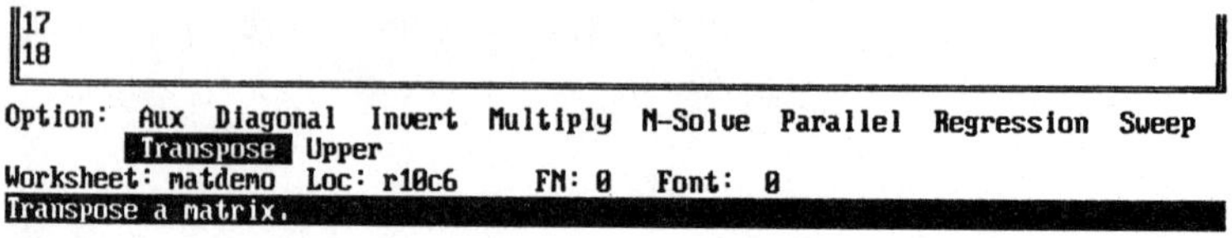

Transposing Columns and Rows

The Transpose option is used to swap columns for rows and rows for columns. The transposition is performed in place; the transposed matrix replaces the original one. If you want to retain the original matrix, first execute the Edit Copy command.

Figure 11.8 shows two examples of the Transpose option. (The Edit Fill command was used to generate the original blocks on the left.)

Fig. 11.8.

Examples of the Sheet Matrix Transpose command.

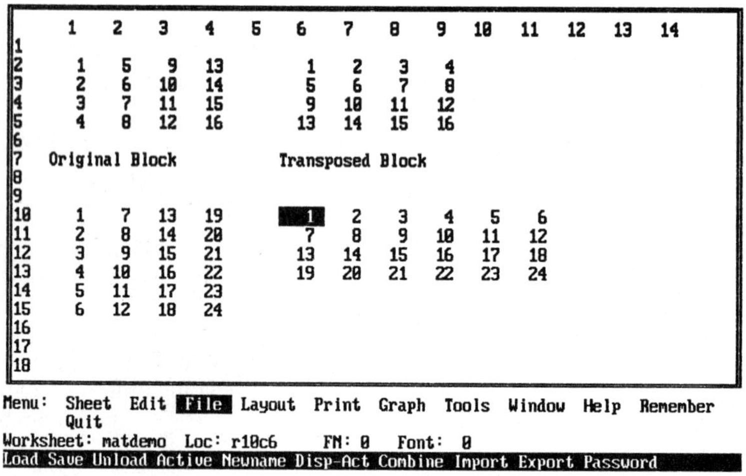

```
       1   2   3   4   5   6   7   8   9  10  11  12  13  14
 1
 2     1   5   9  13          1   2   3   4
 3     2   6  10  14          5   6   7   8
 4     3   7  11  15          9  10  11  12
 5     4   8  12  16         13  14  15  16
 6
 7     Original Block         Transposed Block
 8
 9
10     1   7  13  19          1   2   3   4   5   6
11     2   8  14  20          7   8   9  10  11  12
12     3   9  15  21         13  14  15  16  17  18
13     4  10  16  22         19  20  21  22  23  24
14     5  11  17  23
15     6  12  18  24
16
17
18
Menu:  Sheet  Edit  File  Layout  Print  Graph  Tools  Window  Help  Remember
       Quit
Worksheet: matdemo  Loc: r10c6    FN: 0    Font: 0
Load Save Unload Active Newname Disp-Act Combine Import Export Password
```

The upper blocks are four rows by four columns; notice that the rows have become columns, and vice versa. The lower blocks are rectangular because they do not have the same number of rows as columns; the original block on the left has more rows than columns. Even with a rectangular matrix, the rows and columns can be swapped. In this example, the transposition has created more columns and reduced the number of rows. Any data adjacent to the shorter dimension of a rectangular block also is transposed, so be careful.

The Transpose option can be useful if you want to send the contents of your worksheet to the Data Manager but you want the worksheet rows to represent fields and the columns to be records. Cell references within the block are not adjusted, however, so you may have to perform an Edit Value-Copy command before transposing the block.

Performing Matrix Parallel Operations

The Sheet Matrix Parallel command can be used to add, multiply, subtract, or divide multiple data blocks on a cell by cell basis. When you execute the command, you are prompted:

    Add Div Mult Sub

Regardless of the mathematical operation you select, you are prompted:

    Enter first matrix-block:

You can type the address of the first matrix in row and column notation (*r3:7c5:10*, for example). An easier method is to move the cursor to the upper left corner of the block and press F2 to drop the anchor; then move the cursor to the lower right corner and press Enter to complete the block definition. The block is highlighted as you go. You also can supply the name of a block, as discussed previously in this chapter.

The next prompt is

    Enter second matrix-block, value, or single cell:

Enter the description of the second matrix block. If you enter a single cell address or a value, the value is applied to each cell of the first matrix block. You are then prompted:

    Enter matrix-block for result:

You can enter just the upper left corner of the destination block. Figure 11.9 shows three examples of the use of the Sheet Matrix Parallel command.

Note that the Matrix Parallel calculations are purely arithmetic operations performed on a cell-by-cell basis; they are not true matrix mathematical calculations.

The data sources for the Sheet Matrix Parallel command must be active worksheets. Later in this chapter, you learn about the File Combine command, which enables you to perform addition and subtraction using data in worksheets that are not active.

Fig. 11.9.

Examples of the Sheet Matrix Parallel command.

```
      1   2   3  4   5   6   7  8    9          10         11     12  13  14
  1  Block #1         Block #2                Result Block
  2  ─────────────    ─────────────           ─────────────
  3   1   7  13        5   2  -1         6.000      9.000     12.000
  4   3   9  15   +    4   1  -2   =     7.000     10.000     13.000
  5   5  11  17        3   0  -3         8.000     11.000     14.000
  6
  7  23  44  65       65  59  53         0.354      0.746      1.226
  8  30  51  72   /   63  57  51   =     0.476      0.895      1.412
  9  37  58  79       61  55  49         0.607      1.055      1.612
 10
 11   1  10  19       10   4  -2        10.000     40.000    -38.000
 12   4  13  22   *    8   2  -4   =    32.000     26.000    -88.000
 13   7  16  25        6   0  -6        42.000      0.000   -150.000
 14
 15
 16
 17
 18

Option: Add  Div  Mult  Sub
Worksheet: parallel  Loc: r11c1     FN: 0    Font: 0
Add a matrix, a cell, or an input value to a matrix.
```

Performing Matrix Multiplication

For true matrix multiplication, use the Sheet Matrix Multiply command. When you execute this command, you are prompted for the following blocks:

    Enter first matrix-block:

    Enter second matrix-block:

    Enter matrix-block for result:

Figure 11.10 shows an example of true matrix multiplication.

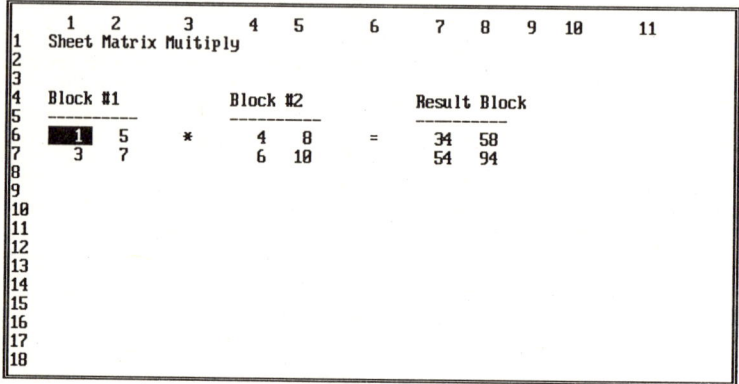

Fig. 11.10.

Result of the Sheet Matrix Multiply command.

Computing Linear Regression

You can use the Sheet Matrix Regression command to compute a linear regression model for developing and testing a forecast. Figure 11.11 shows three columns of data:

- Column 1   Name of month
- Column 2   Number of cars sold in the month
- Column 3   Sequential month number

```
        1      2      3      4      5      6      7      8
                     Month
   1  Month  Cars  Sequence
   2  ------------------
   3
   4  Jan 76  677    1
   5  Feb 76  634    2
   6  Mar 76  764    3
   7  Apr 76  884    4
   8  May 76  914    5
   9  Jun 76  937    6
  10  Jul 76  939    7
  11  Aug 76  848    8
  12  Sep 76  749    9
  13  Oct 76  797   10
  14  Nov 76  763   11
  15  Dec 76  846   12
  16  Jan 77  726   13
  17  Feb 77  717   14
  18  Mar 77  836   15

Menu:  Sheet  Edit  File  Layout  Print  Graph  Tools  Window  Help  Remember
       Quit
Worksheet: cars       Loc: r1c1       FN: 0   Font: 0
Blank Copy Delete Edit-Cell Fill Hide Unhide Insert Move Sort ValueCopy
```

Fig. 11.11.

A linear regression model.

For the purpose of illustrating the regression model, the number of cars is the dependent variable, and the sequential month number is the independent variable. The assumption, then, is that the number of cars registered is dependent on time alone and is not related to other factors.

To begin the calculation of the model, execute the Sheet Matrix Regression command. You are prompted:

    Enter matrix-block for source:

You can type the address of the data in row and column notation (*r4:39c2:3*, for example). An easier method is to move the cursor to the upper left corner of the block and press F2 to drop the anchor; then move the cursor to the lower right corner and press Enter to complete the block definition. The block is highlighted as you go. You also can supply the name of a block, as discussed previously in this chapter.

When you perform a regression, the dependent variable must be positioned in the left column of the matrix block, and the independent variables must be positioned in the columns immediately to the right of the dependent variable. In our model, the source block is r4:39c2:3; it covers 36 months of observations.

The next prompt is

   No-Report Report

If you want a report of the statistics underlying the model, select the Report option. You are then prompted:

   Enter Name or block reference for report:

When identifying an output block, make sure you have at least 6 columns available and 21 rows for the standard report, plus 1 row for each independent variable.

The final prompt asks for a location for the output of the regression coefficients:

   Enter cell or vector for coefficients:

Figure 11.12 shows the regression report and the significant statistics.

Fig. 11.12.

A regression report.

```
 1                    MULTIPLE LINEAR REGRESSION           786.20
 2                                                           4.84
 3  Dependent Variable:
 4
 5                              Parameter Standard  T for H0:
 6  Variable           Mean     Estimate   Error    parameter=0
 7
 8  Intercept                    786.20    36.32     21.64
 9  Variable  1        18.50       4.84     1.71      2.83
10
11                     Sum of    Mean
12  Source       DF    Squares   Square    F-Value
13
14  Model        1.00  90965.87  90965.87    7.99
15  Error       34.00 387173.35  11387.45
16  Total       35.00 478139.22
17
18  Dependent Mean              875.72
19  Root Mean Square Error      106.71

Option:  Aux  Diagonal  Invert  Multiply  N-Solve  Parallel  Regression  Sweep
         Transpose  Upper
Worksheet: cars      Loc: r1c10      FN: 0    Font: 0
Perform multiple linear regression on values in a matrix.
```

Note that the regression coefficients have been displayed in rows 1 and 2 of column 10.

Using Additional Sheet Matrix Options

The other Sheet Matrix options are as follows:

Option	Operation
Aux	Calculates determinant, rank, power, and normalizes.

Diagonal	Calculates sum, product, or copy of diagonal.
Invert	Inverts a matrix.
N-Solve	Solves equations with multiple unknowns.
Sweep	Sweeps a matrix on a pivot.
Upper	Converts to row echelon form.

Combining Files

The File Combine command, new with SmartWare II, enables you to subtract, add, or copy portions of external worksheets to the current sheet. The Add and Subtract options operate only on values and the results of numeric formulas; these options are similar to the Add and Sub options of the Sheet Matrix Parallel command. The Copy option may be used as a substitute for the Edit Copy command. None of the File Combine commands, however, require the source worksheets to be active. If a worksheet is active, the active version is used for the source of the data, not the version on disk.

To combine an external worksheet with the current worksheet, position your cursor at the upper left corner of the destination location and issue the File Combine command. You are prompted:

    Add Copy Subtract

Select Copy to copy all or a portion of an external worksheet to the current sheet. A pop-up window displays the names of the worksheets in the current subdirectory. Move the cursor to the name of the source file and press Enter. You are prompted:

    Block Worksheet

To copy the entire worksheet, select Worksheet. A copy of the source worksheet is inserted in the current sheet, beginning at the cursor position. If you select the Block option, the prompt is

    Enter name or block reference:

Type the name of a block from the source worksheet, or enter the address of the block. When you press Enter, the specified portion of the source worksheet is copied to the current worksheet. The resulting copy includes text and formulas as well as values. Formulas are not adjusted for relative changes in cell locations, however, as they are with the Edit Copy command. If the source contains relative formulas, your current cursor location must be the same as the upper left corner of the source block.

Values or the numeric results of formulas in external worksheets can be added to or subtracted from the current worksheet by selecting the Add or the Subtract option to the File Combine command. The prompts are the same as for the Copy option of the command. If the target range does not contain a number or is not blank, the target remains unchanged. Text and formulas are not overlaid in the target range.

Chapter Summary

After you have built your worksheet, you need to know how to use it effectively. This chapter has covered the commands you need to make the best use of the SmartWare II Spreadsheet. The features covered are sorting, block naming, cursor movement, searching, auditing, recalculation, and the matrix commands.

12

Protecting and Viewing Spreadsheets

Your worksheets can be viewed and changed by anyone unless the worksheets are protected. This chapter focuses on ways to protect your work from inadvertent changes (by you or someone else) and shows you how to save a file so that the formulas are hidden.

This chapter also discusses creating and removing windows. You can create as many as 50 windows in the Spreadsheet module, and in this chapter, you learn how to use these windows to your best advantage.

Protecting Worksheets

You can lock blocks of cells against change; the method you use depends on the type of cell contents. You also can protect entire worksheets with a password to prevent unauthorized persons from loading them.

Locking the Worksheet

If you want to prevent cells or blocks of cells from accidental change, use the Sheet Lock command. (The Quick key Ctrl-L is a toggle that locks or unlocks the current cell.) You can use the Sheet Unlock command to unlock previously locked cells or blocks. The Primary option list for the Sheet Lock command is as follows:

    Blanks Formulas Text Values All Disable Enable Protect

Select the type of cell contents you want to protect. After a cell is protected, you cannot accidentally change or overwrite the contents of that cell.

If you select Blanks or All, there are no further prompts. Selecting Blanks locks all the blank cells in the worksheet; selecting All locks all cells, regardless of type, making the worksheet "read only." You might use this option, for example, with a lookup table whose contents do not change.

By selecting Formulas, Text, or Values, you indicate that cells with contents of that type are to be locked. You are then prompted to select the range to be locked:

    Block   Columns   Rows   All

If you plan to select Columns or Rows, you should first move the cursor to the leftmost column or the uppermost row of the range that you want to protect.

When you select Columns, you are prompted:

    Enter number of columns:

You can type the number of columns to be included in the range, or you can move the cursor to the right so that the system enters the number for you. Press Enter when the number is correct. If you just press Enter without typing a number, the value defaults to 1.

If you select Rows, you are prompted:

    Enter number of rows:

Again, you can enter the number of rows to be included in the range or, by moving the cursor down, have the system enter the number. Press Enter when the number is correct. If you press Enter without typing a number, the value defaults to 1.

If you select Block, you are prompted:

    Enter name or block reference:

You can type the range in row and column notation, such as *r3:7c5:10*. An easier way to indicate the range is to move the cursor to the upper left cell in the block, press F2 to "drop the anchor," and then move the cursor to the lower right corner of the block. The block range is highlighted as you go. Press Enter to complete definition of the block range.

If you select All, no other input is required. Your selected cell type is locked throughout your entire worksheet.

Temporarily Unlocking Worksheet Cells

You can use the Sheet Lock Disable command to temporarily turn off all cell locks throughout your worksheet. Use the Sheet Lock Enable command to reinstate the locks. The lock specifications are retained if you save and unload your file but forget to enable the locks. However, when you reload the file, the locks are not automatically enabled; you must perform the task manually.

Preventing Changes and Hiding Formulas

If you really want to protect the contents of your worksheet against changes, use the Sheet Lock Protect command. When you execute this command, worksheet users are prevented not only from changing but also from viewing your formulas. To provide greater protection, you also should lock your values, text, and blanks if you do not want them to be accidentally changed. However, be aware that the Sheet Unlock and Sheet Lock Disable commands permit access to these cells even if the formulas are protected.

To protect a worksheet, you must first save it if you have made any changes. If you forget to save the worksheet before attempting to protect it, you receive this error message:

    Cannot protect modified worksheet. Changes must be saved first

After you have saved the file and executed the Sheet Lock Protect command, the following prompt appears:

    Are you sure you want to protect this worksheet? (y/n)

You should take great care to maintain a backup copy of your worksheet in its original, unprotected form; give that copy a different name or store it on a different disk. After you have executed the Sheet Lock Protect command and saved the worksheet to disk, you cannot return the worksheet to its original, unlocked form.

After you have protected the formulas, the formula no longer appears on the command line when you are in the Enter mode. Instead, you see the word PROTECTED.

Unlocking the Worksheet

You use the Sheet Unlock command to permanently reverse the effects of the Sheet Lock command. (Use Sheet Lock Disable to unlock the entire sheet temporarily.) The command sequences for Sheet Lock and Unlock are similar. First, you are prompted:

    Blanks Formulas Text Values All

If you select Blanks or All, no further input is required.

If you select one of the other three options, you are prompted to select a range:

    Block Columns Rows All

You identify the appropriate range in the same way you selected a range for the Sheet Lock command. Remember that you cannot reverse the effects of the Sheet Lock Protect command. If you use the protect option, be sure to save a copy of your original worksheet; give the copy a different name or keep it on another disk.

Using Worksheet Passwords

To further secure your worksheets by limiting access, you may assign passwords so that only users who supply the correct password can load the sheet. Passwords can be as long as 16 characters and may contain blanks, letters, numbers, and special characters. Worksheet passwords are case sensitive; *PASS*, for example, is not accepted for *pass*.

Unlike previous versions of Smart, with SmartWare II you cannot assign more than one password to a worksheet. This password allows the file to be loaded for both reading and writing. Passwords encipher the worksheet according to the encryption driver selected in the Tools Preferences Spreadsheet menu.

Attaching a Password to a Worksheet

The options available with the File Password command are

    Attach Remove

When you select Attach, you are prompted:

    Enter new password:

Type the desired password and press Enter. The password you type is not displayed on the screen. To make sure you have typed it correctly, you are prompted:

    Repeat password for verification:

Type the password again and press Enter. (The password does not appear this time either.) If you type the password verification incorrectly, you get the following error message:

    Verification did not match

You are then prompted to begin again by entering a new password. Remembering your password is important; the password is retained with the worksheet when you save it. In a later session, you cannot load the worksheet again without supplying the password.

When you load a worksheet that has been protected with a password, you are prompted:

    Enter password:

Type the password, remembering whether it is upper- or lowercase; press Enter when you have finished. If you type the password incorrectly, the following error message appears:

    Wrong password

Press any key to return to the prompt for the password and try again. You are allowed three attempts to enter the password before the command is aborted.

The process of changing a password is the same as attaching a new one. If you have not saved your worksheet, you will observe no difference; the new password overlays the previous one.

Removing a Password from a Worksheet

To remove a password from a worksheet, select the File Password Remove command. No further input is required, but you must be sure to save the worksheet to make the removal of the password permanent.

Hiding Portions of your Worksheet

To provide flexibility in displaying your worksheet contents, the SmartWare II Spreadsheet provides the capability of hiding portions of your worksheet from view. Once hidden, an area of the worksheet appears blank on the screen and does not print. You should not, however, use this capability as a substitute for the protection provided by the Sheet Lock commands, which prevent accidental change to cell contents and formulas. You also should use the File Password command if you want to prevent unauthorized access.

If you want to hide a portion of a worksheet, execute the Edit Hide command. You are prompted:

    Block Columns Rows All Enable Disable

If you plan to select Columns or Rows, you should first move the cursor to the leftmost column or the uppermost row of the range that you want to hide.

When you select Columns, you are prompted:

    Enter number of columns:

You can type the number of columns to be included in the range, or you can move the cursor to the right so that the system enters the number for you. Press Enter when the number is correct. If you just press Enter without typing a number, the value defaults to 1.

If you select Rows, you are prompted:

    Enter number of rows:

Again, you can enter the number of rows to be included in the range or, by moving the cursor down, have the system enter the number. Press Enter when the number is correct. If you press Enter without typing a number, the value defaults to 1.

If you select Block, you are prompted:

    Enter name or block reference:

You can type the range in row and column notation, such as *r3:7c5:10*. An easier way to indicate the range is to move the cursor to the upper left cell in the block, press F2 to "drop the anchor," and then move the cursor to the lower right corner of the block. The block range is highlighted as you go. Press Enter to complete definition of the block range.

If you select All, no other input is required. Hidden portions of your worksheet appear as if they were blank. However, in the Enter mode, the cell contents are shown on the command line.

Note that column widths remain unchanged when hidden. You also can hide the contents of a column by changing the width to zero using the Layout Cell-Size Width command. For more information on this command, refer to "Changing Column Width and Row Height" in Chapter 9.

You use the Disable option of the Edit Hide command to make hidden portions of your worksheet visible temporarily. When you select this option, you display the hidden areas of your worksheet as if they had never been hidden. Use the Enable option of the Edit Hide command to hide these areas of your worksheet again.

If you hide portions of your worksheet while the hidden attribute is disabled, the newly "hidden" portions remain displayed. If this happens, execute the Edit Hide Enable command to observe the hidden effect you have created.

Using Windows

As in other Smartware II System application modules, you can split your Spreadsheet screen into several different windows. You can load the spreadsheet windows with different worksheets or simultaneously view different sections of the same worksheet in multiple windows.

Creating a Window

You use the Window Split command to divide the current window into two windows. This command has two Quick keys: Alt-H splits the window horizontally, and Alt-V splits it vertically.

Using the Window Split command in the Spreadsheet differs in an important way from using the same command in other SmartWare II modules. In the Spreadsheet module, you must position the cursor *before* issuing the command to split the window. Move the cursor to the row or column *after* the last one you want to retain in the current window, and then issue the Window Split command. The prompt menu is

```
Horizontal Vertical
```

You must allow enough space for at least one row and one column per window.

Figure 12.1 shows a screen that has been split into two windows; notice that the upper left corner of the window shows the window number. (If you remove the row or column numbers from the display, the window number is not shown. Use the Window Numbers command to remove the row or column numbers.) Note that the current window is designated by a double line border, but that all other windows have a single line border. The cursor is located in the current window.

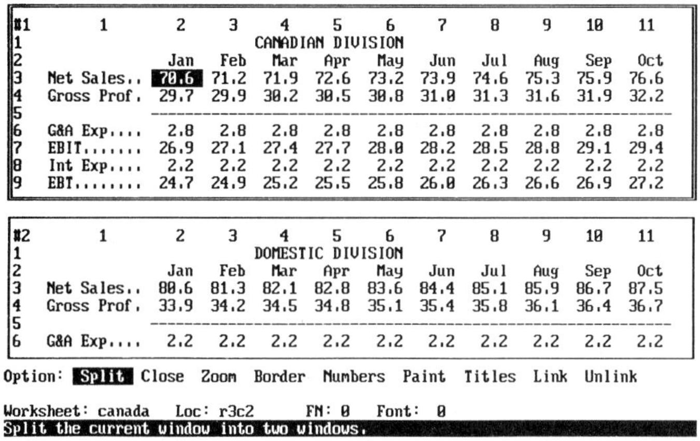

Fig. 12.1.

A screen split into two windows.

To advance to the next sequentially numbered window, use the Quick key Alt-F8; use Alt-F7 to move to the previous window. If you have only two windows, either key combination toggles between the two windows.

A new feature in the SmartWare II Spreadsheet is the capability of moving to another window while the screen is zoomed. In previous versions, you had to unzoom the screen before you could go to a different window.

Removing a Window

You use the Window Close command to remove a window from the screen; the Quick key is Alt-W.

When you select the Window Close command, the current window is removed and a neighboring window is enlarged to fill the void. Worksheets no longer displayed are still active, however; they are not automatically unloaded when you close the windows in which they were displayed.

You cannot close a window if your screen is in the Zoom mode. If you want to close the window, you must first unzoom the screen. The Zoom command is covered next in this chapter.

Filling the Screen with One Window

You use the Window Zoom command to fill the entire screen with the current window; the Quick key is F7. Press F7 once, and the screen is zoomed; press it again, and you restore the multiple-window display.

Use the Window Zoom command when you want to view more of a worksheet than you can see in the current window, yet you do not want to close the remaining windows.

With SmartWare II you can now use the Goto command to move to a different window while your screen is zoomed, but you cannot execute the Window Split and Window Close commands while you are in the Zoom mode.

Scrolling Two Windows Simultaneously

If you want the worksheets in two or more windows to scroll simultaneously, use the Window Link command. As you scroll the view of the worksheet in the current window, the view of the linked window (or windows) also scrolls.

When you select the Window Link command, you are prompted:

    Enter windows to be linked:

Enter the window numbers separated by spaces, as shown in figure 12.2.

Fig. 12.2.

Entering the numbers of windows to be linked.

```
#1      1       2     3     4     5     6     7     8     9     10    11
1                          CANADIAN DIVISION
2              Jan   Feb   Mar   Apr   May   Jun   Jul   Aug   Sep   Oct
3  Net Sales.. 70.6  71.2  71.9  72.6  73.2  73.9  74.6  75.3  75.9  76.6
4  Gross Prof. 29.7  29.9  30.2  30.5  30.8  31.0  31.3  31.6  31.9  32.2

#2      1       2     3     4     5     6     7     8     9     10    11
1                          DOMESTIC DIVISION
2              Jan   Feb   Mar   Apr   May   Jun   Jul   Aug   Sep   Oct
3  Net Sales.. 80.6  81.3  82.1  82.8  83.6  84.4  85.1  85.9  86.7  87.5
4  Gross Prof. 33.9  34.2  34.5  34.8  35.1  35.4  35.8  36.1  36.4  36.7

#3      1       2     3     4     5     6     7     8     9     10    11
1                          INTERNATIONAL DIVISION
2              Jan   Feb   Mar   Apr   May   Jun   Jul   Aug   Sep   Oct
3  Net Sales.. 75.9  76.7  77.4  78.2  79.0  79.8  80.6  81.4  82.2  83.0
4  Gross Prof. 30.4  30.7  31.0  31.3  31.6  31.9  32.2  32.6  32.9  33.2

Enter windows to be linked: 1 2 3
Worksheet: canada   Loc: r3c2     FM: 0   Font: 0
Enter the window numbers (separated by spaces) of windows to link.
```

The screen shown in figure 12.2 was set up to permit easy comparison of comparable line items on statements for three divisions of the company. As you move the cursor down to the next row in window 1, the displays in the other two windows are also advanced to the corresponding rows. Any window in this "network" can be the "driver," causing the other windows to scroll.

You can specify any windows in the Window Link command; you do not have to include the current window. A window can be established in only one link network at a time, but multiple linkages can exist simultaneously. The following table illustrates the effects of successive executions of the Window Link command:

Link	Effect
1 3 5	Windows 1, 3 and 5 are linked.
1 2	Windows 1 and 2 are linked; windows 3 and 5 remain linked to each other, but not to window 1.

If you use the Window Zoom command on a window that is linked, any cursor movement while the window is zoomed also affects the linked windows. The Window Zoom command does not cancel the linkage.

Be aware that the linkage and subsequent simultaneous scrolling are based only on relative positions, row for row or column for column. The linkage is not based on the actual contents of any cell. (By contrast, in the Database, a link is established between two views based on the contents of corresponding fields.)

Removing Links between Windows

You use the Window Unlink command to remove all links or to remove the link for specific windows.

When you select the Window Unlink command, you are prompted:

    Enter window number:

To remove all links, simply press Enter. If you want to remove the link for one or more windows, type the numbers of the windows, separated by spaces, and then press Enter. Any linked windows you did not specifically unlink remain linked.

Chapter Summary

This chapter has covered the methods for protecting your worksheets and for working with windows. You can use the Sheet Lock command to protect your worksheets from inadvertent alteration, locking blank cells, formulas, text, and values in any portion of your worksheet. Furthermore, you can completely protect the worksheet by using the Sheet Lock Protect command.

The new Edit Hide command may be used to hide portions of your worksheet from view; they appear as if they are blank. In addition, you can create as many as 50 windows at one time on your monitor screen. Windows can be linked so that they scroll simultaneously.

13

Using Spreadsheet Graphics

SmartWare II's Graphics command provides you with a complete subsystem that has capabilities rivaling the features of a stand-alone graphics program. However, graphics-only programs do not share SmartWare II's wealth of Spreadsheet commands and functions that help you prepare and manage your data.

The data for Spreadsheet graphics comes from your worksheets; you can send the output to the screen (if you have a compatible monitor), to a printer with graphics capabilities, or to a plotter. You can save a completed graph for inclusion in the body of a Word Processor document or for later display on your monitor.

This chapter provides a description of the Graphics command features, examples of their use and construction, and tips on preparing high quality graphs.

New Features in SmartWare II Spreadsheet Graphics

Smartware II offers you the following new or improved features:

- A new screen-saving format, called *metafile*, enables you to store a graph independently of the computer hardware. After you have stored graphs in this format, you can exchange them with other SmartWare II users with different hardware configurations. Because the metafile format is becoming an industry standard, several other graphics and desktop publishing programs also accept these files. However, because of the introduction of the new metafile format, you no longer can edit the saved screen images as you could do in previous versions of Smart. The Slideshow feature also has been discontinued.

- Composite graphs enable you to arrange up to four graphs in a single image. Composite graphs can even include other composite graphs.
- More text fonts are available. You can specify up to 20 fonts, including serif and sans serif proportional fonts in medium and bold weights, and upright and italic slants. You can specify character height as either Large, Medium, or Small, or by point size.
- You can print your graphs in landscape and portrait orientations.
- You can create text-only graphs to supply additional information or for cover sheets.
- Graph axis labels provide improved date handling.
- Additional scaling options include logarithmic and dual scales on a single graph.
- You can label pie graph slices that represent less than 5 percent.
- Plotting speed has been improved.

The Graphics Command

Eight types of graphs are available through the SmartWare II Graphics command:

    Bar/line
        Vertical Bars
        Horizontal Bars
        Stacked Bars
        Three Dimensional Bars
        Histograms
        Step Charts
    Pie
        Two Dimensional
        Three Dimensional
    Hi-Low
    Layer
    Discrete-Bar
    X-Y
    Text Only
    Composite

The Graphics command is selected from the Command menu of the Spreadsheet module. (You can use the Quick key Ctrl-G to repeat the most recent Graphics Generate command.)

Defining a Graph

After constructing your worksheet, the first step in using Spreadsheet Graphics is to define the graph you want to create.

When you select the Graphics command, you are given three options:

```
Define Generate Undefine
```

As in other modules of the SmartWare II system, you create definitions that are saved to disk for later use. When you select the Define option, you are prompted:

```
Same Bar/line Pie Hi-Low Layer Discrete-Bar Xy Text Composite
```

Select the type of graph you want to define. A pop-up window displays the names of existing graph definitions; you can select one to change, or you can type the name of a new definition and press Enter.

If you modify an existing definition later, you should select Same to retain the same definition selections. If you decide to change the format of the graph, you are prompted:

```
File is a different graph type. Change? (y/n)
```

If you answer *Y*, the portion of the definition that pertained to the previous graph type is cleared.

Creating a Bar/Line Graph

The following discussion takes you through the creation of a bar/line graph using output from the worksheet displayed in figure 13.1. Figure 13.2 shows the general Bar/Line Graph Definition screen, where you begin.

```
            1          2     3     4     5     6     7     8     9    10    11
1                                  DOMESTIC DIVISION
2                     Jan   Feb   Mar   Apr   May   Jun   Jul   Aug   Sep   Oct
3    Net Sales..     80.6  87.2  94.4 102.2 110.7 119.8 129.7 140.4 152.0 164.5
4    Gross Prof.     33.9  36.6  39.7  42.9  46.5  50.3  54.5  59.0  63.8  69.1
5                 ------------------------------------------------------------
6    G&A Exp....      2.2   2.2   2.2   2.2   2.2   2.2   2.2   2.2   2.2   2.2
7    EBIT.......     31.7  34.4  37.5  40.7  44.3  48.1  52.3  56.8  61.6  66.9
8    Int Exp....      1.3   1.3   1.3   1.3   1.3   1.3   1.3   1.3   1.3   1.3
9    EBT........     30.4  33.1  36.2  39.4  43.0  46.8  51.0  55.5  60.3  65.6
10                ------------------------------------------------------------
11   Tax........     14.6  15.9  17.4  18.9  20.6  22.5  24.5  26.6  29.0  31.5
12   Net Income.     15.8  17.2  18.8  20.5  22.4  24.3  26.5  28.8  31.4  34.1
13                ------------------------------------------------------------
14     EPS......     0.04  0.04  0.05  0.05  0.06  0.06  0.07  0.07  0.08  0.09
15   ---------------------------------------------------------------------------
16       Average        Gr Prof     Sales       G&A          Intst       Tax
17       Shares:        Rate %      Grow %      Expense:     Expense:    Rate%
18       400,000           42          99         2.2          1.3         48
Menu:  Sheet  Edit  File  Layout  Print  Graph  Tools  Window  Help  Remember
       Quit
Worksheet: domestic Loc: r1c1      FN:      Font: 0
Load Save Unload Active Newname Disp-Act Combine Import Export Password
```

Fig. 13.1.

Sample worksheet.

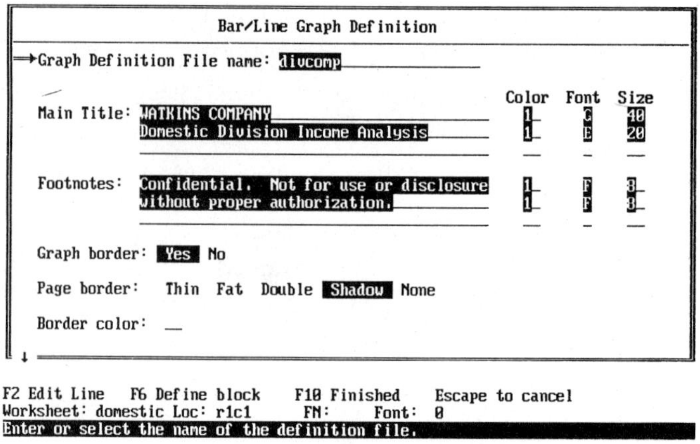

Fig. 13.2.

General graph definition screen.

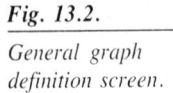

You advance from item to item in graph definition screens by pressing Enter or by using the cursor keys. You can move from page to page by pressing PgDn or PgUp. On the first page, you should make the following entries:

Graph Definition File name. This file name is the same as the name supplied when you defined the graph. This entry automatically is the same as the name you have supplied. (Later, you can make a copy of an existing graph definition if you enter a new name on this line.)

Main Title. Type the title of the graph. You can edit the title by pressing the F2 key; you delete a title by pressing Delete. You can enter up to three title lines of 40 characters each.

For each title, you must enter the color, font, and size. The color you select depends on the capabilities of your monitor screen, printer, and plotter. Select a font from *A* to *T* matching one of the fonts shown in Table 13.1. You specify size in points (at 72 points per inch), or you can specify *L* for Large, *M* for Medium, or *S* for Small; these designations correspond to point sizes 30, 15, and 7 respectively. Graph titles are always centered.

Footnotes. Enter up to three lines of footnotes, specifying color, font, and size. Footnotes are always left-justified and positioned at the bottom of the page.

Graph border. Select Yes or No. The graph border surrounds only the graphical representation inside the axis titles.

Page border. If you want a border around the entire page, select one of the following options:

    Thin Fat Double Shadow None

Border color. If you have chosen a border, you may select a color. The default color is black.

**Table 13.1
Graphics Font Descriptions**

Font	Font Family	Weight	Slant	Proportional
A	Sans Serif	Medium	Upright	Y
B	Sans Serif	Medium	Italic	Y
C	Sans Serif	Bold	Upright	Y
D	Sans Serif	Bold	Italic	Y
E	Serif	Medium	Upright	Y
F	Serif	Medium	Italic	Y
G	Serif	Bold	Upright	Y
H	Serif	Bold	Italic	Y
I	Monospace Serif	Medium	Upright	N
J	Monospace Serif	Medium	Italic	N
K	Monospace Serif	Bold	Upright	N
L	Monospace Serif	Bold	Italic	N
M	Script	Medium	Italic	Y
N	Gothic	Medium	Upright	Y
O	Greek	Medium	Upright	Y
P	Small Caps	Medium	Upright	N
Q	Graphic L	N/A	N/A	N
R	Graphic B	N/A	N/A	N
S	Symbol	Medium	Upright	Y
T	Dingbat 2	N/A	N/A	Y

Press PgDn to proceed to the next definition screen. On the Bar/Line data block definition screen (see fig. 13.3), you may enter definitions for a maximum of 12 data blocks. A data block, in this example, is a row of worksheet data that is represented by a bar on the graph. (Several rows, or bars, can be stacked together.) Columns 2 through 13 of the worksheet define the horizontal dimension of the graph (the x-axis).

You can type the row and column definitions for each block (*r4c2:13*), or you can press F6 to return temporarily to the worksheet. When you are back at the worksheet, position the cursor at the beginning of the block and press F2 to drop the anchor. Then move the cursor to the end of the block and press Enter. The block address is entered into the data block field automatically. You then continue the graph definition with the following entries:

Type. Enter one of the following options:

    B   Bar (A blank also indicates a bar.)
    L   Line
    S   Step
    1-6 If you want to have bars stacked on top of each other, as in this example, enter a number from 1 to 6. Data blocks with identical numbers are stacked together.

Fig. 13.3.

Bar/Line data block definition screen.

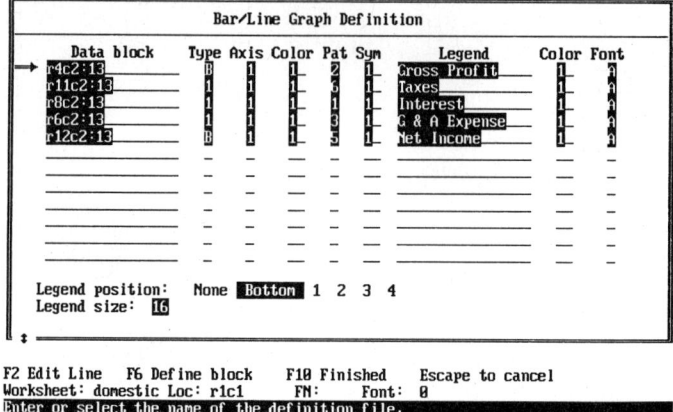

Axis. You can scale a data block versus either y-axis, where 1 is the left y-axis and 2 is the right y-axis; enter the number here. This feature of including two y-axis scales is new with SmartWare II.

Color. Enter the data block color as appropriate.

Pat. When defining a bar/line graph, you can select from six patterns:

1 Solid black
2 Horizontal lines
3 Vertical lines
4 Horizontal and vertical lines
5 Heavy horizontal lines
6 Heavy vertical lines

Sym. If the data item is a line, you may select symbols by number from 0 to 11.

Legend. Enter the wording you want to display in the legend. You can enter a maximum of 20 characters, but only the first 16 appear on the definition screen. Select color and font for each legend.

Legend position. Select a position for the legend from the following options:

None	No Legend
Bottom	Below the x-axis title
1	Upper right corner within graph border
2	Upper left
3	Lower left
4	Lower right

Legend size. Select by point size, or designate *S* (7 points), *M* (15 points), or *L* (30 points).

On the definition screen shown in figure 13.4, you make the following selections:

Chapter 13: Spreadsheet Graphics **271**

```
          Bar/Line Graph Definition
→X-Axis label block: r2c2:13
                                        Color  Font  Size
  X-Axis title: 1987                      1      D    18
  Y1-Axis title: DOLLARS (000)            1      D    18
  Y2-Axis title:                          _      _    _

  Bar Type: 2-dimensional  3-dimensional  Line
  Bar orientation: Vertical  Horizontal

  Values on top of bars: None  Horizontal  Vertical
  Color _       Font _       Size _

  Outline 2-D Bars: Yes  No


F2 Edit Line   F6 Define block   F10 Finished   Escape to cancel
Worksheet: domestic Loc: r1c1    FN:    Font: 0
Enter or select the name of the definition file.
```

Fig. 13.4.

Bar/Line axis and orientation definition screen.

X-Axis label block. Type the block address, or use F6 to return temporarily to the worksheet to help you define the block. In our example, the x-axis label block contains the names of the months from row 2.

Axis titles. You should type a title for the x- and y-axis dimensions of your graph. You may also specify the color, font selection, and size of each title separately. (Previous versions of Smart did not allow a choice of axis title sizes.)

Bar Type. Select one of the following options:

   2-dimensional 3-dimensional Line

Bar orientation. If you have selected a bar graph, indicate whether it is to have vertical or horizontal orientation.

Values on top of bars. If you have selected a bar graph, you may decide t~
the actual values at the tops or at the ends of the bars. You m~··
or Vertical orientation for the values as well as the¡~

Outline 2-D Bars. You may omit tl

You enter axis options on the screen

Division Labels. Specify the color,
and y2-axis division labels. In our exan
division labels, and the dollar values a¡

Axis. Along each axis, you can specify

- Color of the axis.

- Number of tic marks per major divis

- Color of the tic marks.

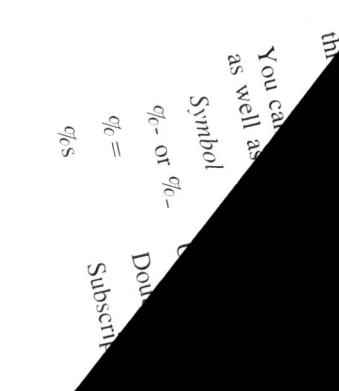

Part II: Using the SmartWare II Spreadsheet

```
┌─────────────────────────────────────────────────────────────┐
│                  Bar/Line Graph Definition                  │
│                                                             │
│  →Division Labels:  Color  Font  Size                       │
│            X-Axis:   __     _    __                         │
│           Y1-Axis:   __     _    __                         │
│           Y2-Axis:   __     _    __                         │
│                                                             │
│       Axis:        Color  Tics/Div.  Tic Color    Grids: (y/n)  Color  Style │
│           X-Axis:   __       __         __                _      __     __  │
│          Y1-Axis:   __       __         __                _      __     __  │
│          Y2-Axis:   __       __         __                _      __     __  │
│                                                             │
│       Scaling:     Type   Minimum    Maximum   Increment    │
│          Y1-Axis:   _    _____   _____  _____      │
│          Y2-Axis:   _    _____   _____  _____      │
│                                                             │
│  ↑                                                          │
│  F2 Edit Line    F6 Define block    F10 Finished    Escape to cancel │
│  Worksheet: domestic  Loc: r1c1      FN:      Font: 0       │
│  Enter or select the name of the definition file.           │
└─────────────────────────────────────────────────────────────┘
```

Fig. 13.5.

Bar/Line axis options definition screen.

- Grid marks to cross the graph. Type *Y* or *N*.
- Color of the grid marks.
- Style of the grid marks; select line pattern 1 through 6.

Scaling. For each of the two y-axis scales, you may indicate the following scaling selections:

Type	Effect and Range Entries
A	Automatic scaling from the minimum value to the maximum. Additional values are ignored.
L	Logarithmic, base 10. Additional values are ignored.
Z	Zero to maximum scaling. You may specify a maximum. If no type is entered, this type is the default.
M	Manual scaling. Specify a minimum, maximum, and division increment amount.

Press F10 to save your graph definition. The graph that was defined in figures 13.2 through 13.5 is shown in figure 13.6.

use the following editing symbols in graph titles, foot notes, and legends, in text graphs:

Effect

Underscore ON

ble Thickness Underscore ON

t ON (note lowercase)

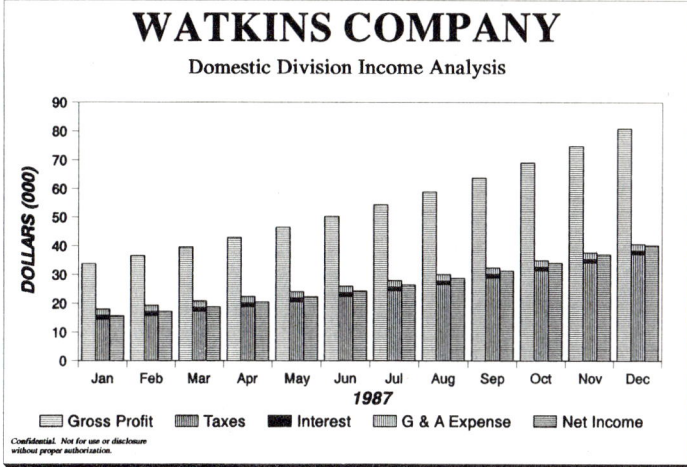

Fig. 13.6.

A sample bar graph.

%S	Superscript ON (note uppercase)
%N	
%n	Cancel underscores, subscript, or superscript
%C<x>	
%c<x>	Change to color x. The brackets (<>) must be included.
%F<x>	
%f<x>	Change to font x
%B<x>	
%b<x>	Insert dingbat-1 bullet x
%%	Insert percent sign

In addition to these text formatting symbols, if you type an equal sign (=) followed by a cell address, the referenced contents of the worksheet are dynamically included at the time the graph prints. You can use only one cell address, and you can not include any text information. If you have any formatting symbols in the referenced cell, they produce the listed result.

Figure 13.7 displays the same data as in figure 13.6, but in a three-dimensional format.

Fig. 13.7.

A three-dimensional bar graph.

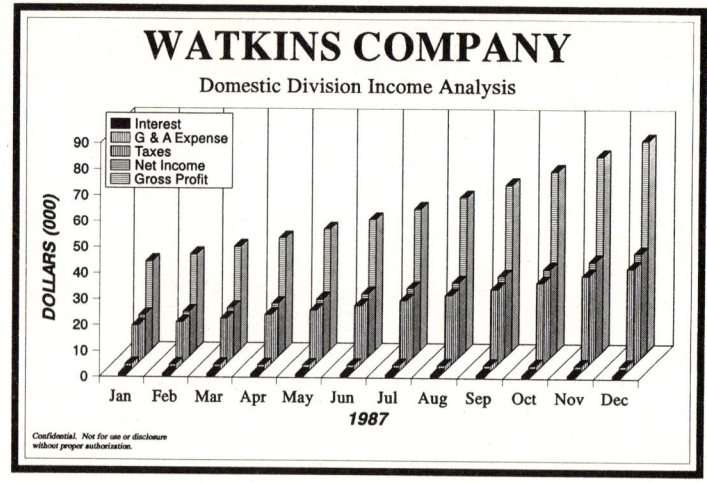

Several additional changes have been made. The page border is Double, and the legend has been moved from the bottom to the number 2 position—the upper left corner. The font of the division labels on the x-axis (the month abbreviations) has been changed to E, the serif, medium upright proportional font.

A discrete-bar graph is similar to a three-dimensional bar graph, except that the bars do not touch each other, and they are displayed in their own individual cells. In previous versions of Smart, a discrete-bar graph was called a histogram.

Creating a Pie Graph

Figures 13.8 and 13.9 show the definition screens for the three-dimensional pie graph in figure 13.10. The Fat border is shown.

Fig. 13.8.

Pie graph data block definition screen.

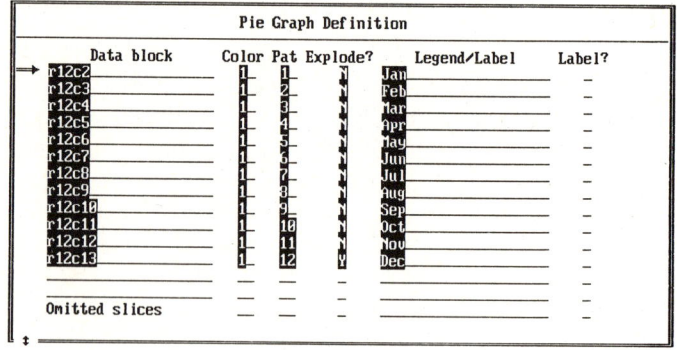

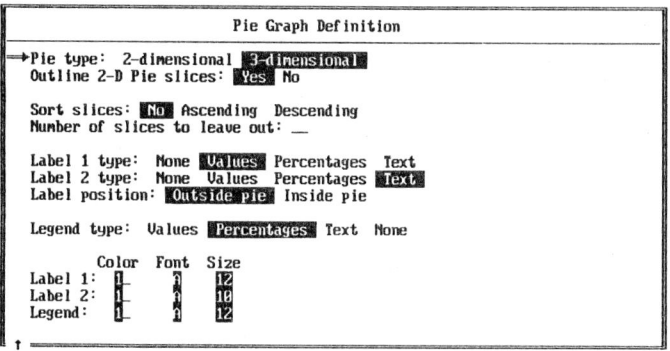

Fig. 13.9.

Pie graph options definition screen.

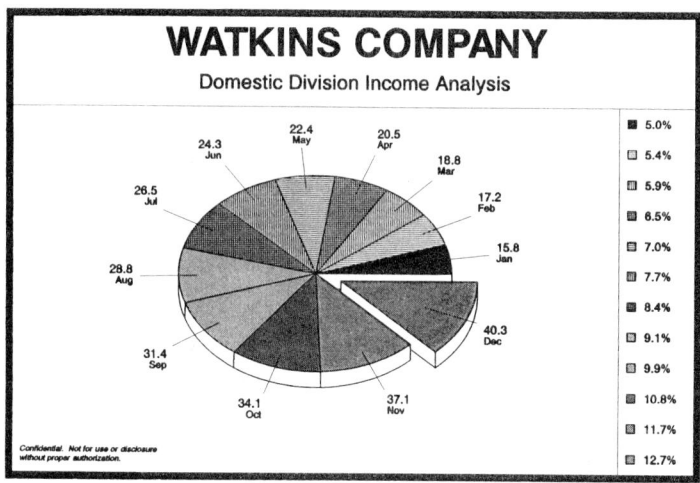

Fig. 13.10.

A sample pie graph.

Notice that patterns 1 through 12 were used for the 12 months of the pie. When you create a pie graph, 14 patterns are available, numbered 0 through 13. The pie slice for December was "exploded" away from the rest of the pie. In figure 13.8, the data blocks for a pie graph are specified individually; alternately, you can specify them as a block for the first data entry, such as *r12c2:13*. If you enter an *N* in the last column of Pie Graph data block definition screen, you suppress the label for an individual pie slice.

You can specify two- or three-dimensional pie graph (see fig. 13.9). You may decide to have the pie slices sorted in ascending or descending order, or you may leave them in the order entered.

Labels in a pie graph identify the individual slices. This example uses Label 1, values, and Label 2, text. Labels may be values, percentages, text, or none. If you have enough space, you may decide to locate the labels inside the pie slices, rather than outside as in the example.

The graph legend is to the right; the example shows the pie percentages. You may select the color, font, and size of the labels and the legend.

Creating a Layer Graph

A layer graph is useful for showing the change in the composition of a total over time. Figures 13.11 and 13.12 show the graph definition screens for the layer graph in figure 13.13. The general definition screen is similar to figure 13.2; in this example, a Thin page border is specified.

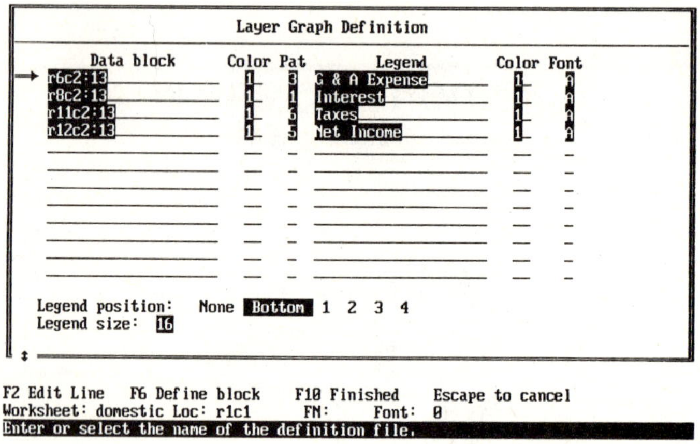

Fig. 13.11.

Layer graph data block definition screen.

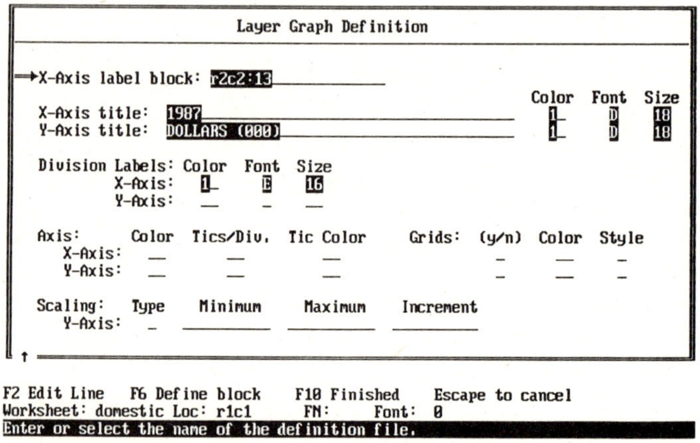

Fig. 13.12.

Layer graph axis and orientation definition screen.

Chapter 13: Spreadsheet Graphics **277**

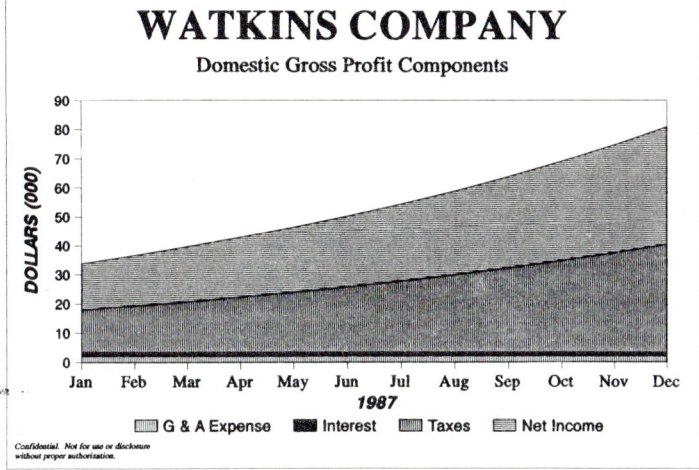

Fig. 13.13.

A sample layer graph.

Creating an X-Y Graph

The previous graphics examples have illustrated the graphing of continuous numeric values (Income) against discrete text (months). Sometimes, however, you need to plot a series of continuous numeric values against another numeric series in order to show the relationships between the sequences. To create this type of graph, select the X-Y graph option.

Figures 13.14, 13.15, and 13.16 show the definitions for the graph in figure 13.17. The general definition screen is similar to figure 13.2; in this example, a Shadow page border is specified.

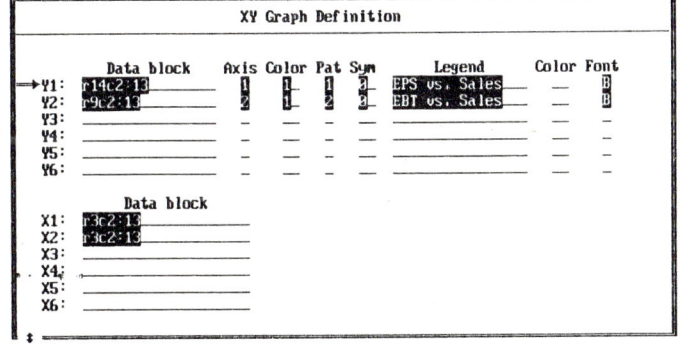

Fig. 13.14.

X-Y graph data block definition screen.

Fig. 13.15.

X-Y graph axis definition screen.

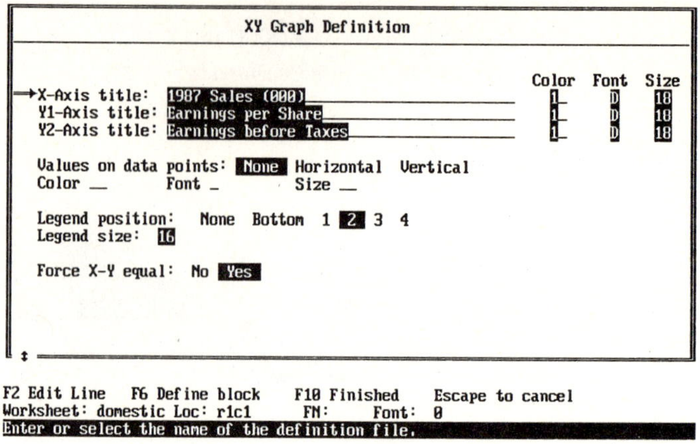

Fig. 13.16.

X-Y graph options definition screen.

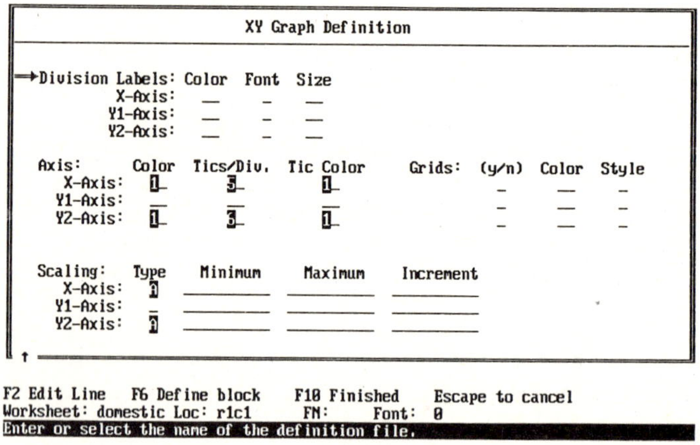

Notice that in the definition screen in figure 13.14, you can define a maximum of six series for the X-Y graph; previous versions of Smart allowed only three. In this example, Earnings per Share is shown on one y-axis and Earnings before Taxes is shown on the other y-axis. Symbols were omitted from the plot lines by entering zero. A maximum of 12 symbols are available to help you identify the lines of complex graphs.

In the definition screen in figure 13.15, you can provide separate titles for the x-axis and the two y-axis scales, and you can specify colors, fonts, and sizes individually. You also can insert values on the data points. Note that the legend has been positioned in quadrant 2, the upper left. If you want a square data area, you can force the x and y dimensions to be of equal size.

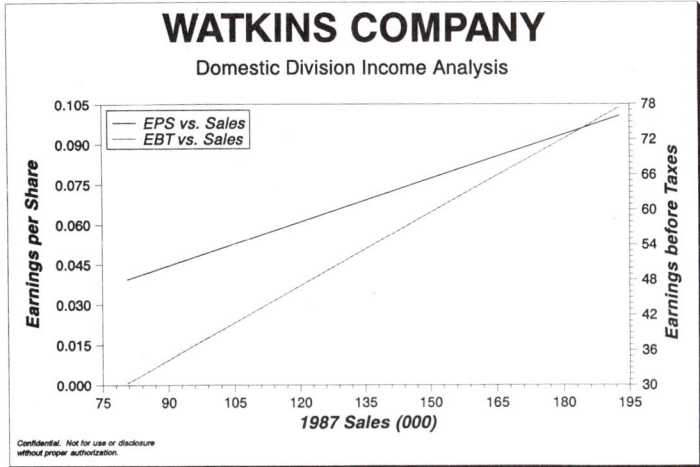

Fig. 13.17.

A sample X-Y graph.

Creating a Text Graph

You can create text graphs from text that you type into the definition or that is pulled from the worksheet. Although you can print a maximum of 40 lines of text at 60 characters per line, only the first 40 characters of each line are displayed in the definition screen. The editing and formatting characters shown in table 13.1 are available for each text line.

Figure 13.18 shows the Text graph definition screen used to create the graph in figure 13.19.

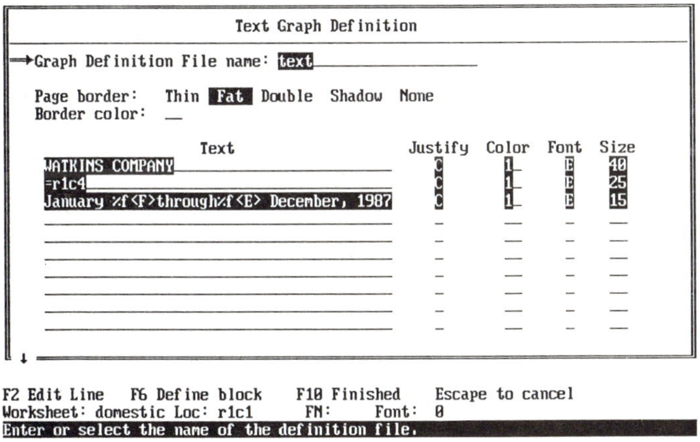

Fig. 13.18.

Text graph definition screen.

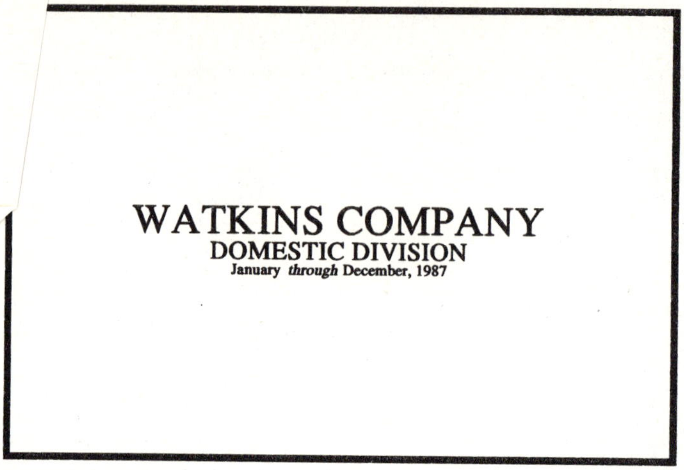

WATKINS COMPANY
DOMESTIC DIVISION
January *through* December, 1987

Justification is entered as *L* for Left, *C* for centered, or *R* for right. Alternatively, you can use the numbers 1 through 9 to indent individual lines from the left margin. The body of text is centered vertically on the printed page.

Combining Graphs

You can combine several graphs into one using the Composite option of the Graph Define command. (You must first have saved the original graphs in the metafile format, which is discussed later in this chapter.) Figure 13.20 shows the graph combination screen.

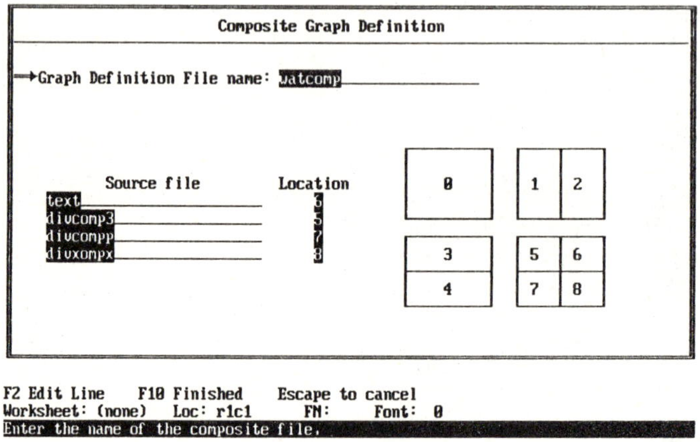

Fig. 13.20.

Composite graph definition screen.

Enter the names of the metafiles you want to combine; you do not need to enter the file extensions. Be sure you know the names of the files before you begin the definition. The location of each graph is indicated by the number you assign to it, as shown on the definition screen. Figure 13.21 shows the composite graph created in this screen.

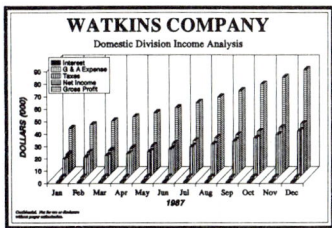

Fig. 13.21.

A sample composite graph.

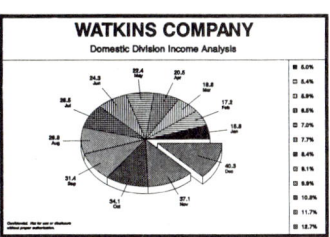
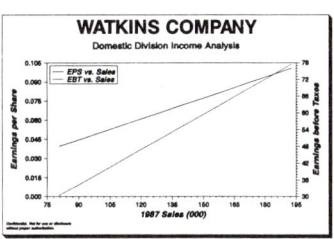

The file extension of a composite definition is .GCF. If you need to edit an existing composite definition, select Composite from the Graph Define menu, and only the .GCF files are displayed. If you select Same, only the .GDF files appear in the pop-up window.

Using the Graphics Generate Command

After you have defined your graph, use the Graphics Generate command to display the graph on the screen if your monitor has graphics capability, to create a metafile, or to print a hard copy of the graph you have created. You don't have to change your hardware preferences; the system handles the switch for you. When you execute the Graphics Generate command, a pop-up window shows the names of any existing graph (.GDF) and metafile (.GMF) files. The file extensions are shown so that you can distinguish the graph definition files from the metafiles. If you select a graph definition file, the worksheet must be loaded. Select the file you want to generate and press Enter. You are prompted:

```
Preview Metafile Hardcopy
```

Displaying the Graph

To view the graph on your monitor screen, select Preview, and the graph is displayed on your screen. Press any key to return to the command level.

Printing Your Graph

When your graph is as you want it, use the Hardcopy option to print it on a suitable printer or plotter. Most dot-matrix printers and laser printers can generate graphics output. When you select this option, you are prompted:

```
Printer Xy-Plot
```

Select Printer to direct the output to your printer. The final prompt is

```
Landscape Portrait
```

In Landscape orientation, the longer dimension of the paper is horizontal; in the Portrait mode, the longer dimension is vertical. The capability of selecting a Portrait orientation is a feature not offered in previous Smart versions.

If you have a plotter, select Xy-Plot instead of the Printer option, and the graph is generated on your plotter.

Generating Metafiles

Instead of generating your graph on your screen (Preview) or on the printer or plotter (Hardcopy), you can select the Metafile option.

When you select Metafile, a disk file representation of your graph and its contents is generated. The new file has the same name as your graph definition, but the file extension is .GMF for Graph MetaFile, rather than .GDF for Graph Definition File. Generation of the metafile has the following benefits:

- You can preview or generate hardcopy output without loading the underlying worksheet.
- You can combine several metafiles into one composite graph. (In fact, you can generate a metafile from a composite graph.)
- You can transmit the metafile to other SmartWare II users with different hardware configurations for viewing or printing on their computers.
- The metafile format is becoming an industry standard; several other graphics and desktop publishing software products can read metafiles.
- You can include metafile graphs in the body of your SmartWare II Word Processor documents.

Chapter Summary

This chapter has described the process of defining and generating graphs from the SmartWare II Spreadsheet module. The graphics capabilities of the SmartWare II system compare favorably with many stand-alone graphics packages. Many examples of graphs have been illustrated in this chapter, along with the definitions for creating them. By comparing the output with the definitions, you can learn how to apply the same techniques in producing your own graphs.

14

Printing Spreadsheet Data and Creating Reports

Up to this point, you have been viewing your spreadsheet on your monitor only. Eventually you will need to print all or part of a spreadsheet on paper so that you can save it for yourself, include it in a report, or show it to someone else. This chapter focuses on printing spreadsheet data.

The SmartWare II Spreadsheet module offers two different levels of spreadsheet printing. The Print Text command provides a quick and easy way to get the information on paper; you use this command when you are not particularly interested in a formal report. With the Print Text command you can take advantage of special fonts by using the Enhanced or Sideways options.

When you need a formal report, you use the Print Report command, which has all the customary options—headings, page numbers, margins, and indenting. Setting up the report may take a little longer, but it is well worth the time when you need to produce a formal document.

In addition to printing the contents of your spreadsheets, you can use the Print Formulas command to produce a listing of all the formulas you have created.

A new feature of SmartWare II is the Print Map command, which allows you to print a map of your spreadsheet. This map is similar to the screen display achieved when you execute the Layout Format Formula-display Map command.

Printing Your Worksheet

You use the Print Text command to produce quick and easy printed output of your entire spreadsheet or of a defined block from the spreadsheet. If you wish, you can direct the output to a disk file rather than to your printer. A feature new with

SmartWare II is the capability of printing your spreadsheet sideways on an appropriate printer.

The Quick key for the Print Text command is Alt-P. Keep in mind that the formatting options you have selected for the screen display are reflected in the printed output. Column widths, percentages, and numbers in dollar, date, and even bar formats are printed exactly as they are formatted in the spreadsheet. On the printed output, columns and rows are aligned as they are on the monitor display.

Compare the printing of a spreadsheet with printing data in the SmartWare II Database. In the Database, you can use the Data Query and Order commands to select certain records or to rearrange the order in which they appear on the printout. You also can specify the fields to be printed and the sequence in which they should appear. But when you print a SmartWare II spreadsheet, what you see is what you get.

When you select the Print Text command, you are prompted:

```
Block Worksheet
```

If you select Worksheet, the entire spreadsheet is printed from row 1, column 1 through the last row and column used, including cells that you have preformatted. If you want to select just a block of the spreadsheet to print, select Block.

If you select Block, you are prompted:

```
Enter name or block reference:
```

You can type the range in row and column notation, such as *r3:7c5:10*. An easier way to indicate the range is to move the cursor to the upper left cell in the block, press F2 to "drop the anchor," and then move the cursor to the lower right corner of the block. The block range is highlighted as you go. Press Enter to complete the definition of the block range.

The next prompt is as follows:

```
Printer Disk
```

If you select Disk, you are prompted for the name of the output file; the file is then created with the name you provide. If you do not provide a file extension, .PRN is used. (Previous versions of Smart did not provide an extension automatically.) If a file with the same name already exists, no prompt asks whether you want to overwrite that file. Be careful!

Unlike previous versions of Smart, the output print file may not consist of entirely ASCII characters. Depending on your printer selection, printer control codes are embedded in the disk file to control the printing of the output. With the control codes embedded in the file, you can print the report to your printer directly from the file outside the SmartWare II environment; the printed output appears just as if you had printed it directly from SmartWare II. (At the DOS level, you can print the file by copying it to your printer.)

Chapter 14: Printing Spreadsheet Data and Creating Reports

The disadvantage of having the control codes embedded is that you cannot edit or view the file easily. If you want to create a disk file without the control codes, select the Generic, Draft printer in the Hardware Preferences menu of the Tools command.

If you select the Printer option, you are prompted:

    Draft Sideways Enhanced

The Draft option provides the quickest printing. Although you can print only your printer's internal fonts, you get the output on paper as quickly as possible. In SmartWare II, you can print underscored and bold standard fonts in the Draft mode. (In earlier versions of Smart, you had to create a report if you wanted to output these features.) However, if you want to print any filled-area, prerasterized, or cartridge fonts, you must specify the Enhanced printing option.

When you specify the Enhanced option, you can print any SmartWare II font, including filled-area or prerasterized fonts. If you want to print rows in nonstandard heights, you must select Enhanced printing. In the Enhanced mode, your printer's internal fonts are rasterized.

If you have a printer with graphics capability, you may elect to print your spreadsheet sideways on the paper. (Most dot-matrix and laser printers can print graphics.) You do not have to make any font or hardware selection changes in order to print sideways.

If you have a great deal of sideways printing to do, you may want to change your hardware preference to specify a landscape orientation, if one is available for your printer. When the printer is defined in the landscape direction, you can use the Print Text...Draft command to print your spreadsheet sideways. Because you are using a font that is internal to your printer, the printing process is faster than using a portrait printer driver with a landscape font.

Even if you do not change to a sideways printer, you can speed the sideways printing of your spreadsheet by generating a 9- or 12-point sideways medium or bold font. Use the Tools New-font command to create this prerasterized font file. You use the 12-point fonts to print at 6 lines per inch and 9-point fonts to print at 8 lines per inch.

The final prompt prior to printing is

    Enter number of copies:

Press Enter if you want just one copy; otherwise, type the number of copies you want.

Selecting Print Options

The options that govern the use of the Print commands, except for the Print Report command, are set in the menu displayed by the Layout Worksheet-Options Current-Sheet command. (Select New-Sheet to set the options for new spreadsheets to be created.) Figure 14.1 shows the Print options portion of the menu.

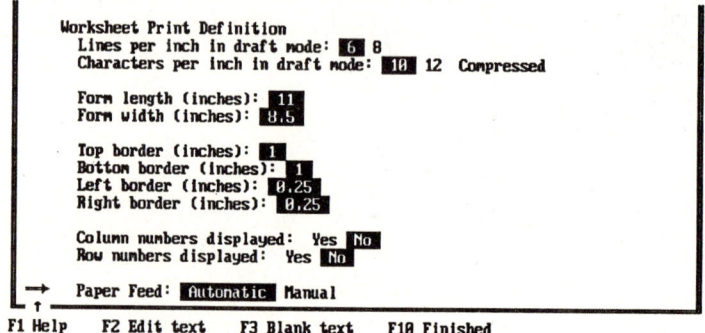

Fig. 14.1.

Worksheet Print options.

In the Draft mode, you can set lines per inch to 6 or 8, and characters per inch to 10, 12, or compressed. In the Enhanced mode, the pitch and point sizes are set by the fonts used in the spreadsheet.

You set the length and width of your form in inches, specifying the dimensions of the paper in your printer. You also set margins or borders surrounding the printed output, in inches. As figure 14.1 illustrates, you can specify fractions of inches.

With SmartWare II, you have the option of printing the row and column numbers when using the Print command. If you want to print the numbers, select *Yes*. Note that this printing option is independent of the screen display. (You control the display of row and column numbers by using the Window Numbers command.)

If your printer does not have an automatic paper feed mechanism and you want it to pause so you can insert a new page, select the Manual option for paper feed.

When you finish setting the options, you are prompted:

    Insert new page, press any key

Position the paper in the printer and press any key to proceed with the printing of the page.

Printing Formulas

Keeping a printout of spreadsheet formulas is valuable for documentation purposes; a printout of the formulas may help you pinpoint possible errors as well.

When you select the Print Formulas command, you are prompted:

    Block Worksheet

If you select Worksheet, the entire spreadsheet is printed, from row 1, column 1 through the last row and column used. If you want to select just a block of the spreadsheet to print, select Block.

If you select Block, you are prompted:

    Enter name or block reference:

You can type the range in row and column notation, such as *r3:7c5:10*. An easier way to indicate the range is to move the cursor to the upper left cell in the block, press F2 to drop the anchor, and then move the cursor to the lower right corner of the block. The block range is highlighted as you go. Press Enter to complete the definition of the block range.

There are no additional prompts. If you want to print the spreadsheet in the Compressed mode, be sure to change the Layout Worksheet-Options for the current sheet. Figure 14.2 shows a printout of some of the formulas in our financial model. Note that the formulas are sorted by row first, and then by column.

ROW	COL	FORMULA
3	3	r3c2*(1+r[18]c[5]/12/100)
	4	r3c3*(1+r[18]c[5]/12/100)
	5	r3c4*(1+r[18]c[5]/12/100)
	6	r3c5*(1+r[18]c[5]/12/100)
	7	r3c6*(1+r[18]c[5]/12/100)
	8	r3c7*(1+r[18]c[5]/12/100)
	9	r3c8*(1+r[18]c[5]/12/100)
4	2	r3c2*r[18]c[3]/100
	3	r3c3*r[18]c[3]/100
	4	r3c4*r[18]c[3]/100
	5	r3c5*r[18]c[3]/100
	6	r3c6*r[18]c[3]/100
	7	r3c7*r[18]c[3]/100
	8	r3c8*r[18]c[3]/100
	9	r3c9*r[18]c[3]/100
6	2	r[18]c[7]
	3	r[18]c[7]
	4	r[18]c[7]

Fig. 14.2.

A sample printout of formulas.

Printing a Worksheet Map

Use the Print Map command to print a map showing the type of data in your spreadsheet cells. (The map is similar to the screen display you get when you execute the command Layout Format Formula-Display Map.) The capability of displaying and printing a spreadsheet map is a new feature in SmartWare II.

The map characters are established in the menu presented in Tools Preferences Spreadsheet. In this menu, you can set the characters to represent the following spreadsheet items:

    Formula character

    Text characters
        Left-justified
        Centered
        Right-justified

    Value characters
        General
        Fixed-decimal
        Scientific notation
        Currency
        Percentage
        Date1
        Date2
        Date3
        Time12
        Time24
        Histogram
        Preformatted blank cells

When you execute the Print Map command, you are prompted:

    `Block Worksheet`

If you select Worksheet, the entire spreadsheet is printed, from row 1, column 1 through the last row and column used. If you want to select just a block of the spreadsheet to print, select Block.

If you select Block, you are prompted:

    `Enter name or block reference:`

You can type the range in row and column notation, such as *r3:7c5:10*. An easier way to indicate the range is to move the cursor to the upper left cell in the block, press F2 to drop the anchor, and then move the cursor to the lower right corner of the block. The block range is highlighted as you go. Press Enter to complete the definition of the block range.

Chapter 14: Printing Spreadsheet Data and Creating Reports

After you select Worksheet or identify the block, you are prompted:

    Printer Disk

If you select disk, you are prompted for the name of the output file; the file is then created with the name you provide. If you do not provide a file extension, .PRN is used. If a file with the same name already exists, no prompt asks whether you want to overwrite that file. Be careful!

If you select the Printer option, you are prompted:

    Draft Sideways

Each column of your spreadsheet takes up two print positions; on an 80-column printout, you can represent a map of 40 spreadsheet columns. If your spreadsheet is wider, you may want to print the map in 12-pitch or condensed print. Printing Sideways enables you to print an even wider contiguous map.

The final prompt prior to printing is

    Enter number of copies:

Press Enter if you want just one copy; otherwise, type the number of copies you want. Figure 14.3 shows a sample printed map for the spreadsheet illustrated in figure 14.4.

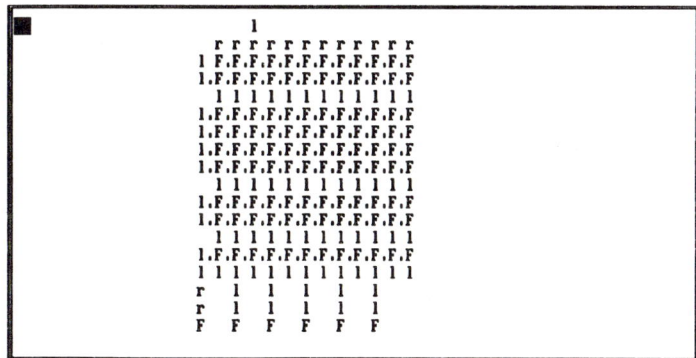

Fig. 14.3.

A spreadsheet map.

In figure 14.3 the following symbols are used:

Character	Symbol used
Formula character	.
Text characters	
Left-justified	l
Right-justified	r
Value characters	
Fixed-decimal	F

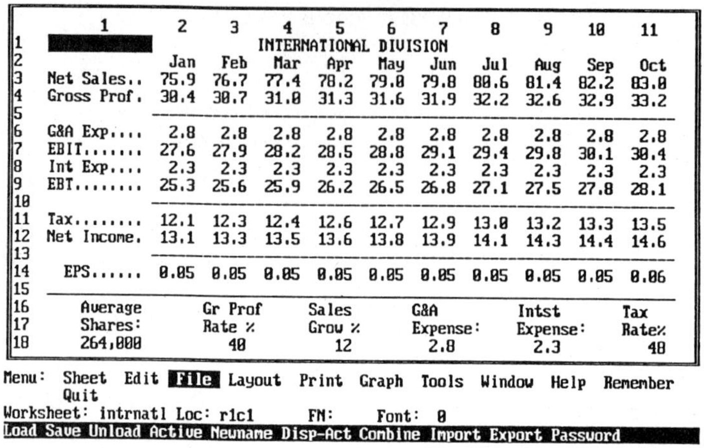

Fig. 14.4.

A sample spreadsheet.

	1	2	3	4	5	6	7	8	9	10	11
1				INTERNATIONAL DIVISION							
2		Jan	Feb	Mar	Apr	May	Jun	Jul	Aug	Sep	Oct
3	Net Sales..	75.9	76.7	77.4	78.2	79.0	79.8	80.6	81.4	82.2	83.0
4	Gross Prof.	30.4	30.7	31.0	31.3	31.6	31.9	32.2	32.6	32.9	33.2
5											
6	G&A Exp....	2.8	2.8	2.8	2.8	2.8	2.8	2.8	2.8	2.8	2.8
7	EBIT.......	27.6	27.9	28.2	28.5	28.8	29.1	29.4	29.8	30.1	30.4
8	Int Exp....	2.3	2.3	2.3	2.3	2.3	2.3	2.3	2.3	2.3	2.3
9	EBT........	25.3	25.6	25.9	26.2	26.5	26.8	27.1	27.5	27.8	28.1
10											
11	Tax........	12.1	12.3	12.4	12.6	12.7	12.9	13.0	13.2	13.3	13.5
12	Net Income.	13.1	13.3	13.5	13.6	13.8	13.9	14.1	14.3	14.4	14.6
13											
14	EPS......	0.05	0.05	0.05	0.05	0.05	0.05	0.05	0.05	0.05	0.06
15											
16		Average		Gr Prof		Sales		G&A		Intst		Tax
17		Shares:		Rate %		Grow %		Expense:		Expense:		Rate%
18		264,000		40		12		2.8		2.3		40

```
Menu:   Sheet   Edit   File   Layout   Print   Graph   Tools   Window   Help   Remember
        Quit
Worksheet: intrnatl Loc: r1c1          FN:      Font: 0
Load Save Unload Active Newname Disp-Act Combine Import Export Password
```

Printing Formal Reports

You use the Print Report command to print formal reports from your spreadsheet directly to the printer or to a disk file for later printing or transmission to another computer. The Print Report capability enables you to print multiple ranges from a single spreadsheet or different spreadsheets. You also can include headings, footings, page numbers, and dates as part of the page format. Because reports tend to be used repeatedly and the specifications for the Print Report command are more complex than those for Print Text, you must first define the report's characteristics before printing.

You cannot print special fonts when using the Print Report command; if you want to use Enhanced printing capabilities, you must use the Print Text...Printer Enhanced command.

Defining a Report

When you execute the Print Report command, you are prompted:

   Define Preset Undefine Execute Template

To build a report definition, select Define from the option list. A pop-up window displays the names of any existing report definitions in the current subdirectory. You also are prompted:

   Enter format definition filename:

Move the cursor to the name of an existing definition in the pop-up menu to edit the definition, or type the name of a new definition. Press Enter when you are ready to continue.

The report definition screens in figures 14.5, 14.6, and 14.7 show the definitions for the printed report in figure 14.8.

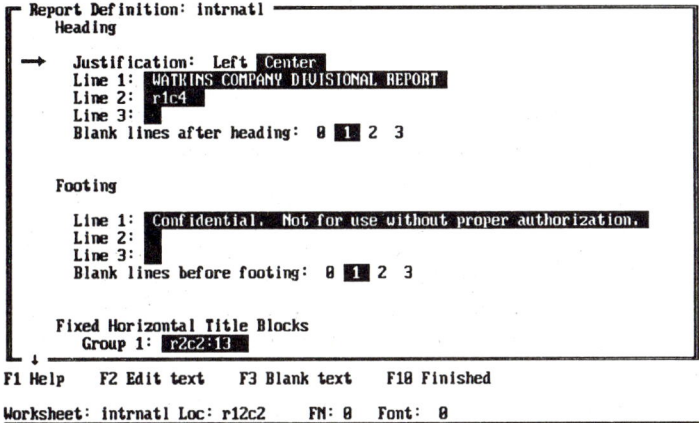

Fig. 14.5.

Defining a report heading and footing.

Fig. 14.6.

Defining title and body blocks.

Your headings and footings can contain a maximum of three lines of 99 characters each; they appear at the top and bottom of each page. You can enter a cell as a block reference in order to use the contents of the cell as the heading or footing. In this case, the width is limited by the margins of the report. In figure 14.5, for example, Line 2 of the heading reads r1c4, picking up the name of the division from the spreadsheet.

Fig. 14.7.

Defining a report layout.

```
┌─ Report Definition: intrnatl ─────────────────────────────────
        Group 2:
        Group 3:
→  Date in heading:  Alpha-Date  Numeric-Date  No-Date
   Lines to enclose report:  Yes  No
   Page numbers:  Left  Right  Center  Left-Right  Right-Left  No-Numbers
   Start page number:  1
   Spacing:  Single  Double
   Paper Feed:  Automatic  Manual
   Lines per inch:  6  8
   Characters per inch:  10  12  Compressed

   Form length (inches):  11
   Form width (inches):  8.5

   Top border (inches):  .6
   Bottom border (inches):  .4
   Left border (inches):  .3
   Right border (inches):  0
└──────────────────────────────────────────────────────────────
 F1 Help      F2 Edit text    F3 Blank text    F10 Finished

 Worksheet: canada     Loc: r3c2      FN: 0    Font: 0
 Enter the name of the file.
```

Fig. 14.8.

A sample report printout.

```
                     WATKINS COMPANY DIVISIONAL REPORT
                            CANADIAN DIVISION

              Jan   Feb   Mar   Apr   May   Jun   Jul   Aug   Sep   Oct   Nov   Dec
Net Sales..  70.6  71.2  71.9  72.6  73.2  73.9  74.6  75.3  75.9  76.6  77.3  78.1
Gross Prof.  29.7  29.9  30.2  30.5  30.8  31.0  31.3  31.6  31.9  32.2  32.5  32.8
           ------------------------------------------------------------------------
G&A Exp....   2.8   2.8   2.8   2.8   2.8   2.8   2.8   2.8   2.8   2.8   2.8   2.8
EBIT.......  26.9  27.1  27.4  27.7  28.0  28.2  28.5  28.8  29.1  29.4  29.7  30.0
Int Exp....   2.2   2.2   2.2   2.2   2.2   2.2   2.2   2.2   2.2   2.2   2.2   2.2
EBT........  24.7  24.9  25.2  25.5  25.8  26.0  26.3  26.6  26.9  27.2  27.5  27.8
           ------------------------------------------------------------------------
Tax........  11.8  12.0  12.1  12.2  12.4  12.5  12.6  12.8  12.9  13.1  13.2  13.3
Net Income.  12.8  13.0  13.1  13.2  13.4  13.5  13.7  13.8  14.0  14.1  14.3  14.4
           ------------------------------------------------------------------------
EPS......   0.04  0.04  0.04  0.04  0.04  0.04  0.04  0.04  0.04  0.04  0.04  0.04
```

Headings (but not footings) can be left-justified or centered relative to the form width. You can specify from 0 to 3 blank lines between the headings or footings and the text of the report itself.

The actual data for the body of the report is specified in the groups under the heading Report Body Blocks (see fig. 14.6). You can define as many as three sets of print groups in a Spreadsheet report. By definition, a print group starts on a new page, giving you some direct control over pagination.

In each print group, you can specify several block references to be printed one after the other without forcing a page break. You can specify as many block references as will fit in the 99-character space allotted on the definition screen. In the following example, the three blocks that are specified derive from different spreadsheets; the references are to named ranges in each spreadsheet:

```
Report Body Blocks
     Group 1:  domestic.dom,intrnatl.inl,canada.can
```

By using short spreadsheet names and block references, you can maximize the number of blocks in the definition.

If the block references are separated by commas, as above, the blocks are printed one above each other vertically on the page. If the references are separated by semicolons, the blocks are printed side by side. Any portions of blocks that do not fit in the page width are continued on successive pages.

To simplify the task of entering block designations in a report definition, you can press F6 to return to the spreadsheet temporarily. Move the cursor to the upper left cell in the block, press F2 to drop the anchor, and then move the cursor to the lower right corner of the block. The block range is highlighted as you go. Press Enter to complete the definition of the block range and insert it in the report definition.

In addition to specifying report body blocks, you also can enter horizontal and vertical title blocks. These blocks appear on each page of the printed report, in much the same way that the Windows Titles command fixes rows or columns on the screen. In figure 14.6, *r2c2:13* is entered as the horizontal title block. (The abbreviations for the months are contained in this row.) If the number of rows in the body of the report causes it to extend to a second page, the horizontal titles print again at the top of the second page.

In figure 14.6, the vertical titles are specified as *r3:14c1*. Note that the title blocks do not overlap, nor do they include the intersection at r2c1. Make sure you do not include any overlap in the title blocks, or the spacing of the report will be altered.

If you specify inclusion of a date in your report heading, the current system date is printed on the right side of the last line of the report heading. If the date is not set automatically when you boot your computer, remember to set the system date before you begin your SmartWare II session.

If you specify lines to enclose the report, dashed lines are drawn at the top and bottom of each page between the body of the report and the heading or footing.

Page numbers are printed at the bottom of the page. The starting page number appears on the first printed page. If you are producing a report to appear in a larger report from another source, you may want to keep page numbering consistent with the larger report; in this case, your starting number would be greater than 1.

You can select single- or double-spacing. This is the only option that enables you to present the body of the spreadsheet in a format different from that of the screen display.

Select paper feed Manual if you want the printer to pause between pages. Vertical lines per inch and horizontal characters per inch can be specified as in figure 14.7, subject to the limitations of your printer.

Enter the actual length of your printer paper in inches. The paper width you specify need not be as great as the actual width of the paper. If you choose to center the heading of your report, it is centered relative to the paper width you have entered.

Enter the width of the borders in inches. Some printers have fixed borders in which you cannot print. If you find that you are losing a portion of your report at the top or on the left, increase the border size.

Printing a Report

After you have created the definition, you are ready to print the report. When you begin the Print Report Execute command, a pop-up window displays the names of your existing report definitions, and you are prompted:

    Enter format definition filename:

Move the cursor to the name of a definition in the pop-up menu, or type the path and name of a definition in another subdirectory. Press Enter when you are ready. The next prompt is

    Printer Disk

If you select disk, you are prompted for the name of the output file; the file is then created with the name you provide. If you do not provide a file extension, .PRN is used. If a file with the same name already exists, no prompt asks whether you want to overwrite that file. Be careful!

Unlike previous versions of SmartWare II, the output print file may not consist of entirely ASCII characters. Depending on your printer selection, printer control codes are embedded in the disk file to control the printing of the output. With the control codes embedded in the file, you can print the report to your printer directly from the file from outside the SmartWare II environment; the printed output appears just as if you had printed it directly from SmartWare II.

If the control codes are embedded in the file, you cannot edit or view the file easily. If you want to create a disk file without the control codes, select the Generic, Draft printer in the Hardware Preferences menu of the Tools command.

If you select Printer, you are prompted for the number of copies you want to print. You can type the number or simply press Enter to print one copy.

Reports in the Spreadsheet module cannot be printed in Enhanced mode; only your printer's internal fonts are available. If you need rasterized or cartridge fonts, use the Print Text...Printer Enhanced command.

Establishing Default Options

You use the Print Report Preset command to establish default options identical to those in the Print Report Define menu. Actually, when you first install the Spreadsheet module, you should bring up the Preset menu and enter the default values you will usually want to have in effect. For instance, if you usually print page numbers on your reports, set this option on the Preset menu. When set, Preset options apply to any new reports you define.

Printing a Page Layout Description

The Print Report Template command prints a description of the page layout for a specified definition. You cannot direct the layout to a file; it must go to the printer.

Erasing a Report Definition

To erase a report definition from your disk, use the Print Report Undefine command. Be careful when executing this command; no prompt asks you to verify that you really want to delete the definition.

Chapter Summary

This chapter has covered the methods of creating printed output from your spreadsheets. The Print Text command is used to create quick and easy reports. Use the Print Map command to print a representative layout of your spreadsheet, and the Print Formulas command to print the formulas. Both commands can help you discover hidden errors or inconsistencies. Use the Print Report command to produce formal reports with headings and footings.

15

Integrating the Spreadsheet with Other Modules

At the heart of the SmartWare II system is the capability of integrating each application module with the other modules. Each module has commands for importing and exporting external (DOS) files and for sending text or data to the other modules. This chapter focuses on using these commands and capabilities within the Spreadsheet.

Importing External Files into the Worksheet

You use the File Import command to read external files into the Spreadsheet. When you import a file, a new spreadsheet is created. You can import five types of files:

    Dif Sylk Text 123 R2-123

A Text file exists in the generic ASCII format. It may be comma or space delimited and may have double quotation marks (") surrounding alphabetic entries; values are *not* enclosed in quotation marks. If an alphanumeric entry in the file has a space (between a last name and first initial, for example), you must enclose the entry in quotation marks. No formulas or formatting codes are contained in a Text file.

When you import files in the Smart or ASCII formats as Text files, each record in the external file creates one row in the Spreadsheet. The data is inserted beginning at the current cursor position, so be sure to position the cursor before you begin executing the command.

With no additional conversion, you can import spreadsheets in the Lotus 1-2-3 Release 1 or 2 formats by selecting the 123 or R2-123 options. Formulas and most functions are maintained, as are formats, underscoring, and column widths. Any macros are read as text, however.

A DIF file is a file in *Document Interchange Format*, a format common to many spreadsheet programs. Use the DIF option to read files in this format; they should have the extension .DIF. SYLK files are in the Multiplan format.

Exporting Worksheet Data to Different Files

You use the File Export command to write the contents of a spreadsheet to a disk file in one of five different formats. When you select the File Export command, you can choose one of two options, Block or Worksheet. If you specify Block, you are prompted:

```
Enter name or block reference:
```

You can type the range in the row and column notation, specify a named block, or press F2 to drop the anchor and move the cursor to the lower right corner of the block. Press Enter to complete the definition of the block range.

When the block specification is complete, or if you have chosen to export the whole spreadsheet, the next prompt is

```
Ascii Dif Wp-Doc Smart Text 123 R2-123
```

Select the type of disk file you want to create as follows:

ASCII	Alphanumeric data is enclosed in quotation marks; numerics are not. Data items are separated by commas. The default extension is .ASC.
DIF	Document Interchange Format. The default extension is .DIF.
WP-DOC	A file used by the SmartWare II Word Processor. The default extension is .DOC.
SMART	Similar to the ASCII format. Data items are separated by a space. The default extension is .DAT.
TEXT	This is a fixed, ASCII format. No quotation marks are used. The file almost looks like the spreadsheet but contains no fonts, underscoring, or boldface attributes. Use this export type if you want to import the spreadsheet to a word processor other than SmartWare II. Data item separation is identical to the view of the spreadsheet. The default extension is .TXT.
123	Lotus 1-2-3 Version 1 format. The default file extension is .WKS.

R2-123 Lotus 1-2-3 Version 2 format. The default file extension is .WK1.

You can edit the ASCII, SMART, and TEXT formats in the Tools Text-Editor; they are in a generic ASCII format. You may supply your own file extensions to override the defaults.

Sending Worksheet Data to Other Application Modules

The Sheet Send command is used to pass data directly from your spreadsheet to another SmartWare II application module and then to transfer control to that module immediately. The first prompt of the Sheet Send command is

    Communications Database Wordprocessor

These options are covered in the sections that follow.

Sending Data to the Communications Module

If you send data to the Communications module, the resulting data set is ready for transmission over your modem to another computer system. The options for the Sheet Send Communications command are

    Document Graphics Smart Text

Use the Document format when the result is to be included in a Smart Word Processor document at the other end of the transmission line. Select Graphics, which sends a metafile that has been created with the Graph Generate...Metafile command, if the graph is to be viewed or included within a document.

Specify the Smart format if the recipient of the file plans to read the spreadsheet data into the SmartWare II Database. If you want to send the file in a format that is almost the same as the spreadsheet, with displayed values instead of formulas, select the Text option.

On the other hand, if your correspondent wants to use the spreadsheet within the SmartWare II Spreadsheet module, do not use the Sheet Send command at all. Simply begin SmartWare II Communications and transmit the spreadsheet file itself. The file name is the spreadsheet name; the extension is .WS.

Be aware that spreadsheets, documents, and graphics contain special control characters; therefore, you must use the Xmodem transmission option. However, Smart and Text files are pure ASCII files and can be sent with or without using the Xmodem protocol.

If you select the Document, Smart or Text options, you are prompted:

    Enter name or block reference:

You can type the range in row and column notation, such as *r3:7c5:10*. An easier way to indicate the range is to move the cursor to the upper left cell of the range, press F2 to drop the anchor, and then move the cursor to the lower right corner of the range. The block range is highlighted as you go. Press Enter to complete the definition of the block range.

If you select Graphics, the prompt is as follows:

    Enter graph filename:

A pop-up menu displays the names of metafiles in the current subdirectory.

The final prompt, regardless of the type of file sent to the Communications module, is

    Enter project file for next application:

If you have already built a project file within the Communications module that you want to initiate, enter the name of the file; if no such file exists or if you don't want to initiate a project file, simply press Enter. (All Sheet Send command sequences terminate with a prompt for a project file.)

Sending Data to the Database

If you choose to send data to the Database, you are prompted:

    Enter name or block reference:

After identifying the block, you are prompted for the name of a project file to initiate within the Database. Press Enter if no file exists.

When a file is sent to the Database, each row from the specified block becomes a record, and each column becomes a field. If a Database with the same name as your spreadsheet does not exist, a new database and standard view are created. Default field names of F001, F002, and so forth are established. Numeric columns create numeric fields; others create alpha fields. Editing characters such as commas, dollar signs, or percent signs are retained. If a matching database already exists, the records are appended to the file.

If you prefer to create one record in the Database for each column in the spreadsheet, use the Sheet Matrix Transpose command to swap the rows for columns and the columns for rows before issuing the Sheet Send command. Deleting unnecessary rows or columns before sending a file to the Database is a good idea.

Sending Data to the Word Processor

If you choose to send data from the Spreadsheet to SmartWare II's Word Processor, you have three options:

```
Document  Graphics  Both
```

If you choose Document, you are first prompted to select a range and then a project file to initiate within the Word Processor. If you select Graphics, a pop-up window displays the names of the graph metafiles in the current subdirectory; select one of them to send. If you select Both, you are prompted for both the metafile name and the range. The final prompt is for the project file.

In the Word Processor, the data from the spreadsheet is displayed in a new document with no name assigned. Each row becomes a line that terminates in a hard carriage return, and the columns are aligned. Underscoring is retained.

When you execute the Graph Insert command in the Word Processor to include a graph in the body of a document, a pop-up menu displays the names of the current graph metafiles. If you send a graph from the Spreadsheet to the Word Processor, that graph file is identified as the default in the pop-up menu.

Chapter Summary

In the SmartWare II Spreadsheet, the capability of importing and exporting data adds to the power of the system greatly. By reading data from an external file, you can interface the Spreadsheet with other software packages without having to retype the data. Similarly, the File Export command enables you to create a file that you later can import to a different system.

The Sheet Send command is used in the SmartWare II Spreadsheet to pass data or graphs to another SmartWare II module and to immediately initiate that module. This feature is the basis of the SmartWare II system integration.

Part III

Using the SmartWare II Word Processor

Includes

Using the Word Processor Module

Manipulating Text

Formatting Text

Using the Spellchecker and Thesaurus

Generating a Table of Contents and Index

Printing and Merging Text

Integrating the Word Processor with other Modules

16

Using the Word Processor Module

If you have never used a word processor, you are in for a treat; if you are converting from another word processing product, you will be delighted with the variety of features and ease of use of SmartWare II. Many new features have been added, which greatly enhance the capabilities of the Word Processor.

A word processor is used to create and edit documents—letters, articles, books, memos, and manuscripts. You can save the documents for later use, edit them by moving sentences or whole paragraphs in the current document or into other documents, and copy or delete portions of your document. Your text can include italics, bold, and underlining and a wide variety of fonts and type styles, if your printer supports them. And because the Word Processor is integrated with the other SmartWare system modules, it can share documents, data, and even graphics. (Yes, you can print a graph in the body of your document.)

This chapter introduces you to SmartWare's Word Processor and explains how to create, load, name, and save document files, making them available for further editing.

New Features of the SmartWare II Word Processor

Several new features are available in SmartWare II. You can now define multiple column areas (MCA) in your document. The columns can be of equal or different widths, whichever you prefer. You can define two types of columns: linked and unlinked. If you create linked columns, the entries in the columns will always remain aligned with each other. The system will insert the necessary blank lines to keep the linked entries opposite each other. If you sort by one of the columns, the linkage will be maintained.

Linked columns are useful, for example, if you are writing a marketing brochure with one column of features and one of benefits. If you declare unlinked columns, the alignment across the columns will not be maintained. This is analogous to the newspaper style of column definition. Your text cannot flow automatically from one column to the next, however.

Rather than having one ruler line that governs the entire document, now you can create different rulers which can apply to individual paragraphs or sections of your text. Rulers are used to establish the following characteristics:

Left and right margins
Indentation
Justification
Spacing
Tabs—normal and decimal
Ruler division (characters per inch)

Rather than reformatting a paragraph, you now edit the ruler which controls the text. As you build your document, you can assign names to rulers so that you can insert them easily.

A thesaurus is now included, in addition to the standard spell checker. If you cannot think of just the right word while you are writing, you can use the thesaurus to look it up. To help you, the thesaurus first looks up the root of the word, then offers several meanings for the root. Once you choose the proper meaning, you can select from among several synonyms or antonyms.

To help manage large documents, you can divide your document into sections. Of particular benefit is the capability to define Print options by section, thus allowing different headings and footings, page numbering style, boundary sizes, and physical form sizes for each section. You can move sections to different locations in the document. You can print footnotes at the end of each section, and you can begin renumbering or have continuous footnote numbers. Similarly, you can select paragraph numbers to either continue or begin again at section breaks. The table of contents can include the section number.

You can mark words or phrases in your document to be entered into a table of contents, which you generate when you have completed the document. When you mark the headings, you indicate a level to determine the number of spaces to indent.

Usually you will generate the table of contents as a final section when your document is complete. You can then move the section to the beginning of the document, if you want.

You can mark phrases or blocks of text in your document and tag them with entries to be included in the index. You can use the phrases as the index entries, or you can supply other text. You also can designate primary and secondary index entries.

Usually you generate your index when you have completed the document. The index is placed at the end of the document and is defined as a new section.

You can hide text in your document to serve as notes or other memoranda.

The size limits of the Word Processor have been increased. Each line can contain 255 characters; each document theoretically can have as many as 64,000 pages, but that depends on the amount of memory in your computer.

The units of measure in the SmartWare II Word Processor are different from those in previous versions. Paper size is measured in inches (in the U.S. and U.K. releases) rather than lines or spaces. Margins, indents, and tabs are also measured in inches.

Linear measures pave the way for proportionally spaced printing. When you use a fixed font, each character uses exactly the same amount of space; the letter *i* takes up as much space as the letter *w*, even though the *i* is much thinner. When you use proportional fonts, each letter uses only the amount of space it needs. Thus, your printed output can be more compact, easier to read, and more professional looking.

You can lock a document with a password to prevent the printing or saving of changes. You can give newly created documents a password and encrypt (scramble) them with one of two encryption algorithms.

Lines of text can be spaced vertically in increments of one-half line from 0.5 to 9.5 lines.

If you want to make sure that a portion of your document is not split between two pages, you can mark text you want to keep intact. This is the Keep feature.

To prevent leftover lines of a paragraph from being on a page by themselves, you can specify the minimum number of lines to allow as widows and orphans.

If you choose, SmartWare II will assign paragraph numbers in one of three formats. This is useful for manuals, proposals, and outlining.

Using the Word Processor

When you begin a Word Processor session, you should be in the Text Entry mode and ready to start typing. Use the Esc key to alternate between the Text Entry mode and Command mode. The beginning screen is shown in figure 16.1.

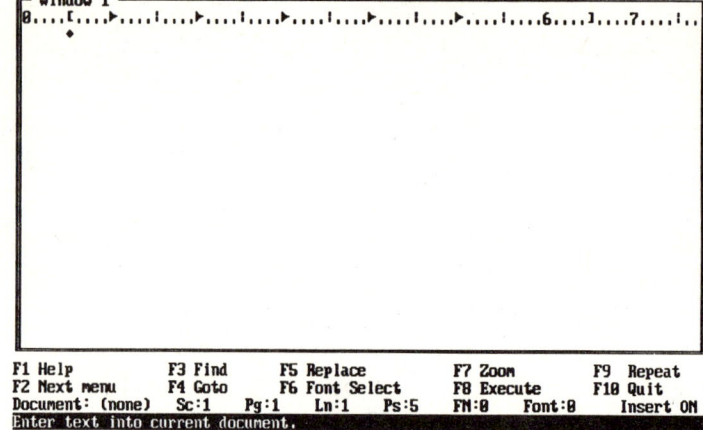

Fig. 16.1.

The Word Processor beginning screen.

Entering New Text

To enter text in the Text Entry mode, just start typing; each character appears on the screen as you type. If you make a mistake, use the Backspace key. If you need to return to a previous part of the line or another part of the document, use one of the cursor-control keys described in the next section. Use the Del key to delete individual characters. If Insert mode is on, you can insert new characters between existing ones. If Insert is off, new characters overwrite what is there. The status of the Insert mode is shown at the right side of the status line.

Several helpful markers appear on the screen (see fig. 16.2). The paragraph marker shows where you have entered a hard carriage return by pressing Enter. The tab markers show where you have pressed the Tab key instead of entering spaces. An automatic page break entered by the program is shown as a solid single line across the screen; if you force a page break with the Layout Newpage Insert command, it appears as a heavy dashed line. The end of the current document is always shown as a diamond.

Several markers new to SmartWare II are shown in figure 16.2. These new marks are as follows:

> Keep
> Hidden text
> Section Break
> Table of Contents
> Index Item

Note that the display of a decimal tab is different from previous SmartWare versions.

Chapter 16: Using the Word Processor Module

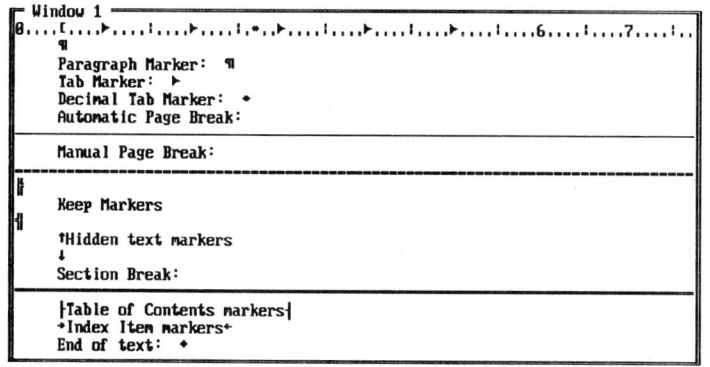

Fig. 16.2.

Use SmartWare's visible markers as a guide.

Moving the Cursor

The cursor indicates the current typing position in the document window. In the Insert mode, the cursor appears as a heavy underscore; when Insert is off, the cursor is a solid block about the height of a lowercase character. When you switch to the command level, the cursor becomes a full-height block.

Several specialized cursor-control keys are available in SmartWare's Word Processor to help you move the cursor in the current document. These keys and their functions are listed in Table 16.1.

Table 16.1
Cursor Control Keys

Key	Function
Ctrl-G	Move cursor right one word
Ctrl-F	Move cursor left one word
Home	Move cursor to top left corner of current window
End	Move cursor to beginning of last line in current window
Tab	Move cursor right to the next tab position, either Normal or Decimal tab
PgUp	Scroll up one screen

PgDn	Scroll down one screen
Ctrl-Left	Move to the beginning of the current line
Ctrl-Right	Move to the end of the current line
Ctrl-Home	Move to beginning of current document
Ctrl-End	Move to end of current document

Switching to Command Mode

To use the Word Processor's commands, press Esc to toggle to the menu. To go back to Text Entry mode, press Esc again, or use the Alt-Y Quick key. (The Esc key is also used to cancel a command and return to a previous menu level.)

Specifying a Range

Certain common concepts and phrases recur throughout the Word Processor. One such concept is that of specifying a range in which an action should take effect. (If you are upgrading from previous versions of Smart, pay particular attention to these changes.) You can specify an area as a block, indicating that the marked area is linear in the document (such as a sentence or a paragraph), or as a set of screen columns, cutting through sentences and paragraphs.

Marking Blocks

Many commands prompt you to specify a range of text. For example, if you want to delete or move a certain portion of text, you are prompted to define the area to which the command applies. Figure 16.3 shows the options offered when you execute the Edit Delete command.

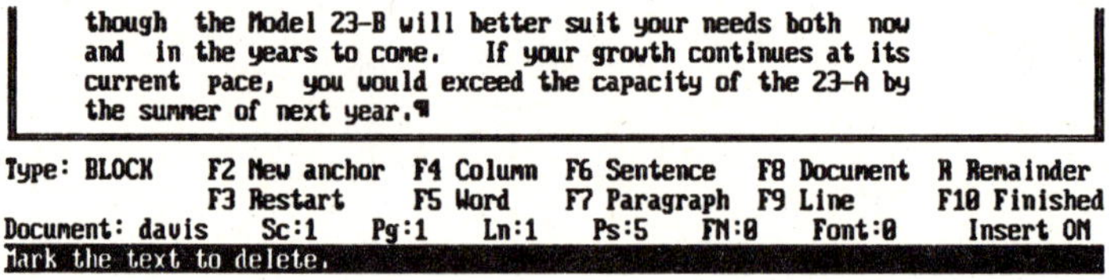

Fig. 16.3.

Block-marking options.

```
        though the Model 23-B will better suit your needs both  now
        and  in the years to come.   If your growth continues at its
        current  pace,  you would exceed the capacity of the 23-A by
        the summer of next year.¶

Type: BLOCK      F2 New anchor  F4 Column  F6 Sentence  F8 Document  R Remainder
                 F3 Restart     F5 Word    F7 Paragraph F9 Line      F10 Finished
Document: davis    Sc:1    Pg:1    Ln:1    Ps:5    FN:0    Font:0    Insert ON
Mark the text to delete.
```

A block must have a beginning and an ending point. As a default, the beginning point is the cursor position at the time you executed the command. Once you are in the Block Definition mode, however, you can designate a new beginning point, or anchor, by moving the cursor and pressing F2. If you move the cursor to a new starting location, even though the text will be highlighted, the highlight will be removed when you press F2 to mark the beginning of the block.

You can designate the ending point simply by moving the cursor; the area affected by your choice is displayed in reverse video. (See fig. 16.4 for an example.)

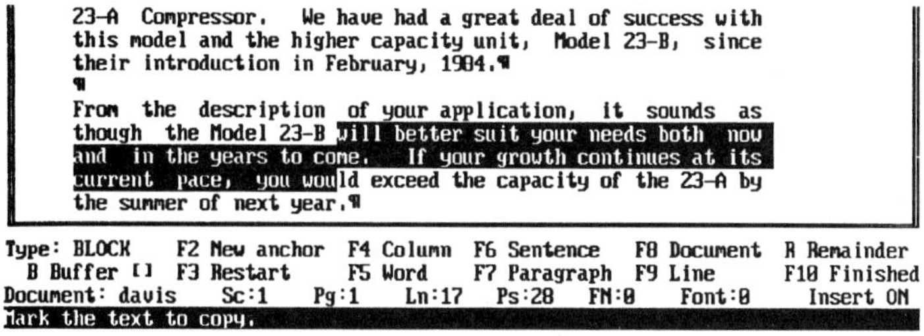

Fig. 16.4.

Block marking.

To make it easier to mark a block, there are several keys you can use:

F5 Word
F6 Sentence
F7 Paragraph
F8 Entire Document
F9 Line
R   Remainder of document

Rather than using the cursor movement keys to move the cursor to the end of the sentence, for instance, you can press F6 to mark the current sentence. To be recognized, a sentence must end with a period or a paragraph marker. The Line option (F9) will specify the current line on which the cursor is positioned. The paragraph marker indicates the current paragraph.

Choosing the Remainder option (R) indicates that the range extends from the current cursor position to the end of the document. Selecting the Word option (F5) specifies the current word, bounded by either blanks or punctuation. Note that the trailing blanks and punctuation are included in the word definition boundary.

Repeated pressing of one of the selection function keys will move the highlight block to the next comparable area. For example, each time you press F6, the next sentence will be highlighted. This method enables you to move through the document more quickly than by using the cursor keys. The effect is not cumulative, however. If you press F6 twice, you will not have marked two sentences, just the second one. Once you have marked an area by using a function key, you can mark an additional area by moving the cursor key.

Pressing F8 marks the entire document, regardless of the current cursor position.

Once you have selected a block, you can change your mind by pressing the restart key, F3. Press F10 or Enter to complete your selection.

Marking Columns

Whereas block marking is linear in the document, you can also mark a rectangular area in the Column mode. In this mode, the exact columns you specify are marked, from the top left corner to the bottom right. Press F4 to switch from the Block mode to the Column mode. The Column mode options are shown in figure 16.5.

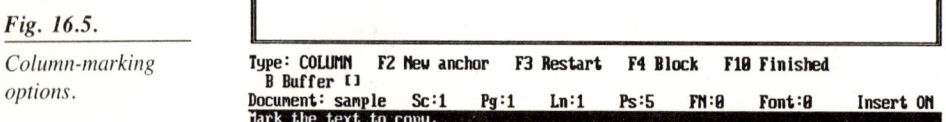

Fig. 16.5.

Column-marking options.

In Column-marking mode, you do not use document-related choices, such as F5 for Word or F6 for Sentence. You simply move the cursor to the lower right and press F10 or Enter. If necessary, reposition the beginning of the block by moving the cursor and pressing F2.

Marking text in Column mode is independent of the capability to define multiple column areas (MCA) in the Word Processor. Column matching refers to screen columns, not MCA's.

Effects of Commands

Certain commands affect existing text, and others affect new text. You should take note of these distinctions because, although the result may be the same and the command may be similar, the method and ease of achieving the result may be different.

For example, you may want a certain sentence in your document underscored. You have two choices: You can enter the sentence and underscore it later with the Layout Font Underscore command, or you can use the Layout Font Select command to choose an underscore font before entering text. (Actually, the Quick key Ctrl-U is the fastest way to indicate that you want to begin entering underscored text.)

Document spacing is another example: You can type a paragraph as single-spaced and then change it to double-spaced by editing the current ruler for the paragraph. Or you can insert a new double-spaced ruler before you begin typing. There is no right or wrong way to perform these tasks; use the method that works best for you.

Setting Defaults

There are several commands in the Word Processor which are used to establish default settings for your session. By establishing the defaults, you can select the settings you want to have in effect each time you begin the Word Processor. Paragraph justification, for instance, can be set initially either justified or left aligned in the Tools Preferences Word Processor menu. At any time during the session, however, you can change the justification by using the Layout Ruler commands.

To set your default options for the entire Word Processor module, execute the Tools Preferences Word Processor command. (See Chapter 28 to learn how to change the Global and Hardware preferences that affect all modules of SmartWare II.)

Several of the settings in the Word Processor Preferences will take effect immediately when you press the F10 to save them:

> Insertion mode
> Paragraph format (new documents only)
> Special character display
> Document auto save
> Dictionary preferences
> Data path
> Exit project file (on exiting current session)

Automatic loading of macros and the execution of an entry project file will not take effect until the next time you initiate a SmartWare Word Processor session.

In addition to the Word Processor Preferences, Layout and Print options can be set to affect new documents when you create them. Refer to the chapters on these commands for an explanation of these options and their effects.

For many of the choices, you move the highlight block among the options with the right and left cursor keys or by pressing the space bar. For other selections, type the number or name of the option and press Enter. To edit an entry, press the right arrow key to begin the Edit mode. To blank an area, press F3.

Figures 16.6, 16.7, and 16.8 show the Word Processor Preferences menus.

Setting Pagination Defaults

For Pagination, from the Word Processor Preferences menu, select Automatic. SmartWare II breaks your document into separate pages; select Manual if you want to paginate it manually, or not at all.

Character Insertion Mode

If you want the Insert on as a default, select On from the Word Processor Preferences menu.

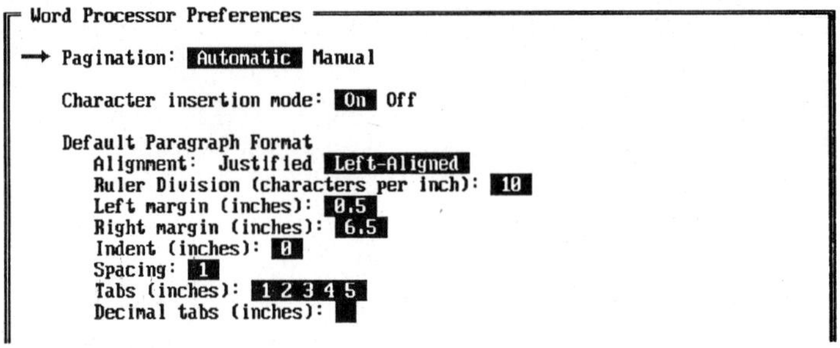

Fig. 16.6.

Word Processor preferences (Pagination, Character Insertion mode, and Default Paragraph Format).

```
┌─ Word Processor Preferences ─────────────────────────────┐
│ → Pagination: Automatic  Manual                          │
│                                                          │
│   Character insertion mode: On  Off                      │
│                                                          │
│   Default Paragraph Format                               │
│      Alignment:  Justified  Left-Aligned                 │
│      Ruler Division (characters per inch): 10            │
│      Left margin (inches):  0.5                          │
│      Right margin (inches): 6.5                          │
│      Indent (inches): 0                                  │
│      Spacing: 1                                          │
│      Tabs (inches): 1 2 3 4 5                            │
│      Decimal tabs (inches):                              │
└──────────────────────────────────────────────────────────┘
```

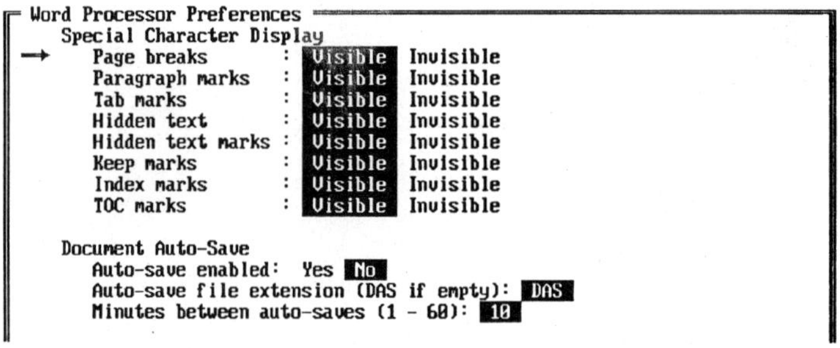

Fig. 16.7.

Word Processor preferences (Special Character Display and Document Auto-Save).

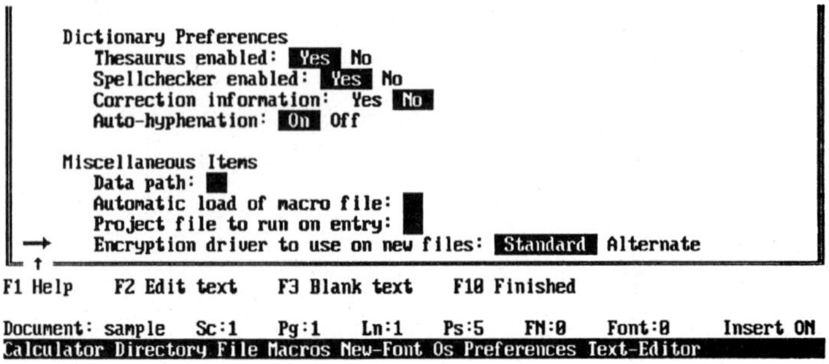

```
┌─ Word Processor Preferences ─────────────────────────────┐
│   Special Character Display                              │
│ →    Page breaks         : Visible  Invisible            │
│      Paragraph marks     : Visible  Invisible            │
│      Tab marks           : Visible  Invisible            │
│      Hidden text         : Visible  Invisible            │
│      Hidden text marks   : Visible  Invisible            │
│      Keep marks          : Visible  Invisible            │
│      Index marks         : Visible  Invisible            │
│      TOC marks           : Visible  Invisible            │
│                                                          │
│   Document Auto-Save                                     │
│      Auto-save enabled:  Yes  No                         │
│      Auto-save file extension (DAS if empty): DAS        │
│      Minutes between auto-saves (1 - 60): 10             │
└──────────────────────────────────────────────────────────┘
```

Fig. 16.8.

Word Processor preferences (Dictionary Preferences and Miscellaneous Items).

```
┌─────────────────────────────────────────────────────────────┐
│   Dictionary Preferences                                    │
│      Thesaurus enabled:   Yes  No                           │
│      Spellchecker enabled: Yes  No                          │
│      Correction information:  Yes  No                       │
│      Auto-hyphenation: On  Off                              │
│                                                             │
│   Miscellaneous Items                                       │
│      Data path:                                             │
│      Automatic load of macro file:                          │
│      Project file to run on entry:                          │
│ →    Encryption driver to use on new files: Standard Alternate │
└─────────────────────────────────────────────────────────────┘
 F1 Help    F2 Edit text    F3 Blank text    F10 Finished
 Document: sample   Sc:1   Pg:1   Ln:1   Ps:5   FN:0   Font:0   Insert ON
 Calculator Directory File Macros New-Font Os Preferences Text-Editor
```

Default Paragraph Format

The following selections control the format of the default ruler for a new document.

- Alignment—Select either Justified (right- and left-justified) or Left-Aligned. In previous versions of SmartWare, you selected justification by choosing the Normal option.

- Ruler Division—Enter the number of characters per inch that you want for the ruler line.

- Right and Left Margins—Enter the value, in inches, of the space you want left blank at the right and left edges of your paper.

- Indent—Enter the value, in inches, for the space you want to indent at the beginning of a paragraph.

- Line Spacing—Enter a number from 1 to 9. You also can enter half-spacing in the decimal (1.5) format or the plus (1+) format.

- Tabs—Enter tab stop locations in inches. Use either spaces or commas between each entry.

- Decimal Tabs—Enter decimal tab stop locations in inches. Use either spaces or commas between each entry.

Special Character Display

Select either Visible or Invisible for the following marks:

- Page breaks
- Paragraph marks
- Tab marks
- Hidden text
- Hidden text marks
- Keep marks
- Index marks
- Table of Contents (TOC) marks

Refer to figure 16.2 for examples of these marks. Don't worry, the marks will never be printed on your finished document; they are merely for guidance while creating or editing your document.

Document Auto-Save

A new feature of SmartWare II enables you to save your document automatically while you are working on it. To take advantage of this capability, select Yes on the Word Processor Preferences menu. When your document is saved automatically, the default file extension is .DAS, but you can change it if needed. A maximum of three characters is allowed for filename extensions. After choosing to use the automatic save capability, enter the number of minutes between automatic saves; the range is one to 60 minutes.

When SmartWare automatically saves a file, not just the current file, but all open, unsaved files will be saved when the interval has elapsed.

In the Tools Preferences Global menu, you are offered the following choices:

```
Automatic file backup: Yes No
```

If you select Yes, each time you perform a manual File Save, a file with the extension .BDC and the same name as your document is created for you. This file contains the second most recent manually saved version. For safety, you can have both the .BDC and the .DAS files created for you.

Dictionary Preferences

If you want to use the dictionary and the thesaurus, you must select Yes from the Word Processor Preferences menu. With the dictionary, you have the option of automatically searching for correction information if a word is found which is not in the dictionary. By selecting No, you must press F8 to search for spelling corrections. If you want automatic hyphenation, select On from the Word Processor Preferences menu.

Miscellaneous Items

You can make four miscellaneous selections from the Word Processor Preferences menu.

- Data Path—If your Word Processor documents are usually stored in a single subdirectory, you should enter the path here. An example of a path is

    c:\smart\wpdata

    However, if you intend to initiate SmartWare from a number of subdirectories, each of which can contain documents, you should leave this entry blank so that the default subdirectory will be the one from which you entered SmartWare.

- Automatic Load of Macro File—A file with macro definitions can be loaded automatically when you begin the SmartWare Word Processor. Enter the name of the macro file here. Be sure to preface its name with the path, if necessary.

- Project File to Run on Entry—You can specify project files to be run each time you enter the SmartWare Word Processor.

- Encryption Driver to Use on New Files—When you save a document to which you have attached a password, it is automatically stored in an encrypted format. Thus, if someone were to examine the file outside of Smart, it could not be read. You should select the standard encryption driver, which contains the encryption rules. If you have a a different encryption driver, contact Informix for instruction on how to use it.

Working with Files

This section covers the creation, loading, saving, and naming of document files in the SmartWare II Word Processor. Regardless of what you do in the Word Processor module, you will need this information to know how to save your documents and how to make them available for editing.

The file handling commands are found under the File command on the Word Processor menu. Figure 16.9 shows the File options.

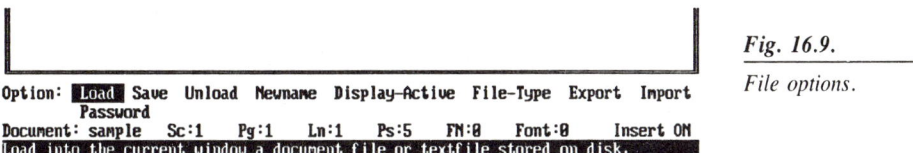

Fig. 16.9.

File options.

Loading Documents

The command to load an existing Word Processor document is File Load; the Quick key is Alt-L. This command is used to retrieve a document from the disk and to make it available for editing in the current window. A pop-up window will display the names of any documents and text files in your current subdirectory (refer to figure 16.10).

Fig. 16.10.

The File Load pop-up window.

Files with the extension .DOC are assumed to be in the Word Processor document format, and those with the extension .TXT are assumed to be in the text file, pure ASCII format. Use the cursor control keys to identify the document you want to edit, and then press Enter.

If the document you want is stored in a different subdirectory, you can enter the path and the file name in response to the prompt:

    Enter a filename:

If you cannot remember the name of the file, press the F4 key to display the prompt:

    Enter the file specification:

In response to this prompt, you should type the path and file name specification to help you locate the file. For example, if you know that the document is in the \office subdirectory, type the following:

    \office*.doc

If there are Word Processor documents in the subdirectory, the following prompt will appear after you press Enter:

    File was found in ‹\office\stenart.doc›—Continue searching? (y/n)

If you have found the file you want, press *N* to end the search. If you press *Y*, the program will continue to search for files matching the specification in your selected subdirectory and any subordinate subdirectories.

If you want to load a file from a different subdirectory but cannot remember its name, press the F5 key. When you press F5, the pop-up window displays \ to indicate the root directory, .. to indicate the subdirectory immediately above the current one, and the names of any subordinate subdirectories.

To display the names of the subdirectories in the root, move the cursor to the \ and press Enter. A directory listing will be displayed in a pop-up window. Now move the cursor to the name of the subdirectory you want and press Enter. Finally, press F5 to display the names of the Word Processor files in the selected subdirectory.

Whatever method you use to locate and display the name of a document to load, if the document is protected by a password, you are given the following prompt:

    Enter password:

You are allowed three attempts to enter the correct password before SmartWare returns you to the menu. Remember that passwords are case sensitive; that is, PASS is different from pass. (The File Password command is discussed later in this chapter.) Because password lengths can vary (to a maximum of 16 characters), you must press Enter after typing the password. Don't use long passwords, however. Although a long password may be more secure, you may find it easier to forget.

SmartWare Word Processor documents are identified by their file extensions. A .DOC extension indicates that the file is a true document file with all the hidden control characters needed for word processing. (If you were to use the DOS TYPE command to view the contents of one of these files, you would see many unusual symbols on the screen. These symbols represent the control characters.) A .TXT extension means that the file is an ordinary text file with no special characters. This is often called an ASCII file. Text files and documents are frequently treated differently in the Word Processor.

In the Word Processor, you can have one document active in the current window and multiple documents active but not displayed. (This is a difference from previous versions of SmartWare.) Use the Document Goto command to switch from one document to another.

Unloading Documents

Unload a document by using the File Unload command if you don't want to view or edit it any more right now. The Quick key for the File Unload command is Alt-U.

If you have changed the document, you are prompted:

    Save modified document first? (y/n).

Press *Y* if you want to save your changes; press *N* if you want to discard them. Note that alterations of Print options or Layout options, as well as changes to the body of the text, constitute changes to the current document.

If you have just created the document and have not named it, SmartWare prompts for a name after the File Unload command. (Refer to the File Newname command, covered later in this chapter.) To name a new document, you respond to the following prompt:

    Current document is unnamed, enter new name:

At this prompt, enter the name of the document; you are allowed a maximum of eight characters. If you already have a file with the same name as what you typed, you are prompted:

    File of that name exists. Overwrite it? (y/n)

If you answer *Y*, the original file is overwritten; if you answer *N*, the File Unload command is aborted.

Saving Files

The SmartWare Word Processor will not let you inadvertently exit the system without giving you a chance to write your modified document to disk. However, you may want to save the document occasionally as you work. Because most (if not all) of your document is kept in RAM as you work, you run the risk of losing the changes you have made if the power is interrupted. Use the File Save command to write the document to disk; after a short wait while the system does its work, you can continue working where you left off. The Quick key for the File Save command is Alt-S.

When you select the File Save command, even if the file already has a name, you are prompted to enter a file name. To save the document under the current name, press Enter. Type a new name if you want to save the document under a different name.

Documents are saved to the current subdirectory unless you provide a path to another subdirectory. If a file with the same name exists in the specified subdirectory, SmartWare displays the following message:

    File of that name exists. Overwrite it? (y/n)

If you answer *Y*, the file is overwritten; if you answer *N*, the File Unload command is aborted.

A feature that is new to SmartWare II is the capability for you to have the system save your file automatically on a schedule you define. In the Word Processor Preferences, you can enable the Document Auto-Save feature. Once enabled, your document will be saved to the disk on a schedule of every one to 60 minutes, as you indicate in the menu. The default extension is .DAS, but you can select a different file extension if you want.

Renaming Documents

You may want to create a new version of an existing document using portions of a previously written, similar file. One way to do this is to load the old document and then assign it a new name. The original document will not be changed when you save or unload the new version.

The File Newname command is used to give a new name to the document in the current window. (The name of the file on disk is left unchanged.) The Quick key for the File Newname command is Alt-N.

After you issue the File Newname command, you are prompted to enter the new document (or text file) name, which can contain as many as eight letters or numbers, and must conform to the DOS file-naming conventions.

Although the Save command also prompts you to enter a new name, giving your document the new name right after you load it is safer—you won't accidentally overwrite the original.

Appending Documents

You already know that the File Load command retrieves a document from the disk and displays it in the current window. Sometimes, however, you may want to append several documents to each other. This technique is useful for documents that contain standard boiler plate sections or paragraphs.

The File Import command is used to append a document onto the one in the current window. To use this command, position the cursor at the character before which you want to insert the new material, then issue the command. You are prompted with a pop-up menu of file names, just as you are with the File Load command. Select the appropriate file and then press Enter. The name of the document in the current window remains unchanged. Note that the new document is inserted before the current character, not just before the current line. Thus, you can insert text in the body of an existing paragraph.

If the document you want to retrieve is protected by a password, you are prompted to enter the password. If the document you want to append onto the current one is located in another subdirectory, you can enter the path and the file name in response to the prompt:

    Enter a filename:

If the file is in another subdirectory or you cannot remember its name, use the F4 or F5 keys to help you.

Protecting Your Files

Word Processor documents can be protected with the File Password command. If a document is protected, you are prompted for the password when you load or read it or when you print it directly from the disk. The options are Attach and Remove.

If you select Attach, you are prompted to enter a new password. Your password can be a maximum of 16 characters in length. Passwords are case sensitive; that is, PASS is different from pass. Be careful; the passwords do not display on your screen as you type them. To ensure you have not made a mistake, you are prompted to type the password again:

    Repeat password for verification:

Type the password again. If you make a mistake either time, the following error message is displayed:

    Verification did not match

You are then prompted to enter the new password again. You must press Enter after typing the password.

If your keyboard does not show the status of the Caps Lock key, and you want to avoid the potential problem of case sensitivity, you can use numbers for the password.

If you forget your password, there is no way to recover the file. The document must be written to disk for the password to be effective. If you quit the Word Processor without saving the document, it will not be protected. The File Password Attach command also can be used to change the password of a document.

To delete a password from a file, use the File Password Remove command. There are no additional prompts to this command. Remember, for the password removal to be permanent, you must save the document to disk.

Locking a Document

If you want to prevent the printing or saving of a document that has been changed, you can lock it with the Document Lock command. When you execute this command, you are prompted for a password:

    Enter a lock password:

Your password must be from one to 16 characters. Type the password in response to the prompt and press Enter. You are then asked to visually verify the password:

    Lock current document with the password "xxxx"? (y/n)

If you answer *Y*, the lock password is accepted. If you answer *N*, the command is aborted.

A lock on a document is not the same as a password. A document with a password cannot be loaded without supplying the password. But if the file is locked, you can load it, and even print it. However, if you change it, you cannot save or print it.

When you load a locked document, the following message is displayed:

    Note: Document is locked; changes cannot be saved or printed.

    Press any key to continue.

If you have changed a locked document and attempt to print it, you receive the following error message:

    A changed, locked document cannot be printed.

If you try to save a changed, locked document the following error message appears:

    A locked document cannot be written to disk.

If you need to print or save a locked document you have changed, you should change the name with the File Newname command.

Unlocking a Document

To unlock a document, execute the Document Unlock com. prompted to enter the lock password:

    Enter the lock password:

At the prompt, type the password and press Enter. You can save or print changed document.

Note that to retain the document lock status, you must save the document to disk after locking it. You will still be able to save changes to the document even after you lock it, but if you unload and load it again, you will not be able to save any changes.

Working with Multiple Columns

In the SmartWare II Word Processor, you can define multiple columns on a page. If you have a list of product features and benefits, for example, you can print them side by side. In this case, you define linked columns so that paragraphs stay together across the page. If you are writing an article that you want to print in multiple columns, you will want the columns unlinked.

To begin a multiple-column area in your document, make sure that at least one blank line exists at the beginning of the document, or you will receive the following error message:

    An MCA cannot be located at the top of a document

If the entire document will have multiple columns, insert a blank line, and then begin the definition of the columns.

To begin a multiple-column area (MCA), select the Document Columns command. You are prompted as follows:

    Define Quick-Define Remove Edit

You can define columns of either equal or varying widths.

Defining Equal-Width Columns

If your columns are to be of equal width, select the Quick-Define option. You are prompted:

    Linked Unlinked

If you want a paragraph in one column to be linked to a paragraph in the next column, select the Linked option. If you plan to enter product names and descriptions, for example, the columns should be linked. If, however, you are writing a company newsletter, you don't need linkage across columns. Regardless of the linkage selection, the next prompt is

```
Enter the number of columns:
```

When using the Quick-Define option, entering the number of columns automatically divides the line into columns of equal size between your existing margins. To complete the definition, you are prompted:

```
Confirm the column definition? (y/n)
```

Press *Y* if the column definition is satisfactory. The minimum space between each column is established in the Layout Document-Options menu for either the current document or for new documents.

Defining Variable-Width Columns

If you want the columns to be different sizes, select the Define option. After indicating either Linked or Unlinked columns, you are prompted:

```
Enter starting position of column 1 (inches), or use cursor keys
```

You can type the position (in inches and fractions) of the left position of the first column. An easier way is to move the cursor to the starting position. Press Enter to complete the left margin. You are then prompted for the ending position of the first column.

Continue with the definition of each column as needed; press F10 when you have defined the desired number of columns and their sizes. You are not prompted to confirm the definition, however.

Entering Multiple Column Text

You should enter text into each column individually. Press Ctrl-F4 to move the cursor to the next column; use Ctrl-F3 to switch to the previous column. (If you have only two columns, the keys work identically, because the cursor wraps around.)

If the columns are not linked, the amount of text in one column is independent of the amount in an adjacent column, just as in a magazine or newspaper. Figure 16.11 shows a document with two unlinked columns of equal size.

The Layout Rulers for the columns are maintained independently. In the example, text is justified in both columns. You must execute the Layout Ruler Edit Current command for each column. Text from one column will not flow automatically to the next column on the page; you must control text continuation manually.

Chapter 16: Using the Word Processor Module 327

```
┌─ Window 1 ─────────────────────────────────────────┐
│0....[....▶....1....▶....1....▶],..1.,[.4....1..,5....1....6..,]1....7....1..│
│    ¶                                                │
│    Who Should Use this Book¶    If you are just now pur-  │
│    ¶                            chasing SmartWare II, you │
│    If you are upgrading from    will need this book. "Us- │
│    Smart to SmartWare II, you   ing SmartWare II" provides│
│    will find this book to be    many    examples,   ex-   │
│    a valuable guide to the      planations, tips, and cau-│
│    differences and benefits     tionary notes that cannot │
│    of SmartWare II. Whenever    be covered in the software│
│    possible, I have pointed     manuals. In each section, │
│    out important dissimilari-   a single model is used to │
│    ties so that you can take    demonstrate the operation │
│    advantage of them ... or     of every command in con-  │
│    avoid some pitfalls. Be      structing and running an  │
│    sure to read Appendix D,     application.   In  the    │
│    covering conversion tech-    Spreadsheet section, for  │
│    niques.¶                     example, a financial model│
│    ¶                            for  a  sample company is │
└─────────────────────────────────────────────────────┘
F1 Help         F3 Find        F5 Replace      F7 Zoom         F9 Repeat
F2 Next menu    F4 Goto        F6 Font Select  F8 Execute      F10 Quit
Document: unlinked  Sc:1   Pg:1    Ln:2    Ps:5    FN:0    Font:0    Insert ON
Enter text into current document.
```

Fig. 16.11.

Unlinked columns.

If the columns are linked, the adjacent paragraphs across the page will always be connected to each other in the same entity. To define the end of one entity and begin the next, use Ctrl-E, the Quick key for the Document Columns Edit Add Entry command. Figure 16.12 shows a document with three linked columns of varying widths.

```
┌─ Window 1 ─────────────────────────────────────────┐
│0....[....],.[.1....2....1....3....1...]4....1[...,5....1....6....1....7.],.1..│
│    ¶                                                │
│    ¶      Feature¶              Benefit¶             │
│           ¶                                         │
│    1.¶    Large Capcity¶        The fact that the D-2 com-│
│                                 pressor has an extra large│
│                                 capacity means that you   │
│                                 will never be without the │
│                                 additional reserve power  │
│                                 needed in critical situa- │
│                                 tions.¶                   │
│    ¶      ¶                     ¶                         │
│    3.¶    Stainless Steel Tank¶ The stainless tank guaran-│
│                                 tees that any of the xr   │
│                                 chemicals may be used     │
│                                 without fear of corrosion │
│                                 or perforation of the tank│
│                                 wall.¶                    │
│    ¶      ¶                     ¶                         │
└─────────────────────────────────────────────────────┘
F1 Help         F3 Find        F5 Replace      F7 Zoom         F9 Repeat
F2 Next menu    F4 Goto        F6 Font Select  F8 Execute      F10 Quit
Document: benny    Sc:1   Pg:1    Ln:4    Ps:5    FN:0    Font:0    Insert ON
Enter text into current document.
```

Fig. 16.12.

Linked columns.

The longest paragraph fills the entity, and the shorter paragraphs extend to only the length of their contents. You can have multiple paragraphs in the entity of an individual column.

Terminating a Multiple Column Area

When you insert an MCA, a blank line is created automatically following the multiple-column area. To continue with your document in the single-column mode, move the cursor past the MCA and continue with text entry. Note, however, that once you have created a multiple-column area, you cannot divide it to insert a single-column area.

Editing a Multiple Column Area

When you select the Document Columns Edit command to change a multiple-column area, you are prompted:

    Add Boundaries Delete Move

Choose one of these options to make alterations to a multiple column area.

Adding a Column

If you want to add a column, select the Add option, and you are prompted:

    Column Entry

When you select Column, a screen similar to that shown in figure 16.13 is displayed.

Fig. 16.13.

Adding a column to an MCA.

```
┌─ Window 1 ──────────────────────────────────────────────────┐
│ 0....[....]..[..!....2....!....3....!...]4....![...5....!....6....!....7.]..!.. │
│    ¶                                                         │
│ 0....<---->..<-!----2----!----3----!--->4....!<---5----!----6----!----7->..!.. │
│    ¶             Feature¶                    Benefit¶        │
│    ¶                                                         │
│   1.¶           Large Capcity¶                               │
│                                              The fact that the D-2 com-│
│                                              pressor has an extra large│
│                                              capacity means that you   │
│                                              will never be without the │
│                                              additional reserve power  │
│                                              needed in critical situa- │
│                                              tions.¶                   │
│    ¶             ¶                           ¶                         │
│   3.¶           Stainless Steel Tank¶                                  │
│                                              The stainless tank guaran-│
│                                              tees that any of the xr   │
│                                              chemicals may be used     │
│                                              without fear of corrosion │
│                                              or perforation of the tank│
│                                              wall.¶                    │
└─────────────────────────────────────────────────────────────┘
 F1 Help  F5 Shift left  F6 Shift right  F7 Add column  F10 Finished   Pos: 0.5
 Document: benny    Sc:1   Pg:1   Ln:2   Ps:5   FM:0   Font:0    Insert ON
 Columns Dictionary Find Goto Math References Send Visible Lock Unlock
```

Before you add the new column, you may want to adjust the position of the current columns. Use the F5 key to shift the existing columns to the left, or F6 to shift them to the right. Each time you press one of these function keys, the current column and any columns to the right of the cursor are shifted by one position. If you want to leave the first column in place while sliding the other columns to the right, position the cursor in the second column and press the F6 key.

Press the F7 key. You are prompted for the starting position and ending position of the new column. This process is similar to defining columns originally. When you have completed the definition of the new column, press F10.

Adding an Entry

If your document has linked columns, you can use the Document Columns Edit Add Entry command (or the Ctrl-E Quick key) to create a new entity. Note that the concept of column entities applies to only linked columns. If you try to add an entry to the MCA of unlinked columns, you will get an error message.

Changing the Column Widths

To alter the left or right margins of the MCA columns, execute the Document Columns Edit command and select the Boundaries option. A screen similar to that in figure 16.14 is shown.

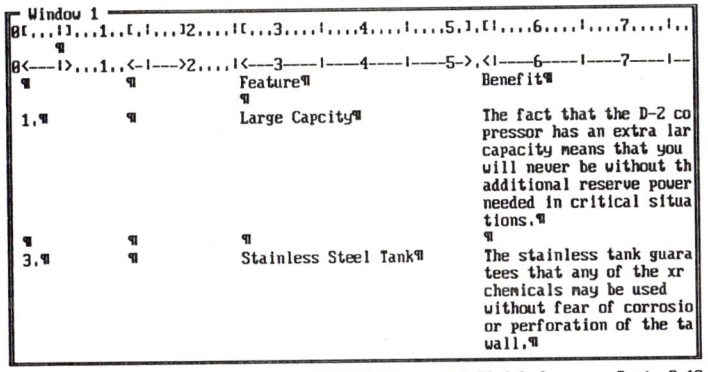

Fig. 16.14.

Editing MCA boundaries.

Just as when you add a column, use the F5 key to shift the existing columns to the left, or F6 to shift them to the right. Each time you press one of these function keys, the current column and any columns to the right of the cursor are shifted by one position. If you want to leave the first column in place but slide the other columns to the right, position the cursor in the second column and press the F6 key.

To adjust the margins of a column, move the cursor to the column to change. Use the F3 key to change the left margin of the column and the F4 key for the right margin. When you press one of these keys, the cursor is automatically moved to the margin, either left or right. Move the cursor in the direction to change the margin and press Enter to complete the adjustment. Press F10 to save your work and return to the menu.

Deleting an MCA Column

To delete one or more MCA columns, execute the Document Columns Edit command and select the Delete option. If the MCA is unlinked, the current column will be highlighted. You press F2 to anchor the range; then you can move the cursor to highlight additional columns to delete. Press F10 to complete the process.

If the MCA is linked, when you execute the command, you see a screen similar to that in figure 16.15.

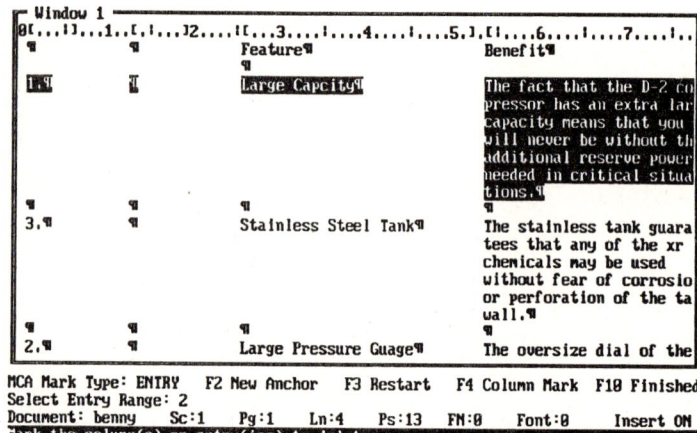

Fig. 16.15.

Deleting linked columns.

When linked columns exist, this same command can be used to delete either a column or an entity.

The default mode is Entry, as can be seen on the command line in figure 16.15. Press F4 to change to Column mode. At this point, the process of deleting one or more linked columns is the same as for unlinked columns. The current column will be highlighted. Press F2 to mark the beginning and move the cursor to highlight additional columns to delete, if necessary. Press the F10 key to complete the process.

Don't confuse the process of deleting one or more columns in an MCA to that of deleting an entire MCA. If you want to eliminate the whole multiple-column area, use the Document Columns Remove command.

Deleting Linked Column Entities

Figure 16.15 shows that the default mode for linked MCA's is Entry when you execute the Document Columns Edit command and select the Delete option. The current entity is highlighted across all the columns. If you want to delete just the current entity, press the F10. You can mark several entities to delete by pressing the F2 key to drop the anchor and then moving the cursor. Press F10 or Enter to complete the process and return to the Word Processor menu.

Moving Columns or Entities

You can move either columns or linked entities by executing the Document Columns Edit command and selecting the Move option. The marking modes are similar to those of the Delete option. If the columns are unlinked, the current column is highlighted; if the columns are linked, the current entity is highlighted. After you mark the columns or entities to move, press Enter. Position the cursor on the column or entity after which the marked areas are to be moved; press Enter to complete the command.

Linked columns also can be rearranged if you sort by the contents of one of the columns.

Deleting a Multiple-Column Area

If you want to erase the whole MCA, execute the Document Columns command and select the Remove option. Before the MCA is deleted, you are prompted:

    Entire column area will be removed. Continue? (y/n)

Press *Y* to erase the multiple column area.

Chapter Summary

Armed with the information in this chapter, you are ready to begin exploring the individual commands of the SmartWare Word Processor. Now that you know how to load, unload, save, rename, and protect your SmartWare Word Processor files, you are ready to learn how to make changes to the documents.

17

Manipulating Text

One of the most important functions of a word processor is the capability to move, copy, insert, and delete portions of a document.

This chapter covers the ways in which you perform these tasks using the SmartWare II Word Processor. It also covers ways to keep yourself out of trouble and how to perform cut and paste operations between documents. You learn how to create and remove windows, as well as how to display them for best usage. Finally, this chapter explains how to move around in your document and find and replace text.

Moving Text

The Edit Move command, as the name implies, is used to transfer portions of text to different places in documents. The Quick key for the Edit Move command is Alt-M.

When you select the Edit Move command, the software moves into the Block-marking mode (see fig. 17.1).

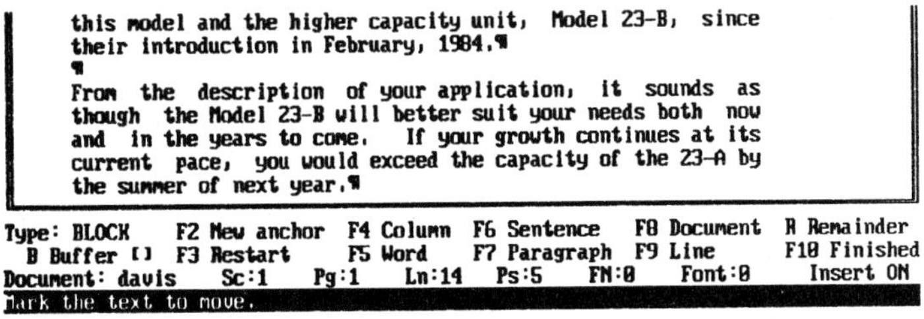

```
         this model and the higher capacity unit, Model 23-B, since
         their introduction in February, 1984.¶
         ¶
         From the description of your application, it sounds as
         though the Model 23-B will better suit your needs both now
         and in the years to come.  If your growth continues at its
         current pace, you would exceed the capacity of the 23-A by
         the summer of next year.¶

Type: BLOCK     F2 New anchor  F4 Column   F6 Sentence   F8 Document   R Remainder
 B Buffer [ ]   F3 Restart     F5 Word     F7 Paragraph  F9 Line       F10 Finished
Document: davis      Sc:1    Pg:1    Ln:14   Ps:5    FN:0    Font:0   Insert ON
Mark the text to move.
```

Fig. 17.1.

Edit Move Block-marking mode.

333

If you want to move a block of text, use the block marking method; if you want to move only certain columns, use column marking.

Using Block Marking

The Edit Move command prompts you to specify a range of text which defines the area over which the command applies.

When you are prompted to identify the range, you must specify a beginning point and an ending point. As a default, the beginning point is the cursor position at the time you execute the command. You can designate a new beginning point, or anchor, by moving the cursor and pressing F2.

You can designate the ending point by moving the cursor; the area affected by your choice is displayed in reverse video (see fig. 17.2 for an example).

Fig. 17.2.

Block marking.

```
┌─ Window 1 ─────────────────────────────────────────────┐
│0....[....▶....I....▶....I....▶....I....▶....I....6....]....7....I..│
│         10/13/86¶                                       │
│         ¶                                               │
│         Mr. Michael Davis¶                              │
│         100 Lewis Avenue¶                               │
│         Covington, LA 70433¶                            │
│         ¶                                               │
│         Dear Mr. Davis:¶                                │
│         ¶                                               │
│         Thank you for your letter of inquiry regarding our Model │
│         23-A Compressor.  We have had a great deal of success with │
│         this model and the higher capacity unit, Model 23-B, since │
│         their introduction in February, 1984.¶          │
│         ¶                                               │
│         From the description of your application, it sounds as │
│         though the Model 23-B will better suit your needs both now │
│         and in the years to come.  If your growth continues at its │
│         current pace, you would exceed the capacity of the 23-A by │
│         the summer of next year.¶                       │
└─────────────────────────────────────────────────────────┘
Type: BLOCK      F2 New anchor  F4 Column   F6 Sentence    F8 Document   R Remainder
      B Buffer [ ] F3 Restart   F5 Word     F7 Paragraph   F9 Line       F10 Finished
Document: davis     Sc:1   Pg:1   Ln:16   Ps:31   FN:0    Font:0       Insert ON
Mark the text to move.
```

To make it easier to mark a block, there are several keys you can use:

- F5 Word
- F6 Sentence
- F7 Paragraph
- F8 Entire Document
- F9 Line
- R   Remainder of document

Rather than moving the cursor through your document to mark text, you can select the Word option (F5), for example, to mark the current word, bounded by either blanks or punctuation, as the block. Note that the trailing blanks and punctuation are included in the word definition boundary. Or you can select F6 to mark the current sentence. To be recognized, a sentence must end with a period or a paragraph marker.

The Paragraph option (F7) indicates the current paragraph as the block. The Line option (F9) specifies the current line on which the cursor is positioned.

Choosing the Remainder option (R) indicates that the range extends from the current cursor position to the end of the document.

Repeated pressing of one of the selection function keys moves the highlight block to the next applicable area. For example, each time you press F6, the next sentence is highlighted. This method enables you to move through the document more quickly than by moving the cursor keys; the effect is not cumulative, however. If you press F6 twice, you will not have marked two sentences, just the second one. Once you have marked an area using a function key, you can mark an additional area by moving the cursor. Pressing F8 specifies the entire document as blocked, regardless of the current cursor position.

Once you have selected a block, you can change your mind by pressing F3 for Restart. Press F10 or Enter to complete your selection.

You immediately can move the text you have marked, or you can store the text in the buffer to be moved at a later time. When you press F10 or Enter to complete the block marking, the following prompt appears:

    Move cursor to desired location and press ENTER (B = Buffer [])

To move the text immediately, move the cursor to the character before which you want the text to appear and press Enter. The Edit Move command is completed, and you are returned to the menu. (If you invoked the Edit Move command with the Quick key Alt-M while in text entry, you are returned to text entry.)

If you want to store the text in the buffer, press B at the prompt. To retrieve the text from the buffer and insert it in your text, use the Edit Copy command, discussed later in this chapter.

Using Column Marking

Although block marking is linear in the document, you also can mark an area in the Column mode. In this mode, the exact columns you specify are marked, from the top left corner to the bottom right. Press F4 to switch from the Block mode to the Column mode. The Column mode options are shown in figure 17.3.

In Column-marking mode, there are no document-related choices, such as F5 to mark a word or F6 for a sentence, because these do not apply. To mark one or more columns, move the cursor to the lower right of the area you want to mark and press F10 or Enter. If the current cursor position is not the beginning of the area, move the cursor to the beginning and press F2.

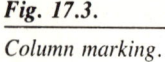

Fig. 17.3.

Column marking.

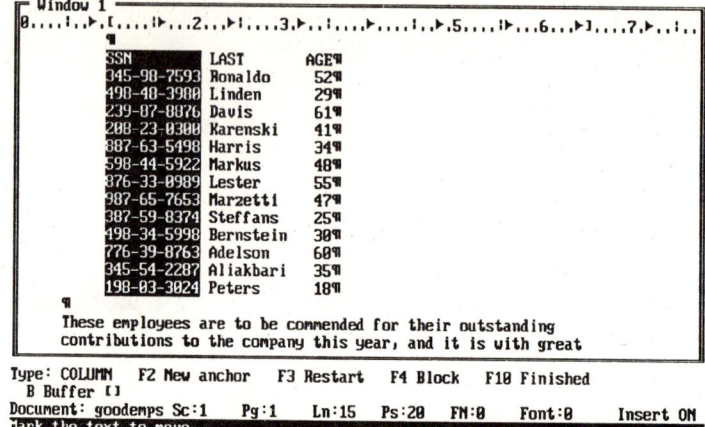

You can move the columns immediately or insert them in the buffer. When you press F10 or Enter, the following prompt appears:

    Move cursor to desired location and press ENTER (B = Buffer [])

To move the columns immediately, move the cursor to the character before which you want the columns to appear and press Enter. The Edit Move command is completed, and you are returned to the menu or the Text Entry mode.

If you want to store the columns in the buffer, press *B* at the prompt. To retrieve the columns from the buffer and insert them in your text, use the Edit Copy command.

Lines in document areas that are moved with the Column option of the Edit Move command end with hard carriage returns after they are moved. If you want to retain the soft returns and the reformatting capability of the Word Processor, use the Block option of the Edit Move command to move text. Even if you are moving a table of numbers, use the Block option if the table goes all the way across the document. However, if you want to rearrange columns of numbers in a table, for example, use the Column option. Note that marking text in the Column mode is independent of the ability to define multiple column areas (MCA) in the SmartWare II Word Processor. Column marking refers to screen columns rather than MCAs.

With the cut and paste capability of the Edit Move command and the buffer, text can be moved in the current document or even between documents. The buffer is unchanged until you store text in it again with the Edit Move or Copy commands. (You can deliberately purge the buffer by pressing Alt-Minus.) When you end your Word Processor session or invoke a different SmartWare module, the buffer is automatically purged. However, if you go to a different window or unload the document, the buffer remains unchanged.

To view the first 23 characters of the copy buffer, press F2 until the characters are displayed. The buffer contents are shown on the command line (see figure 17.4).

```
        776-39-8763 Adelson     60¶
        345-54-2287 Aliakbari   35¶
        198-03-3024 Peters      18¶
   ¶
   These employees are to be commended for their outstanding
   contributions to the company this year, and it is with great
Copied: [387-59-8374 Steffans  ]   Deleted: [345-98-7593 Ronaldo   ]
Document: goodemps Sc:1   Pg:1   Ln:2   Ps:10   FN:0   Font:0   Insert ON
Enter text into current document.
```

Fig. 17.4.

Copy buffer contents.

Note that the contents of the delete buffer also are shown on this line. Deleting text is covered later in this chapter.

Copying Text

The Edit Copy command is used to make a copy of a range of text; the Quick key is Alt-C. Like the Edit Move command, you can complete the execution of the command immediately, or you can insert the copied text into the copy buffer for later retrieval. Unlike the Edit Move command, however, the Edit Copy command does not remove the marked text from your document, but leaves it in place. When you complete the Edit Copy command, you will have an additional copy of the text. If you want to copy a block of text, use the block marking methods; if you want to copy only certain columns, use column marking.

Using Block Marking

The Edit Copy command prompts you to specify a range of text to which the command applies.

When you are prompted to identify a block, you must specify a beginning point and an ending point. As a default, the beginning point is the cursor position at the time you executed the command. Once you are in the Block-definition mode, however, you can designate a new beginning point, or anchor, by moving the cursor and pressing F2.

You can designate the ending point by moving the cursor; the area affected by your choice is displayed in reverse video (see fig. 17.2 for an example).

To make it easier to mark a block, there are several keys you can use:

- F5 Word
- F6 Sentence
- F7 Paragraph
- F8 Entire Document
- F9 Line
- R   Remainder of document

Rather than moving the cursor through your document to mark text, you can select the Word option (F5), for example, to mark the current word, bounded by either blanks or punctuation, as the block. Note that the trailing blanks and punctuation are included in the word definition boundary. Or you can select F6 to mark the current sentence. To be recognized, a sentence must end with a period or a paragraph marker.

The Paragraph option (F7) indicates the current paragraph as the block. The Line option (F9) specifies the current line on which the cursor is positioned.

Choosing the Remainder option (R) indicates that the range extends from the current cursor position to the end of the document.

Repeated pressing of one of the selection function keys moves the highlight block to the next applicable area. Each time you press F6, for example, the next sentence is highlighted. This method enables you to move through the document more quickly than with the cursor keys; the effect is not cumulative, however. If you press F6 twice, you will not have marked two sentences, just the second one. Once you have marked an area using a function key, you can mark an additional area by moving the cursor.

Pressing F8 specifies the entire document as being blocked, regardless of the current cursor position.

Once you have selected a block, you can change your mind by pressing F3 for Restart. Press F10 or Enter to complete your selection.

You can copy the text immediately, or you can store the text in the buffer to be inserted at a later time. When you press F10 or Enter to complete the block marking, the following prompt appears:

    Move cursor to desired location and press ENTER (B = Buffer [])

To copy the text immediately, move the cursor to the character before which you want the text to appear and press Enter. The Edit Copy command is completed, and you are returned to the menu or the Entry mode.

If you want to store the text in the buffer, press *B*. Later, you can retrieve the text from the buffer and insert it in your document by executing the Edit Copy command and pressing *B*. Move the cursor to the character before which you want the text to appear and press Enter. The Quick key for this process is Alt-I. When the information is inserted, the buffer is not emptied so the same data can be inserted elsewhere.

Using Column Marking

Whereas block marking is linear in the document, you also can mark an area in the Column mode. In this mode, the exact columns you specify are marked, from the top left corner to the bottom right. Press F4 to switch from the Block mode to the Column mode. (The Column mode options are shown in figure 17.3.)

In Column-marking mode, there are no document-related choices, such as F5 to mark a word or F6 for a sentence, because these do not apply. To mark one or more columns, move the cursor to the lower right of the area you want to mark and press F10 or Enter. If the current cursor position is not the beginning of the area, move the cursor to the beginning and press F2.

You have the same choices as in block marking: to copy the columns immediately or insert them in the buffer. When you press F10 or Enter, the following prompt appears:

    Move cursor to desired location and press ENTER (B = Buffer [])

To copy the columns immediately, move the cursor to the character before which you want the columns to appear and press Enter. The Edit Copy command is completed, and you are returned to the menu or the Entry mode.

If you want to store the columns in the buffer, press *B* at the prompt. Lines in document areas that are copied with the Column option of the Edit Copy command end with hard returns after they are copied. If you want to retain the soft returns and the reformatting capability of the Word Processor, use the Block option of the Edit Copy command to copy text. Even if you are copying a table of numbers, use the Block option if the table goes all the way across the document. However, if you want to make a copy of a column of numbers in a table, for example, use the Column option.

With the cut and paste capability of the Edit Copy command and the buffer, text can be copied in the current document or even between documents. The buffer is unchanged until you store text in it again with the Edit Move or Copy commands. (You can purge the buffer with the Alt-Minus key.) When you end your Word Processor session or invoke a different SmartWare module, the buffer is automatically purged. However, if you go to a different window or unload the document, the contents of the buffer remain unchanged.

Inserting Text

To extract the contents of the copy buffer, use the Edit Copy command after an Edit Move or Copy command. But rather than marking new text to copy, position the cursor at the character before which you want the text to appear from the buffer and press *B* and Enter. The Quick key for this operation is Alt-I.

Following the insertion of text from the copy buffer, the buffer is not cleared; you can perform successive insertions of the same text. The Edit Move and Copy commands use the same copy buffer.

Deleting Text

The Edit Delete command is used to delete portions of text from the current document. Like Edit Move and Copy, the delete command inserts the contents of the deleted range into a special buffer called the delete buffer. This is not the same buffer as is used by the Edit Move and Copy commands, however. The Quick key for the Edit Delete command is Alt-D. If you want to delete a block of text, use the block marking method; if you want to delete only certain columns, use column marking.

Using Block Marking

The Edit Delete command prompts you to specify a range of text. You are prompted to define the area over which the command applies.

To make it easier to mark a block, there are several keys you can use:

- F5 Word
- F6 Sentence
- F7 Paragraph
- F8 Entire Document
- F9 Line
- R Remainder of document

Rather than moving the cursor through your document to mark text, you can select the Word option (F5), for example, to mark the current word, bounded by either blanks or punctuation, as the block. Note that the trailing blanks and punctuation are included in the word definition boundary. Or you can select F6 to mark the current sentence. To be recognized, a sentence must end with a period or a paragraph marker.

The Paragraph option (F7) indicates the current paragraph as the block. The Line option (F9) specifies the current line on which the cursor is positioned.

Choosing the Remainder option (R) indicates that the range extends from the current cursor position to the end of the document.

Repeated pressing of one of the selection function keys moves the highlight block to the next applicable area. For example, each time you press F6, the next sentence is highlighted. This method enables you to move through the document more quickly than with moving the cursor keys; the effect is not cumulative, however. If you press F6 twice, you will not have marked two sentences, just the second one. Once you have marked an area using a function key, you can mark an additional area by moving the cursor.

Pressing F8 specifies the entire document as being blocked, regardless of the current cursor position.

Once you have selected a block, you can change your mind by pressing F3 for Restart. Press F10 or enter to complete your selection.

Once the Edit Delete command is completed, you are returned to the menu. (If you invoked the Edit Delete command with the Quick key Alt-D while in text entry, you are returned to text entry.)

If you change your mind, you can recover the text from the delete buffer by using the Edit Undelete command. You can undelete only the most recent deletion, however, because your next Edit Delete command overlays the contents of the buffer.

Using Column Marking

Whereas block marking is linear in the document, you also can mark an area in the Column mode. In this mode, the exact columns you specify are marked, from the top left corner to the bottom right. Press F4 to switch from the Block mode to the Column mode. (The Column mode options are shown in fig. 17.3.)

In Column-marking mode, there are no document related choices, such as F5 to mark a word or F6 for a sentence, because these do not apply. To mark one or more columns, move the cursor to the lower right of the area you want to mark and press F10 or Enter. If the current cursor position is not the beginning of the area, move the cursor to the beginning and press F2.

Recovering Deleted Text

If you unintentionally delete text, you can use the Edit Undelete command to retrieve the text from the delete buffer. The Quick key for the Edit Undelete command is Alt-Q. To use the Edit Undelete command, position the cursor at the character before which you want to restore the deleted text and issue the Edit Undelete command. Edit Undelete does not erase the contents of the delete buffer. The command can be used repeatedly to restore the contents of the delete buffer to several positions in the document, in much the same way you might use the Edit Copy command to repeatedly retrieve the contents of the copy buffer.

The delete buffer is overwritten the next time you perform an Edit Delete command. You can clear it by using the Alt-Minus Quick key. The Edit Move and Copy commands use the copy buffer, which is independent of the delete buffer.

Using Windows

Like the other SmartWare II application modules, the Word Processor makes use of windows. As many as 50 windows can be defined at any time in the Word Processor. These windows enable you to edit several documents simultaneously, quickly switching back and forth among them. (With SmartWare II, multiple documents can be loaded simultaneously even with only one window. Use the Document Goto Document command to access them.)

Windows also provide the capability to edit multiple documents and perform cut and paste operations between documents. Using the Edit Copy and Edit Move commands, you can insert text from one document into another. (The buffer holds the text to be moved as you go to another window.) A window is created with the Window Split command and closed with the Window Close command. Use the Window Zoom command to fill the entire screen with the current window.

Creating Windows

The Window Split command is used to create an additional window by dividing the current window into two smaller ones. (You also can create a window for the display of footnotes.) There are two Quick keys for the Window Split command, depending on the orientation you want:

Alt-V Vertical Split
Alt-H Horizontal Split

When you execute the Window Split command, you are prompted to select from the following options:

```
Footnote Horizontal Vertical
```

The Horizontal and the Footnote options divide the screen into an upper part and a lower part. You are prompted to enter a line number or to move the cursor to the position at which the split is to occur:

```
Enter the line number, or use cursor keys to select the location:
```

You must display at least one line in the current window; thus, you must press the down-arrow key at least three times when creating a horizontal document window if you are displaying the main ruler.

If you select Window Split Vertical, you are prompted to enter a column number or to move the cursor to the desired location and press Enter. Figure 17.5 shows the screen after it has been split vertically.

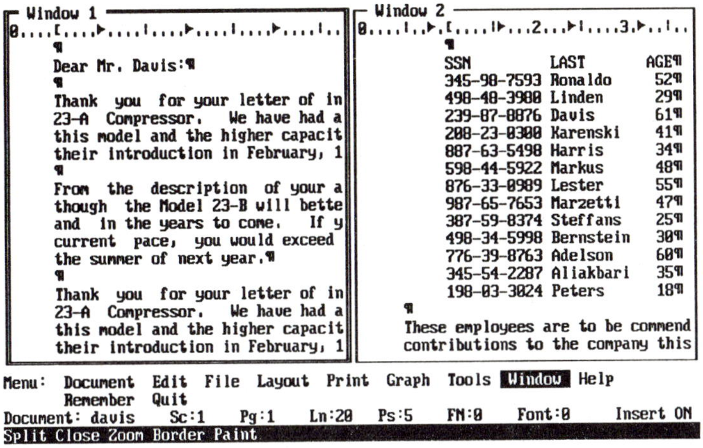

Chapter 17: Manipulating Text **343**

Fig. 17.5.

A vertically split screen.

In figure 17.5, notice that a new document has been loaded into Window 2. When you initially split the current window, the current document is displayed in the new window; this is a difference from previous versions of SmartWare. If you want a different document in the new window, go to the new window and load the document you want, or regain an existing document that is already loaded (using the Document Goto Document command).

If you have not turned off the border display, you must display at least 12 columns in the old window when you execute a vertical split. If your left margin is at column 1, you must press the right-arrow key 13 times. If you do not leave enough space, you receive the following error message:

    Marked area is too small to split.

Many settings are independent from window to window. For example, in each window, ruler lines are displayed according to your choice in the Word Processor Preferences. The Document Visible Rulers command toggles the display of the ruler line at the top of the current window. The command applies individually to each window; you can choose to display the ruler line in one window but not in another, even if the same document is displayed in each window.

When you split your screen into two or more document windows, the current window is surrounded by a double line border; all other windows are bordered by a single line. This helps you to identify your current window at a glance. The Window Split Footnote command creates a special break line across the screen with the word Footnote, followed by a series of single dashes. The footnote referenced in the body of text in the document window is displayed in this footnote area. As you move the cursor to another part of the document, the footnote area displays another footnote or, if there is no footnote, remains blank (see fig. 17.6). Footnotes are covered in depth in Chapter 18.

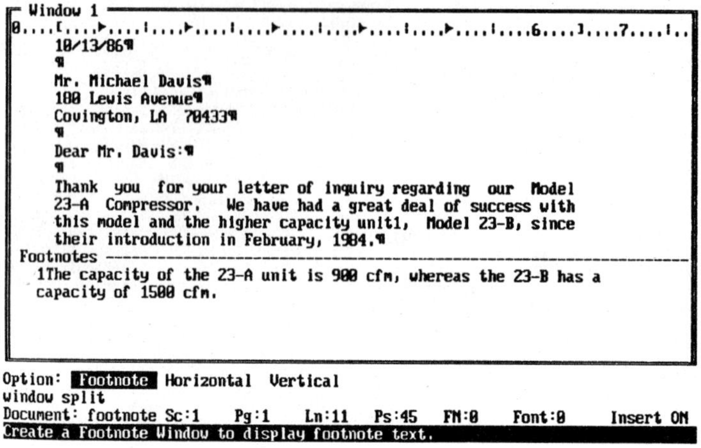

Fig. 17.6.

Displaying a footnote.

```
┌─ Window 1 ─────────────────────────────────────────────┐
│0....[....▶....|....▶....|....▶....|....▶....|....6....]....7....|..│
│  10/13/86¶                                                        │
│  ¶                                                                │
│  Mr. Michael Davis¶                                               │
│  100 Lewis Avenue¶                                                │
│  Covington, LA  70433¶                                            │
│  ¶                                                                │
│  Dear Mr. Davis:¶                                                 │
│  ¶                                                                │
│  Thank you for your letter of inquiry regarding our Model         │
│  23-A Compressor.  We have had a great deal of success with       │
│  this model and the higher capacity unit1, Model 23-B, since      │
│  their introduction in February, 1984.¶                           │
│ Footnotes ────────────────────────────────────────────            │
│  1The capacity of the 23-A unit is 900 cfm, whereas the 23-B has a│
│  capacity of 1500 cfm.                                            │
│                                                                    │
│                                                                    │
│                                                                    │
└────────────────────────────────────────────────────────┘
Option: Footnote  Horizontal  Vertical
window split
Document: footnote  Sc:1   Pg:1   Ln:11  Ps:45  FN:0   Font:0    Insert ON
Create a Footnote Window to display footnote text.
```

Note that you should not split a window for a footnote in the Zoom condition because the results are unreliable. If you attempt to split a window while in the Zoom state, you may receive the following error message:

    A zoomed window cannot be split.

After you unzoom your screen, you can split the window. After you have split your screen into multiple windows, if you want the current window to fill the entire monitor screen, use the Window Zoom command; the Quick key is F7. Window Zoom is a toggle command; when you first execute the command, the current window expands to fill the entire monitor screen. Execute the command again to restore the window to its original size and position.

Removing Windows

The Window Close Doc-Window command is used to remove a document window; the Quick key is Alt-W. When you execute this command, the current document window is closed, and the rest of the windows expand to fill the space available. If there is only one other window, it fills the entire screen.

When you close a window, the document in that window is not unloaded; it remains loaded in memory, but resides in the background. You can use the Document Goto Document command to regain and display the document in the current window. Note that you cannot close a window while in the Zoom condition. Window Zoom is a command to fill your monitor's screen with the current window. If you attempt to close a window while in the Zoom state, you receive the following error message:

    Cannot close a zoomed window.

After you unzoom your screen, you can close the window. To close a footnote window, execute the Window Close Footnote command. The current window will be expanded vertically to fill the available space.

Searching for Text

The Document Find command is used to locate certain words or groups of characters in your document. The Quick key is F3.

When you execute the Document Find command, you are prompted to enter the text to find. (The Document Find command in the Word Processor is similar to the Data Find command in the Database and the Sheet Find command in the Spreadsheet.) If you have not previously executed a Document Find command in the current Word Processor session, you are prompted as follows:

    Enter search text [""]:

If you have previously searched for a string of characters, the most recently issued string is displayed in the prompt. For example, if the last string you sought was 23-B, the following prompt would appear at the next Document Find command:

    Enter search text ["23-B"]:

Enter a new search string, or press Enter if you want to keep the displayed string. To clear the default text and enter a new search string, press F2, or begin typing a new search string. Your search string can have a maximum of 50 characters.

Three directional options are available with the Document Find command (see fig. 17.7). The Forward option causes the search to proceed forward from the current cursor position to the end of the file. If you do not specify, the default direction is forward. The Backward option causes the search to go backward to the beginning of the file. The Global option starts the search at the beginning of the file and proceeds forward, regardless of the current cursor position. This is equivalent to positioning the cursor at the beginning of the file and choosing the Forward option. If you want to start at the end of the document and go backward without having to reposition your cursor, use the Global Backward option.

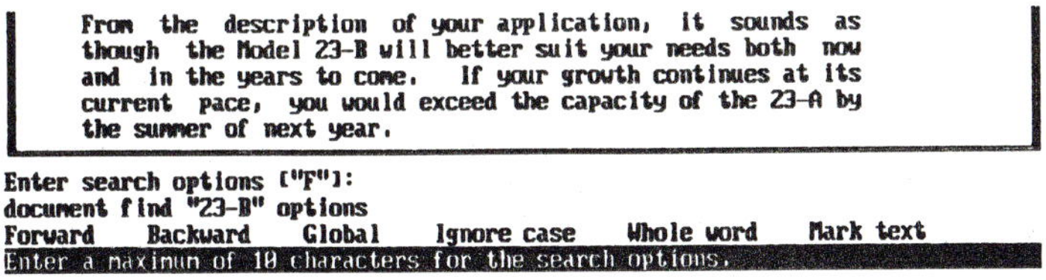

Fig. 17.7.

The Document Find options.

Two other options allow you to further customize your searches. When the Ignore case option is chosen, the case of the string is ignored during the search. The search string will be found regardless of whether the characters appear in the text in upper- or lowercase. The Whole word option searches for whole words only, which are strings bounded by blanks or punctuation marks.

A directional option and the Ignore case or Whole word option can be used at the same time. In addition, a number can be entered to indicate a nonsequential search pattern. For example, entering *4* causes the system to display the fourth occurrence of the string. You can enter Document Find options in either upper- or lowercase.

Both the search string and options are maintained in buffers to simplify repeated use of the Document Find command. The string in the buffer is displayed at the prompt to enter search text:

```
Enter search text ["23-B"]:
```

If the string is acceptable, press Enter to proceed. This same text buffer is used by the Replace command, which is discussed later in this chapter. You will see how useful these buffers are when you do repeated Document Find and Edit Replace commands.

A wild card character also can be used in the search criteria. The search string 198? locates both 1984 and 1985 in your document. You can use the question mark wild card anywhere in the search string.

SmartWare's Word Processor automatically inserts double quotation marks (") around the search string; you should not type them. If you need to search for a string that has a leading or trailing space, enter the space like any other character; the system leaves an appropriate space in the search string. Be careful, however, not to interpret the spacing caused by justification as a true space. The screen may look as though there is more than one space between two words because of the justification, but actually there may be only one space.

To repeat the Document Find command, press the F9 key. (The F9 key repeats the most recent command). If you have performed another intervening command, however, you can use the Alt-R Quick key to repeat the most recent Document Find or Edit Replace command.

An additional option, new with SmartWare II, is Mark text. If you want your Document Find command to search in only a specified area of your document, you can mark a portion of the text in which to search. As with other commands that require you to identify a block, there is a beginning point and an ending point. As a default, the beginning point is the cursor position at the time you executed the command. Once you are in the Block-definition mode, however, you can designate a new beginning point, or anchor, by moving the cursor and pressing F2. If you specify an option combination of Global Mark text, however, the cursor does not return to the beginning of the document prior to entering the Block-definition mode. You can designate the ending point by moving the cursor; the area affected by your choice is displayed in reverse video.

To make it easier to mark a block, there are several keys you can use:

- F5 Word
- F6 Sentence
- F7 Paragraph
- F8 Entire Document
- F9 Line
- R   Remainder of document

Rather than moving the cursor through your document to mark text, you can select the Word option (F5), for example, to mark the current word, bounded by either blanks or punctuation, as the block. Note that the trailing blanks and punctuation are included in the word definition boundary. Or you can select F6 to mark the current sentence. To be recognized, a sentence must end with a period or a paragraph marker.

The Paragraph option (F7) indicates the current paragraph as the block. The Line option (F9) specifies the current line on which the cursor is positioned.

Choosing the Remainder option (R) indicates that the range extends from the current cursor position to the end of the document.

Repeated pressing of one of the selection function keys moves the highlight block to the next applicable area. For example, each time you press F6, the next sentence is highlighted. This method enables you to move through the document more quickly than with the cursor keys; the effect is not cumulative, however. If you press F6 twice, you will not have marked two sentences, just the second one. Once you have marked an area using a function key, you can mark an additional area by moving the cursor.

Pressing F8 specifies the entire document as being marked, regardless of the current cursor position.

If you want to search in certain columns, you can change to the Column-marking mode by pressing F4. Move the cursor to the upper left corner of the search area and press F2 to mark the beginning of the area.

Once you have selected an area, you can change your mind by pressing F3 for Restart. Press F10 or Enter to complete your selection of the area.

If you have marked an area of text and then use Alt-R to execute the previous Document Find command, you are prompted to mark the text area again; the same text area is not maintained automatically.

Replacing Text

The Edit Replace command searches the document for a string of characters and then replaces it with another string. The Quick key for the Edit Replace command is F5.

Search string entry when replacing text is similar to the Document Find command; the two commands even store the string in the same buffer. The text remaining in the buffer from the last Document Find or Edit Replace command is used as a default search string. The first prompt in the Edit Replace command asks for the search text:

    Enter search text [""]:

A wild card character also can be used in the search criteria. The search string 198? locates both 1984 and 1985 in your document. You can use the question mark wild card anywhere in the search string.

If you have executed the Document Find or Edit Replace commands previously in the same Word Processor session, the buffer text is displayed at the prompt:

    Enter search text ["23-B"]:

If the string is acceptable, press Enter to proceed. To clear the default text and enter a new search string, press F2, or simply begin typing a new search string. Your search string can have a maximum of 50 characters.

The second prompt asks for the replacement text:

    Enter replacement text [""]:

If you have executed the Edit Replace command previously in the same Word Processor session, the buffer text is displayed at the prompt:

    Enter replacement text ["23-C"]:

Again, if the string is acceptable, press Enter to proceed. To clear the default text and enter a new replacement string, press F2, or simply begin typing a new string. Your replacement string can have a maximum of 50 characters.

Most of the Edit Replace options are similar to those of the Document Find command (see fig. 17.8).

Fig. 17.8.

The Document Replace options.

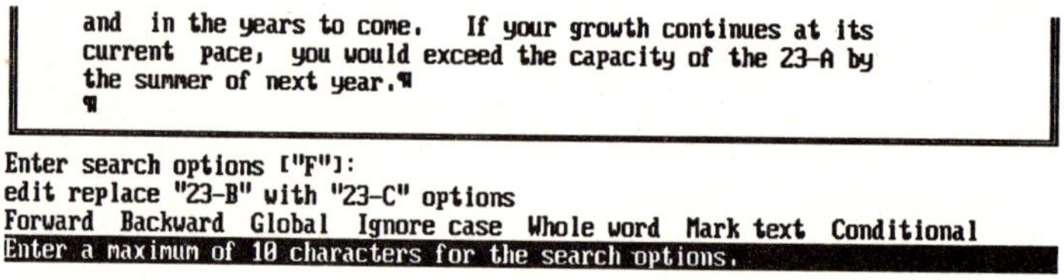

```
   and in the years to come.  If your growth continues at its
   current pace, you would exceed the capacity of the 23-A by
   the summer of next year.¶
   ¶

Enter search options ["F"]:
   edit replace "23-B" with "23-C" options
   Forward  Backward  Global  Ignore case  Whole word  Mark text  Conditional
Enter a maximum of 10 characters for the search options.
```

A new option has been added to the Edit Replace command, however: The Conditional option causes the system to pause and ask whether you want to perform the replacement each time the search string is found. Respond by pressing Enter to perform the replacement; or press the space bar to leave the text unchanged. You can press F10 to terminate the Edit Replace command. If you do not specify conditional replacement, a replacement proceeds without prompting or notification.

Normally, the Edit Replace command ends after all the occurrences of the search string are found and replaced. If you want a specified number of replacements to be made, enter that number as part of the option string. For example, if you want to be prompted for 30 possible replacements, beginning at the current cursor position, the option set is fc30. The 30 does not necessarily mean that 30 replacements will be made, just that you will be prompted 30 times.

To execute the Edit Replace command again, press The Alt-R key. Remember, however, if you had specified Global to begin automatically at the top of the document in your first replacement, successive executions with Alt-R also begin at the top.

Two special search strings, introduced with SmartWare II, can be used with either the Edit Replace or Document Find commands:

%P Paragraph mark
%T Tab mark

If you have a text file, for example, with hard carriage returns at the end of each line, and you would like to transform it into a document file, using only the File File-Type command will not completely change a text file into a document file. Each line will still end with a paragraph mark, indicating a hard return.

To delete the paragraph marks quickly, use the Edit Replace command to replace the %P (paragraph marks) with a single space for every line except the last one in each paragraph. By specifying %T as the search string, for instance, you can substitute spaces for tab characters.

Moving in the Document

One way to move the cursor in your document is by using the arrow keys. The arrow keys move the cursor one position at a time. The PgUp and PgDn keys change the screen display one screen at a time. This method may be satisfactory if the document is short, but it is tedious if you have a long document. The Document Goto command quickly moves the cursor to a location in the current document or to a document in another window. The locations can be specified by section, page number, line number, column positions, or marker. (Markers are discussed later in this chapter.) Windows are referred to by window numbers. The locations can be specified individually or in combination with other window locations.

The Quick key for the Document Goto command is F4. If you are in Text Entry mode and use the Quick key, you will still be in Text Entry mode at the completion of the command. When you execute the Document Goto command, the following prompt is displayed:

    Option: Window Document Marker Location

To go to a specific window, press *W*, or move the highlight block and press Enter.

Changing Windows

If you have split your screen into multiple windows (see the Window Split command), you can use the Window option to change from one window to another. When you select the Window option, you are prompted as follows:

    Enter a window number:

When you type the number of the window you want and press Enter, the selected window becomes the current window. If you are in the Zoom mode, the previous window drops into the background, and the selected window fills your screen. If your screen is not zoomed, the newly selected window is now bordered by a double solid line, indicating that it has become the current window. All other windows are bordered by a single solid line. (Now with SmartWare II, you can go from one window to the next while you are in the Zoom mode.)

To advance sequentially from window to window, use the Quick key F8; the F7 key takes you to the previous window. If you have only two windows open, you can use either key to switch windows, because they wrap around.

Changing Documents

Even with only one window, you can still have multiple documents open simultaneously. Your current document is in the foreground, and all other loaded documents are active in the background. To bring forth one of the background documents, use the Document Goto Document command.

When you execute the command, a pop-up window shows the other active documents, and you are prompted to:

    Enter a document name:

You can type the name of the document you want, or select it by using a cursor movement key and pressing Enter. Refer to figure 17.9.

Note that a document named (none) also is shown in the pop-up window of document names. If you want to start a new document, make this selection.

Rather than using the Document Goto Document command, you can use the Quick key Ctrl-D to switch easily from document to document. Each active document, in turn, is made current. When you go from document to document, the cursor positions are maintained in each.

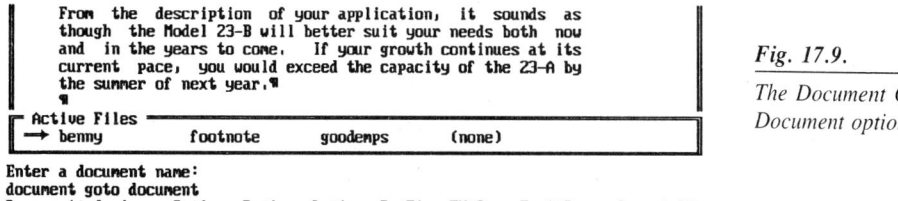

Fig. 17.9.

The Document Goto Document option.

If you have only two documents current, Ctrl-D switches between them. If you want to start a new document, however, you must use the full Document Goto Document command and choose the (none) selection.

In previous versions of SmartWare, when a window containing a document was split, you were asked whether the new window should be left blank. This choice is no longer available, so you must use the Document Goto Document command and select None to get a blank window.

Moving to a Marker

The third option of the Document Goto command is used to reposition the cursor on a marker you have set in your document. (The Document References Marker command is discussed later in this chapter.) If you have a document with multiple tables, for instance, you might mark the tables as TB1, TB2, and so on, to access them quickly.

When you execute the Document Goto Marker command, a pop-up window displays the names of the document markers. You are prompted to:

    Enter a marker name:

Select the marker you want, or type the name and press Enter. The cursor is moved immediately to the marker location.

Moving to a Location

You also can use the Document Goto command to go to a specific location in your document, even though it is not noted by a marker. When you select the Location option of the command, you are prompted for a location:

    Enter a new cursor location:

In response to the prompt, you can enter location identifiers for the following:

Document
Section
Page
Line
Column
Marker

To go to a different document, it is probably easiest to use the Document Goto Document command, but the Location option can be used to specify a different document and a different location at the same time.

To specify a section, type *S* followed by the number of the section. For example, type *S2* in response to the prompt to go to section 2 of the current document. The cursor is moved to the beginning of the section. If there is no section to match the number you type, the cursor is positioned on the last line of the document. To go to a different page in the document or section, type *P* and the page number. For example, type *P3* to go to page 3. If you type a page number higher than the number of pages in your document, the cursor is positioned on the last page of the document.

To go to a new line, type *L* followed by the line number you want to access. For example, *L20* moves the cursor to line 20 of the current page. If the line number you type exceeds the last line on the current page, the cursor is positioned on the last line.

To go to a new character position on the current line, type *C* followed by the number of the character position. For example, you would type *C15* to go to position 15.

Using Location Specifications in Combination

You can specify combinations of locations when you execute the Document Goto Location command. For example, if you want to go to section 2, page 15, line 20, character position 10, you should type the following in response to the location prompt:

　　s2p15l20c10

Note that the prefix letters can be in upper- or lowercase. You can use either the letter prefixes or periods after the leading location indicator. The following response is equivalent to the previous:

　　s2.15.20.10

If you omit leading location specifications, the current values are assumed as a default. If you want to stay in the same section, you do not have to specify the section; you can begin with the specification for the page. Similarly, if the section and page are to remain the same, you can begin with the specification for the line.

If the beginning location for a specification is acceptable, you can omit trailing specifications. For example, if you want to go to line 1, position 1 of a particular section and page, you do not have to enter the line and column designations. Thus, if you respond with *s3.15*, the cursor is positioned on line 1 of page 15 of section 3. When using the letter prefixes, any location specifications must be entered in diminishing order, from section to page to line to character position. If the specifications are out of order, you receive the following error message:

    Variable not found

If you use the period (.) as the separator character, you must be careful to enter the specifications in order. If they are out of order, you may not get an error message, but the location will not be correct. The first specification must always be designated with the letter, however. If you have multiple documents loaded, you can specify the document name along with the location identifier string, as shown in the following example:

    Davis.s2p10l3

Note that the period is used to separate the name of the document from the location specification. Rather than using a section, page, line, and character location specification, you also can use a marker as the target, in combination with the document name:

    Davis.TB2

In this example, TB2 is the name of a marker in the Davis document. If you enter a document and a location specification as the location, the document is made current, and the cursor is moved to the location you have entered. This method combines the Document Goto Document and Document Goto Location commands.

Using Markers

If you have a large document, it may be convenient for you to set markers in various significant locations so that you can quickly go to those locations using the Document Goto Marker Command.

Setting a Marker

To set a marker, position your cursor and execute the Document References Marker Add command. You are prompted to:

    Enter a marker name:

Type the name of a marker you would like to use and press Enter. Marker names must begin with a letter, and can be a maximum of eight characters in length; they are not case sensitive. If you are going to use numbers in the names of the markers, do not use an S, P, L, or C, as the initial letter, because these letters can be interpreted as section, page, line, or character position specifications.

If you try to add a marker that already exists, you receive the following error message:

   The marker name already exists.

Markers do not have to be set at the beginning of a line; you can mark any location on the line.

Finding a Marker

You can find a marker by using the Document References Marker View command. This command causes the system to proceed through the document, stopping at each marker. The name of the marker is displayed on the command line. Press Enter to proceed to the next marker, or press Esc to end the command and leave the cursor positioned at the current marker. When you execute this command, the marker search begins at the beginning of the document, regardless of the current cursor position. If no markers are selected, the cursor is positioned on the final marker.

Removing a Marker

To delete a marker from the text, issue the Document References Marker Remove command. A pop-up window displays the names of all markers. Select the marker you want to remove by using the cursor movement keys or by typing the name of the marker, and press Enter. You do not have to position your cursor on the marker to remove it.

If you delete marked text, the marker also is deleted. (The marker is affixed to the first character of the marked text.) If you use the Edit Undelete command to restore text, the marker also is restored.

Similarly, moving text that contains a marker moves the marker. If you copy marked text, the marker remains associated with the original copy.

Chapter Summary

The larger your document, the more important it is to be able to move quickly from place to place and to find your way around the text. The commands discussed in this chapter can be used to move or copy text, delete material (or restore it), insert new text, locate text in your document, view different portions, and to make changes to selected words or phrases.

18

Formatting Text

Once you have created a document and have moved, copied, inserted, and deleted paragraphs and lines, you must pay attention to the format and fonts in your document. Formatting can affect margin settings, line spacing, and page breaks. The SmartWare II Word Processor even enables you to sort lines of text according to the contents of specified columns. The type styles in SmartWare II include the following:

standard	greek
monospaced	dingbat1
sans serif	dingbat2
script	symbol
serif	b-graphic
small-caps	l-graphic
gothic	internal line printer

Examples of the special fonts are shown in Appendix B of the *Installation and Hardware Guide* that came with your SmartWare II manuals. The actual fonts that you can print depend on your printer's capabilities. Most of the fonts can be printed in underscore, boldface, italics, superscript, or subscript modes.

The SmartWare Word Processor has several complementary sets of commands you can use to change formats and fonts. If you want to underscore a certain passage of text, for example, you can select a command that causes new text to be underscored as it is entered. Or, you can enter your text normally, and then return to it later and specify that you want to underscore it.

The actual changes made to a document are stored when it is saved to disk. Therefore, if you change the spacing of your document to double-spaced before you save it, it will still be double-spaced when you load it the next day. However, if you change your mind and return to single-spaced without saving the double-spaced version, the double-spaced changes are not saved.

Some settings are not saved with the document, however. The command to underscore text, for example, applies to the session, not to the document. Any text entered while this command is active is saved as underscored text, but the underscore entry selection will not be in effect when you call up the document the next day.

Many settings that affect the session apply to all documents you edit or create during that session. For example, if you select tab markings to be visible, they are visible in all windows, regardless of the document.

Using Rulers

To understand text formatting, it is important to grasp the concept of rulers in the SmartWare II Word Processor. A ruler is a configuration setting that governs the appearance and, in some cases, the way in which you can work with a document or the paragraphs in that document. The configuration items specified in a ruler include the following:

Margins—Left and Right
Justification—Left, Right, or Centered
Line spacing—One to nine, with half-spacing available
Indent—Positive: Indent, Negative: Outdent
Tabs—Normal, Decimal
Characters Per Inch—Four to 24

If you are upgrading from a previous version of Smart, you know that most of these configuration items were previously tied to individual paragraphs, and that you could change them through the use of the Reformat command. Now, in SmartWare II, the configurations are maintained in a ruler, which can be changed and even displayed separately by paragraph.

The default ruler, which governs a new document and all the text until another ruler is encountered, is established in the Word Processor Preferences.

When you first begin to type a document, ask yourself if the default ruler reflects the format you want to have at the beginning of your document. If it does, you can type your document. If not, then you should edit the current ruler.

There is a current ruler for each portion of your document. If you want to set the margins independently for a particular paragraph, the ruler for that paragraph will have a configuration different from the default ruler as well as from the ruler for the preceding paragraph. Thus, when the cursor is in the new paragraph, the current ruler is the one which specifies the distinct margin settings.

The format of any portion of your document is governed by the previous ruler. The ruler might be immediately before the current paragraph, or may have been inserted several pages before.

For ease of alternating among formats in your document, you can assign a name to a ruler. Thus, each time you alternate between settings, all you have to do is insert the appropriate ruler by name. The command to insert a ruler actually makes a copy of it; once it is copied, the new version does not retain the name, or any automatic relation to the original. Thus, you can change a named ruler without affecting any of the rulers copied from it.

There are several choices in the display of rulers; you can make them visible or not, depending on your choice. The Document Visible Rulers command has two options:

```
Main Embedded
```

Each option is a toggle; execute the command once, and the display is enabled. Execute it again, and it is disabled. The Main ruler, if enabled, shows at the top line of the window. It represents the ruler current at cursor position. As you move throughout the document, the Main ruler display changes as different rulers are encountered.

If you choose to display Embedded rulers, each ruler is shown in the body of the text at the point where it takes effect. Thus, you can clearly see the rulers governing the formatting of each portion of your document. When displaying both Main and Embedded rulers, the Main ruler is exactly the same as the Embedded ruler for the current paragraph; other Embedded rulers on your screen may be different, however.

Editing the Current Ruler

The Layout Ruler Edit command has three options:

```
Current Default Named
```

To edit the current ruler, type *C*, or move the highlight block and press Enter. When you first begin a document, the current ruler is identical to the default ruler. By editing the current ruler, you are creating a variation of it which will take effect at the beginning of your document. The default ruler will remain unaffected; you can easily change back to the default by inserting it in later portions of your document.

When you edit the current ruler, it is displayed on the second line of your window, and the Ruler Edit mode is invoked. (The top line on the screen represents the default ruler.) Refer to figure 18.1. Several settings can be changed in this mode.

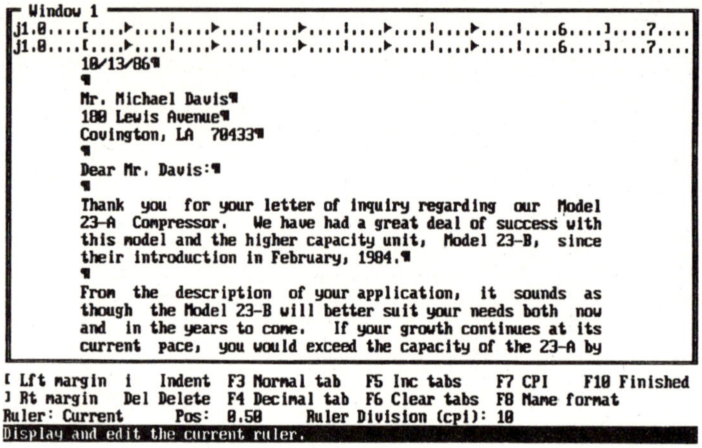

Fig. 18.1.

Editing the current ruler.

```
┌─Window 1─────────────────────────────────────────────────┐
│ ]1.0....[....▶....|....▶....|....▶....|....▶....|....6....]....7....│
│ ]1.0....[....▶....|....▶....|....▶....|....▶....|....6....]....7....│
│   10/13/86¶                                              │
│   ¶                                                       │
│   Mr. Michael Davis¶                                      │
│   100 Lewis Avenue¶                                       │
│   Covington, LA  70433¶                                   │
│   ¶                                                       │
│   Dear Mr. Davis:¶                                        │
│   ¶                                                       │
│   Thank you for your letter of inquiry regarding our Model│
│   23-A Compressor.  We have had a great deal of success with│
│   this model and the higher capacity unit, Model 23-B, since│
│   their introduction in February, 1984.¶                  │
│   ¶                                                       │
│   From the description of your application, it sounds as │
│   though the Model 23-B will better suit your needs both now│
│   and in the years to come.  If your growth continues at its│
│   current pace, you would exceed the capacity of the 23-A by│
│                                                           │
│ [ Lft margin   i    Indent      F3 Normal tab   F5 Inc tabs      F7 CPI       F10 Finished│
│ ] Rt margin   Del Delete      F4 Decimal tab   F6 Clear tabs    F8 Name format│
│ Ruler: Current        Pos:   0.50    Ruler Division (cpi): 10    │
│ Display and edit the current ruler.                       │
└──────────────────────────────────────────────────────────┘
```

Changing Margins

The margins in a ruler are designated by the left square bracket ([) for the left margin, and the right square bracket (]) for the right margin. To change the margin position, move the cursor to the new position and press the appropriate square bracket key. The displayed position of the new margin setting moves immediately to the new location.

Changing Characters Per Inch

You can vary the characters per inch (CPI) selection on the ruler by pressing F7; this setting is also called the ruler division. Ruler settings are always measured in inches, so if you change the CPI selection, you do not have to change the other settings. The current cursor position, in inches, is shown on the status line. For example, if your CPI is 10 characters per inch and you set your margin position at 1.00 inch, the margin will still be at 1.00 even if you change the CPI to 12.

Your CPI can be as low as 4 and as high as 24. When you press F7, you are prompted to enter a CPI value:

        Enter rule division (characters per inch):

The current ruler division is shown at the end of the prompt. Type a number from 4 to 24 and press Enter. The display of the ruler line at the top of your screen changes to reflect the new CPI selection.

Changing Indentation

The letter i is used to position the indent on the ruler line; you must use a lowercase i, not the uppercase I. If you want an indent of one-half inch from your left margin, and if your margin is at position 1.00, move the cursor to position 1.50 and type *i*. A lowercase i is displayed at that position on the ruler line; if the indent mark coincides with a tab stop, an uppercase I is displayed.

To move the indent, reposition the cursor and type *i* again. To delete an indent, you can either position the cursor on the left margin mark ([) and type *i*, or use the Del key to remove the existing indent marker.

If you would like to have an outdent, which extends to the left of the margin, the procedure is the same. Position the cursor at the desired position to the left of the margin and type *i*.

Changing Normal Tabs

To set an individual normal tab, position the cursor where you would like the tab setting and press F3. If the indent setting and a tab setting coincide, an uppercase I is shown on the ruler line.

To delete an individual tab setting, position the cursor on the tab location and press the Del key. If the indent is also located at the same position as the tab, the first time you press the Del key, you delete the indent setting. Press the Del key again to delete the tab.

After you have set tabs, pressing the Tab key on your keyboard when entering text into your document advances the cursor to the next tab setting.

Tabs are displayed on the screen by a triangle symbol. You can hide the symbols by using the Document Visible command. (For more on the Document Visible command, see the "Displaying and Hiding Special Characters" section in this chapter.) A tab character is just like any other single character; it does not represent a series of blank characters. Consequently a tab symbol can be deleted from your text, causing the text to the right of the tab character to move left.

Changing Decimal Tabs

To set an individual decimal tab, position the cursor where you would like the tab setting and press F4. If the indent setting and a tab setting coincide, an uppercase I is shown on the ruler line.

If you want a normal tab and a decimal tab at the same location, just set the decimal tab. A decimal tab stop can function as a normal tab, but the reverse is not true.

To delete a tab setting, position the cursor on the tab location and press the Del key. If an indent is also located at the same position as the tab, the first time you press the Del key, you delete the indent setting. Press the Del key again to delete the tab.

Decimal tabs are used to align columns of numbers on their decimal points. When you enter text, the Tab key is used to locate the cursor at either the decimal tab or the normal tab location. When you type a number from a decimal tab location, the digits to the left of the decimal are pushed to the left as you type them. After you type a period and begin typing the decimal portion of the number, the digits appear to the right of the decimal point. (In previous versions of Smart, you had to press Ctrl-D to tab to a decimal tab stop.)

Changing Incremental Tabs

To set tabs at regular increments between your margins, use the F5 key. You are prompted to select a tab type:

    Select tab type: Normal Decimal

Type either *N* for normal or *D* for decimal. The next prompt asks for an increment:

    Enter tab increment (inches):

Enter a value, in inches, for tab increments. For example, if you want tab stops every one-half inch, type *.5* and press Enter.

Existing tab stops are not be erased, but normal tabs overlay decimal tabs, and decimal tabs overlay normal tabs.

Clearing Tabs

Press F6 to clear all tab stops on the ruler line. Both normal and decimal tabs are cleared.

Changing Justification

Four types of text justification are available in the Word Processor:

Left-Justified	Text is aligned with the left margin, and the right margin is ragged.
Justified	The text material is aligned at both the left and right margins. Space is inserted automatically between words to accomplish the justification. These are only temporary spaces, however, not true spaces equivalent to those caused by pressing the space bar. Justified text was called normal in previous versions of Smart.

Right-Justified   Text is aligned with the right margin; the left margin is ragged.

Centered   Text is centered between the left and right margins.

To specify the justification of the ruler line, change the first character of the ruler line to one of the following:

L Left Justified
R Right Justified
J Justified
C Centered

You can enter the justification abbreviation in either upper- or lowercase.

Changing Spacing

Line spacing can vary from .5 to 9.5. If you want text on every line (single-spaced), type *1* in the second position of the ruler line; if you want double-spacing, type *2*. To accomplish half spacing, type a plus sign, +, in the third position. Thus, if you type *1+* in the second and third positions, your printer will advance 1.5 lines to begin printing each next line of text. Even if half spacing is used, the screen only displays the line count in whole numbers.

A zero is permissible in the second position only if there is a + in the third position. This indicates half-spacing to the next line of text. You must type the plus sign before typing the zero, however.

To change from one spacing to another, type over the number in the second position. If you want to remove half-spacing in the third position, use the Del key.

Naming the Ruler Format

You can assign a name to the ruler format so that you can easily copy it at a later time with the Layout Ruler Insert command. Before you complete the ruler editing process, press F8 to assign a name. You see the following prompt:

    Enter format name:

Type a name of up to eight characters and press Enter. You can include both letters and numbers in the format name; names are not case sensitive.

Once you have named a format, you can copy it (Layout Ruler Insert Named), delete it (Layout Ruler Delete Named), or edit it (Layout Ruler Edit Named). However, keep in mind that a copied ruler is just like text you have copied; changes you make to the original do not affect any copies. Once a format is copied, it does not retain the identity of the original, and thus does not automatically change if the original is changed.

Saving the Ruler

To save your ruler changes and return to the menu, press F10. If you have assigned a name to the ruler, any changes you made after the assignment of the name also is saved under the ruler name.

Editing the Default Ruler

The default ruler is in effect if you do not create another ruler with the Layout Ruler Edit command. The default ruler is established in the Word Processor Tools Preferences. If you decide that you do not want the default conditions to apply in your document, you can edit the ruler by using the Layout Ruler Edit Default command.

The default ruler is similar to a named ruler in that you can copy and edit it. Once copied with the Layout Ruler Insert Default command, the newly copied ruler has no special properties by virtue of having originated from the default ruler. Editing the default ruler, at that time, does not automatically change any rulers generated from it.

If your reason for editing the default is to make changes to it, press F10 when you have completed any modifications. The changes are saved under the name of the ruler you are editing. However, you also can edit the default ruler to create a named ruler similar to the default.

You should design your default ruler to meet your needs for most of your documents. If you find that you are constantly having to edit the current ruler when you begin a document, perhaps you should consider changing the Word Processor Preferences to redesign the default ruler.

To create a similar named ruler, edit the default ruler, make your changes, then press F8 to assign a name to it. You are prompted to

    Enter format name:

Type a name of up to eight characters and press Enter. You can include both letters and numbers in the format name; names are not case sensitive.

The edited ruler is saved under the new name when you press F10, and the new name is displayed on the status line. You can still make any additional changes you want, because when you press F10 to finish the edit process, the named format is saved again.

If you make a similar format by assigning a new name, the default ruler is not changed.

Editing Named Rulers

When editing a current ruler or the default ruler, you have the opportunity to assign a name to your new design. If you want to assign a name to the ruler format so that you can easily copy it at a later time, press F8. You are prompted to

    Enter format name:

Type a name of up to eight characters and press Enter. You can include both letters and numbers in the format name; names are not case sensitive.

Once you have named a format, you can copy it (Layout Ruler Insert Named), delete it (Layout Ruler Delete Named), or edit it (Layout Ruler Edit Named). However, keep in mind that a copied ruler is just like text you have copied; changes you make to the original ruler with this name do not affect any copies. Once a format is copied, it does not retain the identity of the original and does not automatically reformat if the original is changed.

A named ruler is not visible except when you edit it. Even the original ruler you were editing when you assigned the name no longer carries the name assignment, so if you need to edit a named ruler, you do not have to move the cursor back to the original paragraph. You can edit a named ruler from anywhere in the document.

To edit a named ruler, use the Layout Ruler Edit Named command. A pop-up window displays the names of any named rulers associated with your current document. See figure 18.2.

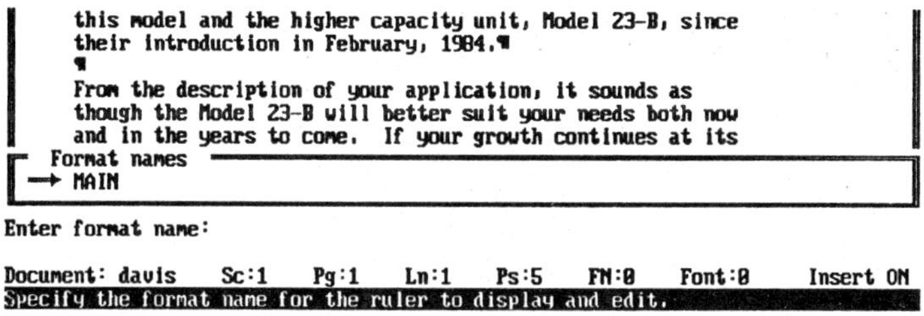

Fig. 18.2.

Editing a named ruler.

Move the cursor to the name you want to edit, or type the name, and press Enter.

The named ruler is displayed on the top line of the window, and the name of the ruler appears on the status line. You can then edit the ruler, using the same ruler edit commands as described in the "Editing the Current Ruler" section in this chapter.

One reason for editing the named ruler is to make changes to it; press F10 when you have completed your changes. The changes are saved under the current name. However, you also can edit a named ruler for the purpose of creating a similar ruler.

To create a similar named ruler, edit the original ruler, make your changes, then press F8 to assign a name to it. You see the following prompt:

    Enter format name:

Enter a name up to eight characters long and press Enter. You can include both letters and numbers in the format name; names are not case sensitive.

The edited ruler is saved under the new name, and the new name is displayed on the status line. You can still make any additional changes you want, because when you press F10 to finish the edit process, the named format is written again.

If you make a similar format by assigning a new name, the original named format is not changed.

Copying Rulers

As you prepare your document, you may want to change the format of a paragraph. If you have used the format previously, the easiest way to change the format is to insert a copy of a previously used ruler prior to the paragraph whose format you want to change. The selected ruler is used as a template for the definition of the new ruler.

The command to copy a format is Layout Ruler Insert. The prompt provides the ability to insert three types of rulers:

    Current Default Named

Select the type of ruler you would like to copy by pressing the initial letter, or move the highlight block and press Enter.

Copying the Current Ruler

To insert a copy of the current ruler immediately prior to the current paragraph, use the Layout Ruler Insert Current command. A copy of the current ruler is inserted just before the current paragraph, and you can make any editing changes. Refer to the instructions on ruler editing in this chapter.

Because the insertion of a ruler is intended to affect only the current paragraph, a copy of the original current ruler is inserted immediately after the paragraph to ensure that the subsequent paragraphs are unaffected by your editing of the ruler for the current paragraph.

If you want to assign a name to the ruler you are inserting, press the F8 key. Press F10 when you have completed editing the ruler.

Note that if you do not make any changes to the template provided by the current ruler, a new ruler is not inserted.

Copying the Default Ruler

To insert the default ruler, issue the Layout Ruler Insert Default command. A copy of the default ruler is inserted prior to the current paragraph, and a copy of the current ruler appears immediately after the current paragraph.

The Layout Ruler Insert Default command does not give you the opportunity to change the ruler at that time. The command inserts the default ruler before the paragraph and the current ruler after the paragraph. If you want to make any changes, you must now edit the current ruler.

Copying a Named Ruler

To insert a named ruler, use the Layout Ruler Insert Named command. A pop-up menu displays the names of any named rulers. Move the cursor to select the ruler you want and press Enter. A copy of the named ruler is inserted prior to the current paragraph, and a copy of the current ruler appears immediately after the current paragraph.

When you insert a named ruler, you are not given the opportunity to change the ruler. The Layout Ruler Insert Named command inserts the named ruler before the paragraph and the current ruler after the paragraph. If you want to make any changes, you must now edit the current ruler.

Changing the Ruler of Multiple Paragraphs

As we just learned, the Layout Ruler Insert command allows you to change the format of one paragraph. To change the format of several paragraphs simultaneously, use the Layout Ruler Reformat command. You can change one or more characteristics of the blocked portion of your document, or you can change all the characteristics to match the ruler of the first paragraph in the block.

Before executing the command, position the cursor in the first paragraph where the reformat is to begin. When you execute the Layout Ruler Reformat command, you must identify the blocked area of your document over which the reformat is to apply.

As described earlier, when you are prompted to identify a block, there is a beginning point and an ending point. As a default, the beginning point is the cursor position at the time you execute the command. Once in the Block-definition mode, however, you can designate a new beginning point, or anchor, by moving the cursor and pressing F2.

You can designate the ending point by moving the cursor; the area affected by your choice is displayed in reverse video.

To make it easier to mark a block, there are several keys you can use:

    F5 Word
    F6 Sentence
    F7 Paragraph
    F8 Entire Document
    F9 Line
    R Remainder of document

Rather than moving the cursor to the end of the sentence, for instance, you can press F6 to mark the current sentence. To be recognized, a sentence must end with a period or a paragraph marker. Selecting the Word option (F5) specifies the current word, bounded by either blanks or punctuation. Note that the trailing blanks and punctuation are included in the word definition boundary.

The paragraph marker (F7) indicates the current paragraph. Press F8 to specify the entire document as blocked, regardless of the current cursor position. The Line option (F9) specifies the current line on which the cursor is positioned.

Choosing the Remainder option (R) indicates that the range extends from the current cursor position to the end of the document.

Repeated pressing of one of the selection function keys moves the highlight block to the next applicable area. Each time you press F6, for example, the next sentence is highlighted. This method enables you to move through the document more quickly than with the cursor keys; the effect is not cumulative, however. If you press F6 twice, you don't mark two sentences, just the second one. Once you have marked an area by using a function key, you can mark an additional area by moving the cursor.

You cannot reformat just a portion of a paragraph. If you select a word, sentence, or line, the entire paragraph is reformatted.

Once you have selected a block, you can change your mind by pressing F3 for Restart. Press F10 or Enter to complete your selection.

The Ruler Edit mode is initiated, and you can make any changes to the displayed ruler line, which is the current ruler. Refer to ruler editing in this chapter for more information.

Any changes you make to the ruler line are displayed in bold type on your screen. If you press F10 after making changes, the changes will be superimposed upon any existing rulers in the area you have blocked. The existing rulers are not be removed, thus retaining their ruler characteristics.

If, after completing the block section, you would like to have the characteristics of the current ruler completely replace the rulers embedded in the blocked area, rather than overlay individual characteristics of the embedded rulers, press F9 (Change

All) before you press F10 to save your changes. Any embedded rulers will be deleted, thus causing the current ruler to control the format of the blocked area.

Note that a copy of the previous current ruler is inserted after following the blocked area, thus preserving its format for the rest of the document.

Deleting a Ruler

A ruler can have two very different purposes. If you delete the current ruler, you change the format of your document. If you delete a named ruler, you make it unavailable for use as a template in the current document.

Deleting the Current Ruler

To delete the current ruler, position the cursor in the document area controlled by the ruler and issue the Ruler Delete Current command. You are asked to confirm your decision:

    Are you sure (y/n)

Type *Y*, and the current ruler is deleted and the area of the document that had been governed by the current ruler is controlled by the preceding ruler.

Deleting a Named Ruler

To delete a named ruler, use the Layout Ruler Delete Named command. A pop-up menu of ruler names is displayed; select the one you want to delete, and press Enter. By deleting a named ruler, you don't affect the format or appearance of your document. You are removing the named ruler template and making it unavailable for further use. Rulers in your document that had been inserted by using the named ruler as a template are unaffected, because once a ruler is inserted, it no longer retains any identification with the original named ruler.

Using Formatting Features

Several other formatting capabilities in the Word Processor affect pagination and the organization of your document.

Using Indent Tabs

Indent Tabs are a new feature in SmartWare II. They work like normal tabs, except that the entire paragraph is aligned with the tab stop, not just the first line. Using an indent tab can achieve results similar to setting a new left margin and an outdent. Indent tabs can be used effectively to change paragraph levels when using automatic paragraph numbering.

Press Ctrl-T to insert an indent tab. The tab symbol displayed on the screen is similar to a squared off 7. Like any other tab, you can remove an indent tab with the Del key.

Using Page Breaks

Normally, as you enter text into a document, page breaks are inserted for you as the document increases in length. The actual location of the page break is controlled by the form length, top and bottom boundaries, headings and footings, and the spacing between lines in the body of the text.

An automatic page break is indicated on your screen by a thin, single line extending the width of the window. (The display of the page breaks can be made invisible as a default in the Word Processor Tools Preferences, or for the individual session by using the Document Visible Newpage command.)

Sometimes, however, it is desirable to force a page break where one would not naturally occur, at the beginning of a new topic, for instance. The Layout Newpage Insert command inserts a page break in your document immediately before the current cursor line. To use the command, position the cursor on the first line that you want on the new page and execute the Layout Newpage Insert command (or the Alt-E Quick key). When you execute Layout Newpage, the following options are offered:

```
Automatic Insert Paginate Remove
```

Select Insert to force a new page. A heavy, dashed line across the entire window indicates that a new page has been inserted at the location.

If you want to remove an inserted page break, position the cursor at the top line of the page after the break and execute the Layout Newpage Remove command.

Automatic Pagination

Whether your document paginates automatically can be controlled as a default in the Word Processor Preferences. For a document, you can control the automatic pagination by executing the Layout Newpage Automatic command. This is a toggle command; if pagination is on, the first time you execute the command, you see the following message:

```
Auto Pagination is off, press any key
```

Execute the command again, and pagination is turned on.

Once pagination is off, page breaks are not inserted automatically as you enter new text. Existing page breaks are not removed, however.

Manual Pagination

If you have entered new text with pagination off, you can manually paginate the existing text with the Layout Newpage Paginate command. This command does not enable the automatic pagination of new text, however.

Using Keep Areas

Often the reason for inserting a new page is to ensure that certain areas of text are not accidentally split between two pages. If you have a table of numbers, for example, you probably would not want the table split onto two pages.

If you force a page break before the table, you may be wasting space in your document and giving it an awkward appearance. The table of numbers may have been able to fit entirely on the page, but you did not know it.

A new concept introduced with SmartWare II is that of keep areas. By defining a keep area, you can guarantee that the area will not be split between pages. If it fits on an existing page, it appears there; if it does not fit, it is printed at the top of the next page.

To insert a keep area, execute the Layout Keep Insert command. If the cursor is already on the first line of the area you want to keep together, press the down arrow to move the cursor to the last line of the keep area and press F10 or Enter. If the cursor is not on the first line, move the cursor to where you want the keep area to begin and press F2. Then move the cursor to the last line of the keep area and press F10 or Enter. The first full paragraph in figure 18.3 has been marked as a keep area.

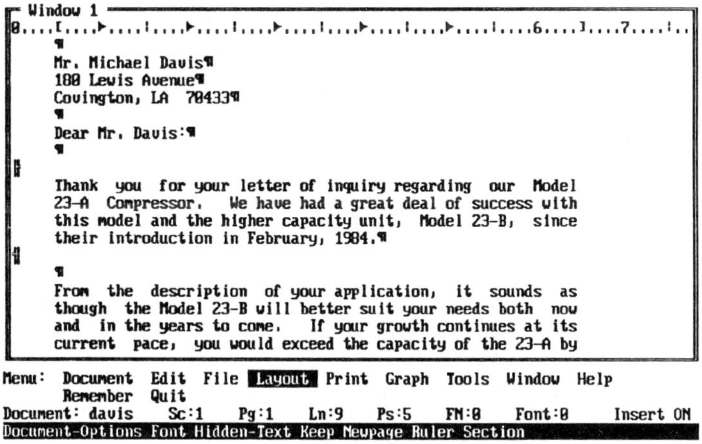

Fig. 18.3.

The keep area.

If the keep area is the current paragraph, you can define the area by pressing F7; you do not have to move the cursor. The keep area boundaries must be entire lines. If the paragraph is the last one in your document, pressing F7 selects the end of document marker. The Keep command will not complete if this marker is selected. The following error message is displayed if the keep area includes the end of document marker:

    A keep area cannot include the end-of-file mark

When you have finished inserting the keep area, the markers are displayed in the left margin. (The keep area markers can be made invisible as a default in the Word Processor Tools Preferences, or for the individual session by executing the Document Visible Marks Keep command.) Although it appears as if the keep markers are displayed on blank lines, these are dummy lines that have been inserted to hold the markers.

To remove a keep area, position the cursor in the keep area and issue the Layout Keep Remove command.

Using Widow and Orphan Settings

Because automatic page breaks can occur anywhere (outside of the keep limits), it is possible that a paragraph could be broken so that just one line exists at the bottom of a page or at the top of a page. In word processing terminology, these conditions are called widows and orphans. If you want to prevent these situations, you can set the minimum number of acceptable lines of a paragraph to remain at the top or bottom of a page. The setting is made in Layout Document-Options, in the Miscellaneous section.

There are two options to the Layout Document-Options command:

    Current-Document New-Document

The widow and orphan settings can apply to just the current document, or to new documents you will create. A specific item on the menu asks for a minimum number of lines:

    Minimum widows/orphans allowed:

If you want to make sure you have at least two lines of a paragraph at the top or bottom of a page, type *2* as the minimum.

To save this setting, as with any other current document layout options, be sure to save the document to the disk, even though you may not have changed the body of the text. If you do not save the document, your options are not retained.

Using Document Sections

With the SmartWare II Word Processor, you can subdivide your documents into sections. The ability to define sections in your document has several advantages. Print Options apply to individual sections. Thus, you can define separate headings and footings by section, as well as page boundaries, length, and number style.

Footnotes can be printed at the end of each section, and you can start the renumbering of footnotes at the end of each section.

Paragraph numbering can start at the section boundaries. The table of contents and index are created as separate sections. The section numbers can be included in the index. Sections can be moved and printed individually. You can go to any section, just as you would go to a specified page.

Creating a Section

To split your document into sections, use the Layout Section Insert command. Position the cursor on the line to be the first line of the new section and execute the command. Unless you have chosen to make section markers invisible, the double-line section marker spans the window where the section begins. (Section markers can be made invisible, by default, by selecting invisible page break markers in the Word Processor Preferences. During the current session, use the Document Visible Newpage command.)

Section numbers are displayed following the document name on the status line:

```
Sc: 1
```

Once you have split your document into multiple sections, the section number changes as you move the cursor from one section to another. A new section always creates a page break.

Removing a Section

If you want to remove a section break, thus joining a section with the previous one, position the cursor immediately above or below the section break and issue the Layout Section Remove command. The second section is joined with the first, and takes on its attributes and options.

Moving a Section

To move an entire section, use the Layout Section Move command. You see the following prompt:

```
Select the section to move:
```

As a default, the current section number is entered for you; if you want to move the current section, press Enter. If you want to move a different section, move the cursor to that section of the document and press Enter, or type the section number and press Enter.

After you have entered the number of the section you want to move, you see the following prompt:

    Select the destination section:

Enter the number of the section before which you want the selected section to appear. If you want to move a section to the end of the document, the destination should be a number higher than any existing section, or the word *end*.

An index or a table of contents is always created as a separate section; to display and print your table of contents at the beginning of the document, use the Layout Section Move command to reposition it.

Using Hidden Text

There may be times when you want to have text hidden in your document. The hidden text can be notes to yourself or confidential paragraphs. Text marked as hidden does not print if you have made it invisible, but it does print if visible. Even though text may be marked as hidden, if you can see it, you can perform Word Processor operations and commands on it.

Hiding Text

To hide text in your document, execute the Layout Hidden-Text Add command. The Block-marking mode is invoked.

As with other commands that require you to identify a block, there is a beginning point and an ending point. As a default, the beginning point is the cursor position at the time you executed the command. Once you are in the Block-definition mode, however, you can designate a new beginning point, or anchor, by moving the cursor and pressing F2.

You can designate the ending point by moving the cursor; the area affected by your choice is displayed in reverse video.

To make it easier to mark a block, there are several keys you can use:

    F5 Word
    F6 Sentence
    F7 Paragraph
    F8 Entire Document
    F9 Line
    R   Remainder of document

Rather than moving the cursor to the end of the sentence, for instance, you can press F6 to mark the current sentence. To be recognized, a sentence must end with a period or a paragraph marker. Selecting the Word option (F5) specifies the current word, bounded by either blanks or punctuation. Note that the trailing blanks and punctuation are included in the word definition boundary.

The paragraph marker (F7) indicates the current paragraph. Press F8 to specify the entire document as being blocked, regardless of the current cursor position. The Line option (F9) specifies the current line on which the cursor is positioned.

Choosing the Remainder option (R) indicates that the range from the current cursor position to the end of the document.

Repeated pressing of one of the selection function keys moves the highlight block to the next applicable area. For example, each time you press F6, the next sentence is highlighted. This method enables you to move through the document more quickly than by moving the cursor; the effect is not cumulative, however. If you press F6 twice, you don't mark two sentences, just the second one. Once you have marked an area by using a function key, you can mark an additional area by moving the cursor.

The marks that identify the boundaries of the hidden area are an up arrow for the beginning, and a down arrow for the end. You can turn off the display of the hidden area marks, as a default condition, by setting Hidden text marks to Invisible in the Word Processor Preferences. During the session, you can toggle the display of the marks with the Document Hidden text marks Visible command.

You can prevent the display of the hidden text itself, as a default, by setting the Hidden text Invisible option in the Word Processor Preferences, or by the toggle command Document Hidden text Visible during the session. (The commands to display or hide the hidden text mark and the hidden text itself seem similar, so try not to confuse them.) If the text is hidden, and the marks are not, a single character that is both an up arrow and a down arrow is displayed.

Unhiding Text

If you want to remove the hidden text marks, either the text itself or the marks must be visible. Position the cursor in the hidden text area and execute the Layout Hidden-Text Remove command. Another way to unhide text is to delete either the beginning or the ending hidden text mark by using the Delete key or the Backspace key. If the text itself is hidden at the time you want to make it visible, delete the single up and down arrow character. The hidden text immediately becomes visible.

You can move hidden text, both while visible and invisible. You must include both the begin and end markers, however. If you move only part of the text, the markers are not moved, but remain where they were.

If you copy hidden text, the markers are copied too, if the entire hidden text area is copied. If only a portion of the hidden area is copied, the new text is not marked as hidden.

You can make changes to the text area in hidden marks while the text is visible. New text can be added, or existing text deleted.

When you hide text by making it invisible, your pagination is adjusted to make up for the loss of the text. You should check your page breaks to make sure they fall in appropriate locations.

Using Fonts

Depending on the capabilities of your printer, you can select from a wide variety of print fonts in different sizes, weights, and slants. The Word Processor selects from among your printer's internal fonts or those supplied with plug-in cartridges. Even without these selectable fonts, if you have a printer that can print graphics, such as a dot-matrix printer or laser printer, SmartWare can form the characters and download them to the printer for printing in the Graphics mode.

The SmartWare system is supplied with several type style or font family outlines, each of which describes the basic shape of a character set. The supplied type styles include the following:

- standard
- monospaced
- sans serif
- serif
- script
- small-caps
- gothic
- greek
- dingbat1
- dingbat2
- symbol
- b-graphic
- l-graphic
- line printer

Figure 18.4 shows examples of these fonts. Depending on your hardware configuration, you can print additional fonts.

Strictly speaking, a font is a type style in a specified height, weight, and slant. Other attributes that can be applied are single- and double-underscoring, strikeout, and baseline shifts (subscript and superscript).

If you use a certain font only occasionally, it can be built during the printing of the document. These types of fonts are called filled-area fonts in SmartWare II. If you find that you use a font repeatedly, you can build it once and store it in a disk file. Then, when you use it, the system needs only to download it to the printer.

Standard	AaBbCcDdEeFfGgHhIiJjKkLlMmNnOoPpQqRrSsTtUuVvWwXxYyZz	*Fig. 18.4.*
Monospaced	AaBbCcDdEeFfGgHhIiJjKkLlMmNnOoPpQqRrSsTtUuVvWwXxYyZz	*Font examples.*
Sans serif	AaBbCcDdEeFfGgHhIiJjKkLlMmNnOoPpQqRrSsTtUuVvWwXxYyZz	
Script	*AaBbCcDdEeFfGgHhIiJjKkLlMmNnOoPpQqRrSsTtUuVvWwXxYyZz*	
Serif	AaBbCcDdEeFfGgHhIiJjKkLlMmNnOoPpQqRrSsTtUuVvWwXxYyZz	
Small-caps	AaBbCcDdEeFfGgHhIiJjKkLlMmNnOoPpQqRrSsTtUuVvWwXxYyZz	
Gothic	AaBbCcDdEeFfGgHhIiJjKkLlMmNnOoPpQqRrSsTtUuVvWwXxYyZz	
Greek	AαBβΓγΔδEε ΞξHηIιΘθKκΛλMμNνOoΠπΦφPρΣσTτYυΨψΩωXχ Zζ	
Dingbat1	✿❁✦✧✶✹✺✻✼✽✾✿❀❁❂❃❄❅❆❇❈❉❊❋●○★☆■□▲△▼▽◆◇◉❋✱❋	
Dingbat2	✕✖✗✘✙✚✛✜✝✞✟✠✡☚☛☜☝☞✍✌✎✏@○◎△∘▽◇◐◑⊗	
Symbol	AαBβXχΔδEεΦφΓγHηIιθφKκΛλMμNνOoΠπΘθPρΣσTτYυζωΩωΞξΨψZζ	
B-graphic	·|·⌐┘└─┴┬┤├┼━┃┏┓┗┛┣┫┳┻╋═║╔╗╚╝╠╣╦╩╬ :	
L-graphic	╟╞╫╪╡╧╤╢╨╖╘╜╙╒╓╔╕╖╗╘╙╚╛╜╝╞╟╠╡╢	
Line Printer	AaBbCcDdEeFfGgHhIiJjKkLlMmNnOoPpQqRrSsTtUuVvWwXxYyZz	

Creating a Font

To build a font and store it on your disk, select the Tools New-Font command; in SmartWare II, this process is referred to as prerasterization. Two options are available:

```
Normal    Sideways
```

The Normal orientation is sometimes called Portrait mode; Sideways orientation is often referred to as landscape. When you select the orientation, the screen in figure 18.5 is displayed.

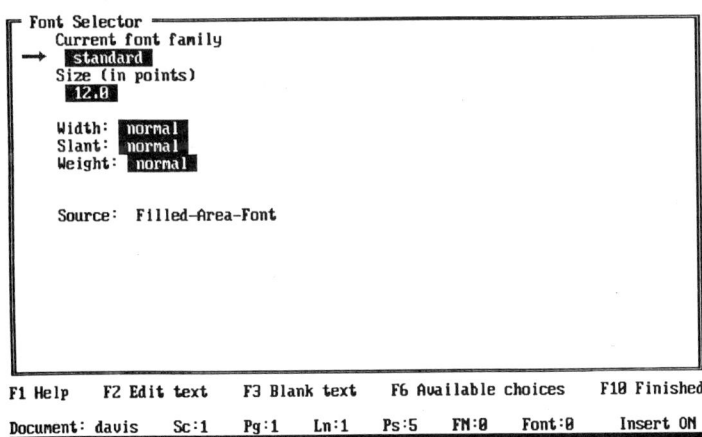

Fig. 18.5.

Building a new font.

With the cursor pointing at the font family selection, press F6 to display a list of the available choices. See figure 18.6.

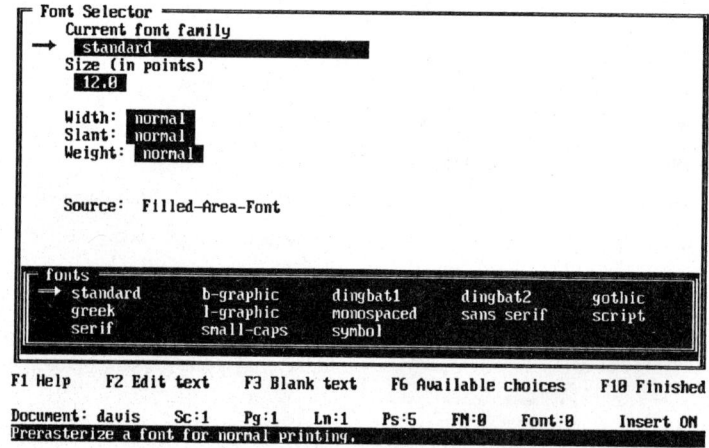

Fig. 18.6.

Available fonts.

Move the cursor to select the type style of the font you would like to create and press Enter. Then move the pointer to your size selection; a default size is displayed. If you want to change the size, type a value for the size you want. Font sizes are specified in points; there are 72 points to an inch. If any fonts of the type style you have selected have been prerasterized, you can use the F6 key to display the sizes in a pop-up window. This is primarily for your information. If you want to rasterize the same font again, you can select the size and press F10.

As you select a font family and size, watch the informational item called Source in the middle of the screen. The following are possible sources for your fonts:

Internal-Font	A font that is built into your printer
Filled-Area-Font	A font that is built as your document is printed
Preraster-Font	A prerasterized font that is built with the Tools New-Font command

If you see that a font is labeled as a Preraster-Font, you do not have to rebuild it.

Select from among any of the options for width, slant, and weight. Press F10 to proceed with the creation of the font file. The actual font file is created in your home subdirectory from which you initiated the SmartWare session. If you want to make it generally available, you can copy it later to the SmartII subdirectory.

Selecting a Font

Regardless of whether you have created a prerasterized font, use the Layout Font command to select or change fonts in your document. The following options are available with this command:

    Select Change Edit Remove Bold Underscore

To set the font for new text, choose the Select option; the Quick key for the Select option is F6. A pop-up window of available fonts is displayed; see figure 18.7.

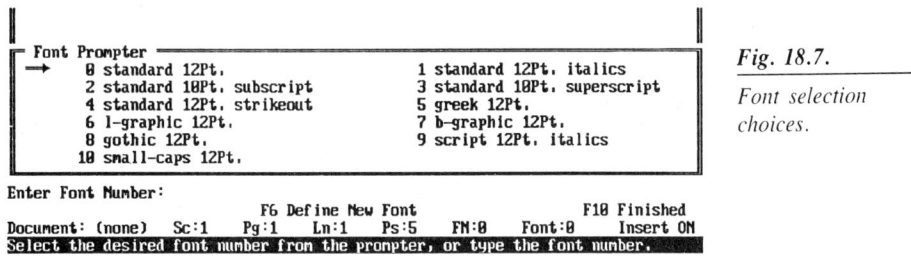

Fig. 18.7.

Font selection choices.

The choices in the window display the standard fonts and any fonts which have been attached to the current document. Move the cursor to select from among the existing fonts. If you want to attach a new font, press F6. See figure 18.8.

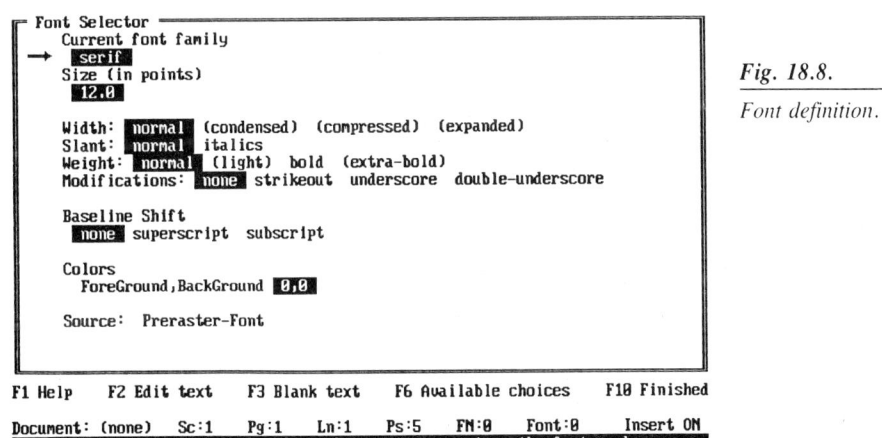

Fig. 18.8.

Font definition.

Select the font family and size by typing the name and size, or press F6 to display the available choices. If you select an attribute in parenthesis, the source is called a Dummy-Font, indicating that the option is not available for your current printer; the closest option is used. Other font sources are as described earlier in this section.

If you select either superscript or subscript, you can select the default offset position, or you can enter your own in point size. Select foreground and background colors for the font, if desired.

Press F10 to complete the font selection. New text you enter is assigned the font you selected, and the font is attached to the current document. Notice that on the status line, the selected font is identified by number:

    Font:11

In this example, the font was assigned the number 11. The other font indicator on the status line, FN:11, indicates the number of the font at the current cursor position.

Changing a Font

To change a font in a portion of your document, select the Change option of the Layout Font command. The Block-marking mode is invoked; use the function keys or cursor movement keys to mark the portion of the document where you want to make the change. When you have completed marking the block, a pop-up window of attached fonts is displayed. You can select from among them, or, as with font selection, you can press F6 to define and attach a new font.

Editing a Font

If you want to change the definition of an existing font, select the Edit option of the Layout Font command. Select one of the two following options, depending on if you want the editing to apply to just the current document, or to new documents you create:

    Current-Document New-Documents

A Definition menu similar to figure 18.8 is displayed.

If you make a change to a font that is already in your document, the change applies to text already entered for that font.

Removing a Font

To remove a font, select the Remove option. A pop-up window shows all the attached fonts; an asterisk indicates any fonts that are not used. You cannot remove a font that is in use.

Using Bold and Underscore

Two of the most common font attributes are bold and underscore. Both of these attributes have Quick keys for selection; use Ctrl-B for bold and Ctrl-U for underscore. It is much faster for you to use Quick keys than to go through the font-selection process.

If you want to add or remove bold or underscore from existing text, select the Bold or Underscore options of the Layout Font command. You have two choices:

    Insert Remove

For either choice, you must mark the area to be affected. Press F10 when you have completed your selection.

Creating and Using Footnotes

If you have ever typed a document that has several footnotes and have had difficulty leaving enough space at the bottom of the page, you will appreciate the easy footnoting capability of the SmartWare Word Processor. Each footnote can have as many as 10 lines of 255 characters each. Each footnote is tied to the text, so the footnote is automatically renumbered if you move it.

When you execute the Document References Footnote command, you have two options:

    Insert Modify

Type *I* to insert a footnote, or *M* to modify an existing footnote; you also can move the highlight block to the appropriate option and press Enter.

Inserting a Footnote

To insert a footnote, place the cursor on the character before which you want the footnote number to appear, then execute the Document References Footnote Insert command. The footnote input area then appears in a pop-up window. If the reference location is in the lower half of the window, the footnote pop-up window will be positioned in the upper half of your screen; if the reference location is in the upper half, then the footnote window will be in the lower half. Even if you have multiple windows displayed on your screen, the footnote pop-up window will span the entire width of the screen.

Type your footnote information on successive lines in the footnote pop-up window. Each of the 10 lines can have as many as 255 characters, but if you enter text that exceeds the printing width capabilities of your printer or the right margin of your document, the text is truncated.

Be aware that there is no word wrapping in the footnote areas; you must press Enter to advance to the next line of the footnote. You can, however, press Enter in the middle of a line to split it onto the next line, or press Delete to append the previous line onto the current.

You can exercise font control in document footnotes by using a code sequence in the following format:

> Format: %[nbu]
> n = Font Number
> B = bold on
> b = bold off
> U = underscore on
> u = underscore off

For example, Line 1: %[12bU]The capacity of the 23-A unit

In a footnote, you don't have to enter text on every line; to leave a blank line, press Enter to go to the next line. When you have completed entering the footnote, press F10.

Note that when you enter your first footnote, the number 1 appears immediately prior to the cursor position. (See the number 1 after the word *unit* in figure 18.9.) The SmartWare Word Processor generates this number automatically.

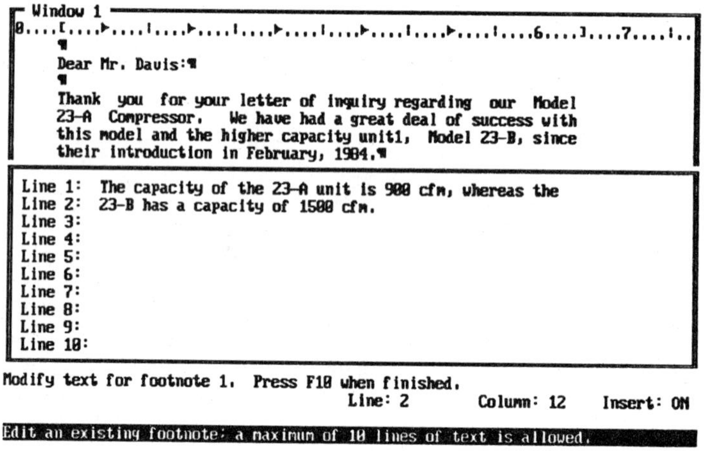

Fig. 18.9.

Footnote modification.

```
┌─ Window 1 ─────────────────────────────────────────────
│0....[....▸....l....▸....l....▸....l....▸....l....6....]....7....l..
│¶
│Dear Mr. Davis:¶
│¶
│Thank you for your letter of inquiry regarding our Model
│23-A Compressor.  We have had a great deal of success with
│this model and the higher capacity unit1, Model 23-B, since
│their introduction in February, 1984.¶
│┌─────────────────────────────────────────────────────┐
││Line 1:  The capacity of the 23-A unit is 900 cfm, whereas the│
││Line 2:  23-B has a capacity of 1500 cfm.             │
││Line 3:                                               │
││Line 4:                                               │
││Line 5:                                               │
││Line 6:                                               │
││Line 7:                                               │
││Line 8:                                               │
││Line 9:                                               │
││Line 10:                                              │
│└─────────────────────────────────────────────────────┘
Modify text for footnote 1.  Press F10 when finished.
                          Line: 2       Column: 12      Insert: ON
Edit an existing footnote: a maximum of 10 lines of text is allowed.
```

In the menu for document options, there are six choices governing the positioning and renumbering of footnotes:

1. End of Page Page
2. End of Page Section

3. End of Page Continuous
4. End of Section Section
5. End of Section Continuous
6. End of Document Continuous

Execute the Layout Document Options command to select the footnote placement and renumbering option. Your selection for renumbering will govern the number assigned to the newly inserted footnote. If you change renumbering methodology, the footnotes are automatically renumbered throughout your document.

If you insert an additional footnote between two existing footnotes, the numbering is automatically adjusted; you never have to enter the footnote number. If you move or copy text that has a footnote, the footnote is carried along with the text, and the renumbering is done for you.

Dictionary Spell Check command does not check footnotes for spelling errors.

Modifying a Footnote

To change the text of a footnote, position the cursor on the footnote number and issue the Document References Footnote Modify command. The footnote text is displayed in a pop-up window. Refer to figure 18.9.

You can edit the text using the cursor-movement keys, the Del key, and the Backspace key. If the Insert mode is off (lower right corner of the screen), any text you type overlays existing text. With the Insert mode on, new text is inserted. Unlike Word Processor text, however, footnote text does not wrap around. You must make any text wrap adjustments by typing the material on the appropriate line.

Deleting a Footnote

The Word Processor has no explicit command to delete a footnote. To remove a footnote, delete the footnote number from the body of the text, just as you would delete any other character. The footnote is deleted, and subsequent footnotes are renumbered.

Moving a Footnote

If you move a footnote number to a new location, the footnote goes along with it, and the footnotes are renumbered to maintain the proper sequence.

Changing between Document and Text Modes

Normally, when you create a document with the SmartWare Word Processor, the document is created as a true document file. All the word processing capabilities can be used to format the text because special control codes are built into the document. Sometimes, however, you may want to use the Word Processor to create a pure text file, such as you might create with a text editor. Text files contain no control codes or formatting characters. Such files are sometimes called ASCII files.

The File File-Type command is used to change between Document mode and Text mode. The command is a toggle command; execute it once, and the document is changed to a text file. If you execute it again, it is changed back to a document file. The first word on the status line indicates the type of the current file. The status line displays either Document or Textfile. The default extension of a file saved as a text file is .TXT; the extension of a document file is .DOC.

When you execute the File Load command, both .TXT and .DOC files are shown in the pop-up menu of file names; if you have both a text file and a document file with the same name, use the cursor to point to the one you want to load and press Enter. (If you type the file name without an extension, you will load the document file.) If there is a text file on your disk with an extension other than .TXT, you must supply both the name and the extension.

Unlike lines in Word Processor documents, text file lines end with a carriage return and a line feed. Changing the rulers of a text file is possible, but remember that each line is a paragraph in itself, because each line ends in a return. Changes in spacing can be accomplished by using the Layout Ruler Reformat command for a block of text, but if you change the margins, you will have unusual results, because word wrapping between lines is not in effect.

If you have a text file, Print Options and Layout Document Options will not be stored with the file, nor will they have an effect while working with the document. Embedded rulers are not saved, either.

If you use the File File-Type command to change a document file into a text file, you will not observe any immediate differences while the document is loaded; in fact, you can change your mind and revert back to a document file without any ill effects. When the file is saved as a text file, however, the soft carriage returns are converted to hard returns; rulers, Print Options, and Layout Document Options are removed; and embedded graphics characters are eliminated. Once the file is saved as a text file, loading it and changing it back to a document will not change the hard returns back to soft returns.

In addition to using the text editing capabilities of the Text mode of the Word Processor, you can also use the Tools Text Editor command. However, the capabilities of the Word Processor far exceed those of the Text Editor.

Displaying and Hiding Special Characters

Several special characters can be shown on your screen to guide you as you construct your document. If desired, you can choose to make these characters invisible. These marks are for reference on your screen only; they are not printed.

In the Word Processor Preferences, you can set the default conditions for the display of these special characters:

    Page Breaks
    Paragraph Marks
    Tab Marks
    Hidden Text
    Hidden Text Marks
    Keep Marks
    Index Marks
    Table Of Contents (TOC) Marks

To set your default conditions, choose either `Visible` or `Invisible` in the preferences.

During a Word Processor session, you can change the display of the marks by using the Document Visible command and selecting from the different options. The first options of the command are:

    Hidden-Text Marks Newpage Paragraphs Rulers Tabs

The following options toggle the display of their respective marks:

    Hidden-Text Marks: The text itself, not the marks

    Paragraphs: Paragraph markers

    Tabs: Tab marks, both normal and decimal

If you select `Hidden-Text Marks`, there is a second set of options:

    All Hidden-Text Index Keep Toc

Select one of these options to toggle the display of the specific guide marks. Note that in this second set of options, the Hidden-Text selection refers to the hidden text marks, not the text itself.

If you select `All`, the four marks in this set of options are toggled off or on simultaneously. They are all set on or all set off each time you issue this command. The visibility of the hidden text, page breaks, paragraph markers, tabs, and rulers is not affected.

If you select `Rulers` from the first set of options, you are prompted to choose from two options:

    Main Embedded

Select Main to toggle the display of the main ruler, and Embedded to change the display of the intermediate, embedded rulers.

Rearranging Lines of Text

The Edit Sort command can be used to rearrange lines of text according to values in specified column ranges. When you execute this command, you are prompted to choose from two options:

Column Text

The operation of the Edit Sort command is different if you are sorting text in multiple column areas (MCA) than if you are sorting text in single column areas.

Sorting NonMCA Document Areas

If you are not sorting multiple column areas, select Text sorting. You must then select one of the following options:

Ascending Descending

An ascending sort goes from A to Z; descending is from Z to A. (Refer to appendix E, "Collation Sort Sequence.")

A Column-marking mode is invoked. If the cursor is already on the upper left corner of the block by which you want to sort, move the cursor to the lower right corner and press F10 or Enter. If you need to reposition the cursor, press the F2 key at the desired starting position, then move the cursor to the lower right corner and press F10 or Enter. Figure 18.10 shows the execution of the Edit Sort command in window 1; the result is shown in window 2.

Fig. 18.10.

Sorting your document.

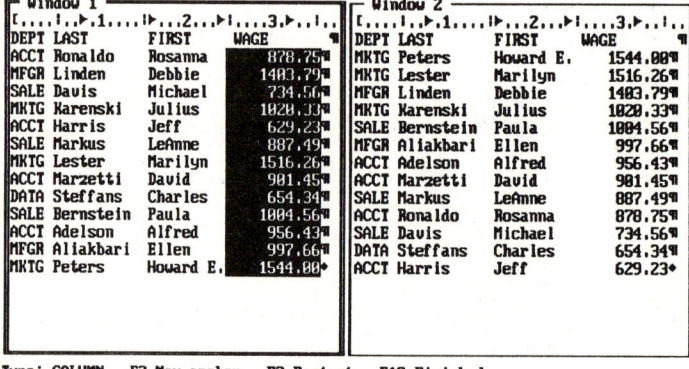

When performing a text sort, each line of your document in the boundaries of the beginning and ending line is kept intact. The order of the lines is rearranged according to the sorting of the text in the marked block.

Be aware that because only one sort range can be defined, complex sorting rules cannot be applied, such as mixed ascending and descending sorting. If you need compound sorting, you should consider using the Database Manager or the Spreadsheet for the sort, then send the text back to the Word Processor.

Sorting Multiple Column Areas

If you are sorting text in an MCA, begin by positioning the cursor in the MCA. You also can position the cursor in the column you want to use as the basis for the sort, or you can reposition it in the marking mode. (Use Ctrl-F4 to go to the next column, or Ctrl-F3 to go to the previous column.) When you execute the Edit Sort command, select the Column option. You must then select one of the following options:

    Ascending Descending

An ascending sort goes from A to Z; descending is from Z to A. (Refer to appendix E, "Collation Sort Sequence.") The MCA Column-marking mode is then invoked. If the cursor is in the column you want to use as the basis for the sort, press F10 or Enter. If you need to move the cursor to another column, use the right- or left-arrow keys and then press the F10 key or Enter. Refer to figure 18.11.

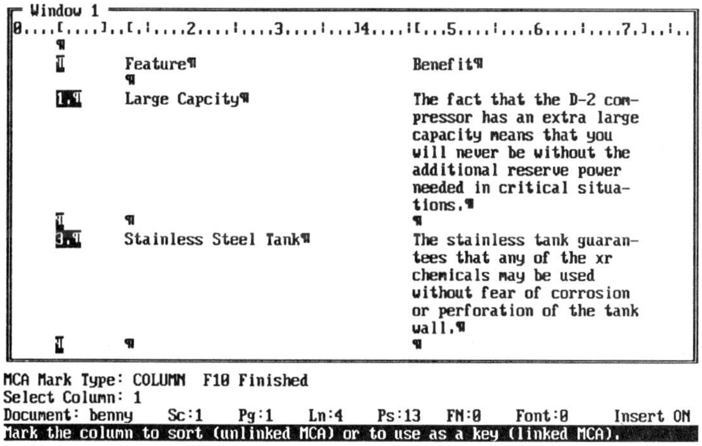

Fig. 18.11.

Sorting a Multiple Column Area.

Notice that you cannot specify the beginning or ending line in the column to sort when you are sorting an MCA; you must sort the entire column. If the columns in the MCA are linked, then the columns retain their relation to the sort basis column. If the columns are not linked, sorting one column does not affect the others. In either case, only one column can be sorted at a time.

Chapter Summary

Both the content and appearance of your documents are important. The formatting commands covered in this chapter can be used to improve the appearance of your Word Processor output. You have the choice of setting formatting characteristics before or after you enter the text. If you have many different formats, you may find it easier to set them all at one time, rather than constantly switching back and forth.

19

Using the Spellchecker and Thesaurus

When you are producing important documents and it is imperative that each word in your document be spelled correctly, you will want to use the SmartWare II Spellchecker in the Word Processor module. In addition, you may want to use the Thesaurus, which provides a built-in reference for synonyms and antonyms for words in the text. A display of root words and meanings guide you to the exact word you need for what you are trying to say.

Using the Spellchecker and Thesaurus require additional computer resources. Together, they consume an additional 75K of memory. On your disk, you will need more than 1M of memory to store the necessary files. Note, however, that the Spellchecker and Thesaurus are included with your purchase of the SmartWare II system; you do not have to pay extra for them. You enable the Spellchecker and Thesaurus in the Dictionary Preferences section of the Tools Preferences Word Processor menu.

The Smart Spellchecker

Although the Smart Word Processor can make writing and rewriting easier and can improve the appearance of your letters and documents, output that is sprinkled with misspellings is going to lose some of its impact. Despite all the spelling drills in grade school, let's face it—some of us still cannot remember whether *independent* is spelled with an *e* or an *a*.

Because the Smart Spellchecker is integral to the Word Processor, it checks your spelling in the module itself. You do not have to save your document and then run a separate program. This feature speeds the processing of your documents and may prevent additional misspellings in later parts of the same document.

In addition to the extensive standard dictionary, you can create your own custom dictionaries and attach as many as five of them to any document. The standard dictionary contains about 60,000 words, which grows to over 140,000 if you count prefixes, suffixes, and other word forms. There is no design limitation to the size of a custom dictionary.

Operating the Smart Spellchecker

To initiate the Spellchecker, use the Document Dictionary command. The Quick key for this command is Alt-F2; additional dictionary Quick keys are discussed later in this chapter.

There are four options to the Document Dictionary command:

```
Erase  Hyphenate  Spellcheck  Thesaurus
```

To check the spelling of your current document, select Spellcheck and press Enter. When checking the spelling, you have the option of either writing the results to a file or displaying the results on the screen so that you can correct any misspellings. Two options are displayed:

```
File   Screen
```

Selection of either option requires you to select the document area to spell check.

In every instance when you are prompted to identify a block, there is a beginning point and an ending point. As a default, the beginning point is the cursor position at the time you execute the command. Once you are in the Block-definition mode, however, you can designate a new beginning point, or anchor, by moving the cursor and pressing F2.

You designate the ending point by moving the cursor; the area affected by your choice is displayed in reverse video. To make it easier to mark a block, there are several keys you can use:

- F5 Word
- F6 Sentence
- F7 Paragraph
- F8 Entire Document
- F9 Line
- R   Remainder of document

Rather than moving the cursor through your document to mark text, you can select the Word option (F5), for example, to mark the current word, bounded by either blanks or punctuation, as the block. Note that the trailing blanks and punctuation are included in the word definition boundary. Or you can select F6 to mark the current sentence. To be recognized, a sentence must end with a period or a paragraph marker.

The Paragraph option (F7) indicates the current paragraph as the block. The Line option (F9) specifies the current line on which the cursor is positioned.

Choosing the Remainder option (R) indicates that the range extends from the current cursor position to the end of the document.

Repeated pressing of one of the selection function keys moves the highlight block to the next applicable area. Each time you press F6, for example, the next sentence is highlighted. This method enables you to move through the document more quickly than with the cursor keys; the effect is not cumulative, however. If you press F6 twice, you don't mark two sentences, just the second one. Once you have marked an area using a function key, you can mark an additional area by moving the cursor.

Press F8 to specify the entire document as marked, regardless of the current cursor position.

Once you have selected a block, you can change your mind by pressing F3 for Restart. Press F10 or Enter to complete your selection.

From the menu level, there are three additional Quick keys which can help you to correct your spelling:

- Alt-F3   Spell check current word
- Alt-F5   Spell check remainder of document
- Alt-F6   Spell check entire document

All three of these Quick keys display any misspellings on your monitor. (The Alt-F4 key, which was used in previous versions of Smart to spell check a paragraph to the screen, is now used to look up a word in the thesaurus.)

Setting Spellcheck Preferences

Pressing the F8 key displays the pop-up menu of suggested spelling corrections. If you want the menu to appear automatically each time the Spellchecker highlights a misspelled word, however, you can set Correction Information to Yes in the Tools Preferences Word Processor.

You may not want the correction information to appear automatically every time an unknown word is encountered, however. You may, for example, have mistyped a word that you really know how to spell. The Spellchecker usually takes a few seconds to search the dictionaries and display the menu of suggested corrections, while simply finding the misspelled word takes only about a second. You also know that some words, such as some proper nouns or product names, will not be found in the standard dictionary. You would not want a menu of meaningless alternative spellings for these words. Thus, this automatic correction feature may slow you down by checking proper nouns or elementary misspellings that are easily corrected.

The Spellchecker works phonetically; if you do not know how to spell a word, just type it as it sounds. It will probably be found in the dictionary. The word most likely to match the misspelled word is listed first in the menu; if that is the word you want, press Enter. If you want another word in the menu, use the cursor movement keys to move the cursor to that word, and then press Enter. If the word you want is not on the menu, however, you must look it up in your own dictionary (the book on your desk) and type the correctly spelled word as the replacement. With any luck, you may never have to type any corrections. But because the search for correct spellings is phonetic, you may get some unusual suggestions!

Correcting Misspellings

The Spellchecker reads each word in the selected range, checking it against the words in the standard dictionary. Any custom dictionaries attached to the document are also checked. If the Spellchecker finds a word in your document not contained in any available dictionary, that word is highlighted (see fig. 19.1).

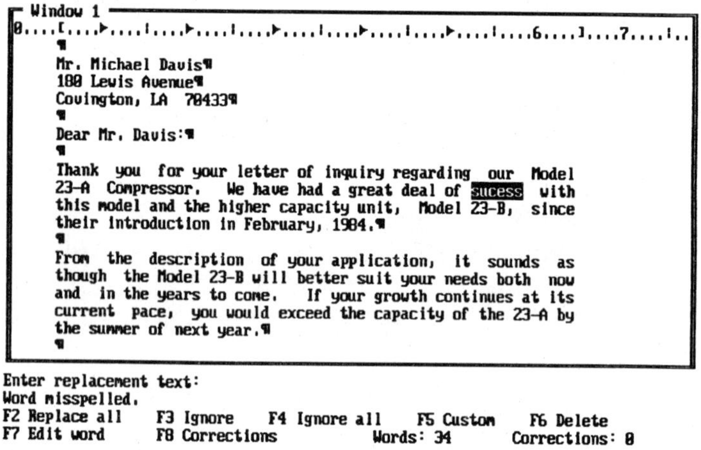

Fig. 19.1.

Highlighting a misspelled word.

```
┌─ Window 1 ──────────────────────────────────────────
0....[....▶....I....▶....I....▶....I....▶....I....6....]....7....I.
    ¶
    Mr. Michael Davis¶
    180 Lewis Avenue¶
    Covington, LA 70433¶
    ¶
    Dear Mr. Davis:¶
    ¶
    Thank you for your letter of inquiry regarding  our  Model
    23-A  Compressor.   We have had a great deal of sucess  with
    this model and the higher capacity unit, Model 23-B,  since
    their introduction in February, 1984.¶
    ¶
    From  the  description  of your application, it  sounds  as
    though  the  Model 23-B will better suit your needs both  now
    and  in the years to come.   If your growth continues at its
    current  pace,  you would exceed the capacity of the 23-A by
    the summer of next year.¶
    ¶

Enter replacement text:
Word misspelled.
F2 Replace all    F3 Ignore    F4 Ignore all    F5 Custom    F6 Delete
F7 Edit word      F8 Corrections            Words: 34      Corrections: 0
```

If you know the spelling of the word, you can retype it and press Enter to replace the original word in the text. You also can select a course of action by pressing the appropriate function key:

F2 Replace All
F3 Ignore
F4 Ignore All
F5 Custom
F6 Delete
F7 Edit Word
F8 Corrections

Use F2, the Replace All option, if you have misspelled the same word several times in your document. As each occurrence of the highlighted word is encountered, it is replaced with the word you supply. Replace All is a useful option if you are consistent in your misspellings. If you use this option, the Spellchecker does not pause for corrections of the same misspelling later in the document; they are corrected automatically. When the first occurrence of the misspelled word is highlighted, you should correct the spelling and then press F2. Do not press Enter, because that corrects just the one occurrence.

Use F3, Ignore, to ignore what the program interprets as the misspelling of the current highlighted word and proceed to the next one. Select Ignore for a special word that you would not expect to find in the dictionary, such as the name of a person or a product. Any word you accept by pressing F3 is highlighted again the next time you check this portion of your document or if the same word is encountered later in the document. There is no record of your approval of the word.

The effect of F4, the Ignore All option, is similar to that of F3, except that all occurrences of the highlighted word are accepted as correctly spelled. Use F4 if the same word appears throughout the document and you don't want the Spellchecker to stop at every occurrence. After you press F4, the Spellchecker skips over this word during the current operation of the Document Dictionary Spellcheck command.

The memory table of words approved with the F4 key is cleared at the completion of spellchecking. When you check the spelling again, you must once again identify acceptable words with the F4 key.

Use the Custom option, F5, to add a frequently used word to one of your custom dictionaries. If no custom dictionary exists, the Spellchecker creates one for you and attaches it to your document. Any capitalization is retained in the custom dictionary; syllabication is determined through an algorithm. (More later about custom dictionaries.)

The Delete option, F6, which is equivalent to the Edit Delete Word command, deletes the highlighted word from the document. This function key is useful if you have typed the same word twice and want to delete the second occurrence.

If you want to edit the misspelled word, press F7, the Edit Word option, to display the word on the command line. You can edit it, using the Del key to eliminate individual letters, or you can type characters to insert or overlay, according to the position of the Ins key. Note that the setting of the Ins key is not shown while you are checking your spelling. If Insert was on before you began checking, it will still be on. If you turn it off so that you can easily edit a misspelled word, it will be off when the spell check is completed. Once you have finished editing the word, press Enter to replace the original word in the document.

Press F8, the Corrections option, to view as many as 20 suggested correct spellings in a pop-up menu (see fig. 19.2).

Fig. 19.2.

Suggested spelling corrections.

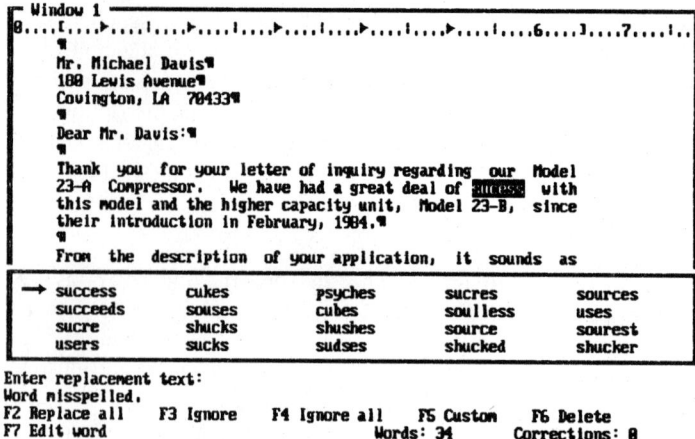

If the Spellchecker locates words in the standard dictionary (or any attached custom dictionaries) that are similar to the misspelled word, those words are displayed when you press F8. Select the correct word by moving the cursor and pressing Enter; the word you select is substituted for the misspelled word. If you want to perform a global substitution, use the Replace option, F2, instead of Enter.

Note that in previous versions of the Smart Word Processor, you pressed F7 to display suggested spelling corrections. In SmartWare II, you press F8.

Correcting Other Errors

The Spellchecker also finds many errors in capitalization of proper nouns and punctuation of abbreviations. The standard dictionary contains the names and abbreviations of the 50 states, the months, and the days of the week, for example. Identical, adjacent words are also flagged. As shown in figure 19.3, the message Word is repeated is displayed and the second occurrence of the word is highlighted. To delete the repeated word, press F6.

Previous versions of the Smart Spellchecker verified the capitalization of each sentence; this feature is not available in SmartWare II.

Creating Dictionary Files

If you want to write the misspelled words to a file, execute the Document Dictionary Spellcheck command, and select the File option instead of Screen. You are prompted for a file name:

    Enter the output filename:

```
┌─ Window 1 ─────────────────────────────────────┐
│0....[....▸....I....▸....I....▸....I....▸....I....6....]....7....I..│
│         ¶                                                            │
│         From the description of your application, it sounds as       │
│         though the Model 23-B will better suit your needs both now   │
│         and in the years to come. If your growth continues at its    │
│         current pace, you would exceed the capacity of the 23-A by   │
│         the summer of next year.¶                                    │
│         ¶                                                            │
│         I am planning on having Mr. Julius Karenski, our sales rep-  │
│         resentative in [in] New Orleans, call you as soon as possible.¶│
│         ¶                                                            │
│         I wish you every success in your new company.◆               │
│                                                                      │
│                                                                      │
│                                                                      │
│                                                                      │
└──────────────────────────────────────────────────┘
Enter replacement text:
Word is repeated.
F2 Replace all    F3 Ignore      F4 Ignore all   F5 Custom     F6 Delete
F7 Edit word      F8 Corrections                 Words: 111   Corrections: 0
```

Fig. 19.3.

Repeated words are flagged.

Type the name of the file to which you want the misspelled words written and press Enter. The file you have designated will contain the address of the misspelled word (section, page, line and position) and the misspelled word itself. A summary displays the number of words checked and the number misspelled. An example of such a file is shown in figure 19.4.

```
s1.1.3.9     Michael
s1.1.20.44   Karenski

SPELL CHECK SUMMARY

Number of words checked:              128
Number of misspellings:                 2
```

Fig. 19.4.

The Dictionary Spellcheck file.

Because custom dictionaries are in ASCII format, you can delete the extraneous data from the spellcheck output file and append only the new words onto one of your dictionaries. Use the Tools Text-Editor to edit a custom dictionary, and Alt-F3 to insert a file. Similarly, you can use the editor to delete any unneeded words from a custom dictionary. Make sure the custom dictionary is sorted in ASCII sequence before saving it. Also, you can use the UDC-Conv command to guarantee that a custom dictionary is in the proper format; refer to Appendix D.

Observing Counts

At the end of the spellcheck, the Spellchecker displays a count of the number of words checked and the number of corrections made. A pop-up menu displays a summary of the total number of words read, corrections made, and words added to any custom dictionaries (see fig. 19.5).

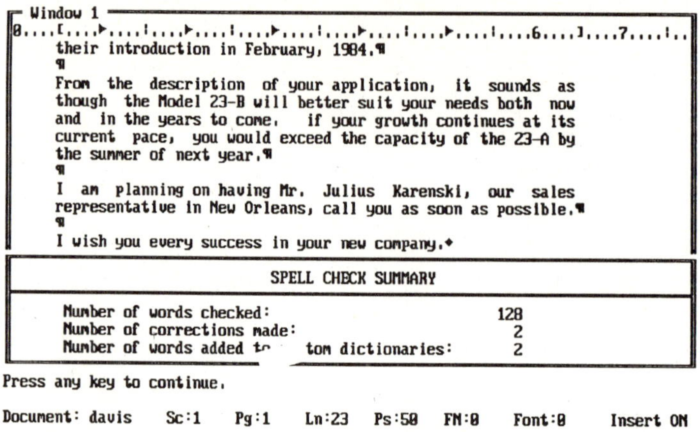

Fig. 19.5.

The Spellcheck summary.

```
┌─Window 1─────────────────────────────────────────────────┐
│0....[....▶....|....▶....|....▶....|....▶....|....6....].....7....|..│
│      their introduction in February, 1984.¶              │
│      ¶                                                   │
│      From the description of your application, it sounds as│
│      though the Model 23-B will better suit your needs both now│
│      and in the years to come. If your growth continues at its│
│      current pace, you would exceed the capacity of the 23-A by│
│      the summer of next year.¶                           │
│      ¶                                                   │
│      I am planning on having Mr. Julius Karenski, our sales│
│      representative in New Orleans, call you as soon as possible.¶│
│      ¶                                                   │
│      I wish you every success in your new company.♦      │
│     ┌──────────────SPELL CHECK SUMMARY──────────────┐    │
│     │ Number of words checked:              128     │    │
│     │ Number of corrections made:             2     │    │
│     │ Number of words added to  tom dictionaries:  2│    │
│     └───────────────────────────────────────────────┘    │
│ Press any key to continue.                               │
│ Document: davis    Sc:1   Pg:1   Ln:23  Ps:50  FN:0  Font:0    Insert ON│
└──────────────────────────────────────────────────────────┘
```

Creating Custom Dictionaries

In addition to the standard dictionary that comes with the SmartWare II Spellchecker, you can create custom dictionaries and attach them to your document so that they are consulted along with the main dictionary. A custom dictionary can be used to store legal terms for a law office, medical words for a doctor's office, or any terms specific to your company or industry. (Legal and medical dictionaries specifically for use with SmartWare II are sold separately.)

If you have a readily available source of terms, you can create a custom dictionary with the Tools Text-Editor. A custom dictionary is an ASCII file with a .UDC extension. The file should have one word per line; the words must be in ASCII order, with all the uppercase words before the lowercase ones. Proper nouns should be entered capitalized; enter other custom words in lowercase.

Hyphenation

Use the Document Dictionary Hyphenate command to hyphenate all of your document or portions of it if hyphens were not inserted initially. When you execute this command, a modified Block-marking mode is initiated in which you can mark an area by pressing F2, or mark a paragraph by pressing F7.

Once inserted, a hyphen can be removed only by deleting the word. Remember that automatic hyphenation can be controlled only through the Tools Preferences Word Processor command; you cannot establish a setting for an individual document. If automatic hyphenation is on and you retype a word, hyphens are inserted automatically if the word does not fit in the margins of the paragraph. If you edit the ruler that governs the paragraph margins, automatic hyphenation takes effect as required. For more precise control over hyphenation, set automatic hyphenation to off in the Word Processor Preferences and use the Document Dictionary Hyphenate command as needed. Use the Layout Document Options menu to control the allowable number of consecutive hyphenated lines.

Hyphenation of words in your custom dictionaries is handled through a formula that determines the correct syllabication.

Special Spellchecker Parameters

Several settings and preferences throughout the Word Processor govern the operation of the Spellchecker. These settings are summarized here.

The settings of the Tools Preferences Word Processor pertain to the entire Word Processor environment and all documents you create or change while the settings are in effect. Changing one of the settings does not alter existing work, but does affect new documents you type or alterations you make to existing documents. Changes to the Preferences settings take effect immediately, without having to quit the Word Processor module.

	`Spellchecker enabled.` If you want to use the Spellchecker, make sure that this option is set to Yes.

	`Correction information.` If you want a pop-up menu of suggested spellings automatically displayed for all unknown words, set this option to Yes. Unknown words are any that do not match the standard dictionary or any of the attached custom dictionaries. If you set this option to No, you can still display a list of suggested spelling corrections when you spell check your document by pressing F8.

	`Auto-hyphenation.` Set to On to have words hyphenated automatically at the end of a line if they do not fit.

The Layout Document-Options Current-Document options apply to the document in the current window. For the settings to be stored with the document, you must save the document to disk.

A similar collection of settings is found in the menu provided by the Layout Document-Options New-Documents command. Any selections in this menu affect new documents you create, but do not override selections you have made for the current document.

	`Spellchecker language.` The options are American, English, French, German, and Spanish.

	`Maximum consecutive hyphen breaks.` Enter the number of lines you would permit to be consecutively hyphenated. The value must be between 1 and 100. If you do not want any hyphen breaks, set the automatic hyphenation to Off in the Preferences menu.

Custom dictionary names. If you want certain custom dictionaries to be attached to the current document, enter the names. If the dictionaries do not reside in the current subdirectory, you should enter the full path, including the drive specification if necessary.

When you spell check a document, if you decide to enter a word into a custom dictionary that is not attached, the dictionary is automatically attached for you.

A maximum of five custom dictionaries can be attached to a document.

The Smart Thesaurus

The SmartWare II Word Processor includes a thesaurus to help you select the right words for your document. Before you use the Document Dictionary Thesaurus command, make sure the words in your document are spelled correctly. The Thesaurus has no capability to correct or recognize misspelled words. The ability to use the Thesaurus is controlled by an option on the Tools Preferences Word Processor menu. The Thesaurus Enabled option on the menu must be set to Yes for you to be able to use the Thesaurus.

If you have entered a word into your document that does not seem to convey the exact meaning you want, use the Thesaurus to help you. The Quick key for looking up the current word in the Thesaurus is Alt-F4. (In previous versions of the Smart Word Processor, this Quick key was used to spellcheck the current paragraph.)

If the cursor is on the word you want to look up, use the Alt-F4 Quick key. If the cursor is not on the word you want to look up, you can execute the Document Dictionary Thesaurus command. You are prompted to:

   Move the cursor to the desired word and press ENTER.

When you move the cursor and press Enter, the word is searched in the Thesaurus. If it is possible that the word derives from multiple roots, a pop-up window displays a list of root words. Select the appropriate root and press Enter. If the root is unambiguous, this step is bypassed. A choice of root words may be displayed if you have attached a prefix or suffix to a word which you would normally find in a dictionary or thesaurus. For the word *preordained*, for example, the Thesaurus would retrieve the possible root words *preordain* and *ordained*. Some plurals of nouns or certain tenses of verbs will probably result in the display of root words. If root words are displayed, select the correct word and press Enter.

A list of meanings is displayed after you have chosen a root word or if it was unnecessary to prompt you for a root. In figure 19.6, the word *application* is searched in the Thesaurus. A pop-up window displays five possible meanings.

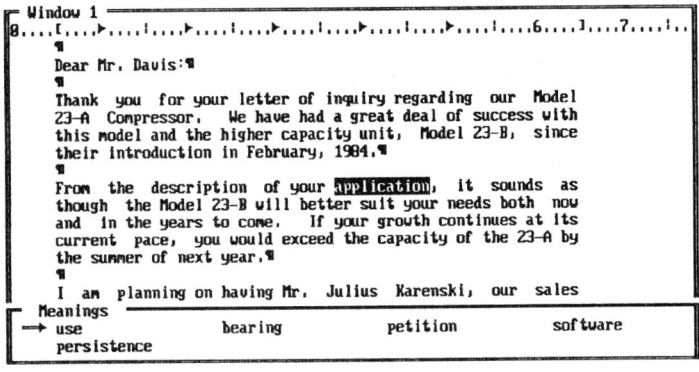

Fig. 19.6.

Pop-up Thesaurus meanings.

There are several function key options available at this time:

F2 View the synonyms for the meaning. You also can use the Enter key.

F3 Replace the search word in the document with the current word. The highlighted word in your document is immediately replaced with the meaning word.

F4 Display a list of meanings for one of the words in the pop-up window. A new pop-up window of meanings for the selected meaning word is displayed.

F5 Display a list of antonyms for the word marked in your text.

F6 Return to the original search for the roots and meanings of the word in the document. Because you can continually search for new meanings and new synonyms, you can end up going down the wrong path. Use F6 to return to the original search.

If you press F2, a pop-up window displays a list of synonyms for the selected meaning (see figure 19.7).

The following function keys are available for use with the synonym list:

F2 Return to the list of meanings.

F3 Replace the search word in the document with the word at the current cursor position in the pop-up menu. The highlighted word in your document is replaced with the synonym. Because the plurals of some nouns or certain tenses of verbs are not displayed in the pop-up window, you may want to edit the word before entering it into the document. Press Enter to display the synonym on the command line, allowing you to edit it.

Fig. 19.7.

Synonym list.

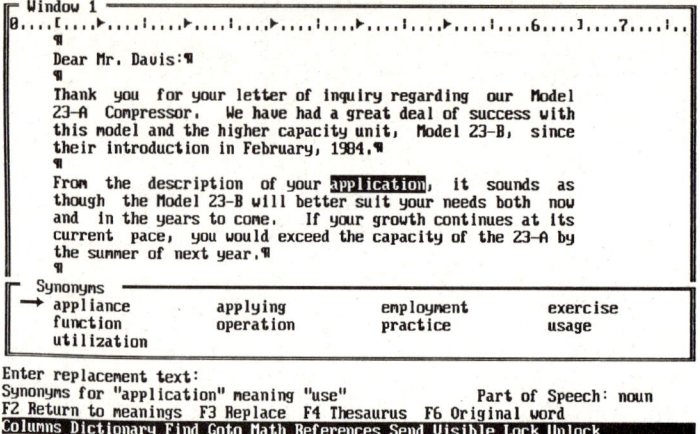

F4 Display a list of meanings for the word at the current cursor position in the pop-up menu. A new pop-up window of meanings for the selected meaning word is displayed.

F6 Return to the original search for the roots and meanings of the word in the document. Because you can continually search for new meanings and new synonyms, you can end up going down the wrong path. Use F6 to return to the original search.

Chapter Summary

The Smart Spellchecker is a valuable feature of the SmartWare II Word Processor. The Spellchecker is as easy to use as the other Word Processor features; it operates quickly, especially if the pop-up menu of suggested spelling corrections is not invoked automatically.

The capability to search custom dictionaries as well as the standard dictionary is a desirable feature which allows you to check the spelling of proper nouns and industry-specific terms.

With the Thesaurus, you can quickly look up synonyms and antonyms for words in your documents. By selecting words according to their roots and meanings, you can select just the right word to convey the exact message you want.

20

Generating a Table of Contents and Index

Three major reference features introduced with the SmartWare II Word Processor are Table of Contents (TOC), index generation, and paragraph numbering. If you have ever produced a long proposal, thesis, or even a book, you know how difficult it is to produce an accurate table of contents and index. If you have followed an outline carefully, the table of contents should closely follow it. But if you add or delete portions of the document, the outline and table of contents may not match up. In either case, you must type the TOC and make sure all the page numbers are accurate.

Preparing an accurate index is even more tedious and time-consuming. A good index makes a reference book or document easier to use. The index must be complete and accurate, and have multiple entries for the same topic, and must be accurate.

The new Table of Contents and Index features of the Word Processor make the creation of these valuable document sections quick, easy, and accurate. And, because you tag the references in the body of the document itself, you can enter them as you go along, rather than having to wait until the document is completed. Don't worry about page numbers, because the system keeps track of them for you.

Automatic paragraph numbering can be useful in the preparation of proposals or technical documentation. You can use this feature to help you create outlines.

Table of Contents

A well-ordered table of contents can be a valuable guide to a proposal or long document. The SmartWare II Word Processor provides the capability of generating a table of contents from special markers embedded in your document.

Selecting Table of Contents Options

The options for the Table of Contents are set in the menu displayed by the Layout Document Options command. Select either the Current Document or New Document option, depending on whether your selections are to apply to the current document only or to all new documents. The menu of choices is shown in figures 20.1 and 20.2.

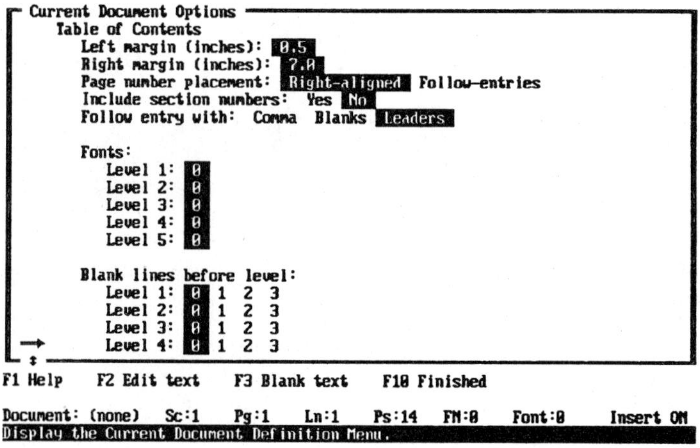

Fig. 20.1.

Layout Document options.

```
┌─ Current Document Options ──────────────────────────────────┐
│    Table of Contents                                        │
│       Left margin (inches):  0.5                            │
│       Right margin (inches): 7.0                            │
│       Page number placement: Right-aligned  Follow-entries  │
│       Include section numbers: Yes  No                      │
│       Follow entry with:  Comma  Blanks  Leaders            │
│                                                             │
│       Fonts:                                                │
│          Level 1:  0                                        │
│          Level 2:  0                                        │
│          Level 3:  0                                        │
│          Level 4:  0                                        │
│          Level 5:  0                                        │
│                                                             │
│       Blank lines before level:                             │
│          Level 1:  0  1  2  3                               │
│          Level 2:  0  1  2  3                               │
│          Level 3:  0  1  2  3                               │
│ →        Level 4:  0  1  2  3                               │
└─────────────────────────────────────────────────────────────┘
 F1 Help    F2 Edit text    F3 Blank text    F10 Finished
 Document: (none)   Sc:1   Pg:1   Ln:1   Ps:14   FM:0   Font:0   Insert ON
 Display the Current Document Definition Menu.
```

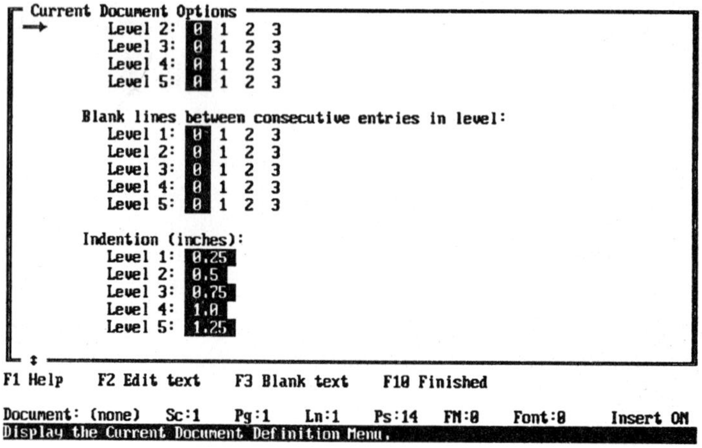

Fig. 20.2.

Layout Document options.

```
┌─ Current Document Options ──────────────────────────────────┐
│ →        Level 2:  0  1  2  3                               │
│          Level 3:  0  1  2  3                               │
│          Level 4:  0  1  2  3                               │
│          Level 5:  0  1  2  3                               │
│                                                             │
│       Blank lines between consecutive entries in level:     │
│          Level 1:  0  1  2  3                               │
│          Level 2:  0  1  2  3                               │
│          Level 3:  0  1  2  3                               │
│          Level 4:  0  1  2  3                               │
│          Level 5:  0  1  2  3                               │
│                                                             │
│       Indention (inches):                                   │
│          Level 1:  0.25                                     │
│          Level 2:  0.5                                      │
│          Level 3:  0.75                                     │
│          Level 4:  1.0                                      │
│          Level 5:  1.25                                     │
└─────────────────────────────────────────────────────────────┘
 F1 Help    F2 Edit text    F3 Blank text    F10 Finished
 Document: (none)   Sc:1   Pg:1   Ln:1   Ps:14   FM:0   Font:0   Insert ON
 Display the Current Document Definition Menu.
```

Your selections in this menu govern the generation of the TOC for the current or new documents. Changing one of the selections in the menu has no effect on a TOC you have already generated; the changes affect the generation of the next TOC for the document. You can change the TOC selection on the Layout Document Options menu either before or after you have added the TOC markers in the document, however.

From the menu, select left and right margins, in inches. Note that both selections are entered relative to the left side of the paper.

Page numbers can be positioned right-aligned or immediately following the TOC entries. If you choose page numbers aligned to the right, your table of contents will look like the following:

```
VIEWING FILES AND ARRANGING DATA . . . . . . . . . . . . . . . . . . . . . . .1
    Arranging your data for best results . . . . . . . . . . . . . . . . . . . . . . . .2
        Using keys . . . . . . . . . . . . . . . . . . . . . . . . . . . . . . . . . . . . . . . . .3
            Keys that do not match. . . . . . . . . . . . . . . . . . . . . . . . . . . . . .4
```

If you want the page numbers to follow the entries, your TOC will look like the following:

```
VIEWING FILES AND ARRANGING DATA...1
    Arranging your data for best results...2
        Using keys...3
            Keys that do not match...4
```

If you have chosen to include section numbers in addition to the page numbers, a hyphen will separate the section and page numbers. If your document has multiple sections, and unless you have specifically designated that the page numbering is to continue from section to section, you will want to include section numbers in your TOC. For more information on page numbering, refer to Chapter 21. The following example shows the use of section numbers:

```
VIEWING FILES AND ARRANGING DATA. . . . . . . . . . . . . . . . . . . . .1-1
    Arranging your data for best results . . . . . . . . . . . . . . . . . . . . . . .1-2
        Using keys. . . . . . . . . . . . . . . . . . . . . . . . . . . . . . . . . . . . . . . .1-3
            Keys that do not match . . . . . . . . . . . . . . . . . . . . . . . . . . . .1-4
```

The previous illustrations use periods to separate the TOC entries from the section or page numbers. You also can follow the entry with blanks, or just a single comma, as shown in the following example:

```
VIEWING FILES AND ARRANGING DATA,   1
    Arranging your data for best results,   2
        Using keys,                         3
            Keys that do not match,         4
```

There are five levels of TOC entries which you can specify; for each level, you can select several options:

1. Fonts. To select a font for a TOC level, move the cursor to the menu entry for the level and press F6 to display a pop-up menu of available fonts. The font selections displayed as a default are the eleven fonts supplied with the Word Processor; any fonts you had previously attached to the current document by using the Layout Font Select Change or Edit command are also displayed.

2. Blank lines before level. The number of blanks lines before the first occurrence of a level in the TOC can be zero through three.

3. Blank lines between consecutive entries in level. When there are consecutive entries of the same level, you can specify that you want zero through three blank lines between them.

4. Indention, in inches. Specify the number of inches to indent each level from the left margin. Note that you are not selecting the space to indent from the previous level, but rather from the left margin, as set by your margin selection for the TOC. Figure 20.2 shows indentations in increments of 0.25 inch.

Press F10 to save the Layout Document Options for the current or new documents.

Adding Table of Contents References

You must add TOC reference entries to your document before you can generate the TOC. It does not matter if you add the TOC markers before or after you make the Layout Document Options selections. Once you have added the reference entries, the system keeps track of the page numbers for you.

To add a reference entry to the TOC, use the Document References Toc Add command. (Use the Quick key Shift-F7 to issue the partial command, Document References Toc.) The Block-marking mode is invoked, allowing you to mark the text to be included in the table of contents. Note that the exact text you mark will appear in the TOC, including capitalization and punctuation.

Once you have selected the text for the TOC, you are prompted to supply a TOC level:

```
Enter Table of Contents level (1 - 5):
```

Type a number from 1 to 5 and press Enter. The level you select appears as you specified in the Layout Document Options menu when you generate the TOC. Be careful, however, if you move text that you have chosen to be included in your TOC. If you move the entire entry, there is no problem because the TOC designation remains with the text. If you move only a portion of the text, the TOC text will consist of only the portion that remains in the original location. If you copy TOC text, the copied material is not automatically designated as TOC material.

Figure 20.3 shows text with the TOC markings. If you do not want to display the TOC markers, use the Document Visible Marks Toc command to hide them. The marks do not indicate the TOC level; you must keep track of the levels on your own. Once text has been selected for TOC marking, you cannot change the level; you must remove the TOC selection from the text and add it again at the new level.

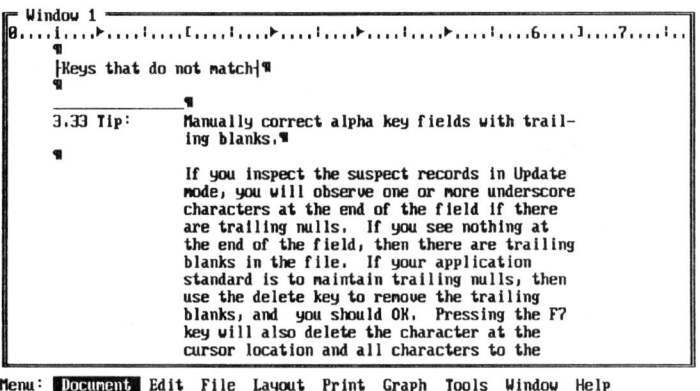

Fig. 20.3.

Text marked as table of contents entry.

TOC entries cannot overlap. If you accidentally add overlapping entries, you receive the following error message:

    Partial spanning of other table of contents items is not allowed.

Press any key to abort the command.

Generating a Table of Contents

Once you have created your document, added the TOC text markers, and made your selections on the Layout Document Options menu, you are ready to generate the TOC. The command to create the TOC is Document References Toc Generate. When you issue this command, the TOC is generated as a separate section at the end of your document. Each new level in the TOC will have a separate ruler, with the margins and indent selection you have chosen. If you need to make any changes, it is easier to regenerate the TOC than to change the rulers.

If you want to have your table of contents appear at the beginning of the document, you can move the text in the section.

Because the text in the TOC is generated from the text in the body of your document, make sure you perform your spellchecking prior to generating the TOC.

Successive generations of a TOC are easily accomplished because the TOC section is recognized by the Word Processor as being special. If you generate another TOC, you are reminded:

    The previously generated TOC section will be deleted. Continue? (y/n)

When you respond with *Y*, the old TOC section is replaced with the new table of contents. If you remove the section break between the TOC and any other section, however, the special quality of the TOC section is not recognized.

Removing a Table of Contents Marker

If you want to unmark TOC text, position the cursor in the text area and issue the Document References Toc Remove command. The next time you generate a TOC, the previously marked text does not appear in it. Note that the text is not deleted from the body of the document, nor is it deleted from the currently existing TOC. You also can remove a TOC marker using the Del key rather than using the Document References Toc Remove command.

When you delete a TOC entry, the successive entries do not automatically advance to the next level. TOC entries retain their level designation regardless of the addition or deletion of previous entries. No sorting of the entries by level takes place. Therefore, if you move a level 1 entry after a level 2 entry, the level 2 appears first in the TOC.

Indexing your Document

A thorough index is invaluable for a reference document. The SmartWare II Word Processor provides the capability of automatically generating an Index with multiple cross references and page numbers.

Selecting Index Options

The options for the Index capability are set in the menu offered by the Layout Document Options command. Select the Current Document or New Documents option, depending on whether your selection is to apply to only the current document or to all new documents. The menu of choices is displayed in figure 20.4.

Your selections in this menu govern the generation of the index for the current document or new ones. If you have already generated an index for the current document, changing one of the selections in the menu has no effect until you generate another index. You can change the index selection on the menu before or after you have added the index markers in the document, however.

From the menu, select left and right margins, in inches. Note that both selections are entered relative to the left side of the paper.

Chapter 20: Generating a Table of Contents and Index

```
┌─ Current Document Options ──────────────────────────────┐
│   Index                                                 │
│ → Left margin (inches): 0.5                             │
│     Right margin (inches): 7.0                          │
│                                                         │
│     Alphabetic headings:  None  Lowercase  Uppercase    │
│     Alphabetic heading alignment:  Left-aligned  Right-aligned  Centered │
│     Alphabetic heading font: 0                          │
│     Blank lines before alphabetic heading:  0  1  2  3  │
│     Blank lines after alphabetic heading:   0  1  2  3  │
│                                                         │
│     Primary entries font: 0                             │
│     Subordinate entries font: 0                         │
│     Blank lines between primary entries:  0  1  2  3    │
│     Subordinate entries indention (inches): 0.25        │
│                                                         │
│     Page number placement:  Right-aligned  Follow-entries │
│     Include section numbers:  Yes  No                   │
│     Follow entry with:  Comma  Blanks  Leaders          │
└─────────────────────────────────────────────────────────┘
F1 Help    F2 Edit text    F3 Blank text    F10 Finished
Document: ttttocr  Sc:2  Pg:5  Ln:1  Ps:8  FN:0  Font:0  Insert ON
Display the Current Document Definition Menu.
```

Fig. 20.4.

Index options.

If you want individual letters as alphabetic headings, you can select them to be generated in upper- or lowercase, or you can omit them altogether. The headings can be aligned to the left, the right, or centered.

Select the font you want to use for the alphabetic headings. To select the font, position the cursor on the menu entry and press F6 to display a pop-up menu of available fonts. The font selections displayed as a default are the eleven fonts supplied with the Word Processor; any fonts you had previously attached to the current document by using the Layout Font Select, Change, or Edit command are also displayed.

Select the number of blank lines you would like to have before and after the alphabetic headings. The range is zero to three lines.

Select fonts for the primary and subordinate index entries. To select a font, position the cursor on the menu entry and press F6 to display a pop-up menu of available fonts. The font selections displayed as a default are the eleven fonts supplied with the Word Processor; any fonts you had previously attached to the current document by using the Layout Font Select, Change, or Edit command are also displayed.

Select the number of blank lines you would like to have between the primary entries. The range is zero to three lines.

Enter the number of inches to indent the subordinate entries from the left margin. The minimum number of inches is zero; you must allow at least one inch between the indent and the right margin.

Page numbers must be right-aligned or immediately follow the index entries. If you want the page numbers to be aligned to the right, your index will look like the following:

K

Key
    Nonmatch 5, 6, 7
    Trailing blanks 5

Q

Query
    Blank elimination 7
    Trim function 7

If you want the page numbers immediately after the index entries, your index will look like the following:

K

Key
    Nonmatch...5, 6, 7
    Trailing blanks...5

Q

Query
    Blank elimination...7
    Trim function...7

If you choose to include section numbers in addition to the page numbers, they will be separated by a hyphen. If your document has multiple sections, and unless you have specifically designated that the page numbering is to continue from section to section, you will want to include sections in your index. For more information on page numbering, refer to Chapter 21.

The previous examples of the index use periods to separate the index entry from the page number. You also can select blanks as separators, or use commas as follows:

K

Key
    Nonmatch, 5, 6, 7
    Trailing blanks, 5

Q

Query
    Blank elimination, 7
    Trim function, 7

When you have completed the menu selections for the format of your document index, press F10 to return to the command level of the Word Processor.

Adding an Index Marker

To add an index marker to your document, use the Document References Index Add command. (Use the Quick key Shift-F6 to mark the current word. Use Shift-F5 to execute the partial command, Document References Index.)

When you execute the command, the Block mode is invoked. In every instance when you are prompted to identify a block, there is a beginning point and an ending point. As a default, the beginning point is the cursor position at the time you execute the command. Once you are in the Block-definition mode, however, you can designate a new beginning point, or anchor, by moving the cursor and pressing F2.

You can designate the ending point by moving the cursor; the area affected by your choice is displayed in reverse video (see fig. 20.5).

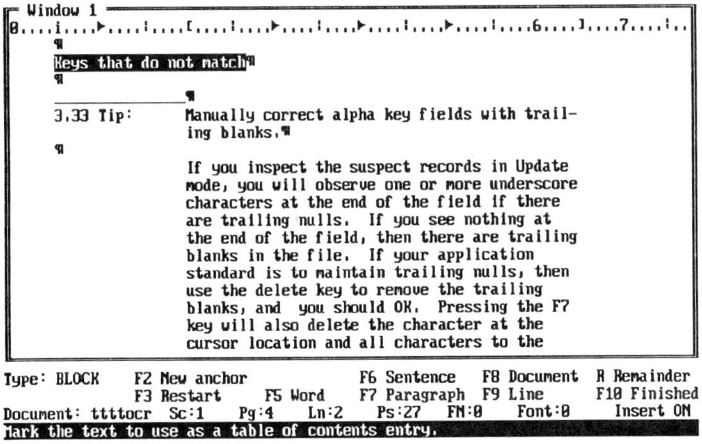

Fig. 20.5.

Block marking.

To make it easier to mark a block, there are several keys you can use:

    F5 Word
    F6 Sentence
    F7 Paragraph
    F8 Entire Document
    F9 Line
    R Remainder of document

Rather than moving the cursor through your document to mark text, you can select the Word option (F5), for example, to mark the current word, bounded by either blanks or punctuation, as the block. Note that the trailing blanks and punctuation are included in the word definition boundary. Or you can select F6 to mark the current sentence. To be recognized, a sentence must end with a period or a paragraph marker.

The Paragraph option (F7) indicates the current paragraph as the block. Use the Line option (F9) to specify the current line on which the cursor is positioned.

Choosing the Remainder option (R) indicates that the range extends from the current cursor position to the end of the document.

Repeated pressing of one of the selection function keys moves the highlight block to the next applicable area. For example, each time you press F6, the next sentence is highlighted. This method enables you to move through the document more quickly than with the cursor movement keys; the effect is not cumulative, however. If you press F6 twice, you don't mark two sentences, just the second one. Once you have marked an area using a function key, you can mark an additional area by moving the cursor.

Press F8 to specify the entire document as marked, regardless of the current cursor position.

Once you have selected a block, you can change your mind by pressing F3 for Restart. Press F10 or Enter to complete your selection.

By marking a block of text, you identify the text with which the index reference is to be associated. Once you have identified the block, you are prompted for the index entries:

    Enter index entries:

You can respond to this prompt in several ways, depending on how you want your index to appear.

1. The easiest response is to simply press Enter. The text you have blocked becomes a primary index entry. If you use this method, clearly you do not want to block anything more than a word or a phrase. If you use Shift-F6 to mark the current word, the word is blocked for you and is used as the index entry.

2. If you want to use the blocked text as a secondary entry, you must supply your own primary entry. In the following example, the word *Query* is the primary entry, followed by the two secondary entries:

    Query
        Blank elimination, 7
        Trim function, 7

    If you had marked *Trim function* in the body of the text as the index entry, to specify *Query* as the primary entry, in response to the Enter index entries: prompt, you would type

    Query:

Type the name of the primary index entry followed by a colon to use the default blocked text as the secondary index entry.

3. If you want to maintain the marker in the text but want to supply your own secondary entry rather than accepting the marked block, you must type the secondary entry after the colon:

   Query:Removing Blanks

   The text following the colon will be used as the secondary entry, rather than the blocked text.

4. Often you would like the same text to be referenced multiple times in the index. If you want to use the default blocked text as both a primary entry and a secondary entry, use a leading forward slash (/) as a separator:

   /Query:

   The slash is used to enter multiple responses to the entry of the index reference. Because no text precedes the slash, it is interpreted as an Enter, which, of course, accepts the blocked text as a primary reference. Following the slash, a primary entry is specified before the colon, and the default secondary entry is taken from the blocked text.

   If the blocked text in the paragraph had been *Trim function*, the response to the preceding prompt would produce the following index entries:

   Q

   Query
       Trim function 7

   T

   Trim function. 7

   Notice that the default text is entered into the index as both secondary to the primary heading *Query* and primary unto itself.

5. The same default secondary can be used under multiple primary headings at the same time, using the slash (/) as the separator:

   Query:/Function:/Blank removal:/Link problems:

   The slash is used to separate the specification of multiple primary headings.

6. You can also specify the default text as primary in its own right, as well as being secondary to several specified primary headings:

   /Query:/Function:/Blank removal:/Link problems:

In this example, a leading slash indicates the use of the blocked text as its own primary heading, similar to example 4. (The slash can be leading or trailing to accomplish this effect.) The result of this specification is as follows:

> B
>
> Blank removal
>   Trim function 7
>
> F
>
> Function
>   Trim function 7
>
> L
>
> Link problems
>   Trim function 7
>
> Q
>
> Query
>   Trim function 7
>
> T

Trim function 7

Notice that each entry is delineated by a slash and followed by a colon that designates another primary entry, with the default text as the secondary entry. The leading slash creates a primary entry of the default text.

Be sure to include the colon after the primary entry; if you don't, you will create a primary entry of the text you have typed, but the default secondary entry will not be entered into the index.

7. Finally, if you do not want to use the default blocked text as your index entry but you still want to have multiple primary and secondary references, you can enter pairs of primary and secondary index entries, separated by the slash character:

   Query:trim blanks/Trim:blank removal function/Link:hidden blanks

If you use this index specification, the result is as follows:

> L
>
> Link
>   hidden blanks 7

Q

Query
      trim blanks...7

T

Trim
      blank removal function..................................7

If you add a leading or trailing slash, the default text also is used as a primary entry. Instead of the default primary, you can also type your own primary entry, without the trailing colon.

Editing your Index Entry

If you want to change the specifications for the index entries, position the cursor on the blocked text and issue the Document References Index Edit command. The index specification is displayed on the command line, preceded by the following prompt:

    Enter index entries:

Notice that any default text has been added to what you originally specified. If you had marked *Trim function* in the body of the text as the index entry and specified *Query* as the primary entry, for example, you would have typed the following in response to the preceding prompt:

    Query:

Type the name of the primary index entry followed by a colon to specify the default blocked text as the secondary index entry. You don't have to type the secondary entry. When you edit the index entry, however, the specification will appear as follows:

    Query:Trim function

Notice that the default blocked text is filled in, as if you typed it.

To edit any index entry, use the right- and left-arrow keys to position the cursor as needed on the line; use the Delete key or the Backspace key to delete characters from the line. You can toggle the Insert mode on and off with the Ins key. Press Enter when your editing is complete.

Deleting an Index Reference

If you want to delete an index reference, position your cursor on the blocked text and issue the Document References Index Remove command. Or you can use the Delete key while in Text Entry mode to remove one of the markers. The text will no longer be identified as an index reference.

Generating an Index

After you have added and edited the index references, you will want to create the index itself. To make the index, use the Document References Index Generate command.

The index you generate is always appended to your current document as a separate section. Your selections in the Layout Document Options menu, for new documents or the current document, govern the appearance of your index.

Once the index is generated, it is like any other text—almost. You can edit the index or add other material to it. If you generate another index for the same document during the same session, however, the new version of the index overlays the previous version, obliterating any changes you may have made. You are prompted as follows:

        The previously generated Index section will be deleted. Continue? (y/n)

Press *Y* to generate the new index. If you do not want to overlay your previous index, press *N*. Thus, although you can edit an index section after it has been generated, it retains the special index attribute that makes it different from other sections of your document.

Paragraph Numbering

Along with the table of contents and indexing capabilities, another feature new with the SmartWare II Word Processor is the capability to number paragraphs automatically. Being able to generate paragraph numbers, rather than simply typing them, has several advantages:

1. Consistency. If the numbers are generated for you, you can be certain that the numbering scheme is consistent throughout your document. You can also be sure you have not duplicated or skipped the numbers of any paragraphs.

2. Flexibility. If you had simply typed paragraph numbers, you would also have to change them if you decided to insert an additional paragraph. If you use the paragraph numbering feature of the Word Processor,

paragraphs are automatically renumbered for you if you insert a new one. If you move a paragraph, the numbers are automatically adjusted, too.

3. Format changes. If you decide to switch from one numbering style to another, you simply change the Layout Document Option for the current document; the changes are made for you. The style of the paragraph numbers can follow one of three different formats, as governed by the menu choices in the Layout Document Options you have chosen for new documents or for the current document. The portion of the Document Options menu dealing with paragraph numbering is shown in figure 20.6.

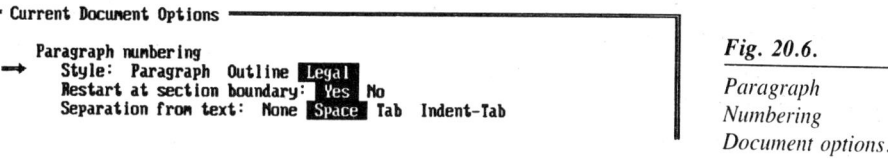

Fig. 20.6.

Paragraph Numbering Document options.

Selecting Paragraph Number Options

You can choose a Paragraph, Outline, or Legal numbering style. Paragraph numbers themselves can be nested to a maximum level of 15 deep. Table 20.1 shows the format for each level of the three styles:

**Table 20.1
Level Formats**

Level	Outline	Paragraph	Legal
1	I.	1.	1.
2	A.	a.	1.1
3	1.	i.	1.1.1
4	a)	(1)	1.1.1.1
5	(1)	(a)	1.1.1.1.1
6	(a)	(i)	1.1.1.1.1.1
7	i)	1)	1.1.1.1.1.1.1
8	a.	a)	1.1.1.1.1.1.1.1
9	i.	i)	1.1.1.1.1.1.1.1.1
10		i)	1.1.1.1.1.1.1.1.1.1
11		i)	1.1.1.1.1.1.1.1.1.1.1
12		i)	1.1.1.1.1.1.1.1.1.1.1.1
13		i)	1.1.1.1.1.1.1.1.1.1.1.1.1
14		i)	1.1.1.1.1.1.1.1.1.1.1.1.1.1
15		i)	1.1.1.1.1.1.1.1.1.1.1.1.1.1.1

Although there are theoretically 15 levels of paragraph numbers, the tags are unique only through level 11 for the Outline mode, level 9 in the Paragraph Numbering mode, and level 15 in the Legal mode. Because you specify the desired mode on the Layout Document Option menu, only one mode can be used in any given document.

As shown in figure 20.6, you can select the paragraph numbers to restart at the section boundaries.

The separation of the paragraph number from the body of the text can be None if you do not want any separation at all, Space if you want one space, or Tab if you want to tab over to the next tab stop automatically. If you want every line of your paragraph to align with the first tab stop after the paragraph number, select Indent-Tab on the menu. (The tab symbol inserted on the screen in this case is similar to a square 7, rather than the normal triangular tab symbol.)

The following is an example of the use of the Indent-Tab option:

1. This is an example of aligning the body of a paragraph with the first tab stop when using paragraph numbers.

The alignment of the paragraph body with the first tab stop is similar to the results you achieve using the Indent Tab key, Ctrl-T. If only some paragraphs are numbered, you may achieve better results with this Indent Tab. An alternative method is to use a negative indent, or outdent, and select the Tab option when using paragraph numbers.

Inserting Paragraph Numbers

To insert a paragraph number, use the Document References Paragraph Number Insert command. (The Quick key Shift-F8 can be used for the Document References Paragraph Number portion of the command.) If you select Insert, the two options are:

    Automatic Fixed

If you select Automatic, you can increase the level of the paragraph by inserting an Indent Tab (Ctrl-T) before the paragraph number; if you select Fixed, inserting an Indent Tab does not change the number. In either case, paragraph numbers are adjusted automatically if you insert a new numbered paragraph.

Removing Paragraph Numbers

To remove a paragraph number, position the cursor on the number and issue the Document References Paragraph Number Remove command. You also can use the Del key to delete the paragraph number. Even though the number may appear to be more than one character in length, in fact it is only one character; position the cursor on the number and press the Del key once.

Moving and Copying Paragraphs with Numbers

An advantage of using the automatic paragraph numbering feature of the SmartWare II Word Processor lies in the capability of having the system keep track of the numbers for you. If you change your mind about the order of importance of your paragraphs and move them around, the numbers are adjusted automatically for you. Even if you copy a paragraph that is numbered, the new version of the paragraph is assigned a new number, and the remaining paragraph numbers are altered.

Be aware that paragraph numbers referenced in the body of your document are not automatically adjusted as you add or delete paragraphs. If you have a reference to paragraph number 5.2.3 in your document, and you later insert a new numbered paragraph in front of 5.2.3, so that it is now 5.2.4, the original reference will be incorrect. You must manually locate any paragraph references and make sure they are still correct before you print your document.

Chapter Summary

Several powerful new reference features have been added to the SmartWare II Word Processor. The Table of Contents (TOC) feature can be used to create a separate TOC section, based on text you have marked throughout the body of your document. Complete control of the format of the TOC is provided in the Layout Document Options, including margins, alignment, fonts, and indentation. Up to five levels of TOC entries can be specified.

The Index capability allows you to mark text to be included in an index which you can create as a separate section at the end of your document. You can use the text in the document as the basis for the index entries, or you can supply your own wording. Both primary and secondary index entries can be specified. Control over the format of the index is selected from the Layout Document Options menu. You also can elect to have your paragraphs automatically numbered. Three types of numbering schemes are available: Paragraph, Outline, and Legal. Up to 15 levels of paragraph numbers can be entered and maintained. As numbered paragraphs are inserted or moved, the numbering is automatically adjusted.

21

Printing and Merging Text

In the SmartWare II Word Processor, printing a document involves sending it from the current window or from a disk file to the printer, or to another disk file for later printing. Documents can be printed in either of two modes: Enhanced or Draft. Draft mode uses the built-in fonts and other capabilities of your printer. Enhanced mode allows you to include graphs in your documents or to print special fonts, depending on the capabilities of your printer.

You select the Print command from the menu; the Quick key is Alt-P. There are four initial options to the Print command, shown in figure 21.1.

```
          though the Model 23-B will better suit your needs both now
          and in the years to come.  If your growth continues at its
          current pace, you would exceed the capacity of the 23-A by
          the summer of next year.¶

Option: Document Merge Options Preset
print
Document: davis   Sc:1   Pg:1   Ln:11   Ps:53   FM:0   Font:0   Insert ON
Print an enhanced or draft version of the specified document.
```

Fig. 21.1.

Selecting the Print command.

Setting Default Print Options

Even before you create any documents, you may want to set the Print Preset defaults. The Print Preset command is used to establish default settings that apply to all documents you create in the Word Processor unless you override the defaults for a single document or section of a document. The selections for Print Options, which apply to the individual sections of the current document, are identical to the Print Preset selections. The default settings of Print Preset are shown in figures 21.2, 21.3, and 21.4.

Fig. 21.2.

Screen 1 of Print Preset.

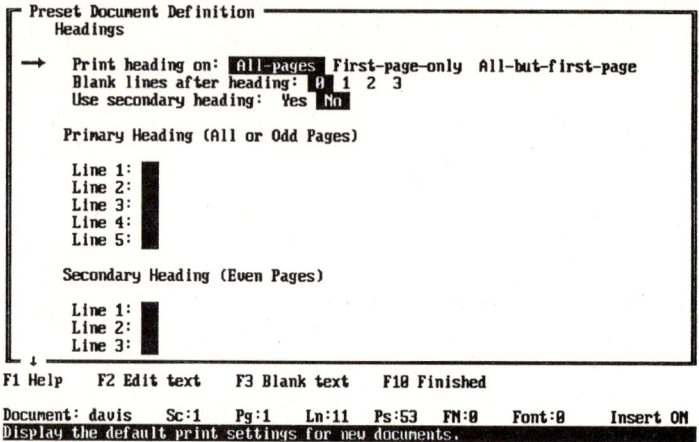

Fig. 21.3.

Screen 2 of Print Preset.

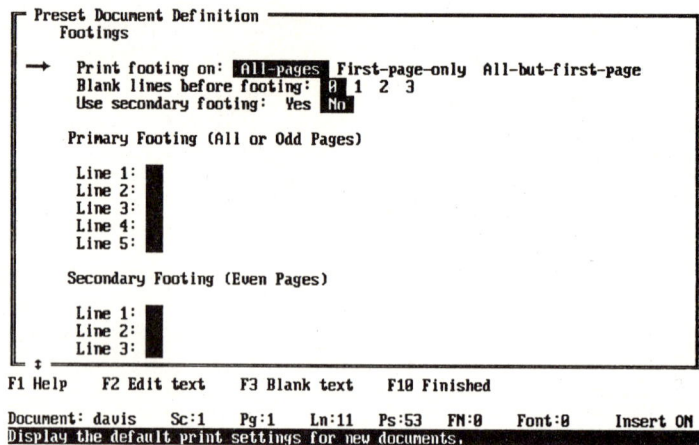

You should change any of the following preset entries to establish the default options you want apply to any newly created documents.

Using Headings and Footings

As many as five lines of primary and secondary headings and footings can be printed on each page. Primary headings and footings are printed on all pages; if secondary headings or footings are selected, they are printed only on even-numbered pages.

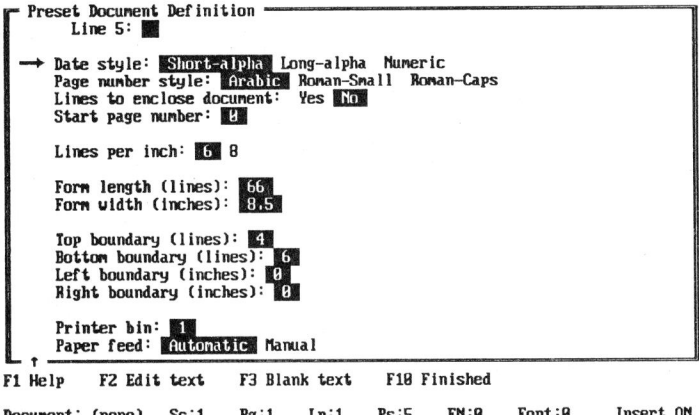

Fig. 21.4.

Screen 3 of Print Preset.

A maximum of 255 characters can be entered on one heading or footing line. You can insert the following special print codes to control the format or contents of heading or footing lines:

Format Control

%L Left-Justify
%C Center
%R Right-Justify

Line Contents

%P Page Number
%D Date
%T Time
%F Name of file being printed

Print control codes must be entered in uppercase letters. The codes can be used in combination with other control codes on the same line, or with text literals. Separating the control codes with a blank space is not necessary unless you want to print a blank character.

You can exercise font control in headings and footings by using a code sequence in the following format:

%[*n*bu]

where

n = Font Number
B = Bold on

b = Bold off
U = Underscore on
u = Underscore off

The following format:

%[12bU]%CTHE WATKINS COMPANY

prints the words THE WATKINS COMPANY in font number 12, underscored and centered.

This format is similar to the specification of fonts in a footnote. Be sure to enter the centering code, %C, after the symbols for the font, because even though they will not print, the font markings are counted in the number of characters to center.

If you select secondary heading or footings, the number of lines allocated for them will be the greater of the number of lines of either, so that the text is evenly spaced on both odd and even pages. If you have two heading lines on odd pages, for example, a second, blank heading line will be inserted on the even pages. Ordinarily, you can print a blank line in a heading or a footing only if a nonblank line follows it.

To edit your heading or footing line entries, move the cursor to the line you want to change and press F2 or the right-arrow key. You can then use the right- and left-arrow keys and the Delete and Insert keys to control alterations you may want to make. To delete a line of text, move the cursor to the line and press F3.

If you want to enclose the body of your text with lines, select *Yes* for the option (see fig. 21.4). The lines are printed below the heading and above the footing.

Printing Dates

If you choose to include a date in the heading or footing of your document, make sure that you set the system date when you first turn on your computer.

Dates can be printed in one of three formats:

Date Style	*Example*
Short Alpha	20 Jun 65
Long Alpha	June 20, 1965
Numeric	06/20/65

Printing Page Numbers

To include a page number in a heading or footing, use the % P control code. The following control code format prints and centers the word Page:, followed by a space and the page number:

%CPage: %P

The starting page number is that which appears on the first page of the document when it is printed—not on the first page you want to print. If you change the starting page number to three, for example, the first page will have the number 3 on it. (The choice of beginning a print beyond the start of your document is made when you issue the Print Document command.)

Page numbers can be printed in Arabic numerals (such as 4), lowercase Roman numerals (iv), or uppercase Roman numerals (IV).

Printing Page Format

Your selection of the number of vertical lines per inch may be affected by the characteristics of your printer. You may not be able to change this attribute if your printer does not support variable line spacing.

The prompts for Form length (lines) and Form width (inches) refer to the physical size of the paper. If, for example, your paper is 11 inches long and you set the lines per inch at 6, the form length is 66 lines.

The top and bottom boundary selections control the number of blank lines that appear between the edge of the paper and the first or last printed line.

The left boundary selection specifies the distance (in inches) between the left edge of the paper and the left margin of your text. If you specify a left boundary of one inch on this screen and the ruler has a left margin of 0.5 inches, then 1.5 inches will separate the edge of the paper from the first character of the printed line.

At the Printer bin selection, enter the number of the printer bin from which the paper is to be selected, if your printer supports this option.

Select Manual paper feed if you want your printer to pause so that you can use single sheets of paper.

Press F10 to save the Print Preset changes to your disk. The default options of any newly created documents will conform to the selections in the Preset menu.

Printing Footnotes

Note that footnote placement is now selected in the Layout options for the current document. In previous versions of SmartWare, footnotes were controlled in the Print Options menu.

Setting Section Options

To set the options for an individual section of your document, position the cursor in the section and execute the Print Options command. The choices are the same as for the Print Preset menu. Print Preset, however, establishes the default options for newly created documents, and Print Options is used to set or change the options for individual sections of the current document.

Note that if you have multiple sections, you can establish different options for each of them. An important difference between Print Preset and Print Options is that you should set the starting page number to zero if you want the page numbers in later sections to follow those of the previous section. Press F6 to copy the Print options from another section. The prompt asks you to:

    Enter the number of the section to be copied:

Enter a valid section number and press Enter.

Printing your Document

Once you have chosen the Print Preset and the Print Options settings and have created your document, you are ready to print it.

When you execute the Print Document command, a pop-up window displays the names of both the .DOC and .TXT files in the current subdirectory. Use the cursor to select a file to be printed. If you want to print the document in the current window, select [default] (see figure 21.5); otherwise, select a file from the disk by moving the arrow in the pop-up menu. Remember that there may be two versions of the same file; one in memory and the other on disk. If you have made changes to your document but have not saved it, the two versions will be different.

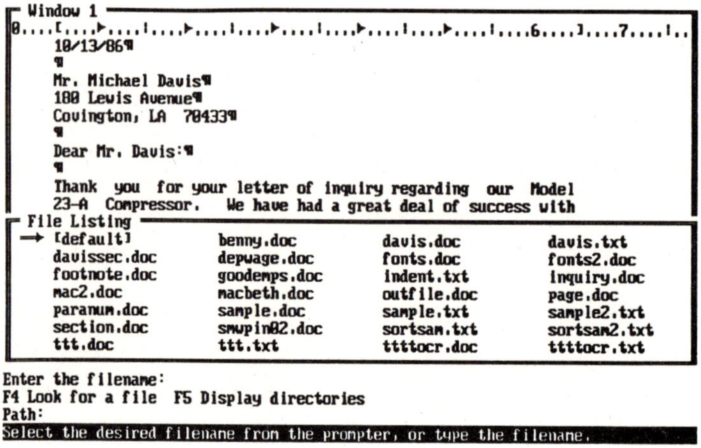

Fig. 21.5.

Selecting a file to print.

```
┌─ Window 1 ─────────────────────────────────────────────────────────┐
│0....[....►....I....►....I....►....I....►....I....6....]....7....I..│
│   10/13/86¶                                                        │
│   ¶                                                                │
│   Mr. Michael Davis¶                                               │
│   100 Lewis Avenue¶                                                │
│   Covington, LA  70433¶                                            │
│   ¶                                                                │
│   Dear Mr. Davis:¶                                                 │
│   ¶                                                                │
│   Thank you for your letter of inquiry regarding our Model         │
│   23-A Compressor.  We have had a great deal of success with       │
├─ File Listing ─────────────────────────────────────────────────────┤
│ → [default]      benny.doc       davis.doc       davis.txt         │
│   davissec.doc   depwage.doc     fonts.doc       fonts2.doc        │
│   footnote.doc   goodemps.doc    indent.txt      inquiry.doc       │
│   mac2.doc       macbeth.doc     outfile.doc     page.doc          │
│   paranum.doc    sample.doc      sample.txt      sample2.txt       │
│   section.doc    smupin02.doc    sortsam.txt     sortsam2.txt      │
│   ttt.doc        ttt.txt         ttttocr.doc     ttttocr.txt       │
└────────────────────────────────────────────────────────────────────┘
 Enter the filename:
 F4 Look for a file    F5 Display directories
 Path:
 Select the desired filename from the prompter, or type the filename.
```

Note that as you move the cursor from name to name in the pop-up menu, the date, time, and size of the file are displayed on the status line. If the file you want to print is not in the current subdirectory, you can type the path and name of the file in response to the following prompt:

    Enter the filename:

Chapter 21: Printing and Merging

You also can use the F4 key to search for a file, or the F5 ke˙
tory and file.

Once you have selected the file to print, the next prompt asks 1ͺ
you want to use:

    Enhanced Draft

Select Draft to use your printer's built-in fonts and print attributes. All printers can print draft text. Most printers also have the built-in capability of underscoring text and printing in boldface. Increasing numbers of dot-matrix and laser printers have built-in or downloadable fonts. If your printer is fully supported by the SmartWare II system, several of the fonts may be available even when selecting Draft mode.

Whenever possible, use the Draft mode to take advantage of the printer's built-in fonts, because Draft mode is faster. When you use special fonts or include a graph in a document, however, the Enhanced mode is required.

Once you have selected Draft or Enhanced, you see the following prompt:

    Enter the number of copies:

If you want just one copy, press Enter. If you want more than one copy, type the number you want and press Enter. The next prompt asks for the starting point as follows:

    Enter the starting section and page:

If you want to start on page 1 of section 1, press Enter. You can, however, specify the starting section or page or both. Sample responses to the prompt for the starting point include the following:

Response	*Meaning*
s2p3	Section 2, page 3
s3	Section 3, page 1
8	Section 1, page 8
s5.4	Section 5, page 4

Note that to specify a section, you must type an *S*, but to specify the page in a section, you can use a *P* or a period. A number by itself specifies a page number.

The page number represents a physical page in the document, not necessarily a logical page number. If, for example section 1 has three pages, section 2 has five pages numbered 1 through 5, and you print beginning at page 5, you will get pages 2 through 5 of section 2 (the fifth through the eighth pages of the entire document).

Next, you see the prompt for the final page to print:

    Enter the ending section and page:

Enter the section and page number, using the same set of rules as with the starting page prompt. The final prompt asks where you want the document sent:

```
Printer Disk
```

Press either *P* or *D*, depending on whether the output is to go directly to your printer or to a disk file.

If you select Printer, printing begins immediately. If you send your document to disk so that you can produce your hard copy printout at a later time or transmit the output to another computer, you are prompted as follows:

```
Enter the output filename:
```

Enter a file name (up to eight characters long) and press Enter. A file is created with the name you have supplied; no extension is added. If you would like an extension, you must supply your own. If a disk file with that name already exists, the Word Processor writes over the file only after asking for your approval:

```
File of that name exists. Overwrite? (y/n)
```

Answer *Y* if you want to write over the file. If you answer *N*, the command is aborted and you must begin the Print command again; you are not prompted for an alternative output file name.

If your printer is other than generic and you are printing to a disk file, all the control codes your printer requires will be embedded in the file. You probably will not be able to view this file successfully with an editor, because of the escape codes and the lack of the customary carriage returns and line feeds. If you want to view your printed output as a file, set your printer to Generic in the Tools Preferences Hardware menu. Previous versions of Smart always created ASCII print files.

If you are printing a file from the disk (not [default]), you are prompted for a password if the file is protected.

Printing in Enhanced Mode

If you are printing special fonts that are not built into your graphics printer, or if you are including a graph in your document, you must use the Enhanced mode. Enhanced printing is slower than Draft mode printing because each letter is treated as if it were part of a graph. The results, however, can be outstanding, especially when you include a graph in the body of a document.

The prompts for the Enhanced mode are the same as for draft printing. A new feature of SmartWare II allows you to print Enhanced mode to a disk file, not just to the printer. Because all your printer's control codes will be written to the disk file, you can create the actual hard copy at a later time. At the DOS prompt, you can copy the file to your printer:

   Copy text.prt prn

This DOS command will copy the output print file to your printer.

Merging Text

To produce multiple copies of a letter with embedded text taken from an input data file, use the Print Merge command. Mass mailings and personalized form letters can easily be produced with this command. Instead of using a data file as the source of the data, you also can enter the variable data directly from the keyboard. The Print Merge command works well with external files in the Smart format that have been created from databases in the Database.

Merging Data from a File

When merging data from a file, the document you create in the Word Processor is the main document; the external file you send from your database is called the input file. Before you use the Print Merge command, make sure that your input file is properly prepared. If the input data file is coming from one of the other Smart-Ware application modules, you should export it in the Smart format, or use one of the Send commands.

Notice that a Smart file contains the field names in quotation marks on the first line, and the actual data on the successive lines of the file. Alphanumeric fields are bounded by double quotation marks ("), and spaces are used to separate the individual fields. If you send data from the database, numeric fields will be bounded by quotation marks; they will not have quotation marks around them if you use the File Export command. Figure 21.6 shows a sample data file exported from the Database. It is ready for use as input for the Print Merge command.

```
"SSN" "FIRST" "LAST" "WAGE" "PHONE" "EMPDATE"
"345-98-7593" "Rosanna" "Ronaldo" 878.75 "(312) 439-8760" "10/01/1959"
"498-48-3980" "Debbie" "Linden" 1403.79 "(413) 886-3498" "06/20/1975"
"239-87-8876" "Michael" "Davis" 734.56 "(318) 997-6621" "05/25/1969"
"208-23-0300" "Julius" "Karenski" 1020.33 "(606) 779-5000" "08/20/1971"
"887-63-5498" "Jeff" "Jarris" 629.23 "(614) 776-3398" "07/01/1970"
"598-44-5922" "LeAnne" "Markus" 887.49 "(303) 797-5939" "10/30/1965"
"876-33-8989" "Marilyn" "Lester" 1516.26 "(617) 873-0979" "09/05/1975"
"987-65-7653" "David" "Marzetti" 901.45 "(704) 472-0042" "10/30/1985"
"387-59-8374" "Charles" "Steffans" 654.34 "(207) 878-4880" "10/15/1981"
"498-34-5998" "Paula" "Bernstein" 1004.56 "(916) 475-4220" "06/15/1975"
"776-39-8763" "Alfred" "Adelson" 956.43 "(203) 739-3095" "07/23/1945"
"345-54-2287" "Ellen" "Aliakbari" 997.66 "(201) 727-9242" "08/15/1972"
"198-03-3024" "Howard E." "Peters" 1544 "(318) 729-5060" "10/01/1985"
```

Fig. 21.6.

A SmartWare text file with data for the Merge command.

In the input file, there can be as many as 50 different fields in each record; the total of all the characters in a data file record cannot exceed 1,025. In the document, the maximum length of a merge variable is 50 characters.

In the body of the text shown in figure 21.7, the substituted variables are enclosed in double angle brackets. The marker on the left of a variable is entered by pressing Ctrl-J, and the brackets on the right of the variable are entered by pressing Ctrl-K. You must press the Ctrl-J and Ctrl-K to enter the double brackets; do not use the angle bracket keys on your keyboard.

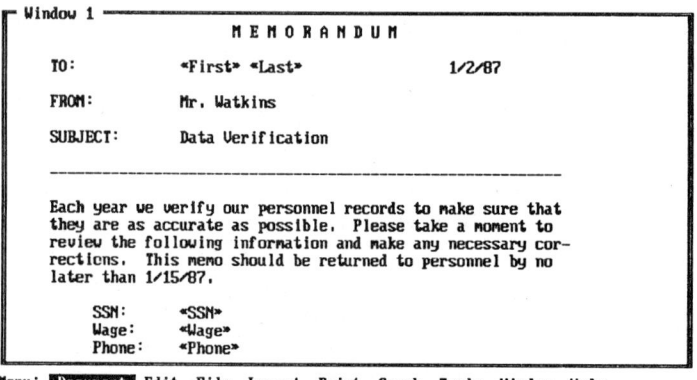

Fig. 21.7.

A merge document.

The names of the variables must match the names on the first line of the data file. The document need not use all the fields in the input file, nor do the document variables and data file fields need to be in the same order. One data field can be used many times throughout the document.

If a certain field in the data file can be blank in some records of the file, you can insert a plus sign (+) in front of the field name to prevent the printing of the blank line where that variable ordinarily would appear. Blank fields such as these are common in addresses, where some records in your data file might not have data in all possible address fields.

When you issue the Print Merge command, one complete document is printed for each record in the data file. If the fields are of varying lengths, the document is reformatted for each printing so that the proper justification is maintained. As a result, you can end up with a different number of lines or pages for each printing.

Figure 21.8 shows a memo printed with the Print Merge command; the text is shown in figure 21.7, and the data file is displayed in figure 21.6.

```
                       M E M O R A N D U M

        TO:          Julius Karenski              1/2/87
        FROM:        Mr. Watkins
        SUBJECT:     Data Verification
        ------------------------------------------------------------
        Each year we verify our personnel records to make sure that
        they are as accurate as possible.  Please take a moment to
        review the following information and make any necessary cor-
        rections.  This memo should be returned to personnel by no
        later than 1/15/87.
             SSN:       208-23-0300
             Wage:      1020.33
             Phone:     (606) 779-5088
             Employed:  08/20/1971
```

Fig. 21.8.

The results of a Print Merge command.

In SmartWare II, you can include formulas in your merge text. In the Ctrl-J and Ctrl-K delimiters, you can include any formula containing constants, literals, functions, and project processing variables. The first character after the Ctrl-J must be an equal sign (=) to designate the variable as a formula. At least one of your merge variables must be ordinary data; they cannot all be formulas.

Merging Data from the Screen

If you have a standard letter you send frequently but you have no input data file, you can issue the Print Merge Screen command and enter the data from the keyboard. With this command, you are prompted to enter the variable values on an input screen similar to that shown in figure 21.9. Once you have typed entries for each variable, press F2 to print the document. The entry for each variable can be as long as 49 characters.

```
First  : Byron
Last   : Phylkin
SSN    : 443-87-7765
Wage   : 1287.67
Phone  : 887-9839
Empdate: 6/28/65




F2 Print Merged Document     F3 Clear All Variables
F10 Quit                     F8 Clear Current Variable
Document: inquiry  Sc:1    Pg:1   Ln:1   Ps:26   FN:0   Font:0   Insert ON
Output a draft version of the merge to the selected "default" printer.
```

Fig. 21.9.

Merge from screen input.

Unlike previous versions of the Smart Word Processor, the screen entries are not cleared after printing. To edit the contents of the variables, use the cursor movement keys and the Ins and Del keys to insert, overlay, or delete text. Press F8 to erase the contents of an individual variable, or F3 to clear all the variables. Press F10 to terminate the command.

You can print in either Draft or Enhanced mode, regardless of whether your data originates from an input file or the screen. Use the Print Options command to establish options to apply to the output. A new feature of SmartWare II offers direct output to a disk file from the Print Merge command.

Chapter Summary

All of your work in the SmartWare Word Processor would be fruitless if you could not print high quality output. This chapter explained how to use the Print commands to print your documents in Draft mode, taking advantage of your printer's built-in fonts, or in Enhanced mode, using your printer's graphics and rasterized font capabilities.

Using the Print Merge command, you can incorporate data from the SmartWare Database into the body of your documents. You also can supply data directly from the keyboard using the Print Merge command.

22

Integrating the Word Processor with Other Modules

Part of the beauty of the SmartWare II system lies in the integration of its application modules. You know, for example, that you can produce customized letters by using the Word Processor's Print Merge command with an input file sent from the Database. Text files also can be read into the SmartWare Word Processor when you want to include data from the Database or portions of worksheets. With the right kind of printer, you can use SmartWare's unique Graphics command to include a spreadsheet graph in your document.

Files read into the Word Processor do not necessarily have to come from other application modules; you might have created them with the Word Processor itself. This feature gives you the capability of assembling a document from separate, smaller boilerplate document files.

Word Processor text can be sent (with the Document Send command) or written (with the File Export command) to other application modules. If you have created a document that contains a table, for instance, you may want to send that table to the Spreadsheet module for further analysis.

Reading Files into Text

The File Import command is used to insert a document file or a text file into the document in the current window. The file is read into the current document at the position immediately preceding the cursor location.

The imported file can be either a Word Processor document, which can be reformatted by changing the ruler, or a text file with hard carriage returns at the end of each line. Remember, if you import a text file into a document, the carriage returns and line feeds are not automatically removed. Refer to the Edit Replace command to learn a quick way to transform text paragraphs into document paragraphs.

If you insert standard phrases or paragraphs in many documents, the capability to assemble a document from smaller ones will appeal to you. You are prompted for a password if the imported file is protected; you have three attempts to enter the password before the File Import command is aborted.

Unlike some other popular word processing programs, the SmartWare II Word Processor does not have the capability of referencing different subsidiary documents from your main document. (A referenced document is printed directly from disk; it is not actually stored with the main document in the computer's memory.) To save disk space, after you finish printing, you may decide to save only the main document, without the files imported into it.

When you execute the File Import command, a pop-up menu displays the names of the documents and text files in the current subdirectory. Move the cursor and press Enter to select a file. If the file you want to import is neither a .DOC nor .TXT file, or is outside the current subdirectory, you must type the name of the file, preceded by the path, if different from the current subdirectory. The following prompt appears when you must type a file name:

```
Enter a filename:
```

You also can use the F4 key to look for a file, or the F5 key to change subdirectories at this time. If you type just the name of the file, a .DOC file will be retrieved, if it exists, rather than a .TXT file with the same name.

Writing Text to a File

The File Export command writes all or part of your document to a disk file. As shown in figure 22.1, when you execute the File Export command, you select a block of your document to be written to disk.

Using Block-Marking

As in all commands where you are prompted to identify a block, there is a beginning point and an ending point. As a default, the beginning point is the cursor position at the time you execute the command. Once you are in the Block-definition mode, however, you can designate a new beginning point, or anchor, by moving the cursor and pressing F2. You can designate the ending point simply by moving the cursor; the area affected by your choice is displayed in reverse video.

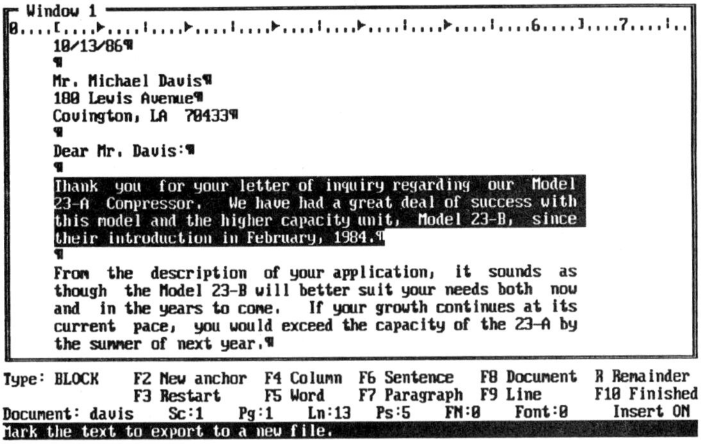

Fig. 22.1.

Select a block to write to disk.

To make it easier to mark a block, you can use several keys:

    F5   Word
    F6   Sentence
    F7   Paragraph
    F8   Entire Document
    F9   Line
    R   Remainder of document

Rather than actually moving your cursor to the end of the sentence, for instance, you can select F6 to mark the current sentence. To be recognized, a sentence must end with a period or a paragraph marker. The Line option (F9) specifies the current line on which the cursor is positioned. The Paragraph option (F7) indicates the current paragraph.

Choosing the Remainder option (R) indicates that the range extends from the current cursor position to the end of the document. Selecting the Word choice (F5) specifies the current word, bounded by either blanks or punctuation. Note that the trailing blanks and punctuation are included in the word definition boundary.

Press F8 to specify the entire document as blocked, regardless of the current cursor position.

Repeated pressing of one of the selection function keys moves the highlight block to the next applicable area. Each time you press F6, for example, the next sentence is highlighted. This method enables you to move through the document more quickly than with the cursor keys, but the effect is not cumulative. If you press F6 twice, you don't mark two sentences, just the second one.

Once you have marked an area by using a function key, you can mark an additional area by moving the cursor key.

Once you have selected a block, you can change your mind by pressing F3 for Restart. Press F10 or Enter to complete your selection.

Using Column Marking

Whereas block marking is linear in the document, you also can mark an area in the Column mode. In this mode, the exact columns you specify are marked, from the top left corner to the bottom right. Press F4 to switch from the Block mode to the Column mode.

In Column-marking mode, you do not use document-related choices, such as F5 for Word or F6 for Sentence, because these do not apply. You simply move the cursor to the lower right and press F10 or Enter. If the current cursor position is not to be the beginning of the area, move the cursor and press F2 to mark the beginning.

Lines in document areas that are exported with the Column option of the Edit Move command end with hard returns after they are written. If you want to retain the soft returns and the reformatting capability of the Word Processor, use the Block option of the File Export command to write a portion of your document to a disk file. Even if you are writing a table of numbers, use the Block option if the table goes all the way across the document.

Regardless of whether you used block or column marking, the File Export command always writes a true document file if the current file is a document, and a text file if the current file is a text file. After you specify the range, you are prompted for a destination file:

    Enter an output filename:

Enter a file name without an extension at this prompt. If a file of that name already exists, you are asked whether you want to overwrite it. Answer *Y* or *N*.

Sending Text to Other Application Modules

To transfer the contents of a document to another application module, you could, of course, export the data to a file, quit the Word Processor, enter the other module, and import the newly created file into that module. Using the Document Send command is much simpler. The Document Send command transfers the data and initiates the new module for you. Each module has a similar send capability to transfer data and initiate a new module.

Chapter 22: Integrating the Word Processor with Other Modules

You can send the contents of your current file or a disk file to any of the other three applications modules. When you execute the Document Send command, the following prompt is displayed:

```
Communications  Database  Spreadsheet
```

If you choose to send to the Communications, the following prompt is displayed:

```
Document  Text
```

If the file you want to send is a document and you select the Document option, the file is sent as a true SmartWare II Word Processor document. In all other cases, a text file is sent.

For all destination modules, the following prompt appears next:

```
Enter document or textfile name:
```

Type the name of the file you want to send; there is no pop-up menu to display the names of the files in your subdirectory. If you want to send the current document, just press Enter; type the name of any other document you want to send. The Document Send command, unlike the File Export command, applies to the entire document or text file; you cannot specify a range.

Regardless of the module you send to, the following prompt is displayed:

```
Enter project file for next application:
```

You have the option of supplying a name of a project file to be initiated in the new module. Type the name of the project file, if any, and press Enter. If you do not want to execute a project file in the new module, simply press Enter.

Sending Data to the Data Manager

Typically, the only data you will send to the Data Manager from the Word Processor is a document that contains a table of numbers or alphanumeric strings. You probably will not want to send a free-form paragraph.

When you send to the Data Manager, each separate word becomes a field in a database. The number of fields is governed by the number of words in the first line of the file: five words in the first line creates five fields in the database, even though a greater number of words may be on successive lines. Insert quotation marks around a group of words that you want considered as one word.

The first line of the document is used to determine the structure of the database that is created. Numeric fields are created from Word Processor words that contain only numbers; alphanumeric fields are created for all other types. If an existing data file has the same name as the Word Processor document, the assumption is that the format of the data you send is compatible, and the records from the Word

Processor are appended to the database. If no database has a matching name, one is created with a standard view. (If you send a document that has not been given a name, the database is created and named NONAME.)

The Data Manager assigns field names of F001, F002, and so on, as the database is created. To create more meaningful field names and to correct data types, you may want to create a new file and then transfer the data from the old file to the new one. Although you cannot change field names after a file is created, you can change field types from numeric to alphanumeric when you create your new file. As an alternative, you can create a custom view that has more meaningful names for fields.

Sending Data to the Spreadsheet

The format of the data you will probably send from the Word Processor to the Spreadsheet module will be a table of numbers or alphanumeric strings. As with sending to the database, you probably will not want to send a free-form paragraph.

When you send to the Spreadsheet, each word becomes a column in the worksheet. You can enclose groups of words in quotation marks to insert them into one cell. The number of rows is governed by the number of lines you send from the document. Numeric entries create values in the spreadsheet; all other entries create text cells. The column widths are assigned automatically to accommodate the number of characters in each column.

Sending Data to the Communications Module

If you want to use your modem to transmit a file to another computer, you must first use the Document Send Communications command to send your file to the Communications module. The file can be sent as either a document (with all the embedded control codes) or as a pure text (ASCII) file.

If you intend to transmit to other SmartWare II users, use the Document option so that they can load the file into their Word Processor to change it, add to it, or print in Enhanced mode. (Remember, however, that you must transmit the document using the Xmodem option to be able to send the embedded codes. Refer to Chapter 23.)

If the receiving party does not own SmartWare II, you should send the document to the Communications module as a text file, without any of the embedded Word Processor codes. You can make the actual transmission using either Xmodem or Text-File protocol.

Chapter 22: Integrating the Word Processor with Other Modules **435**

Of course, if you want to transmit a document that is already in a file, you don't have to send it to the Communications module at all. You can simply exit to the Communications module and transmit the file with the Data Transmit command.

Sending a document to a different module does not automatically save it for you. As your Word Processor session is terminated, you are prompted to save a document that you have modified but not saved. If the document has no name, you are prompted to supply one.

Importing Graphics into Text

A Spreadsheet graph saved in the metafile format can be inserted into the body of a Word Processor document and printed in the Enhanced mode. A metafile format can be identified by the .GMF file extension.

You can insert a graph in one of three sizes, aligned to either the right or the left of the document. The actual graph, as positioned in the document, is not displayed on the screen (refer to figure 22.2), but appears as a shaded area indicating its location.

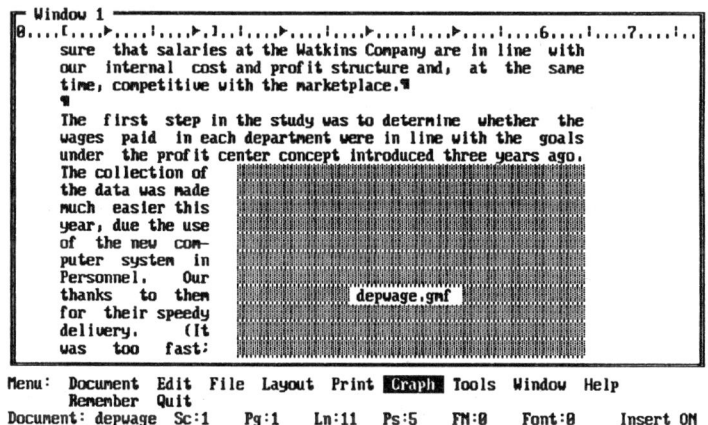

Fig. 22.2.

A Graph embedded in a document.

When you execute the Graph command, the following prompt is displayed:

    Insert   Remove   View

To make sure you are inserting the correct graph, you can select the View option. View displays the graph without requiring you to leave the Word Processor.

Inserting a Graph

To insert a graph in your document, position the cursor on the line where you want the top of the graph, and then execute the Graph Insert command. From a pop-up menu of graph metafile names, select the name of the graph to be inserted. (The default choice inserts the graph sent most recently from the Spreadsheet module, if any.) For a graph file name to be displayed in the pop-up window, you must have saved it in the metafile format in the Spreadsheet module. For more information on the metafile format, refer to Chapter 13.

After you have selected a graph to insert, you are prompted to select a graph size. You can choose from the following options:

Large	Extends from margin to margin
Medium	Half of the page width
Small	One-third of the page width

If you select the Medium or Small size, you are prompted for a justification selection:

```
Right-Aligned   Left-Aligned
```

If you select a Large graph, there is no justification prompt.

A shaded area, which represents the position of the graph, is then inserted into the body of the document. The surrounding text is reformatted to compensate for the graph.

Figure 22.2 illustrates the appearance of the graph on the screen. The final document, as printed, is shown in figure 22.3. (Remember to print the document in Enhanced mode when the document includes a graph.) The document in figure 22.3 resulted from choosing the Medium and Right-Aligned options.

Displaying a Graph

Although you cannot view the contents of a graph while it is positioned in the document on the screen, you can use the Graph View command to display any graph in a metafile. Use the Graph View File command to view a graph in the metafile format on disk. A pop-up menu displays the names of the files in the current subdirectory. Use the cursor to select a file name, and then press Enter. The document on your screen is replaced by the graph, which appears exactly as it did when you created it in the Spreadsheet. You cannot change a graph in the metafile format, however. Press any key to return to your document.

The Graph View Document command is used to display a graph you have already inserted into your document. Position the cursor on any line on which the graph occurs (or immediately above or below it), and then execute the Graph View Document command to display the graph. Press any key to return to the document.

WATKINS COMPANY
Personnel Department
Annual Salary Study

The annual wage and salary study was conducted this year under the supervision of our auditors, Parkenfarquer, Muckenfuss, and Plattsblatt. The purpose of the study is to insure that salaries at the Watkins Company are in line with our internal cost and profit structure and, at the same time, competitive with the marketplace.

The first step in the study was to determine whether the wages paid in each department were in line with the goals under the profit center concept introduced three years ago. The collection of the data was made much easier this year, due the use of the new computer system in Personnel. Our thanks to them for their speedy delivery. (It was too fast; made the rest of look slow.)

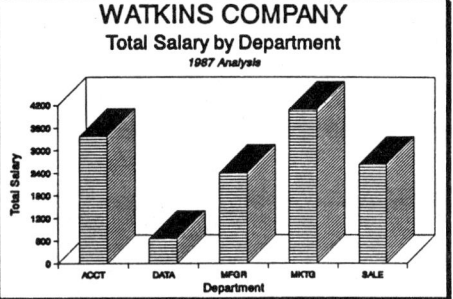

The total wages are shown in figure 1, by department. As you can see, the marketing department again leads the company in total salaries paid. The fact that the accounting department is second is certainly a surprise, but this figure must be compared to the cost and profit ratio table on page 2.

Wages in the manufacturing department have increased, but we must view this variance in light of the new product line, the second shift operations in the spring and summer, and the new union contract in our country plants. Variable manufacturing costs are analyzed in section two.

Fig. 22.3.

A graph in a printed document.

Removing a Graph from your Document

To remove a graph from your document, position the cursor on a line adjacent to the graph (or immediately above or below it) and select the Graph Remove command. When the command executes, the text area is restored to the format as defined by the current ruler.

Certain restrictions apply if you have embedded a graph in your document. If, for example, you edit the current ruler of an area of your document containing an embedded graph, the graph remains in the same position, even though you may have changed the margins. The text adjacent to a Small or Medium graph shifts to match the new margins. If you need to change the margins of the area in which the graph is embedded, it is best to remove the graph and insert it again after you have edited the ruler.

If you delete a paragraph that contains a graph, the graph is embedded in the next paragraph. (In previous versions of SmartWare, the graph would be deleted along with the paragraph.) If the paragraph surrounding the graph is moved, the graph is not moved with it. As with the Edit Delete command, the graph is embedded in the next paragraph.

Chapter Summary

The true power of the SmartWare II system becomes evident when you realize how easily the different applications modules can share data, text, and graphics. Each module has the capability to import and export external files. The Document Send command transfers data to another module and immediately transfers control to that module. In the SmartWare Word Processor, the Graph command provides the capability to embed graphs from the Spreadsheet into the body of a document.

Part IV

Using SmartWare II Communications

Includes

Using the Communications Module

23

Using the Communications Module

The Communications module enables you to connect your computer to your company's mainframe computer, to one of the on-line services such as Dow Jones News/Retrieval or CompuServe, or to another microcomputer also running SmartWare II.

New Features of SmartWare II Communications

1. SmartWare II Communications now supports 9600 baud transmissions.
2. Approximately 30 modems are supported directly. If your modem is not on the list, you can define your own.
3. You can debug the commands your computer sends to your modem, and the responses.
4. You can display a clock to keep track of the time you are on-line.
5. Tools macros are available in Terminal mode during communications sessions.

SmartWare II Communications

In the simplest form of communication, you type a command that is sent to the remote computer, and you receive the response on your screen. If you are making a simple inquiry and the answer is short, this form of communication is adequate. But if the answer is long, you may want to save the output, directing it to your printer, a disk file, the Communications module buffer, or all three at once. The following Quick keys toggle the capture modes:

F5 Buffer
F6 Printer
F7 File

Being able to capture received data in a file is certainly an advantage. Sometimes, however, you may want to receive files from the remote computer. Smart's Communications commands enable you to send and receive both text and data files. A text file in the Smart system contains only numbers and letters, without control characters. (You can type a text file to the screen at the DOS level without seeing "smiling faces" or the other strange-looking control characters.)

To create a text file containing data from one of the other applications modules, you can export a file in the text, ASCII, or Smart formats. Files other than text files, however, have structures specific to the SmartWare system; they contain special control characters that are used by the programs of the application modules. These files include .DOC files in the Word Processor and .WS files in the Spreadsheet; these files also can be transmitted by the Communications module, but you must use a special protocol.

The Communications module can transmit and receive both text and internal format files, but the two types must be treated differently. You must use the Xmodem protocol to transmit internal files because of the special characters they contain. The Xmodem protocol provides additional error checking and retransmission facilities. Data in the file is broken into blocks, and a number called a checksum is transmitted along with the data block. By comparing the data block and the checksum, the receiving computer can determine whether the data block was received error-free. Transmission with the Xmodem protocol usually takes longer than with other protocols. Both the sending and receiving computers must use Xmodem protocol if it is needed for the transmission.

If you are transmitting a text file, you need not use the Xmodem protocol. In fact, you have no choice but to use text file transmission if the other computer cannot handle Xmodem. If there is noise on the phone line during the transmission, however, you may find some errors in the received file.

Like the other modules, the Communications module has two modes of operation. Command mode is used to control your computer; Terminal mode sends typed characters to the computer at the other end of the phone line.

Understanding the Status Screen

When you first enter the Communications module, the status screen is displayed (see fig. 23.1).

Chapter 23: Using the Communications Module

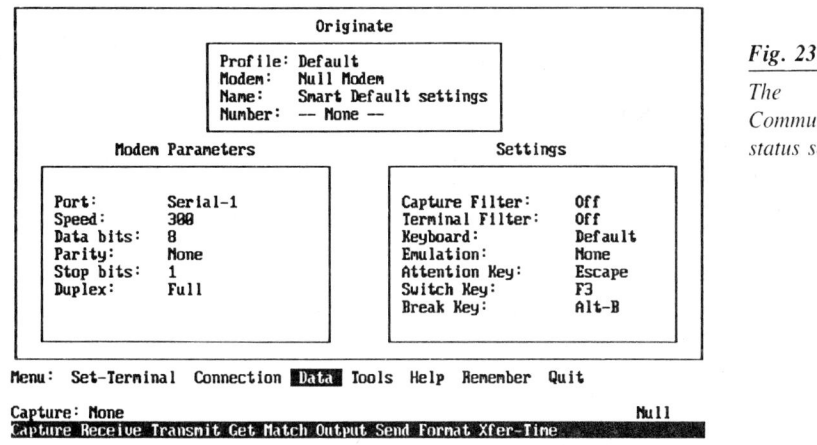

Fig. 23.1.

The Communications status screen.

The status screen shows the status of various communications settings. From this screen, you can issue any of the Communications commands.

To switch to the terminal screen (which is initially blank), press F3. The terminal screen displays all the information you type for transmission to the other computer and all the information sent back to you. To return to the status screen, press F3 again. If you have just one command to execute, you can press Esc; at the completion of the command, you are returned to the Terminal mode.

To place a call to another computer, you must be in the Originate mode. If your modem is an autodial type (meaning that it can dial the phone for you), you can include the phone number in the setting files and use the Connection Dial command to initiate the call. For repeated usage, you can store the correct communications settings for several remote computers or services in settings files. When you want to connect with one computer or another, you just load the proper settings file and issue the Connection Dial command.

You can change many Communications parameters, but the ones you will change most often are baud rate (roughly equivalent to bits per second), parity, data length (in bits), number of stop bits, and duplex selection (full or half).

The process of originating a call and transmitting a file is sometimes called "uploading to the host computer." The host computer is the one you call, such as your company's mainframe or a local bulletin board. However, the capabilities of the Smart Communications module can be used to set up your machine as a host computer so that other users in your company can call into your machine to send or receive files. For example, a typical application might be one in which sales representatives send you files of new orders and receive order confirmations or stock status reports.

Setting the Communications Parameters

Settings are the parameters needed for correct communications with the other computer. The Set-Terminal Settings Define command is used to define and undefine, edit, load, and save a set of parameters for each computer you call. If you want, you can specify a settings profile to be loaded automatically each time you enter the Communications module.

Creating and Using Terminal Settings

The Set-Terminal Settings command allows you to create, maintain, and load terminal settings files. The Quick key is Alt-P. When you execute the command, the following options are available:

```
Define Edit Load Save Undefine
```

To create a new profile, select Define and press Enter. If any profiles have been previously defined, their names are displayed in a pop-up window. If you want to change a profile, select it and press Enter; if you want to create a new profile, enter a new name.

The screens of the settings definitions are shown in figures 23.2 through 23.5.

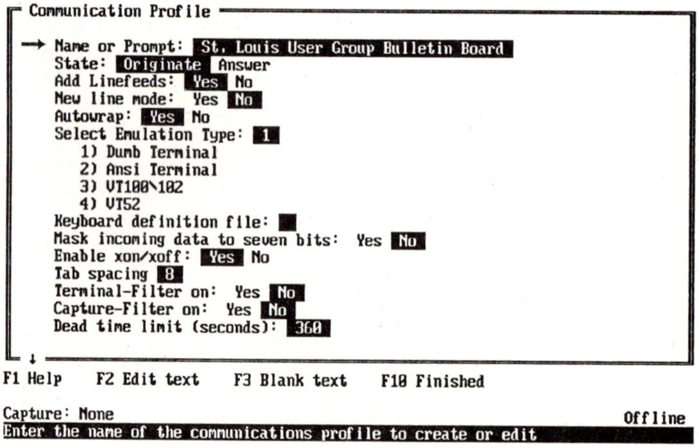

Fig. 23.2.

Communications Settings screen 1.

Chapter 23: Using the Communications Module

```
┌─ Communication Profile ─────────────────────────────┐
│         Originate Settings                          │
│                                                     │
│   Number: 920-9993                                  │
│   Originate Password:                               │
│   Dial Prefix: AT DP                                │
│   Dial Suffix: T                                    │
│   Seconds to wait between re-dials: 20              │
│   Maximum Number of re-dial attempts: 3             │
│   Seconds to wait for carrier: 45                   │
│                                                     │
│         Answer Settings                             │
│                                                     │
│   Receive/Transmit Password:                        │
│   Receive Password:                                 │
│   Transmit Password:                                │
│   Connect-Only Password:                            │
│   Number of rings: 3                                │
│ → Connection time limit (minutes): 60               │
└─────────────────────────────────────────────────────┘
 F1 Help   F2 Edit text   F3 Blank text   F10 Finished
 Capture: None                                Offline
 Enter the name of the communications profile to create or edit
```

Fig. 23.3.

Communications Settings screen 2.

```
┌─ Communication Profile ─────────────────────────────┐
│   Connection time limit (minutes): 60               │
│                                                     │
│         Modem Settings                              │
│                                                     │
│   Modem Type: d:\smart4\cmmodem.mdu   Hayes 1200    │
│                                                     │
│   Modem port: Serial-1  Serial-2                    │
│   Baud rate:  110  300  600  1200  2400  4800  9600 │
│   Data Bits:  5  6  7  8                            │
│   Parity:  Odd  Even  None  Mark  Space             │
│   Stop bits:  1.5  1  2                             │
│   Duplex: Full  Half                                │
│                                                     │
│         Text File Transmission                      │
│                                                     │
│   Expand tabs:     Yes  No                          │
│   Pad blank lines: Yes  No                          │
│   Filter Linefeeds: Yes  No                         │
│ → Select Character Delay: 0                         │
└─────────────────────────────────────────────────────┘
 F1 Help   F2 Edit text   F3 Blank text   F10 Finished
 Capture: None                                Offline
 Enter the name of the communications profile to create or edit
```

Fig. 23.4.

Communications Settings screen 3.

```
┌─ Communication Profile ─────────────────────────────┐
│   Select Character Delay: 0                         │
│       0) No Delay                                   │
│       1) Wait for Echo                              │
│       #) Delay Time in 1/10 seconds                 │
│   Select Line Delay: 0                              │
│       0) No Delay                                   │
│       1) Wait for CR                                │
│       2) Wait for User                              │
│       3) Wait for Prompt                            │
│       #) Delay Time in 1/10 seconds                 │
│   Prompt to wait for:                               │
│   End of File delay time (seconds): 360             │
│                                                     │
│         Advanced User Settings                      │
│                                                     │
│   Debug mode: Off  Decimal  Hex  Character          │
│   Forced local echo: Off  On                        │
│   Maximum number of xmodem retries: 9               │
│ → Break signal length (in 1/100 seconds): 0         │
└─────────────────────────────────────────────────────┘
 F1 Help   F2 Edit text   F3 Blank text   F10 Finished
 Capture: None                                Offline
 Enter the name of the communications profile to create or edit
```

Fig. 23.5.

Communications Settings screen 4.

The following are the six major groups of Communications profile settings:

General
Originate
Answer
Modem
Text File Transmission
Advanced User

In the SmartWare II Communications module, the General settings, shown in figure 23.2 and described next, are used in both answer and originate modes.

Name or Prompt. Serves as an identifier in Originate mode or as a sign-on message in Answer mode.

State. If you initiate the call, select Originate. If you answer the call, select Answer.

Add Linefeeds. Some systems require the local computer to add linefeeds at the end of each line of text. If you find that you are getting an extra linefeed, change this setting to *No*; if received lines of text overlay each other, change this setting to *Yes*.

New line mode. If you want a carriage return added to the linefeeds, select *Yes*.

Autowrap. If you want long lines to wrap around to the beginning of the next line, leave the selection at *Yes*.

Emulation Type. Four choices are available:

1) Dumb Terminal
2) Ansi Terminal
3) VT100\102
4) VT52

A dumb terminal provides no special screen handling characteristics; when in doubt, select this one. If special ANSI characters are to be received and interpreted to emulate an ANSI terminal, select number 2. (Be sure to include the statement DEVICE = ANSI.SYS in your CONFIG.SYS file if you use selection 2.) If the remote computer system requires a special terminal type, you may need one of the VT terminal keyboard definition files (selections 3 and 4). These are used to indicate a file in which you can redefine your keyboard. Refer to the Set-Terminal Keyboard command.

Mask incoming data to seven bits. You should probably leave this set to *No*; a setting of *Yes* strips the high order bit from all received characters except Xmodem transmissions.

`Enable xon/xoff`. This setting depends on the protocol the remote computer uses to start and stop transmissions. To begin with, you should leave this set at *Yes*.

`Tab spacing`. This setting specifies the number of spaces between received tab characters. The range is three to 20.

`Terminal-Filter on`. Select *Yes* if you are using terminal filters, which can prevent the display of selected characters on your screen. For more information, see the Set-Terminal Filter Terminal command in this chapter.

`Capture-Filter on`. Select *Yes* if you are using capture filters, which can block the capturing of certain characters to the buffer, file, or printer when using the Data Capture command. For more information, see the Set-Terminal Filter Capture command in this chapter.

`Dead time limit (seconds)`. Determines the maximum number of seconds of inactivity before terminating the connection.

Originate settings, shown in figure 23.3, determine the operation of Originate mode.

`Number`. You can enter the phone number with or without hyphens.

`Originate Password`. In the Originate mode, if SmartWare receives a Ctrl-E, this password is sent.

`Dial Prefix` and `Dial Suffix`. These settings depend on the autodial features of your modem. (Some modems, for example, adhere to the AT command convention, and require all modem commands to be preceded by these two characters.) A vertical bar (|) is used for a carriage return.

`Seconds to wait between re-dials`. Number of seconds you would like to wait before your modem redials the remote computer, in case the connection is unsuccessful.

`Maximum Number of re-dial attempts`. Number of times to redial automatically.

`Seconds to wait for carrier`. Number of seconds to wait for receipt of carrier signal after dialing has begun.

In the Answer settings (see fig. 23.3), four levels of password protection can be established to guard against unauthorized access. The remote originator of the call can issue the appropriate commands, depending on the level of access granted by the password response.

`Receive/Transmit Password`. Allows uploading and downloading of files.

`Receive Password`. Allows downloading only.

`Transmit Password`. Allows uploading only.

Connect-Only Password. Disallows both uploading and downloading.

Number of rings. Number of rings before the phone is to be answered.

Connection time limit (minutes). Maximum number of minutes allowed a remote user.

The settings used to identify your modem are shown in figure 23.4.

Modem Type. Press F6 for a list of available modem choices. Move the cursor to your choice and press Enter. If a custom modem definition file exists in the current subdirectory, the definitions are appended to the standard list appearing in the pop-up window. For more information about custom modem definitions and how to specify them in your settings, refer to the section on defining your own modem.

Modem port. Select *Serial-1* or *Serial-2*.

Baud rate. Select from one of the baud rates shown in figure 23.4. Note that 9600 baud is new in SmartWare II.

Data Bits. Select either *5*, *6*, *7*, or *8*. You must select *8* if you plan to transmit or receive files using the Xmodem protocol.

Parity. Parity is used for error checking. Select *Odd*, *Even*, *None*, *Mark*, or *Space*. Select *None* if the data bits setting is 8.

Stop bits. Select either *1.5*, *1*, or *2*. The most common selection is 1.

Duplex. You should select *Full* if you originate the call, *Half* if you answer the call.

The Text-File Transmission settings govern the transmission of text files:

Expand tabs. Select *Yes* if you want to transmit blanks instead of tab characters.

Pad blank lines. Some receiving computers require that blank lines be padded out with spaces.

Filter Linefeeds. Select *Yes* to send only carriage returns instead of carriage return linefeed combinations.

Select Character Delay. This setting governs the delay between transmitted characters. Enter 0 for no delay or 1 to wait for complete echo from remote. If you enter any other value, it represents the number of tenths of seconds between characters.

Select Line Delay. This setting determines the delay between each transmitted line:

   0) No delay
   1) Wait for carriage return from remote

```
2) Wait for you to press a key
3) Wait for a prompt of your designation
#) Delay time in 1/10 seconds
```

Prompt to wait for. Enter the prompt here, if you have selected number 3 in the Select Line Delay settings.

End of File delay time (seconds). Number of seconds to wait to terminate the text file transmission.

Advanced User settings enable you to further customize Smart communications.

Debug mode. This mode allows you to diagnose communications problems. The following display choices are available:

```
Off Decimal Hex Character
```

In this mode, terminal filter and masking to 7 bits are disabled.

Forced local echo. Set to *On* to force echo to screen, regardless of duplex setting.

Maximum number of xmodem retries. This setting governs the number of retransmissions for Xmodem protocol. If you have a particularly noisy telephone line and are using the Xmodem protocol, your transmission is normally terminated after 10 attempts at retransmission. If you want to keep trying to transmit the data after 10 tries, enter the number of retries. The range must be between 9 and 9999. Often, you can obtain a less noisy line if you hang up and redial.

Break signal length (in 1/100 seconds). Enter the duration of the break signal.

Loading the Definition

Once you have used the Set-Terminal Settings Define command to create the initial definition or to change an existing definition, you must load it with the Set-Terminal Settings Load command. (The Quick key is Alt-L.) A pop-up window displays the names of your existing definitions; select the desired definition and press Enter.

Make sure that your modem is plugged in and turned on, because during the Load process, it is initialized with the profile settings of your definition. A message appears across the command line, indicating that the modem is being initialized, followed by a series of asterisks as the process takes place:

```
Initializing Modem * * * * * * * * *
```

If your modem is not plugged in or not attached correctly, you receive the following error messages:

```
Modem is not responding.
Is the modem on? Are the switches set correctly?
```

Press any key to clear the error message. Then correct the problem and load the profile again. Once you have successfully loaded a profile and the modem has been initialized, the configuration status screen changes to reflect your settings. Figure 23.6 shows the settings from the selections in figures 23.2 through 23.5.

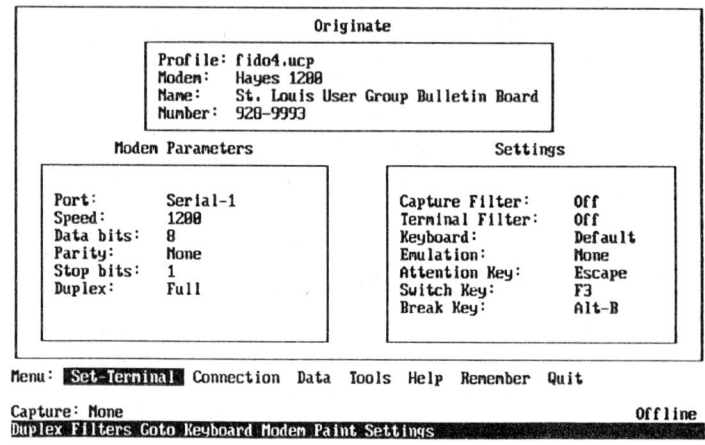

Fig. 23.6.

Configuration status screen.

Changing the Current Settings

Once your settings are loaded, you can edit them with the Set-Terminal Settings Edit command. The Quick key is Alt-S. The selections are the same as in figures 23.2 through 23.5. Any changes you make take effect immediately, and remain in effect for the duration of only the current session. If you want to save your changes, use the Set-Terminal Settings Save command. Either type a new name under which to save the settings, or press Enter to save your changes under the current name.

If you want to erase a settings profile from your disk, use the Set-Terminal Settings Undefine command.

Changing Duplex Settings

The Set-Terminal Duplex command is used to switch between full and half duplex without editing the current settings. The Quick key is Alt-U. Changing this setting has the same effect as changing the Duplex setting with the Set-Terminal Settings Edit command, but this method is faster.

In Full Duplex mode, the characters you see on your screen are actually echoed back to your machine by the receiving computer. The characters do not appear on screen until they have been received by the remote computer and transmitted back to you. You should probably use this setting when you are in the Originate mode. You can force local echo by selecting this option from among the advanced user settings. When this option is on, characters appear as soon as they are transmitted to the remote computer.

If duplex is set to half, the characters you type appear on the screen as soon as they are transmitted, instead of being echoed back from the other computer. You will probably use this setting in the Answer mode. If you see double characters on your screen, try switching to half duplex.

Dialing a Remote Computer

Once you have defined and loaded your profile settings, you are ready to begin communicating.

The Connection Dial command is used to dial the phone number automatically through the modem. You can either enter a phone number from the keyboard or use the number you defined in the profile. The Quick key to dial the number for carrier connection is Alt-D. If you execute the Connection Dial command, you have two options:

     Carrier   Voice

You should select Voice if you need to talk to a person at the other end before establishing the connection for data transmission. (In the profile, do not specify a wait for a carrier longer than five seconds when establishing voice communications.) If you are going to establish a computer connection immediately, select Carrier.

The second prompt asks for a phone number:

     Enter a phone number:

Type the phone number to be dialed, or press Enter to use the number in your settings. If your modem does not support autodial, bring up the terminal screen and manually dial your phone. When you hear the carrier (the high-pitched "modem tone"), press the button on your modem and begin your Communications session.

The number of seconds to wait for a carrier, the number of automatic redials, and the time between redials are established in your settings.

If you have selected Voice, you can use the Set-Terminal Goto command to establish carrier connection after you have completed your conversation. This is discussed later in this chapter.

If your modem does not automatically hang up the phone, use the Connection Hangup command.

Handling Data

Defining your terminal settings and making the connection are steps necessary in preparation for sending and receiving data. This section covers the commands you need to send and receive data in both the Text and Xmodem protocols. You also learn how to capture screen text and how to filter the capture.

Receiving Data

The Data Receive command is used to accept transmitted files and store them on your disk; the data is not echoed to the screen as the file is received. The Quick key for the Data Receive command is Alt-R.

The Data Receive command has two options:

    Text-File   Xmodem

If the data file contains special control characters, such as those found in the SmartWare Word Processor document files (.DOC) and Spreadsheet files (.WS), you must use the Xmodem protocol. Remember, however, that Xmodem can be used only if the other computer also has the capability of transmitting with Xmodem.

Select Xmodem to use this special error correcting protocol. Any type of file, not just data files, can be transmitted with Xmodem. The advantage of using Xmodem is its error correcting capabilities: the receiving computer double checks each block of 128 bytes for errors. If any errors are detected, the sending computer is automatically asked to transmit the data block again. This process can take longer than Text-File transmission, but greater accuracy is guaranteed.

After selecting Xmodem, you are prompted to enter a name for the received file:

    Enter a receiving filename:

A pop-up window displays the names of your files; you can select an existing file name, or type a new one and press Enter. Because of the special "handshaking" that takes place between the two computers, the receiving computer waits until the sending computer begins to transmit. Your computer waits for up to two minutes for the file transmission to begin. As the file is being received, the system displays a count of the number of blocks received and errors corrected. In figure 23.7, the right side of the screen shows the transfer information.

Note that the name of the file is displayed along with the number of the current block being received. If there are any errors detected and corrected, a count of the errors in the current block and in the total file is shown. If you see that the number of errors is high, your file transmission will take longer than normal because of the automatic retransmission. You may decide to terminate the connection and try to get a phone line with less noise. Line noise is a particular problem when you dial long distance.

Chapter 23: Using the Communications Module

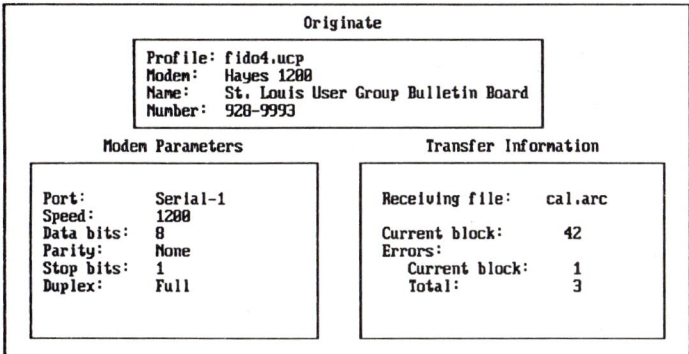

Fig. 23.7.

The transfer information.

Using the Text-File option is similar to using the Xmodem option, except that with Text-File, you cannot receive a file containing special control characters. Only pure ASCII text files can be sent or received with the Text-File option. No error checking is performed, apart from the regular parity checking of your system, so transmission errors can occur. With text files, however, such errors are generally not as troublesome as they are with other kinds of files.

Because no special handshaking is performed between the sending and the receiving computers when the Text-File option is used, starting the transmission at just the right time may be a little tricky. You don't want your file to end up with extra characters you would have to edit out later.

In addition to supplying a name for the received file, you also can enter an optional expression to be sent to the computer that initiates the transmission. This expression is used to try to eliminate noise characters that might produce garbage in your file. Your computer won't actually begin recording until the expression is echoed from the other system.

You will probably have the best success if you can begin the transmission from the remote computer and then immediately type Alt-R to start file receipt. If the receiving file already exists, the following message appears:

```
File already exists. Overwrite or Append (o/a)
```

Press *O* to replace the file, or *A* to append.

Sending Data

If you are sending a file to another computer, use the Data Transmit command; the Quick key is Alt-T. Like the Data Receive command, there are two options:

```
Text-File   Xmodem
```

Remember that the receiving computer must use the same communications protocol that your computer is using. You cannot transmit with Xmodem and receive with Text-File, for example. If your file contains special control characters, you cannot use the Text-File option.

Whichever protocol you select, you are then prompted for the name of the file to transmit. If a file was sent to the Communications module, choose the [default] filename on the pop-up menu.

If you are transmitting with Xmodem, the following information is displayed on your screen:

```
Sending file: filename.ext
Xmit time (mins.): estimated number of minutes
Total blocks: number of blocks to send
Current block: number of the current block
Complete: percent complete
```

If the phone line is particularly noisy, a great deal of error correction may be necessary. If an individual block cannot be sent in 10 attempts, the transmission is aborted, however. You can set the total number of allowable block retransmissions in the profile settings. If the phone line is extremely noisy, you may want to terminate the call and try to obtain a less noisy line by calling again.

Because Xmodem transmission requires an extra bit to transmit special control characters, the system automatically switches to a data length of eight bits, regardless of the settings you have defined. Your settings are restored after the completion of the transmission. The settings also are changed for you, if necessary, if you receive in the Xmodem mode.

Estimating the Transfer Time

The Data Xfer Time command can be used to estimate the number of minutes needed to transmit a given file at the current data transmission speed. The Quick key is Alt-Q. After selecting the command, a pop-up window of file names is displayed. Select a file, or type the name and press Enter. The following message is displayed on the command line:

```
Transmission time at 1200 baud = x minutes (approximate), press
any key
```

Based on the baud rate in your settings (1200 in this case), the approximate transmission time is calculated as follows:

$$\frac{\text{number of characters in the file}}{((\text{bits per second}/10)*60)}$$

The x in the transmission time message reflects the approximate number of minutes needed for transmission of the file. Be aware, however, that these calculations reflect Text-File transmission times and do not take into account the additional time required for Xmodem error checking or for retransmission of incorrect data blocks.

Capturing to the Screen

Whereas the Data Receive command can accept a file transmitted from the remote computer, you can use the Data Capture command to record anything that appears on your screen during the communications session. You may decide to capture the text to the RAM buffer, or you can direct it to the printer or to a file.

The Quick keys for the capture commands are:

F5 Toggle Buffer Capture
F6 Toggle Printer Capture
F7 Toggle File Capture

If you are capturing to the buffer, use Alt-V to display the buffer contents; pressing Esc returns you to the Terminal mode.

When you issue the Data Capture command, the prompt offers you three options:

    Buffer File Printer

Received data can be captured to any of these destinations simultaneously.

Capturing to the Buffer

If you select the Buffer option, you are presented with another set of options:

    Begin Clear End Save View

The buffer is an area of memory that can store received characters. By choosing the appropriate option, you can view the contents of the buffer or save its contents to a disk file. Selecting Begin starts the capturing of received characters to the buffer; selecting End stops the capture process. If you select Begin again, new text is appended to the existing contents of the buffer.

Use the Clear option to erase the contents of the buffer; you then have an opportunity to write the buffer to a file prior to clearing, if you choose. To avoid losing data because you have exceeded the size of the buffer, you should periodically write the buffer to a file or capture to both a file and the buffer simultaneously or capture to the file only. While you are capturing to the buffer, a message similar to the following is displayed on the status line:

```
Capture: Buffer[ 112 K]
```

The amount of free memory remaining is displayed in the square brackets.

To write the buffer contents to a disk file, use the Save option. You are prompted to enter a file name:

```
Enter a filename for captured text:
```

Type the name of a file, and press Enter. If the file already exists, you have the option to overwrite it or append to it.

Capturing to a File

If you want the screen text to be saved directly to a file, select the File option. The following prompt is displayed:

```
Begin   End
```

By selecting either Begin or End, you can control the text written to the file. If you select Begin, you are prompted for a file name. No file extension is automatically supplied; you must furnish your own.

If the file already exists, you have the option to overwrite or append to it.

Capturing to the Printer

To send output directly to the printer, select the Printer option. The choices are the same as capturing to a file:

```
Begin   End
```

When you select Begin, the current date is printed; the time is printed when you end the capture.

Filtering Characters

If you do not want certain characters to go to the printer, file, screen, or capture buffers, use the Set-Terminal Filters command to specify the characters you do not want to receive.

The two options are Terminal and Capture.

Select Terminal if you want to filter out characters going to your screen, or Capture for characters destined for the buffer, printer, or disk file. In either case, a screen similar to figure 23.8 is displayed.

Terminal Filter Table

[0]	1	2	3	4	5	6	7	8	9	10	11	12	13	14	15
16	17	18	19	20	21	22	23	24	25	26	27	28	29	30	31
32	33	34	35	36	37	38	39	40	41	42	43	44	45	46	47
48	49	50	51	52	53	54	55	56	57	58	59	60	61	62	63
64	65	66	67	68	69	70	71	72	73	74	75	76	77	78	79
80	81	82	83	84	85	86	87	88	89	90	91	92	93	94	95
96	97	98	99	100	101	102	103	104	105	106	107	108	109	110	111
112	113	114	115	116	117	118	119	120	121	122	123	124	125	126	127
128	129	130	131	132	133	134	135	136	137	138	139	140	141	142	143
144	145	146	147	148	149	150	151	152	153	154	155	156	157	158	159
160	161	162	163	164	165	166	167	168	169	170	171	172	173	174	175
176	177	178	179	180	181	182	183	184	185	186	187	188	189	190	191
192	193	194	195	196	197	198	199	200	201	202	203	204	205	206	207
208	209	210	211	212	213	214	215	216	217	218	219	220	221	222	223
224	225	226	227	228	229	230	231	232	233	234	235	236	237	238	239
240	241	242	243	244	245	246	247	248	249	250	251	252	253	254	255

Filtered Non-Filtered

F2 Toggle Filter Mark F3 Toggle Display Type ESC Abort F10 Finished
2:09:45

Fig. 23.8.

Terminal Filter Table Decimal.

Move the cursor to the indicator of the character you want to eliminate. The cursor is represented by the square brackets as shown in the upper left corner of figure 23.8.

In figure 23.8, the characters are identified by their decimal representations. Press F3 to change the display to hexadecimal and then again to change to Character Display mode. If you are getting funny little characters on your screen, it is frequently easier to identify them by the way they appear than by looking them up in a table. The characters highlighted in figure 23.8 are the control characters disallowed from text files. Press F10 to save the changes to the Filter settings.

Because filters are stored with a profile setting file, you must edit the current settings and change the appropriate filter selection to On. Be sure to save the settings when you have finished the edit.

Communications Project Processing

You can execute the Data Match, Output, and Get commands individually at the command level, but they are most useful in project files.

The Data Get Command

The Data Get command is used to insert a received character or line into a variable. The Quick key for the command is Alt-G. Two options are available:

```
Character  Line
```

If you select Character, only the next character is inserted into the variable; selecting Line causes the entire line to be saved. The destination of the received character or line is determined by your response to the following prompt:

```
Enter a variable name:
```

If you are working at the command level, the variable will be declared Public if it does not already exist.

The Data Match Command

The Data Match command is used to suspend the execution of a project file until certain characters are received. The match characters can be literals, which must be enclosed in double quotation marks, or decimal or hexadecimal representations of ASCII characters. The character types can be used in combination. The Quick key for the Data Match command is Alt-M.

When you issue the Data Match command, you are prompted for a character expression:

```
Enter a character expression to match:
```

Note that any filtering you have specified takes place before the system matches the string. If the filter removes the characters you are looking for, they will never be matched. Any high bit masking also precedes the match.

Even though processing has been suspended, capturing to the buffer, printer, or a file can continue, allowing you to diagnose any problems with your Match condition.

The Data Output Command

Use the Data Output command to send a literal string or the contents of a variable to the receiving computer. The command is useful in project processing and can be used to initiate commands on the other computer or to send a logon sequence. The Quick key is Alt-C.

When you execute the command, the following prompt appears:

```
Enter a character expression to output:
```

You can enter the expression as a literal enclosed in double quotation marks, or you can enter a variable name. Multiple variables can be used together as output; their names must be separated by the vertical bar (|). In contrast to previous Smart versions, a carriage return line feed combination is not automatically issued following the expression; if you need these characters, you must supply your own, as in the following project file example:

```
public @lf
'following is carriage return, line feed
let @lf = chr(13)|chr(10)
connection dial carrier number
data output " "
data match "NEW:"
data output "182"|@lf
data match "Password:"
data output "Spridle"|@lf
data match "######"
data output "3100"|@lf
```

You also can use the Keys command, instead of the Data Output command, to generate output. The Keys project file command is new with SmartWare II.

Customizing the Communications Module

You can use the keyboard definition facility and format structure to customize the Communications module to meet your needs. And if you find that your modem is not among those directly supported, you can create your own definition.

Keyboard Definition

The Set-Terminal Keyboard command can be used to establish keyboard macros in the Communications module or to redefine the system keys (Attention, Break, and Switch). The Quick key for the Set-Terminal Keyboard command is Alt-J. In previous versions of Smart, regular macros (see the Tools Macros command) would not operate in the Terminal mode; you were required to use keyboard macros. Now, with SmartWare II, the use of regular macros is permissible in Terminal mode, so there is less of a need for keyboard macros. If you tend to use a number of different keyboard layouts on different computers, you may find that by redefining the keyboards, you can simplify your work.

When you execute the Set-Terminal Keyboard command, you are given two options:

```
Define   Undefine
```

When you select Define, a pop-up window displays the names of existing keyboard definition files, and the following prompt appears:

```
Enter a keyboard definition filename
```

If you want to change a file, select it with the cursor, or type a new name and press Enter.

After you select Define, a menu of available keys is displayed (see fig. 23.9). Enclose literals in double quotation marks, precede hexadecimal representations with the letter *H*, and enter ASCII codes as decimal numbers.

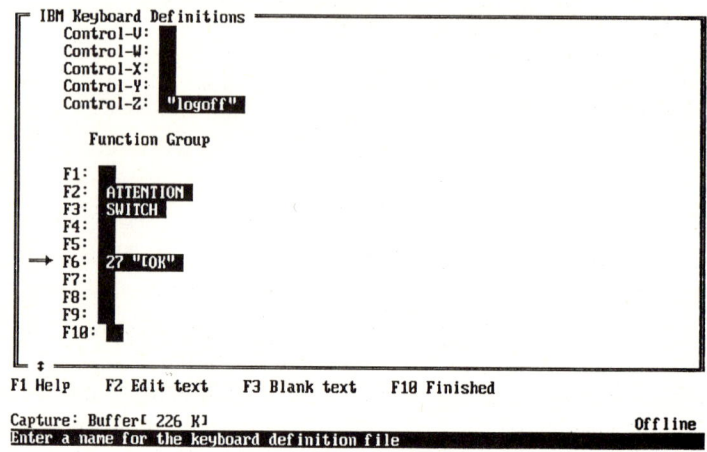

Fig. 23.9.

Using Set-Terminal Keyboard definitions.

To reassign the system keys, type the words *ATTENTION*, *BREAK*, or *SWITCH* after the keys you want to use; don't enclose these words in quotation marks. Press F3 to delete any entry from the original key assignment. Press F10 to save the keyboard settings. The method in which these settings are coupled with a profile differs from the way in which filters are attached to a profile. The Set-Terminal Keyboard command creates a separate file which can be used with one or more profiles. Enter the name of the keyboard file in the profile; when the setting is loaded, the keyboard file also is loaded (see fig. 23.2). To use the keyboard settings in the current session, edit the settings; the new definitions take effect immediately. (In previous versions of Smart, you had to save the settings and then reload them.) Be sure to save the settings if you want the keyboard definitions to be in place during your next communications session.

Regular macros take precedence over keyboard macros in the Communications module; keyboard macros supersede Quick keys. Make sure that your definitions do not overlap, or you will lose some of your system's capability. A note of warning: Do not name a keyboard definition the same as a database in the same subdirectory. In SmartWare II, the files for both Database keys and Communications keyboard definitions use the extension .KEY. If you must use the same name, store the database and keyboard definition files in different subdirectories.

File Format Definition

If you receive a text file you want to send to either the Database or Spreadsheet, it may already be in an acceptable format. Realistically speaking, however, this is not always the case. Suppose that you received a file containing data in the following format:

Rosanna
Ronaldo
546 Olive Hill
Oak Park
IL 60301 (312) 4398760

Debbie Linden
409 Pleasant St
Amherst
MA 01002 (413) 8863498

Clearly, you would have difficulty sending this data to the Database to be read into two new records. Each logical record, in this example, has five physical records; the last record contains three different fields: State, ZIP Code, and Phone Number. There also is a blank line between each set of data.

The Data Format command is used to establish the format description of a data file that is received in the Communications module and sent to either the Database or the Spreadsheet. The Quick key for the Data Format command is Alt-E.

With the Data Format command, you can define field types as Text or Values, split one input line into several output lines, or combine several input lines into one logical record. The following information may be entered for as many as 25 fields:

```
Field start column: start column
Field type: Ignored, Text, or Value
Read next input line: Yes or No
Start new output line: Yes or No
```

To format the previous sample data into one logical record, you would use the definition in figure 23.10.

The complete definition for the sample data file is summarized as follows:

Field		Start Col	End Col	Data Type	Read Next Line	Start New Line	Physical Record
1	First	1	9	Text	Yes	No	1
2	Last	1	10	Text	Yes	No	2
3	Street	1	15	Text	Yes	No	3
4	City	1	10	Text	Yes	No	4

Fig. 23.10.

Data Format Definition.

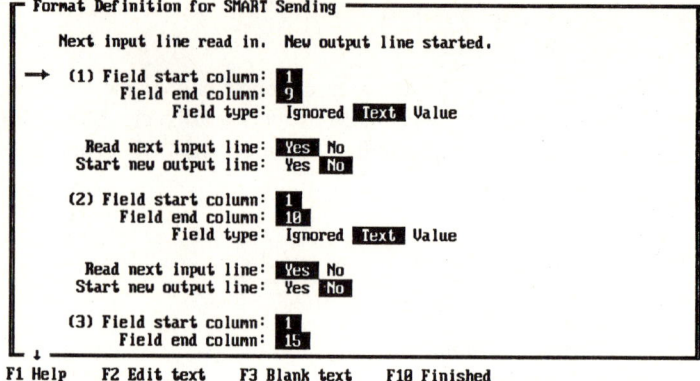

Field		Start Col	End Col	Data Type	Read Next Line	Start New Line	Physical Record
5	State	1	2	Text	No	No	5
6	blank	3	3	Ignore	No	No	5
7	Zip	4	8	Text	No	No	5
8	blank	9	9	Ignore	No	No	5
9	Phone	10	23	Text	Yes	No	5

Format definitions can be used to structure multiple record format files. Within each record, however, the fields must be in a fixed format. If the first name and last name fields had been on the same line with only a single space between them, the format definition would not have been able to identify the fields individually. A defined format file is specified in the Data Send command.

Modem Definition

A new feature of SmartWare II allows you to define your own modem characteristics. Thirty modem definitions are supplied with the system; these are contained in a file called CMMODEM.MDV, which is installed in your SmartWare II subdirectory. If you redefine one of the standard modems, a new file called REDEFINE.MDV is created for you; the original is not altered. If you decide to create a modem definition from scratch, the modem definition file (.MDV) may have any name you choose.

Whether you are redefining one of the standard modem definitions or creating your own, make sure that you have your modem manual handy; many of the selections are technical.

Chapter 23: Using the Communications Module

When you select the Set-Terminal Modem Define command, the first prompt asks for a file name:

    Enter filename:

If you have previously created a modem definition in the current subdirectory, the name is displayed in the pop-up window. You can select it if you want to change the definition, or you may type a new definition file name. If you want to create a new definition from scratch, type a new name for the definition. If you want to use an existing modem definition as a template, type the file name in a format similar to the following:

    C:\SMARTII\CMMODEM

By specifying the CMMODEM file, a new definition named REDEFINE.MDV is created in your current subdirectory. If you type a name of your own choice, it is used instead.

The next prompt asks for a modem name:

    Enter modem name:

If you have specified that CMMODEM.MDV is to be used as a template, you should respond to this prompt with the exact name of the modem you want to copy. (The names are displayed when you press F6 in Set-Terminal Settings Define or Edit at the Modem Type line.) Be sure to maintain the same spacing and spelling, including parenthesis; upper- or lowercase does not matter. If you have typed the name correctly, you will see a display of that modem's configuration on the screen. Figure 23.11 shows the first screen of the definition for the Hayes 1200 modem.

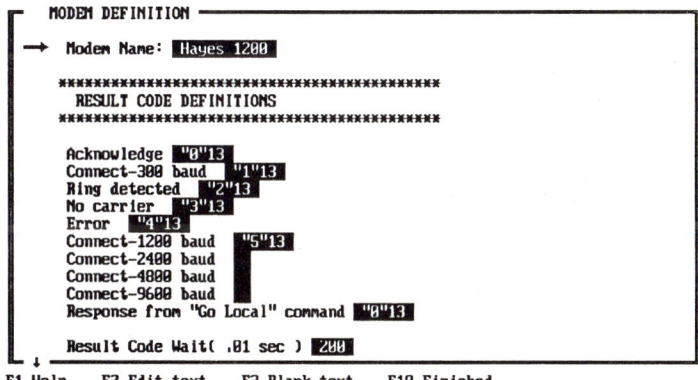

Fig. 23.11.

Modem Definition Hayes 1200.

If you decide to start from scratch by supplying your own file name, press Enter when prompted for the modem name. Of course, you will not be able to use any existing modem definitions as a template; you will have to fill in all the entries manually. Note that on the screen, literal characters are enclosed in quotation marks, and that numbers outside of quotation marks are decimal ASCII representations.

After making your entries and changes, press F10 to save your new modem definition. Remember, if you had decided to use CMMODEM.MDV as a template, the new file automatically is named REDEFINE.MDV; otherwise, your own file name is used.

If you have to change your custom modem definition, use the Set-Terminal Modem Define command and select the desired modem definition from the pop-up window. Press Enter when prompted for the modem name; the name is immaterial, because the definition for only one modem may be stored in a custom .MDV file.

Modem definitions in the current subdirectory are automatically appended to the display of the standard CMMODEM definitions when you are editing or defining your settings; when you press F6, your own definitions are found at the end of the list. Independent of the current subdirectory, you can directly specify the modem definition file you would like to use by entering the full path and file name and the modem name. For example, the following modem type definition would be valid from any subdirectory:

    C:\COMM\REDEFINE.MDV DICOMM 1200

This definition specifies a modem you called *Dicomm 1200* in the REDEFINE modem definition file in the C:\COMM subdirectory. Make sure that you maintain the same spacing and spelling, including any parenthesis; upper- or lowercase does not matter.

Communications Preferences

The default Communications module settings are established in the menu provided by the Tools Preferences Communications command (see fig. 23.12). If you often initiate communications from different subdirectories, you should specify the full path in the options which call for file names:

> Automatic load of settings. If you want a settings profile loaded automatically for you when you enter the Communications module, insert the name here.
>
> Automatic load of macro file. Enter the name of a macro file to load automatically when you begin a Communications session.

Chapter 23: Using the Communications Module

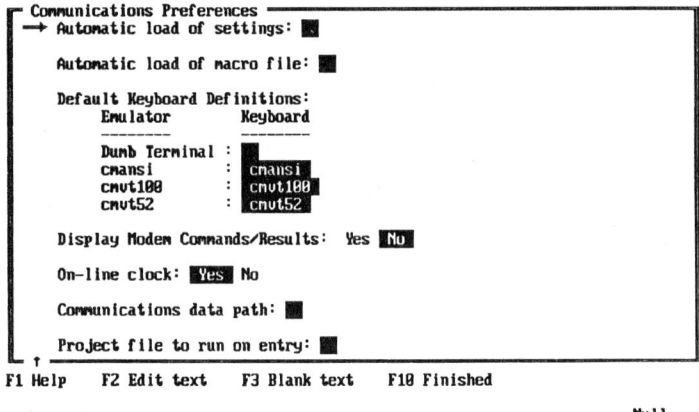

Fig. 23.12.

Communications Preferences.

Default Keyboard Definitions. Select the default keyboard definition files to be used, depending on the emulation type you have selected in the settings. If you have defined a new keyboard and want to have it in effect as a default, you should enter the name for the appropriate emulator.

Display Modem Commands/Results. If you select *Yes*, this is helpful in debugging your modem commands. A display similar to that in figure 23.13 is shown when you send output through your modem.

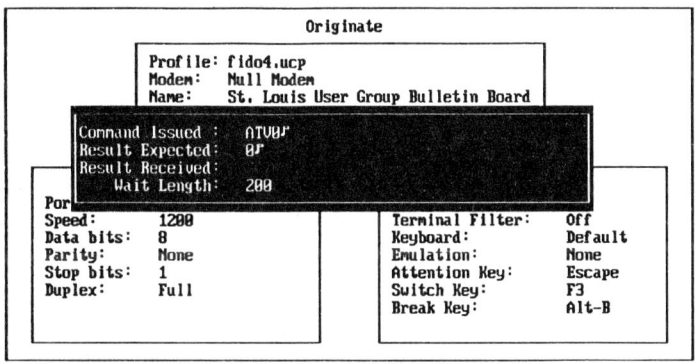

Fig. 23.13.

Modem commands and results.

In the window, you see the following information:

```
Command Issued by your computer
Result Expected from the modem
Result Received actual characters received from modem
Wait Length
```

You should watch the screen closely, because as multiple commands are sent from your computer, the contents of the window change. Press any key to clear the command results.

Online clock. Set to *Yes* to display a call elapsed time counter in the lower right corner of your screen.

Communications data path. Set to the default path for all your communications sessions. If you want the path to default to the subdirectory from which you initiated the communications session, you should leave this blank. The entry of a path here will override a path you may have specified in the Global Preferences. Remember, no matter how you have set a default path, you can always override it with the Tools Directory New Directory command.

Project file to run on entry. If you want to run a certain project file each time you begin the communications module, enter the name here.

Integrating with other Smart Modules

The Data Send command is used to integrate the Communications module with the other SmartWare II modules. You can use the Data Send command to send data from the buffer or a file to another module, and then transfer control to that module.

When you execute the Data Send command, the first prompt asks you to specify a module to which you want to send data:

```
Database  Spreadsheet  Wordprocessor
```

Data can be sent from one of two sources, as indicated by the next prompt:

```
Buffer    File
```

If you have captured screen output to the buffer, you can send the buffer contents without first writing the data to a file. Data may be entered into the buffer only with the Data Capture Buffer command. A text file, however, can be created with either the Data Capture File or Data Receive Text-File commands. If you select File at the preceding prompt, you are prompted to enter the name of the file containing the information you want to send.

The next prompt asks how you want the information sent:

    Formatted-By Un-Formatted

Your selection determines whether the information in the file is to be sent exactly as it was received (Un-Formatted) or modified in accordance with a format definition (Formatted-By). Refer to the Data Format command for an explanation and demonstration of the formatting capabilities. If you select Formatted-By, you are prompted for a format definition file name.

You are then prompted to enter the name of a project file for the next application. If you want to initiate a project file automatically, enter the name of the file; otherwise, press Enter. The Communications session is terminated, and the new module started.

Chapter Summary

The commands in the Communications module offer you the ability to link your computer to other computers or online services. If the receiving computers are operating under the SmartWare II system, you can easily share internal files, such as SmartWare Word Processor document files or Spreadsheet worksheets, by transmitting them with the error correcting Xmodem protocol. Even if the other computer is not running Smart, you can upload or download text files for integration with your applications.

Communications commands can be issued interactively from the keyboard, or you can include the commands in project files for unattended operation.

PART V

Using SmartWare II Project Processing

Includes

Project Processing

24

Project Processing

Although the capability to issue Smart commands individually from the keyboard provides flexibility for the knowledgeable user, this method of operating the Smart system has disadvantages. Frequently, repetitive processes call for several steps to be performed in succession every time. These processes may be simple utilities or complete applications.

In addition, not all users of the Smart system have equal levels of expertise. If you are a system designer, you may need to develop an application for use by people who don't need (or want) to know anything about Smart. Not only must you ensure that all steps are executed in the right order, but also that the application is error free.

The Project Processing feature of the SmartWare II system provides the capability of developing and executing sequences of commands contained within a project file. Some of the commands in a project file can be issued from the menu of a Smart application module; other commands are available only in the Project Processing environment and in particular modules. Each of the Project Processing commands is discussed in this chapter.

A Project Processing file can contain commands specific to only one module at a time; you cannot have both Data Manager and Word Processor commands in one file, for example. Project file execution control can be transferred between modules by a direct statement or by using one of the Send commands.

Project File Operations

Project Processing commands are initiated by selecting Remember from the menu. The following options are available after selecting Remember:

```
Start  Finish  Tools  Execute  Load  Unload
```

The Start and Finish options can be used to help you create project files in a recording mode that requires no programming. The Tools option makes available a set of project file utilities. Select Execute when you want to run a project file. Load installs a project file in RAM and Unload removes it; use this facility if you develop your own functions.

Creating and Editing a Project File

Project Processing files can be created in several ways. The Smart Text-Editor in the Tools command (or another text editor outside of Smart) can be used to create a file. You can also use the Remember Tools Edit editor that is specifically designed for project files and is similar to the Tools Text Editor. But the easiest way to create a project file is by using the Remember Start command.

Remember Start Command

There are three options to the Remember Start command:

    Commands   Keys   Both

If you select Commands, all the commands you issue interactively are recorded in a file you select. Instead of referring to the Smart manual (or even this book) for the format of the commands and then typing them into your project file, you can issue the commands you need and the system writes them to the file for you. Even if you make a mistake, you don't need to end the recording mode; just enter the correct command and continue. Later, you can use the Remember Tools Edit command to correct errors.

When you have selected the Recording option, a pop-up window displays the names of your existing project files. If you want to create a new project file, type a new name and press Enter. If you want to append statements to an existing project file, select the file from the menu and press Enter.

The following is a Spreadsheet project file that closes two windows and unloads all worksheets:

    window close
    window close
    file unload "all"

This simple project file was created with the Remember Start Commands command. Of course, with an elementary project file like this, it is just as easy to create it in the Remember Edit mode. However, if you have a project file containing several steps or unfamiliar commands, the Remember Start mode can be a real time-saver.

Even if your project file will ultimately require commands that you cannot issue from the menu level, you can create the nucleus of the program, containing the application commands, and then use the Remember Tools Edit command to insert the remaining commands.

Remember Finish Command

To terminate the recording mode, use the Remember Finish command. The application commands you execute while in the Start mode are written to the specified file, and the project file is automatically compiled. It is now ready to run. (Of course, if you made some mistakes along the way, use the Remember Tools Edit command to correct them.) Use the Ctrl-F10 key to suspend temporarily and resume the Recording mode.

If you would like both the applications commands and the keystrokes contained in the file, select the Both option under the Remember Start command. This option is useful for executing a command and selecting options in a menu. The following project file was created with the Both option to replicate a data file in the Database module:

```
file create "temp" similar standard-view "person3" no password
keys "rdperson3",Enter,"person4",Enter,"fn"
keys F10
```

This example demonstrates that project files in SmartWare II offer a Keys command, enabling you to issue keystrokes as if they originated from your keyboard. The Keys command is covered in detail later in this chapter. If you record only the keystrokes (the Keys option), the same steps would record the following project file:

```
suspend command
keys "fctemp",Enter,"ssperson3",Enter,"nrdperson3",Enter,"person4"
keys Enter,"fn"
keys F10
keys "rf"
```

Note that literals are contained in the quotation marks. Note also that the last line of the Keys-only project file contains the keystrokes rf, that represent the execution of the Remember Finish command needed to terminate the recording mode. Make sure to delete this line if you record only the keys.

Editing a Project File

Whether you write your project files in the Remember Start mode or write them from scratch, you need to know how to use the project file editor. Select the Remember Tools Edit command to display a pop-up window of project file names. If you want to edit an existing project file, select it from the menu; if you are creating a new one, type the name and press Enter.

The project file editor commands are the same as those of the Tools Text-Editor. Refer to Chapter 28 for a complete discussion of these capabilities. There are two important differences, however, between the project file editor and the Tools Text Editor.

When you use the Remember Tools Edit command, you do not have to specify the file extension. Smart relies on the following DOS file extensions to identify project source files:

Module	Extension
Spreadsheet	Pf1
Word Processor	Pf2
Database	Pf3
Communications	Pf4
Main Menu	Pf0

Because the Remember Tools Text Editor is used specifically for project files, you do not have to type the extension; it is assumed.

When you save your work at the completion of a Remember Tools Edit session, your project file is automatically compiled into the executable form needed by the system. (The extensions of these compiled files begin with Rf instead of Pf.) Many types of errors are identified by the compiler; you can correct them immediately. If you want to correct them later, press Esc to return to the command level; your source file will be written to the disk, and you can edit your project file at a later time.

Not all errors are caught at the completion of the Remember Tools Edit session. Following are some of the types of errors that are not caught during the compile process:

Logic Errors. If you type *if r1c1 > 100* instead of *if r1c1 < 100*, both are valid statements, but they have very different meanings. Your program may run without any execution errors, but the results will be wrong.

Typing Errors. If you mistype the name of a field, for example, an execution error will result. Similarly, if you have forgotten to define a query that is to be used in the program, you will get an error when the program runs.

Data Type Errors. If an alpha field contains a number, you must test it with a quoted comparison (if [code] = "2") not with a numeric comparison (if [code] = 2).

Only those statements that clearly violate the syntax requirements of project processing are detected as errors at the time of compilation.

As you develop your project file, if you find that you need more room on the line than is available, use the backslash key (\) at the end of the line to indicate that the project file line continues on the next physical line of the file.

Running a Project File

To run a project file, select the Remember Execute command, or press F8. A popup window displays the names of the project files in the current subdirectory; you can type the name, or use the cursor to point to the one you want to run. Press Enter to display the following options:

    In-Memory From-File

If you select In-Memory, the whole project file is loaded into RAM before execution. This option usually makes the project run faster, particularly if the program contains loops in which the same line is executed repeatedly. If the project file is too large to fit into memory, and you select In-Memory, it will run as though the From-File option was chosen.

If you elect to execute the project file with the From-File option, each line of the file will be read from the file as it is needed for execution.

During the execution of your project file, you can stop processing by pressing Ctrl-Z. You must respond to the following prompt:

    Cancel or suspend execution? (c/s)

Press *C* to cancel execution of the project file. If you want to suspend execution, press *S*. Once you are in the suspend mode, you are returned to the command level temporarily, where you can execute almost all of the application module commands. You may want to check on the records being processed, or the accumulation of amounts in variables. However, before resuming execution of the project, you must be sure to restore all conditions (window, records, etc.) to the state they were in when you suspended execution.

You are reminded that a project has been suspended by the following display in the lower right corner of your screen:

    Project suspended...

To resume execution, issue the Remember Execute command, or press F8. Execution begins from the point at which it was suspended.

Using Other Project File Tools

You can use several other tools to compile, print, and debug your project files.

Compile

If you use a text editor other than the Remember Tools Edit command, you must compile your program in a separate step. (If you use the SmartWare Word Processor, you must save your file as a Text-File, not a Document.) From the Remember Tools option list, select Compile to create the object file that Smart requires for execution. You have the choice of two modes of compiling:

No-Debug Debug

While you are developing your program, select the Debug mode; once you are certain there are no more bugs or errors, you can recompile the program in the No-Debug mode. Programs compiled in the No-Debug mode run faster, but will not contain the codes necessary for helping you detect errors during execution.

Trace

To help you track down bugs in your programs, you can use the Trace option of the Remember Tools command. When you select Trace, the menu shown in figure 24.1 is displayed.

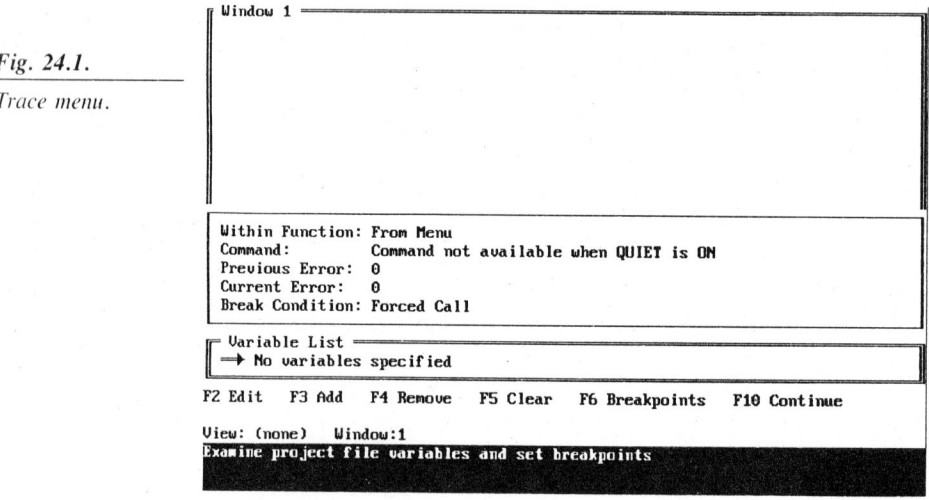

Fig. 24.1.

Trace menu.

By specifying certain conditions that you expect to occur in your program, you can cause the execution to be suspended and the trace screen displayed. For example, suppose you display the trace screen when the [dept] field equals DATA in the following project file:

```
public $accum $count
clear public

data goto record record-number 1
for $count = 1 to records
    let $accum = $accum + [wage]
    data goto record next
end for

message "Total wage is: " | fixed($accum,2)
```

When the trace screen is displayed, press F3 to add a variable you want to see at the trace breakpoint. If you want to see all of them, enter an asterisk (*).

Press F6 to edit, add, or remove the breakpoint conditions at which the trace screen is to be displayed. The type of breakpoint can be one of the following four:

0 = Each line
1 = Only on error
2 = On a specified condition
3 = Upon function execution

In this example, press 2 to specify the following condition:

[dept] = "DATA"

When specifying conditions (type 2), use the following function keys:

F2   Edit existing condition
F3   Add a new condition
F4   Remove a condition
F5   Clear all conditions
F10 Finished

Figure 24.2 shows the condition specification.

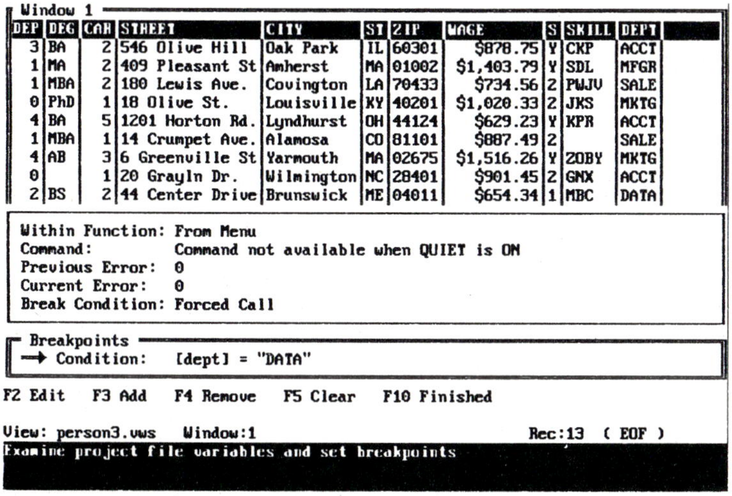

Fig. 24.2.

Trace condition specification.

Press F10 to save the trace specification. Now, when you execute your project file, each time the designated condition occurs, the trace screen appears (see fig. 24.3).

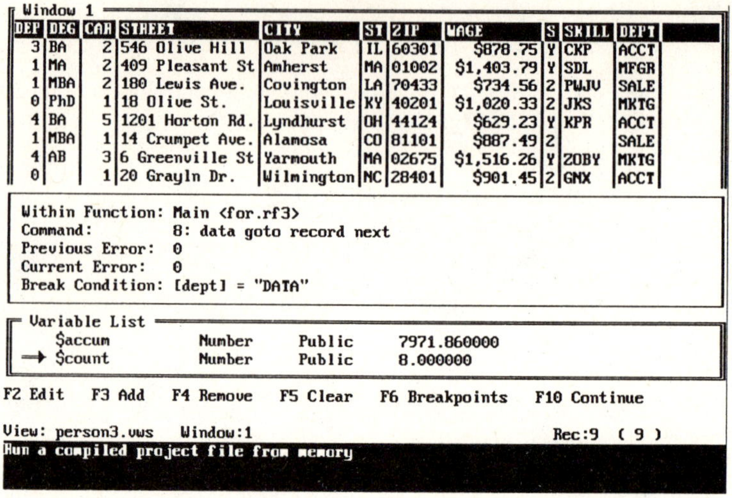

Fig. 24.3.

Trace screen during program execution.

```
┌ Window 1 ─────────────────────────────────────────────────────────────┐
│DEP│DEG│CAR│STREET         │CITY      │ST│ZIP  │WAGE      │S│SKILL│DEPT│
│  3│BA │  2│546 Olive Hill │Oak Park  │IL│60301│   $878.75│Y│CKP  │ACCT│
│  1│MA │  2│409 Pleasant St│Amherst   │MA│01002│ $1,403.79│Y│SDL  │MFGR│
│  1│MBA│  2│180 Lewis Ave. │Covington │LA│70433│   $734.56│2│PWJV │SALE│
│  0│PhD│  1│18 Olive St.   │Louisville│KY│40201│ $1,020.33│2│JKS  │MKTG│
│  4│BA │  5│1201 Horton Rd.│Lyndhurst │OH│44124│   $629.23│Y│KPR  │ACCT│
│  1│MBA│  1│14 Crumpet Ave.│Alamosa   │CO│81101│   $887.49│2│     │SALE│
│  4│AB │  3│6 Greenville St│Yarmouth  │MA│02675│ $1,516.26│Y│ZOBY │MKTG│
│  0│   │  1│20 Grayln Dr.  │Wilmington│NC│28401│   $901.45│2│GNX  │ACCT│
├───────────────────────────────────────────────────────────────────────┤
│ Within Function: Main <for.rf3>                                       │
│ Command:             8: data goto record next                         │
│ Previous Error:      0                                                │
│ Current Error:       0                                                │
│ Break Condition: [dept] = "DATA"                                      │
├───────────────────────────────────────────────────────────────────────┤
│ Variable List                                                         │
│     $accum            Number      Public     7971.860000              │
│  → $count            Number      Public        8.000000               │
└───────────────────────────────────────────────────────────────────────┘
 F2 Edit    F3 Add    F4 Remove    F5 Clear    F6 Breakpoints    F10 Continue

 View: person3.vws   Window:1                              Rec:9  ( 9 )
 Run a compiled project file from memory
```

When the trace screen is displayed, you can add or remove breakpoints or variables as needed. If you want to alter the contents of any of your selected variables, move the cursor to the variable and press F2. You can enter any expression or constant. Press F10 to continue execution of the program.

To display the line number and command being executed, you must compile the program in the Debug mode. All other trace operations function in both Debug and No-Debug mode.

If you want to force the display of the trace screen, insert the Trace command at the desired point in your program. If you have invoked the trace facility but do not want the screen displayed in certain sections of your program, turn it off with the Trace Off command, and back on again with Trace On.

Remember Tools Print

To print a copy of a project file, use the Remember Tools Print command. Line numbers are printed for reference purposes.

Using Project File Commands

A project file can contain two types of commands. *Application commands* work at the command level of applications, and *Project File commands* execute in only a project file.

Application commands can be recorded in a project file using the Remember Start command; project file commands must be typed while in the Remember Tools editor or another text editor. The following section discusses the structure of project files and presents each of the project file commands.

Using Project File Structure

Project files in SmartWare II are more highly structured than in previous versions of Smart. If you plan to use functions (they replace procedures), you must specify a main section of your program, in which the processing of the project file takes place from beginning to end. Any functions that are used during execution appear outside of the main area.

Declaring a Program Main Section

The main section of your program is delimited by the key words, Main and End Main. The declaration of a main section is necessary only if you refer to functions. For example, the following project file does not need a main section:

```
global $name
screen shortinput $name "Your Name:"
message "Hello,"| $name
```

The project file asks for your name on the first command line, and then displays it along with a greeting. Note that the variable, $name, must be declared before its use. Variables are discussed later in this chapter. Note also that literals are enclosed in double quotation marks. (Previous versions of the Smart project processing language used a special parameter, denoted with a percent sign (%), to display the name on the message line; parameters are not used in SmartWare II.)

The following project file, on the other hand, requires the notation of a main section because it declares a function:

```
global $name upname()

main
   screen shortinput $name "Your Name:"
   upname ($name)
end main

function upname (upstr)
   message "Hello,"|upper(upstr)
end function
```

The demarcation of the main section, beginning with Main and ending with End Main, indicates the extent of the primary program. Once the End Main statement is encountered, the program terminates.

Functions

Functions are new in SmartWare II. They can be used like procedures were used in previous versions of Smart, they can be used like commands, or they can act like built-in Smart functions. Functions must be declared outside the Main section of your program, and they must begin with the word `function` and end with `End Function`. Each function must have a name, and can have as many as 25 arguments to be used during the execution of the function.

The function statement used in the previous example took the following form:

    function upname (upstr)

The name of the function in this example is Upname, and the argument used for reference inside the function is called Upstr. The function argument name has no usage outside the function itself; it is used in the function to refer to the values passed to the function.

Using a Function as a Procedure

You can use a function in the same way that you may have used procedures in previous Smart versions.

```
'Function as a procedure
global $name upname()

main
   screen shortinput $name "Your Name:"
   upname ($name)
   message "Hello, "|$name
end main

function upname (upstr)
   let $name = upper(upstr)
end function
```

In this example, the procedure is called by entering it on a line by itself. In the function, the case of the argument is changed to uppercase, and assigned to the variable, *$name*. Here, the function changes the case of only the $name variable; it does not have the flexibility to convert the case of a different variable.

Using a Function as a Command

In this example, the function operates like a command:

```
'Function as a command
global $name upname()

main
```

```
    screen shortinput $name "Your Name:"
    upname ($name)
end main

function upname (upstr)
    message "Hello,"|upper(upstr)
end function
```

In this example, the case of the $name variable is not changed; the name is passed to the argument, Upstr, of the function, in which the uppercase of the argument is printed. Note that you have the independence of the variable and the function itself. The name of the variable passed to the function does not always have to be $name; it is specified in the parentheses on the call line.

Using a Function as a Function

You can use a project file function to act as if it were a built-in Smart function. You can use it wherever you would use a regular Smart function, whether in a project file, Query, or Report.

```
'Function as a function
global $name upname ()

main
    screen shortinput $name "Your Name:"
    message "Hello, "|upname($name)
end main

function upname (upstr)
    return upper(upstr)
end function
```

Here, the function is completely independent of both the argument variable and the usage of the result. Any variable could have been passed as an argument to the Upname function, and the result could have been used anywhere, not just in a message statement.

Variables

Unlike previous Smart versions, you must now declare your variables before you can use them. This is because of the expanded variable capabilities in SmartWare II projects, the dimensionality that a variable can assume, and the ambiguity that might exist between a variable name and other project file elements.

A variable is a scratch pad in RAM where you can jot down something for later retrieval, or accumulate values as you proceed through a project file. The rules for variable names are as follows:

- A variable name can begin with a letter from A to Z, a number, or the symbols $, #, or _ (underscore).
- No spaces are allowed in a variable name.
- You can use a maximum of 31 characters in a name.
- Variable names are not case sensitive.

Previous versions of Smart offered a special type of variable called a parameter. Parameters are useless in SmartWare II, so they are unavailable.

The standard project variables TEXT1, TEXT2, VALUE1, and VALUE2 also have been removed from SmartWare II. You can, however, declare these as user-defined variables.

Variables can contain either numeric or text data; the data type is not assigned at the time of declaration, but is determined by the type of data entered. The following statement, for example, defines a variable as numeric because both fields will obviously contain numeric data:

```
let $extension = [quantity] * [price]
```

Similarly, the following defines a different variable as text:

```
let #dept = "ACCT"
```

A text variable also can contain a number, if it is assigned as text:

```
let Status = "2"
```

In this instance, however, even though there is a number in the variable, you will not be able to perform calculations with it. You can calculate with only numeric variables.

Variables fall into four classes, depending on the extent to which you want them to span program sections, programs, or modules. The declaration of a class of variable is made at the beginning of the section to which it applies.

Local

Local variables apply to only the main section or a function in the individual project files in which they are declared. Once the program or function terminates, the variables are unassigned. If your project stands alone and you don't want to retain the values of your variables once the project file has terminated, declare the variables as Local:

```
LOCAL $dept #total_wage Employee_Name
```

Spaces or commas can delimit the variable names on the declaration line. Variables local to the main section must be declared in that section; local variables for functions must be declared in the functions to which they apply.

Global

If you want to use the same variable throughout an individual project file, making its contents available to both the main section and any functions, declare the variable as Global. Global variables must be declared at the beginning of the project file. Like Local variables, once the project file terminates, the variable is automatically deallocated—unavailable for use in other project files.

Public

To allow a variable to carry over beyond the project file in which it is declared, allocate it as a Public variable, so it remains allocated during execution of the project file or any project files subordinate to it. Thus, if you have a series of project files that pass control to each other, with either Execute or Transfer commands, Public variables will remain allocated. As a default, once control is returned to the command level, Public variables are deallocated.

You can retain the allocation of Public variables in the module by one of the following statements:

```
LOCK MODULE $test
LOCK MODULE public
```

A Lock Module statement following the declaration of Public variables prevents them from becoming automatically deallocated when you return to the command level. As in these examples, you can lock either individual variables or all of the public variables at once. If, however, you change to another Smart module, the variables are cleared. To retain the value of variables from module to module, use one of the following commands:

```
LOCK SYSTEM $test
LOCK SYSTEM public
```

Public variables with system lock are equivalent to the level of variable retention in previous versions of Smart. Only about 6,000 bytes can be transferred from one module to another, however. The Lock and Unlock statements are covered in greater detail later in this chapter.

External

Even though you declare a variable as Public, any subordinate or successive project files that use the variable must include a statement indicating to the compiler that the variable is expected to have been allocated elsewhere:

```
External $test
```

This statement, at the beginning of a project file, before the main section, indicates that the Public variable $test was allocated in a previous project file.

Variable Dimensions

Up to now, the discussion of variables has centered around single content variables, containing only one number or string. Now, with SmartWare II, you can declare multiple dimension variables and store multiple contents.

Arrays

A variable with multiple dimensions, called an array, can have one, two, or three dimensions. The method of declaring an array is similar to declaring a scalar (single content) variable:

```
Local $amount[5,3]
Global #Account[20]
```

The $amount variable is given the dimension 5 by 3; you can think of it as 5 rows by 3 columns. The #account variable can hold as many as 20 accounts. In a project file, you reference individual cells of an array as $amount[3,2], #account[2], and so on. Of course, in your program, a scalar variable can be used to reference an individual cell:

```
#account[accno]
```

In this example, if the variable accno were equal to 5, the reference would be the fifth element of the #account array.

Redimensioning an Array

Once you have declared an array, you can change its size by using the Redimension command. Although you cannot change an array from two-dimensional to three, for example, you can change the sizes of the existing dimensions.

```
global $totals[1] $nracts
lock module $nracts $totals[]
screen shortinput $nracts "Number of Accounts:"
redimension $totals[$nracts]
```

You cannot, in this case, perform the following command:

```
redimension $totals[$nracts,5]
```

This would be an attempt at changing the number of dimensions, rather than the size of an existing dimension. Be careful: If you change the size of an array with the redimension command, the previous contents of the array are discarded.

Just as with scalar variables, array variables can be locked in the module; they cannot be system locked, however.

Display Commands

Display commands are used to provide instructions or information to you as you run your project file.

Beep

The Beep command can be used to alert the project file operator; it also can be used to turn on or off the capability of producing any tone at all.

To alert the operator, you can issue the command in any of the following formats:

```
Beep
Beep 5
Beep 3 "Insert Disk"
Beep $nrbeeps $message
```

The first example produces a single beep; the second produces five beeps. You can follow the number of beeps with an optional message. Both the number of beeps and the message can be variables.

New with SmartWare II is the capability of turning your computer's speaker on and off as follows:

```
Beep On
Beep Off
```

The default beep setting, even outside project files, is controlled in the Tools Preferences Global menu. Using the Beep Off command in a project file will override the preferences, and remain in effect for the duration of the session.

Sound

To alert the operator with something a bit fancier than beeps, use the Sound command to produce a tone you control by frequency and duration. The format of the command is the following:

```
sound $frequency $duration
sound 440 2
```

The duration is optional; it defaults to .1 seconds. You can produce multiple tones by inserting pairs of values following the Sound command:

    Sound 262 .3 262 .1 294 .6 262 .6 349 .6 330 .6

Multiple executions of the Sound command can produce short tunes or songs. The Soundblock command produces even more sophisticated legato musical productions.

Message

To issue a message in the control area without sounding a tone, use the Message command. Execution is suspended until you press a key. Examples of the Message command are the following:

    Message "Insert disk ... press a key to continue"
    Message $warning
    Message "Phase 1 completed at " | time

Note that text, variables, and functions can be concatenated to produce a compound message.

Wait

The Wait command suspends execution for a specified number of seconds and displays an optional message. If you press any key before the time is exhausted, execution continues immediately.

    Wait 10 "Phase 1 Completed"
    Wait 5

The message portion of the Wait command is optional. The numeric portion of the command represents seconds; for more precise control, you can specify both an integer and decimal argument:

    Wait 7.5 "End of Job"

The Milli-Wait command can be used to provide even greater pause control, because the arguments to the command are specified in thousands of a second:

    Milli-Wait 750

The command in this example waits for 3/4 of a second. If you combine the Sound command with the Milli-Wait command, you can produce some interesting musical compositions.

Because the Beep command doesn't pause to allow you to read a message, you may want to use the Beep command followed by the Wait command to alert the user and display an important message.

Locate

If you want to position the cursor at a specific spot on the screen, use the Locate command. You must supply a row and column location, followed by a cursor size number. The cursor sizes are the following:

1   Heavy Underscore
2   Square
3   Vertical Rectangle

Use the command as follows:

Format: Locate row column cursor
Example: Locate 5 10 1

The following project file allows you to type a line across the screen. Press Enter to terminate the line.

```
public $col , $letter

lock system $col , $letter

screen clear 7 0
let $col = 10

label nextltr
locate 5 $col 1
let $letter = inchar
if $letter <> {enter}
    screen print 5 $col 7 0 chr($letter)
    let $col = $col + 1
    jump nextltr
end if
```

Note that a variable $col is used for the column location in the Locate command. The value of $col is increased by 1 each time you type a letter.

Repaint

If you want to keep your screen from displaying new records, windows, or spreadsheet areas as your project file executes, use the command Repaint Off at the beginning of a Project file. The project file will look cleaner and run faster. At certain points, however, you must use the Repaint On command. Before updating a record in the database, for example, you certainly want the screen to be repainted so you can see what's going on.

Preventing the repainting of the screen also allows you to maintain the display of a menu during execution of a project file. If you want to force the screen to be repainted, use the Repaint command by itself.

Control Commands

Control commands are used to control termination of a project file and execution of subsequent project files.

Execute

If you want to execute another project file from in the current project, and then return to the original, use the Execute command. The arguments are similar to the Remember Execute command in each application module.

Format: Execute "f"
 f = project file name
 Execute "f" in-memory
 Execute "f" from-file
 Execute "f"

Example: Execute "INVOICE" in-memory

If the subordinate project file can fit in the available RAM, you can specify In-Memory for faster execution. If there isn't enough memory, don't worry; the project file will execute From-File, reading each line as needed. (The default execution mode is From-File if you do not specify.)

If you have nested project files, where the first one executes the second, control is returned to the first when the second terminates with an End Main statement. However, if the second project file encounters a Stop or Quit statement, control does not return to the first.

Transfer

If you want to execute a second project file from in the first, but you do not want the first to continue after the completion of the second, use the Transfer command.

Format: Transfer "f"
 f = project file name
 Transfer "f" in-memory
 Transfer "f" from-file
 Transfer "f"

Example: Transfer "INVOICE" in-memory

Keys

Besides being able to execute module commands in a project file, you can also generate keystrokes as if you had typed them at the keyboard. Thus, you can stack a series of responses to a menu or prompt sequence, provided, of course, you know the answers in advance. (Use the Remember Keys facility to create a project file of only keystrokes.) For example, the following project file turns the system beep on or off:

```
suspend command
keys "tpg",Down,Right,F10,F8
```

From the command level, the command Tools Preferences Global is executed. On line 2, the status of the Beep setting is switched.

Note that for the duration of the Keys command, normal command execution is suspended in the Command mode with the statement Suspend Command. Normal control is resumed by the inclusion of the F8 (Execute) key; if you want your project file to resume normal command execution automatically, you must have this key stroke as the final key in the sequence. If you do not include the F8, you must press it manually to continue processing.

Screenon and Screenoff

If you do not want to change the display during Keys execution, you can use the terms SCREENON and SCREENOFF. For example, to avoid displaying the Preferences Global menu in the previous example, include the Screenoff keyword:

```
suspend command
keys Screenoff, "tpg",Down,Right,F10,F8
```

The Screenon and Screenoff key words are analogous to the Repaint On and Repaint Off commands.

Until and Waitfor

In the previous Keys command examples, the keystrokes are embedded in the command; the commands execute the same way every time. If you want to supply your own keystrokes at the execution time, use the term Until to cause the Keys command to pause and accept additional keystrokes. Regular execution resumes when the key after the Until term is encountered.

The following example can be used to change the title in the table portion of a report named Deplist:

```
suspend command
keys "prmdeplist",Enter,"tt",Down,Down,Down,Until,enter
keys F10,F10,F10,F8
```

Note that you are allowed to type the title until you press the Enter key; at that point, execution of the Keys command resumes.

The Waitfor term is similar to the Until term, except that your keystrokes during the pause are ignored. You cannot use Waitfor to change anything; you can use it for viewing an existing menu setting or file contents. Waitfor is similar to the Pause term, discussed later in this chapter.

Handling Macro Keys

An existing key redefined as a macro will not normally continue to act as a macro when used in a Keys statement. You must use the Look or Lookon terms in the Keys command if you want to use a macro. (At the command level, the opposite is true; you must preface the use of a Macro key with a Shift-F10 if you want to temporarily revert to the original key meaning for the next keystroke.)

If, for example, you have redefined Alt-E as a macro, you must preface its usage in the Keys command with the term Look:

```
Keys Look, Alt-E
```

If you have a series of macro keys you want to use, Lookon enables you to use them without having to specify Look before each one. Use Lookoff to end the Lookon condition. Even while Lookon is in effect, if you want to ignore the macro redefinition of the next keystroke, you can preface the individual keystroke with the term Nolook.

Key Execution Timing

The execution of the Keys command is fast—sometimes too fast. If it is necessary to slow down the process, perhaps for instruction or demonstration purposes, you can use Delayon. Delayon requires an argument, the number of hundredths of seconds to delay between each output keystroke. In the following example, the command delays each keystroke by 1 second:

```
Keys Delayon, #100
```

Note that you must separate the delay argument from the Delayon term with a comma, and that the number symbol (#) must precede the value.

To resume normal, fast execution of your keylist, use Delayoff.

If you want to pause during the Keys command, use Pause. The system halts until you press a key; the key is not processed as part of the command. If you want only a specific key to be allowed to resume processing, use the Waitfor term discussed previously.

If you do want the next keystroke to be processed after a pause, use Key instead of Pause. Thus, you can allow some manual variability in menu selection even while processing the majority of a command sequence from your project file.

Other Keys Terms

To repeat the output of a keystroke multiple times, such as an F10 or a cursor key, use Repeat.

    Keys Repeat, #5, F10

This command repeats F10 five times.

To insert the result of the most recent Tools Calculator command, use Result. This is equivalent to pressing Ctrl-C outside of a project file.

If an error is encountered during the processing of your Keys command, the remainder of the keylist is discarded and not processed. If you want to prevent the rest of the list from being lost, use Nokey before the keys you want to retain.

You also can include comments in a Keys command, but because comments consume RAM, you should probably just use Project file comments on adjacent lines; refer to the Comment command.

Reply

Many commands that you issue at the command level have a standard prompt that you must answer before the command can be completed. In the Database, if you are writing a report to an existing disk file, you are prompted:

    File filename.ext already exists. Continue? (y/n)

If you want to continue, you press *Y*; otherwise, press *N*. In either case, you do not press the Enter key after your response.

In a project file, most of these interactive prompts have default responses; you are not prompted for an answer as you are at the command level. Using the Reply command, however, you can force the prompt or change the default answer for individual prompts. You can reset the prompt condition for just the next execution of the command, or for all commands generating the prompt throughout the current or subordinate project files. (The prompts, their numbers, and the default answers are found in Appendix B in your *Project Processing* manual.)

To reset the default for a particular prompt, the statement immediately preceding the prompt-generating command would be:

    Reply char "character" to prompt-number

For example, if you want to change the default response for the previous prompt about overwriting a report output file, you would use this command:

    Reply char "n" to 3014

This command changes the response for only the next command, however. If you want to change the default for the duration of the current project file and for any subordinate project files, use this command:

    Reply ON char "n" to 3014

The additional word On causes the change in the default to apply throughout the current project file and any subordinates. Once control is returned to the command level, any changes to the responses are reset to the defaults.

Besides changing the default response character, you also can issue an escape:

    Reply {on} escape to prompt-number

Use the additional word On to cause the change in the default to apply throughout the current project file and any subordinates.

If you want to force the prompt to appear, just as it does when you execute the command from the command level, use the following format:

    Reply {on} nothing to prompt-number

You can selectively reset an individual response back to its original default value with the command:

    Reply off to prompt-number

To reset all responses to their original default values, use the following command:

    Reply off to all

The number of active Reply commands is limited to 20 in any project file; if you exceed the limit, any additional commands are ignored.

Command Level Control

You can use any of several commands to terminate or suspend execution of a project file.

The Suspend Command

To suspend execution of a project file and temporarily pass control to the keyboard, use the Suspend command. (This command has the same effect as pressing Ctrl-Z to suspend the execution.) While execution is suspended, you can perform any operation except those Remember commands that would compile, start, or execute another project file. Be careful not to disturb anything that was created or established by the project file. If you change the order of a database, for example, the project file does not automatically return the file to desired order when execution is resumed.

Remember Execute Command

To resume execution of the program, press F8, or issue the Remember Execute command.

I used the Suspend command before a Keys command earlier in this chapter. To make sure that the system is in the Command mode when execution is suspended, use the argument Command, as in this example:

   Suspend Command

If you want to be in the Enter mode when suspended, use the command:

   Suspend Enter

In the Suspend mode, you can execute any number of commands before you press F8 to continue with the project file. If you want to execute only one command, use the Suspendone statement. Execution of the project file is resumed automatically at the completion of the individual command. Do not press F8 to continue.

As with the Suspend command, you also can specify an argument of Command or Enter to the Suspendone command.

The Exit Command

An Exit command by itself causes an immediate termination of the current section of the current project file and causes execution of the next command following the end of the section. For example, if encountered in a function, the Exit command operates the same as an End Function command.

To avoid ambiguity, don't use the Exit command by itself; use the structure identifiers as follows:

   Exit Main
   Exit Function
   Exit While
   Exit For
   Exit Case

Exit While is the same as the Break command in previous Smart versions. When encountered, execution begins immediately with the command following End While.

The Exit Main command acts the same as an End Main, terminating the current project file, or returning control to a previous project file, if any.

The Stop Command

To stop the execution of all project files, regardless of their status as subordinate or primary, use the Stop command. When this statement is encountered, you are returned to the command level. The following series of statements halts execution if the field [wage] is less than zero.

```
if [wage] < 0
    stop
end if
```

When the Stop command is encountered, control is not returned to a previous project file, even if the current project file is subordinate to another.

The Quit Command

To terminate Smart and return to the operating system, use the command Quit Quit. (Yes, you must have the word *Quit* twice; you're not seeing double.)

You also can quit to another module. From the Word Processor, for example, the Quit command by itself at the menu level displays the following options:

    Quit Main-Menu Communications Database Spreadsheet

Naturally, to quit to the Operating system, you must use the Quit option. If you want to begin execution of one of the other modules, or the Main Menu, you would perform the appropriate selection. The command to invoke the spreadsheet is the following:

    Quit Spreadsheet

To begin execution of a project file in another module, the entire command is as follows:

    Quit Spreadsheet Project-File "proj-file"

This format of the Quit command replaces the corresponding format of the Jump command in previous Smart versions.

Execution Order Commands

The Jump and Label commands can be used to change the order in which a Project file is executed.

The Jump Command

The Jump command is used to transfer execution to a different line in your project file. The line at which execution continues is identified by a label.

Format: Jump l
             l = label

Example: Jump step3

In this example, step3 is a label. When the Jump statement is encountered, execution transfers to the line labeled step3. If the label does not exist, the error is detected during compilation of the project file.

The Jump command can, of course, be part of a conditional statement:

```
if [dept] = "ACCT"
    jump depac
end if
```

To use the Jump command, you must have a label—the next subject.

The Label Command

Label is not really a command, but the identifier of a line designated in a Jump command. The following rules apply to labels:

- The word Label and the label itself must be on a line by themselves.

- The label can have a maximum of 31 characters. Any characters beyond the 31st are ignored.

- Any combination of letters or numbers is permitted, but spaces in the label are not.

- Label names are no longer case sensitive, as they were in previous versions of Smart.

- If you attempt to jump to a nonexistent label, your project file will not compile, and you will be given the opportunity to make the necessary corrections.

Operating System Commands

You can execute operating system commands automatically from in a Project file. The Osexit command can be used to prevent manual execution of DOS comands while a Project file is suspended.

The Tools OS Command

At the command level, or if you execute Smart manually, you can access the operating system by pressing the quick key Ctrl-O, invoking a secondary command processor. You also can use the Tools OS command. When you do this, the Smart System is temporarily interrupted so that you can execute DOS commands or other programs from the operating system. If you do not have enough available memory for executing DOS commands, you may need to use the -r option when you enter SmartWare II at the beginning of the session. (The -r option is explained at the beginning of this book.)

The Tools OS command can also provide DOS access from in project files. On a line by itself, Tools OS invokes the secondary processor. Execution is transferred to the DOS level, where you can run DOS commands. When you type *Exit*, the Smart session is resumed, and the processing of the project continues.

If you want to execute a DOS command without manual intervention, use the following format:

    Tools OS "DOS Command"

The command in quotation marks is executed, and on completion, the project file continues. This format may be preferable to manual execution if you are building an application to be used by novice users. If you do not specify a DOS command to be executed, once the project accesses DOS, users have complete control of the computer.

The Osexit Command

If you suspend processing of a project file, with either a Suspend command or by pressing Ctrl-Z, you can drop to the operating system level by using the Tools OS command or by pressing Ctrl-O. If you want to prevent access to the operating system from the Suspend mode, however, use the following command in your project file:

    Osexit Off

This command blocks access if anyone tries to get out to DOS while the project file is suspended, displaying the following error message instead:

    DOS access is disabled

To allow access, use the command Osexit On. When the project file finishes, and control is returned to the command level, DOS access is automatically enabled. Even with Osexit Off, however, you are not prevented from the execution of a DOS command or exiting to DOS with the Tools Os command.

Peripheral Commands

Several project processing commands directly access the hardware of your computer. These commands allow you to print free form lines of text, write directly to DOS files, and even examine and change data in RAM.

Printer Commands

There are two commands you can use to write directly to your printer from a project file: Lprint and Lprintraw. To use either, you must first open the printer with the Open-Printer command.

The Lprint and Lprintraw Commands

Use the Lprint command to write text to your printer from variables, literals, database fields, or spreadsheet cells. The Lprint command uses the driver of the current printer, and thus may include escape and other controlling codes that your printer would normally need. If you want to avoid generating escape codes, use the Lprintraw command because it bypasses the printer driver.

Lprint and Lprintraw are used primarily for sending text directly to the printer.

Format: Lprint e
                e = expression or literal in quotation marks

Example: `Lprint "Last Name: " | [last]`

Note that in SmartWare II, you use the vertical bar (|) to concatenate separate expressions on the Lprint command line; in previous versions, you used a semicolon. To suppress the line feed, use the term No-Linefeed after the Lprint command; you cannot use the semicolon at the end of the line for this purpose:

`Lprint No-Linefeed "Last Name: " | [last]`

At the completion of the project file in which you use the Lprint command, a form feed may be issued automatically, depending on the characteristics of your printer definition. The Lprintraw will not force a form feed.

If you want to print a number, you should convert it to a text expression with either the STR or FIXED functions. If you try to print it as a numeric expression, it is interpreted as an ASCII representation of a single letter, and the letter itself will print.

The Open-Printer and Close-Printer Commands

To be able to use either the Lprint or Lprintraw commands, you first must issue the Open-Printer command. If you do not open the printer, you receive the following error message:

`Printer not open`

When you have completed using the Lprint or Lprintraw commands, issue the command Close-Printer. Both the Open-Printer and Close-Printer commands are new to SmartWare II.

File Commands

There are six file commands that you can use to access operating system files directly. In previous versions of Smart, you were limited to pure ASCII files, those that you can edit with the Tools Text-Editor or type at the DOS command level. Now with SmartWare II, you can read and write both ASCII and binary files.

The Fopen Command

The Fopen command is used to open a file for reading or writing; you must issue this command before any other of the project processing file access commands can be used. After the file has been opened, it is referenced by the file number you assign to it.

Format: Fopen f AS n {OPTIONS option1 option2}
f = file name
n = number from 1 to 30

Example: Fopen "account.dat" as 1
Fopen $filename as 2
Fopen $filename as data

Note that you can use variables in the command; in the examples, a file name would previously have been assigned to the variable $filename and a number to the variable data. If a file with the given name already exists, the Fopen command does not automatically erase its contents. If you know the format of the file, such as its record, field lengths, and the number of records, you can use the Fseek command to locate the file pointer, which controls the position at which data is either read or written.

The Fopen command has two options. The first option (1-7) indicates the path, or subdirectory, in which the file is to be created (see Table 24.1). As an alternative, you can specify the path in the file specification of the Fopen command:

Fopen "\account\summary.dat" as 1

The second option (10-13) indicates the file mode, and is useful on local area networks. Either option can be specified by name or ID number.

**Table 24.1
Fopen Command Option List**

ID	Name and Meaning
0	DATAPATH. Directory identified through Tools Directory New-Directory, or the Data Path setting in the Tools Preferences menu for the appropriate module.
1	SYSPATH. Your Smart subdirectory.
2	PAGEPATH. Paging path of temporary files; see Tools Preferences Global.
3	NOPATH. Directory at the time you initiated the Smart session. Same as CURPATH, number 7.
4	HOMEPATH. Same as CURPATH in DOS.
5	DEFPATH. Same as CURPATH, unless you override the default data path in Tools Preferences Global or with the -D switch upon entry into Smart.
6	CMDPATH. Selection made by -D entry switch.
7	CURPATH. Directory at the time you initiated the Smart session.
10	RW_MODE. Read/Write. Cannot be opened by other users until you close the file.
11	RO_MODE. Read only exclusive. Cannot be opened by other users until you close the file.
12	RO_SHARE. Read only/share. Can be shared by others.
13	RW_SHARE. Read write/share. Can be shared by others.

When you open a file, the current pointer is positioned at the beginning of the file (position zero). If you want the pointer positioned at a different location, use the Fseek command, discussed later in this chapter.

The Fclose Command

Use the Fclose command to close a file before using it for another purpose.

Format: Fclose n
               n = file number

Example: Fclose 5
               Fclose data

You can use a variable for the file number.

The Fread Command

The Fread command is used to read parts of an external file into a variable. You specify the number of characters to be read with LENGTH. A new feature of SmartWare II is the capability to read binary as well as text files with the Fread command.

Format: Fread n INTO v
Fread n LENGTH l INTO v
Fread n BINARY l INTO v
n = file number
v = variable name
l = length, in bytes

Example: Fread 2 INTO $account
Fread data LENGTH 6 INTO $account
Fread 10 BINARY 2 INTO size

The first example reads data from file 2, beginning with the current position in the external file up to—but not including—the next carriage return or line feed. The result is placed into the variable $account. The second example also reads from the current position, but only 6 bytes are read into the $account variable. In both examples, the pointer is repositioned at the character following the last character read.

In the third example, two binary bytes are read from the file into the variable called size. If you read binary data, use the Unpack command to convert the data for use in your project file.

The Fwrite Command

Use the Fwrite command to write to an external file from a project file. The file pointer indicates the starting location of the write. The pointer is advanced to the next position following the end of the previous write.

Format: Fwrite n FROM v
Fwrite n LENGTH l FROM v
Fwrite n BINARY l FROM v
n = file number
v = variable name
l = length, in bytes

Example: Fwrite 2 FROM $account
Fwrite data LENGTH 6 FROM $account
Fwrite 10 BINARY 2 FROM size

In the first example, the contents of the variable $account is written to the file, followed automatically by a carriage return and line feed. The file pointer advances to the beginning of the new line.

In the second example, the contents of the $account variable, which is six characters long, is written to the file. The pointer is advanced to the first character past the length, and no carriage return or line feed is issued. You can use this format if you are writing Fixed-Format external files.

The third example writes a binary variable called size to the file for a length of 2.

The Fwrite command can be used to overwrite the contents of an existing file or to append data to the end of a file. You must know the format of the file, the lengths of records and fields, and the number of records. Use the Fseek command to position the file pointer.

The Fseek Command

You use the Fseek command with the Fread and Fwrite commands to position the pointer in an external file.

Format: Fseek n p
            n = file number
            p = position pointer

Example: Fseek 5 25
            Fseek EOF

The first example places the pointer of file number 5 at position 25. Remember to count each carriage return and line-feed combination as two characters when you calculate the pointer position. Positions are numbered relative to the beginning of the file, not relative to the current pointer position. In other words, you cannot advance the pointer ahead five positions; you must specify the exact location.

The second example moves the pointer to the end of the file.

If you know the format of the file, you can overwrite the contents of an existing file or append to the end of a file, using the Fseek command to position the pointer, and the Fwrite command to write the data.

The Fposition Command

To insert the number of the current file position into a variable, use the Fposition command.

Format: Fposition n INTO v
            n = file number
            v = variable

Example: Fposition 5 INTO 5spot

In the example, the number of the pointer in file 5 is inserted into the variable called 5spot. Remember, only the address of the pointer is inserted into the variable; to read the actual contents of the file at that location, use the Fread command. To change the pointer location, use the Fseek command.

Memory Access Commands

Two sets of commands can be used to access memory.

The Peek and Poke Commands

You can use the Peek command to examine the contents of the random access memory of your computer. You can use the Poke command to change the value at a specified RAM location.

Both of these commands are designed for the advanced user who is familiar with the memory structure of 80286 and 80386 computers. **Be aware, however, that using the Poke command incorrectly can change your data or freeze your computer.**

Experienced programmers can use the Interrupt command to execute an 80286 or 80386 software interrupt.

The Smartpeek and Smartpoke commands

Use the Smartpeek command to determine the status or value of many of the Smart System settings. You can determine screen colors, beep setting, or encryption driver usage, among other things. You can change many of the settings with the Smartpoke command, or you can use the appropriate Smart commands.

The format of the Smartpeek command is as follows:

    Smartpeek setting_name variable

In this command, the value or text of the setting name is inserted into the variable, that can then be tested or displayed. You cannot test or display the setting name directly. The following command,

    `Smartpeek $_nodos $dosaccess`

inserts a 1 into the $dosaccess variable if DOS access is denied and a 0 is inserted if it is allowed. A complete list of the setting names is included in your *Project Processing* manual.

You can use the Smartpoke command to change many of the Smart settings. The following command,

    Smartpoke $_nodos 1

assigns a 1 to the $_nodos setting, thus preventing access to DOS while in the Suspend mode.

Assignment Statements

Assignment statements are those that assign a value to a variable, database field, or spreadsheet cell. Some assignments take place without manual intervention; other assignments are made at the time of keyboard entry.

The Let Command

The Let command is used to assign a value to a variable, field, or cell. The Let command is optional, as indicated by the braces {} in the following examples:

Format: {Let} t = s
t = target variable, field or cell
s = source expression, variable, field or cell

Example: Let $newsal = [salary] * [pct]
[ssn] = $ssn
value1 = r5c10
Let [person3.wage] = $newsal
$accum = $accum + [wage]

Note that in an assignment statement, the Let command is optional, but can be used for clarity. The equal sign is mandatory. In the fourth example, both the view name and the field can be specified in the database module if the view is not current in the window. In the last example, note that the variable $accum can be used on both sides of the equation.

The Pack and Unpack Commands

To assign data to a buffer variable in binary format, use the Pack command. You must perform this step before you can use the Fwrite command to write to a binary file:

    Pack buffer-variable template source

Use the Unpack command to extract binary data from a buffer variable and store it in a regular variable for processing.

Keyboard Assignment Statements

Some assignments are made when you respond to a prompt from the keyboard. The Screen Shortinput and Screen Input commands are designed to provide a screen prompt and accept input into variables.

The Screen Shortinput Command

The Screen Shortinput command accepts input from the keyboard, assigns the input to a project variable, and displays an optional message on the command line.

Format: Screen Shortinput v m
               v = variable name
               m = message, in quotes

Example: Screen Shortinput $newsal "Enter New Salary:"
               Screen Shortinput acct "Account Number:"

Be aware that the result of the Screen Shortinput command is *always* text, even if you respond with a number. If you want the variable to be numeric, you should follow the Screen Shortinput command with an assignment statement similar to the following:

Let $newsal = val($newsal)

Be aware, however, that if the response to the prompt is text, the result of the function will be zero.

The Screen Input Command

The Screen Input command accepts input from the keyboard and assigns the result to a variable. Whereas the Screen Shortinput command always prompts on the command line with an optional prompt message, the Screen Input command can accept the input anywhere on the screen, so you must use a separate Screen Print command to generate the prompt message:

Format: Screen Input r c fg bg l v
               r = prompt row
               c = prompt column
               fg = foreground color
               bg = background color
               l = length of the input
               v = variable name

Example: Screen Input 5 10 7 0 4 $dept

Chapter 24: Project Processing

The following example uses the Screen Print command to display the prompt and the Screen Input command to accept the value:

```
screen print 5 10 7 0 "Department Code:"
screen input 5 27 9 17 4 $dept
```

Again, the result of the Screen Input command is always text, even if you respond with a number. When you use the Screen Input command, however, you can specify a mask to help validate the input. Use the following mask if the department code in the previous example must be uppercase alphabetic:

```
screen input 5 27 9 17 4 $dept mask "*4{au}"
```

In this example, the {au} option indicates that the input must be alphabetic and will be forced to uppercase; the *4 repeats the option for each of the four input characters. Here are some other mask examples, with comments embedded at the beginning of each:

Numeric, positive or negative, with decimals, variable length:

```
screen input 05 10 9 17 10 $value mask "[0-9-.]*9{[0-9.]}"
```

Numeric, positive integer, fixed length:

```
screen input 07 10 9 17 3 $value mask "*3[0-9]"
```

Numeric integer, positive or negative, variable length:

```
screen input 09 10 9 17 10 $value mask "[0-9-]*9{[0-9]}"
```

Alpha, uppercase converted, variable length:

```
screen input 11 10 9 17 8 $value mask "*8{au}"
```

Social Security Number:

```
screen input 13 10 9 17 11 $ssn mask "###-##-####"
```

North American Phone:

```
screen input 15 10 9 17 14 $phone mask "(###) ###-####"
```

Date2 format as mm/dd/yy. Years 1988 to 1991:

```
while isdate($date) = 0
  screen input 17 10  9 17 8 $date mask "[0-1][0-9]/[0-3][0-9]/[8-9][8901]"
end while
```

X, Y or Z, forced lowercase:

```
screen input 19 10 9 17 1 $code mask "[x-zX-Z]L"
```

Mask literals, such as the hyphens in a Social Security number, are inserted into the variable. The rules for masking in project processing Screen Input statements are the same as for view fields in the Database.

Input Screens

One of the Remember Tools options is called Input Screen. This Input Screen facility is another means of entering data into project variables. You can enter data directly into fields in the Database or into cells in the Spreadsheet.

In addition to entering data, you can use the Input Screen option to select from a list of alternatives by moving the highlight block from one item to another.

When you select the Input Screen option, you are prompted:

```
Define   Load   Undefine
```

As with other commands of this nature, you must define a screen before you can load it.

Selecting the Remember Tools Input-Screen Load sequence initiates the execution of a previously defined input screen. Select Undefine to delete the screen definition from the disk.

The definition screen looks very much like the definition screen used to create views in the Database. You can include text, boxes, and lines in the screen. The default order of input is top to bottom, but you can change the order by pressing F7. You can use function keys to change the colors as follows:

- F2   Text Foreground/Background
- F3   Input Item
- F4   Box/Line
- F5   Highlighted Item

You can use the Input-Screen facility to define a screen from which you select an item by moving a highlight block in a list of choices, just as you do with the command lists. While defining the screen, press F5 to define an area to display the names of items to be entered. When you load the Input-Screen, use the space bar to select an item from the menu.

Several new commands, such as Screen Menu, Screen Shortmenu, and Screen Prompt, also can be used to create point-and-shoot menus; these commands are covered in the next section.

Screen Commands

Screen commands can be used to input data into variables, as you have seen with the Screen Input and Screen Shortinput commands; the Screen Print command is used to display text on your monitor. You also can clear the screen, either entirely or in a drawn box.

Screen Clear

You can clear the whole screen with the Screen Clear command, or you can clear the screen in a box. To clear the whole screen, use the following:

Format: Screen Clear fg bg {no-border}
fg = foreground color
bg = background color

Example: Screen Clear 9 0
Screen Clear 7 0 no-border

The foreground and background colors you specify will define the appearance of the screen border. If you do not want a border, specify no-border at the end of the command.

To clear just a portion of the screen, use the Screen Clear Box command:

Format: Screen Clear Box r c r c fg bg {no-border}
r = row
c = column
fg = foreground color
bg = background color

Example: Screen Clear Box 10 5 15 70 2 9 no-border
Screen Clear Box 5 70 10 79 9 0

When clearing a box, you must specify a pair of row and column markers, denoting the upper left and the lower right corners.

If you want to draw a box, use the Screen Draw Box command:

Screen Draw Box 5 70 10 79 9 0

The foreground and background colors you specify will define the appearance of the box border.

The Screen Menu Command

The Remember Tools Input-Screen facility can create a menu for cursor selection. Another way to create such a menu is the Screen Menu command.

Format: Screen Menu r c r c fg bg hfg hbg dc ls ac exp
r = row
c = column
fg = foreground color
bg = background color
hfg = foreground color of highlight block
hbg = background color of highlight block

```
                    dc  = default choice number
                    ls  = list of choices
                    ac  = actual choice number
                    exp = title expression (optional)
```

Example:

```
public $list , $choice , $title

let $list = "Detail-Inventory Summary-Inventory Order-Status \
             Back-orders Company-Transfers Goods-Damaged \
             Work-in-Progress Productions-Delayed"

let $title = "Select Desired Report:"

screen clear box 9 3 16 77 9 0
screen menu 10 5 15 75 9 0 9 17 1 $list $choice $title
```

This project file produces the menu shown in figure 24.4.

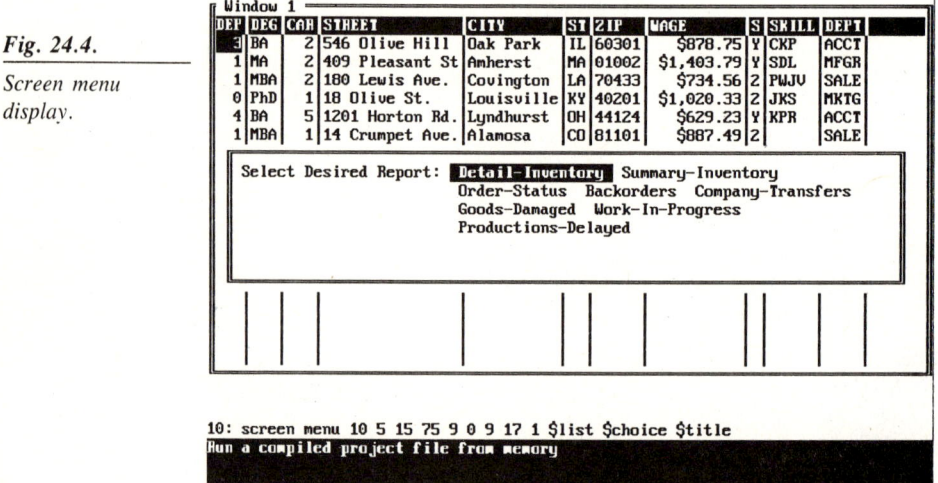

Fig. 24.4.

Screen menu display.

Notice that the title appears on the first line of the menu to the left of the initial entry. The default choice, on which the highlight block is initially positioned, is selected by the item immediately before the list of choices. If your menu items begin with unique letters of the alphabet, you can select from the list using just the initial letter of the selection. You also can use the space bar, plus sign and minus sign to move the highlight block. Press Enter to complete the selection. The number of the items selected is inserted into the actual choice number variable.

You must allow enough space in your defined area to accommodate the complete menu selection list. If you do not, you receive an error; the list cannot be scrolled. If you have too many items to be displayed conveniently, use the Screen Prompt command.

The Screen Shortmenu Command

If you want to create a menu similar to the Smart menu and don't need to specify your own row, column, or color choices, use the Screen Shortmenu command.

Format: Screen Shortmenu dc ls ac exp

dc = default choice number
ls = list of choices
ac = actual choice number
exp = title expression (optional)

Example:

```
public $list , $choice

let $list = "Detail-Inventory Summary-Inventory Order-Status \
            Back-orders Company-Transfers Goods-Damaged \
            Work-in-Progress Productions-Delayed"

let $choice = 1

screen shortmenu $choice $list $choice
```

By using the same variable for both the default and actual choice number, you can return to the same choice if the variable is not initialized again. The menu is shown in figure 24.5.

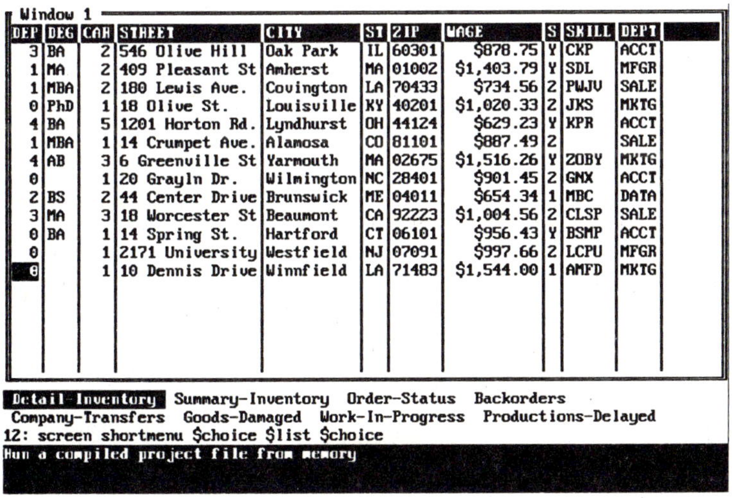

Window 1

DEP	DEG	CAR	STREET	CITY	ST	ZIP	WAGE	S	SKILL	DEPT
3	BA	2	546 Olive Hill	Oak Park	IL	60301	$878.75	Y	CKP	ACCT
1	MA	2	409 Pleasant St	Amherst	MA	01002	$1,403.79	Y	SDL	MFGR
1	MBA	2	180 Lewis Ave.	Covington	LA	70433	$734.56	Z	PWJV	SALE
0	PhD	1	18 Olive St.	Louisville	KY	40201	$1,020.33	Z	JKS	MKTG
4	BA	5	1201 Horton Rd.	Lyndhurst	OH	44124	$629.23	Y	KPR	ACCT
1	MBA	1	14 Crumpet Ave.	Alamosa	CO	81101	$887.49	Z		SALE
4	AB	3	6 Greenville St	Yarmouth	MA	02675	$1,516.26	Y	ZOBY	MKTG
0		1	20 Grayln Dr.	Wilmington	NC	28401	$901.45	Z	GNX	ACCT
2	BS	2	44 Center Drive	Brunswick	ME	04011	$654.34	1	MBC	DATA
3	MA	3	18 Worcester St	Beaumont	CA	92223	$1,004.56	Z	CLSP	SALE
0	BA	1	14 Spring St.	Hartford	CT	06101	$956.43	Y	BSMP	ACCT
0		1	2171 University	Westfield	NJ	07091	$997.66	Z	LCPU	MFGR
0		1	10 Dennis Drive	Winnfield	LA	71483	$1,544.00	1	AMFD	MKTG

Detail-Inventory Summary-Inventory Order-Status Backorders
Company-Transfers Goods-Damaged Work-In-Progress Productions-Delayed
12: screen shortmenu $choice $list $choice
Run a compiled project file from memory

Fig. 24.5.

Screen shortmenu display.

The control area has limited space. The longer the title or the names of the choices, the fewer choices you can display. If you have too many choices, you see the following error message:

```
Menu area too small
```

You may want to omit the title to increase the available menu area.

The Screen Prompt Command

To produce a pop-up window that shows a list with items which are selected by moving the cursor and pressing Enter, use the Screen Prompt command.

Format: Screen Prompt r c r c fg bg ls ac exp
r   = row
c   = column
fg = foreground color
bg = background color
ls = list of choices
ac = actual choice number
exp = title expression (optional)

Example:

```
public $list , $choice , $title

let $list = "Detail-Inventory Summary-Inventory Order-Status \
            Back-orders Company-Transfers Goods-Damaged \
            Work-in-Progress Productions-Delayed"

let $title = "Select Desired Report:"

screen prompt 17 5 20 75 9 0 $list $choice $title
```

This example produces the pop-up selection window shown in figure 24.6; you must use the cursor keys to make your selection, then press Enter.

The number of the item selected is inserted into the actual choice number variable.

With the Screen Prompt command, you can scroll down to display additional selections; you are not limited to just the selections that can be displayed, as you are with the Screen Menu or Screen Shortmenu commands. You cannot make your selection by using the initial character of the choice, however.

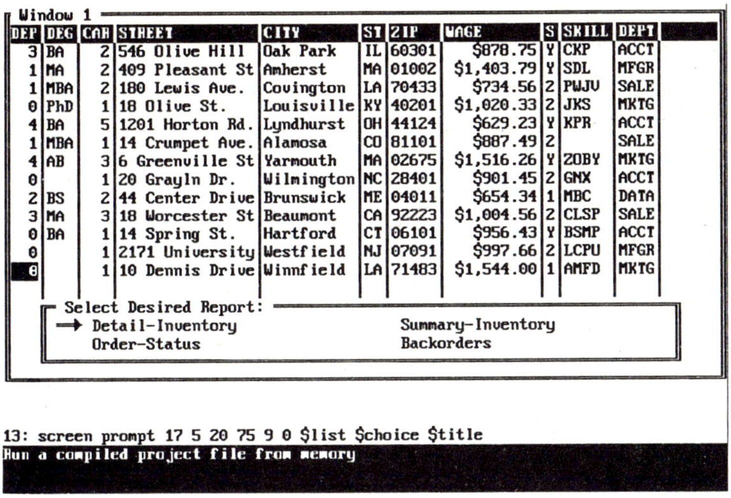

Fig. 24.6.

Screen prompt display.

The Screen Print Command

To print text on the screen, use the Screen Print command:

Format: Screen Print r c fg bg v
Screen Print r c fg bg FORMAT f v

    r   = row
    c   = column
    fg = foreground color
    bg = background color
    f   = format expression
    v   = variable or literal text to print

Example: Screen Print 5 10 9 0 "Department:"
Screen Print 10 20 7 0 $depcode

Beginning at the selected row and column, the Screen Print command prints the literal text or the contents of the variable with the colors you select. Numeric variables can be printed directly, without first being converted to text; however, if you want to concatenate a numeric variable to a literal or text variable, you must convert it to text with either the STR or FIXED functions.

A second form of the Screen Print command enables you to format the output so that you can easily center text or add decimals, commas or currency signs to numbers. In the format expression, you can specify the following:

Precision	Number of decimals
Alignment	Left (L), Right (R) or Center (M)
Width	Width of field
Options	Display of negatives, * fill
Data Types	Commas, $ sign, % sign, date format

The following example displays a number as having two decimal postions, right-justified in a field 10 characters wide, with commas to separate the thousands, and a leading dollar sign:

```
screen print 10 10 9 17 FORMAT "2r10,$" $value
```

The next example prints the heading centered on the screen; you do not have to count print positions:

```
screen print 2 2 9 0 format "m78" "Scott's Tennis Camp"
```

Additional data types and options are available; consult your manual for a complete list.

Screen Save and Restore

The Screen Save command is used to take a snapshot of a portion of your screen and hold it aside for later display. Sometimes you need to change the screen display temporarily, but you do not want to lose the appearance of your screen.

Format: Screen Save r c r c v
                     r   = row
                     c   = column
                     v   = variable to save snapshot

Example:

```
public $dept , $name , $saveit , $wage

screen clear 7 0
screen print 5 10 7 0 "Department:"
screen input 5 25 9 17 4 $dept
screen print 7 10 7 0 "Name:"
screen input 7 25 9 17 25 $name
screen save 1 1 25 80 $saveit

data browse all
suspend

screen restore 1 1 $saveit
screen print 9 10 7 0 "Wage:"
screen input 9 25 9 17 8 $wage
```

In the example, the screen showing the prompts for the department code and name are saved in the variable $saveit. Although the command Data Browse All overlays the screen display, it is restored after the completion of the Suspend by the Screen Restore statement.

You do not have to restore the screen to the same location; you can specify a different upper left row and column location if desired. However, if you want to restore to exactly the same location, use the Screen Shortrestore command in the following format:

Screen Shortrestore v
v = variable

The Screen Scroll Command

If you want to move a portion of the screen, rather than saving and restoring it, use the Screen Scroll command. You can scroll up or down by rows, and right or left by columns.

Format: Screen Scroll d r c r c fg bg n
                d   = direction: Up, Down, Right, Left
                r   = row
                c   = column
                fg = foreground color of blanked area
                bg = background color of blanked area
                n   = number of rows or columns

Example:

```
public $dept , $name , $wage
screen clear 7 0

screen print 5 10 7 0 "Department:"
screen input 5 25 9 17 4 $dept
screen print 7 10 7 0 "Name:"
screen input 7 25 9 17 25 $name
screen print 9 10 7 0 "Wage:"
screen input 9 25 9 17 8 $wage
screen scroll down 5 5 11 79 7 0 2
```

The area abandoned by the scroll resets to the foreground and background colors specified. Once the destination area is overlaid, you cannot restore it by scrolling back to the original location. Because the command scrolls in the defined boundaries, you will lose part of the display if the area is not large enough to accommodate the newly scrolled text.

Command Line Substitution

As you know, variables can substitute for names of files, definitions, responses, or print elements in project processing commands; these are your contributions to a command. Variables cannot, however, substitute for the reserved words which the Smart system needs to execute the commands. Among these reserved command elements are those you select from the command line menus.

If you want to write a project file in which actual elements of a command line are substituted, you must use the Evaluate statement to build the command line at execution time. For example, suppose that you want to have the choice of loading either a custom or standard view in the Database module. You build the following project file:

```
public $viewtype , $viewname

screen shortinput $viewtype "Type of View:"
screen shortinput $viewname "Name of View:"

file load $viewtype $viewname
```

When you try to compile this project file, you receive the following error message:

```
Bad syntax
file load $viewtypel $viewname
```

You get the error because the File Load command must be followed by the command element custom-view or standard view; variables are not allowed.

However, if you use the Evaluate command, you can construct the File Load command with the proper view type:

```
evaluate ( "file load " | $viewtype | " $viewname" )
```

The Evaluate statement is used to build a command after any reserved word variables have been assigned. In this example, your answer to the prompt for the view type and view names would be substituted in the variables; the command string would then be built and the resulting command executed. The arguments to the Evaluate command must be text (string) characters, even if they are numbers. Be sure to leave spaces so that the elements of the command line are interpreted as distinct words.

In previous versions of Smart, the parameters %0 through %9 performed command line substitution, limiting you to 10 parameters. In SmartWare II, command line substitution is limited by only the available memory.

Commands used to create or reference program memory addresses cannot be used in Evaluate statements. These commands include the following:

Label, Jump
Main, Function
Global, Public, Local, External
Lock, Unlock
While, For
End If, End Main, End Function, End While, End For, Return, Exit,
  Continue While
Case, If, Clear, Comment, Debug

Remember that Evaluate statements are processed twice because they are initially built, and then executed. Because of this extra processing, they take longer than normal to run. Use them only when you must.

Avoiding Limitations

As your project files get larger, you may run up against some system or memory limitations. There are a series of commands which can help you manage your system resources and circumvent some of the restrictions.

The Clear Command

If you have assigned values or text to variables you no longer need, use the Clear command to free this memory:

Format: Clear class list-of-variables

Examples: `Clear $amount, $depsal[]`
           `Clear public[], global`

The Clear statement sets the value of a single element or array variable to zero, but the variable name exists for later use if the name is in the class and lock declarations. You must use the square brackets [] to distinguish an array variable from a single-element variable.

You can clear several variables at once by using one of the following class arguments to the clear command:

```
Public or Public[]
External or External[]
Global or Global[]
Local or Local[]
```

You can clear all local variables in the current section of the project file by using either of the Local class arguments to the Clear command. The other three classes of arguments clear variables from the current project file according to their class.

You will find less need to use the Clear command in SmartWare II than in previous versions because you assign a variable to a class with an optional lock condition. For instance, even if you declare a public variable, unless you specifically lock it in the module or system, the variable is cleared automatically at the completion of the project file.

The Clear statement by itself does nothing; you must provide a list of variables or classes.

The Lock and Unlock Statements

As previously stated, unless you lock a variable, the declaration and contents are removed from memory at the completion of the project file. The range over which you can lock a variable is module, system, or both.

Format: Lock range list

Example:
```
Lock Module $amount , $depsal[]
Lock System $ssn
Lock Module Public , External[]
```

The following rules apply to the lock statement:

- You do not have to list variables individually; you can refer to them by class.
- If you lock a variable with the Module range, it will remain allocated while you are in the same SmartWare II module, even after the project file is completed.
- If you lock a variable with the System range, you can reference scalar variables in other modules until you Quit to the operating system.
- You cannot lock array variables with the System range.
- If a variable is locked, declaring it again in a subsequent project file does not automatically reset it to 0. Use the Clear or Let commands to reset a variable to 0.

The SmartWare II commands that declare and lock variables are consistent with the previous Smart versions:

Public variable-list
Lock System Public

If you want to unlock a variable, use the Unlock command. The format and options of this command are similar to the Lock command.

Logical Decision Commands

Several project processing commands evaluate conditions to vary the commands to execute.

The IF Statement

Use the IF statement to evaluate a condition and, depending on the result of the condition, execute one or more commands.

Format: IF (logical condition)
             (command 1)
             (command 2)
          END IF

Example:
```
public $number

screen shortinput $number "Number:"

if $number = "1"

     beep
end if

message "All Done"
```

Notice that the beep statement executes only if the condition is true ($number = "1"). This form of the IF statement is the simplest; if the condition is true, any statements encountered before the END IF statement are executed. If the condition is false, the enclosed statements are ignored. In either case, execution continues with the next statement following the END IF.

You can indent the command lines between the IF and the END IF to make the program more readable, but the indentation serves no other purpose.

Note that in SmartWare II, the form of the IF command using the term THEN no longer is valid.

In the preceding examples of the IF command, any commands between the logical expression and the key words End If are disregarded if the logical expression is false. If you have certain statements to be executed only if the condition is false, use the Else construction:

Format: IF (logical expression)
             (command 1)
             (command 2)
          ELSE
             (command 3)
          END IF

Example: public $number

screen shortinput $number "Number:"

if $number = "1"

    beep

else

    message "Value was not 1"

end if

message "All Done"

In this format, the statements between the Else and the End If are executed if the condition is false, but are ignored if the condition is true.

You can construct even more complicated conditional statements with multiple expressions and the keyword ElseIf:

Format: IF (logical expression 1)
    (command 1)
ELSEIF (logical expression 2)
    (command 2)
ELSEIF (logical expression 3)
    (command 3)
ELSE
    (command 4)
END IF

Example: public $number

screen shortinput $number "Number:"
if $number = "1"
    beep
elseif $number = "2"
    beep 2
elseif $number = "3"
    beep 3
else
    message "Value was not 1, 2 or 3"
end if

message "All Done"

Make sure an If statement is terminated with a matching End If statement; you can nest sets of If...End If statements, but be careful to match the pairs of statements correctly. You are allowed use just an End statement instead of End If. For clarity, use the full statement.

The WHILE Command

The While command is used to loop in a project file while a logical condition is true. (You can think of this command as a special form of an If test and a Jump statement.)

Format: WHILE (logical expression)
                (command 1)
                (command 2)
            END WHILE

Example:

```
public $number

while $number <> "9"
    screen shortinput $number "Number:"
    beep val($number)
end while
```

The logical expression is reevaluated each time the End While statement is encountered. If the expression is still true, the loop is executed again, beginning with the statement after the While. If the expression is false, however, execution continues with the statement following the End While. In this example, the system will beep for a number of times matching your response. If you enter 9, the system beeps nine times, then terminates the loop.

You can use two special subcommands with the While statement. The Exit While command exits the While loop immediately. (This command was named Break in previous Smart versions.) The remainder of the statements in the loop will not be executed when this statement is encountered:

```
public $number

while $number <> "9"
    screen shortinput $number "Number:"
    if val($number) < 0
        exit while
    end if
    beep val($number)
end while
```

In this example, if you enter a negative number, the While loop is terminated immediately; the system does not attempt to beep a negative number of times.

If you want the remaining commands in the loop to be ignored but the While loop to continue, use the Continue While command:

```
public $number

while $number <> "9"
    screen shortinput $number "Number:"
```

```
    if val($number) › 9
        continue while
    end if
      beep val($number)
end while
```

In this example, if you enter a number greater than 9, the system will not beep. The loop continues, and you are prompted to enter a new number. When you enter 9, the system beeps nine times and the While loop terminates.

The Case Command

The Case Command is similar to the If command, frequently simplifying your project files.

Format: Case (expression)
                When (value 1)
                     (command 1)
                When (value 2)
                     (command 2)
              Otherwise
                     (command 3)
              End Case

Example:

```
public $marital $status $name
let $marital = "Single Married Widow/Widower Divorced"

screen shortmenu 1 $marital $status "Marital Status: "

case ($status)
  when 2
    screen shortinput $name "Spouse's Name:"
  when 3
    screen shortinput $name "Name of deceased Spouse:"
  when 4
    screen shortinput $name "Ex-spouse's Name:"
  otherwise message "I'd like you to meet my sister"
end case
```

If you don't include an expression after the Case statement, you can have an expression after each When statement:

```
public $marital $status $name
let $marital = "Single Married Widow/Widower Divorced"
```

```
screen shortmenu 1 $marital $status "Marital Status: "

case
  when ( $status = 2 or $status = 3 )
    screen shortinput $name "Spouse's Name:"
  when ( $status = 4 )
    screen shortinput $name "Ex-spouse's Name:"
  otherwise
    message "I'd like you to meet my sister ..."
end case
```

If you don't have an Otherwise statement, execution continues with the statement following the End Case. To break out of a Case series of statements, use the Exit Case command.

The FOR Command

To perform a series of commands repetitively for a certain number of times, use the For command:

```
For counter = low TO high STEP step
    (command)
End For
```

For example:

```
public $accum $count

for $count = 1 to records
    let $accum = $accum + [wage]
    data goto record next
end for

message "Total wage is: " | fixed($accum,2)
```

The example steps through each record of a file and accumulates the [wage] field into a variable.

In the For command, the low end of the range, the high end, and the step can be variables. If you do not specify a step, the default is 1. If you had wanted to accumulate the wages of every other employee in the database, the For command would have been:

```
for $count = 1 to records STEP 2
```

To break out of the loop immediately, use the Exit For command. If you want to skip the execution of the remainder of the commands in the loop but continue with the next iteration, use the Continue For command.

Project File Execution Control

Certain project execution control commands will help you with debugging and documenting your project files.

The Autohelp Command

If you want to make sure the Autohelp line is off during project file execution, use the command Autohelp Off.

Use Autohelp On if you want to have it on. The default is governed by the setting in the Tools Preferences Global menu.

The Single-step Command

If you are writing a complicated project file, you may want to pause the system before the execution of each statement, so that you can examine what is happening. The Single-step command is used for this purpose. You can turn on and off single-step processing during execution by including the command in an If statement.

When single-step is on, the prompt and the command appear on the command line and status line:

```
Execute the following command? (y/n)
4: let $accum = $accum + [wage]
```

Notice that the execution line number is shown. To use the Single-step capability, do not include the Debug Off statement or compile your project file with the No-Debug option. If you don't allow Debug mode, Single-step On will not cause the current project file to pause. The On condition does carry over to later project files, however.

If you want to see the execution of the entire project file, place the Single-step On command at the beginning. If you want to inspect just one routine, set Single-step On at the beginning of the section of code you want to examine, and turn it off at the end. You may want to set Single-step On as a result of a logical expression. You can easily do so by means of an If statement:

```
If [dept] = "ACCT"
    single-step on
end if
```

Once you change the Single-step mode in one project file, the setting remains until you change it in another. If you want the default mode of execution to be Single-step, change the setting in Tools Preferences Global to *Yes*.

The Quiet Command

If you do not want the project file to pause at each statement during execution, but you want to display lines as they are executed and any error lines, use the command Quiet Off. If Quiet is off, commands are displayed on the status line as they are executed, and any error lines will be identified. Once you have all the bugs out of your program, you can use the Quiet On statement to improve both the appearance and the execution speed.

The menu in Tools Preferences Global controls the default Quiet setting. To use the Quiet Off capability successfully, do not use the Debug Off statement or compile your project file with the No-Debug option. If you inhibit the debug mode, Quiet off will not cause the statements to be displayed. The Off condition carries over to later project files.

You can turn Quiet On and Off at difficult sections throughout your project file, or you can issue the commands based on logical criteria.

The Debug Statement

Under normal (Debug) circumstances, the original source project file statements are contained in the object file as well as the source file. However, if you compile a project file with the No-Debug option, the source statements are omitted. For this reason, if you intend to use Single-step On or Quiet Off, you must compile with the Debug option.

If you would like to have some of the source statements contained in the object file, and others omitted, use the Debug Off and Debug On commands in the project file. The sections of code for which you do not want source code included in the object file should begin with the Debug Off command and end with the Debug On command. Then, when you execute a Remember Tools Compile Debug command or complete the Remember Tools Edit by pressing F10, the marked section of source code will be omitted from the object file. For example:

```
        (Difficult Section of Code)
Debug Off
        (Easy Section of Code)
Debug On
        (Difficult Section of Code)
```

If you were to begin the project file with Debug Off and end with Debug On, this would have the same effect as compiling the project file with the No-Debug option.

Comments

The Comment statement is used to make notations in the body of your project file so that you (or someone else looking at the project file) can better understand the logic. A project file with comments will execute just as fast as one without comments, but it may take a bit longer to compile:

    Comment Loading the Invoice file here
    'This is the end of the processing section

At least one space must separate the comment command from the text. You can use a single quotation mark (') in place of the Comment command. In many instances, you can insert the comment on the same line as another command if you use the single quotation mark:

    file load standard-view "person3.vws" 'personnel file

In this example, a comment is inserted on the same line as the File Load command.

Czbreak

During execution, you can press Ctrl-Z to halt a project file. When you do, you are prompted:

    Cancel or suspend execution? (c/s)

If you are still developing the application, Ctrl-Z should be enabled. However, once the application is in production, you may want to turn off the Ctrl-Z Break. With Ctrl-Z off, a user cannot inadvertently interrupt the execution of the project file.

The Czbreak Off command disables the use of Ctrl-Z; use Czbreak On to enable it again. The Czbreak condition carries forward to subordinate project files. When you return to the command level, the default Czbreak On is automatically reinstated, however.

Application Module Specific Commands

Some project processing commands pertain to only certain modules of SmartWare.

Database Commands

The following commands apply to only the Database module.

Entering and Updating Records

You can use the Data Enter and Data Update commands to initiate the entry or update of records in a view; both commands enable the processing of multiple records.

Data Enter Blank

If you want to create a new record while in a project file, use the Data Enter Blank command:

```
let $last = [last]
data goto window 1
data enter blank
let [last] = $last
```

This statement is useful when you have stored values in variables, and you want to create a new record with fields equal to these values.

Data Update Only-One

Once you initiate the Data Update mode, you can change as many records as you want. Under control of a project file, however, you may want to set a restriction so that a user can update only one record. The Data Update Only-One statement is used for this purpose:

```
Data Update Only-One
```

After the single record is updated, the project file continues with the next statement. If you want to build a new record manually, use the following sequence of commands:

```
Data Enter Blank
Data Update Only-One
```

In this example, the Data Update Only-One command enables you to update the individual blank record just entered.

The Let Command

Together with the Data Enter Blank command, you can use the Let command to build a new record entirely under project file control. The source of the data can be variables, as shown in the example for the Enter Blank command. These variables can be assigned their values manually in Screen Input commands, or calculated during the execution of your project file. The following example,

```
let [last] = $last
```

assumes that the destination view is in the current window. If the destination view is in a different window, you may be able to simplify your project file by specifying both the destination view and field in the same statement:

```
let [person3.last] = $last
```

In this example, the destination view is Person3 and the field is [last]. Using this construction may prevent having to switch back and forth between windows several times. It also enables you to use a field as the source of the data:

```
let [person3.last] = [last]
```

In this example, the source of the data is the field called [last] in the current file; the destination is in a different window.

Note that in SmartWare II, the destination view name is contained in the square brackets; in previous versions, the file name was outside of the brackets.

The Lock-Record Command

In a network environment, two users cannot update the same record of the same view simultaneously, although viewing or reading the same view records creates no problem. Before you can update a record, you must issue the Lock-Record command.

The current record is automatically unlocked when a different record becomes current. (If you are updating the record from the command level, record locking is automatic.)

Even in a single-user environment, the Lock-Record command can be beneficial if you are performing a series of field assignments. By locking the record, some processing is postponed until all the assignments have been completed, thus improving execution speed.

On a network, you can avoid the possibility of any file contention by loading the file exclusively:

```
file load standard-view "person3.vws" exclusive
```

While you have the view open exclusively, others cannot load it. In this instance, you do not have to lock the record to be able to update it.

The Cancel-Record Command

When you use the Lock-Record command, field assignments are posted to the data file together. Only when you access a different record is the set of assignments completed. While you are still addressing the original record, you can use the Cancel-Record command to cancel the previous assignments if you find that a later condition invalidates them.

The Cancel-Record command also cancels the Lock-Record condition.

Record Deletion

The regular Data Delete Record command will mark a record for deletion if it is active, or activate a deleted record; the command is a toggle. To delete a record without the possibility of activation, use the Data Delete Yes command.

To force a record active, use the command Data Delete No.

Special Data Goto Commands

In project processing in the Database module, there are several special forms of the Data Goto command.

In addition to being able to specify the number of a window, you can use the Data Goto Window Next and the Data Goto Window Previous commands.

These are the commands generated by pressing the Alt-F8 or Alt-F7 function keys at the command level.

In addition to being able to specify the number of a record to address, or the next or previous record, you can use the Data Goto Record First and the Data Goto Record Last commands.

These commands perform the same functions as the Ctrl-Home and Ctrl-End keys at the command level. However, the commands themselves are not generated by the keystrokes and cannot be recorded in a project file.

If you want to change the pointer of a file in a different window, you can use the Data Goto Record Next View "viewname.vw" and the Data Goto Record Previous View "viewname.vws" commands. For example:

```
data goto record next view "person4.vws"
```

This command causes the pointer to go to either the next or previous record of the specified file. The current window remains unchanged. Assuming that the file whose pointer you wanted to change was in the next window, the effect of the example is the same as the following commands:

```
data goto window next
data goto record next
data goto window previous
```

Make sure that you specify the view extension, either .VWS for standard view or .VW for custom view.

Line

Use the Data Goto Line command to display alternate pages of a custom screen. The effect of the command depends on the number of lines your screen can display; on a standard screen, the following command displays the second page of a custom screen:

    Data Goto Line 29

If you try to address a line beyond the last line of the screen, the system goes to the last line.

Field Calculation

In the manual enter or update mode, the performance of a field calculation can be either immediate, wait, or manual, according to the specification of the calculation. Under project file control, calculations are normally performed when the record is written to the disk. If you want to control recalculation, use the Recalc command. Any calculated fields will be recalculated when this command is encountered.

Spreadsheet

The following commands apply only to the Spreadsheet module.

Cursor Location

Several project processing commands affect the positioning of the cursor.

You can position the cursor with the AT command, followed by a row and column address. For example:

    at r5c34

You also can use the full command:

    Sheet Goto cell cell-location

In previous versions of Smart, when recording commands in the Remember Start mode, the cell address was preceded by the at sign (@); this notation is no longer valid in SmartWare II. You must use the word *at*, followed by a space and the address. This command to locate the cursor must appear on a line by itself; you cannot follow it by another command on the same line, as in previous Smart versions.

Sheet Goto Commands

The Sheet Goto commands can specify not only a cell, name, or worksheet, but also a direction:

Command	*Command Level Equivalent*
Sheet goto next-right	Sheet Goto Other right-arrow
next-down	down-arrow
next-left	left-arrow

```
           next-up                    up-arrow
           upper-edge                 Ctrl-Home
           lower-edge                 Ctrl-End
           right-edge                 Ctrl-right-arrow
           left-edge                  Ctrl-left-arrow
```

If you record your commands using Remember Start, the project processing equivalents of the command level cursor movements will be entered into the project file.

Cursor Command

Using the Cursor command, followed by a direction name, you can move the cursor one cell at a time:

```
Cursor down
Cursor up
Cursor right
Cursor left
```

If the cursor cannot be moved because it is already at a worksheet boundary, there is no error message.

Data Entry

You can use several commands to enter data into cells of your worksheet.

Cursor

At a specific cell, you can issue the Cursor command, followed by an optional data type and a prompt message:

```
Cursor {data type} prompt-message
```

For example:

```
Cursor text "Your Name:"
Cursor "Amount:"
```

If you specify a data type, the valid entries are:

Value
Text
Formula
Date1
Date2
Date3
Time12
Time24

By using the Cursor command and a prompt, the data in your project file can vary each time you run it.

Assignment

If you want to enter worksheet data that will not vary from execution to execution, use the Enter command, followed by a data type and the value to enter into each cell:

```
enter value 44.5
enter text "Eric"
enter formula "r7c4/r3c3"
enter date1 "5/20/89"
enter date2 "5/20/89"
enter date3 "5/20/89"
enter time12 ".75"
enter time24 ".75"
```

Instead of the Enter command, you can use the Let command to perform cell assignment:

```
Let r7c4 = "Indiana"
let r3c3 = count
```

Because the specific cell is identified in the Let command, you do not need to reposition the cursor before each command.

You also can use the Ssput function to make an entry into a worksheet cell:

Format: ssput(e,w,r,c)
        e = entry item
        w = optional spreadsheet name
        r = row number
        c = column number

Example: ssput("Maria",1,2)
           ssput(3.0,"Spridle",5,6)

Locked Cells

You can use the following special commands to affect the lock status of portions of the worksheet:

Command	Function
Sslock Cell	Locks current cell
Ssunlock Cell	Unlocks current cell
Ssunlock Blanks	Unlock all blanks

You also can use the Sheet Lock commands in a project file.

Word Processor

Several project processing commands are designed to be used with only Word Processor applications.

Commands that Mark Text

At the command level, commands in which you can mark text, such as Edit Copy and Edit Move, display the following menu:

Type: BLOCK
F2 New anchor   F4 Column   F6 Sentence   F8 Document
R Remainder   B Buffer []   F3 Restart   F5 Word   F7 Paragraph
F9 Line   F10 Finished

You can execute text marking commands in project files by including key words to display the prompts and direct the operation of the commands:

```
edit copy block to point
edit copy block to []
edit copy [] to point
edit move block to point
edit delete block
document find "Model" options "m" block
edit replace "Model" with "Style" options "m" block
file export block "outfile"
layout font change block 3
document references index add block "23-B"
document references toc add block 1
document dictionary spellcheck screen block
layout hidden-text add block
layout ruler reformat block
document dictionary hyphenate lines
layout keep insert lines
edit sort text ascending column
```

Note that most of the text-marking commands allow specification of a block, but others will work on only whole lines or only columns. The key word Point is used to indicate the current cursor position. The insertion into or retrieval from the buffer is indicated by the square brackets [].

You can achieve a greater degree of automation if you specify the exact document range, rather than just Block. The options are as follows:

Word   Sentence   Line   Paragraph   Remainder   Document

For example:

```
edit copy sentence to point
edit copy line to []
edit move paragraph to point
edit delete remainder
document find "Model" options "m" document
edit replace "Model" with "Style" options "m" sentence
file export line "outfile"
layout font change paragraph 3
document references index add remainder "23-B"
document references toc add sentence 1
document dictionary spellcheck screen line
layout hidden-text add paragraph
layout ruler reformat document
```

When you specify the exact range, the range selection menu is omitted; you cannot deviate from the selection of the marked text.

If you know the exact locations of text in the document, you can use the section, page, line and column numbers to indicate specific addresses:

```
edit copy "block:p1.15.5:p1.17.55" to point
edit move "block:p1.5.5:p1.10.5" to *
edit delete "block:p1.10.5:p1.10.15"
document dictionary hyphenate "lines:p1.15.5"
```

Note that the asterisk (*) can also be used to indicate the current position of the cursor.

Editing Rulers

You can edit ruler lines under project file control by specifying a string of changes as arguments to the following Layout Ruler commands:

```
Edit Current
Edit Default
Edit Named
Reformat
```

For example:

```
layout ruler edit current "l1 r6 i.5 ninc.5"
layout ruler reformat block "clear(*) dinc.5"
```

The specifications you can include in the string are as follows:

L#:	Left margin, in inches
R#:	Right margin, in inches
I#:	Indent, in inches

NTAB#:   Individual, normal tab stops, in inches
DTAB#:   Individual, decimal tab stops, in inches
CPI#:   Characters per inch
NINC#:   Increment normal tab stops every $ns inches
DINC#:   Increment decimal tabs every $ns inches
CLEAR(#):   Clear specific tabs
CLEAR(*):   Clear all tabs
NAME(string): Name the ruler format (max. 8 characters)

There are no specific options to change the spacing or the justification; you can use the Keys command to make these changes.

Toggle Commands

Those commands that toggle from on to off and back again can be forced to one condition or the other by the addition of On or Off to the command:

    document visible paragraphs off
    document visible rulers main on document visible tabs off
    file file-type text

Other toggle commands are used to alter the display of hidden text, index markers, table of contents markers, new pages, embedded rulers, and window borders.

Communications

The following commands are used in project files in the Communications module.

The Data Match Command

Use the Data Match command to pause processing until the specified characters are received from the remote station:

    Data Match "User Name:"

The matched characters are not stored, as with the Data Get command.

The Data Get Command

If you want to store received screen data, either a character or a line, use the Data Get command:

    Data Get Line Variable $inline
    Data Get Character Variable #getchar

In the first example, the contents of the next line received will be entered into the designated variable.

The Data Output Command

To send characters to the serial port, use the Data Output command as follows:

    Data Output "password"

The Data Match and Data Output commands can be paired to create a fixed conversation, such as a log in session. Note that a carriage return and line feed are not automatically sent at the conclusion of the Data Output command as in previous versions of Smart. To issue a return and line feed, you can use either of the following structures to append the appropriate ASCII characters to the output text:

    Data Output "password" | chr(13) | chr(10)

    Data Output "password" | chr({aCr}) | chr({aLf})

The Empty Command

The Empty command can make sure that all characters have been sent. The project file pauses until the buffer is empty, Ctrl-Z is pressed, or three minutes elapse.

The Break-Key Command

To send a break key signal to the modem during transmission, use the Break-Key command. Some computer systems use this signal to interrupt processing. This signal is similar to pressing Alt-B or another key sequence defined as the break in your keyboard definition.

Project Processing Error Handling

Naturally, you want your project files to run as error free as possible. Occasionally, however, an error condition occurs. This section of the project processing chapter covers the subject of error detection, handling and correction.

The Cerror Function

The Cerror function returns the error number of the most recently executed command. If Cerror is 0, the previous command executed without error; if it is not 0, an error occurred. Refer to Appendix A in the project processing section of your manual for a complete list of error codes. An example of using the Cerror function is as follows:

    order sort now "ind1.idx" fields "[dept;laast]" ascending
    if cerror <> 0
        beep
        message "Sort Failed   ..press any key to continue ..."
        stop
    end if

If it is sufficient to determine that a command failed, test for a non-zero Cerror; if you need to know why it failed, you should check for a specific error code.

The Lerror Function

To determine the most recent non-zero error, test the Lerror function. Rather than testing the Cerror code after each command, it may be preferable to check Lerror after a series of commands that comprise one routine. If Lerror is not zero, then an error has occurred.

Lerror is initially set to zero during the current Smart session; it will retain its value from module to module. To reset it, use the Clearerror command.

The Error Command

To inhibit the display of the Smart error messages, turn them off with the Error Off command. The default condition is Error On. When the project file is completed and control is returned to the command level, Error is automatically set back On.

The Errormessage Command

If you have decided to suppress the Smart error messages, you can substitute your own with the Errormessage command:

```
clearerror
error off
file load custom-view "bowdoin.vw"
if lerror <> 0
      errormessage lerror "Load of Bowdoin failed"
      stop
end if
```

The substitution of the error message is not permanent; it exists only for the execution of the command. If the error condition returns you to the command level—as in this case—you can execute Help On-Error to display context sensitive help.

On Error

If an error occurs, you can execute a function which you have designed:

```
on-error function "special ()"
```

Once you have issued this command, all errors will call the designated function. If Error is On, the standard error message displays before the function is executed; if Error is Off, the function is executed immediately. The Cerror code will accurately reflect the error condition even after the function has executed.

Chapter Summary

The SmartWare II project processing capabilities can automate repetitive tasks and develop detailed applications. If you are using the applications yourself, you will find that project processing can save time and reduce mistakes. If others use the applications, they can do so with little knowledge of the inner workings of SmartWare II.

Project files can be self-contained or transfer control to other project files.

Part VI

Using Functions

Includes

Date, Time, and Text Functions
Business and Mathematical Functions
Module Specific and Special Functions
Tools: Commands Common to All Modules

Date, Time, and Text Functions

Throughout the SmartWare II system, you may need to use formulas and functions to perform calculations, table lookups, evaluations for branching, or string concatenations. The SmartWare II system provides several types of operators and a whole library of functions.

The SmartWare II Operators

Operators fall into different categories, reflecting the types of data they work with and the results they return.

Numeric Operators

The most common operators are numeric—the familiar operators for addition, subtraction, and so forth. The numeric operators are as follows:

Operator	Function
+	Addition
−	Subtraction
*	Multiplication
/	Division
^	Exponentiation

539

You use these operators only when you work with numbers and expect the answer to be a number. Remember the order of precedence when you use these operators:

1. Parentheses
2. Exponentiation
3. Multiplication and division
4. Addition and Subtraction
5. Left to right

You may want to use parentheses to clarify the meaning of a formula, even when the standard order of precedence does not make the parentheses necessary. Extra parentheses, inserted for readability, do not affect the calculation.

Text Operators

The text operators, which are used to concatenate text items, are as follows:

Operator	Function
&	Concatenate with a space separator
|	Concatenate without a space

An example of the use of these operators is:

$city|","&$state&$zip

This formula concatenates the contents of the variables $city, $state, and $zip. The comma, entered as a text literal enclosed in double quotation marks, is concatenated with the contents of $city. No space separates the two items. The contents of the other variables are concatenated with spaces.

Relational Operators

Both numeric and text operators return a value or a result that can be either printed or inserted in a cell or field. Relational operators, on the other hand, are used to evaluate expressions; these operators return a value of true or false. The true or false is used to make a decision in a database query or a spreadsheet formula, for instance. The relational operators are as follows:

Operator	Function
=	Equal to
>	Greater than
<	Less than
>=	Greater than or equal to
<=	Less than or equal to
<>	Unequal

In the Database, for example, if you want to query for records of individuals earning more than $750.00, the statement is as follows:

[wage] > 750

These relational operators can be used for text as well as for numeric data. (If you are comparing values in alphanumeric text fields, you do not have to specify trailing blanks.) Three additional operators can be used with data that contains only text:

Operator	Function
!	Contains
!!	Does not contain
==	Compare, ignoring case

A reverse operator (NOT) can be used when it is easier to state the negative, rather than the positive:

NOT ([state] = "MO")

In this query example, it is certainly much easier to exclude the one state than to list all the remaining 49 states.

Logical Operators

Logical operators are used to specify multiple logical conditions at the same time. The operators are as follows:

Operator	Function
AND	Both expressions must be true
OR	One expression must be true

For example:

[state] = "MA" and [wage] > 750

Be careful when you use AND and OR; we sometimes say AND when, in computer terms, we really mean OR. For example, to find all residents of Texas and Maine, you might be tempted to write:

[state] = "TX" AND [state] = "ME"

This query would retrieve no records, because one individual cannot reside in both states simultaneously. The correct form is:

[state] = "TX" OR [state] = "ME"

Sometimes you do want to use the AND operator on a single field. Consider the following example:

[zip] >= 63000 AND [zip] <= 63999

Both conditions must be met for the record to be selected; only those ZIP codes greater than or equal to 63000 and less than or equal to 63999 are selected. If you used OR, all records would be selected because all ZIP codes would meet at least one condition.

Functions

Functions can be used in any expression in the SmartWare II System. They can save you time by enabling you to do, in one step, what would otherwise take several steps. In fact, functions can provide capabilities that otherwise might not be possible at all. Most functions operate throughout the SmartWare II system, but some are limited to a particular module. In examples using the Spreadsheet module, the format of the formula cell may determine whether the results of these functions are displayed as number, or as dates and time.

The remainder of this chapter is devoted to an explanation of the date, time, and text functions and their uses. Examples are provided where appropriate.

Date Functions

SmartWare II System date functions are used to manipulate dates and times. Dates are actually stored as the number of days since December 31, 1899. Time values are stored as a fraction of a day. The use of date functions can save you many hours of work.

Name:	ADATE
Description:	Alpha date
Module(s):	All
Format:	adate(d1) d1 = original date
Explanation:	Converts a date expression or number to an alpha date.
Example:	adate(r14c2) adate("8/20/71") adate(26164)
Original:	08-20-71
Result:	August 20, 1971

Chapter 25: Date, Time, and Text Functions

Name: **ADDDAYS**

Description: Add days

Module(s): All

Format: adddays(d1,n1)
d1 = original date
n1 = number of days to add or subtract

Explanation: Returns a date (or a sequential number representing a date) as the original date plus or minus the number of days added or subtracted.

Example: adddays(r14c2,90)

Original: 08-20-71

Result: 11-18-71

Name: **ADDMONTHS**

Description: Add months

Module(s): All

Format: addmonths(d1,n1)
d1 = original date
n1 = number of months to add or subtract

Explanation: Returns a date (or a sequential number representing a date) as the original date plus or minus the number of months added or subtracted.

Example: addmonths(r14c2,23)

Original: 08-20-71

Result: 07-20-73

Name: **ADDYEARS**

Description: Add years

Module(s): All

Format: addyears(d1,n1)
d1 = original date
n1 = number of years to add or subtract

Explanation: Returns a date (or a sequential number representing a date) as the original date plus or minus the number of years added or subtracted.

Example:	addyears(r14c2,16)
Original:	08-20-71
Result:	08-20-87

Name:	**DATE1**
Description:	Date 1 format
Module(s):	All
Format:	date1(d1) d1 = date in text format
Explanation:	Converts a date to date 1 format.
Example:	date1(r14c2)
Original:	08-20-71
Result:	20-Aug-71
Notes:	The format of date1 is determined in the Tools Preferences Global menu.

Name:	**DATE2**
Description:	Date 2 format
Module(s):	All
Format:	date2(d1) d1 = date in text format
Explanation:	Converts a date to date 2 format
Example:	date2(r14c2)
Original:	20-Aug-71
Result:	08-20-71
Notes:	The format of date2 is determined in the Tools Preferences Global menu.

Name:	**DATE3**
Description:	Date 3 format
Module(s):	All
Format:	date3(d1) d1 = date in text format

Explanation: Converts a date to date 3 format

Example: date3(r14c2)

Original: 20-Aug-71

Result: Aug 71

Notes: The format of date3 is determined in the Tools Preferences Global menu.

Name:	DAY (or @DAY)
Description:	Day of the month
Module(s):	All
Format:	day(d1) d1 = original date
Explanation:	Returns a value representing the day of the month of the given date.
Example:	day(r14c2)
Original:	20-Aug-71
Result:	20
Notes:	The value returned is numeric

Name:	DAYNAME
Description:	Name of the day of the week
Module(s):	All
Format:	dayname(d1) d1 = original date
Explanation:	Returns a text string with the name of the day of the week of the given date.
Example:	dayname(r14c2)
Original:	20-Aug-71
Result:	Friday
Notes:	The result is a text string.

Name:	DAYS
Description:	Number of days since 12/31/1899
Module(s):	All

Format:	days(d1) d1 = original date
Explanation:	Returns the number of days since 12/31/1899
Example:	days(r14c2)
Original:	25-May-69
Result:	25,347.00
Notes:	Especially useful for checking date ranges: days([empdate]) >= days("1/1/50") and days([empdate]) <= days("12/31/59"). The days2 and Datevalue functions provide a similar result: days2(n1,n2,n3) n1 = year, n2 = month, n3 = day.

Name:	MONTH
Description:	Number of the month
Module(s):	All
Format:	month(d1) d1 = original date
Explanation:	Returns the numeric number of the month
Example:	month(r14c2)
Original:	27-Jun-43
Result:	6

Name:	MONTHNAME
Description:	Name of the month
Module(s):	All
Format:	monthname(d1) d1 = original date
Explanation:	Returns the name number of the month as a text string.
Example:	monthname(r14c2)
Original:	27-Jun-43
Result:	June

Chapter 25: Date, Time, and Text Functions

Name:	TODAY
Description:	Today's date
Module(s):	All
Format:	today
Explanation:	Returns computer system date in the date2 format
Example:	today
Result:	02-10-1986
Notes:	The @today function returns a sequential number representing the number of days between today and December 31, 1899.

Name:	YEAR
Description:	Number of the year
Module(s):	All
Format:	year(d1) d1 = original date
Explanation:	Returns the number of the year as a number
Example:	year(r14c2) @year(r14c2)
Original:	05-May-40
Result:	1940 40
Notes:	The @year function returns only the last two digits of the year.

Name:	NOW
Description:	A number representing the current date and time.
Module(s):	All
Format:	NOW
Result:	32,719.41
Notes:	In this example, the current date was 07/31/1989 and the time was 09:48:39. The integer portion of the number is the same as the value returned in the @today function. The fractional portion represents the fraction of the day.

Time Functions

The time functions are used to add, subtract, and otherwise manipulate time fields and cells. Throughout the SmartWare II system, time values are stored as a fraction of a day—0.50 represents 12:00 Noon. You have the option of displaying the value in either the 12-hour or 24-hour format. The default format is established in the Tools Preferences Global menu.

Name:	ADDHOURS
Description:	Add hours
Module(s):	All
Format:	addhours(t1,n1) t1 = a date or a time expression n1 = number of hours (integer)
Explanation:	Adds the number of hours (n1) to the date or time represented by t1. If t1 is a date, the result is a date or a sequential number representing a date; if t1 is time, the result is time or a fraction representing time.
Example:	addhours(r14c2,36) addhours(r14c5,.255)
Original:	11-22-63 10:04:48A
Result:	11-23-63 10:20:06A
Notes:	You can add either integer hours or fractions of hours. Time values wrap around in either the 12- or 24-hour clock display mode.

Name:	ADDMINUTES
Description:	Add minutes
Module(s):	All
Format:	addminutes(t1,n1) t1 = a date or a time expression n1 = number of minutes
Explanation:	Adds the number of minutes (n1) to the date or time represented by t1. If t1 is a date, the result is a date or a sequential number representing a date; if t1 is time, the result is time or a fraction representing time.
Example:	addminutes(r14c2,22) addminutes(r14c5,95.25)

Original:	03:45:37P	23:57:32
Result:	04:07:37P	01:32:47
Notes:	You can add either integer minutes or fractions of minutes. Time values wrap around in either the 12- or 24-hour clock display mode.	

Name:	ADDSECONDS
Description:	Add seconds
Module(s):	All
Format:	addseconds(t1,n1) t1 = time or date expression n1 = number of seconds
Explanation:	Adds the number of seconds (n1) to the date or time represented by t1. If t1 is a date, the result is a date or a sequential number representing a date; if t1 is time, the result is time or a fraction representing time.
Example:	addseconds(r14c2,5280)
Original:	07:37:22A
Result:	09:05:22A
Notes:	Time values wrap around in either the 12- or 24-hour clock display mode.

Name:	ATIME	
Description:	Elapsed time in AM/PM format	
Module(s):	All	
Format:	atime(n1) n1 = number of minutes since the beginning of the day.	
Explanation:	The result of the expression is the time in the AM/PM format represented by the number of minutes.	
Example:	atime(r14c2)	atime(r14c4)
Original:	500	1300
Result:	08:20:00A	09:40:00P
Notes:	Function wraps to PM or to the next day.	

Name:	ATIME24
Description:	Elapsed time in 24-hour format
Module(s):	All
Format:	atime24(n1) n1 = number of minutes since the beginning of the day.
Explanation:	The result of the expression is the time in the 24-hour format represented by the number of minutes.
Example:	atime24(r14c2) atime24(r14c4)
Original:	500 1300
Result:	08:20:00 21:40:00
Notes:	The function wraps to the next day.

Name:	HOURS
Description:	Number of hours elapsed
Module(s):	All
Format:	hours(t1 {,t2}) t1 = date or time t2 = time
Explanation:	If t1 is time, the function returns the number of integer hours since the beginning of the day. If t1 is a date, the function yields the number of hours since the beginning of the century. Optional time t2 can be added to the elapsed time.
Example:	hours(r14c2) hours(r14c4) hours(r14c4,r14c6)
Original:	10:45 01-01-33 "1/1/33","14:40:00"
Result:	10 289296 289310
Notes:	Result is an integer number of hours.

Name:	MINUTES
Description:	Number of minutes elapsed
Module(s):	All
Format:	minutes(t1 {,t2}) t1 = date or time t2 = time

Chapter 25: Date, Time, and Text Functions

Explanation:	If t1 is time, the function returns the number of minutes since the beginning of the day. If t1 is a date, function yields the number of minutes since the beginning of the century. Optional time t2 can be added to the elapsed time.
Example:	minutes(r14c2) minutes(r14c4) minutes(r14c4,r14c6)
Original:	10:45:33 01-Jan-09 1/1/09,14:40:17
Result:	645 4734720 4735600
Notes:	Result is an integer value.

Name:	SECONDS
Description:	Number of seconds elapsed
Module(s):	All
Format:	seconds(t1 {,t2}) t1 = date or time t2 = time
Explanation:	If t1 is time, function returns the number of seconds since the beginning of the day. If t1 is a date, function yields the number of seconds since the beginning of the century. Optional time t2 can be added to the elapsed time.
Example:	seconds(r14c2) seconds(r14c4) seconds(r14c4,r14c6)
Original:	10:45:33 01-Feb-01 14:40:17
Result:	38733 34300800 34353617

Name:	TIME and TIME24
Description:	System time
Module(s):	All
Format:	time time24
Explanation:	The Time function returns the current system time in the configuration you have selected in the Tools Preferences Global menu. The Time24 function will always return the system time in the 24-hour format.
Example:	time time24
Result:	05:30:58P 17:30:58

Name:	HOUR
Description:	Hour of the day
Module(s):	All
Format:	Hour(n1) n1 = fraction of a day, in the range 0 to 1.
Explanation:	The function yields the hour portion of a time decimal number as an integer number from 0 to 23.
Example:	Hour([login])
Original:	.15
Result:	3
Notes:	The formula is evaluated as: int(n1 * 24)

Name:	MINUTE
Description:	Minute in the hour
Module(s):	All
Format:	Minute(n1) n1 = fraction of a day, in the range 0 to 1.
Explanation:	The function yields the minute portion of a time decimal number as an integer number from 0 to 59.
Example:	Minute($fraction)
Original:	.35
Result:	24

Name:	SECOND
Description:	Second in the minute
Module(s):	All
Format:	Second(n1) n1 = fraction of a day, in the range 0 to 1.
Explanation:	The function yields the second portion of a time dec number as an integer number from 0 to 59.
Example:	Second($fraction)
Original:	.3456
Result:	40

Chapter 25: Date, Time, and Text Functions **553**

Name:	TIMEVALUE
Description:	Time decimal
Module(s):	All
Format:	Timevalue(t1) t1 = time in either 12- or 24-hour format
Explanation:	The function yields the time decimal represented by time string.
Example:	Timevalue("03:24:39A")
Result:	0.142118055556

Name:	@TIME
Description:	Time decimal
Module(s):	All
Format:	@time(h,m,s) h = hours m = minutes s = seconds
Explanation:	The function yields the time decimal represented by the hour, minutes and seconds.
Example:	@time(3,24,39)
Result:	0.142118055556

Text Functions

The functions in this sections are used to manipulate text.

Name:	ASC		
Description:	ASCII value		
Module(s):	All		
Format:	asc(t1) t1 = text field or cell		
Explanation:	Returns the decimal ASCII value of the first character of the text t1.		
Example:	asc(r14c2)	asc(r14c3)	asc(r14c6)
Original:	A	a	ABC
Result:	65	97	65

Name:	CHR
Description:	Character
Module(s):	All
Format:	chr(n1) n1 = decimal ASCII representation of a character
Explanation:	Returns a text character corresponding to the numerical argument n1.
Example:	chr(r14c2) chr(r14c4)
Original:	65.00 353.00
Result:	A a
Notes:	Original value is interpreted as mod 256; thus chr(353) returns 97. In some cases, SmartWare II will print a representation of ASCII characters different from that which appears on your screen or is printed in ASCII tables. Refer to Appendix B of the *Installation and Hardware Guide* for a complete display of the Smart special character set.

Name:	CURRENCY
Description:	Currency conversion
Module(s):	All
Format:	currency(n1) n1 = numeric expression
Explanation:	Function returns text expression in currency format.
Example:	currency(r14c2)
Original:	19.95
Result:	$19.95

Name:	FIXED
Description:	Number-to-text conversion
Module(s):	All
Format:	fixed(n1,n2) n1 = original number n2 = number of decimal places
Explanation:	Converts a number to a text string. The number of decimal places is determined by the second argument, n2.

Chapter 25: Date, Time, and Text Functions **555**

Example:	fixed(r14c2,2)	fixed(r14c2,0)	fixed(r14c2.3)
Original:	19.956		
Result:	19.96	20	19.956
Notes:	Result is rounded to the specified number of decimal places.		

Name:	VAL
Description:	Value from text
Module(s):	All
Format:	val(t1) t1 = text string containing digits
Explanation:	Converts a text string to a value. Conversion is from left to right, and is halted at the first non-numeric character. If the argument is not a string, the result is always zero.

Example:	val(r14c2)	val(r14c4)	val(r14c6)	val(r14c8)
Original:	19.95	25%	23 Skidoo	−55
Result:	19.95	25.00	23.00	−55.00
Notes:	The % character is not considered part of the numeric set, and halts the conversion. The minus sign is interpreted as part of the number.			

Name:	VALUE
Description:	Value from text
Module(s):	All
Format:	value(t1) t1 = text string containing digits or numeric value
Explanation:	Converts a text string or value to a value. If the argument is a string, conversion is from left to right, and is halted at the non-numeric character, similar to the Val function. If the argument is a value, the result is the value of the argument.

Example:	value("19.95%")	value(19.95)
Result:	19.95	19.95
Notes:	The primary difference between VAL and VALUE is that if the argument is numeric, VALUE will return the argument unchanged; VAL will always yield zero if the argument is not a string.	

Name:	STR
Description:	Numeric-to-string conversion
Module(s):	All
Format:	str(n1 {,n2}) n1 = numeric expression n2 = optional number of significant digits
Explanation:	Converts a number to text. If n2 is omitted, the entire number is converted, regardless of the numeric display. If n2 is entered, it specifies the number of significant digits. Rounding may take place.
Example:	str(r14c2,2) str(r14c2) (str(r14c2,6)
Original:	5280.345
Result:	5300 5280.345 5280.35
Notes:	Compare to the Fixed function, in which you specify the number of decimal places. STR can be used to specify the number of significant digits. Rounding takes place.

Name:	LEFT
Description:	Left portion of string
Module(s):	All
Format:	left(t1,n1) t1 = text string n1 = number of characters to extract
Explanation:	Extracts the leftmost portion of a string of text. The argument n1 specifies the number of characters to be extracted.
Example:	left(r14c2,4)
Original:	Dogs and Cats
Result:	Dogs

Name:	RIGHT
Description:	Right portion of a string
Module(s):	All
Format:	right(t1,n1) t1 = text string n1 = number of characters to extract

Chapter 25: Date, Time, and Text Functions

Explanation:	Extracts the right portion of a string of text. The argument n1 specifies the number of characters to be extracted.
Example:	right(r14c2,4)
Original:	Dogs and Cats
Result:	Cats
Name:	MID and @MID
Description:	Right portion of a string
Module(s):	All
Format:	mid(t1, n1 {,n2}) t1 = text string n1 = starting position n2 = optional length of returned string
Explanation:	Extracts the middle portion of a string of text. N1 specifies the beginning position within the string. The optional second numeric argument n2 specifies the length of the returned string. If n2 is omitted, the entire portion of the string to the right of n1 is returned.
Example:	mid(r14c2,6,3) mid(r14c2,6)
Original:	Dogs and Cats
Result:	and and Cats
Notes:	If argument n2 is omitted, Mid functions like Right, except that you specify the starting position instead of the length of the string. The @MID function is similar to MID, except that you cannot omit the length (n2); in @MID, the first character is zero rather than one.
Name:	LEN
Description:	Length of string
Module(s):	All
Format:	len(t1) t1 = text expression
Explanation:	Returns the length of the text as an integer number.
Example:	len(r14c2) len("2345")
Original:	Dogs and Cats
Result:	13.00 4.00

Name:	MATCH
Description:	Matches a string
Module(s):	All
Format:	match(t1,t2{,n1}) t1 = text string to search in t2 = text string to search for n1 = optional starting position in t1
Explanation:	Function returns a number, which is the starting location of t2 in t1; n1 indicates the point in t1 at which the search begins. If n1 is omitted, n1 defaults to 1. If the string t2 is not found, the function returns a zero.
Example:	match(r14c2,".")
Original:	Debbie A. Linden
Result:	9

Name:	FIND
Description:	Matches a string
Module(s):	All
Format:	find(t1,t2{,n1}) t1 = text string to search for t2 = text string to search in n1 = starting position in t1
Explanation:	Function returns a number, which is the starting location of t1 in t2; n1 indicates the point in t2 at which the search begins. If the string t1 is not found, the function returns a zero.
Example:	find(".",r14c2,0)
Original:	Debbie A. Linden
Result:	8
Notes:	The Find function is similar to the Match function, except that in Find, the starting position is zero and the order of the arguments is reversed.

Name:	REPLACE
Description:	Replace a portion of a string
Module(s):	All

Chapter 25: Date, Time, and Text Functions

Format:	Replace(t1,n1,n2,t2) t1 = existing string n1 = starting position in existing string n2 = number of characters to delete t2 = string to insert
Explanation:	Deletes a specified portion of the existing string and then inserts the new string. Strings need not be of identical length, since you specify the number of characters to delete.
Example:	replace("make no law",8,3,"ordinance")
Result:	"make no ordinance"
Notes:	The first position in the existing string is zero.

Name:	**TRIM**
Description:	Trims leading and trailing spaces
Module(s):	All
Format:	trim(t1) t1 = text string
Explanation:	Removes all leading and trailing spaces from a text string. Returns a text string.
Example:	trim("St. Louis")|","&trim("Missouri")&"63132"
Result:	St. Louis, Missouri 63132
Notes:	This function is useful when concatenating strings.

Name:	**LOWER**
Description:	Lowercase conversion
Module(s):	All
Format:	lower(t1) t1 = text string
Explanation:	Converts text to lowercase. Returns text.
Example:	lower(r14c2)
Original:	WATKINS
Result:	watkins
Notes:	Only alphabetic characters are affected. Numbers in the text string are unchanged.

Name:	UPPER
Description:	Uppercase conversion
Module(s):	All
Format:	upper(t1) t1 = text string
Explanation:	Function converts text to uppercase. Returns text.
Example:	upper(r14c2)
Original:	watkins
Result:	WATKINS
Notes:	Only alphabetic characters are affected. Numbers in the text string are unchanged.

Name:	PROPER
Description:	Proper Name conversion
Module(s):	All
Format:	proper(t1) t1 = text string
Explanation:	Converts the text string so that the first letter of each word is uppercase and the rest are lowercase.
Example:	proper(r14c2)
Original:	horton a. watkins
Result:	Horton A. Watkins
Notes:	Be careful: If a Roman numeral follows the name, III becomes Iii. The name "McNutt" will become "Mcnutt."

Name:	CELLTEXT
Description:	Cell-contents display format
Module(s):	Spreadsheet
Format:	celltext(t1) t1 = text expression representing cell address
Explanation:	Function returns a text expression that is an exact representation of what is displayed in the cell, including blanks and format characters. Individual cells or horizontal blocks of cells can be addressed.

Example:	celltext("r15c2") celltext("r15c5:7")
Original:	$2.33 01/01/86 34.56% 10:16pm
Result:	$2.33 01/01/86 34.56% 10:16pm
Notes:	Celltext can be used with Length to calculate the width of a column.
Example:	len(celltext("r15c2"))
Result:	10.00

Name:	MAKECELL
Description:	String cell-reference
Module(s):	Spreadsheet
Format:	makecell(n1,n2) n1 = row number expression n2 = column number expression
Explanation:	Creates a cell-reference text string in the form r1c2.
Example:	makecell(r14c5,r14c6)
Original:	5.00 18.00
Result:	r5c18

Name:	MAKEBLOCK
Description:	Block reference string
Module(s):	Spreadsheet
Format:	makeblock(n1,n2,n3,n4) n1 = starting row number n2 = ending row number n3 = starting column number n4 = ending column
Explanation:	Creates a block-reference text string in the form r1:2c5:18.
Example:	makeblock(r14c2,r14c3,r14c4,r14c5)
Original:	1.00 2.00 5.00 18.00
Result:	r1:2c5:18

Name:	REPEAT
Description:	Repeats a text string
Module(s):	All
Format:	repeat(t1,n1) t1 = text string n1 = number of occurrences
Explanation:	Repeats a text string a number of times, as determined by the value of n1.
Example:	repeat("=*",5)
Result:	=*=*=*=*=*

Name:	CURRFILES
Description:	Names of currently loaded files
Module(s):	All
Format:	Currfiles(n1) n1 = filespec argument 0 = file names only 1 = file names and extensions 2 = file names, extensions, and path
Explanation:	The result of this text function will be the names of the files currently loaded, whether they are spreadsheet worksheets, word processor documents, or database views.
Example:	currfiles(1)
Result:	domestic.ws intrnatl.ws canada.ws (none).ws

Name:	GETFNAMES
Description:	Names of files matching a file specification
Module(s):	All
Format:	Getfnames(t1,n1) t1 = file specification n1 = integer indicating degree of information 0 = file names only 1 = file names and extensions
Explanation:	The function returns a text string containing the names of the files matching the file specification; the * and ? wild cards are permissible in the file specification. The numeric argument should be zero if you want only the file names; use any other number if you want the extensions too.

Example:	getfnames("Int?.ws",1)
Result:	int2.ws int3.ws int5.ws
Name:	GROUP
Description:	Select a word from a text string based on position.
Module(s):	All
Format:	Group(t1,n1) t1 = text string n1 = word position
Explanation:	Returns a word from a text string, based on a numeric argument of the position of the word in the string. Spaces must separate the words. A null string is returned if the argument exceeds the number of words.
Example:	Group("Snoops Spooky Spridle",3)
Result:	Spridle
Name:	PATH
Description:	Displays path names
Module(s):	All
Format:	Path(n1 or t1) n1 = path type number t1 = path type name

Explanation:	The function creates a text string containing the indicated path. Argument options are:
	
	  0 Datapath
	  1 Syspath
	  2 Pagepath
	  3 Nopath
	  4 Homepath
	  5 Defpath
	  6 Cmdpath
	  7 Curpath
	
	For a complete discussion of the meanings of these path names and identifiers, refer to Chapter 24.

Example:	path(syspath)
Result:	d:\smart4\

Name:	FORMAT
Description:	Format an expression
Module(s):	All
Format:	format(e1,t1,n1) e1 = expression, either numeric or date text t1 = formatting specification n1 = optional width
Explanation:	With the Format function, you can apply any of the SmartWare formatting characteristics to a numeric or date text expression. The formatting specifications are the same as used in field declarations in the Database module. You can specify the following formatting options: *Precision* (number of decimal places) *Alignment* (L=Left, R=Right, M=Center) *Width* from 1 to 255 *Asterisk* fill —F *Zero Blank* —Z *Negative number treatment* (P=parenthesis, B=use "cr" and "db", C=use "cr") *Currency, percent, date or time representation*

Example:	*Result:*
format(32145,"d3")	January 04, 1988
format("June 20, 1965","d1")	20 June 65
format(0.54,"%")	54%
format(−99,"2rc")	99.00cr
format(−99,"2rp")	(99.00)
format(250,"2r$f",15)	*******$250.00*
format(0.8345,"t24")	20:01:41
format(0.8345,"t12")	08:01:41P

Name:	PHONEX
Description:	Generate a number representing a sound
Module(s):	All
Format:	Phonex(t1) t1 = text string

Explanation: The function returns a number representing the sound of a word or group of words. You can use the function to test for words that sound alike or in applications in which the exact spelling of a name may not be known, for example.

Example: Phonex("Slide Rule") Phonex("Sly Drool")

Result: 6430 6430

26

Business and Mathematical Functions

This chapter presents SmartWare II's business and mathematical functions. The relational operators that are usable with the date, time, and text functions discussed in Chapter 25 also can be used with these functions.

Some of these functions also can be entered with a leading @ sign to provide compatibility with Lotus 1-2-3. If the results are the same as the function without the @, the @ is not stored with the formula.

Business Functions

Following are examples of the business functions available in the SmartWare II System. When you use these functions, make sure that the interest rate and the term are expressed in the same units of time. If the term is expressed in years, the interest should be expressed as an annual rate. If the term is expressed in months, the interest rate should be the annual rate divided by 12.

Name:	FV
Description:	Future value
Module(s):	All
Format:	fv(n1,n2,n3)
	n1 = payment amount
	n2 = term
	n3 = interest rate

Explanation:	Calculates the future value of a current one-time payment at a specified interest rate over a term expressed in years.
Example:	fv(159.66,3,.5)
Result:	538.85
Notes:	This is not the same function as @FV or FVA, which follow. Compare this function to PV, which calculates present rather than future value.

Name:	FVA (or @FV)
Description:	Future value annuity
Module(s):	All
Format:	fva(n1,n2,n3) n1 = equal payment amount n2 = term years n3 = interest rate
Explanation:	Calculates the future value of a series of equal payments, given the term in years and the annual interest rate.
Example:	fva(100, 5.5, .1)
Result:	689.12
Notes:	If you use @FV, n2 equals interest and n3 equals term.

Name:	INTEREST
Description:	Interest rate
Module(s):	All
Format:	interest(n1,n2,n3) n1 = principal n2 = payment n3 = term years
Explanation:	Calculates interest rate from principal, payment, and term
Example:	interest(12462.21, 1000, 20)
Result:	0.05
Notes:	Payment is annual.

Chapter 26: Business and Mathematical Functions

Name:	IRR (or @IRR)
Description:	Internal rate of return
Module(s):	All
Format:	irr(n1, block) n1 = first approximation block = income series
Explanation:	Calculates the internal rate of return for a series of positive and negative payments. The calculation is iterated 20 times.
Example:	irr(.10, r14c2:7)
Result:	0.08
Series:	−100 50.00 25.00 10.00 15.00 20.00

Name:	NPV
Description:	Net present value
Module(s):	All
Format:	npv(n1, block) n1 = interest rate block = cash flow series block = income series
Explanation:	Calculates the net present value of a series of cash flows, assuming a constant interest rate.
Example:	npv(.07, r14c2:6)
Result:	303.28
Series:	25 50 25 70 200
Notes:	The results of the NPV function are slightly different from the @NPV formula.

Name:	PMT (or @PMT)
Description:	Payments
Module(s):	All
Format:	pmt(n1,n2,n3) n1 = principal n2 = term n3 = interest rate

Explanation:	Calculates the equal payments required to pay back the principal at the specified rate over the term.
Example:	pmt(12462.21, 20, .05)
Result:	1,000.00
Notes:	See PRINCIPAL, INTEREST, and TERM.

Name:	PRINCIPAL
Description:	Principal
Module(s):	All
Format:	principal(n1,n2,n3) n1 = payment amount n2 = term n3 = interest rate
Explanation:	Calculates the beginning principal amount needed to produce the payment over the term at the interest rate.
Example:	principal(1000,20 .05)
Result:	12,462.21
Notes:	See PMT, INTEREST, and TERM.

Name:	PV
Description:	Present value
Module(s):	All
Format:	pv(n1,n2,n3) n1 = future lump-sum payment n2 = term n3 = interest rate
Explanation:	Calculates the value today of a lump-sum payment in the future, given the term and the interest rate.
Example:	pv(538.85, 3, .5)
Result:	159.66
Notes:	Compare to FV, which calculates the future value of a lump sum payment.

Chapter 26: Business and Mathematical Functions 571

Name: PVA (or @PV)

Description: Present value annuity

Module(s): All

Format: pva(n1,n2,n3)
n1 = payment amount
n2 = term
n3 = interest rate

Explanation: Calculates today's value of a set of equal annuity payments over a specified term at a given rate.

Example: pva(1000, 20, .05)

Result: 12,462.21

Notes: Same as @PV and PRINCIPAL functions. For @PV n2 = interest and n3 = term.

Name: TERM

Description: Calculates term

Module(s): All

Format: term(n1, n2, n3)
n1 = principal
n2 = payment
n3 = interest rate

Explanation: Calculates the term, given the principal, the payment amount, and the interest rate.

Example: term(12462.21, 1000, .05)

Result: 20.00

Notes: See PRINCIPAL, PMT, and INTEREST.

Name: CTERM

Description: Number of compounding periods of an investment.

Module(s): All

Format: Cterm(n1,n2,n3)
n1 = interest rate
n2 = future value of the investment
n3 = present value

Explanation:	The function will determine the length of time for the present value to reach the future value at the specified interest rate.
Example:	cterm(.10/12 , 20000 , 2000)
Result:	277.46
Notes:	The length of time returned in the function is not necessarily months or years. In this example, because the 12 percent (.12) is divided into 12 parts, the answer represents months. If the interest had been expressed as just 12 percent, this would have indicated an annual compounding. The RATE function is a counterpart to the CTERM function.

Name:	RATE
Description:	Interest rate of an investment
Module(s):	All
Format:	Rate(n1,n2,n3) n1 = future value n2 = present value n3 = number of periods
Explanation:	The function returns the rate of return of an investment, knowing the future value you want to achieve, the present value, and the number of periods.
Example:	rate(20000,2000,277.46)
Result:	.008333
Notes:	In this example, if you want to make $2,000 into $20,000 over 277.46 periods, the rate will have to be .00833, or .833 percent. If each period represents a month, the annual rate is .833 * 12, or 10 percent. The CTERM function is a counterpart to the RATE function.

Name:	@TERM
Description:	Term of an annuity
Module(s):	All
Format:	@TERM(n1,n2,n3) n1 = payment amount n2 = interest rate n3 = future value amount

Explanation:	The function yields the number of periods for which you would have to save the payment amount at the specified interest rate to attain the future value amount.
Example:	@term(200 , .10/12 , 20000)
Result:	73.04
Notes:	Notice that the annual rate of 10% has been divided by 12, resulting in a number of months. The @TERM function assumes that you save your money at the end of the month. If you are able to save at the beginning of the month, the formula would be: @term(200 , .1/12 , 20000 / (1 + .10/12)) In this example, you would have to save for only 72.59 months.
Name:	SLN
Description:	Straight-line depreciation
Module(s):	All
Format:	sln(n1, n2, n3) n1 = original cost basis n2 = salvage value n3 = useful life of asset, in years
Explanation:	Returns the straight-line annual depreciation of an asset over its useful life.
Example:	sln(r14c2, r14c3, r14c4)
Original:	12,000 5,000 3
Result:	2,333.33
Notes:	Result is the same as (n1 − n2)/n3.
Name:	SYD
Description:	Sum of the year's digits depreciation
Module(s):	All
Format:	SYD(n1,n2,n3,n4) n1 = original cost basis n2 = salvage value n3 = useful life of asset, in years n4 = year of the life of the asset

Explanation:	Accelerated depreciation using the sum of the year's digits method over the useful life of the asset.
Example:	In this example, a $15,000 asset is depreciated over 10 years. It is expected to have a salvage value of $1,000. In the first year, the depreciation is $2,545.45.

    syd(15000,1000,10,1) = 2,545.45
    syd(15000,1000,10,2) = 2,290.91
    syd(15000,1000,10,3) = 2,036.36
    syd(15000,1000,10,4) = 1,781.82

Notes:	If you prefer to do the actual calculation, the formula for the first year is:

$$((15000 - 1000) * (10 - 1 + 1)) / (10 * (10 + 1)/2)$$

Name:	DDB
Description:	Double declining balance depreciation
Module(s):	All
Format:	ddb(n1,n2,n3,n4) n1 = original cost basis n2 = salvage value n3 = useful life of asset, in years n4 = year of the life of the asset
Explanation:	Accelerated depreciation using the double declining balance method over the useful life of the asset.
Example:	In this example, a $15,000 asset is depreciated over 10 years; it is expected to have a salvage value of $1,000. In the first year, the depreciation is $3,000.

    ddb(15000,1000,10,1) = 3,000.00
    ddb(15000,1000,10,2) = 2,400.00
    ddb(15000,1000,10,3) = 1,920.00
    ddb(15000,1000,10,4) = 1,536.00

Explanation:	If you want to do the calculation yourself, the formula is:

$$\frac{(\text{cost basis} - \text{sum of prior depreciations}) * 2}{(\text{life of the asset})}$$

Double declining balance depreciation will drop to zero once the total depreciation equals the life of the asset, less salvage value.

Numeric Functions

Numeric Functions operate on numeric values only. These functions can be used in a variety of applications.

Name:	ABS (or @ABS)
Description:	Absolute value
Module(s):	All
Format:	abs(n1) n1 = numeric value
Explanation:	Returns the absolute value of a numeric value in a field, cell, or expression.
Example:	abs(r14c2) abs(r14c4) abs(r14c2*r14c4)
Original:	−5.00 5.00
Result:	5.00 5.00 25.00

Name:	INT
Description:	Integer value
Module(s):	All
Format:	int(n1) n1 = numeric field, cell or expression
Explanation:	Returns the integer value that is less than or equal to n1.
Example:	int(r14c2) int(r14c4) @int(r14c6)
Original:	23.40 −3.50 −3.50
Result:	23.00 −4.00 −3.00
Notes:	Function @int returns a different value for negative numbers.

Name:	MOD
Description:	Modulus
Module(s):	All
Format:	mod(n1,n2) n1 = first numeric value n2 = second numeric value

Explanation:	Returns the remainder when n1 is divided by n2.
Example:	mod(r14c2, r14c3)
Original:	9.00 7.00
Result:	2.00

Name:	PI
Description:	Pi
Module(s):	All
Format:	pi
Explanation:	Function returns value of pi.
Example:	pi
Result:	3.141592654

Name:	ROUND (or @ROUND)
Description:	Rounds a Numeric Expression
Module(s):	All
Format:	round(n1,n2) n1 = numeric field, cell, or expression n2 = number of decimal places
Explanation:	Returns a numeric value rounded to the specified number of decimal places.
Example:	round(r14c2,2) round(r14c2,1)
Original:	5.245
Result:	5.250 5.200
Notes:	Remember that the decimal precision feature in the Spreadsheet displays a value as though it were rounded, although it is not really rounded. The Round function actually rounds the value.

Name:	HEX
Description:	Hexadecimal number
Module(s):	All
Format:	HEX(n1) n1 = decimal number from 0 to 4,294,967,295 (2^32).

Explanation: HEX returns the hexadecimal string representation of the decimal argument.

Example: HEX(250)

Result: FA

Name: BITAND, BITOR, BITXOR

Description: Binary functions

Module(s): All

Format: Bitand(n1,n2) Bitor(n1,n2) Bitxor(n1,n2)
n1 = integer number
n2 = integer number

Explanation: These three functions compare the two numeric arguments on a bit-by-bit basis, yielding a number whose binary makeup is derived from the following set of rules:

BITAND. The resulting bit is 1 if the corresponding bits of the argument numbers are both 1.

BITOR. The resulting bit is 1 if either of the corresponding bits of the argument numbers is 1.

BITXOR. The result is 1 if one and only one of the corresponding bits of the argument numbers is 1. The result is 0 if both bits are the same, either 1 or 0.

Example: See figure 1.

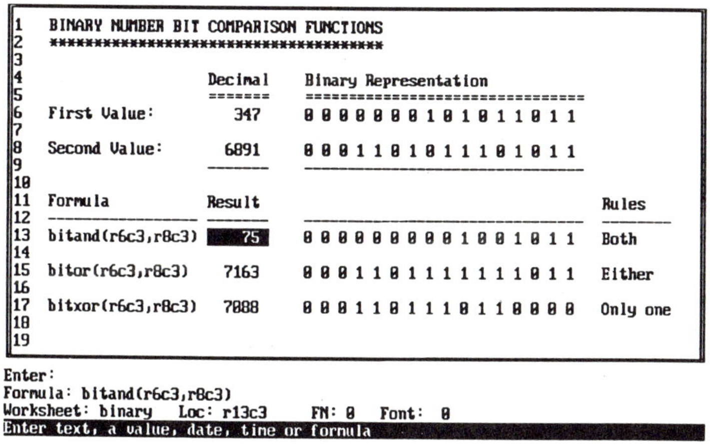

```
1  BINARY NUMBER BIT COMPARISON FUNCTIONS
2  ****************************************
3
4                    Decimal   Binary Representation
5                    =======   =================================
6  First Value:        347     0 0 0 0 0 0 1 0 1 0 1 1 0 1 1
7
8  Second Value:      6891     0 0 1 1 0 1 0 1 1 1 0 1 0 1 1
9
10
11 Formula           Result                                      Rules
12 _____  _____    _____ _____
13 bitand(r6c3,r8c3)   75      0 0 0 0 0 0 0 0 1 0 0 1 0 1 1     Both
14
15 bitor(r6c3,r8c3)   7163     0 0 0 1 1 0 1 1 1 1 1 1 1 0 1 1   Either
16
17 bitxor(r6c3,r8c3)  7088     0 0 0 1 1 0 1 1 1 0 1 1 0 0 0 0   Only one
18
19
Enter:
Formula: bitand(r6c3,r8c3)
Worksheet: binary   Loc: r13c3   FN: 0   Font: 0
Enter text, a value, date, time or formula
```

Fig. 26.1.

Binary number bit comparison functions.

Notes: In this example, the "n1" in each of the functions is the number 347 and "n2" is the number 6891. These figures are labeled as First Value and Second Value, and are displayed in r6c3 and r8c3 of the spreadsheet. The binary representation of each number is shown at the right.

The actual functions are in formulas in column 3, rows 13, 15, and 17. Note that r13c3 is highlighted, and the formula shown on the command line at the bottom. (The text of the calculation is shown to the left of the actual formula.)

Each function performs a bit-by-bit comparison between the binary representations of the integer numbers. The BITAND function compares each bit and yields a value of 1 if both corresponding bits in the argument are 1, but will result in 0 if either bit is 0. Thus, working from the right-hand, low-order bits, both the bits in the 1's and 2's positions are 1, so the resulting bits are each 1. In the 4's position, both are 0, so the result is 0. But in the 16's position, the bit for the first value is 1, but the bit for the second value is 0. Because the rule for the BITAND function requires that both bits be 1 for the result to be 1, the result must be 0.

With the BITOR function (row 15), if either bit is 1, the result will be 1. Thus, only when both bits are 0 will the result be 0, as in the 4's position of the function arguments.

When you use the BITXOR function, the exclusive OR, the resulting bit will be 1 if one and only one bit is 1. Thus, the first four bits (from the right) of the result are 0 because the corresponding bits of the arguments are identical to each other—either 1 or both 0. In the 16's position, however, the bit of the first value is 1 and the bit of the second value is 0. Thus, the 16's position of the result is 1.

Random Functions

Random functions return random values that fall within a specified range according to one of several distribution patterns. These functions are used most often in modeling and simulation applications.

Name: EXPONENTIAL

Description: Random number from an exponential curve

Module(s):   All

Format: exponential(n1)
              n1 = numeric mean of curve

Chapter 26: Business and Mathematical Functions **579**

Explanation:	Returns a number randomly selected from an exponential distribution.
Example:	exponential(5)
Result:	0.74
Notes:	The value changes every time you recalculate the worksheet.
Name:	NORMAL
Description:	Random number from a normal distribution
Module(s):	All
Format:	normal(n1) n1 = standard deviation
Explanation:	Returns a number randomly selected from a normal distribution.
Example:	normal(8.3)
Result:	−9.16
Notes:	The value changes every time you recalculate the worksheet.
Name:	RAND (or @RAND)
Description:	Random number between 0 and 1
Module(s):	All
Format:	rand
Explanation:	Returns a random number in the range 0 to 1.
Example:	rand
Result:	0.32
Notes:	Same as the UNIFORM function with an argument of 1.
Name:	UNIFORM
Description:	Random number
Module(s):	All
Format:	uniform(n1) n1 = top end of uniform range
Explanation:	Returns a number at random in the range 0 to n1.

Example:	uniform(75)
Result:	66.95
Notes:	Value changes every time you recalculate the worksheet.

Statistical Functions

The following statistical functions are available in all modules of the SmartWare II System.

Name:	AVERAGE (or @AVG)
Description:	Average
Module(s):	All
Format:	average(n1, n2, n3 ... nn) n1 = numeric
Explanation:	Returns the arithmetic mean. Empty fields or cells are not averaged; zero values are averaged.
Example:	average(r14c2:6)
Result:	15.00
Notes:	Same as SUM/COUNT.

Name:	COUNT (or @COUNT)			
Description:	Counts items in list			
Module(s):	All			
Format:	count(n1, n2, n3...nn) n1 = numeric			
Explanation:	Returns a count of items in a list. Empty fields or cells are not counted; zero values are counted.			
Example:	count(r14c2:6)			
Original:	5.00	15.00	0.00	25.00
Result:	4.00			

Name:	FACTORIAL
Description:	Factorial calculation
Module(s):	All
Format:	factorial(n1) n1 = positive number

Chapter 26: Business and Mathematical Functions

Explanation:	Calculates the product of the integer numbers between 1 and n1.	
Example:	factorial(4)	1 * 2 * 3 * 4
Result:	24.00	24.00

Name: MAX (or @MAX)
Description: Maximum value in a list
Module(s): All
Format: max(n1, n2 ... {,nn})
n1 = numeric
Explanation: Returns the maximum value in a list of values.
Example: max(r14c2:6)

Original:	1.00	5.00	3.00	7.00	8.00

Result: 8.00
Notes: Non-numeric entries are ignored.

Name: MIN (or @MIN)
Description: Minimum value in a list
Module(s): All
Format: min(n1, n2 ... {,nn})
n1 = numeric
Explanation: Returns the minimum value from a list of values.
Example: min(r14c2:6)

Original:	1.00	5.00	3.00	7.00	8.00

Result: 1.00
Notes: SmartWare II non-numeric entries are ignored.

Name: STD (or @STD)
Description: Standard deviation in a population
Module(s): All
Format: std(n1, n2 ... {,nn})
n1 = numeric
Explanation: Returns the standard deviation of the population in a list.

Example:	std(r14c2:6)
Original:	12.34 32.50 9.78 45.99 21.44
Result:	13.41
Notes:	Non-numeric values are ignored. The list must have a minimum of two entries. Returns the square root of the value returned by @VAR.

Name:	STDEV
Description:	Standard deviation of a sample
Module(s):	All
Format:	stdev(n1, n1 ... {,nn}) n1 = numeric
Explanation:	Returns the standard deviation of the sample for a list of items.
Example:	stdev(r14c2:6)
Original:	12.34 32.50 9.78 45.99 21.44
Result:	15.00
Notes:	Non-numeric values are ignored. The list must have a minimum of two entries. Returns the square root of the value returned by the VAR function.

Name:	VAR
Description:	Sample variance
Module(s):	All
Format:	var(n1,n1 ... {,nn}) n1 = numeric
Explanation:	Returns the variance of a sample for the list of items.
Example:	var(r14c2:6)
Original:	12.34 32.50 9.78 45.99 21.44
Result:	224.92
Notes:	Non-numeric values are ignored. The list must have a minimum of two entries. Use @VAR for variance of the population.

Name: SUM (or @SUM)

Description: Sum of numeric values

Module(s): All

Format: sum(n1,n1...{,nn})
n1 = numeric

Explanation: Returns the arithmetic sum of the values in a list.

Example: sum(r14c2:6)

Original: 12.34   32.50   9.78   45.99   21.44

Result: 122.04

Notes: Non-numeric values are ignored.

Name: SUMSQ

Description: Sum of squares

Module(s): All

Format: sumsq(n1,n1 ... {,nn})
n1 = numeric

Explanation: Returns the sum of the squares of items in a list.

Example: sumsq(r14c2:6)

Original: 12.34   32.50   -9.78   45.99   21.44

Result: 3,878.93

Notes: Non-numeric values are ignored.

Logical Functions

Logical functions provide varying forms of abbreviated table-lookup facilities, If..Then..Else capabilities, and True/False evaluations.

Name: CASE

Description: Case match

Module(s): All

Format: case v1 (s1,r1)(s2,r2)...(sn,rn) else v2
v1 = original value
s1 = search match 1
r1 = return value 1
v2 = default value

Explanation:	Case works like a short table-lookup function. The function matches the original value against s1, s2, etc. If a match is found, the corresponding r value is returned. If no match is found, the default v2 is returned.
Example:	case r14c2 (1,2390)(2,3540)(3,1770)(4,2390) else 999
Original:	2.00
Result:	3,540.00
Notes:	There must be an exact match between the original value and a search value. Either numeric values or text items are acceptable. Search items do not have to be in order. For range matches, use @HLOOKUP or @VLOOKUP.

Name:	SELECT
Description:	Selection
Module(s):	All
Format:	select(e1, r1)(e2,r2)...(en,rn) else v1 e1 = original value s1 = search match 1 r1 = return value 1 v1 = default value
Explanation:	Each logical expression is evaluated in turn. For the first one found to be true, the corresponding r value is returned. If no expression is true, the default value v1 is returned.
Example:	select(r14c2>2,100)(r14c3<5,20)(r14c4=10,55) else 999
Original:	2.00 4.00 10.00
Result:	20.00
Notes:	Logical expressions do not have to refer to the same set of fields or cells. Numeric and text values may be mixed. If multiple conditions are met, the function returns the result of the first true condition.

Name:	IF
Description:	If..Then..Else
Module(s):	All
Format:	if (e1) then v1 else v2 e1 = logical expression v1, v2 = result expressions

Chapter 26: Business and Mathematical Functions

Explanation: The logical expression e1 is evaluated. If it is true, v1 is returned; if it is false, v2 is returned. Expressions may be nested; the first true expression terminates the function. Values or expressions can be returned.

Example: See figure 26.2.

```
┌─ Formula Editor ──────────────
│ if r14c2 > 2  then 100 else
│ if r14c3 < 5  then 20  else
│ if r14c4 = 10 then 55  else 999
│
```

Fig. 26.2.

An If..Then..Else test.

Original:	2.00	4.00	10.00
Result:	20.00		

Notes: Then If..Then..Else expression corresponds to the example for the SELECT function. If multiple conditions are met, the function returns the result of the first true condition.

Name:	CHOOSE (OR @CHOOSE)
Description:	Ordinal match
Module(s):	All
Format:	choose (v1, i1, i2, i3...in) v1 = original value i1 = item one
Explanation:	Choose function is similar to the case function, except that the item returned is determined by the value of v1. If v1 evaluates to 2, the third item in the list is returned.
Example:	choose(r14c2, "north", "south", "east","west")
Original:	2.00
Result:	east
Notes:	If the original value is zero, blank, or text, the first item in the list is returned. There is no Else condition, as there is with the CASE function.

Name:	FALSE (or @FALSE)
Description:	False condition
Module(s):	All
Format:	false
Explanation:	Returns the false indicator (0) for use with logical expressions.
Example:	if r14c2<10 then false else true
Original:	5.00
Result:	0.00

Name:	TRUE (or @TRUE)
Description:	True condition
Module(s):	All
Format:	true
Explanation:	Returns the true indicator (1) for use with logical expressions.
Example:	if r14c2<10 then false else true
Original:	55.00
Result:	1.00

Name:	LOGICAL
Description:	Logical evaluation
Module(s):	All
Format:	logical (e1) e1 = expression containing logical operator(s) and operands
Explanation:	Returns true (1) if the expression is true, or false (0) if the expression is false
Example:	logical(r14c2>0)
Original:	5.72
Result:	1.00

Chapter 26: Business and Mathematical Functions

Name:	NOT
Description:	Test of opposite
Module(s):	All
Format:	not (e1) e1 = logical expression
Explanation:	Returns false (0) if the expression is true, or true (1) if the expression is false.
Example:	not(r14c2 = "ACCT") not(r14c2<>"ACCT")
Original:	ACCT
Result:	0.00 1.00

Name:	ISNUMBER
Description:	Tests for numeric value
Module(s):	All
Format:	isnumber (v1) v1 = value
Explanation:	Returns true (1) if the value v1 is a number, or false (0) if the value is not a number.
Example:	snumber(r14c2) isnumber(r14c4) isnumber(r14c7)
Original:	ACCT 55.00 01-01-86
Result:	0 1 1

Name:	ISSTRING
Description:	Tests for string value
Module(s):	All
Format:	isstring (v1) v1 = value
Explanation:	Returns true (1) if the value v1 is a string, or false (0) if the value is not a string.
Example:	isstring(r14c2) isstring(r14c4)
Original:	ACCT 55.00
Result:	1 0

Name:	ISDATE
Description:	Tests for a valid date
Module(s):	All
Format:	ISDATE(t1) d1 = text date field or cell
Explanation:	Returns 1 if the argument is a valid date; 0 if it not a date.
Example:	isdate("5/25/69")
Result:	1
Notes:	Make sure the argument to the function is text; a numeric argument will always yield a true result, even if it does not represent a valid number of days from 12/31/1899.

Name:	ISVAR
Description:	Verify existence of a public variable
Module(s):	All
Format:	Isvar(v1) v1 = variable name
Explanation:	Function will yield 1 if the variable exists or 0 if it does not.
Example:	Isvar("$amount")
Result:	1
Notes:	Be sure to enclose the name of the variable in quotation marks.

Name:	COLLATE	
Description:	Compares text expressions	
Module(s):	All	
Format:	collate(t1,t2) t1 = first text expression t2 = second text expression	
Explanation:	The two expressions are compared, ignoring case. If t1 < t2, result is −1; if t1 = t2, result is 0; if t1 > t2, result is 1.	
Example:	collate(r14c2, r14c3)	collate(r14c3, r14c6)
Original:	McAliffe MCALIFFE	McCarthy
Result:	0.00	−1.00
Notes:	All punctuation characters are evaluated as being equal.	

Name:	EXACT
Description:	Determine if two strings are identical
Module(s):	All
Format:	Exact(t1,t2) t1 = first text string t2 = second text string
Explanation:	The function returns 1 if the strings are identical, or 0 if they are different.
Example:	Exact("McNutt","Mcnutt")
Result:	0
Notes:	This function yields the same result as the formula:

if "McNutt" = "Mcnutt" then 1 else 0

Transcendental Functions

The following transcendental functions, used primarily in scientific and mathematical applications, are available in the SmartWare II system:

Function	Description
COSH	Hyperbolic cosine
EXP	Value of the natural logarithm e
LN	Natural logarithm base e
LOG10	Logarithm base 10
POWER	Raise to a power
SINH	Hyperbolic sine
SQRT	Square root

Trigonometric Functions

The following trigonometric functions are available in the SmartWare II system:

Function	Description
ACOS	Arccosine calculation
ASIN	Arcsine calculation
ATAN	Arctangent calculation
ATAN2	Tangent with quadrant identification by the angle
COS	Cosine
SIN	Sine
TAN	Tangent

Input Functions

The following functions are used for input in the SmartWare II system.

Name:	ASK
Description:	Asks for input
Module(s):	All
Format:	ask(t1) t1 = text for prompt
Explanation:	Causes the text to be displayed on the command line and the value of the response to be entered into the cell or field.
Example:	ask(r14c2)
Original:	Enter the number of employees:
Result:	20.00

Name:	FILE	
Description:	Tests for existence of file	
Module(s):	All	
Format:	file(f1), f1 = file name and extension	
Explanation:	Used to test for the existence of a file on disk. You must supply both the file name and the extension; a path is required if the file is not in the current subdirectory. The result is 1 if the file exists, or 0 if it does not exist.	
Example:	file(r14c2)	file(r14c4)
Original:	account.ws	canada.ws
Result:	0.00	1.00
Notes:	Can be used in project files to make them more foolproof.	

Name:	NULL
Description:	Empty or default string
Module(s):	All
Format:	Null
Explanation:	Returns a string equal to the default value, (ASCII 0).
Example:	if [account] = "110" then [amount] else null

Notes:	A null field, cell or variable contains an ASCII zero (0). Do not confuse this with a space (ASCII 32), the number zero (ASCII 48), or a blank (ASCII 0.)
	In the spreadsheet, a cell with a NULL formula does not display a value, even if you use the Layout Format command to try to force the display of a zero. A cell with a BLANK formula will display a zero value unless you specify Zero-blank in the Layout Format command. A cell with a BLANK formula is counted in the AVERAGE function, but the NULL and space are not. A space is a text field.
	In the Database, a field into which nothing has been entered is BLANK; this is true for both text and numeric fields. If you assign a NULL value to a field, it will yield a zero to the ISBLANK function, but will have the same appearance and ASCII value as a blank field. Unlike the Spreadsheet, if you specifically assign a BLANK value to a Database field, it will yield a 1 as a result of the ISBLANK function.
Name:	BLANK
Description:	Blank status
Module(s):	All
Format:	Blank
Explanation:	Refer to the NULL function.
Example:	if r15c1 = blank then 1 else 0
Result:	1
Notes:	As shown in the example Spreadsheet formula, a cell is BLANK before you enter anything into it. However, if you specifically enter a BLANK formula into the cell, the example formula will yield zero. Also, refer to the ISBLANK function.
Name:	NOCHANGE
Description:	No change
Module(s):	All
Format:	nochange
Explanation:	Used to prevent the change of a field in a Database or cell in a spreadsheet.

Example: if [quote] = null then [price]*[quant] else nochange

Notes: The example prevents the change of the original contents of the quote field, even if price or quantity change.

Module Specific and Special Functions

Some of the functions in SmartWare II are applicable to only certain modules or will operate only in a project file. These special functions are covered in this chapter.

Spreadsheet Functions

Name:	COLUMN
Description:	Column number
Module(s):	Spreadsheet
Format:	Column
Explanation:	Returns column number of spreadsheet cell.
Example:	column
Result:	2

Name:	ROW
Description:	Row number
Module(s):	Spreadsheet
Format:	row
Explanation:	Returns row number of spreadsheet cell.
Example:	row
Result:	14

Name:	ROWS
Description:	Number of rows in a block
Module(s):	Spreadsheet
Format:	rows(block specification)
Explanation:	Returns number of rows in specified worksheet block. The block may be identified by row and column numbers or by name.
Example:	rows(r87:532c3:47) or rows(data)
Result:	446

Name:	HLOOKUP (or @HLOOKUP)
Description:	Horizontal lookup
Module(s):	Spreadsheet
Format:	hlookup(s1, b1 {,o1}) s1 = item to search for b1 = block to search in o1 = offset from top row of block (optional)
Explanation:	Function searches the top row of the block for a value less than or equal to the search item. If no offset is provided, the function returns the value from the corresponding column on the last row of the block. If the offset is provided, it represents the number of rows from the top of the table.
Example:	hlookup(3, r16:19c2:6) @hlookup(6.2,r16:19c2:6, 2)
Result:	5.20 4.47
Table:	0.50 3.00 5.00 7.00 9.00 0.71 1.73 2.24 2.65 3.00 1.41 3.46 4.47 5.29 6.00 2.12 5.20 6.71 7.94 9.00
Notes:	If you expect to find an exact match, the items in the top row need not be in order. The Hlookup function cannot handle a nonmatching element whose value lies between items in the top row of the table. If you expect that the value of a search item might lie between the values in the top row, you must use @HLOOKUP and make sure that the values in the top row

Chapter 27: Module Specific and Special Functions 595

are in order. If no match is found, the column with the value less than s1 is used. In the example, the column for value 5.00 is used because the value 6.2 lies between 5 and 7.

Both Hlookup and @hlookup can operate on values or text items.

Name:	VLOOKUP (or @VLOOKUP)
Description:	Vertical lookup
Module(s):	Spreadsheet
Format:	vlookup(s1, b1 {,o1}) s1 = item to search for b1 = block to search in o1 = offset from top row of block (optional)
Explanation:	The function searches the left column of the block for a matching value that is less than or equal to s1. If no offset is provided, the value from the row containing the matching item is returned. If an offset is provided, the offset value indicates the number of columns to the right of the left column; the value in that column is returned.
Example:	vlookup(3,r16:19c2:5) @vlookup(6.2,r16:19c2:5,2)
Result:	5.20 4.47
Table:	0.50 0.71 1.41 2.12 3.00 1.73 3.46 5.20 5.00 2.24 4.47 6.71 7.00 2.65 5.29 7.94
Notes:	The Vlookup function must find an exact match, or an error occurs. With @vlookup, however, a range is permissible: the value is retrieved from the row whose value matches or is less than the search item. In the example, 5.00 is the last item in the column that is less than or equal to the search value 6.2. Both Vlookup and @vlookup work with text values as well as numeric values.
Name:	INDEX (and @INDEX)
Description:	Offset cell contents
Module(s):	Spreadsheet

Format:	index(b1, r1, c1) b1 = block r1 = offset rows c1 = offset columns
Explanation:	Returns the contents of a cell in the designated block, offset from the upper left corner by r1 rows and c1 columns.
Example:	index(r15:17c2:4, 1, 2)
Result:	8:00
Table:	1.00 4.00 7.00 2.00 5.00 8.00 3.00 6.00 9.00
Notes:	The offset values indicate the number of rows down or columns over, but do not indicate the number of the row or column in the block. A row offset of zero returns a value from the first row. The @index function will yield results similar to the Index function, but the arguments are in a different order: @index(b1, c1, r1) Note that the row offset and column offset are reversed.

Name:	N
Description:	Numeric value of upper left corner of block
Module(s):	Spreadsheet
Format:	N(block identifier)
Explanation:	Function returns the numeric value of the upper left corner of a block. The block can be identified by row and column notation or by name. The function yields zero if the cell is text.
Example:	N(r1:14c1:7) or N(data)
Notes:	Formula will be circular if contained in the block; the value will be correct, however.

Name:	S
Description:	Text of upper left corner of block
Module(s):	Spreadsheet
Format:	S(block identifier)

Chapter 27: Module Specific and Special Functions

Explanation:	Function returns the text of the upper left corner of a block. The block can be identified by row and column notation or by name. The function yields NULL if the cell is numeric.
Example:	S(r1:14c1:7) or S(data)
Notes:	Formula will be circular if contained in the block. However, the text will be correct.

Name:	ISERR
Description:	Test for error
Module(s):	Spreadsheet
Format:	iserr(r1) r1 = cell reference
Explanation:	Returns true (1) if the cell contains an error, or false (0) if it does not.
Example:	iserr(r14c2)
Original:	Error 29
Result:	1

Name:	ISCALC
Description:	Tests for spreadsheet calculation
Module(s):	Spreadsheet
Format:	iscalc
Explanation:	Returns true (1) if the worksheet needs to be recalculated, or false (0) if it does not.
Example:	iscalc
Result:	1

Name:	ISNA
Description:	Tests for N/A
Module(s):	Spreadsheet
Format:	isna(r1) r1 = cell reference
Explanation:	Returns true (1) if the cell contains N/A, or false (0) if not. A cell contains N/A if the cell refers to a block name that has been undefined or to a worksheet that has been unloaded.

Example:	isna(r14c2)
Original:	N/A
Result:	1

Name:	NA
Description:	Not available
Module(s):	Spreadsheet
Format:	if e1 then na else v1 e1 = logical expression v1 = value
Explanation:	Returns N/A if e1 is true, or v1 if not.
Example:	if r14c2 < 1000 then na else r14c2
Original:	100.00
Result:	N/A

Name:	ISBLANK
Description:	Tests for blank cell or field
Module(s):	Spreadsheet and Database
Format:	isblank(r1) r1 = cell reference or field
Explanation:	Returns true (1) if the argument is blank, or false if is not blank.
Example:	isblank(r14c2)
Result:	1
Note:	A blank cell or field is one which has never had an entry. In the Spreadsheet, you can blank a cell with the Edit Blank command, but the BLANK or NULL functions contained in a cell will not yield a true result from the ISBLANK function. In the Database, you can test for a blank field with the function isblank([fieldname]). In previous Smart versions, you needed to test: "if [fieldname] = null"

The function is similar to the equation:

if [fieldname] = blank then 1 else 0

In this example, a 1 is returned if the field is blank; you could also test a cell in the spreadsheet module.

Name:	BLANK
Description:	Blank status
Module(s):	All
Format:	blank
Explanation:	Returns a blank status. This function can often be used instead of the ISBLANK function.
Example:	let [fieldname] = blank if r6c1 = blank then 1 else 0
Result:	In the first example, the field assumes its original blank status, prior to any assignment. The second example is identical to using the Isblank function.

Name:	NULL
Description:	Null value
Module(s):	All
Format:	null
Explanation:	Returns a text value of null, an ASCII 0. This is not the same as BLANK, which does not have a value.
Example:	if r6c1 = null then 1 else 0
Result:	In this example, if the cell is null, then the result is 1. Note that there is no ISNULL function to test for Null in SmartWare II.

In project processing, a variable can be set to null by either of two commands:

let $text = null
let $text = ""

The two adjacent quotation marks are equivalent to null. In the Spreadsheet, a null value can be entered into a cell by pressing a quotation mark (to indicate text) and then an immediate Enter.

Statistical Database Functions

In some cases, you can build a small database in the Spreadsheet module and use special functions to analyze the data. The following functions can be used in a worksheet block of a spreadsheet database:

Average
  @Daverage—Ignores blanks and text, comparable to the average function.
  @Davg—Ignores blanks; text is zero.

Count
  Dcount—Ignores blanks and text, comparable to the Count function.
  @Dcount—Ignores blanks, counts text.

Minimum
  @Dmin

Maximum
  @Dmax

Standard Deviation
  @Std

Sum
  @Dsum

Sum of Squares
  @Dsumsq

Variance
  Dvar—sample variance
  @Dvar—population variance

Statistical database calculations are performed only on rows meeting specified criteria. The search criteria operate similar to a Query in the Database module.

The spreadsheet in figure 27.1 is an example. The database is in the block r1:13c1:11. Note that this block must include the column titles, because they are referenced in the criteria block.

The criteria block is in r15:17c1:11, which contains a copy of the column titles in the data base block plus two extra rows. The extra rows are used to hold the criteria for selection of rows from the data base. The statistical functions take the following form:

  function(database block, offset value, criteria block)

The offset value represents the number of columns to the right of the leftmost column of the data base block upon which the operation is to be performed. In figures 27.1 and 27.2, the offset is two columns, which is the AGE column. Thus, the function calculates an average age for the rows meeting the criteria.

```
        1          2       3    4   5    6   7    8        9    10     11
1  FIRST      LAST      AGE  SEX  MS  DEP  CAR  ST      WAGE  STATUS  DEPT
2  Rosanna    Ronaldo   52   M    M   3    2    IL      878.75   Y    ACCT
3  Debbie     Linden    29   F    S   1    2    MA    1,483.79   Y    MFGR
4  Michael    Davis     61   M    M   1    2    LA      734.56   2    SALE
5  Julius     Karenski  41   M    D   0    1    KY    1,020.33   2    MKTG
6  Jeff       Harris    34   M    M   4    5    OH      629.23   Y    ACCT
7  LeAnne     Markus    48   F    W   1    1    CO      887.49   2    SALE
8  Marilyn    Lester    55   F    M   4    3    MA    1,516.26   Y    MKTG
9  David      Marzetti  47   M    D   0    1    NC      901.45   2    ACCT
10 Paula      Bernstein 30   F    S   3    3    CA    1,004.56   2    SALE
11 Alfred     Adelson   60   M    M   0    1    CT      956.43   Y    ACCT
12 Ellen      Aliakbari 35   F    S   0    1    NJ      997.66   2    MFGR
13 Howard E.  Peters    18   M    S   0    1    LA    1,544.00   1    MKTG
14
15 FIRST      LAST      AGE  SEX  MS  DEP  CAR  ST      WAGE  STATUS  DEPT
16                           F
17                                S
18 Average:   31.33
Enter:
Formula: @daverage( r1:13c1:11, 2, r15:17c1:11 )
Worksheet: person1  Loc: r18c2   FM: 0   Font: 0
Enter text, a value, date, time or formula
```

Fig. 27.1.

An example spreadsheet database.

```
        1          2       3    4   5    6   7    8        9    10     11
1  FIRST      LAST      AGE  SEX  MS  DEP  CAR  ST      WAGE  STATUS  DEPT
2  Rosanna    Ronaldo   52   M    M   3    2    IL      878.75   Y    ACCT
3  Debbie     Linden    29   F    S   1    2    MA    1,483.79   Y    MFGR
4  Michael    Davis     61   M    M   1    2    LA      734.56   2    SALE
5  Julius     Karenski  41   M    D   0    1    KY    1,020.33   2    MKTG
6  Jeff       Harris    34   M    M   4    5    OH      629.23   Y    ACCT
7  LeAnne     Markus    48   F    W   1    1    CO      887.49   2    SALE
8  Marilyn    Lester    55   F    M   4    3    MA    1,516.26   Y    MKTG
9  David      Marzetti  47   M    D   0    1    NC      901.45   2    ACCT
10 Paula      Bernstein 30   F    S   3    3    CA    1,004.56   2    SALE
11 Alfred     Adelson   60   M    M   0    1    CT      956.43   Y    ACCT
12 Ellen      Aliakbari 35   F    S   0    1    NJ      997.66   2    MFGR
13 Howard E.  Peters    18   M    S   0    1    LA    1,544.00   1    MKTG
14
15 FIRST      LAST      AGE  SEX  MS  DEP  CAR  ST      WAGE  STATUS  DEPT
16                                S
17                           F
18 Average:   35.83
Enter:
Formula: @daverage( r1:13c1:11, 2, r15:17c1:11 )
Worksheet: person1  Loc: r18c2   FM: 0   Font: 0
Enter text, a value, date, time or formula
```

Fig. 27.2.

Criteria equivalent to a logical OR.

In this example, the criteria are specified as F for Sex and S for MS (Marital Status). The @Daverage function calculates the average age of the individuals who are both female and single. Because the criteria are on the same row, both conditions must be met simultaneously; placement of the criteria on the same row is equivalent to a logical AND. When the criteria are on separate rows, the effect is that of a logical OR, as in figure 27.2.

Rather than just specifying a literal test value, you can enter a formula in a criterion cell to form the basis for the selection. In figure 27.3, the following formula has been entered in r16c3 to select only those records in which the age is less than 35:

   r2c3 < 35

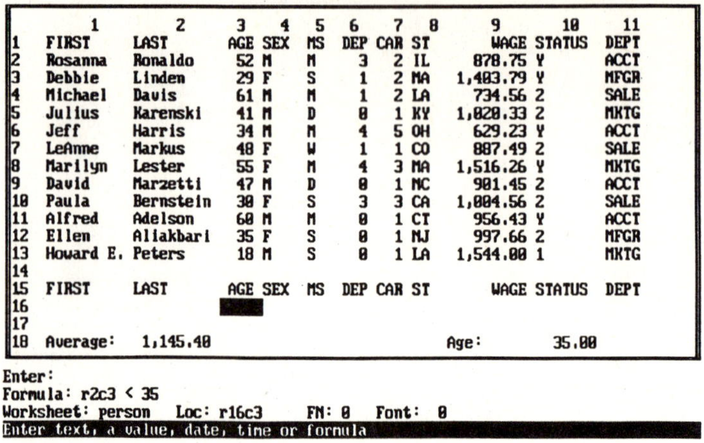

Fig. 27.3.

Selection by a formula criterion.

```
        1          2        3   4   5   6    7   8     9      10    11
 1 FIRST      LAST       AGE SEX MS  DEP CAR ST     WAGE STATUS DEPT
 2 Rosanna    Ronaldo     52 M   M   3   2   IL    878.75 Y     ACCT
 3 Debbie     Linden      29 F   S   1   2   MA  1,483.79 Y     MFGR
 4 Michael    Davis       61 M   M   1   2   LA    734.56 2     SALE
 5 Julius     Karenski    41 M   D   0   1   KY  1,020.33 2     MKTG
 6 Jeff       Harris      34 M   M   4   5   OH    629.23 Y     ACCT
 7 LeAnne     Markus      48 F   W   1   1   CO    887.49 2     SALE
 8 Marilyn    Lester      55 F   M   4   3   MA  1,516.26 Y     MKTG
 9 David      Marzetti    47 M   D   0   1   NC    981.45 2     ACCT
10 Paula      Bernstein   30 F   S   3   3   CA  1,004.56 2     SALE
11 Alfred     Adelson     60 M   M   0   1   CT    956.43 Y     ACCT
12 Ellen      Aliakbari   35 F   S   0   1   NJ    997.66 2     MFGR
13 Howard E.  Peters      18 M   S   0   1   LA  1,544.00 1     MKTG
14
15 FIRST      LAST       AGE SEX MS  DEP CAR ST     WAGE STATUS DEPT
16                         ■
17
18 Average:  1,145.40                        Age:     35.00

Enter:
Formula: r2c3 < 35
Worksheet: person   Loc: r16c3    FN: 0    Font: 0
Enter text, a value, date, time or formula
```

The formula has been changed to calculate average wages. Although the cell containing the criterion will normally display a zero, you can reformat it to suppress a zero display.

Note that only the first data row in the database block has been selected for measurement in the formula. Do not, however, select the first actual row of the block; this is the field title row. You may combine formula criteria with literal criteria as needed.

Rather than embedding a constant in a criterion formula, you may reference a cell. In figure 27.4, the formula in r16c3 has been changed to reference the target age in r18c10:

   r2c3 < r[18]c10

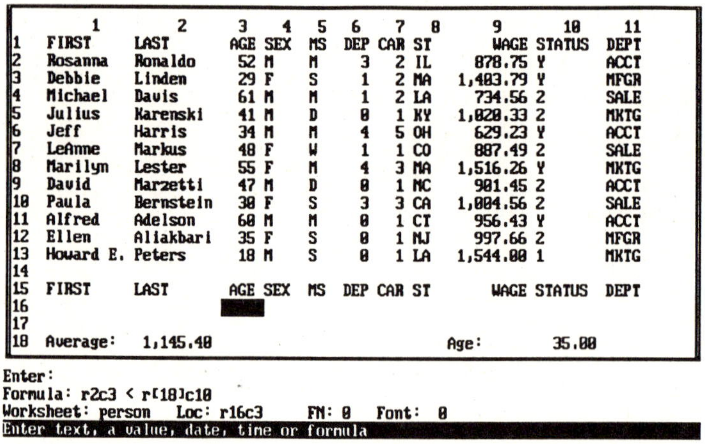

Fig. 27.4.

An absolute cell reference in a formula criterion.

```
        1          2        3   4   5   6    7   8     9      10    11
 1 FIRST      LAST       AGE SEX MS  DEP CAR ST     WAGE STATUS DEPT
 2 Rosanna    Ronaldo     52 M   M   3   2   IL    878.75 Y     ACCT
 3 Debbie     Linden      29 F   S   1   2   MA  1,483.79 Y     MFGR
 4 Michael    Davis       61 M   M   1   2   LA    734.56 2     SALE
 5 Julius     Karenski    41 M   D   0   1   KY  1,020.33 2     MKTG
 6 Jeff       Harris      34 M   M   4   5   OH    629.23 Y     ACCT
 7 LeAnne     Markus      48 F   W   1   1   CO    887.49 2     SALE
 8 Marilyn    Lester      55 F   M   4   3   MA  1,516.26 Y     MKTG
 9 David      Marzetti    47 M   D   0   1   NC    981.45 2     ACCT
10 Paula      Bernstein   30 F   S   3   3   CA  1,004.56 2     SALE
11 Alfred     Adelson     60 M   M   0   1   CT    956.43 Y     ACCT
12 Ellen      Aliakbari   35 F   S   0   1   NJ    997.66 2     MFGR
13 Howard E.  Peters      18 M   S   0   1   LA  1,544.00 1     MKTG
14
15 FIRST      LAST       AGE SEX MS  DEP CAR ST     WAGE STATUS DEPT
16                         ■
17
18 Average:  1,145.40                        Age:     35.00

Enter:
Formula: r2c3 < r[18]c10
Worksheet: person   Loc: r16c3    FN: 0    Font: 0
Enter text, a value, date, time or formula
```

Chapter 27: Module Specific and Special Functions **603**

In this example, the formula evaluation takes place for each row in the database. Be sure to use the absolute reference, as shown in figure 27.4.

When using the statistical database features of the Spreadsheet, do not include any extraneous text rows, such as dashes, in the database block; formula criteria will be evaluated against these extra rows and will yield erroneous results. Literal criteria, as in figures 27.1 and 27.2, will be unaffected.

Name:	SSGET
Description:	Retrieve cell contents
Module(s):	Spreadsheet
Format:	ssget({t1,},r,c) t1 = optional worksheet name r = row number c = column number
Explanation:	Retrieves the value of a cell from the specified worksheet or the current sheet. The row and column arguments may be variables or cell references. This function should probably be used in project files only, because automatic minimal recalculation will not recognize a change in the source cell.
Example:	ssget(r9c1,r9c3)
Result:	If r9c1 = 5 and r9c3 = 2, the result of the function will be the contents of r5c2.
Notes:	In this example, you could also use the formula indirect(makecell(r9c1,r9c3)).
Name:	INDIRECT
Description:	Return contents of a cell whose address is contained in another cell
Module(s):	All
Format:	indirect(t1) t1 = cell address (or field reference)
Explanation:	Function returns the contents of the cell whose address is specified as the argument to the function.
Example:	indirect(r10c1)
Result:	If r10c1 contains r14c1 and r14c1 contains 33.94, then the function will return 33.94.
Notes:	Refer to the Makecell and SSget functions.

Name:	SSPUT
Description:	Assign a value to a cell
Module(s):	Spreadsheet
Format:	ssput(e1,{t1,},r,c) e1 = expression t1 = optional worksheet name r = row number c = column number
Explanation:	Inserts the value of the expression into the cell at the designated row and column in the specified worksheet or in the current worksheet. The row and column arguments may be variables or cell references. If the as signment is successful, the function returns True (1); if not, it returns False (0). SSPUT cannot be used directly in a cell; it must be used in a project file.
Example:	SSPUT(33.94,r2c2,r3c2)
Result:	If r2c2 = 13 and r3c2 = 4, then cell r13c4 will contain 33.94 after statment execution.

Name:	GOAL
Description:	Solve an equation in one unknown
Module(s):	All
Format:	goal(n1,n2,GUESS formula) n1 = estimated value n2 = desired result
Explanation:	You can use the Goal function to solve an equation by iteration until the difference in successive calculations is less than $1E-7$ (.0000001) or until 20 iterations have been calculated. Although you might be able to rewrite an equation algebraically to solve it, using the Goal function is often more convenient and faster. Figure 27.5 shows a complicated quadratic equation that would take more than a few minutes to solve manually, but the Goal function solves the equation almost instantly. The function is shown in row 5, the formula is in the command area below, and row 17 contains a formula to verify the Goal function's accuracy.

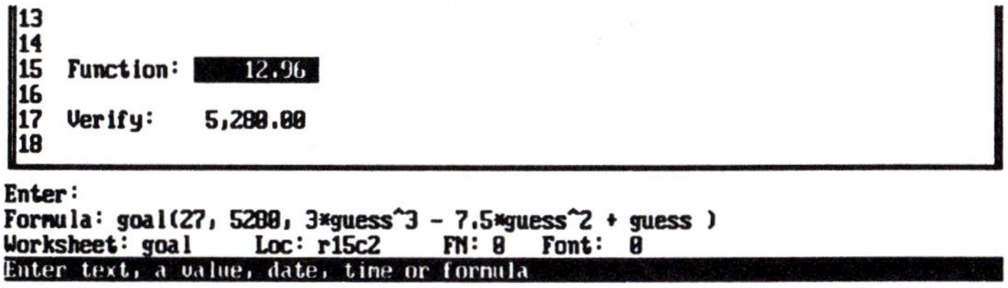

```
13
14
15  Function:  12.96
16
17  Verify:    5,280.00
18
Enter:
Formula: goal(27, 5280, 3*guess^3 - 7.5*guess^2 + guess )
Worksheet: goal     Loc: r15c2    FN: 0    Font: 0
Enter text, a value, date, time or formula
```

Fig. 27.5.
Seeking a goal.

In some formulas, the unknown may have more than one possible value. An example is

$$guess^2 + 6*guess = -8$$

The two possible values for the unknown are -2 and -4. In these cases, the screen displays an Error 30 message:
No convergence.

For safety, you should perform your own calculation to verify the accuracy of the Goal function until you're satisfied that the formula and constants are in the satisfactory range of solution.

Word Processor Functions

The following functions apply to only the Word Processor module.

Name:	WPGET
Description:	Retrieve text from document
Module(s):	Word Processor
Format:	wpget(n1,n2) n1 = number of characters to retrieve n2 = 0 to retrieve only text; non-zero to retrieve font and special character information.
Explanation:	Retrieves text from the current document, beginning at the current cursor position. You can specify a maximum of 240 characters to retrieve. If the second argument is zero, only text is retrieved; if the second argument is not zero, font and special information is retrieved, preceded by a percent sign.
Example:	wpget(30,0)

Name:	WPPUT
Description:	Insert text into a document
Module(s):	Word Processor
Format:	wpput(t1) t1 = text to insert
Explanation:	Use this function in a project file to enter text into a document. The currently selected font is used unless you specify a font in the format %[*f*], where *f* is the font number. Use uppercase *U* or *B* to initiate underscore and bold. If the command is successful, a 1 is returned; otherwise, a 0 is returned.
Example:	wpput("%[1U]This is font 1, underscored")

Name:	WPINFO
Description:	Retrieve information about the current document.
Module(s):	Word Processor
Format:	wpinfo(n1), n1 = information identifier

n1	Name	Content
1	wp_cursect	Section Number
2	wp_curpage	Page Number
3	wp_curline	Line Number
4	wp_curcol	Column Position
5	wp_filename	File name
6	wp_filespec	File specification
7	wp_curfont	Current character font
8	wp_newfont	Selected font
9	wp_mcacol	MCA column number
10	wp_mcaent	MCA entry number

Explanation:	The function returns selected information about the current document or the cursor position in the document. You may use either the number or the name as the argument to the function.
Example:	wpinfo(wp_curpage) or wpinfo(2)

Database Functions

The following functions apply to only the Database module.

Name:	DELETED
Description:	Record deleted
Module(s):	Database
Format:	deleted
Example:	[last] = "Kirby" and not (deleted)
Explanation:	Useful in Database Query command or in project files to determine whether the current record is deleted.

Name:	Record Numbers
Module(s):	Database
Explanation:	Returns a physical or logical record number as indicated.

Physical record numbers are returned relative to the entire file, regardless of the order of the file:

> PRECORD Physical number of the current record
>
> PRECORDS Total number of records in file

Logical record numbers are returned relative to the current Index order of the file.

> RECORD Logical number of the current record.
>
> RECORDS Total number of logical records available through the Index

Note: In previous versions of Smart, when ordered by a key, the Record function returned the logical record number. In SmartWare II, this function returns the physical record number. When the file is in either physical or key order, Record and Precord are equal.

Name:	FETCHFIELD
Description:	Field from previous record
Module(s):	Database
Format:	fetchfield([f1]) f1 = field name

Explanation:	Function returns contents of the field from the previous record in the current order. The result is the same as retrieved when you press the F9 key for a field while in the Data Enter or Update modes.
Example:	fetchfield([dept])

Name:	INVERT
Description:	Reverse text so that last word is first
Module(s):	Database
Format:	Invert(t1) t1 = text field
Explanation:	The Inverted field type in the Database allows you to sort on the last word, such as a last name. Thus, in an inverted field, the name Michael Lybron would sort by *Lybron*, rather than the first name *Michael*. If you want to display an inverted field with the last name first, use the Invert function.
Example:	Invert([name]), Invert("Michael Lybron")
Result:	Lybron Michael
Notes:	If the name has a suffix, such as Jr. or IV, a backslash (\) must precede the word which is to be considered last. Thus, to correctly invert *Michael Lybron Jr.* the string would have to be *Michael \Lybron Jr.* In previous Smart versions, a reference to an inverted field would give you the last name first; this was necessary for sorting and field comparisons. If you wanted to view the first name first, you needed to use the Reinvert function. In SmartWare II, a reference to an inverted field gives you the first name first, as you see it on-screen. When sorting or performing comparisons, however, the system recognizes the unique properties of an Inverted field and will perform the operation correctly. The Reinvert function is no longer available in SmartWare II; it has been replaced by the Invert function.

Chapter 27: Module Specific and Special Functions **609**

Name:	File Reference Functions:

FILEAVERAGE	Field average
FILECOUNT	Count of entries
FILEMAX	Field maximum
FILEMIN	Field minimum
FILESTD	Field standard deviation, population
FILESTDEV	Field standard deviation, sample
FILESUM	Field sum
FILESUMSQ	Field sum of squares
FILEVAR	Field variance

Description: These nine file functions perform their calculations throughout the current or specified file. Optional criteria may be specified.

Module(s): Database

Format: fileFUNCTION([f1]{,c1})
f1 = field
c1 = optional criteria

Explanation: For the specified field, each of the nine functions will return the calculation, based on the non-blank fields in the file. Because these functions are numeric, only numeric fields can be specified (except for Count). The entire file will be used, unless you have performed a Data Query to restrict the number of records. If the function is to operate on a file other than the current one, you can specify the view name as part of the first argument.

Examples: filesum([wage] , [sex] = "F")
fileaverage([wage])
filemax([person3.wage])
filemin([person3.wage], [dept]= "ACCT" and [age] > 30)

Note: The Totals function from previous versions of Smart has been replaced by the Filesum function.

Name: FILELOOKUP

Description: Retrieve data from file by key field match

Module(s): Database

Format:	filelookup([f1],[f2],e1) f1 = key field to search f2 = data field to return e1 = data to match in key field
Explanation:	The function searches the file for the text or value in the expression in the key field. If a matching field is found, the value of the data field is returned. If duplicate keys exist, only the first encountered record is used. The file can be ordered by the key field or another key; it can be in physical order, or can be ordered by an Index. If ordered by an index, you can still retrieve data outside the boundaries of the index.
Examples:	filelookup([last],[wage],"Markus") filelookup([person3.ssn],[last],"498-48-3980")
Result:	In the first example, the [last] field is searched for "Markus"; the wage is returned when the record is found. In the 2nd example, the [ssn] field is searched for the specified ssn; the last name is returned. The search value must be an equality; you cannot specify "less than" or "greater than." You cannot specify an abbreviation and you must specify the correct case of the search text.
Name:	Table Reference Functions: TABLEAVERAGE — Field average TABLECOUNT — Count of entries TABLEMAX — Field maximum TABLEMIN — Field minimum TABLESTD — Field standard deviation, population TABLESTDEV — Field standard deviation, sample TABLESUM — Field sum TABLESUMSQ — Field sum of squares TABLEVAR — Field variance
Description:	These nine table functions perform their calculations throughout the table of the current or specified view. Optional criteria may be specified.
Module(s):	Database
Format:	tableFUNCTION([f1]{,c1}) f1 = field c1 = optional criteria

Chapter 27: Module Specific and Special Functions

Explanation:	For the specified field, each of the nine functions will return the calculation, based on the non blank fields in the table. Since these functions are numeric, only numeric fields may be specified (except for Count). If the function is to operate on a view other than the current one, you may specify the view name as part of the first argument.
Examples:	tablesum([wage] , [sex] = "F") tableaverage([wage]) tablemax([depper.wage]) tablemin([depper.wage], [dept]= "ACCT" and [age] > 30)

Name:	TABLEREC
Description:	Current table record position
Module(s):	Database
Format:	tablerec(t1) t1 = field name in table
Explanation:	Returns the logical number of the current record in the table. The table is identified by the field used as the function argument.
Examples:	tablerec([sold])

Name:	TABLELOOKUP
Description:	Retrieve data from table by criterion
Module(s):	Database
Format:	tablelookup([f1],e1) f1 = data field to return e1 = logical expression
Explanation:	The function searches the table for the first record in which the expression is true. When a qualifying record is found, the value of the data field is returned. If duplicate records would meet the criteria, only the first encountered record is used.
Examples:	tablelookup([wage],[last] = "Markus") tablelookup([depper.last],[ssn] = "498-48-3980") tablelookup([ssn],[wage] >= 1000)
Result:	In the first example, the [last] field is searched for "Markus"; the wage is returned when the record is found. In the second example, the [ssn] field is searched for the specified ssn; the last name is returned. The third example

	returns the [SSN] of the first record in which the wage is greater than or equal to 100.
Note:	Notice the important difference between the Filelookup and Tablelookup specifications. In the Filelookup function, you must search for an exact match to the key field. In Tablelookup, you may specify a condition on any field; not just a key. The condition must include a relational operator, and may include any of the SmartWare II functions.
Name:	DBGET
Description:	Get field contents
Module(s):	Database
Format:	dbget(f1) f1 = database field
Explanation:	Returns the contents of a field. The function argument is a database field reference in quotation marks.
Example:	dbget("[last]") dbget("[person3.last]")
Name:	DBPUT
Description:	Field assignment
Module(s):	Database
Format:	dbput(f1,v1) f1 = database field v1 = field contents
Explanation:	Assigns the value of the second argument to the field as specified in the 1st argument.
Example:	dbput("[person3.last]","Ronaldo")
Result:	If the function is successful, the result is 1; if the assignment fails, the result is 0.

Project Processing Functions

The following functions can be used in project processing only.

Name:	INCHAR
Description:	Input character
Module(s):	Project Files, all modules

Format:	inchar
Explanation:	Returns key value of next key pressed.
Example:	inchar
Result:	114
Notes:	Particularly useful in project files for rapid execution. In previous Smart versions, INCHAR returned the ASCII value of the key. In SmartWare II, the function returns the special Key Value, which may or may not be the ASCII value. Although there are unique numerical key values, you do not have to memorize them or look them up. You can use the braces ({}) to evaluate the results of the INCHAR function, as demonstrated in the following example:

```
public $key

label next
let $key = inchar
if $key = {enter}
   message "Key is Enter"
elseif $key = {Bs}
   message "Key is Backspace"
elseif $key = {^F12}
   message "Key is Ctrl-F12"
elseif $key = {Del}
   message "Key is Delete"
else
   message "All Done"
      jump alldone
end if

jump next

label alldone
```

A complete list of the reserved key code terms is in Appendix B of the *Formula Reference* manual. Using the braces to evaluate a return from INCHAR is preferable to using the ASC function, the KEYVALUE function, or the actual key value itself. Not only is the project file more readable, but the project file will run faster, because the braces notation is interpreted during compilation. Refer to the KEYVALUE and OLDKEY functions for additional information.

Name:	**KEYVALUE**
Description:	Key value of a character or key stroke
Module(s):	All
Format:	keyvalue(t1) t1 = character or key combination
Explanation:	Returns the numerical value of the text argument, a character or key stroke combination. The result is identical to the result of enclosing the argument in braces {} in a project file, not using the KEYVALUE function. Refer to the discussion of the INCHAR function.
Example:	keyvalue("Bs") or {Bs}
Result:	744
Notes:	A complete list of the reserved key code terms is in Appendix B of the *Formula Reference* manual. Refer to the INCHAR and OLDKEY functions for more information.

Name:	**OLDKEY**
Description:	Value returned by INCHAR in previous Smart versions.
Module(s):	All
Format:	oldkey(n1)
Explanation:	If you are converting project files created in previous Smart versions to SmartWare II and have tested for specific INCHAR values, you can save time by using the OLDKEY function to convert the results of SmartWare II INCHAR back to the old values.

Example:	let $key = inchar
	
	'insert this statement here to convert value
	
	let $key = oldkey($key)
	
	if $key = 17408 'F10 keystroke
	   .
	   .
	elseif $key = 17152 'F9 keystroke
	   .
	   .

In fact, however, your project file will be easier to read and will probably run faster if you change the old key value numbers to braces and key codes:

let $key = inchar

if $key = {F10}   'F10 keystroke
    .
    .
elseif $key = {F9}   'F9 keystroke
    .
    .

Notes: Refer to the Inchar and Keyvalue functions for more information on this topic.

Name:	NEXTKEY
Description:	Next key pressed
Module(s):	Project files, all modules
Format:	nextkey
Explanation:	Returns the ASCII value of the next key waiting in the keyboard buffer. Program execution does not pause. Buffer is not automatically cleared.
Example:	let $key = nextkey

The Nextkey function is useful in project files in which you want the program to continue to execute while waiting for a keystroke. The following example demonstrates the use of the Nextkey function to accept a part number, display it on-screen, and flash a prompt message while waiting for the next character:

```
public $col $letter $color $partno

screen clear 7 0
let $partno = null
let $col = 10

label next

    if nextkey <> 0                 'if a key is pressed
       let $letter = inchar         'empty nextkey buffer
       if $letter = {enter}         'terminate prompting
          jump alldone
       end if
```

```
            screen print 5 $col 7 0 chr($letter)
            let $col = $col + 1        'advance to next column
            locate 5 $col 1            'locate the cursor
            let $partno = $partno | chr($letter) 'part number
         end if

         screen draw box 7 10 12 30 $color 0
         screen print 9 12 9 0 "Enter Part Number"
         let $color = abs($color-9)      'alternate flash

      jump next

      label alldone
```

Name:	**CERROR**
Description:	Error number generated by preceding command
Module(s):	Project files, all modules
Format:	if cerror = n1 ... n1 = error number
Explanation:	Returns any error number resulting from the preceding command in a project file. The error numbers are found in Appendix A of the SmartWare II Project Processing Manual. Value will be 0 if the preceding command did not result in an error.

Name:	**LERROR**
Description:	Most recent error number
Module(s):	Project files, all modules
Format:	if Lerror = n1 ... n1 = error number
Explanation:	Returns most recent error number resulting from the preceding commands in a project file. The error numbers are found in Appendix A of the SmartWare II Project Processing Manual. Use this function to check for the failure of a series of commands. Reset the Lerror function to 0 with the Clearerror project file command.

Name:	**ERRORTEXT**
Description:	Text of an error code
Module(s):	Project files, all modules

Chapter 27: Module Specific and Special Functions

Format:	errortext(n1) n1 = error number
Explanation:	Returns the text of an error identified by number. The error numbers are found in Appendix A of the SmartWare II Project Processing Manual. Most errors are specific to the individual module.
Example:	errortext(1618)
Result:	Insufficient body area

Name:	ERROR
Description:	User-defined error
Module(s):	All
Format:	if e1 then v1 else error e1 = logical condition v1 = value
Explanation:	Used to create a user-defined error condition, based on the specifications of the logical condition. The error is displayed as error 35.
Example:	If r35c72 <> 33.94 then error else "OK"
Result:	Error 35

Name:	Foreground colors:	
	FGSTANDARD	Smart module menu
	FGINVSTANDARD	Highlight on menu
	FGBACKGROUND	Labels on status line
	FGPLEASING	Definition menus
	FGINVPLEASING	Selected items in definitions
	FGERROR	Error message
Description:	The functions return the various colors in use by the current screen driver. With these functions, you can guarantee consistency with the colors of any screen display.	
Module(s):	All	
Notes:	Refer to background color functions.	

Name:	Background Colors

BGSTANDARD	Smart module menu
BGINVSTANDARD	Highlight on menu
BGBACKGROUND	Labels on status line
BGPLEASING	Definition menus
BGINVPLEASING	Selected items in definitions
BGERROR	Error message

Description:	The functions return the various colors in use by the current screen driver. With these functions, you can guarantee consistency with the colors of any screen display.
Module(s):	All
Notes:	Refer to foreground color functions.

Name:	Screen Information

Message and screen print commands:
   SCRCOLUMN Column after last character on-screen.
   SCRLINE Last line on-screen.

Screen Dimensions:
   SCRHEIGHT Screen height, lines
   SCRWIDTH Screen width, columns
   SCRMODE 0 = character, 1 = graphics

Description:	These functions provide information about the location of data generated on-screen by the message and screen print commands, and about screen driver in use.
Module(s):	All

Name:	FACTUAL
Description:	Number of bytes in preceding Fread command
Module(s):	All
Format:	factual
Explanation:	Returns the number of bytes in the most recent Fread command. If you are reading the entire line, Factual will be two bytes more than the length of the destination variable, due to the Carriage Return and Line Feed.
Example:	Fread 1 into $bear let $actual = Factual

Chapter 27: Module Specific and Special Functions **619**

Name: EOF

Description: End of file

Module(s):   All

Format:
eof(n1)
n1 = file number from Fopen command

Explanation: Function returns one when end of file is encountered in an Fread command; function will be zero otherwise.

Example:
if eof(1) = 1
    jump alldone
end if

Notes: In previous Smart versions, an End of File condition could be detected only by checking for Cerror greater than 0.

Name: MEMLEFT

Description: Amount of memory remaining

Module(s):   All

Format: memleft

Explanation: Function returns the amount of memory available to be used; quantity is in bytes.

Example:
If memleft < 5000
    beep
    message "You are low on memory"
end if

Notes: The value of Memleft is the same as displayed on your screen when you press Ctrl-F1.

28

Tools: Commands Common to All Modules

Certain common utility commands (Tools) are available in each of the applications modules of the SmartWare II system and in the Main Menu. You can use these commands to do the following:

- Perform calculations on-screen
- Display file names
- Make and change directories
- Copy, delete, erase, rename, and print files
- Create, remove, load, save, view, and edit macro definitions
- Create a font file
- Execute operating system commands
- Change your system configuration
- Develop and edit macros
- Edit text files

Except for the setting of module-specific preferences, which are covered in the individual module sections of this book, the Tools commands work identically in each module.

Execute the Tools command from the menu to display the different options, as shown in figure 28.1.

Fig. 28.1.

The Tools command options.

621

Directory Commands

The Directory commands of the SmartWare II system are similar to their counterparts in DOS. Because these commands are used so frequently, they have been included in SmartWare II. Of special significance is the capability to create or change to a new subdirectory from in the SmartWare II system. Without this capability, you would have to terminate your Smart session to perform these functions.

The Tools Directory commands are shown in figure 28.2.

```
Option: Display Make New-Directory Remove
tools directory
View: person3.vws    Window:1                    Rec:1 ( 1 )
Display file information for a directory
```

Fig. 28.2.

The Tools directory commands.

Display Option

To display information about selected files on your disk, use the Display option; the Quick key is Alt-O. You can search for files by name or extension; even portions of names or extensions can be used to locate a file if you use wild card characters. The asterisk (*) substitutes for any characters beginning with this position of the file specification, and the question mark (?) means any single character in this position.

Figure 28.3, for example, illustrates the result of the Display option, using the following search criterion:

    D*.BAT

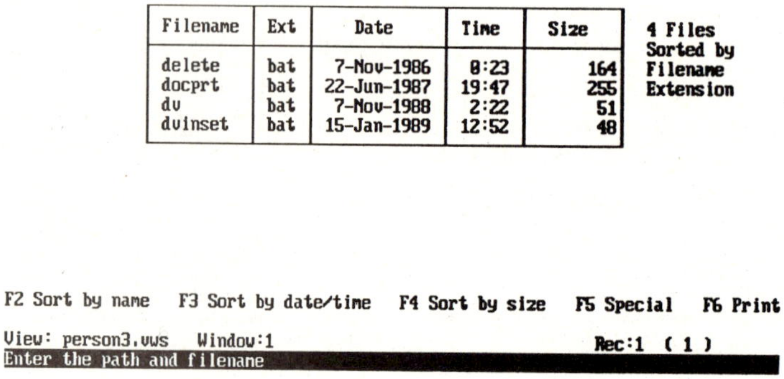

Fig. 28.3.

Displaying file names.

Filename	Ext	Date	Time	Size	
delete	bat	7-Nov-1986	8:23	164	4 Files Sorted by Filename Extension
docprt	bat	22-Jun-1987	19:47	255	
dv	bat	7-Nov-1988	2:22	51	
dvinset	bat	15-Jan-1989	12:52	48	

```
F2 Sort by name   F3 Sort by date/time   F4 Sort by size   F5 Special   F6 Print
View: person3.vws    Window:1                              Rec:1 ( 1 )
Enter the path and filename
```

Chapter 28: Tools: Commands Common to All Modules 623

Notice that four files were found in the current subdirectory that had D as the first letter, and .BAT as the extension. If necessary, you can preface the file specification with a drive letter and subdirectory name. The file name, extension, date and time of creation or last change, and the size in bytes are displayed.

To change the order of the display, use the following function keys:

    F2 File name (This is the default)
    F3 Date and time, ascending
    F4 File size, ascending
    F5 Special two-key sort
        F2 Name
        F3 Extension
        F4 Date and time
        F5 Size
    F6 Print the directory listing as shown

To use the special two-key sort feature, you press one of the listed function keys to select a primary sort, and another as a secondary sort. If, for example, you want your files listed first by extension, and then by date and time in extension, press F5 to select the special sort, F3 to select extension as the primary sort, and F4 for the date and time secondary sort.

On standard-sized screens, only 17 files can be displayed at one time. If a greater number of files match your search criteria, the following symbol appears to the left of the first entry:

    First ⇒

Use the down-arrow or PgDn keys to view the remainder of the entries. When there are no more entries to view, you see the following symbol to the left of the final entry:

    Last ⇒

Press Esc to return to the menu. If there are no files matching your search criteria, you receive the following error message:

    `No matching files, press any key`

When you press a key to clear the message, the system returns to the top command level.

Making A New Subdirectory

To make a new directory, use the Tools Directory Make command. You are prompted:

    Enter a directory name:

Type a new directory name and press Enter. (Names of directories must not exceed eight characters; generally, subdirectory names do not have an extension.) Make sure that the subdirectory does not already exist, or you receive the following error message:

    Unable to create the directory

If the directory you want to create is subordinate to the current directory, you can type the name without the preceding backslash (\). If, however, the desired directory is on a different path, you must use the full path identifiers. Some examples are as follows:

    \taxes
    \office\wordp
    d:\view1\data

Note that if the drive is different from the current drive, it must be included.

Changing to a New Directory

Use the Tools Directory New-Directory command to select a new subdirectory. If you store files in different subdirectories, this command is a valuable time-saving feature to change your current directory without leaving SmartWare II. An example of the screen display is shown in figure 28.4.

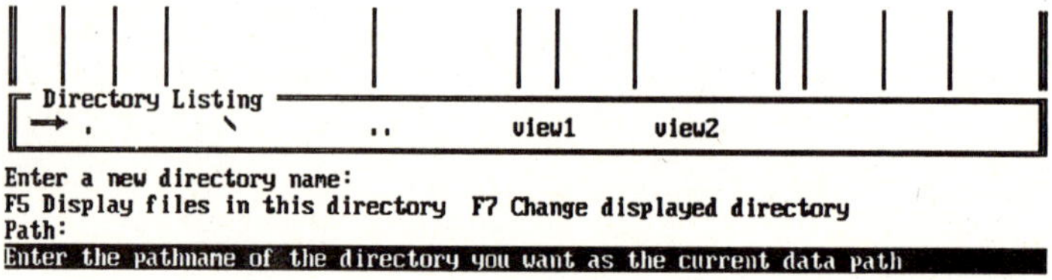

Fig. 28.4.

Directory selection.

```
┌─ Directory Listing ──────────────────────────────┐
│ →  .                                             │
│    .  .                          view1    view2  │
└──────────────────────────────────────────────────┘
Enter a new directory name:
F5 Display files in this directory  F7 Change displayed directory
Path:
Enter the pathname of the directory you want as the current data path
```

The current subdirectory is shown on the status line if you have previously changed subdirectories during the current SmartWare II session. The pop-up window shows you the names of the subdirectories that are descendent from the current directory. Also shown are the following three entries:

  .   Current subdirectory
  ..   Subdirectory immediately above current subdirectory
  \   Root directory

To change to a new directory, you type the name of the directory after the following prompt:

    Enter a new directory name:

If the directory you want is subordinate to the current directory, you can type the name without the preceding backslash (\), or you can move the cursor and press Enter. If the desired directory is on a different path, however, you must use the full path identifiers. Some examples are as follows:

    \taxes
    \office\wordp
    d:\view1\data

Note that you must specify the drive if it is different from the current drive.

If you misspell a directory name, you receive the following error message:

    Path not accessible (\path\)

In SmartWare II, you cannot change to a directory that does not exist, which is an improvement over previous Smart versions.

Rather than type the names of the subdirectories, you can use the cursor key. Move the cursor to highlight the directory that you want and press Enter. Upon completion of the command, the system returns to the menu.

You can use the F7 key to display subdirectory names as you traverse your hard disk. Move the cursor to the name of the subdirectory which is the parent of the one you want and press F7. The names of the subdirectories in the newly selected subdirectory are displayed in the pop-up window. Move the cursor to the name of the subdirectory you want and press Enter.

If the subdirectory you are trying to find follows those listed, press F7 again. A new set of directory entries is displayed. Continue this process until you have selected the directory you want, then highlight it and press Enter.

Selection of a new subdirectory is maintained as you change from module to module, unless you have specifically entered a data path in the preference menu for an individual module.

Removing a Directory

To remove a directory, use the Tools Directory Remove command. The current subdirectory is shown on the status line if you previously have changed subdirectories during the current SmartWare II session. The pop-up window shows you the names of the subdirectories subordinate to the current directory. Also shown are the following three entries:

    .   Current subdirectory.
    ..   Subdirectory immediately above current subdirectory
    \\   Root directory

You cannot remove any of these directories. To remove any other directory, you move the cursor to select a directory and press Enter, or type the name of the directory after the following prompt:

    Enter a new directory name:

If the directory you want to remove is subordinate to the current directory, you type the name without the preceding backslash (\\). If, however, the directory is on a different path, you must use the full path identifiers. Some examples are as follows:

    \\taxes
    \\office\\wordp
    d:\\view1\\data

If the drive is different from the current drive, you must specify it.

Make sure that the subdirectory already exists, or you will receive the following error message:

    Unable to remove the directory

You cannot remove a directory that contains files, the current directory, or a directory from which the current directory is descendent. To erase files in a subdirectory, use the Tools File Erase command. If the current directory is empty and you want to remove it, change to the next higher directory by choosing the .. selection in the pop-up menu of the New-Directory command. Then execute the Tools Directory Remove command.

Tools File Command

The Tools File command has four options. These options enable you to copy, erase, rename, and print files in much the same way as you can at the operating-system level. SmartWare II provides you with extra protection, which is beneficial. You cannot, for example, erase a file currently in use or copy onto an existing file.

Copying a File

The Copy option is used to make an exact duplicate of a file and store it under a different name, under the same name in a different subdirectory, or on a different disk. You can copy individual or multiple files with one command.

Chapter 28: Tools: Commands Common to All Modules **627**

When you execute the Tools File Copy command, a pop-up window displays the names of the files in the current subdirectory (see fig. 28.5). The prompt is as follows:

    Enter the source filename:

```
┌─ File Listing ──────────────────────────────────────────────┐
│ → countf.bas    docprt.bas      dosexec.bas    jeff.bas     │
│   lablprt.bas   leah.bab        que.bas        today.bas    │
│   tprint.bas    tqcnvrt.bas                                 │
└─────────────────────────────────────────────────────────────┘
Enter the source filename:
F4 Look for a file   F5 Display directories   F6 Mark or Unmark
Path: \dog\              Date: Oct 13, 1987   Time: 16:34   Size: 980
Copy a file to the specified file.
```

Fig. 28.5.
Tools File Copy command.

The status line shows the name of the current subdirectory. As you move the cursor from file to file, the date and time of file creation or last change, and the size of the file is shown on the status line for each file.

If you want to copy one file, highlight the name with the F6 key and press Enter. You can type the name of the file instead. You are prompted:

    Enter the destination path or filename:

If the new copy is not going to be stored in the current subdirectory, you must supply the full path name. Type the name of the new file and press Enter.

You can copy multiple files with one command if you use the asterisk and question mark wild card specifications for the source files. If you want to select the files to copy by using the selection wild cards, enter them in your specification of the source file name. To copy all files with an extension of .BAS, for example, you should type the source file name as:

    *.BAS

When using this technique, you cannot assign new names to the files, and you must copy them to another subdirectory or another drive. When prompted for the destination path or filename, follow these steps:

1. Move the cursor in the window to highlight the displayed subdirectories. If the destination subdirectory is displayed, highlight it and press Enter. If the parent of the destination subdirectory is displayed, highlight it and proceed to step 2. To access the root directory, select the backslash (\).

   Three subdirectory entries have a special significance:

   .   Current subdirectory
   ..   Subdirectory immediately above current subdirectory
   \   Root directory

   Actual subdirectory names may be listed also.

2. Press F7 to display the names of the subdirectories preceding and following the new subdirectory you just selected.

3. Continue steps 1 and 2 until you have located the destination subdirectory. Press Enter to complete the Tools File Copy command.

Rather than using the wild card file identification method, you can use the F6 key to highlight individual files to copy. If you don't remember the location or the exact name of the source file, you can use the F4 key to help you. When you press F4, you are prompted:

```
Enter the file specification:
```

You can enter the specification with wild card characters and a path. The specified directory and all subordinate subdirectories are searched for files that match the selection criteria. Each subdirectory is searched in turn, and if a matching file is found, the following message is displayed:

```
File was found in directory name\filename.ext
Continue Searching (y/n)
```

Once you have located the correct subdirectory, respond *N*; press *Y* to continue the search. Now that you know the subdirectory name, follow these steps:

1. Press the F5 key to display the subdirectories preceding and following the current subdirectory.

2. Type the name of the subdirectory from which you want to copy the files.

3. Press F5 to display the names of the files in the selected subdirectory.

If you can recognize the name of the source subdirectory, you can use the function keys to help you locate it.

1. After you execute the Tools File Copy command, press the F5 key to display the subdirectories preceding and following the current subdirectory.

2. Move the cursor in the window to point to one of the displayed subdirectories. To access the root directory, select the backslash.

3. Press F7 to display the names of the subdirectories preceding and following the new subdirectory you just selected.

4. Continue steps 2 and 3 until you have located the source subdirectory.

5. Press F5 to display the names of the files in the selected subdirectory.

The methods of searching for files and changing subdirectories are common throughout the Tools Files commands and the SmartWare II system.

Erase Option

To erase one or more files from your disk, use the Tools File Erase command. When you execute this command, a pop-up window shows you the names of the files in the current subdirectory. You are prompted as follows:

    Enter the filename:

The status line shows the current subdirectory. For the file highlighted by the cursor, the date and time of the file creation or last change, and the size of the file in bytes are also shown on the status line.

To erase an individual file, move the cursor to the name of the file and press Enter. If you want to erase several files at one time, use the F6 key to mark the files you want; they are highlighted as shown in figure 28.6.

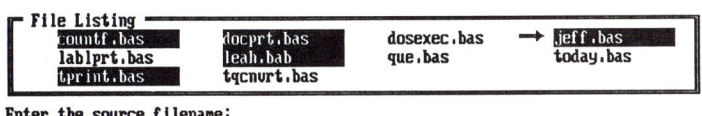

Fig. 28.6.
Erasing files.

If you want to select the files to erase by using the selection wild cards, enter the wild cards in your specification of the file name. To erase all files with an extension of .BAS, for example, you should type the source file name as:

    *.BAS

The rest of the files in the subdirectory are not be disturbed.

If you enter the file name as *.* to indicate that you want all files erased, you are prompted:

    Are you sure (y/n)

Press *Y* if you want to erase all files; press *N* if you don't want to erase all files.

Renaming Files

To rename a file, use the Tools File Rename command. When you execute this command, a pop-up window shows you the names of the files in the current subdirectory. The prompt is as follows:

    Enter the filename:

The status line shows the current subdirectory. For the file highlighted by the cursor, the date and time of the file creation or last change, and the size of the file in bytes are also shown on the status line.

To rename an individual file, move the cursor to the name of the file and press Enter. You cannot use the wild cards to rename several files at once or use the F6 to mark several files.

Once you have selected a file to rename, you are prompted:

    Enter a new filename:

You can enter any name not currently in use in the current subdirectory. If you enter an existing name, you receive the following the error message:

    Rename was not successful

Besides renaming a file in the current subdirectory, you can change the subdirectory in which the file is located, in effect moving the file to another subdirectory. To "move" the file, enter the path name preceding the file name. In this case, you need not change the name of the file. The original date of the file remains unchanged.

Note that when renaming a file, you are changing entries in the directory table of your disk; the file itself remains in the original physical location. Thus, although you are able to rename a file to a different subdirectory, you cannot rename it to a different disk drive. To move a file to a different disk, use the Tools File Copy command.

Printing Files

To print a file, use the Tools File Print command. When you execute this command, a pop-up window shows you the names of the files in the current subdirectory. The prompt is as follows:

    Enter the filename:

The status line shows the current subdirectory. For the file highlighted by the cursor, the date and time of the file creation or last change and the size of the file in bytes are also shown on the status line.

To print an individual file, move the cursor to the name of the file and press Enter. You cannot use the wild cards to print multiple files at once or use the F6 to mark several files to be printed at the same time.

It is very important that you select only ASCII files to print; an ASCII file is one which has been created in a text editor, such as the SmartWare II Tools Text-Editor or the Textfile mode of the Word processor. If you can view the file successfully on your computer screen by using the DOS Type command, then you can print it using the Tools File Print command. If, however, the file is a program file or even a word processing document, printing the file probably will send your printer into spasms.

Preferences

The settings in the Tools Preferences fall into three categories:

    Global
    Hardware
    Application-specific preferences

Global preferences are those which apply to the entire SmartWare II system and which can provide continuity and uniformity throughout all applications modules.

Hardware preferences refer to the physical hardware of your computer and the equipment connected to it. Both Global and Hardware preferences may be changed from the Main Menu or from any of the applications modules.

Application-specific preferences pertain to those selections that affect only the individual module (there are no applications preferences for the Main Menu).

Use either the space bar or the Backspace key to move the highlight block to indicate preference type. Press F10 to save your preferences selections.

Global Preferences

Select Tools Preferences Global to display the screens shown in figures 28.7 and 28.8.

```
┌─Global Preferences ─────────────────────────────────────┐
│→ Autohelp:  On  Off                                     │
│  Beeper:    On  Off                                     │
│                                                         │
│     Display of file names for file prompting: Yes  No   │
│     Automatic file backup: Yes  No                      │
│                                                         │
│     Quiet execution of project files:  Yes  No          │
│     Single-step execution of project files:  Yes  No    │
│                                                         │
│     Time format:  AM/PM  24 hour                        │
│                                                         │
│     Date style:  MMDDYY  DDMMYY  YYMMDD                 │
│     Date1 format:  dd month yy                          │
│     Date2 format:  mm/dd/yyyy                           │
│     Date3 format:  month dd, yyyy                       │
│                                                         │
│     Currency symbol: $                                  │
│     Currency symbol location: Before-amount After-amount│
│     Decimal separator: Period  Comma                    │
│ ↓                                                       │
│ F1 Help    F2 Edit text   F3 Blank text   F10 Finished  │
│ View: person3.vws   Window:1              Rec:1 ( 1 )   │
│ View or change the default operation settings for the system │
└─────────────────────────────────────────────────────────┘
```

Fig. 28.7.

The Tools Preferences Global preferences.

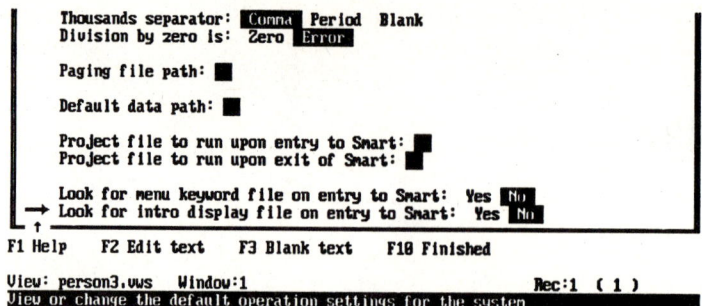

Fig. 28.8.

The Tools Preferences Global preferences.

Autohelp

Select Autohelp On if you want a one-line description of the commands to appear at the bottom of your screen; choose Autohelp Off if you prefer no command description. The Autohelp line provides information about the commands at each level in the command tree structure; more detail is provided as you progress into the execution of a command and move down the tree.

Beeper

Select Beeper On if you want the computer to beep when errors or warnings are encountered; choose Beeper Off if you (or your neighbors) prefer not to hear the beeps.

Display of File Names for File Prompting

If you prefer not to see the names of files in pop-up windows as you execute your commands, set this selection to *No*.

Automatic File Backup

Several of the critical files can be backed up for you automatically in the SmartWare II system. Specifically, the document files in the Word Processor, the worksheet files in the Spreadsheet, and the text files you edit in the Tools Text-Editor may all be backed up for you if you choose *Yes*. (Refer to Appendix B for a list of file extensions, including backup files.) Note that databases in the Database module are not backed up automatically; you must use a backup program.

Quiet execution of project files

Select *Yes* if you want to have your project files executed in the Quiet mode. A project file executed in the Quiet mode does not display the commands as they are executed. If your project files run in the Quiet mode, you will not be able to detect

Chapter 28: Tools: Commands Common to All Modules 633

most types of errors; however, the files generally run faster. You can control the Quiet settings of your project files individually by the statements Quiet On or Quiet Off. For more discussion on this subject, refer to Chapter 24.

Single-step execution of project files

If you select *Yes*, your project files will execute one statement at a time, and prompt you if the statement is to be executed. Normally, this setting is used only for debugging purposes, and would not be chosen as a global setting. As with the Quiet settings, you can control single-step execution individually in each project file, and can even choose to turn single step on and off based on logical conditions. For more discussion on this subject, refer to Chapter 24.

Time format

Select AM/PM if you plan to enter and view time values on a 12-hour basis. Select 24-hour if you plan to enter time on a 24-hour basis.

Date style

Select the order in which you plan to enter dates. The abbreviations represent months (MM), days (DD), and years (YY). If you select MMDDYY, an entry of *07/20/89* results in July 20, 1989.

Date formats. In SmartWare II, you can select the formats for the display of dates in three different styles. Some examples are as follows:

Format	*Example*
mm/dd/yy	07/20/89
mm-dd-yy	07-20-89
mm/dd/yyyy	07/20/1989
dd month yy	07 July 89
dd mon yyyy	07 Jul 1989
month dd, yyyy	July 07, 1989

The three date format selections are fields in which you must type or edit your choices. The key word month represents the full name of the month. You can select either a two-digit year YY or a four-digit year YYYY; these features are new with SmartWare II.

Currency symbol

The dollar sign is used as the currency symbol in the United States. The sign for the British pound (£) can be entered as an Alt-156. To enter, hold the Alt key down while you type *156* on the numerical key pad. (If you use this procedure, make sure that your printer can recognize this symbol.)

Currency Symbol Location

Select either Before-Amount or After-Amount.

Decimal Separator

Select either Period or Comma.

Thousands Separator

Select either Comma, Period, or Blank.

Division by Zero

If you want division by zero to result in an error which will halt the execution of project files, select Error. Alternately, you can allow division by zero to yield a zero result.

Paging File Path

As SmartWare II executes, there are processes which must create temporary files for sorting or work files. If you would like to designate a specific path or drive, you should make the entry for this selection. If you leave the entry blank, the home subdirectory will be used for paging. Normally, you should not have to make an entry here. You can designate a RAM drive as the paging drive. The home subdirectory is the one from which you initiated the current session.

Default Data Path

If a data path is not specified in the individual module preferences, the data path entered here will be the default. If you would like the data path to default to the current subdirectory, leave this entry blank, as well as the corresponding entry in the module preferences.

Running Project Files Automatically

Enter the names of the Main Menu project files that should execute automatically. If you will be entering SmartWare II from different subdirectories, be sure to enter the full path name as well as the project file name.

For totally customized applications, you can elect to ignore the standard SmartWare II menu keyword and introductory displays upon entry into SmartWare II.

If you elect to look for a menu keyword file or entry into SmartWare II, the system searches for a file named SMART.MNU in both the current and system directories. This optional menu keyword file contains additional keywords to be added to the SmartWare II menus.

Chapter 28: Tools: Commands Common to All Modules **635**

If you choose to look for an introduction display file on entry into SmartWare II, the system searches for a file named START.MSG in both the current and system directories. This ASCII file contains text and optional control sequence codes used to display an introduction screen after the normal introduction screen but before entry into the specified module.

Hardware Preferences

You can establish hardware preferences from the Tools Preferences Hardware command in any module of the SmartWare II system; you do not have to return to the Main Menu to change your hardware choices. The ability to change your hardware configuration in the SmartWare II environment is new with SmartWare II. Figures 28.9 and 28.10 show the input screens for hardware choices.

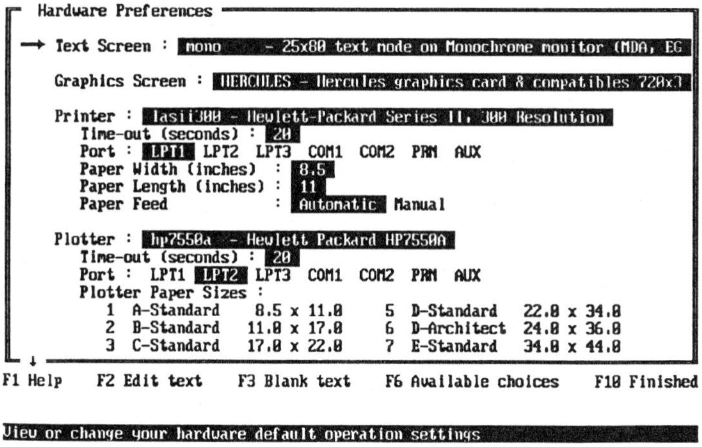

Fig. 28.9.

The Tools Preferences Hardware preferences.

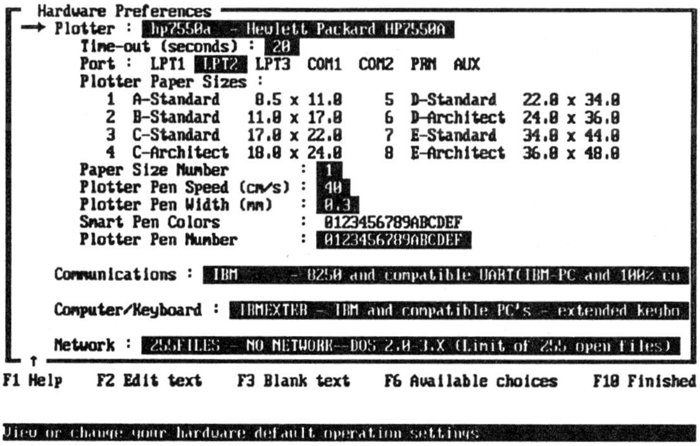

Fig. 28.10.

The Tools Preferences Hardware preferences.

The available alternatives are displayed in this menu by pressing the F6 key while your cursor is beside the selection. Many of the hardware choices are not "hard coded" into the preferences menu, but rather are stored individually in files on your disk. Greater hardware selection flexibility is provided by having the options available in individual files. As new printers are manufactured, they can be supported without any software changes by installing the driver files on your disk. The hardware devices and driver files available in the Tools Preferences Hardware command are those you selected during installation of the SmartWare II system. For additional selections, execute the Install program again.

Text Screen

Press F6 to display the choices available to you. Your screen display should be the one you choose for normal text usage. Figure 28.11 shows the pop-up window with some of the screen display choices.

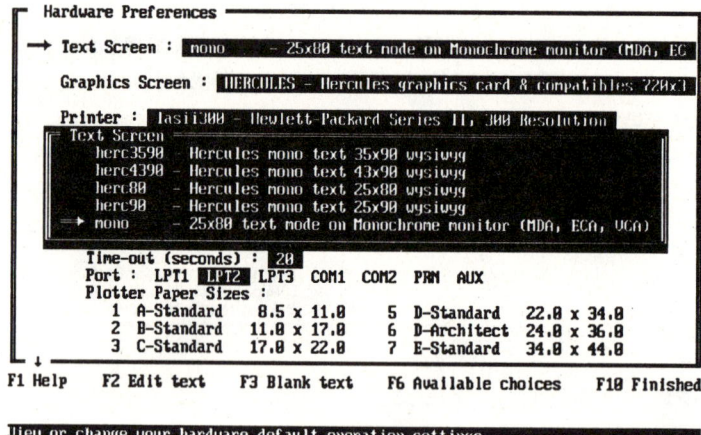

Fig. 28.11.

Text screen display choices.

Scroll the cursor up or down to find the correct display for your computer, and press Enter when the cursor arrow is beside your choice. Changing your text screen will sometimes require you to initiate a new SmartWare II session.

Graphics Screen

The graphics screen choice should reflect the Display mode needed to display spreadsheet graphs. Press F6 to display the available drivers, and press Enter.

Printer

Select from among the list of printers by pressing F6 to display a pop-up window of printer drivers.

Time Out (seconds)

Enter the number of seconds for the time out.

Port

Select the appropriate port to which your printer is attached. If your printer has a parallel interface, you should specify LPT1, LPT2, or LPT3, depending on the port to which you have attached it. If it is a serial printer, select either COM1 or COM2, again depending on the port.

SmartWare II addresses your computer hardware directly when you select one of the LPT or COM ports. With some networks or certain printers, however, interfacing to the printer through DOS is mandatory. If printer output must be directed through DOS, select PRN. Similarly, select AUX to address COM1 through DOS.

Paper Width and Length

Enter the actual width and length of the paper in your printer in inches. The default sizes are 8.5 inches wide and 11 inches long, the normal size for office paper in the United States. Sizes must be in the range of 1 to 100 inches. The width and length specified in hardware preferences will apply in printing operations in which you do not specifically select the paper dimensions.

Note that paper size is not specified in number of characters or lines of print. If you are using proportional fonts, the number of characters you can print on a line will vary, depending on their width.

Paper Feed

Select either Automatic or Manual paper feed. If you want printer to pause so that you can hand feed each sheet of paper, you should select Manual. If your printer feeds paper continuously, even if the sheets are already cut (as in a laser printer), select Automatic.

Plotter

If you are using a plotter, you should complete the following section. If you do not have a plotter, you need not be concerned with this area.

Select the appropriate port to which your plotter is attached. If your plotter has a parallel interface, you should specify LPT1, LPT2 or LPT3, depending on the port to which you have attached it. If it is a serial plotter, select either COM1 or COM2, again, depending on the port.

If you select either COM1 or COM2, the display will change to show the options in figure 28.12.

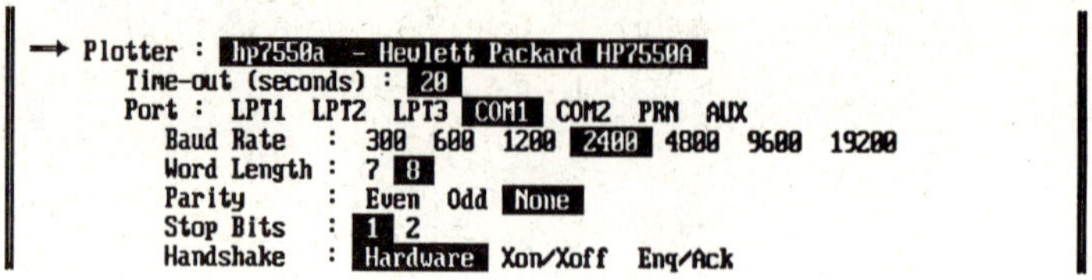

Fig. 28.12.

Serial options.

```
→ Plotter     : hp7550a  - Hewlett Packard HP7550A
  Time-out (seconds) : 20
  Port  : LPT1  LPT2  LPT3  COM1  COM2  PRN  AUX
  Baud Rate    :  300  600  1200  2400  4800  9600  19200
  Word Length  :  7  8
  Parity       :  Even  Odd  None
  Stop Bits    :  1  2
  Handshake    :  Hardware  Xon/Xoff  Enq/Ack
```

You should enter the settings as specified in your plotter's user manual.

Plotter Paper Size

Enter a number 1 through 8 to indicate the plotter paper size as shown in figure 28.10.

Pen Speed

Enter a plotter pen speed, in centimeters per second. The value must be between 1 and 100.

Plotter Pen Width

Enter the width of the pen you are using in your plotter. The range is 0.1 millimeters to 2.0 millimeters.

SmartWare II Pen Colors

The following two lines represent a table to indicate the relationship between the 16 SmartWare II colors and those drawn by your plotter. On the line labeled Pen Number, you should enter the number of the pen you would like to have used to represent the SmartWare II color immediately above on the previous line.

Communications

Select the type of hardware and the type of communications chip and protocol used. Normally, this will not change.

Computer/Keyboard

Select the correct computer type. Normally, this will not change.

Network

The available network options are shown in figure 28.13.

```
┌─ Network ─────────────────────────────────────────────────────┐
│ → 255files  - NO NETWORK--DOS 2.0-3.X (Limit of 255 open files)│
│   antts3p1  - DOS 3.1 Novell Advanced Netware 2.1 SFT Lvl 2 TTS│
│   antts3p2  - DOS 3.2 Novell Advanced Netware 2.1 SFT Lvl 2 TTS│
│   antts3p3  - DOS 3.3 Novell Advanced Netware 2.1 SFT Lvl 2 TTS│
│   net_3p1   - DOS 3.1 Compatible Network (20 Open Files)       │
│   net_3p2   - DOS 3.2 Compatible Network (255 Open Files)      │
│   net_3p3   - DOS 3.3 Compatible Network (254 Open Files)      │
│   net_n46   - DOS 3.1 (and up) Novell Netware Version 4.6      │
└────────────────────────────────────────────────────────────────┘
```

Fig. 28.13.

Network options.

If you are using SmartWare II on a single-user system, select the 255files option. This will allow you to open as many as 255 files simultaneously.

Once you have selected or changed your hardware preferences, press F10 to return to the Menu.

Macro Keys

The Tools Macros commands can be used to establish a set of keystrokes that can be issued by pressing just one key. This feature can be a great time-saver if you have to perform repetitive tasks. When you execute a macro, the commands are executed as though you were entering them from the keyboard, so you must be careful to be in the correct mode. If, for example, you are in the Text Entry mode of the Word Processor, you would not want to invoke a macro that executes commands without first switching to the Command mode.

Macro keys are defined separately by application module. You could, for example, assign one macro to Ctrl-Q in the Spreadsheet, and another macro to Ctrl-Q in the Word Processor. If, however, the same macro would work correctly in both modules, you are not required to create two different definitions.

When assigning a macro, make sure that you are not accidentally using a Quick Key that has already been defined for you. Although this does not create an error, it does reduce the selection of Quick keys that are available. For a complete list of the Quick keys by module, refer to Appendix A.

Creating a Macro

The easiest way to create a macro is to record your keystrokes as you type the exact series of keystrokes you want to store in the macro.

Select Tools Macros Remember command to begin the Recording mode. You are prompted:

```
Press key to define:
```

You need to enter a key that is to be used as the shorthand for the other keystrokes. Don't choose a commonly used key, such as A or B; use a Ctrl or Alt key combination that is not used for anything else in your application. You may want to try the key combination first just to make sure that it is not currently being used. To identify the key to define, press the key (or key combination), but don't press Enter. The Recording mode is now on.

Now proceed to execute the exact series of strokes you want in your macro. If it is important that you make sure that you are in either the Entry or Command mode, your first keystroke in the application should be one of the following:

    Alt-Y   Entry mode
    Alt-Z   Command mode

If you want to temporarily suspend the recording of your key strokes, use the Ctrl-F10 key; this same key combination will restart the recording. When you have completed recording the macro, return to the menu and execute the Tools Macros Finish command.

Editing A Macro

You can edit your macro, once you have recorded it, to remove any extra keystrokes you typed by mistake. Figure 28.14 shows the macro that was recorded to sum sets of five rows in a spreadsheet column.

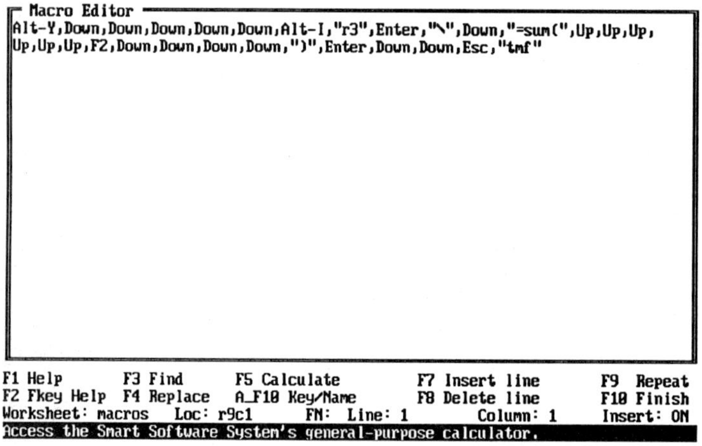

Fig. 28.14.

A recorded macro.

```
Macro Editor
Alt-Y,Down,Down,Down,Down,Down,Alt-I,"r3",Enter,"\",Down,"=sum(",Up,Up,Up,
Up,Up,Up,F2,Down,Down,Down,Down,")",Enter,Down,Down,Esc,"tmf"




F1 Help        F3 Find      F5 Calculate      F7 Insert line    F9 Repeat
F2 Fkey Help   F4 Replace   A_F10 Key/Name    F8 Delete line    F10 Finish
Worksheet: macros   Loc: r9c1      FN:  Line: 1      Column: 1    Insert: ON
Access the Smart Software System's general-purpose calculator.
```

Figure 28.15 shows a spreadsheet with two columns. The macro in figure 28.14 was used to alter column 2, which was originally identical to column 1.

Chapter 28: Tools: Commands Common to All Modules

```
        1        2       3      4      5      6      7
 1     1.00     1.00
 2     2.00     2.00
 3     3.00     3.00
 4     4.00     4.00
 5     5.00     5.00
 6     6.00   -------
 7     7.00    15.00
 8     8.00
 9     9.00     6.00
10    10.00     7.00
11    11.00     8.00
12    12.00     9.00
13    13.00    10.00
14    14.00   -------
15    15.00    40.00
16    16.00
17    17.00    11.00
18    18.00    12.00

Menu:  Sheet  Edit  File  Layout  Print  Graph  Tools  Window  Help  Remember
       Quit
Worksheet: macros    Loc: r1c1    FM: 0    Font: 0
```

Fig. 28.15.

Result of using a macro.

In figure 28.14, notice that keystrokes are separated by commas, and that the series can span multiple lines. Those entries which are literals or command keys are enclosed in double quotation marks ("). Cursor direction keys, the Enter key, and the Esc keys each have their own representative words in the macro language. Alt, Ctrl, and Function keys are represented without quotation marks.

Notice that the macro begins with an Alt-Y, to ensure that you are in the Entry mode. You should edit your macro to delete any mistakes, and to remove the final keystrokes that finish the macro (,"tmf").

Because the Tools Macros Finish command is used to terminate the Recording mode, you easily can record even difficult keystrokes, such as F10. You must return to the menu, however, to finish the recording.

Rather than recording your macros, you also can create them in the Macro Editor. If a macro does not currently exist for the key you select, you receive the message:

```
No macro defined for that key — Continue (y/n)
```

Be sure to follow the same format as in the recorded macros.

Clearing Macros

To clear one or all macros from memory, issue the command Tools Macros Clear. You are prompted:

```
One    All
```

Move the highlight block to indicate your choice and press Enter, or press *O* or *A*. If you select one macro, you are prompted:

```
Press key of macro to remove:
```

When you press the proper key sequence, the macro is removed from memory. If you have saved your macro definitions in a file, the macro is not automatically erased from the file.

If you elect to clear all macros, you are prompted:

    Clear all macros (y/n)

You should answer Y if you really want to clear all your macros from memory.

Viewing Macros

To see a list of the active macros you have defined, issue the Tools Macros View command. An example is shown in figure 28.16.

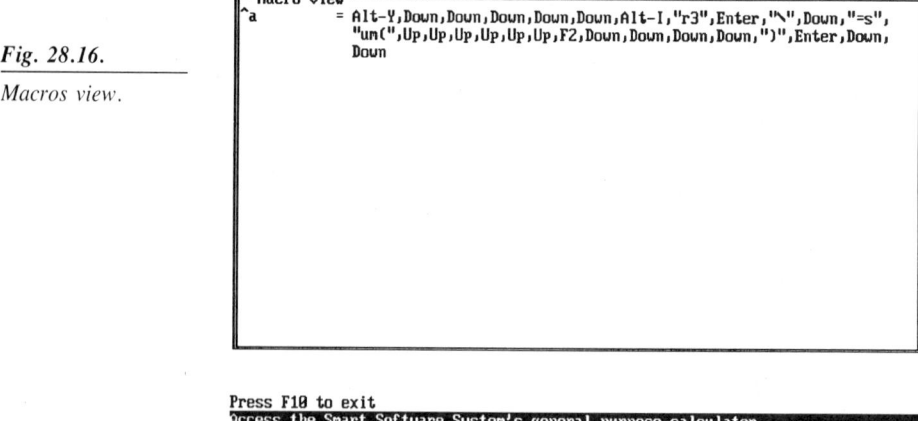

Fig. 28.16.

Macros view.

To return to the command level, press Esc or F10.

Saving Macros

After you have defined a set of macros during one session, you can save them for use in subsequent sessions. To do so, issue the Tools Macros Save command. You are prompted:

    Enter a macro filename:

Type a name under which to save the macros. At the completion of the command, the macros in memory are written to a disk file; the macros in memory remain as they were. The macro file has an extension of .MAC, regardless of the module in which it was created. If the file already exists, you are asked if you want to overwrite it.

To delete an individual macro definition from the MAC file, load the macro file and execute the Tools Macros Clear command to remove the one you no longer need. Now save the macros into the original file again; the macros in memory will overlay the macros in the disk file, minus the one you just cleared.

Loading Macros

To retrieve macro definitions you have saved in a file, execute the Tools Macros Load command. A pop-up menu displays the names of the macro files in the current subdirectory; select the file you want to use and press Enter.

You can load several macro files in succession and add to the set of macros stored in memory. If a later macro file contains a definition for a macro already in memory, the second occurrence will take precedence, and replace the first. There will, however, be no warning about this.

Erasing Saved Macros

No explicit command is used to delete macros files from your disk. You can use the Tools File Erase command to accomplish the task. The file extension of a macro file is .MAC. (For a complete list of file extensions, refer to Appendix B.) All macro files, regardless of the current module, have an extension of .MAC, thus allowing you to use the same macros in different modules.

Creating New Fonts

The Tools New-Font command is used to create font files from the font outlines supplied with the SmartWare II system. If you want a new size, slant (italics or normal), or weight (bold or normal), you can use one of the typeface outlines as a template for the creation of a new font.

To understand how this is accomplished, a few words about fonts, typefaces, internal, and rasterized fonts are appropriate. No matter which printer(s) you selected at the time you installed SmartWare II, there is at least one resident font in the printer if it is a dot matrix or laser printer. (The daisy-wheel or other formed-character printers are not covered in this discussion, because of their lack of graphics capability.)

At the very least, every printer has a standard resident font. When the signal is sent from your printer to print the letter *A* in the standard font, the arrangement of the tiny dots that make up the letter is already stored in read only memory in the printer. The computer does not have to calculate the location of each dot.

In addition to the standard font, many printers have other resident fonts, such as italics, letter quality, or even script. Because you identify your printer by manufacturer and model when you install the system, the list of resident fonts is available to the SmartWare II system. Whenever possible, resident fonts will be used rather than using your computer to construct each letter dot by dot. Resident fonts can be printed in the Draft mode of the Word Processor, for example.

In addition to the printer's standard resident fonts, several other fonts are offered with the SmartWare II system. These other fonts can be printed without being resident in the printer because they are drawn by the computer, dot by dot. This process of drawing the individual dots of a letter is called *rasterization*. In rasterization, a typeface or font outline (supplied with SmartWare II) is used as the template to generate a specific font. In typesetting terms, a font represents not only the shape of the letter, but also the size, slant, and weight.

You can rasterize a font that is not internal in your printer in two ways. One way saves space on your hard disk, the other saves time.

As you construct a Word Processor document, you can specify different fonts to be used at the time of printing. (Refer to the Word Processor Layout Font commands to find out how to select, change, and edit fonts). When you print your document, your computer will rasterize the new fonts needed for that printing. The rasterized fonts are not saved; if you print the document again immediately, the same fonts must be rasterized again. For occasional usage, rasterizing the needed fonts "on the fly" is probably preferable. A reference in the SmartWare II system to a "filled-area font" pertains to a font which is rasterized as it is needed.

If you need to use the same fonts repeatedly, and if you have enough space on your hard disk, you can prerasterize the fonts you intend to use most frequently. When you use them, your computer does not draw the fonts, but simply selects from among the inventory of existing characters, and sends them to the printer. The Tools New-Font command is used to create these prerasterized fonts.

One final word about fonts. Some printers have font cartridges containing prerasterized fonts in ROM. The SmartWare II system supports many of these cartridges for the most popular printers. Your printer installation must specify not only the manufacturer and model of printer, but the font cartridges you will be using. When the appropriate driver and cartridge are installed, the cartridge fonts are selected as if they were internal to the printer.

Many of the newer laser printers support downloadable fonts; these are prerasterized fonts which are stored in volatile memory in your printer. You must copy them or install them from your computer each time you turn it on and want to use these software fonts. Because SmartWare II printer support is provided at the hardware level only, downloadable fonts are not supported in SmartWare II.

To make a variation of an existing font, or prerasterize a new font, select the command Tools New-Font. The first set of options is as follows:

    Normal   Sideways

The Normal orientation is sometimes called *portrait*, because the longer side of the paper is vertical, as you usually see in a portrait. The Sideways orientation is frequently referred to as *landscape*. For best results, use the 12 or 9 point standard typefaces. If you select Normal, you can specify any other fonts.

The font selector menu (see fig. 28.17) provides a list of options.

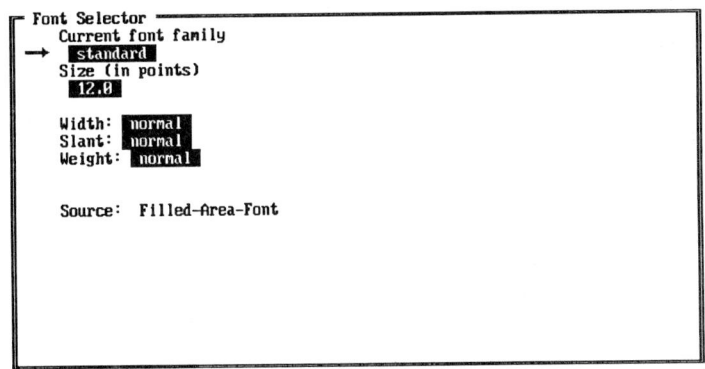

Fig. 28.17.

Font selector menu.

The name of the current font family or typeface is displayed on the first line. To display a pop-up window of alternate typefaces, press F6. Note that in figure 28.18 there are 13 typefaces provided with SmartWare II.

To select a typeface to use as the template for the font you want to prerasterize, move the cursor to the appropriate name and press Enter.

Select the size (height) of the font you want, in points. There are 72 points to the vertical inch, so a character that is 18 points is one fourth of an inch high. If the point size is too small, you will not be able to read the printed text. If the point size is too large, the SmartWare II system may not be able to prerasterize it. Point sizes must be between 1.0 and 99.9.

With your cursor at the size field, you can simply type a new point size. If the F6 option is listed at the bottom of the screen, press this function key to display a list of sizes already created for this font.

The Width, Slant, and Weight of the selected typeface are displayed in the center of the screen. Not all fonts are available in every variation. For some typeface selections, there is a choice of weights, or thickness of the letters. The Sans Serif

Fig. 28.18.

Alternate typefaces.

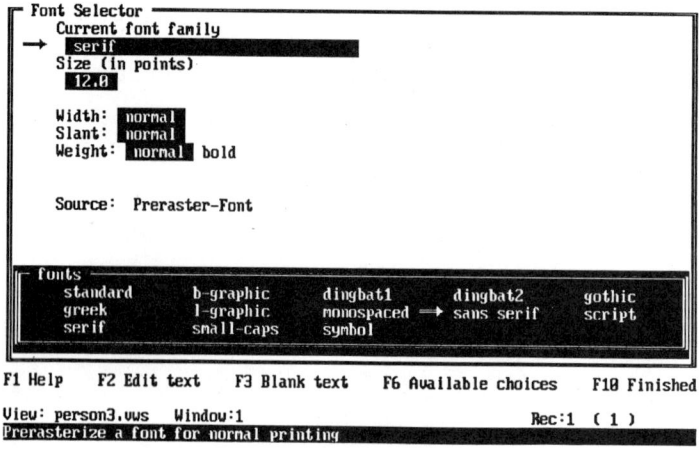

font, for example, is available in both Normal and Bold weights. Where options are available, you can move the highlight block to the one you want.

The last line on-screen in figure 28.17 shows the source of the typeface. If you have already prerasterized the font, the source will be Preraster-Font. If the template has not been rasterized already, the source will read Filled-Area-Font. The display of the source depends on your choice of typeface and point size, and whether you have created a preraster font file.

Press F10 to proceed with the rasterization process. A message on the command line reads:

   Rasterizing character *ccc* of *ttt*

In this message, *ccc* is the character number, which increments as the process takes place. The *ttt* shows you the total number of characters to be rasterized.

Once the rasterization is complete, a disk file is created which contains the exact specifications for each character in the font. (The file is created in your home directory, not in the SmartII directory; you can move it later.) When you print the document that contains the font, the complete set of dots for each character is sent to your printer. Remember you must print your document in the Enhanced mode in the Word Processor and the Spreadsheet. You can use the Draft mode only when printing fonts that are internal to your printer.

Editing Text Files

A general purpose text editor is available by executing Tools Text-Editor. You are prompted:

   Enter the filename:

A pop-up menu shows the names of the files in the current subdirectory with an extension of .TXT. If you want to edit one of these files, use the cursor to point to the name of the file and press Enter. You can also type the name of the file on the command line and press Enter. If the extension of the file you want to edit is .TXT, you do not need to specify the extension; if the file has a different extension, you must type it. Specify the full path if the file is in a subdirectory other than the current one.

The following function keys are available in the Text Editor:

F1 Help.

F2 Toggle between function key menus at the bottom of the screen.

F3 Find a text string.

F4 Replace one text string with another. The replacement can be either Conditional or Global.

    If you specify conditional, you are prompted:

```
Replace (y/n)
```

    Enter Y to perform the replacement. Only one replacement is performed at a time; to continue throughout the file, press F9 to repeat the replacement command. A global replacement affects the entire file, regardless of your cursor position; a conditional replacement will begin at the current cursor position toward the end of the file.

F5 Calculate. An expression on the first line of the file can be calculated and the result displayed on the status line. Any variables or functions can be included in the expression.

F7 Insert a line before the current line. If you have previously deleted a line with the F8 key, the deleted line is inserted at the cursor position. This is one way to duplicate lines. If you have not deleted a line previously, a blank line is inserted.

F8 Delete the current line.

F9 Repeat the last command.

F10 Save the work to the current file and return to the menu. Note that there is no opportunity to supply an alternative file name.

Alt-F2 Delete all data in the editor, beginning at the top of the file. This command does not depend on the current cursor position.

Alt-F3 Read a text file into the editor at the current cursor position. You must specify the extension, even for a .TXT file.

Ctrl-Y Delete the current line without storing the line in the buffer.

Alt-G   Go to a line. You are prompted to supply the line number. Every line has an implied number, even though it is not shown in the text area. The number of the current line is shown on the status line of the text editor.

Alt-P   Print the file.

Alt-C   Copy the marked area into the copy buffer. When you press Alt-C, additional function key choices are available:

    F2   Drop the anchor to mark the beginning of the area
    F10   Finished

To copy a marked area, position the cursor anywhere on the first line to be copied, and press F2. Then move the cursor down to the last line to be copied, and press Enter. All the lines in the boundaries are inserted into the buffer.

Alt-I   To insert the contents of the buffer into a new area of your file, position the cursor on the line before which you want to insert the text and press Alt-I.

Alt-D   To delete several lines of your text file, press Alt-D and follow the same procedure as with the Alt-C: position the cursor anywhere on the first line to be deleted, and press F2. Then move the cursor down to the last line to be deleted, and press Enter. All lines in the boundaries are inserted into the buffer.

To move several lines, first delete them with the Alt-D, and then insert them in the new position with the Alt-I.

Alt-W   Write the current file (or blocked portion) to a new file. Use Alt-W to write your entire file to a new file. If you block a portion of the text when you use Alt-C or Alt-D, you can write just the highlighted lines. The output file must not already exist, or you will receive the following message:

    Error creating file

Alt-P   Print the current file.

Only true ASCII text files can be edited with the Tools Text-Editor. If you were to type your file at the DOS operating system level and you saw all kinds of funny characters and smiling faces, and your computer beeped at you unmercifully, this would be your indication that the file was not pure ASCII, and thus not able to be edited with the Text-Editor.

Using the Calculator

The SmartWare II Calculator is accessed with the Tools Calculator command, or the Alt-K Quick key. The default calculator screen is shown in figure 28.19.

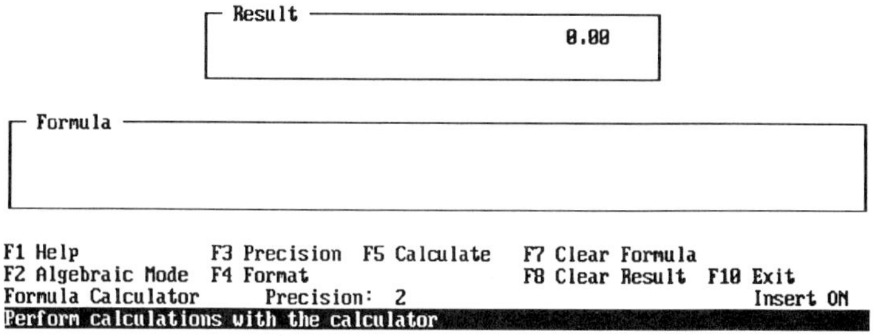

Fig. 28.19.

SmartWare II calculator.

The calculator has both a Formula mode and an Algebraic mode. To reference fields from the current database or spreadsheet, project or system variables, or to use any of the SmartWare II functions, use the Formula mode. Type your formula in the formula window and press F5 to display the result in the result window. An example of the use of the Formula mode is shown in figure 28.20.

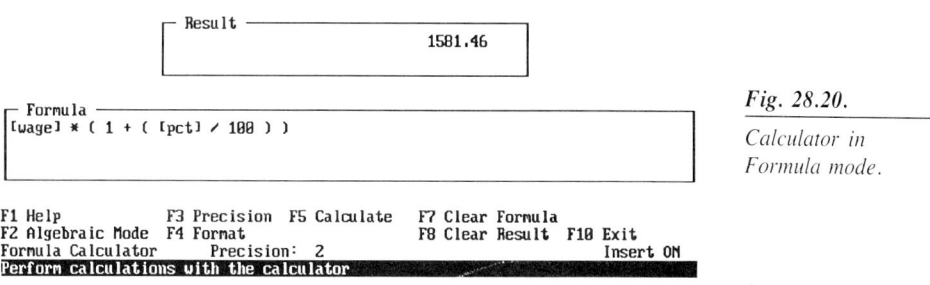

Fig. 28.20.

Calculator in Formula mode.

You can use the following function keys in the SmartWare II calculator:

- F1 Help.
- F2 Switch to Algebraic mode.
- F3 Set the decimal Precision. The range is 0 to 15 decimal places.
- F4 Change the format of the display from decimal, to scientific, to hexadecimal, to octal, and back to decimal.
- F5 Display the results of the calculation in the result window.

F7   Clear the formula from the formula window; retain the result in the result window.

F8   Clear the result from the result window; retain the formula in the formula window.

F10 Exit to the application level.

If you want to use the calculator just like a pocket calculator, switch to the Algebraic mode by pressing the F2 key. A screen similar to figure 28.21 is displayed:

```
┌─ Result ─────────────────────┐
│                     63360.00 │
└──────────────────────────────┘
```

Fig. 28.21.

Calculator in Algebraic mode.

```
F1 Help           F3 Precision  F5 Mem Store   F7 Inverse      F9 Change sign
F2 Formula Mode   F4 Format     F6 Mem Recall  F8 Clear Result F10 Exit
Algebraic Calculator    Precision: 2    Memory 0.00
Perform calculations with the calculator
```

In the Algebraic mode, enter each number, followed by the arithmetic symbol (+, −, /, or *). Press either the Enter key or the equal sign to complete the series. If you know the number of yards in a mile (1,760), for example, and knowing that there are 3 feet to a yard and 12 inches to a foot, you can calculate the number of inches in a mile by entering the following keystrokes:

1760* 3* 12=

(or Enter, instead of =). Note the use of the following function keys when you are in the Algebraic mode:

F1   Help.

F2   Switch to Formula mode.

F3   Set the decimal Precision. The range is 0 to 15 decimal places.

F4   Change the format of the display from decimal, to scientific, to hexadecimal, to octal, and back to decimal.

F5   Store the current results in the calculator memory.

F6   Retrieve the value of the calculator memory.

F7   Change the current result to its inverse. This is what you would get if you divided the current result into 1.

F8   Clear the current result.

F9   Change sign of the current result.

F10   Exit.

You can invoke the SmartWare II calculator from not only the command level, but also from the Entry mode of the Spreadsheet or Word Processor. (The Database uses the Field Text editor, Alt-T.) Once you return to the application module, use Ctrl-C to retrieve the most recent calculator result and insert the value in the cell, document, or field.

Chapter Summary

The Tools commands provide commonly used capabilities that you can call from any SmartWare II module. Some of the Tools are substitutes for their DOS equivalents; others pertain to just the SmartWare II environment. Once you have mastered the Tools commands in one module, you will know how to use the same commands in every module.

Quick Keys

Many of the commands in SmartWare II can be executed using Quick keys. Mastery of these Quick keys will increase your efficiency in using the system. Particularly in the Word Processor and the Spreadsheet modules, using the Quick keys can be very beneficial because they can be executed while you are in the Enter mode.

Frequently, you must use either the Alt or the Ctrl keys along with an action key. For best results, do not try to press the keys simultaneously. Just press the Alt or Ctrl key and then press the action key.

This appendix lists the Quick key, the executed command (if any), and an explanation of the action.

System-Wide Quick Keys

You can use these Quick keys throughout the system.

Quick Key	Executed Command	Explanation
Alt-K	Tools Calculator	Activate Formula Calculator
Alt-O	Tools Directory Display	Display a list of file names, with extension, date, time, and size. The display may be sorted
Alt-X	—	Edit the most recent command

653

Quick Key	Executed Command	Explanation
Alt-Z	—	Return immediately to the Command mode. Can be used from the Entry mode of the Word Processor or the Spreadsheet, or can be used to escape from a command option list
Ctrl-O	Tools Os	Exit to the DOS operating system temporarily and invoke a secondary command processor
Ctrl-Z	—	Cancel the operation of a project file or many commands
Ctrl-F1	—	Display product serial number, disk, and random access memory remaining
Ctrl-F10	—	Suspend or resume the Remember mode during the recording of a macro
F1	Help	Provide context sensitive help information
F2	—	Display the next Quick key menu on the control lines at the bottom of your screen
F8	Remember Execute	Execute a project file
F9	—	Repeat the execution of the previous command
F10	Quit	Quit to DOS or begin a different SmartWare II module
Shift-F10	—	Suspend a macro temporarily so that the keystroke reverts to its original value

Spreadsheet Quick Keys

You use these Quick keys in the Spreadsheet module.

Quick Key	Executed Command	Explanation
Alt-A	File Display Active	Display a list of active worksheets
Alt-B	Edit Blank	Blank rows, columns, a block, or entire worksheet

Appendix A: Quick Keys

Quick Key	Executed Command	Explanation
Alt-C	Edit Copy	Copy text, values or formulas down, across or from a block
Alt-D	Edit Delete	Delete block, columns, or rows
Alt-E	Edit Edit-Cell	Edit the current cell
Alt-F	—	Edit the current cell, using the full-screen formula editor
Alt-G	Graph	Define, undefine, or generate a graph
Alt-H	Window Split Horizontal	Split current window horizontally
Alt-I	Edit Insert	Insert new columns, rows, or a block
Alt-J	Layout Justify	Change the justification of existing cells
Alt-L	File Load	Open a worksheet for processing
Alt-M	Edit Move	Move text, values, or formulas down, across, or from a block
Alt-N	File Newname	Assign a new name to the current worksheet
Alt-P	Print	Print text, formulas, map, or a report
Alt-Q	Layout Format	Change the format of values or numeric formulas
Alt-R	—	Repeat the most recent Sheet Find command
Alt-S	File Save	Save a worksheet to disk
Alt-T	Window Titles	Fix or drop title areas
Alt-U	File Unload	Unload a worksheet from memory
Alt-V	Window Split Vertical	Split the current window vertically
Alt-W	Window Close	Close the current window
Alt-Y	—	Access Entry mode. Similar to pressing Esc at the command level

Quick Key	Executed Command	Explanation
Alt-Z	—	Access the Command mode. Similar to pressing Esc at the Entry mode
Alt-F7	Sheet Goto Window X	Go to the previous sequentially numbered window
Alt-F8	Sheet Goto Window X	Go to the next sequentially numbered window
Ctrl-B	Layout Set-Font Select	Toggle on/off the bold attribute of newly entered text
Ctrl-C	—	Insert computation resulting from the Tools Calculator command
Ctrl-G	Graphics Generate	Execute the most recent Graphics Generate command
Ctrl-L	Sslock Cell or Ssunlock Cell	Toggle the lock or unlock condition of the current cell
Ctrl-U	Layout Set-Font Select	Toggle on/off the underscore attribute of newly entered text
Ctrl-End	—	Go to lower edge of worksheet
Ctrl-Home	—	Go to Row 1, Column 1
F3	Sheet Find	Find a calculation error, empty or highlighted cell, value, or text in your worksheet or in a block
F4	Sheet Goto	Go to a worksheet, cell, window, or "other"
F5	Recalc	Recalculate necessary portions of the worksheet; unchanged worksheet areas are not recalculated
F6	Layout Set-Font Select	Select font for newly entered text
F7	Window Zoom	Enlarge current window to fill the screen
Shift-F5	Recalc	Recalculate the entire worksheet, whether or not required

Word Processor Quick Keys

The following Quick keys make your word processing chores easier.

Quick Key	Executed Command	Explanation
Alt –	—	Purge contents of the Copy or Delete buffers
Alt-A	File Display-active	Display a list of active documents
Alt-B	Layout Ruler Insert Current ''ac''	Insert a centered ruler for the current paragraph
Alt-C	Edit Copy	Copy document text
Alt-E	Layout Newpage	Insert or remove a fixed page break, toggle the automatic pagination of your document, or insert soft page breaks
Alt-F	Document References Footnote	Insert or modify a footnote
Alt-G	Graph	Insert, remove or view a graph
Alt-H	Window Split Horizontal	Split current window horizontally into two windows
Alt-I	Edit Copy [] to *	Insert the contents of the copy buffer at the current location
Alt-L	File Load	Open a document or text file for processing
Alt-M	Edit Move	Move document text
Alt-N	File Newname	Assign a new name to the current document
Alt-P	Print	Print or merge a document; establish or preset options
Alt-Q	Edit Undelete	Insert the contents of the delete buffer at the current location
Alt-R	—	Repeat the most recent Document, Find, or Edit Replace command

Quick Key	Executed Command	Explanation
Alt-S	File Save	Save the current document
Alt-T	—	Transpose the two characters preceding cursor; Entry mode only
Alt-U	File Unload	Unload the current document
Alt-V	Window Split Vertical	Split current window vertically into two windows
Alt-W	Window Close	Close the current window
Alt-Y	—	Access Entry mode
Alt-F1	Tools Preferences Wordprocessor	Change Word Processor preferences
Alt-F2	Document Dictionary	Erase custom dictionary, hyphenate the current paragraph, Spellcheck portions of your document, or invoke the thesaurus
Alt-F3	Document Dictionary Spellcheck Screen Word	Check the spelling of the current word
Alt-F4	Document Dictionary Thesaurus Word	Check the current word in the thesaurus
Alt-F5	Document Dictionary Spellcheck Screen Remainder	Check the spelling of the remainder of the document, beginning with the current cursor position
Alt-F6	Document Dictionary Spellcheck Screen Document	Check the spelling of the entire document
Alt-F7	Document Goto Window X	Go to the previous sequentially numbered window
Alt-F8	Document Goto Window X	Go to the next sequentially numbered window
Ctrl -	—	Insert a soft hyphen
Ctrl-B	—	Begin or end Bold for new text
Ctrl-C	—	Insert computation resulting from the Document Math or the Tools Calculator commands

Appendix A: Quick Keys **659**

Quick Key	Executed Command	Explanation
Ctrl-E	Document Columns Edit Add Entry	Start a new entry in a multiple column area (MCA)
Ctrl-F	—	Move cursor left one word
Ctrl-G	—	Move cursor right one word
Ctrl-J	—	Mark the beginning of a merge variable. Must be in Enter mode
Ctrl-K	—	Mark the end of a merge variable. Must be in Enter mode.
Ctrl-P	Edit Delete Paragraph	Delete the current paragraph
Ctrl-S	Edit Delete Sentence	Delete the current sentence
Ctrl-T	—	Insert an indent tab. Remainder of text in the paragraph aligns with the tab, rather than the left margin. Must be in Enter mode
Ctrl-U	—	Begin or end underscore of newly entered text
Ctrl-W	Edit Delete Word	Delete the current word
Ctrl-X	—	Insert a hard space
Ctrl-Y	Edit Delete Line	Delete the current line. Deleted text is inserted into the delete buffer
Ctrl-PgDn	—	Move cursor to the first character of next paragraph
Ctrl-PgUp	—	Move cursor to the first character of previous paragraph
Ctrl-End	—	Go to end of document
Ctrl-Home	—	Go to beginning of document
Ctrl-F3	—	Go to previous column in an MCA
Ctrl-F4	—	Go to the next column in an MCA
Ctrl-F5	—	Move cursor to the first character of current sentence or to previous sentence depending on location of cursor

Quick Key	Executed Command	Explanation
Ctrl-F6	—	Move cursor to the first character of the next sentence
Ctrl-F7	Layout Ruler Edit	Edit the current, default or named ruler
Ctrl-F8	Layout Ruler Insert	Insert the current, default, or named ruler prior to current paragraph
Ctrl-F9	—	Turn on the Character Insert mode
Ctrl-F10	—	Turn off Character Insert mode; not a toggle
F3	Document Find	Locate a string of characters
F4	Document Goto	Go to a window, document, marker, or location
F5	Edit Replace	Find a string and replace it with another
F6	Layout Font Select	Select a font for new text
F7	Window Zoom	Enlarge the current window to fill the screen
Shift-F3	Layout Font Bold	Insert or remove boldface from existing text
Shift-F4	Layout Font Underscore	Insert or remove underscore from existing text
Shift-F5	Document References Index	Add, Edit, Generate, or Remove an index item
Shift-F6	Document References Index Add Word	Add the current word as a primary index item
Shift-F7	Document References TOC	Generate a Table of Contents, or add or remove an item
Shift-F8	Document References Paragraph-number	Insert or remove paragraph number
Tab	—	Insert a tab

Database Quick Keys

You can use the following Quick keys in the Database module.

Quick Key	Executed Command	Explanation
Alt-A	File Display-active	Display a list of active views
Alt-B	Data Browse All	Activate/deactivate the Browse mode for all fields in the view
Alt-C	File Create	Create a view
Alt-D	Data Delete Record	Delete or undelete current record
Alt-E	Data Enter	Enter new records
Alt-F	Data Utilities Information	Display specifications about the current view and the fields
Alt-G	Order Key	Add, delete, or rebuild a key
Alt-H	Window Split Horizontal	Split current window horizontally into two windows
Alt-I or Alt-Y	Data Update	Update the current record
Alt-J	Order Sort	Create, modify, execute, or remove a sort definition
Alt-L	File Load	Load a custom or standard view
Alt-M	Tools Macro	Clear, remember, load, save, view, edit, or finish a macro definition
Alt-N	Data Relate	Create, modify, execute, or remove a relate definition
Alt-P	Print	Print the current record, view, or a report
Alt-Q	Data Query	Create, modify, execute, or remove a query definition
Alt-R	—	Repeat the most recent Data Find command
Alt-S	File Save	Save the databases in the current view

Quick Key	Executed Command	Explanation
Alt-T	Data Transact	Create, modify, execute, or remove a transaction definition
Alt-U	File Unload	Unload one or more views
Alt-V	Window Split Vertical	Split current window vertically into two windows
Alt-W	Window Close	Close the current window
Alt-F7	Data Goto Window Previous	Go to the previous sequentially numbered window
Alt-F8	Data Goto Window Next	Go to the next sequentially numbered window
Ctrl-End	—	Go to the last logical record of the view
Ctrl-Home	—	Go to the first logical record of the view
F3	Data Find	Find a field or other view item
F4	Data Goto	Go to a Page, Record, Table, View, or Window
F5	—	Go to the previous record
F6	—	Go to the next record
F7	Window Zoom	Enlarge the current window to fill the screen

Communications Quick Keys

The following Quick key short cuts will help you while you are in the Communications module.

Quick Key	Executed Command	Explanation
Alt-A	Connection Answer	Answer an incoming call from a remote computer
Alt-B	—	Signal a Break; ANSI communications default
Alt-C	Data Output	Send one or more characters to the communications port

Appendix A: Quick Keys

Quick Key	Executed Command	Explanation
Alt-D	Connection Dial Carrier Number	Dial the phone number (through the modem) to originate a call to a remote system
Alt-E	Data Format	Define or undefine a file for conversion of text
Alt-F	Tools File	Copy, erase, print, or rename an ASCII file
Alt-G	Data Get	Insert the next character or line into a project processing variable
Alt-H	Connection Hangup	Terminate the telephone connection
Alt-I	Remember Tools Input-screen	Define, load, or undefine an input screen
Alt-J	Set-terminal Keyboard	Define or undefine a keyboard definition file
Alt-L	Set-Terminal Settings Load	Load a communications profile
Alt-M	Data Match	Pause until the specified character is received
Alt-N	Tools Macros	Clear, remember, load, save, view, edit, or finish a macro definition
Alt-P	Set-terminal Settings	Define, undefine, load, edit, or save a communications profile
Alt-Q	Data Xfer-time	Estimate the time to transmit a specified file
Alt-R	Data Receive	Receive a text or binary file from a remote computer
Alt-S	Set-Terminal Settings Edit	Edit the current communications profile
Alt-T	Data Transmit	Send a text or binary file to a remote computer
Alt-U	Set-terminal Duplex	Set your computer for either half or full duplex

Quick Key	Executed Command	Explanation
Alt-V	Data Capture Buffer View	View the contents of the capture buffer
Alt-W	Tools Text-Editor	Edit an ASCII file
F3	—	Switch between communications and Command mode; ANSI communications default
F4	Set-terminal Goto	Switch between voice and data communications
F5	Data Capture Buffer Begin or End	Toggle on/off capturing screen text to the buffer
F6	Data Capture Printer Begin or End	Toggle on/off capturing screen text to the printer
F7	Data Capture File Begin or End	Toggle on/off capturing screen text to a file

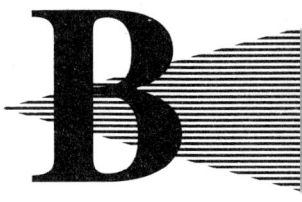

File Extensions

The SmartWare II system relies heavily on the use of extensions for file identification. Most commands that prompt for a file name do not require you to enter an extension, because the proper extension is always associated with the command.

In the list of file extensions in this appendix, the modules are identified as follows:

Module Code	Name
MM	Main Menu
SS	Spreadsheet
WP	Word Processor
DB	Database
CM	Communications
All	Used by all modules
System	Used by the SmartWare II system

Following is a list of the file extensions used in SmartWare II.

Extension	Module	Description
AIF	System	Application Interface File (program overlay)
ASC	SS	Export file in ASCII format
BDC	WP	Backup Document
BDF	All	Backup Options Definition
BFR	DB	Backup Report Definition
BFS	DB	Backup Sort Definition
BFT	DB	Backup Transaction Definition
BFW	DB	Backup Cross-Tab Definition
BFX	DB	Backup Relate Definition
BKY	CM	Backup Keyboard Definition
BP0	MM	Backup Project Source
BP1	SS	Backup Project Source
BP2	WP	Backup Project Source
BP3	DB	Backup Project Source

Extension	Module	Description
BP4	CM	Backup Project Source
BTX	All	Backup Text
BVS	DB	Backup Standard View
BVW	DB	Backup Custom View
BWS	SS	Backup Worksheet
CDV	CM	Communications Driver
CSF	CM	Send Format
DAS	WP	Document Automatic Save (Default Extension)
DAT	All	Text file, usually in the Smart format
DB	DB	Database
DBQ	DB	Query Definition Backup
DEF	All	Options Definition
DFQ	DB	Query Definition
DFR	DB	Report Definition
DFS	DB	Sort Definition
DFT	DB	Transaction Definition
DFW	DB	Cross-Tab Definition
DFX	DB	Relate Definition
DIF	SS	Document Interchange Format
DOC	WP	Document
DSC	System	Printer Descriptor
EXC	WP	Dictionary Exception
EXE	System	Program
GCF	SS	Graph Composite Definition
GDF	SS	Graph Definition
GDV	SS	Graphics Driver
GMF	SS	Graph Metafile
HDV	System	Hardware Driver
HUD	WP	Dictionary
HYP	WP	Dictionary
IDX	DB	Index
IFF	All	Temporary Send File
IS0	MM	Input Screen
IS1	SS	Input Screen
IS2	WP	Input Screen
IS3	DB	Input Screen
IS4	CM	Input Screen
KEY	DB	Key File
KEY	CM	Keyboard Definition
LEX	WP	Thesaurus
LSC	System	"Like" Printer Descriptor
MAC	All	Macro File
MBK	All	Backup Macro File
MDV	CM	Modem Definition
MNU	System	Menu Keyword

MSG	System	Introductory Message
NDV	System	Network or File Driver
PDV	System	Printer Driver
PF0	MM	Project File—Source
PF1	SS	Project File—Source
PF2	WP	Project File—Source
PF3	DB	Project File—Source
PF4	CM	Project File—Source
PIX	DB	Physical Record Index
PRN	SS	Print File
PRT	DB	Print File
PS	System	PostScript Prolog
PSC	System	Plotter Descriptor
RDF	SS	Report Definition
RF0	MM	Project File—Object
RF1	SS	Project File—Object
RF2	WP	Project File—Object
RF3	DB	Project File—Object
RF4	CM	Project File—Object
SDV	System	Text Screen Driver
SFF	System	Screen Fonts
THS	WP	Thesaurus
TMP	All	Temporary File
TXT	All	Text File
UCP	CM	Communications Profile
UDC	WP	Custom Dictionary
USR	System	User Registration
VUD	WP	Temporary Custom Dictionary
VW	DB	Custom View
VWS	DB	Standard View
WKS	SS	Lotus 1-2-3 Worksheet (Version 1)
WK1	SS	Lotus 1-2-3 Worksheet (Version 2)
WS	SS	Worksheet
$$$	SY	Temporary Network Backup

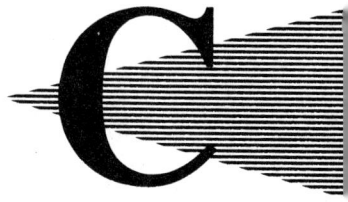

Command Comparison: Smart 3.10 versus SmartWare II

This appendix provides a translation table between the commands in Smart 3.10 and SmartWare II. In some cases, certain supplementary words or phrases that make up the complete command are automatically inserted by the command processor when you execute commands manually. In project files, however, you must be sure to include these contributory words.

The Communications Module

Smart 3.10 Command	SmartWare II Command
ANSWER	CONNECTION ANSWER
AUTOHELP	None. Set Autohelp On or Off in the menu offered by the command TOOLS PREFERENCES GLOBAL.
BEEP	None. Set Beep On or Off in the menu offered by the command TOOLS PREFERENCES GLOBAL.
CAPTURE BUFFER BEGIN	DATA CAPTURE BUFFER BEGIN
CAPTURE BUFFER CLEAR	DATA CAPTURE BUFFER CLEAR
CAPTURE BUFFER END	DATA CAPTURE BUFFER END
CAPTURE BUFFER SAVE filename.ext	DATA CAPTURE BUFFER SAVE filename.ext
CAPTURE BUFFER VIEW	DATA CAPTURE BUFFER VIEW

Smart 3.10 Command	SmartWare II Command
CAPTURE FILE BEGIN filename.ext	DATA CAPTURE FILE BEGIN filename.ext
CAPTURE FILE END	DATA CAPTURE FILE END
CAPTURE PRINTER BEGIN	DATA CAPTURE PRINTER BEGIN
CAPTURE PRINTER END	DATA CAPTURE PRINTER END
CONFIDENCE level 1-5	None. Concept of confidence levels does not exist.
DIAL CARRIER NUMBER Phone-Number	CONNECTION DIAL CARRIER NUMBER Phone-Number. Although the word "NUMBER" is inserted automatically by the command processor, you must be sure to include it in a project file statement.
DIAL VOICE NUMBER Phone-Number	CONNECTION DIAL VOICE NUMBER Phone-Number. Although the word "NUMBER" is inserted automatically by the command processor, you must be sure to include it in a project file statement.
DIRECTORY file specification	TOOLS DIRECTORY DISPLAY file specification
DISPLAY BLACK/WHITE	None. You can select a new Text Screen or Graphics screen from the Tools Preferences Hardware menu, but you may need to exit SmartWare for the change to work.
DISPLAY COLOR	None. You can select a new Text Screen or Graphics screen from the Tools Preferences Hardware menu, but you may need to exit SmartWare for the change to work.
DISPLAY GRAPHICS	None. You can select a new Text Screen or Graphics screen from the Tools Preferences Hardware menu, but you may need to exit SmartWare for the change to work.
DUPLEX FULL	SET-TERMINAL DUPLEX FULL
DUPLEX HALF	SET-TERMINAL DUPLEX HALF

Smart 3.10 Command	SmartWare II Command
EXECUTE project-file	REMEMBER EXECUTE project-file {IN-MEMORY/FROM-FILE }
FILE COPY file1.ext TO file2.ext	TOOLS FILE COPY file1.ext TO file2.ext. At the command level, don't type TO; it is inserted automatically by the command processor. In a project file, however, you must use TO to separate the file names.
FILE ERASE filename.ext	TOOLS FILE ERASE filename.ext
FILE NEW-DIRECTORY \directory	TOOLS DIRECTORY NEW-DIRECTORY \directory
FILE RENAME file1.ext TO file2.ext	TOOLS FILE RENAME file1.ext TO file2.ext. At the command level, don't type TO; it is inserted automatically by the command processor.
FILTERS CAPTURE	SET-TERMINAL FILTERS CAPTURE
FILTERS TERMINAL	SET-TERMINAL FILTERS TERMINAL
FORMAT DEFINE Def-Name	DATA FORMAT DEFINE Def-Name
FORMAT UNDEFINE Def-Name	DATA FORMAT UNDEFINE Def-Name
F-CALCULATOR	TOOLS CALCULATOR
GET CHARACTER PARAMETER Parameter	DATA GET CHARACTER VARIABLE Variable
GET CHARACTER Standard-Variable	DATA GET CHARACTER VARIABLE Variable
GET CHARACTER VARIABLE User-Variable	DATA GET CHARACTER VARIABLE variable
GET LINE PARAMETER Parameter	DATA GET LINE VARIABLE variable
GET LINE Standard-Variable	DATA GET LINE VARIABLE Variable
GET LINE VARIABLE User-Variable	DATA GET LINE VARIABLE variable

Smart 3.10 Command	SmartWare II Command
GOTO CARRIER	SET-TERMINAL GOTO CARRIER
GOTO VOICE	SET-TERMINAL GOTO VOICE
HANGUP	CONNECTION HANGUP
HELP	HELP ABOUT-HELP
INPUT-SCREEN DEFINE filename	REMEMBER TOOLS INPUT-SCREEN DEFINE filename
INPUT-SCREEN LOAD filename	REMEMBER TOOLS INPUT-SCREEN LOAD filename
INPUT-SCREEN UNDEFINE filename	REMEMBER TOOLS INPUT-SCREEN UNDEFINE filename
KEYBOARD DEFINE Def-Name	SET-TERMINAL KEYBOARD DEFINE Def-Name
KEYBOARD UNDEFINE Def-Name	SET-TERMINAL KEYBOARD UNDEFINE Def-Name
MACRO CLEAR	TOOLS MACROS CLEAR ALL
MACRO DEFINE key	TOOLS MACROS EDIT or TOOLS MACROS REMEMBER
MACRO LOAD filename	TOOLS MACROS LOAD filename
MACRO REMOVE key	TOOLS MACROS CLEAR ONE
MACRO SAVE filename	TOOLS MACROS SAVE filename
MACRO VIEW	TOOLS MACROS VIEW
MATCH Character-String	DATA MATCH Character-String
OUTPUT Expression	DATA OUTPUT Expression
PAINT MAIN-WINDOW BORDER value	SET-TERMINAL PAINT STATUS-WINDOW BORDER FOREGROUND value
PAINT MAIN-WINDOW SETTINGS value	SET-TERMINAL PAINT STATUS-WINDOW SETTINGS FOREGROUND value
PAINT MAIN-WINDOW WINDOW value1 value2	SET-TERMINAL PAINT STATUS-WINDOW WINDOW BACKGROUND value1 FOREGROUND value2

Appendix C: Command Comparison: Smart 3.10 versus SmartWare II

Smart 3.10 Command	SmartWare II Command
PAINT TERMINAL-WINDOW value1 value2	SET-TERMINAL PAINT TERMINAL-WINDOW BACKGROUND value1 FOREGROUND value2
PARAMETERS	TOOLS PREFERENCES COMMUNICATIONS
PROFILE DEFINE Def-Name	SET-TERMINAL SETTINGS DEFINE Def-Name
PROFILE UNDEFINE Def-Name	SET-TERMINAL SETTINGS UNDEFINE Def-Name
RECEIVE TEXT-FILE filename.ext AFTER expression	DATA RECEIVE TEXT-FILE filename.ext AFTER expression. Although the word "AFTER" is inserted automatically by the command processor, you must be sure to include it in a project file statement.
RECEIVE XMODEM filename.ext	DATA RECEIVE XMODEM filename.ext
REMEMBER COMPILE LINE-NUMBERS Proj-Name	REMEMBER TOOLS COMPILE DEBUG Proj-Name
REMEMBER COMPILE NO-LINE NUMBERS Proj-Name	REMEMBER TOOLS COMPILE NO-DEBUG Proj-Name
REMEMBER DELETE Proj-Name	REMEMBER TOOLS DELETE Proj-Name
REMEMBER EDIT Proj-Name	REMEMBER TOOLS EDIT Proj-Name
REMEMBER FINISH	REMEMBER FINISH
REMEMBER HELP	None
REMEMBER PRINT Proj-Name	REMEMBER TOOLS PRINT Proj-Name
REMEMBER START Proj-Name	REMEMBER START COMMANDS Proj-Name. In addition to recording commands, you also can record KEYS or BOTH commands and keys.

Smart 3.10 Command	SmartWare II Command
SEND DATA-MANAGER BUFFER DATA PROJECT-FILE Proj-File	DATA SEND DATABASE FROM BUFFER UN-FORMATTED PROJECT-FILE Proj-File. Although the words "FROM" and "PROJECT-FILE" are inserted automatically by the command processor, you must be sure to include them in project file statements.
SEND SPREADSHEET FILE filename.ext DATA PROJECT-FILE Proj-File	DATA SEND SPREADSHEET FROM FILE filename.ext UN-FORMATTED PROJECT-FILE Proj-File. Although the words "FROM" and "PROJECT-FILE are inserted automatically by the command processor, you must be sure to include them in project file statements.
SEND WORDPROCESSOR BUFFER FORMATTED Def-Name PROJECT-FILE Proj-File	DATA SEND WORDPROCESSOR FROM BUFFER FORMATTED-BY Def-Name PROJECT-FILE Proj-File. Although the words "FROM" and "PROJECT-FILE" are inserted automatically by the command processor, you must be sure to include them in project file statements.
SEND WORDPROCESSOR FILE filename.ext FORMATTED Def-Name PROJECT-FILE Proj-File	DATA SEND WORDPROCESSOR FROM FILE filename.ext FORMATTED-BY Def-Name PROJECT-FILE Proj-File. Although the words "FROM" and "PROJECT-FILE" are inserted automatically by the command processor, you must be sure to include them in project file statements.
SETTINGS EDIT	SET-TERMINAL SETTINGS EDIT
SETTINGS LOAD Def-Name	SET-TERMINAL SETTINGS LOAD Def-Name
SETTINGS SAVE Def-Name	SET-TERMINAL SETTINGS SAVE Def-Name

Appendix C: Command Comparison: Smart 3.10 versus SmartWare II

Smart 3.10 Command	SmartWare II Command
TEXT-EDITOR filename.ext	TOOLS TEXT-EDITOR filename.ext
TRANSFER-TIME filename.ext	DATA XFER-TIME filename.ext
TRANSMIT TEXT-FILE filename.ext	DATA TRANSMIT TEXT-FILE filename.ext
TRANSMIT XMODEM filename.ext	DATA TRANSMIT XMODEM filename.ext

The Database Module

Smart 3.10 Command	SmartWare II Command
ACTIVATE filename SCREEN Screen-Name	FILE ACTIVATE CUSTOM-VIEW Screen-Name
AUTOHELP	None. Set Autohelp On/Off in the Tools Preferences Global menu.
BEEP	None. Set Beep On/Off in the Tools Preferences Global menu.
BORDER	WINDOW BORDER
BROWSE ALL	DATA BROWSE ALL
BROWSE FIELDS [field1;field2;field3]	DATA BROWSE FIELDS [field1;field2;field3]
BROWSE OFF	DATA BROWSE OFF
CLOSE	WINDOW CLOSE
CONFIDENCE level 1-5	None. The concept of confidence levels does not exist.
CREATE FILE filename FIXED-LENGTH NO-PASSWORD NEW	FILE CREATE viewname NEW NO-PASSWORD. You must create both a custom view and a new database file. Once you have created the view name, you can create the file: CREATE DATA-FILE filename FIXED-LENGTH NO-PASSWORD. You also can create a data file in a variable-length format and with a password.

Smart 3.10 Command	SmartWare II Command
CREATE filename1 FIXED-LENGTH NO-PASSWORD MATCHING FILE filename2	FILE CREATE viewname1 SIMILAR CUSTOM-VIEW viewname2 NO-PASSWORD. Once you have created a similar view, you may then create a matching database: REPLICATE DATA-FILE filename1 filename2 FIXED-LENGTH NO-PASSWORD. You also can create a data file in a variable-length format and with a password.
CREATE filename1 FIXED-LENGTH NO-PASSWORD SIMILAR FILE filename2	FILE CREATE viewname1 SIMILAR CUSTOM-VIEW viewname2 NO-PASSWORD. Once you have created a similar view, you can create a matching database: REPLICATE DATA-FILE filename1 filename2 FIXED-LENGTH NO-PASSWORD. To change the structure, you can edit or delete fields that vary from the original. You also can use the Query command to create a similar database.
CREATE SCREEN Screen-Name	FILE CREATE View-Name NEW NO-NEW PASSWORD. You also can create a view with a password.
CREATE SCREEN Screen-Name1 NO-PASSWORD SIMILAR SCREEN Screen-Name 2	FILE CREATE View-Name1 SIMILAR CUSTOM-VIEW View-Name2 NO-PASSWORD
DELETE	DATA DELETE RECORD
DIRECTORY file specification	TOOLS DIRECTORY DISPLAY file specification
DISPLAY BLACK/WHITE	None. You can select a new Text Screen or Graphics screen in the Tools Preferences Hardware menu, but you may need to exit SmartWare for the change to work.

Appendix C: Command Comparison: Smart 3.10 versus SmartWare II

Smart 3.10 Command	SmartWare II Command
DISPLAY COLOR	None. You can select a new Text Screen or Graphics screen in the Tools Preferences Hardware menu, but you may need to exit SmartWare for the change to work.
ENTER	DATA ENTER
EXECUTE project-file	REMEMBER EXECUTE project-file {IN-MEMORY/FROM-FILE}
FILE COPY file1.ext TO file2.ext	TOOLS FILE COPY file1.ext TO file2.ext. At the command level, you don't type TO; it is inserted automatically by the command processor. In a project file, however, the TO must separate the file names.
FILE ERASE filename.ext	TOOLS FILE ERASE filename.ext
FILE NEW-DIRECTORY \directory	TOOLS DIRECTORY NEW-DIRECTORY \directory
FILE RENAME file1.ext TO file2.ext	TOOLS FILE RENAME file1.ext TO file2.ext. At the command level, you don't type TO; it is inserted automatically by the command processor.
FILE-SPECS CALCULATED-FIELDS	DATA UTILITIES INFORMATION
FILE-SPECS DATA-RANGES	DATA UTILITIES INFORMATION
FILE-SPECS FIELD-INFO	DATA UTILITIES INFORMATION
FILE-SPECS GENERAL	DATA UTILITIES INFORMATION
FILE-SPECS KEY-FIELDS	DATA UTILITIES INFORMATION
FILE-SPECS RUNNING-TOTALS	None. Use the Tablesum function in a calculated field to display the total of any numeric field.
FIND [field] EQUAL "search" OPTIONS	DATA FIND [field] EQUAL "search" OPTIONS. You also can specify GREATER-THAN, LESS-THAN, and PARTIAL.
F-CALCULATOR	TOOLS CALCULATOR

Smart 3.10 Command	SmartWare II Command
GOTO FILE filename SCREEN Screen-Name	DATA GOTO VIEW Screen-Name.vw
GOTO RECORD NEXT	DATA GOTO RECORD NEXT
GOTO RECORD PREVIOUS	DATA GOTO RECORD PREVIOUS
GOTO RECORD REC-NUMBER #	DATA GOTO RECORD RECORD-NUMBER #
GOTO WINDOW #	DATA GOTO WINDOW #
HELP	HELP ABOUT-HELP
INDEX	FILE DISPLAY-ACTIVE
INPUT-SCREEN DEFINE filename	REMEMBER TOOLS INPUT-SCREEN DEFINE filename
INPUT-SCREEN LOAD filename	REMEMBER TOOLS INPUT-SCREEN LOAD filename
INPUT-SCREEN UNDEFINE filename	REMEMBER TOOLS INPUT-SCREEN UNDEFINE filename
KEY ADD [field]	ORDER KEY ADD [field]
KEY DELETE [field]	ORDER KEY DELETE [field]
KEY ORGANIZE ALL	ORDER KEY REBUILD
KEY ORGANIZE ONE [field]	ORDER KEY REBUILD
KEY UPDATE	None. Keys are updated automatically in SmartWare II.
LINK WINDOW # FIELD [field]	WINDOW LINK [field1] viewname [field2]. Use the command WINDOW UNLINK to break the link. Field1 is the "link from" field and Field2 is the "link to."
LOAD filename SCREEN FILE Screen-Name	LOAD CUSTOM-VIEW Screen-Name
LOOKUP DEFINE Lookup-Name LINK [field1] FILE filename LINK [field2]	None. The concept of the LOOKUP command has been superseded by the ability to attach multiple files to a custom screen.
LOOKUP INDEX	None

Appendix C: Command Comparison: Smart 3.10 versus SmartWare II

Smart 3.10 Command	SmartWare II Command
LOOKUP LOAD Lookup-Name	None
LOOKUP REMOVE Lookup-Name	None
LOOKUP UNDEFINE Lookup-Name	None
MACRO CLEAR	TOOLS MACROS CLEAR ALL
MACRO DEFINE key	TOOLS MACROS EDIT or TOOLS MACROS REMEMBER
MACRO LOAD filename	TOOLS MACROS LOAD filename
MACRO REMOVE key	TOOLS MACROS CLEAR ONE
MACRO SAVE filename	TOOLS MACROS SAVE filename
MACRO VIEW	TOOLS MACROS VIEW
ORDER INDEX indexfile	ORDER CHANGE INDEX indexfile
ORDER KEY [field]	ORDER CHANGE KEY [field]
ORDER SEQUENTIAL	ORDER CHANGE PHYSICAL
PAINT BORDER FOREGROUND #	WINDOW PAINT BORDER #
PAINT DATA FOREGROUND #	WINDOW PAINT DATA #
PAINT GRAPHICS FOREGROUND #	WINDOW PAINT GRAPHICS #
PAINT TITLES BACKGROUND # FOREGROUND #	WINDOW PAINT TITLES # #
PAINT WINDOW BACKGROUND #	WINDOW PAINT WINDOW-AREA #
PARAMETERS	TOOLS PREFERENCES DATABASE
PRINT FILE LIST [field1;field2;field3] PRINTER	PRINT VIEW LIST [field1;field2;field3] PRINTER
PRINT FILE LIST [field1;field2;field3] SCREEN	PRINT VIEW LIST [field1;field2;field3] SCREEN
PRINT FILE REPORT [field1;field2;field3] PRINTER	PRINT VIEW REPORT [field1;field2;field3] PRINTER

Smart 3.10 Command	SmartWare II Command
PRINT FILE REPORT [field1;field2;field3] SCREEN	PRINT VIEW REPORT [field1;field2;field3] SCREEN
PRINT PAGE ALL	PRINT CURRENT-RECORD PAGE ALL
PRINT PAGE DATA	PRINT CURRENT-RECORD PAGE DATA
PRINT RECORD LIST	PRINT CURRENT-RECORD LIST
PRINT RECORD SCREEN ALL	PRINT CURRENT-RECORD VIEW ALL
PRINT RECORD SCREEN DATA	PRINT CURRENT-RECORD VIEW DATA
QUERY COUNT [field1;field2]	None. To count occurrence of key fields, create a report to count breakpoints, report only totals.
QUERY DEFINE filename DATA QUERY	CREATE filename NEW. To change existing Query Definition, use DATA QUERY MODIFY filename. To create a definition similar to one that already exists, use DATA QUERY CREATE filename SIMILAR.
QUERY HIGH-LOW BOTH ALL # FIELD [field] INDEX indexfile	Use the HIGH# or LOW# specifications in the Query by Example expressions.
QUERY HIGH-LOW BOTH CATEGORY # FIELD [field] INDEX indexfile	Use the HIGH# or LOW# specifications in the Query by Example expressions.
QUERY HIGH-LOW HIGH ALL # FIELD [field] INDEX indexfile	Use the HIGH# or LOW# specifications in the Query by Example expressions.
QUERY HIGH-LOW HIGH CATEGORY # FIELD [field] INDEX indexfile	Use the HIGH# or LOW# specifications in the Query by Example expressions.
QUERY MANUAL INDEX indexfile	ORDER MANUAL indexfile. Use the F7 key to manually select or deselect records to enter into the index.

Appendix C: Command Comparison: Smart 3.10 versus SmartWare II

Smart 3.10 Command	SmartWare II Command
QUERY NOW INDEX indexfile	DATA QUERY NOW. The index QNOW is automatically created and is used to order the file.
QUERY NOW NEITHER	DATA QUERY NOW
QUERY NOW SCREEN	DATA QUERY NOW. The results of the Query are visible on-screen, because the file is automatically ordered by the QNOW index.
QUERY PREDEFINED Define-Name INDEX indexfile	DATA QUERY EXECUTE Define-Name INDEX indexfile
QUERY PREDEFINED Define-Name NEITHER	DATA QUERY EXECUTE Define-Name. If the Query definition contains the word replace, you are not prompted for an index file name.
QUERY PREDEFINED Define-Name SCREEN	DATA QUERY EXECUTE Define-Name INDEX indexname. The file is automatically ordered by the resulting index.
QUERY UNDEFINE Define-Name	DATA QUERY REMOVE Define-Name
READ ASCII filename.ext FIELDS [field1;field2;field3]	FILE IMPORT ASCII filename.ext FIELDS [field1;field2;field3]
READ DBASE filename	FILE IMPORT DBASE filename
READ FIXED filename.ext FIELDS [field1;field2;field3]	FILE IMPORT FIXED filename.ext FIELDS [field1;field2;field3]
READ SMART filename.ext FIELDS [field1;field2;field3]	FILE IMPORT SMART filename.ext FIELDS [field1;field2;field3]
RELATE DEFINE Relate-Def FILE file2	DATA RELATE CREATE Relate-Def
RELATE PREDEFINED Relate-Def INTERSECT filename	DATA RELATE EXECUTE Relate-Def. The relate type and output file name are contained within the Relate definition.
RELATE PREDEFINED Relate-Def NOT-INTERSECT filename	DATA RELATE EXECUTE Relate-Def. The relate type and output file name are contained within the Relate definition.

Smart 3.10 Command	SmartWare II Command
RELATE PREDEFINED Relate-Def SUBTRACT filename	DATA RELATE EXECUTE Relate-Def. The relate type and output file name are contained within the Relate definition.
RELATE PREDEFINED Relate-Def UNION filename	DATA RELATE EXECUTE Relate-Def. The relate type and output file name are contained within the Relate definition.
RELATE UNDEFINE Relate-Def	DATA RELATE REMOVE Relate-Def
REMEMBER COMPILE LINE-NUMBERS Proj-Name	REMEMBER TOOLS COMPILE DEBUG Proj-Name
REMEMBER COMPILE NO-LINE-NUMBERS Proj-Name	REMEMBER TOOLS COMPILE NO-DEBUG Proj-Name
REMEMBER DELETE Proj-Name	REMEMBER TOOLS DELETE Proj-Name
REMEMBER EDIT Proj-Name	REMEMBER TOOLS EDIT Proj-Name
REMEMBER FINISH	REMEMBER FINISH
REMEMBER HELP	None
REMEMBER PRINT Proj-Name	REMEMBER TOOLS PRINT Proj-Name
REMEMBER START Proj-Name	REMEMBER START COMMANDS Proj-Name. In addition to recording commands, you also can record KEYS or BOTH commands and keys.
REPORT DEFINE Report-Def	PRINT REPORT CREATE Report-Def NEW. To change an existing report definition, use the command PRINT REPORT MODIFY Report-Def. If you want to make a variation of an existing report, use the command PRINT REPORT CREATE Report-Def SIMILAR Report-Def.

Appendix C: Command Comparison: Smart 3.10 versus SmartWare II

Smart 3.10 Command	SmartWare II Command
REPORT PRINT Report-Def PRINTER	PRINT REPORT EXECUTE Report-Def PRINTER DETAIL START # END # COPIES #. Note that now you may specify the beginning and ending page numbers and the number of copies. If you want to see all the detail that goes into the report body, select the DETAIL option; if you want only the totals, select TOTALS-ONLY.
REPORT PRINT Report-Def DISK filename	PRINT REPORT EXECUTE Report-Def DISK filename DETAIL START # END # COPIES #
REPORT PRINT Report-Def SCREEN	PRINT REPORT EXECUTE Report-Def SCREEN DETAIL START # END # COPIES #
REPORT UNDEFINE Report-Def	PRINT REPORT REMOVE Report-Def
SAVE	FILE SAVE
SCROLL NEXT	None
SCROLL PREVIOUS	None
SEND ALL COMMUNICATIONS [field1;field2] DATA PROJECT-FILE proj-File	DATA SEND COMMUNICATIONS DATA ROW-FORMAT [field1;field2] PROJECT-FILE Proj-File
SEND ALL COMMUNICATIONS [field1;field2] TEXT PROJECT-FILE Proj-File	DATA SEND COMMUNICATIONS TEXT ROW-FORMAT [field1;field2] PROJECT-FILE Proj-File
SEND ALL SPREADSHEET [field1;field2] DATA PROJECT-FILE Proj-File	DATA SEND SPREADSHEET ROW-FORMAT [field1;field2] PROJECT-FILE Proj-File
SEND ALL WORDPROCESSOR [field1;field2] DATA PROJECT-FILE Proj-File	DATA SEND WORDPROCESSOR DATA ROW-FORMAT [field1;field2] PROJECT-FILE Proj-File
SEND ALL WORDPROCESSOR [field1;field2] TEXT PROJECT-FILE Proj-File	DATA SEND WORDPROCESSOR TEXT ROW-FORMAT [field1;field2] PROJECT-FILE Proj-File

Smart 3.10 Command	SmartWare II Command
SEND SUMMARIZED DEFINE Summary-Name ROW COMPLETE	DATA CROSS-TAB CREATE Summary-Name
SEND SUMMARIZED DEFINE Summary-Name COLUMN/ROW PARTIAL	DATA CROSS-TAB CREATE Summary-Name
SEND SUMMARIZED DEFINE Summary-Name ROW COMPLETE	DATA CROSS-TAB CREATE Summary-Name
SEND SUMMARIZED DEFINE Summary-Name ROW PARTIAL	DATA CROSS-TAB CREATE Summary-Name
SEND SUMMARIZED PREDEFINED Summary-Name COMMUNICATIONS	DATA CROSS-TAB EXECUTE Cross-Tab-Definition SMART PROJECT-FILE
DATA PROJECT-FILE Proj-File	Proj-File. Write your summarized data to a disk file in the Smart format to be read into another Smart module.
SEND SUMMARIZED PREDEFINED Summary-Name COMMUNICATIONS TEXT PROJECT-FILE Proj-File	DATA CROSS-TAB EXECUTE Cross-Tab-Definition SMART PROJECT-FILE Proj-File
SEND SUMMARIZED PREDEFINED Summary-Name SPREADSHEET DATA PROJECT-FILE Proj-File	DATA CROSS-TAB EXECUTE Cross-Tab-Definition SMART filename. Write your summarized data to a disk file in the format to be read into another Smart module.
SEND SUMMARIZED PREDEFINED Summary-Name WORDPROCESSOR DATA PROJECT-FILE Proj-File	DATA CROSS-TAB EXECUTE Cross-Tab-Definition SMART filename. Write your summarized data to a disk file in the format to be read into another Smart module.
SEND SUMMARIZED PREDEFINED Summary-Name WORDPROCESSOR TEXT PROJECT-FILE Proj-File	DATA CROSS-TAB EXECUTE Cross-Tab-Definition SMART filename. Write your summarized data to a disk file in the format to be read into another Smart module.
SEND SUMMARIZED UNDEFINE Summary-Name	DATA CROSS-TAB REMOVE Summary-Name

Appendix C: Command Comparison: Smart 3.10 versus SmartWare II

Smart 3.10 Command	SmartWare II Command
SORT DEFINE Sort-Def FIELDS [field1;field2]	ORDER SORT CREATE Sort-Def FIELDS [field1;field2]
SORT NOW Index-File FIELDS [field1;field2] ASCENDING	ORDER SORT NOW Index-File FIELDS [field1;field2] ASCENDING
SORT NOW Index-File FIELDS [field1;field2] DESCENDING	ORDER SORT NOW Index-File FIELDS [field1;field2] DESCENDING
SORT PREDEFINED Sort-Def INDEX Index-File	ORDER SORT EXECUTE Sort-Def INDEX Index-File
SORT UNDEFINE Sort-Def	ORDER SORT REMOVE Sort-Def
SPLIT HORIZONTAL	WINDOW SPLIT HORIZONTAL
SPLIT VERTICAL	WINDOW SPLIT VERTICAL
TEXT-EDITOR filename.ext	TOOLS TEXT-EDITOR filename.ext
TRANSACTIONS DEFINE Trans-Def. SRC filename SC D-DRIVER	DATA TRANSACT CREATE Trans-Def. The Transact definition contains the specifications for the driver and driver fields and the audit selections.
TRANSACTIONS DEFINE Trans-Def SRC filename SC S-DRIVER	DATA TRANSACT CREATE Trans-Def
TRANSACTIONS PREDEFINED Trans-Def AUDIT FILE auditfile	DATA TRANSACT EXECUTE Trans-Def
TRANSACTIONS PREDEFINED Trans-Def AUDIT PRINTER	DATA TRANSACT EXECUTE Trans-Def
TRANSACTIONS PREDEFINED Trans-Def NO-AUDIT	DATA TRANSACT EXECUTE Trans-Def
TRANSACTIONS UNDEFINE Trans-Def	DATA TRANSACT REMOVE Trans-Def
UNLINK	WINDOW UNLINK
UNLOAD ALL	FILE UNLOAD ALL
UNLOAD FILE filename	FILE UNLOAD VIEW filename.vws
UNLOAD SCREEN Screen-Name	FILE UNLOAD VIEW viewname.vw

Smart 3.10 Command	SmartWare II Command
UPDATE	At the command level, press Esc to update the current record. In a project file, use the DATA UPDATE command.
UTILITIES ALTER-COUNT count NEXT	DATA UTILITIES CHANGE-COUNT count NEXT filename
UTILITIES ALTER-COUNT count RENUMBER	DATA UTILITIES CHANGE-COUNT count RENUMBER filename
UTILITIES CONCATENATE Source-File	DATA UTILITIES APPEND Source-File
UTILITIES DUPLICATES DELETE	None
UTILITIES DUPLICATES REPORT	None
UTILITIES ERASE FILE filename	None. You must use the command TOOLS FILE ERASE and manually select the database, key and view files you want to erase. If there are no other files with the same file name, you can use the "*" in place of the file extension.
UTILITIES ERASE SCREEN Screen-Name	None. Use the TOOLS FILE ERASE command to erase the desired "vw" file.
UTILITIES FILE-FIX DATA filename	DATA UTILITIES FILE-FIX DATA-FILE filename
UTILITIES FILE-FIX SCREEN filename	DATA UTILITIES FILE-FIX VIEW filename
UTILITIES NEW-PASSWORD FILE NO-PASSWORD	FILE PASSWORD DATA-FILE REMOVE filename
UTILITIES NEW-PASSWORD FILE PASSWORD Password	FILE PASSWORD DATA-FILE ATTACH filename NO-ENCRYPTION password. You also can select ENCRYPTION.
UTILITIES NEW-PASSWORD SCREEN NO-PASSWORD	FILE PASSWORD VIEW REMOVE
UTILITIES NEW-PASSWORD SCREEN PASSWORD Password	FILE PASSWORD VIEW ATTACH

Smart 3.10 Command	SmartWare II Command
UTILITIES PURGE filename	DATA UTILITIES PURGE filename
UTILITIES RESTRUCTURE Source-File	DATA UTILITIES APPEND Source-File
UTILITIES TOTALS-RECALC	None
WRITE ALL [field1;field2;field3] 3-DBASE filename	FILE EXPORT 3-DBASE [field1;field2;field3] FILE filename
WRITE ALL [field1;field2;field3] ASCII filename	FILE EXPORT ASCII ROW-FORMAT [field1;field2;field3] FILE filename. You also can Export a file in the COLUMN-FORMAT if you want each database record to create a column in the external file.
WRITE ALL [field1;field2;field3] DIF filename	FILE EXPORT DIF ROW-FORMAT [field1;field2;field3] FILE filename
WRITE ALL [field1;field2;field3] M-SYLK filename	FILE EXPORT M-SYLK ROW-FORMAT [field1;field2;field3] FILE filename
WRITE ALL [field1;field2;field3] SMART filename	FILE EXPORT SMART ROW-FORMAT [field1;field2;field3] FILE filename
WRITE ALL [field1;field2;field3] TEXT filename	FILE EXPORT TEXT ROW-FORMAT [field1;field2;field3] FILE filename
WRITE SUMMARIZED DEFINE Summary-Name COLUMN/ROW COMPLETE	DATA CROSS-TAB CREATE Cross-Tab-Definition
WRITE SUMMARIZED DEFINE Summary-Name COLUMN/ROW PARTIAL	DATA CROSS-TAB CREATE Cross-Tab-Definition
WRITE SUMMARIZED DEFINE Summary-Name ROW COMPLETE	DATA CROSS-TAB CREATE Cross-Tab-Definition
WRITE SUMMARIZED DEFINE Summary-Name ROW PARTIAL	DATA CROSS-TAB CREATE Cross-Tab-Definition

Smart 3.10 Command	SmartWare II Command

In SmartWare II, you cannot directly create a summarized file in the 3-Dbase, DIF, or M-SYLK formats. You should execute the SmartWare II commands as follows to create a SmartWare II data file:

Smart 3.10 Command	SmartWare II Command
WRITE SUMMARIZED PREDEFINED Summary-Name 3-Dbase PROJECT-FILE Proj-File	DATA CROSS-TAB EXECUTE Cross-Tab-Definition DATA-FILE filename
WRITE SUMMARIZED PREDEFINED Summary-Name DIF PROJECT-FILE Proj-File	DATA CROSS-TAB EXECUTE Cross-Tab-Definition DATA-FILE filename
WRITE SUMMARIZED PREDEFINED Summary-Name M-SYLK PROJECT-FILE Proj-File	DATA CROSS-TAB EXECUTE Cross-Tab-Definition DATA-FILE filename
WRITE SUMMARIZED PREDEFINED Summary-Name SMART PROJECT-FILE Proj-File	DATA CROSS-TAB EXECUTE Cross-Tab-Definition SMART PROJECT-FILE Proj-File

Next, use the FILE EXPORT command to write the new, summarized file in the desired format.

WRITE SUMMARIZED UNDEFINE Summary-Name	DATA CROSS-TAB REMOVE Cross-Tab-Definition
ZOOM	WINDOW ZOOM

The Main Menu

Smart 3.10 Command	SmartWare II Command
AUTOHELP	None. Set Autohelp On/Off in the Tools Preferences Global menu.
BEEP	None. Set Beep On/Off in the Tools Preferences Global menu.
CONFIDENCE levels 1-5	None. The concept of confidence levels does not exist.
CONFIGURE	TOOLS PREFERENCES GLOBAL or TOOLS PREFERENCES HARDWARE
DIRECTORY filename.ext	TOOLS DIRECTORY DISPLAY file specification

Appendix C: Command Comparison: Smart 3.10 versus SmartWare II

Smart 3.10 Command	SmartWare II Command
DISPLAY BLACK/WHITE	None. You can select a new Text Screen or Graphics screen in the Tools Preferences Hardware menu, but you may need to exit SmartWare for the change to work.
DISPLAY COLOR	None. You can select a new Text Screen or Graphics screen in the Tools Preferences Hardware menu, but you may need to exit SmartWare for the change to work.
DISPLAY GRAPHICS	None. You can select a new Text Screen or Graphics screen in the Tools Preferences Hardware menu, but you may need to exit SmartWare for the change to work.
EXECUTE project-file	REMEMBER EXECUTE project-file {IN-MEMORY/FROM-FILE}
FILE COPY file1.ext TO file2.ext	TOOLS FILE COPY file1.ext TO file2.ext. At the command level, you don't type TO; it's inserted automatically by the command processor. In a project file, TO must separate the file names.
FILE ERASE filename.ext	TOOLS FILE ERASE filename.ext
FILE NEW-DIRECTORY \directory	TOOLS DIRECTORY NEW-DIRECTORY \directory
FILE RENAME file1.ext TO file2.ext.	TOOLS FILE RENAME file1.ext TO file2.ext. At the command level, you don't type TO; it is inserted automatically by the command processor.
FONT-DESIGN PRINTER	TOOLS NEW-FONT
FONT-DESIGN SCREEN	None
G-CALCULATOR	TOOLS CALCULATOR
HELP	HELP ABOUT-HELP
MACRO CLEAR	TOOLS MACROS CLEAR ALL
MACRO DEFINE key	TOOLS MACROS EDIT or TOOLS MACROS REMEMBER

Smart 3.10 Command	SmartWare II Command
MACRO LOAD filename	TOOLS MACROS LOAD filename
MACRO REMOVE key	TOOLS MACROS CLEAR ONE
MACRO SAVE filename	TOOLS MACROS SAVE filename
MACRO VIEW	TOOLS MACROS VIEW
PRINTER-SETUP FONT-PARAMETERS	None
PRINTER-SETUP INIT-SEQUENCES	None
PRINTER-SETUP PRINTER-CODES	None
REMEMBER COMPILE LINE-NUMBERS Proj-Name	REMEMBER TOOLS COMPILE DEBUG Proj-Name
REMEMBER COMPILE NO-LINE NUMBERS Proj-Name	REMEMBER TOOLS COMPILE NO-DEBUG Proj-Name
REMEMBER DELETE Proj-Name	REMEMBER TOOLS DELETE Proj-Name
REMEMBER EDIT Proj-Name	REMEMBER TOOLS EDIT Proj-Name
REMEMBER FINISH	REMEMBER FINISH
REMEMBER HELP	None
REMEMBER PRINT Proj-Name	REMEMBER TOOLS PRINT Proj-Name
REMEMBER START Proj-Name	REMEMBER START COMMANDS Proj-Name. Plus recording just commands, you also can record KEYS or BOTH commands and keys.
TEXT-EDITOR filename.ext	TOOLS TEXT-EDITOR filename.ext

Project Processing

Smart 3.10 Command	SmartWare II Command
BEEP Number-of-beeps message	BEEP Number-of-beeps ''message''
BREAK	EXIT WHILE. This command will exit the WHILE loop immediately.

Appendix C: Command Comparison: Smart 3.10 versus SmartWare II

Smart 3.10 Command	SmartWare II Command
BREAK-KEY	BREAK-KEY
CALL Procedure-Name	Procedure-Name()
CLEAR	CLEAR PUBLIC, CLEAR EXTERNAL, CLEAR GLOBAL, or CLEAR LOCAL. You also can separately specify that only the arrays should be cleared by inserting square brackets after the key word: CLEAR PUBLIC[]
CLEAR $var1 , $var2	CLEAR $var1 , $var2
COMMAND	TOOLS OS
COMMAND /c DOS Command	TOOLS OS ''DOS Command''
COMMENT Your Comment Here	COMMENT Your Comment Here
CONTINUE	CONTINUE WHILE
CURSOR LEFT (RIGHT, UP, DOWN)	CURSOR LEFT (RIGHT, UP, DOWN)
CURSOR VALUE Prompt Message	CURSOR VALUE ''Prompt Message''
EMPTY	EMPTY
END	END MAIN
ENDWHILE	END WHILE
ENTER BLANK	DATA ENTER BLANK
ENTER ONLY-ONE	This command is invalid in SmartWare II. Use ENTER BLANK followed by DATA UPDATE ONLY-ONE.
EXECUTE Proj-File	EXECUTE ''Proj-File'' FROM-FILE
EXECUTE Proj-File IN-MEMORY	EXECUTE ''Proj-File'' IN-MEMORY
FCLOSE File-Number	FCLOSE File-Number
FOPEN filename AS file-number	FOPEN ''Filename.exe'' AS File-Number
FREAD File-Number INTO r	FREAD File-Number INTO r

Smart 3.10 Command	SmartWare II Command
FREAD File-Number LENGTH Length INTO r	FREAD File-Number LENGTH Length INTO r
FSEEK File-Number File-Location	FSEEK File-Number File-Location
FWRITE File-Number FROM r	FWRITE File-Number FROM r
FWRITE File-Number LENGTH Length FROM r	FWRITE File-Number LENGTH Length FROM r
IF condition THEN command1 IF condition/command1/ENDIF	IF condition/command1/END IF IF condition/command1/END IF
IF condition1/command1/ELSE/ command2/ENDIF	IF condition1/command1/ELSE/ command2/END IF
IF condition1/command1/ ELSEIF/command2/ELSE/ command3/ENDIF	IF condition1/command1/ELSEIF/ command2/ELSE/command3/ENDIF
INPUT 1 Prompt Message	SCREEN SHORTINPUT 1 "Prompt Message" Note: The result will always be text.
JUMP Label-Name	JUMP Label-Name
JUMP WORDPROCESSOR PROJECT-FILE Proj-File	QUIT WORDPROCESSOR PROJECT-FILE "Proj-File"
LABEL Label-Name	LABEL Label-Name
LET Destination = Source	LET Destination = Source
LET filename.[field] = r	LET [filename.field] = r NOTE: The name of the view is inside the square brackets.
LOCK-RECORD	LOCK-RECORD
LPRINT Text to go to printer	LPRINT Text to go to printer Note: LPRINT must be preceded by OPEN-PRINTER and followed by CLOSE-PRINTER commands.
MENU CLEAR (foreground color) (background color)	SCREEN CLEAR (foreground color) (background color)
MENU CLEAR (foreground color) (background color) NO-BORDER	SCREEN CLEAR (foreground color) (background color) NO-BORDER

Appendix C: Command Comparison: Smart 3.10 versus SmartWare II

Smart 3.10 Command	SmartWare II Command
MENU CLEAR BOX (line #) (column #) (line #) (column #) (foreground color) (background color)	SCREEN CLEAR BOX (line #) (column #) (line #) (column #) (foreground TEXT PROJECT-FILE Proj-File
MENU CLEAR BOX (line #) (column #) (line #) (column #) (foreground color) color) (background color) (background color)NO-BORDER	SCREEN CLEAR BOX (line #) (column #) (line #) (column #) (foreground color) (background color) NO-BORDER
MENU DRAW BOX (line #) (column #) (line #) (column #) (foreground color)	SCREEN DRAW BOX (line #) (column #) (line #) (column #) (foreground color) (background color)
MENU INPUT (line #) (column #) (foreground color) (background color) (variable length) $var	SCREEN INPUT (line #) (column #) (foreground color) (background color) (variable length) $var The variable will aways be text.
MENU PRINT (line #) (column #) (foreground color) (background color) message	SCREEN PRINT (line #) (column #) (foreground color) (background color) ''message''
MESSAGE Message	MESSAGE ''Message''
PROCEDURE Procedure-Name	FUNCTION Procedure-Name()
QUIET OFF	QUIET OFF
QUIET ON	QUIET ON
QUIT	QUIT QUIT
REPAINT	REPAINT
REPAINT {OFF/ON}	REPAINT {OFF/ON}
RETURN	RETURN
SINGLESTEP {ON/OFF}	SINGLE-STEP {ON/OFF}
STOP	STOP
SUSPEND	SUSPEND
TRANSFER Proj-File	TRANSFER ''Proj-File''
TRANSFER Proj-File IN-MEMORY	TRANSFER ''Proj-File'' IN-MEMORY
UPDATE	DATA UPDATE

Smart 3.10 Command	SmartWare II Command
UPDATE ONLY-ONE	DATA UPDATE ONLY-ONE
WAIT Number-of-seconds Message	WAIT Number-of-seconds "Message"
WHILE condition	WHILE condition
%1 Prompt Message (parameters)	SCREEN SHORTINPUT $var "Prompt"
@r#c# CURSOR Prompt Message	AT r#c# CURSOR "Prompt Message"
'Your Comment Here	'Your Comment Here

The Spreadsheet Module

Smart 3.10 Command	SmartWare II Command
ACTIVATE filename	FILE ACTIVATE filename
AUTOHELP	None. Set Autohelp On/Off in the Tools Preferences Global menu.
AUTO-RECALC AUTOMATIC	SHEET CALC-MODE AUTOMATIC
AUTO-RECALC DISPLAY	SHEET CALC-MODE DISPLAY
AUTO-RECALC ITERATE COUNT count	SHEET CALC-MODE ITERATE COUNT count
AUTO-RECALC ITERATE REMOVE	AUTO-RECALC ITERATE REMOVE
AUTO-RECALC ITERATE TEST Cell-Ref DELTA value COUNT count	SHEET CALC-MODE ITERATE TEST Cell-Ref DELTA value COUNT count
AUTO-RECALC MANUAL	SHEET CALC-MODE MANUAL
BEEP	None. Set Beep On/Off in the Tools Preferences Global menu.
BLANK ALL	EDIT BLANK ALL
BLANK BLOCK block	EDIT BLANK BLOCK block
BLANK COLUMNS # of columns	EDIT BLANK COLUMNS columns
BLANK ROWS # of rows	EDIT BLANK ROWS rows
BORDER	WINDOW BORDER

Appendix C: Command Comparison: Smart 3.10 versus SmartWare II

Smart 3.10 Command	SmartWare II Command
CLOSE	WINDOW CLOSE
COLNUMBERS	WINDOW NUMBERS COLUMN
CONFIDENCE levels 1-5	None. The concept of confidence levels does not exist.
COPY DOWN ROW LENGTH length COPIES copies	EDIT COPY DOWN ROW LENGTH length COPIES copies
COPY DOWN SINGLE-CELL COPIES copies	EDIT COPY DOWN SINGLE-CELL COPIES copies
COPY FROM block TO block	EDIT COPY FROM block TO block
COPY RIGHT COLUMN LENGTH length COPIES copies	EDIT COPY RIGHT COLUMN LENGTH length COPIES copies
COPY RIGHT SINGLE-CELL COPIES copies	EDIT COPY RIGHT SINGLE-CELL COPIES copies
DELETE BLOCK block	EDIT DELETE BLOCK block
DELETE COLUMNS # of columns	EDIT DELETE COLUMNS columns
DELETE ROWS # of rows	EDIT DELETE ROWS rows
DIRECTORY file specification	TOOLS DIRECTORY DISPLAY filename.ext
DISPLAY BLACK/WHITE	None. You can select a new Text Screen or Graphics screen in the Tools Preferences Hardware menu, but you may need to exit SmartWare for the change to work.
DISPLAY COLOR	None. You can select a new Text Screen or Graphics screen in the Tools Preferences Hardware menu, but you may need to exit SmartWare for the change to work.
DISPLAY GRAPHICS	None. You can select a new Text Screen or Graphics screen in the Tools Preferences Hardware menu, but you may need to exit SmartWare for the change to work.
EDIT	EDIT EDIT-CELL
EXECUTE project-file	EXECUTE project-file

Smart 3.10 Command	SmartWare II Command
FILE COPY file1.ext TO file2.ext	TOOLS FILE COPY file1.ext TO file2.ext. At the command level, you don't type TO; it is inserted automatically by the command processor. In a project file, the TO must separate file names.
FILE ERASE filename.ext	TOOLS FILE ERASE filename.ext
FILE NEW-DIRECTORY \directory	TOOLS DIRECTORY NEW-DIRECTORY \directory
FILE RENAME file1.ext TO file2.ext	TOOLS FILE RENAME file1.ext TO file2.ext. At the command level, you don't type TO; it is inserted automatically by the command processor.
FILL BLOCK block START number INCREMENT number	EDIT FILL BLOCK block START number INCREMENT number
FILL COLUMNS columns START number INCREMENT number	EDIT FILL COLUMNS columns START number INCREMENT number
FILL ROWS rows START number INCREMENT number	EDIT FILL ROWS rows START number INCREMENT number
FIND ERROR	SHEET FIND ALL CALC-ERROR
FIND TEXT text	SHEET FIND ALL TEXT text
FIND VALUE value	SHEET FIND ALL VALUE value
FONT CHANGE Font-Number attribute ALL	LAYOUT SET-FONT CHANGE attribute ALL
FONT CHANGE Font-Number attribute BLOCK block	LAYOUT SET-FONT CHANGE attribute BLOCK BLOCK
FONT CHANGE Font-Number attribute COLUMNS columns	LAYOUT SET-FONT CHANGE attribute COLUMNS COLUMNS
FONT CHANGE Font-Number attribute ROWS rows	LAYOUT SET-FONT CHANGE attribute ROWS ROWS
FONT SELECT Font-Number attribute	LAYOUT SET-FONT SELECT attribute
F-CALCULATOR	TOOLS CALCULATOR

Appendix C: Command Comparison: Smart 3.10 versus SmartWare II

Smart 3.10 Command	SmartWare II Command
GOTO window #	SHEET GOTO WINDOW #
GOTO cell-location	SHEET GOTO CELL cell-location
GOTO name	SHEET GOTO CELL name
GOTO worksheet	SHEET GOTO SHEET worksheet
GOTO (cursor movement)	SHEET GOTO OTHER (cursor movement). Use any of the arrow keys, the Home or End keys, or the Ctrl-Right or Ctrl-Left keys.
GRAPHICS DEFINE Graph-Definition	GRAPH DEFINE Graph-Type Graph-Definition
GRAPHICS EDIT Graph-Screen-File	None
GRAPHICS GENERATE Graph-Definition BLACK/WHITE SCREEN Graph-Screen-File	GRAPH GENERATE Graph-Definition METAFILE
GRAPHICS GENERATE Graph-Definition COLOR SCREEN Graph-Screen-File	GRAPH GENERATE Graph-Definition METAFILE
GRAPHICS MATRIX-PRINT Graph-Definition	GRAPH GENERATE Graph-Definition HARDCOPY PRINTER LANDSCAPE
GRAPHICS PLOT Graph-Definition FULL-PAGE	GRAPH GENERATE Graph-Definition HARDCOPY XY-PLOT
GRAPHICS PLOT Graph-Definition QUADRANT Quadrant-Nr	GRAPH GENERATE Graph-Definition HARDCOPY XY-PLOT
GRAPHICS SLIDESHOW	None
GRAPHICS UNDEFINE Graph-Definition	GRAPH UNDEFINE GRAPH Graph-Definition
GRAPHICS VIEW Graph-Screen-File CURTAIN Curtain-type	GRAPH GENERATE Graph-Screen-File PREVIEW
GRAPHICS VIEW Graph-Screen-File FADE-IN	GRAPH GENERATE Graph-Screen-File PREVIEW
GRAPHICS VIEW Graph-Screen-File INSTANT	GRAPH GENERATE Graph-Screen-File PREVIEW
HELP	HELP ABOUT-HELP

Smart 3.10 Command	SmartWare II Command
INPUT-SCREEN DEFINE filename	REMEMBER TOOLS INPUT-SCREEN DEFINE filename
INPUT-SCREEN LOAD filename	REMEMBER TOOLS INPUT-SCREEN LOAD filename
INPUT-SCREEN UNDEFINE filename	REMEMBER TOOLS INPUT-SCREEN UNDEFINE filename
INSERT BLOCK block	EDIT INSERT BLOCK block
INSERT COLUMNS columns	EDIT INSERT COLUMNS columns
INSERT ROWS rows	EDIT INSERT ROWS rows
JUSTIFY direction ALL	LAYOUT JUSTIFY direction ALL
JUSTIFY direction BLOCK block	LAYOUT JUSTIFY direction BLOCK block
JUSTIFY direction COLUMNS # of columns	LAYOUT JUSTIFY direction COLUMNS columns
JUSTIFY direction ROWS # of rows	LAYOUT JUSTIFY direction ROWS rows
LINK 1 2 3 4	WINDOW LINK 1 2 3 4
LOAD worksheet	FILE LOAD worksheet
LOCK ALL	SHEET LOCK ALL
LOCK BLANKS	SHEET LOCK BLANKS
LOCK DISABLE	SHEET LOCK DISABLE
LOCK ENABLE	SHEET LOCK ENABLE
LOCK FORMULAS ROWS rows	SHEET LOCK FORMULAS ROWS rows
LOCK PROTECT	SHEET LOCK PROTECT
LOCK TEXT COLUMNS columns	SHEET LOCK TEXT COLUMNS columns
LOCK VALUES ALL	SHEET LOCK VALUES ALL
MACRO CLEAR	TOOLS MACROS CLEAR ALL

Smart 3.10 Command	SmartWare II Command
MACRO DEFINE key	TOOLS MACROS EDIT or TOOLS MACROS REMEMBER
MACRO LOAD filename	TOOLS MACROS LOAD filename
MACRO REMOVE key	TOOLS MACROS CLEAR ONE
MACRO SAVE filename	TOOLS MACROS SAVE filename
MACRO VIEW	TOOLS MACROS VIEW
MATRIX AUX DETERMINANT block RESULT cell	SHEET MATRIX AUX DETERMINANT block RESULT cell
MATRIX AUX NORMALIZE STANDARD ROW LENGTH number	SHEET MATRIX AUX NORMALIZE STANDARD ROW LENGTH number
MATRIX AUX NORMALIZE UNIT COLUMN LENGTH number	SHEET MATRIX AUX NORMALIZE UNIT COLUMN LENGTH number
MATRIX AUX POWER block EXPONENT number	SHEET MATRIX AUX POWER block EXPONENT number
MATRIX AUX RANK ROW LENGTH number	SHEET MATRIX AUX RANK ROW LENGTH number
MATRIX DIAGONAL COPY block1 NEW-MATRIX block2	SHEET MATRIX DIAGONAL COPY block1 NEW-MATRIX block2
MATRIX DIAGONAL PRODUCT block RESULT cell	SHEET MATRIX DIAGONAL PRODUCT block RESULT cell
MATRIX DIAGONAL SUM block RESULT cell	SHEET MATRIX DIAGONAL SUM block RESULT cell
MATRIX EIGEN block1 VALUES block2 VECTORS block	None
MATRIX INVERT block1 NEW-MATRIX block2	SHEET MATRIX INVERT block1 NEW-MATRIX block2
MATRIX MULTIPLY block1 BY block2 NEW-MATRIX block3	SHEET MATRIX MULTIPLY block1 BY block2 NEW-MATRIX block3
MATRIX N-SOLVE block1 RESULT block2	SHEET MATRIX N-SOLVE block1 RESULT block2
MATRIX PARALLEL block1 DIV cell NEW-MATRIX block2	SHEET MATRIX PARALLEL DIV block1 BY cell NEW-MATRIX block2

Smart 3.10 Command	SmartWare II Command
MATRIX PARALLEL block1 MULT value NEW-MATRIX block2	SHEET MATRIX PARALLEL MULT block1 BY value NEW-MATRIX block2
MATRIX PARALLEL block1 SUB block2 NEW-MATRIX block3	SHEET MATRIX PARALLEL SUB block1 BY block2 NEW-MATRIX block3
MATRIX REGRESSION block1 NO-REPORT RESULTS block2	SHEET MATRIX REGRESSION block1 NO-REPORT RESULTS block2
MATRIX REGRESSION block1 REPORT block2 RESULT block3	SHEET MATRIX REGRESSION block1 REPORT block2 RESULT block3
MATRIX SWEEP block PIVOTS rows	SHEET MATRIX SWEEP block PIVOTS rows
MATRIX TRANSPOSE block	SHEET MATRIX TRANSPOSE block
MATRIX UPPER block RESULT block	SHEET MATRIX UPPER block RESULT block
MOVE BLOCK block1 TO block2	EDIT MOVE BLOCK block1 TO block2
MOVE COLUMNS number TO column	EDIT MOVE COLUMNS number TO column
MOVE ROWS number TO row	EDIT MOVE ROWS number TO row
NAME DEFINE name block	SHEET NAME DEFINE name block
NAME EDIT	SHEET NAME EDIT
NAME PRINT	SHEET NAME PRINT
NAME UNDEFINE name	SHEET NAME UNDEFINE name
NEWNAME worksheet	FILE NEWNAME worksheet
PAINT BORDER BACKGROUND value1 FOREGROUND value2	WINDOW PAINT BORDER BACKGROUND value1 FOREGROUND value2
PAINT CURSOR BACKGROUND value1 FOREGROUND value2	WINDOW PAINT CELLS CURSOR BACKGROUND value1 FOREGROUND value2

Appendix C: Command Comparison: Smart 3.10 versus SmartWare II

Smart 3.10 Command	SmartWare II Command
PAINT FORMULAS BACKGROUND value1 FOREGROUND value2	WINDOW PAINT CELLS FORMULAS BACKGROUND value1 FOREGROUND value2
PAINT LOCKED-CELLS BACKGROUND value1 FOREGROUND value2	WINDOW PAINT CELLS LOCKED-CELLS BACKGROUND value1 FOREGROUND value2
PAINT TEXT BACKGROUND value1 FOREGROUND value2	WINDOW PAINT CELLS TEXT BACKGROUND value1 FOREGROUND value2
PAINT VALUES BACKGROUND value1 FOREGROUND value2	WINDOW PAINT CELLS VALUES BACKGROUND value1 FOREGROUND value2
PAINT WINDOW BACKGROUND value1 FOREGROUND value2	WINDOW PAINT WINDOW BACKGROUND value1 FOREGROUND value2
PARAMETERS	TOOLS PREFERENCES SPREADSHEET
PASSWORD ATTACH	FILE PASSWORD ATTACH
PASSWORD REMOVE	FILE PASSWORD REMOVE
PRINT FORMULAS BLOCK block COMPRESSED	PRINT FORMULAS BLOCK block
PRINT FORMULAS BLOCK block NORMAL	PRINT FORMULAS BLOCK block
PRINT FORMULAS WORKSHEET COMPRESSED	PRINT FORMULAS WORKSHEET
PRINT FORMULAS WORKSHEET NORMAL	PRINT FORMULAS WORKSHEET
PRINT TEXT BLOCK block DISK filename.ext	PRINT TEXT BLOCK block DISK filename.ext
PRINT TEXT BLOCK block PRINTER COMPRESSED COPIES number	PRINT TEXT BLOCK block PRINTER DRAFT COPIES number
PRINT TEXT BLOCK block PRINTER NORMAL COPIES number	PRINT TEXT BLOCK block PRINTER DRAFT COPIES number

Smart 3.10 Command	SmartWare II Command
PRINT TEXT WORKSHEET DISK filename.ext	PRINT TEXT WORKSHEET DISK filename.ext
PRINT TEXT WORKSHEET PRINTER COMPRESSED COPIES number	PRINT TEXT WORKSHEET PRINTER DRAFT COPIES number
PRINT TEXT WORKSHEET PRINTER NORMAL COPIES number	PRINT TEXT WORKSHEET PRINTER DRAFT COPIES number
READ 123 filename.ext	FILE IMPORT 123 FILE filename
READ DIF filename.ext	FILE IMPORT DIF FILE filename
READ R2-123 filename.ext	FILE IMPORT R2-123 FILE filename
READ SYLK filename.ext	FILE IMPORT SYLK FILE filename
READ TEXT filename.etx	FILE IMPORT TEXT FILE filename
REFORMAT ALL DATE DATE-FORMAT 1-3	LAYOUT FORMAT ALL DATE 1-3
REFORMAT ALL NUMERIC NORMAL COMMAS PRECISION number	LAYOUT FORMAT ALL NUMERIC COMMAS MINUS SHOW-ALL PRECISION number
REFORMAT BLOCK block BAR	LAYOUT FORMAT BLOCK block BAR
REFORMAT BLOCK block DATE3	LAYOUT FORMAT BLOCK block DATE 3
REFORMAT BLOCK block NUMERIC E-NOTATION PRECISION number	LAYOUT FORMAT BLOCK block E-NOTATION SHOW-ALL PRECISION number
REFORMAT COLUMNS number CURRENCY NORMAL COMMAS PRECISION number	LAYOUT FORMAT COLUMNS number CURRENCY COMMAS PARENS SHOW-ALL PRECISION number
REFORMAT COLUMNS number PERCENT PRECISION number	LAYOUT FORMAT COLUMNS number PERCENT NOCOMMAS MINUS SHOW-ALL PRECISION number
REFORMAT COLUMNS number RESET	LAYOUT FORMAT COLUMNS number RESET

Appendix C: Command Comparison: Smart 3.10 versus SmartWare II

Smart 3.10 Command	SmartWare II Command
REFORMAT FORMULA-DISPLAY TEXT	LAYOUT FORMAT FORMULA-DISPLAY TEXT
REFORMAT FORMULA-DISPLAY VALUES	LAYOUT FORMAT FORMULA-DISPLAY VALUES
REFORMAT ROWS number CURRENCY NORMAL COMMAS PRECISION number	LAYOUT FORMAT ROWS number CURRENCY COMMAS MINUS SHOW-ALL PRECISION number
REFORMAT ROWS number DATE DATE-FORMAT (1-3)	LAYOUT FORMAT ROWS number DATE (1-3)
REMEMBER COMPILE LINE-NUMBERS Proj-Name	REMEMBER TOOLS COMPILE DEBUG Proj-Name
REMEMBER COMPILE NO-LINE NUMBERS Proj-Name	REMEMBER TOOLS COMPILE NO-DEBUG Proj-Name
REMEMBER DELETE Proj-Name	REMEMBER TOOLS DELETE Proj-Name
REMEMBER EDIT Proj-Name	REMEMBER TOOLS EDIT Proj-Name
REMEMBER FINISH	REMEMBER FINISH
REMEMBER HELP	None
REMEMBER PRINT Proj-Name	REMEMBER TOOLS PRINT Proj-Name
REMEMBER START Proj-Name	REMEMBER START COMMANDS Proj-Name. In addition to recording commands, you can record KEYS or BOTH commands and keys.
REPORT DEFINE Report-Name	PRINT REPORT DEFINE Report-Name
REPORT ENHANCED Report-Name DISK filename	PRINT REPORT EXECUTE Report-Name DISK filename
REPORT ENHANCED Report-Name PRINTER COPIES number	PRINT REPORT EXECUTE Report-Name PRINTER COPIES number
REPORT NORMAL Report-Name DISK filename	PRINT REPORT EXECUTE Report-Name DISK filename

Smart 3.10 Command	SmartWare II Command
REPORT NORMAL Report-Name PRINTER COPIES number	PRINT REPORT EXECUTE Report-Name PRINTER COPIES number
REPORT PRESET	PRINT REPORT PRESET
REPORT TEMPLATE Report-Name	PRINT REPORT TEMPLATE Report-Name
REPORT UNDEFINE Report-Name	PRINT REPORT UNDEFINE Report-Name
ROWNUMBERS	WINDOW NUMBERS ROW
SAVE worksheet	FILE SAVE worksheet
SCROLL DOWN rate	None
SCROLL UP rate	None
SEND COMMUNICATIONS DOCUMENT BLOCK block PROJECT-FILE Proj-File	SHEET SEND COMMUNICATIONS DOCUMENT BLOCK block PROJECT-FILE Proj-File
SEND COMMUNICATIONS GRAPHICS Screen-File PROJECT-FILE Proj-File	SHEET SEND COMMUNICATIONS GRAPHICS Screen-File PROJECT-FILE Proj-File
SEND COMMUNICATIONS SMART BLOCK block PROJECT-FILE Proj-File	SHEET SEND COMMUNICATIONS SMART BLOCK block PROJECT-FILE Proj-File
SEND COMMUNICATIONS TEXT BLOCK block PROJECT-FILE Proj-File	SHEET SEND COMMUNICATIONS TEXT BLOCK block PROJECT-FILE Proj-File
SEND DATA-MANAGER BLOCK block PROJECT-FILE Proj-File	SHEET SEND DATABASE BLOCK block PROJECT-FILE Proj-File
SEND WORDPROCESSOR BOTH Screen-File BLOCK block PROJECT-FILE Proj-File	SHEET SEND WORDPROCESSOR BOTH Screen-File BLOCK block PROJECT-FILE Proj-File
SEND WORDPROCESSOR DOCUMENT BLOCK block PROJECT-FILE Proj-File	SHEET SEND WORDPROCESSOR DOCUMENT BLOCK block PROJECT-FILE Proj-File
SEND WORDPROCESSOR GRAPHICS Screen-File PROJECT-FILE Proj-File	SHEET SEND WORDPROCESSOR GRAPHICS Screen-File PROJECT-FILE Proj-File

Smart 3.10 Command	SmartWare II Command
SORT block ASCENDING USING COLUMN Column-Numbers	EDIT SORT block ASCENDING USING COLUMN Column-Numbers
SORT block ASCENDING USING ROW Row-Numbers	EDIT SORT block ASCENDING USING ROW Row-Numbers
SORT block DESCENDING USING COLUMN Column-Numbers	EDIT SORT block DESCENDING USING COLUMN Column-Numbers
SORT block DESCENDING USING ROW Row-Numbers	EDIT SORT block DESCENDING USING ROW Row-Numbers
SPLIT HORIZONTAL	WINDOW SPLIT HORIZONTAL
SPLIT VERTICAL	WINDOW SPLIT VERTICAL
TEXT-EDITOR filename.ext	TOOLS TEXT-EDITOR filename.ext
TEXT-FORMAT CENTER	LAYOUT DEFAULT TEXT CENTER
TEXT-FORMAT LEFT	LAYOUT DEFAULT TEXT LEFT
TEXT-FORMAT RIGHT	LAYOUT DEFAULT TEXT RIGHT
TITLES DROP	WINDOW TITLES DROP
TITLES FIX COLUMNS # of columns	WINDOW TITLES FIX COLUMNS number
TITLES FIX ROWS # of rows	WINDOW TITLES FIX ROWS number
UNLINK Window-Numbers	WINDOW UNLINK Window-Numbers
UNLOAD worksheet	FILE UNLOAD worksheet
UNLOCK ALL	SHEET UNLOCK ALL
UNLOCK BLANKS	SHEET UNLOCK BLANKS
UNLOCK FORMULAS BLOCK block	SHEET UNLOCK FORMULAS BLOCK block
UNLOCK TEXT COLUMNS number	SHEET UNLOCK TEXT COLUMNS number
UNLOCK VALUES ROWS number	SHEET UNLOCK VALUES ROWS number
VALUE-FORMAT BAR LEFT	LAYOUT DEFAULT VALUES BAR LEFT

Smart 3.10 Command	SmartWare II Command
VALUE-FORMAT DATE DATE-FORMAT CENTER	LAYOUT DEFAULT VALUES DATE 1 CENTER
VALUE-FORMAT DATE DATE-FORMAT RIGHT	LAYOUT DEFAULT VALUES DATE 2 RIGHT
VALUE-FORMAT DATE DATE-FORMAT LEFT	LAYOUT DEFAULT VALUES DATE 3 LEFT
VALUE-FORMAT E-NOTATION CENTER PRECISION # of decimals	LAYOUT DEFAULT VALUES E-NOTATION SHOW-ALL CENTER PRECISION # of decimals
VALUE-FORMAT NORMAL CENTER NUMERIC NOCOMMAS PRECISION # of decimals	LAYOUT DEFAULT VALUES NUMERIC NOCOMMAS MINUS SHOW-ALL CENTER PRECISION # of decimals
VALUE-FORMAT NORMAL LEFT PERCENT PRECISION # of decimals	LAYOUT DEFAULT VALUES PERCENT NOCOMMAS MINUS SHOW-ALL LEFT PRECISION # of decimals
VALUE-FORMAT NORMAL RIGHT CURRENCY COMMAS PRECISION # of decimals	LAYOUT DEFAULT VALUES CURRENCY COMMAS PARENS SHOW-ALL RIGHT PRECISION # of decimals
VCOPY DOWN ROW LENGTH length COPIES copies	EDIT VALUE-COPY DOWN ROW LENGTH length COPIES copies
VCOPY DOWN SINGLE-CELL COPIES copies	EDIT VALUE-COPY DOWN SINGLE-CELL COPIES copies
VCOPY FROM block TO block	EDIT VALUE-COPY FROM block TO block
VCOPY RIGHT COLUMN LENGTH length COPIES copies	EDIT VALUE-COPY RIGHT COLUMN LENGTH length COPIES copies
VCOPY RIGHT SINGLE-CELL COPIES copies	EDIT VALUE-COPY RIGHT SINGLE-CELL COPIES copies
WIDTH width ALL	LAYOUT CELL-SIZE WIDTH width ALL
WIDTH width COLUMNS # of columns	LAYOUT CELL-SIZE WIDTH width COLUMNS # of columns
WRITE BLOCK block 123 FILE	FILE EXPORT BLOCK block 123 FILE filename.ext

Smart 3.10 Command	SmartWare II Command
WRITE BLOCK block DIF FILE	FILE EXPORT BLOCK block DIF FILE filename.ext
WRITE BLOCK block DOCUMENT FILE	FILE EXPORT BLOCK block DOCUMENT FILE filename.ext
WRITE BLOCK block R2-123 FILE	FILE EXPORT BLOCK block R2-123 FILE filename.ext
WRITE BLOCK block SMART FILE	FILE EXPORT BLOCK block SMART FILE filename.ext
WRITE BLOCK block TEXT FILE	FILE EXPORT BLOCK block TEXT FILE filename.ext
WRITE WORKSHEET 123 FILE	FILE EXPORT WORKSHEET 123 FILE filename.ext
WRITE WORKSHEET DIF FILE	FILE EXPORT WORKSHEET DIF FILE filename.ext
WRITE WORKSHEET DOCUMENT FILE	FILE EXPORT WORKSHEET DOCUMENT FILE filename.ext
WRITE WORKSHEET R2-123 FILE	FILE EXPORT WORKSHEET R2-123 FILE filename.ext
WRITE WORKSHEET SMART FILE	FILE EXPORT WORKSHEET SMART FILE filename.ext
WRITE WORKSHEET TEXT FILE	FILE EXPORT WORKSHEET TEXT FILE filename.ext
ZOOM	WINDOW ZOOM

The Word Processor Module

Smart 3.10 Command	SmartWare II Command
AUTOHELP	None. Set Autohelp On/Off in the Tools Preferences Global menu.
BEEP	None. Set Beep On/Off in the Tools Preferences Global menu.
BOLD INSERT BLOCK	LAYOUT FONT BOLD INSERT
BOLD INSERT CHARACTER	LAYOUT FONT BOLD INSERT
BOLD INSERT DOCUMENT	LAYOUT FONT BOLD INSERT

Smart 3.10 Command	SmartWare II Command
BOLD INSERT LINE	LAYOUT FONT BOLD INSERT
BOLD INSERT PARAGRAPH	LAYOUT FONT BOLD INSERT
BOLD INSERT REMAINDER	LAYOUT FONT BOLD INSERT
BOLD INSERT SENTENCE	LAYOUT FONT BOLD INSERT
BOLD INSERT WORD	LAYOUT FONT BOLD INSERT
BOLD REMOVE BLOCK	LAYOUT FONT BOLD REMOVE
BOLD REMOVE CHARACTER	LAYOUT FONT BOLD REMOVE
BOLD REMOVE DOCUMENT	LAYOUT FONT BOLD REMOVE
BOLD REMOVE LINE	LAYOUT FONT BOLD REMOVE
BOLD REMOVE PARAGRAPH	LAYOUT FONT BOLD REMOVE
BOLD REMOVE REMAINDER	LAYOUT FONT BOLD REMOVE
BOLD REMOVE SENTENCE	LAYOUT FONT BOLD REMOVE
BOLD REMOVE WORD	LAYOUT FONT BOLD REMOVE
BORDER	WINDOW BORDER
CHANGE-TYPE	FILE FILE-TYPE
CLOSE FOOTNOTE	WINDOW CLOSE FOOTNOTE
CLOSE WINDOW	WINDOW CLOSE DOC-WINDOW
COMPUTE FORMULA	DOCUMENT MATH FORMULA
COMPUTE SUM	DOCUMENT MATH SUM
CONFIDENCE level 1-5	None
COPY BLOCK	EDIT COPY BLOCK. You can insert the copied text immediately, or you can insert it into the buffer for later retrieval.
COPY LINE	EDIT COPY LINE
COPY PARAGRAPH	EDIT COPY PARAGRAPH
COPY REMAINDER	EDIT COPY REMAINDER
COPY SENTENCE	EDIT COPY SENTENCE
COPY WORD	EDIT COPY WORD
DELETE BLOCK	EDIT DELETE BLOCK

Appendix C: Command Comparison: Smart 3.10 versus SmartWare II

Smart 3.10 Command	SmartWare II Command
DELETE LINE	EDIT DELETE LINE
DELETE PARAGRAPH	EDIT DELETE PARAGRAPH
DELETE REMAINDER	EDIT DELETE REMAINDER
DELETE SENTENCE	EDIT DELETE SENTENCE
DELETE WORD	EDIT DELETE WORD
DICTIONARY CUSTOM CREATE language INPUT filename.ext Dictionary-Name	None
DICTIONARY CUSTOM ERASE Dictionary-Name	DOCUMENT DICTIONARY ERASE Dictionary-Name
DICTIONARY CUSTOM LIST INPUT Dictionary-Name OUTPUT filename.ext	None
DICTIONARY CUSTOM UPDATE Dictionary-Name	None
DICTIONARY HYPHENATE DOCUMENT	DOCUMENT DICTIONARY HYPHENATE LINES
DICTIONARY HYPHENATE PARAGRAPH	DOCUMENT DICTIONARY HYPHENATE PARAGRAPH
DICTIONARY HYPHENATE REMAINDER	DOCUMENT DICTIONARY HYPHENATE LINES
DICTIONARY OPTIONS	LAYOUT DOCUMENT-OPTIONS CURRENT-DOCUMENT
DICTIONARY SPELL-CHECK DOCUMENT FILE filename.ext	DOCUMENT DICTIONARY SPELLCHECK FILE DOCUMENT filename.ext
DICTIONARY SPELL-CHECK DOCUMENT SCREEN	DOCUMENT DICTIONARY SPELLCHECK SCREEN DOCUMENT
DIRECTORY file specification	TOOLS DIRECTORY DISPLAY file specification
DISPLAY BLACK/WHITE	None. You can select a new Text Screen or Graphics screen in the Tools Preferences Hardware menu, but you may need to exit SmartWare for the change to work.

Smart 3.10 Command	SmartWare II Command
DISPLAY COLOR	None. You can select a new Text Screen or Graphics screen in the Tools Preferences Hardware menu, but you may need to exit SmartWare for the change to work.
DISPLAY GRAPHICS	None. You can select a new Text Screen or Graphics screen in the Tools Preferences Hardware menu, but you may need to exit SmartWare for the change to work.
DRAW	None
EXECUTE project-file	REMEMBER EXECUTE project-file {IN-MEMORY/FROM-FILE}
FILE COPY file1.ext TO file2.ext	TOOLS FILE COPY file1.ext TO file2.ext. At the command level, you don't type TO; it is inserted automatically by the command processor. In a project file, TO must separate the file names.
FILE ERASE filename.ext	TOOLS FILE ERASE filename.ext
FILE NEW-DIRECTORY \directory	TOOLS DIRECTORY NEW-DIRECTORY \directory
FILE RENAME file1.ext TO file2.ext	TOOLS FILE RENAME file1.ext TO file2.ext. At the command level, you don't type TO; it is inserted automatically by the command processor.
FIND	DOCUMENT FIND ''search text'' OPTIONS
FONT CHANGE Font-number attribute option	LAYOUT FONT CHANGE option font
FONT SELECT Font-number attribute	LAYOUT FONT SELECT font
FOOTNOTE INSERT	DOCUMENT REFERENCES FOOTNOTE INSERT
FOOTNOTE MODIFY	DOCUMENT REFERENCES FOOTNOTE MODIFY

Appendix C: Command Comparison: Smart 3.10 versus SmartWare II

Smart 3.10 Command	SmartWare II Command
F-CALCULATOR	TOOLS CALCULATOR
GOTO window #	DOCUMENT GOTO WINDOW window #
GOTO column #	DOCUMENT GOTO LOCATION column #
GOTO line #	DOCUMENT GOTO LOCATION line #
GOTO marker	DOCUMENT GOTO MARKER marker
GOTO page #	DOCUMENT GOTO LOCATION page #
GOTO page #, column #, line #	DOCUMENT GOTO LOCATION page #, column #, line #
GOTO P+number of pages from current page	DOCUMENT GOTO LOCATION P+number of pages from current page
GRAPHICS INSERT filename LARGE	GRAPH INSERT filename LARGE
GRAPHICS INSERT filename MEDIUM LEFT-JUSTIFIED	GRAPH INSERT filename MEDIUM LEFT-ALIGNED
GRAPHICS INSERT filename SMALL RIGHT-JUSTIFIED	GRAPH INSERT filename SMALL RIGHT-ALIGNED
GRAPHICS REMOVE	GRAPH REMOVE
GRAPHICS VIEW DOCUMENT	GRAPH VIEW DOCUMENT
GRAPHICS VIEW FILE filename	GRAPH VIEW FILE filename
HELP	HELP ABOUT-HELP
INDENT spaces	LAYOUT RULER EDIT CURRENT indent
INDEX	FILE DISPLAY-ACTIVE
INPUT-SCREEN DEFINE filename	REMEMBER TOOLS INPUT-SCREEN DEFINE filename
INPUT-SCREEN LOAD filename	REMEMBER TOOLS INPUT-SCREEN LOAD filename

Smart 3.10 Command	SmartWare II Command
INPUT-SCREEN UNDEFINE filename	REMEMBER TOOLS INPUT-SCREEN UNDEFINE filename
INSERT	EDIT COPY BUFFER TO location
JUSTIFY CENTERED	LAYOUT RULER
JUSTIFY LEFT-JUSTIFIED	LAYOUT RULER
JUSTIFY NORMAL	LAYOUT RULER
JUSTIFY RIGHT-JUSTIFIED	LAYOUT RULER
LOAD filename.ext	FILE LOAD document
MACRO CLEAR	TOOLS MACROS CLEAR ALL
MACRO DEFINE key	TOOLS MACROS EDIT or TOOLS MACROS REMEMBER
MACRO LOAD filename	TOOLS MACROS LOAD filename
MACRO REMOVE key	TOOLS MACROS CLEAR ONE
MACRO SAVE filename	TOOLS MACROS SAVE filename
MACRO VIEW	TOOLS MACROS VIEW
MARGIN LEFT number	LAYOUT RULER
MARGIN RIGHT number	LAYOUT RULER
MARGIN TEMP-RELEASE	LAYOUT RULER EDIT
MARKER DIRECTORY	DOCUMENT GOTO MARKER
MARKER SET name	DOCUMENT REFERENCES MARKER ADD name
MARKER UNSET name	DOCUMENT REFERENCES MARKER REMOVE name
MARKER VIEW	DOCUMENT REFERENCES MARKER VIEW
MERGE FILE ENHANCED filename	PRINT MERGE FILE ENHANCED filename PRINTER
MERGE FILE NORMAL filename	PRINT MERGE FILE DRAFT filename PRINTER
MERGE SCREEN ENHANCED	PRINT MERGE SCREEN ENHANCED PRINTER

Appendix C: Command Comparison: Smart 3.10 versus SmartWare II

Smart 3.10 Command	SmartWare II Command
MERGE SCREEN NORMAL	PRINT MERGE SCREEN DRAFT PRINTER
MOVE BLOCK	EDIT MOVE BLOCK TO POINT
MOVE LINE	EDIT MOVE LINE TO POINT
MOVE PARAGRAPH	EDIT MOVE PARAGRAPH TO POINT
MOVE REMAINDER	EDIT MOVE REMAINDER TO POINT
MOVE SENTENCE	EDIT MOVE SENTENCE TO POINT
MOVE WORD	EDIT MOVE WORD TO POINT
NEWNAME document	FILE NEWNAME document
NEWPAGE INSERT	LAYOUT NEWPAGE INSERT
NEWPAGE REMOVE	LAYOUT NEWPAGE REMOVE
PAINT BORDER FOREGROUND value	WINDOW PAINT BORDER FOREGROUND value
PAINT TEXT-BLOCK BACKGROUND value FOREGROUND value	WINDOW PAINT MARKED-TEXT BACKGROUND value FOREGROUND value
PAINT WINDOW BACKGROUND value FOREGROUND value	WINDOW PAINT WINDOW BACKGROUND value FOREGROUND value
PARAMETERS	TOOLS PREFERENCES WORDPROCESSOR
PASSWORD ATTACH password	FILE PASSWORD ATTACH password
PASSWORD REMOVE	FILE PASSWORD REMOVE
PRINT ENHANCED document PRINTER COPIES number START-PAGE number END-PAGE number	PRINT DOCUMENT document ENHANCED COPIES number START-PAGE number END-PAGE number PRINTER
PRINT NORMAL document DISK output-file	PRINT DOCUMENT document DRAFT COPIES 1 START-PAGE 1 END-PAGE * DISK output-file

Smart 3.10 Command	SmartWare II Command
PRINT NORMAL document PRINTER COPIES number START-PAGE number END-PAGE number	PRINT DOCUMENT document DRAFT COPIES number START-PAGE number END-PAGE number PRINTER
PRINT OPTIONS	PRINT OPTIONS
PRINT PRESET	PRINT PRESET
PRINT TEMPLATE CURRENT-DOCUMENT	None
PRINT TEMPLATE PRESET	None
READ document	FILE IMPORT document
REFORMAT DOCUMENT CENTERED LEFT number RIGHT number INDENT number SPACING number	LAYOUT RULER EDIT or REFORMAT
REFORMAT DOCUMENT NORMAL LEFT number RIGHT number INDENT number SPACING number	LAYOUT RULER EDIT or REFORMAT
REFORMAT PARAGRAPH LEFT-JUSTIFIED LEFT number RIGHT number INDENT number SPACING number	LAYOUT RULER EDIT or REFORMAT
REFORMAT PARAGRAPH SAME LEFT number RIGHT number INDENT number SPACING number	LAYOUT RULER EDIT or REFORMAT
REFORMAT REMAINDER RIGHT-JUSTIFIED LEFT number RIGHT number INDENT number SPACING number	LAYOUT RULER EDIT or REFORMAT
REMEMBER COMPILE LINE-NUMBERS Proj-Name	REMEMBER TOOLS COMPILE DEBUG Proj-Name
REMEMBER COMPILE NO-LINE NUMBERS Proj-Name	REMEMBER TOOLS COMPILE NO-DEBUG Proj-Name
REMEMBER DELETE Proj-Name	REMEMBER TOOLS DELETE Proj-Name
REMEMBER EDIT Proj-Name	REMEMBER TOOLS EDIT Proj-Name

Appendix C: Command Comparison: Smart 3.10 versus SmartWare II

Smart 3.10 Command	SmartWare II Command
REMEMBER FINISH	REMEMBER FINISH
REMEMBER HELP	None
REMEMBER PRINT Proj-Name	REMEMBER TOOLS PRINT Proj-Name
REMEMBER START Proj-Name	REMEMBER START COMMANDS Proj-Name. Plus recording just commands, you also can record KEYS or BOTH commands and keys.
REPLACE	EDIT REPLACE "search text" WITH "replace text" OPTIONS options
RULER	DOCUMENT VISIBLE RULERS MAIN
SAVE document	FILE SAVE document
SCROLL DOWN rate	None
SCROLL UP rate	None
SEND COMMUNICATIONS DOCUMENT document PROJECT-FILE Proj-File	DOCUMENT SEND COMMUNICATIONS DOCUMENT document PROJECT-FILE Proj-File
SEND COMMUNICATIONS TEXT document PROJECT-FILE Proj-File	DOCUMENT SEND COMMUNICATIONS TEXT document PROJECT-FILE Proj-File
SEND DATA-MANAGER document PROJECT-FILE Proj-File	DOCUMENT SEND DATABASE document PROJECT-FILE Proj-File
SEND SPREADSHEET document PROJECT-FILE Proj-File	DOCUMENT SEND SPREADSHEET document PROJECT-FILE Proj-File
SPACING number	LAYOUT RULER
SPLIT FOOTNOTE	WINDOW SPLIT FOOTNOTE
SPLIT HORIZONTAL	WINDOW SPLIT HORIZONTAL
SPLIT VERTICAL	WINDOW SPLIT VERTICAL
TABS DECIMAL	LAYOUT RULER
TABS NORMAL	LAYOUT RULER

Smart 3.10 Command	SmartWare II Command
TEXT-SORT ASCENDING	EDIT SORT TEXT ASCENDING COLUMN
TEXT-SORT DESCENDING	EDIT SORT TEXT DESCENDING COLUMN
UNDELETE	EDIT UNDELETE
UNDERSCORE INSERT BLOCK	LAYOUT FONT UNDERSCORE INSERT BLOCK
UNDERSCORE INSERT CHARACTER	LAYOUT FONT UNDERSCORE INSERT
UNDERSCORE INSERT DOCUMENT	LAYOUT FONT UNDERSCORE INSERT DOCUMENT
UNDERSCORE INSERT LINE	LAYOUT FONT UNDERSCORE INSERT LINE
UNDERSCORE INSERT PARAGRAPH	LAYOUT FONT UNDERSCORE INSERT PARAGRAPH
UNDERSCORE INSERT REMAINDER	LAYOUT FONT UNDERSCORE INSERT REMAINDER
UNDERSCORE INSERT SENTENCE	LAYOUT FONT UNDERSCORE INSERT SENTENCE
UNDERSCORE INSERT WORD	LAYOUT FONT UNDERSCORE INSERT WORD
UNDERSCORE REMOVE BLOCK	LAYOUT FONT UNDERSCORE REMOVE BLOCK
UNDERSCORE REMOVE CHARACTER	LAYOUT FONT UNDERSCORE REMOVE
UNDERSCORE REMOVE DOCUMENT	LAYOUT FONT UNDERSCORE REMOVE DOCUMENT
UNDERSCORE REMOVE LINE	LAYOUT FONT UNDERSCORE REMOVE LINE
UNDERSCORE REMOVE PARAGRAPH	LAYOUT FONT UNDERSCORE REMOVE PARAGRAPH
UNDERSCORE REMOVE REMAINDER	LAYOUT FONT UNDERSCORE REMOVE REMAINDER
UNDERSCORE REMOVE SENTENCE	LAYOUT FONT UNDERSCORE REMOVE SENTENCE

Smart 3.10 Command	SmartWare II Command
UNDERSCORE REMOVE WORD	LAYOUT FONT UNDERSCORE REMOVE WORD
UNLOAD	FILE UNLOAD
VISIBLE NEWPAGE	DOCUMENT VISIBLE NEWPAGE
VISIBLE PARAGRAPH-MARKS	DOCUMENT VISIBLE PARAGRAPHS
VISIBLE TABS	DOCUMENT VISIBLE TABS
WRITE BLOCK filename	FILE EXPORT BLOCK filename
WRITE DOCUMENT filename	FILE EXPORT DOCUMENT filename
WRITE PARAGRAPH filename	FILE EXPORT PARAGRAPH filename
WRITE REMAINDER filename	FILE EXPORT REMAINDER filename
XLATE DCA filename	None
XLATE EDIT	None
XLATE SMART filename TO DCA filename USING	None
ZOOM	WINDOW ZOOM

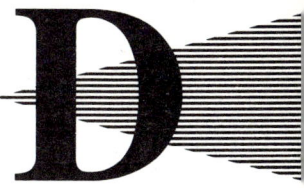

Converting from Smart 3.10

This appendix covers techniques for converting from Smart Version 3.10 to SmartWare II. Some of the modules will convert very easily; others will require more work. Several modules have pitfalls to avoid. You will have few problems converting the Word Processor, Communications and Spreadsheet modules. There are some techniques to observe and some things to watch out for.

Converting a database application (data files and associated files such as report definition, project files, and so on) may provide some challenges. Should you simply convert a Smart Version 3.10 database application to run identically under SmartWare II, or should you rewrite the application? If you convert an existing application, you will be able to take advantage of many of the enhancements, but you will be missing others. For example, under SmartWare II, you do not have to worry about updating keys. However, if your application performs several Relate commands to pull together data from multiple files to print a report, you could probably accomplish the same result by attaching the files to a single view in SmartWare II. In many instances, you may find that elaborate data input project files in the Database module can be eliminated by using a view with field masks, pop-up windows, error and jump rules, project variable fields and multiple file attachments.

A "soft" conversion from Smart 3.10 will most certainly take less time than a "hard" conversion, in which the application is completely rewritten. The requirements of the task ultimately determine the course of action you will take.

Try to keep Smart 3.10 files separate from those of SmartWare II, because once you convert, you cannot go back. When converting database applications and project files, if you want to keep the same names, it is mandatory that the files of the two versions be kept in separate subdirectories during the conversion process.

Converting the Database

One way to convert a Smart 3.10 data file to SmartWare II is to use the File Import 310-Smart command. This command reads a Smart 3.10 data file and creates a SmartWare II data file and a standard view. You are prompted for the names of both the 3.10 data file and the new data file to create; the new SmartWare II data file must not already exist. For more information on the use of this command, refer to Chapter 7.

A conversion utility has been provided with SmartWare II which converts the data file; each custom screen will be converted to a custom view. To execute this utility project file, select the Remember Execute command (or press F8). When you are prompted to enter a project file name, type the following:

```
c:\smartii\dbs_conv
```

(This example assumes that you have installed the SmartWare II software on your C drive in the subdirectory SMARTII. If necessary, you should alter the response for your own configuration.) When you press Enter, you are prompted:

```
In-Memory  From-File
```

You should select From-File, because this conversion is very memory intensive. You are then prompted:

```
Enter the complete path to your Smart 3.10 Database data directory:
```

You should type the path and press Enter. Next, a pop-up window displays the names of the databases in the specified subdirectory (see fig. D.1).

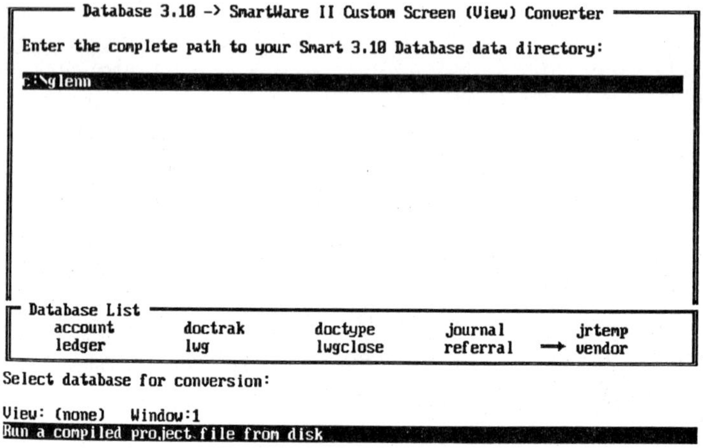

Fig. D.1.

A pop-up window that displays the names of the databases in the specified subdirectory.

Appendix D: Converting from Smart 3.10

Select the file to convert and press Enter. The next prompt is as follows:

```
Select conversion option for "filename":

(1) Import Database and Convert Custom Screens
(2) Convert Custom Screens only
```

Select *1* to convert both the database and the custom screens. If you have already converted or imported the database, you can select *2* to convert just the custom screens. If you are converting the database, you are prompted:

```
Enter name for SmartWare II Database:
```

The default is the same name as the original; press Enter to accept it, or type a new name and press Enter. If you are converting the screens, you are prompted:

```
Select conversion screens for "filename":

(1) Convert All Screens
(2) Select Screens to Convert
```

If the database is converted, the following message is displayed on the screen during conversion:

```
Importing filename ... Please Wait
```

A record count, along with progress messages, is displayed on the command line. If you have chosen to select the screens to convert, for each screen, you are prompted:

```
Processing views for "filename"...

Process View "viewname" (y/n)?
```

If you select *Y*, the conversion program develops a project file to create the new view. When the new project file is ready to run, you are prompted:

```
Hit any key to continue. (ESCAPE to cancel)
```

The conversion program uses the Smart 3.10 screen names for the SmartWare II custom view names. Because 3.10 screen names can be as long as 20 characters, it is possible to exceed the eight-character limit for the view names. If this happens, you receive the following error message:

```
Not text variable, or character offset outside text
```

When you press Esc to clear the error, you are prompted for a new view name.

Next, you will see the automatic creation of the custom view on the monitor screen. At the completion, the message is displayed:

```
Conversion complete...hit any key.
```

Press any key to continue. At this point, both the data file and the custom screens have been converted. You are returned to the menu level of SmartWare II, but the new file is not automatically loaded for you.

Although the conversion process will recreate your keys for you, the program will probably run more smoothly if you delete the keys from the Smart 3.10 file before converting. The conversion process is very complex, and the more you can simplify it, the faster and better it will run. Besides, you may want to set up the keys in SmartWare II to disallow duplicates. If you do, you would have to delete the keys and then add them again.

If you have several databases to convert, the process may go more smoothly in separate SmartWare II Database sessions. Again, due to the complexity of the conversion process, working storage memory is used most efficiently if it is clear of any leftover variables or buffers.

Other Database Files

What about all the definition files used in database applications? Can they be used or converted? In most cases, you will have to re-create your definitions, such as relates, transactions, sorts, and so forth. Input screen definitions (IS3) and most Query definitions can be copied and used as they are.

Converting the Spreadsheet

To convert a spreadsheet from a previous Smart version to SmartWare II, load the worksheet with the File Load command. Specify the path from which to load, if necessary. Once it is loaded, press the Shift-F5 to force a total recalculation of the worksheet. Saving the worksheet to the disk completes the conversion process. If you have loaded the worksheet from a subdirectory other than the current one and want to keep the same worksheet path and name, type the name when you are prompted for a file name; do not just press Enter. Then unload the worksheet and go to the next one.

Only one password can be attached to a worksheet in SmartWare II. The "save permission" password of a worksheet from previous versions will be the new password in SmartWare II.

Converting the Word Processor

To convert a document from a previous Smart version to SmartWare II, simply load it with the File Load command. When you save the document, the conversion is complete. If you have loaded the document from a subdirectory other than the current one and want to keep the same document name, type the name when you are prompted for a file name; do not just press Enter.

Custom Dictionaries

If the document has a custom dictionary attached, when you load it, the following warning message appears:

    Version 3.10 dictionary files omitted. They are no longer valid.

You will need to use the Layout Document-Options Current-Document to attach new custom dictionaries to the document.

There is a Word Processor command that is not on the menu which you can use to convert Smart 3.10 custom dictionaries to SmartWare II. The procedure is as follows:

1. In the Smart 3.10 Word Processor, write the contents of the custom dictionary to an ASCII file, using the Dictionary Custom List command. When you execute the command, you are prompted to enter the name of the custom dictionary to convert. Enter the name, providing the path, if necessary.

   The second prompt asks for the name of the output file. Enter a file name and the extension UDC, which is the extension of custom dictionaries in SmartWare II. Enter a destination path if necessary.

2. Quit Smart 3.10 and begin a SmartWare II Word Processor session. Press Alt-X to be able to enter your own command. This will display the previous Word Processor command on the command line, if there was one.

3. Press F8 to clear the command line, or simply hold down the Delete key.

4. Type the following on the command line:

   Udc-Conv "filename"

The file name must include the path, if it is different from the current. Do not include the .UDC extension of the custom dictionary, however.

In the conversion process, the custom dictionary entries are sorted into ASCII sequence, and commas, which separate syllables, are removed. Any words longer than 22 characters will be removed, and you will be warned.

Use the Layout Document-Option Current-document command to attach the new custom dictionary to a document. If the document has been loaded from the Smart 3.10 format, you must save it as a SmartWare II document and reload it to be able to use the custom dictionary.

Converting the Communications Module

To convert a communications profile from Smart 3.10 to SmartWare II, execute the Set-Terminal Settings Load command (in SmartWare II). You are prompted:

    Enter the settings filename:

Type the path and name of the Smart 3.10 profile and press Enter. The following error message will be displayed:

    Modem definition not found. Check pathname and/or Modem name.

This error message is normal; now execute the Set-Terminal Settings Edit command to select the modem you want to use. Move the cursor down to the Modem Type: entry and press F6. (For more information on modem selection, refer to Chapter 23.) Press F10 to exit the edit menu. Use the Set-Terminal Settings Save command to save the definition to the disk.

Custom key definitions from Smart 3.10 may also be carried over to SmartWare II. Use the Set-Terminal Keyboard Define command on an existing definition to make it compatible with SmartWare II.

Converting Project Files

The conversion of project files is accomplished at the DOS level using a program called TRANLAT, which you will find in your SmartWare II system subdirectory. This program converts Smart 3.10 statements to SmartWare II statements and can save you many hours of work.

In some instances, there will be no equivalent command in SmartWare II. In those cases, the statement will be flagged, as in the following example:

    'key update   '*** msg# 1: ***`no counterpart in smartware II
    for the above command

The total number of such messages written will be displayed both at the conclusion of the translation and at the end of the project file.

The format of the translation command is

    \smartii\Translat   \path1\Old.Pf#   \path2\New.Pf#

You can use wild cards to translate a group of files in one command as follows:

    \smartii\Translat   \path1*.Pf3   \path2\

Be sure to specify the closing slash (\) on the destination path. Note that only the source project files (PFx) are translated; after translation, you must still compile them in the appropriate module with either the Remember Tools Edit or Remember Tools Compile commands. (You will probably want to edit the programs to review any messages.)

You must specify the source file extensions for both the old and the new files. Note that the extension for project files in the Communications module have changed from PF6 in Smart 3.10 to PF4 in SmartWare II.

Summary

There are a number of utilities that can help you convert from Smart 3.10 to SmartWare II. The Database module will probably require the most extensive modifications, because it has been changed or been improved more than the other modules. The new features of the Database will make the conversion well worth the while. To take full advantage of the new features, you may decide to redesign your Database applications and rewrite parts of them.

You should try to keep Smart 3.10 files in a different subdirectory from those of SmartWare II. In most cases, the file-naming conventions remain the same; you would undoubtedly get a number of error messages in SmartWare II if you tried to use Smart 3.10 files.

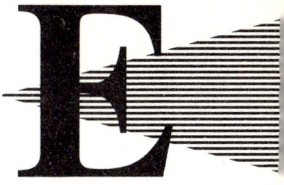

Collation Sort Sequence versus ASCII Sort Sequence

The majority of the SmartWare II system uses the collation sorting sequence, in which corresponding upper- and lowercase letters of the alphabet are intermingled with each other. Letters having the same collation weight are grouped together. Uppercase B and lowercase b, for example, have the same collation sort value, and thus will be commingled. In a group, however, the sequence of individual characters is random. Some of the special characters are reshuffled from the ASCII sequence and are sometimes interspersed among the letters of the alphabet.

In the Database module, however, when you create a key for a file, the ASCII sort sequence is used. This difference results from the revised key maintenance procedures introduced with SmartWare II, permitting instantaneous key updating.

Figures E.1, E.2, E.3, and E.4 show the two sorting sequences. In each figure there are several pairs of columns. In each pair, the first column shows the decimal ASCII value; the second column displays the matching character symbol. Figures E.1 and E.2 show the collation sequence; figures E.3 and E.4 show the ASCII sequence.

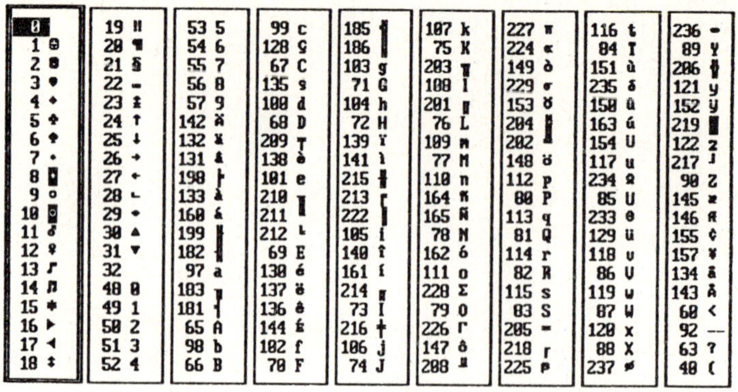

Fig. E.1.

Collation sequence, page 1.

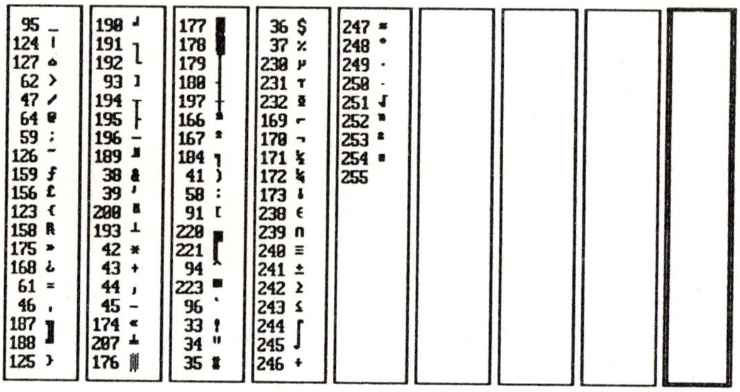

Fig. E.2.

Collation sequence, page 2.

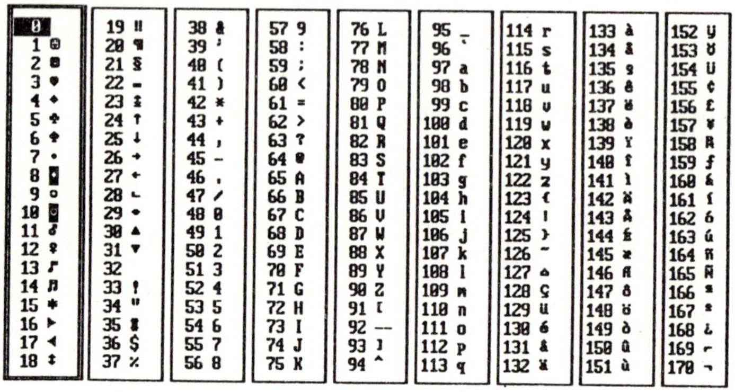

Fig. E.3.

ASCII sequence, page 1.

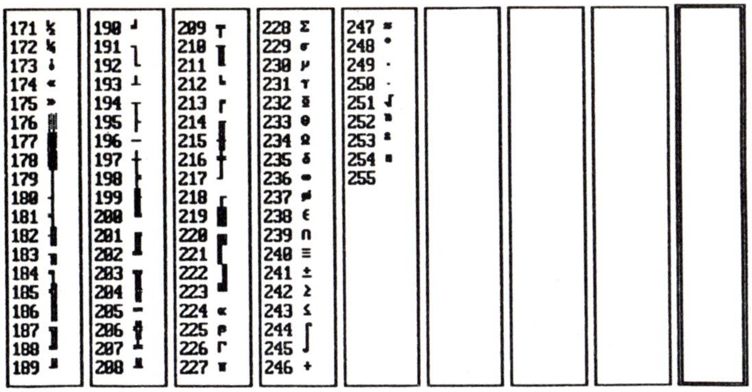

Appendix E: Collation Sort Sequence versus ASCII Sort Sequence

Fig. E.4.

ASCII sequence, page 2.

Index

A

absolute cell references, spreadsheet, 170-171
ADATE date function, 542
ADDDAYS date function, 543
ADDHOURS time function, 548
ADDMINUTES time function, 549
ADDMONTHS date function, 543
address, spreadsheet cell, 166
ADDSECONDS time function, 549
ADDYEARS date function, 543-544
Algebraic mode, function keys, 650-651
Alpha Field Options menu, 133
alpha fields, 133
alphanumeric fields, 16
Alt key, 6
arrays, project file, 484-485
ASC text function, 553
ASCII
    files, 299-301
        importing, 144
    sort sequence vs. collation sort sequence, 727-729
    text files, editing, 648
ATIME time function, 549
ATIME24 time function, 550
Attach Data-File (DB) command, 37
Attach Field (DB) command, 37
Autohelp (PP) command, 522
Autohelp options, 632
Automatic File Backup options, 632

B

background colors function, 617
Backspace key (WP), 310
bar graph, 266-273
Bar/Line Graph Definition screen, 267
bar menu, 31-32
bar notation format, 186
BDC file extension, 318
Beep (PP) command, 485
Beeper options, 632
BLANK function, 599
block names, printing, 236
blocks
    clearing spreadsheet, 231
    deleting spreadsheet, 229-230
    editing definition, 236-237
    inserting in spreadsheet, 227-228
    marking word processor, 312-314
    moving spreadsheet, 223-225
    removing a name, 237
    spreadsheet, 169
boldface, word processor, 379
book
    overview, 7
    users, 2
Breakpoint Totals Options menu, 136-137
breakpoints
    choosing fonts, 138
    editing, 138
    report, 135-138
Browse mode, 65-67
buffer, capturing, 455-456

C

Calculated Field Option menu, 127-128
calculated fields, 33
calculations, report, 134
calculator
    built-in, 59-60
    function keys, 649-650
    using, 649-651
Caps Lock key, 23
Case (PP) command, 520-521
cell address, spreadsheet, 166
cells
    editing worksheet, 231-232
    formatting spreadsheet, 181-212
    naming a block, 235
    spreadsheet, 163
    unlocking worksheet, 256
CELLTEXT text function, 560-561
CERROR project processing function, 616
Change option, 130
CHR text function, 554
Clear (PP) command, 515-516
Close-Printer (PP) command, 497-498
collation sort sequence vs. ASCII sort sequence, 727-729
colors, changing database, 46
column fonts, using in reports, 135
COLUMN spreadsheet function, 593
column summary definition, 152-153
columns
    adding word processor, 328-329
    changing
        spreadsheet width, 204-205
        word processor widths, 329-330
    clearing spreadsheet, 230
    deleting
        linked word processor, 330-331
        spreadsheet, 228
    inserting in spreadsheet, 226

marking word processor, 314
moving
    spreadsheet, 222-223
    word processor, 331
retaining spreadsheet, 243-244
sizing spreadsheet, 187-188
word processor, 325-326
command comparison
    communications module, 669-675
    database module, 675-688
    main menu, 688-690
    project processing, 690-694
    Smart 3.10 vs. Smartware II, 669-718
    spreadsheet module, 694-707
    word processor, 707-718
Command mode
    spreadsheet, 167
    word processor, 312
commands
    common to all modules, 621-651
    Directory, 622-626
    execution of, 5
Comments statement, 524
communication module, 441-470
    command comparison, 669-675
    converting from Smart 3.10, 724
    importing spreadsheet data, 301-302
    sending database data to, 157-158
communication quick keys, 662-664
communications
    buffer capture, 455-456
    calling another computer, 443, 451
    capturing data, 455-456
    communications module, 442
    customizing, 459-466
    default preferences, 464-466
    duplex settings, 450-451
    estimating data transfer time, 454-455
    file format definition, 461-462
    filtering characters, 456-457
    handling data, 452
    keyboard definition, 459-460
    loading terminal settings, 449-450
    modem definition, 462-464
    new features, 441
    parameters, 444
    receiving data, 452-453
    screen capture, 455
    sending data, 453-454
    status screen, 442-443
    terminal screen, 443
    terminal settings, 444-450
    Xmodem protocol, 452
Communications options, 638
Computer/keyboard options, 638

computers, calling another, 443, 451
concepts (DB), 13
configuring program, 3
Connection Dial (CM) command, 443, 451
control commands, project file, 488-490
Copy options, 626-628
count fields, 54
counter numeric field, 17
Create Box (DB) command, 30-31
Create Calculation (DB) command, 33
Create command options, 23-24
Create Menu (DB) command, 31-33
Create Note (DB) command, 30
Create Rule (DB) command, 34-35
Create Table (DB) command, 35
Cross-Tab command options, 151
Cross-Tab definition screen, 149-150
Cross-tab feature (DB), 13
cross-tabs, 148-157
Ctrl-End keys, 19
Ctrl-Home key, 19
Ctrl key, 6
currency format, 184
Currency symbol location options 634
Currency symbol options, 633
CURRENCY text function, 554
CURRFILES text function, 562
cursor control keys, 19
    spreadsheet module, 167
    word processor, 311-312
cursor, moving, 19
custom view, 15

D

DAS file extension, 317, 322
data
    arranging database, 93
    browsing database, 65-67
    entering database, 57-60
    files, repairing damages, 54
    replacing in database, 88-89
    sending/receiving in communications mode, 452-454
    summarized, 159
    types, 16-17
    updating database, 60-62
    viewing database, 64-65
Data Browse (DB) command, 65-66
Data Capture (CM) command, 455
Data Capture Buffer (CM) command, 466
Data Cross-Tab (DB) command, 148-152, 159
Data Cross-Tab Execute (DB) command, 156
Data Delete (DB) command, 64
Data Delete Record (DB) command, 62-64
Data Enter (DB) command, 57, 60-61

Index 733

Data Entry mode, 59-61
Data Find (DB) command, 73-78
Data Find (DB) command options, 75-77
Data Format (CM) command, 461
Data Get (CM) command, 457
Data Goto (DB) command, 70-72
Data Goto View (DB) command, 50
Data Match (CM) command, 458
Data Output (CM) command, 458-459
data path, setting word processor, 318
Data Query (DB) command, 63, 78-79, 86, 88, 119
Data Query Create (DB) command, 91
Data Query Execute (DB) command, 91
Data Query Modify (DB) command, 92
Data Query Now (DB) command, 79-80
Data Query Remove (DB) command, 92
Data Receive (CM) command, 452
Data Relate (DB) command, 105-108
Data Relate Execute (DB) command, 108
Data Relate Modify (DB) command, 109
Data Relate Remove (DB) command, 109
Data Send (CM) command, 466
Data Send (DB) command, 157
Data Transact (DB) command, 110
Data Transact Execute (DB) command, 114
Data Transact Modify (DB) command, 114
Data Transact Remove (DB) command, 114
Data Transmit (CM) command, 453
Data Update mode, 60-62
Data Utilities Append (DB) command, 114-115
Data Utilities Change-Count (DB) command, 54
Data Utilities File-Fix (DB) command, 54
Data Utilities Information (DB) command, 52
Data Utilities Purge (DB) command, 62, 64
Data Xfer Time (CM) command, 454
Database
   concepts, 13-14
   new features, 12-13
   quick keys, 661-662
database functions
   BLANK, 599
   DBGET, 612
   DBPUT, 612
   DELETED, 607
   FETCHFIELD, 607-608
   File Reference functions, 609
   FILELOOKUP, 609-610
   INVERT, 608
   Record Numbers, 607
   see also functions
   Table Reference functions, 610-611
   TABLEREC, 611
   TAVLELOOKUP, 611-612
Database module, 11-20
   command comparison, 675-688

importing spreadsheet data, 302
databases
   activating views, 50
   adding
      box to a view, 30-31
      key, 93-96
      view notes, 30
   alpha fields, 133
   Alt-E (Data Enter), 57
   arranging
      data, 93
      views, 101
   changing
      a transaction definition, 114
      colors, 46
      order of views, 100
      passwords, 55
      to index order, 102
      to key order, 101-102
      to original view order, 101
   character-specific input mask fields, 60
   column summary definitions, 152-153
   converting from Smart 3.10, 720-722
   copying data from one view to another, 114-115
   creating, 21-29
      a view, 22-23
      fields, 24-29
      passwords, 24
      sort definitions, 97-98
      temporary index files, 102
      transaction definition, 110-114
   data replacement, 88-89
   defining relationships, 106-108
   deleting
      keys, 96
      multiple linked files, 63
      records, 62-64
   designing, 30-46
   duplicating
      fields, 46
      files, 45
   editing
      a view, 42
      field declarations, 42-43
   entering
      data, 57-60
      date in fields, 59
      search criterion, 75
      time in fields, 59
   erasing
      query definition, 92
      relation definition, 109-110
      transaction definition, 114
   exporting files, 147-148
   field rules, 34-35

fields, adding a menu, 31-33
file keys, 93-96
fixing keys, 96
getting information about a view, 52-54
immediate sorts, 99-100
importing files, 143-147
key fields, 93-96
linking
    files, 39-41
    windows, 69-70
loading views, 48-50
logical operators in searches, 74-75
making backup files, 64
mandatory fields, 60
marking records for deletion, 63-64
match equations, 152-156
modifying
    a query definition, 92
    files, 46
    relation definition, 109
multiple files, 105-116
naming conventions, 24
numeric fields, 133
printing, 117-121
printing mailing labels, 128-129
query optimization, 90
query view expressions, 84-86
read-only fields, 60
rearranging a view, 43
relating two views, 105-110
removing a file password, 55
repairing damages to data file, 54
report breakpoints, 135-138
running saved query definition, 91-92
saving a query definition, 91
saving files, 52
selecting
    field names, 74
    records, 73-74
    records manually, 92
    report fields, 133-134
sending
    data to
        communications module, 157-158
        spreadsheet module, 158
        word processor module, 159
    summarized data to other modules, 159
setting preferences, 46-48
sorting a view, 96-97
summarizing fields, 148-149
summary file statistics, 86-88
table reports, 132-135
tables, 35-41
transacting views, 110
unloading views, 50-52

updating data, 60-62
using cross-tabs, 148-157
viewing data, 64-65
windows, 67-70
working with, 17-18
date, entering in database field, 59
date fields, 17
date format, 184-185
date functions
    ADATE, 542
    ADDDAYS, 543
    ADDMONTHS, 543
    ADDYEARS, 543-544
    DATE1, 544
    DATE2, 544
    DATE3, 544-545
    DAY, 545
    DAYNAME, 545
    DAYS, 545-546
    MONTH, 546
    MONTHNAME, 546
    NOW, 547-548
    TODAY, 547
    YEAR, 547
Date style options, 633
DATE1 date function, 544
DATE2 date function, 544
DATE3 date function, 544-545
dates
    entering in spreadsheet, 171
    printing word processor, 420
DAY date function, 545
DAYNAME date function, 545
DAYS date function, 545-546
dBASE files, converting, 147
DBGET database function, 612
DBPUT database function, 612
Debug statement, 523
Decimal separator options, 634
decimal tabs, word processor, 359-360
Default data path options, 634
default value format options, 182
Del key (WP), 310
Delete (DB) command, 43-44
DELETED database function, 607
dictionaries
    converting from Smart 3.10, 723
    custom spellcheck, 394
directories
    changing, 624-625
    making new, 624
    removing, 625-626
Directory commands, 622-626
display commands, project file, 485-488
Display of File Names options, 632

Index

Display option, 622-623
Division by zero options, 634
DOC file extension, 320
document auto-save word processor, 317-318, 322
Document Columns (WP) command, 325
Document Columns Edit (WP) command, 328-331
Document Columns Edit Add Entry (WP) command, 327, 329
Document Dictionary (WP) command, 388
Document Dictionary Hyphenate (WP) command, 394
Document Dictionary Spellcheck (WP) command, 392-393
Document Dictionary Thesaurus (WP) command, 396
Document Find (WP) command, 345
Document Goto (WP) command, 349-352
Document Goto Document (WP) command, 350
Document Goto Location (WP) command, 352
Document Goto Marker (WP) command, 353
Document Interchange Format (DIF) file, 300
Document Lock (WP) command, 324
Document References Footnote Insert (WP) command, 379
Document References Footnote Modify (WP) command, 381
Document References Index Add (WP) command, 407
Document References Index Edit (WP) command, 411
Document References Index Generate (WP) command, 412
Document References Index Remove (WP) command, 412
Document References Marker Add (WP) command, 353-354
Document References Marker Remove (WP) command, 354
Document References Marker View (WP) command, 354
Document References Paragraph Number Insert (WP) command, 414
Document References Paragraph Number Remove (WP) command, 414
Document References Toc Add (WP) command, 402
Document References Toc Generate (WP) command, 403
Document References Toc Remove (WP) command, 404
Document Send (WP) command, 432
Document Send Communications (WP) command, 434
Document Unlock (WP) command, 325
documents
    adding index marker, 407-411
    appending word processor, 323
    changing between, 350-351
    displaying graphs, 436-437
    finding markers, 354
    importing graphics, 435
    indexing, 404-412
    inserting graphs, 436
    inserting paragraph numbers, 414
    loading word processor, 319-320, 324
    moving around in, 349-353
    moving to a marker, 351
    printing word processor, 422-424
    reading files into text, 429-430
    removing graphs, 437
    removing markers, 354
    removing paragraph numbers, 414
    renaming word processor, 322
    sections, 371
    setting markers, 353-354
    specifying combinations of locations, 352-353
    unloading word processor, 321, 325
    using markers, 353-354
dot-matrix printers, defining mailing labels, 129
Dupe (DB) command, 130

E

Edit Blank (SS) command, 230
Edit Blank All (SS) command, 231
Edit Blank Block (SS) command, 231
Edit Blank Columns (SS) command, 230
Edit Blank Rows (SS) command, 231
Edit Copy (SS) command, 215-216
Edit Copy (WP) command, 337
Edit Copy Down (SS) command, 216-217
Edit Copy From (SS) command, 220-221
Edit Copy Right (SS) command, 217-219
Edit Copy Right Column (SS) command, 217-219
Edit Copy Right Single-Cell (SS) command, 217-219
Edit Delete (SS) command, 228
Edit Delete (WP) command, 312, 340
Edit Delete Block (SS) command, 229-230
Edit Delete Rows (SS) command, 229
Edit Edit-Cell (SS) command, 231-232
Edit Fill (SS) command, 246-247
Edit Hide (SS) command, 259
Edit Insert (SS) command, 226
Edit Insert Block (SS) command, 227-228
Edit Insert Columns (SS) command, 226
Edit Insert Rows (SS) command, 227
Edit Links (DB) command, 39
Edit Move (SS) command, 222
Edit Move (WP) command, 333, 336
Edit Move Block (SS) command, 223-225
Edit Move Columns (SS) command, 222-223
Edit Move Rows (SS) command, 223
Edit Replace (WP) command, 347
Edit Sort (SS) command, 233-235
Edit Sort (WP) command, 384
Edit Table (DB) command, 38
Edit Undelete (WP) command, 341

Edit Value-Copy (SS) command, 221
editing macros, 640-641
encryption driver, word processor, 318
Enhanced mode, printing, 424-425
Enter mode, spreadsheet, 167
EOF function, 619
Erase options, 629
ERROR project processing function, 617
errors, correcting in word processor, 310
ERRORTEXT project processing function, 616-617
Esc key (WP), 312
Execute (PP) command, 488
Exit (PP) command, 493
exporting, 143

F

F1 (Help) key, 6
F10 key, 6
FACTUAL function, 618
Fclose (PP) command, 499
FETCHFIELD database function, 607-608
field declarations
    deleting, 43-44
    editing, 42-43
Field Declarations options, 26-29
field names, 18
    selecting database, 74
field rules, 34-35
Field Text Editor screen, 59
Field title placement option, 26
Field type option, 25
Field width option, 25
fields, 14
    alpha, 133
    alphanumeric, 16
    attaching to database table, 41-42
    counter numeric, 17
    database, 24-29
        adding a menu, 31-33
        calculated, 33
        character-specific input mask, 60
        count, 54
        duplicating, 46
        entering date in, 59
        entering time in, 59
        key, 93-96
        quotation marks in, 60
        setting input order, 44-45
    date, 17
    identifying, 18
    inverted, 17
    key, 16
    mandatory, 60
    numeric, 133

numeric data, 17
read-only, 60
reformatting multiple-line alphanumeric, 59
selecting, 18
selecting report, 133-134
time, 17
File Activate (DB) command, 50
File Activate (SS) command, 175
File Combine (SS) command, 253-254
File Create (DB) command, 22
File Creation Edit options, 42
File Display Active (DB) command, 50
File Display-Active (SS) command, 175
File Export (DB) command, 147-148
File Export (SS) command, 300-301
File Export (WP) command, 430
file extensions
    BDC, 318
    DAS, 317, 322
    DOC, 320
    GDF, 281
    GMF, 281
    GMF, 435
    IFF, 157-158
    list of, 665-667
    MAC, 643
    MDV, 462
    PRT, 140
    TXT, 320, 647
    UDC, 394
    VW, 22
    VWS, 22
File File-Type (WP) command, 382
File Import (DB) command, 143-146
File Import (SS) command, 299-300
File Import (WP) command, 323, 429-430
file keys, 93-96
File Load (DB) command, 48
File Load (SS) command, 173
File Load commands, WP, 319-321
File Modify (DB) command, 46
file naming conventions, word processor, 322
File Newname (WP) command, 322
file operations, project processing, 471-475
File Password (DB) command, 55
File Password (SS) command, 258-259
File Password (WP) command, 323-324
File Password Attach (WP) command, 324
File Password Data-File Remove (DB) command, 55
File Password Remove (SS) command, 259
File Password Remove (WP) command, 324
File Password View Attach (DB) command, 55-56
File Password View Remove (DB) command, 56
file paths, paging, 634
File Reference functions, database, 609

File Save (DB) command, 52
File Save (SS) command, 175-176
File Save (WP) command, 322
File Unload (DB) command, 51
File Unload (SS) command, 176-177
File Unload (WP) command, 321
File Unload All (DB) command, 51
File Unload View (DB) command, 51
FILELOOKUP database function, 609-610
files
    adding keys to database, 94-96
    ASCII, 299-300
    attaching
        password to, 55
        to database table, 41-42
    capturing, 456
    combining, 253-254
        spreadsheet, 253-254
    converting
        dBASE, 147
        Smart Version 3.10, 146-147
    copying, 626-628
    creating, 23-24
        temporary index, 102
    database, saving, 52
    deleting multiple linked database, 63
    DIF, 300
    duplicating database, 45
    editing text, 646-648
    exporting, 147-148
    fixed-format, 144-146
    importing
        ASCII, 144
        database, 143-147
        into spreadsheet, 299-300
    in database, 13
    KEY, 93
    linking database, 39-41
    Lotus 1-2-3, 299-301
    making database backup, 64
    merging data from screen, 427-428
    modifying database, 46
    multiple database, 105-116
    PIX, 54
    printing, 630-631
    printing to, 118
    protecting word processor, 323-324
    removing a password, 55
    renaming, 629-630
    repairing data, 54
    saving word processor, 321-322
    smart, 145
    spreadsheet, 172-177
    supported export, 300-301
    supported import, 299-300

    SYLK, 300
    text, 299-300
    WP-DOC, 300
    writing text to, 430-432
filled area font, 207
FIND text function, 558
fixed-format files, 144-146
FIXED text function, 554-555
Font Definition menu, 131-132
Font Selection menu, 206
fonts
    attaching/editing worksheet, 209-210
    available types, 207-208
    breakpoint, 138
    changes, 644
    changing word processor, 378
    creating
        new, 643-646
        word processor, 375
    downloadable, 644
    editing word processor 378
    filled area, 207
    internal, 207
    prerasterized, 207
    removing
        spreadsheet, 211
        word processor, 378
    selecting
        report, 130-132
        spreadsheet, 205-209
        word processor, 377
    styles, 374
    table report, 140
    unsupported, 644
footers, printing word processor, 418-420
footnotes
    printing word processor, 421
    word processor, 379-381
Fopen (PP) command, 498-499
FOR (PP) command, 521
Foreground colors function, 617
form declarations
    editing, 130
    moving, 130
    removing, 130
form report, 126
formal reports, printing, 292, 296
FORMAT text function, 564
formats
    bar notation, 186
    changing spreadsheet default, 189
    currency, 184
    date, 184-185
    general, 184
    numeric, 183

percent, 186
recalculation order, 182
scientific notation, 186
time, 185-186
worksheet default, 182-188
forms, 121
formulas
    hiding worksheet, 257
    printing worksheet, 289
    viewing worksheet, 200-201
Fposition (PP) command, 501-502
Fread (PP) command, 500
Fseek (PP) command, 501
function keys, 6
    Algebraic mode, 650-651
    Calculator, 649-650
    Text Editor, 647-648
functions, 542-565
    background colors, 617
    database, 600-605, 607-612
    date, 542-547
    (DB), 13
    EOF, 619
    FACTUAL, 618
    foreground colors, 617
    GOAL, 604-605
    INDIRECT, 603
    module specific, 593-619
    project file, 480
    project processing, 612-619
        error handling, 534-535
    screen information, 618
    spreadsheet, 593-599
    statistical database, 86, 600-605
    text, 553-565
    time, 548-553
    using, 539-565
    word processor 605-606
Fwrite (PP) command, 500-501

G

GDF file extension, 281
general format, 184
GETFNAMES text function, 562-563
Global Preferences, 631
GMF file extension, 281, 435
GOAL function, 604-605
Graph (WP) command, 435
Graph Define (SS) command, 279
Graph Insert (WP) command, 436
graph, inserting into document, 436
Graph Remove (WP) command, 437
Graph View (WP) command, 436-437
Graph View Document (WP) command, 436-437

Graph View File (WP) command, 436-437
graphics fonts descriptions, 268
Graphics Generate (SS) command, 280-281
graphics, importing into word processor, 435
Graphics Screen options, 636
Graphics (SS) command, 266
graphics, spreadsheet, 265-284
graphs
    bar, 266-273
    combining, 279-280
    defining, 266
    displaying, 281, 436-437
    layer, 275-276
    line, 266-273
    pie, 273-275
    printing, 281
    removing from documents, 437
    text, 278-279
    x-y, 276-277
GROUP text function, 563

H

Hardware Preferences, 635-639
headings, printing word processor, 418-420
Help key, 6
Hidden-Text Remove (WP) command, 373
hidden text, work processor, 372-374
HLOOKUP spreadsheet function, 594-595
HOUR time function, 552
HOURS time function, 550
hyphenation, word processor, 394-395

I

IF statement, 516
IFF file extension, 157-158
importing, 143
INCHAR project processing function, 612-613
incremental tabs, word processor, 360
indent tabs, word processor, 367-368
INDEX spreadsheet function, 595-596
indexes
    adding marker, 407-411
    deleting reference, 412
    files, creating database, 102
    selecting options, 404-406
INDIRECT function, 603
Input-Order (DB) command, 44
input order, database field, 44-45
Input Screen option, 506
Ins key, 59-60
Insert mode, 59-60
    word processor, 315-316
installing program, 3

internal font, 207
INVERT database function, 608
inverted field, 17
ISBLANK spreadsheet function, 598-599
ISCALC spreadsheet function, 597
ISERR spreadsheet function, 597
ISNA spreadsheet function, 597-598

J

Jump (PP) command, 495
justification
    changing, 203-204
    word processor text, 360-361

K

keep areas, word processor, 369-370
key combinations, 6
key fields, 16
KEY file, 93
keys
    adding to a database file, 94-96
    Alt, 6
    Caps Lock, 23
    Ctrl, 6
    Ctrl-End, 19
    Ctrl-Home, 19
    cursor control, 19
    deleting database, 96
    F1 (Help), 6
    F10, 6
    file, 93-96
    fixing database, 96
    function, 6
    Ins, 59
    macro, 639
    Num Lock, 19
    project file macro, 490
    quick, 6
    updated, 12
    WP
        Backspace, 310
        cursor control, 311-312
        Del, 310
        Esc, 312
        Tab, 310
Keys (PP) command, 489-491
Keys Repeat (PP) command, 491
KEYVALUE project processing function, 614

L

Label (PP) command, 495
Label option, 128

labels, printing, 128-129
landscape orientation, 645
laser printers, defining mailing labels, 129
layer graph, 275-276
Layout Cell-Size Width (SS) command, 187, 201, 204, 260
Layout Default (SS) command, 189
Layout Default Text (SS) command, 195
Layout Default Values (SS) command, 189
Layout Default Values command options, 190-195
Layout Document-Options (WP) command, 370, 400, 404
Layout Document-Options Current-Document (WP) command, 395
Layout Document-Options New-Documents (WP) command, 395
Layout Font (WP) command, 377-378
Layout Font Select (WP) command, 314
Layout Format (SS) command, 195
Layout Format command options, 196-200
Layout Format Formula-Display (SS) command, 200-201
Layout Format Formula-Display Values (SS) command, 203
Layout Hidden-Text Add (WP) command, 372
Layout Justify (SS) command, 203
Layout Keep Insert (WP) command, 369
Layout Newpage Automatic (WP) command, 368
Layout Newpage Insert (WP) command, 310
Layout Newpage Paginate (WP) command, 369
Layout Newpage Remove (WP) command, 368
Layout Ruler (WP) command, 315
Layout Ruler Delete Named (WP) command, 367
Layout Ruler Edit (WP) command, 357, 362
Layout Ruler Edit Current (WP) command, 326
Layout Ruler Insert (WP) command, 361, 364
Layout Ruler Reformat (WP) command, 365
Layout Section Insert (WP) command, 371
Layout Section Move (WP) command, 371
Layout Section Remove (WP) command, 371
Layout Set-Font (SS) command, 205-206, 209-210
Layout Set-Font Change (SS) command, 209
Layout Set-Font Edit Current-Sheet (SS) command, 210
Layout Set-Font Edit New-Sheet (SS) command, 210
Layout Set-Font Remove (SS) command, 211
Layout Set-Font Select (SS) command, 206
Layout Worksheet-Options Current-Sheet (SS) command, 189, 288
LEFT text function, 556
LEN text function, 557
LERROR project processing function, 616
Let (PP) command, 503
line graph, 266-273
linear regression, computing in spreadsheets, 251-252
Link Definition menu, 39

Locate (PP) command, 487
Lock statement, 516
logical operators, 541-542
    database search, 74-75
Lotus 1-2-3 files, 299-301
LOWER text function, 559
Lprint (PP) command, 497
Lprintraw (PP) command, 497

M

MAC file extension, 643
macro files, automatic load of word processor, 318
macro keys, 639
    project file, 490
macros
    clearing, 641-642
    creating, 639-640
    editing, 640-641
    erasing saved, 643
    loading, 643
    saving, 642-643
    viewing, 642-643
mailing labels, printing, 128-129
main menu, command comparison, 688-690
MAKEBLOCK text function, 561
MAKECELL text function, 561
mandatory fields, 60
maps, viewing worksheet, 200-201
markers
    finding, 354
    index, 407-411
    removing, 354
    setting, 353-354
    using word processor, 353-354
MATCH text function, 558
matrix multiplication, 250
MDV file extension, 462-463
memory, clearing worksheet, 176-177
menu level, returning to, 6
menus
    Alpha Field Options, 133
    bar, 31-32
    Breakpoint Totals Options, 136-137
    Calculated Field Option, 127-128
    Font Definition, 131-132
    Font Selection, 206
    Link Definition, 39
    New Font Definition, 208
    Numeric Field Options, 133
    pop-up, 6-7, 32-33
    Relate Definition, 107
    Report Definition, 123-126
    Table Definition, 132
    Tools Preferences Global, 171, 317
    Tools Preferences Spreadsheet, 202
    Tools Preferences Word Processor, 315
    Trace, 476
    Transaction Definition, 111
    View Table Options, 36
    Word Processor Preferences, 318
Message (PP) command, 486
messages
    A changed, locked document cannot be printed, 324
    A keep area cannot include the end-of-file mark, 370
    A locked document cannot be written to disk, 324
    An MCA cannot be located at the top of a document, 325
    data-entry, 57
    End of search, press any key, 174
    File already exists. Overwrite or Append (o/a), 453
    Index file does not match main data-file, 92
    Invalid field entered, 99
    Invalid number of keys in sort definition, 99
    Invalid password, 49
    Key field is in use. Cannot delete the key, 96
    Mandatory entry. Please enter something into field, 60
    No error found below current cell, 240
    Document is locked; changes cannot be saved or printed, 324
    Variable not found, 353
    Verification did not match, 258, 323
    View 2 is not a key field, 107
    View screen already exists, 22
    Wrong password, 49, 258
metafile format, 265
metafiles, generating, 281
MID text function, 557
MINUTE time function, 552
MINUTES time function, 550-551
misspellings, correcting, 387-396
modems, defining, 462-464
modes
    Browse, 65-67
    changing between word processor document/text, 382
    Data Entry, 59-61
    Data Update, 60-62
    Enhanced, 424-425
    Insert, 59-60
    Originate, 443
    Quiet, 632-633
    recording, 639
    WP
        Command, 312
        Text Entry, 309-310
module codes, 665
module specific functions, 593-619
modules
    common features, 5-6

communications, 441-470
database, 11-20
project processing, 471-536
selecting, 4
spreadsheet, 161-305
word processor, 305-435
MONTH date function, 546
MONTHNAME date function, 546
Move (DB) command, 43, 130

N

N spreadsheet function, 596
NA spreadsheet function, 598
named blocks, 236-237
Network options, 638
New Font Definition menu, 208
NEXTKEY project processing function, 615-616
normal tabs, word processor, 359
NOW date function, 547-548
NULL spreadsheet function, 599
Num Lock key, 19
Numeric Field Options menu, 133
numeric
    data fields, 17
    fields, 133
    format, 183
    operators, 539-540
        spreadsheet, 168
    values, formatting, 189

O

OLDKEY project processing function, 614-615
Open-Printer (PP) command, 497-498
operators
    logical, 541-542
    numeric, 539
    relational, 540-541
    text, 540
option switches, 4-5
options
    Autohelp, 632
    Automatic File Backup, 632
    Beeper, 532
    canceling, 5
    Change, 130
    Computer/keyboard, 638
    Copy, 626-628
    Create command, 23-24
    Cross-Tab command, 151
    Currency symbol, 633
    Currency symbol location, 634
    Data Find (DB) command, 75-77
    Date style, 633
    Decimal separator, 634
    Default data path, 634
    default value format, 182
    Display, 622-623
    Display of File Names, 632
    Division by zero 634
    Erase, 629
    Field Declarations, 26-29
    Field title placement, 26
    Field type, 25
    Field width, 25
    File Creation Edit, 42
    Graphics Screen, 636
    Input Screen, 506
    Label, 128
    Layout Default Values command, 190-195
    Layout Format command, 196-200
    Network, 638
    Paging file path, 634
    Paper Feed, 637
    Paper Width and Length, 637
    Pen colors, 125
    Pen Speed, 638
    Plotter, 637
    Plotter Paper, 638
    plotter Pen Width, 638
    Port, 637
    Printer, 636
    Quiet execution of project files, 632-633
    Running project files automatically, 634-635
    Set-Font, 130
    Sheet Matrix command, 252-253
    Single step execution of project files, 633
    Text Screens, 636
    Thousands separator, 634
    Time format, 633
    Time Out, 637
Order Change (DB) command, 50, 100-101
Order Change Index (DB) command, 102
Order Change Key (DB) command, 101-102
Order Change Physical (DB) command, 101
Order Key (DB) command, 94
Order Key Add (DB) command, 94
Order Key Rebuild (DB) command, 96
Order Manual (DB) command, 92
Order Sort (DB) command, 97-98
Order Sort Execute (DB) command, 98-99
Order Sort Now (DB) command, 99-100
Order Sort Remove (DB) command, 100
orientation, 645
Originate mode, 443
Osexit (PP) command, 496

P

Pack (PP) command, 503
page breaks
    forcing, 310
    word processor, 368
page format, printing word processor, 421
page layout description, printing, 297
page numbers, printing word processor, 420-421
pagination defaults, setting word processor, 315
pagination, word processor, 368-369
Paging file path, 634
Paging file path options, 634
Paint (DB) command, 46
Paper Feed option, 637
paper size, 309
Paper Width and Length options, 637
paragraph format, word processor, 316-317
paragraph marker, word processor, 310
paragraph numbers, removing, 414
paragraphs, numbering word processor, 412-415
passwords
    attaching
        to a database view, 55-56
        to a file, 55
    changing, 55
    database, 24
    removing
        from a database view, 56
        from files, 55
    spreadsheet, 258-259
    view, 23
    word processor, 323-324
PATH text function, 563
Peek (PP) command, 502
Pen Colors options, 638
Pen Speed options, 638
percent format, 186
PHONEX text function, 564-565
pie graph, 273-275
PIX file, 54
Plotter options, 637
Plotter Paper Size options, 638
Plotter Pen Width options, 638
Poke (PP) command, 502
pop-up menu, 6-7, 32-33
Port options, 637
portrait orientation, 645
Preferences, 631-632
prerasterized font, 207
Print Current-Record Page All (DB) command, 121
print definitions, setting spreadsheet, 188
Print Document (WP) command, 422
Print Formulas (SS) command, 289
Print Formulas Worksheet (SS) command, 201
Print Map (SS) command, 290-291
Print Merge (WP) command, 425-427
Print Merge Screen (WP) command, 427-428
Print Options (WP) command, 421-422
print options, spreadsheet, 288
Print Preset (WP) command, 417-418
Print Report (DB) command, 118, 121
Print Report (SS) command, 292
Print Report Create (DB) command, 132
Print Report Execute (DB) command, 140
Print Report Execute (SS) command, 296
Print Report Modify (DB) command, 141
Print Report Preset (SS) command, 297
Print Report Remove (DB) command, 141
Print Report Template (SS) command, 297
Print Report Undefine (SS) command, 297
Print Text (SS) command, 285-286
Print View (DB) command, 117-119
Print View Report (DB) command, 118
Printer options, 636
printers
    canceling output, 118
    capturing to, 456
    dot-matrix, defining mailing labels, 129
    laser, defining mailing labels, 129
printing
    databases, 117-121
    Enhanced mode, 424-425
    files, 630-631
    formal reports, 292
    graphs, 281
    mailing labels, 128-129
    page layout description, 297
    reports, 140-141
        to disk, 140-141
    spreadsheet block names, 236
    to a file, 118
    word processor documents, 422-424
    worksheet formulas, 289
    worksheet map, 290-291
    worksheets, 285-298
project file
    arrays, 484-485
    command line substitution, 514-515
    Comments statement, 524
    compile tool, 475-476
    control commands, 488-490
    converting from Smart 3.10, 724-725
    creating, 472-473
    Debug statement, 523
    display commands, 485-488
    editing, 473-474
    execution of, 633
    functions, 480
        as commands, 480-481
        as a function, 481
        as procedures, 480
    IF statement, 517-518
    Lock statement, 516
    macro keys, 490
    main section, 479
    running, 475

Index 743

structure, 479
trace, 476-478
Unlock statement, 516
variable dimensions, 484
variables, 481-484
project processing
    command comparison, 690-694
    communications commands, 533-534
    database commands, 524-528
    error handling functions, 534-535
    file operations, 471-475
    module, 471-536
    spreadsheet commands, 528-530
    word processor commands, 531-533
project processing functions, 612-619
    see also functions
    CERROR, 616
    ERROR, 617
    ERRORTEXT, 616-617
    FACTUAL, 618
    INCHAR, 612-613
    KEYVALUE, 614
    LERROR, 616
    NEXTKEY, 615-616
    OLDKEY, 614-615
PROPER text function, 560
PRT file extension, 140

Q

queries, summary statistics, 86-88
query by example (QBE), 80-84
query definition
    erasing, 92
    modifying, 92
    running saved, 91-92
    saving, 91
Query facility, 13
query, immediate, 79-80
Query Summary (DB) command, 87
Query Summary screen, 81
Query Summary statistics screen, 87
Query View Expression Editor screen, 84
query view expressions, 84-86
Quick keys, 6
    Alt-C (Edit Copy), 337
    Alt-C (File Create), 22
    Alt-D (Connection Dial), 451
    Alt-D (Data Delete Record), 63
    Alt-D (Edit Delete), 340
    Alt-E (Data Enter), 60
    Alt-E (Data Format), 461
    Alt-E (Edit Edit-Cell), 231-232
    Alt-F (Data Utilities Information), 52
    Alt-F2 (Document Dictionary), 388
    Alt-F4 (Document Dictionary Thesaurus), 396
    Alt-F5 (Calculate), 33
    Alt-G (Data Get), 457
    Alt-G (Order Key), 94
    Alt-H (Horizontal Window Split), 342
    Alt-H (Vertical Split), 67
    Alt-H (Window Split Horizontal), 260
    Alt-I (Extract Text), 339
    Alt-J (Order Sort), 97
    Alt-J (Set-Terminal Keyboard), 459
    Alt-L (File Load), 48, 173, 319-321
    Alt-L (Set-Terminal Settings Load), 449
    Alt-M (Edit Move), 333
    Alt-N (Data Relate), 105
    Alt-N (File Newname), 322
    Alt-P (Print Text), 286
    Alt-P (Print), 117
    Alt-P (Set-Terminal Settings), 444
    Alt-Q (Data Query), 78-79
    Alt-Q (Edit Undelete), 341
    Alt-Q (Data Xfer Time), 454
    Alt-Q (Layout Format), 195
    Alt-Q (View Expression), 84
    Alt-R (Data Receive), 452
    Alt-R (Sheet Find), 239-240
    Alt-S (File Save), 52, 175-176
    Alt-T (Data Transact), 110
    Alt-T (Data Transmit), 453
    Alt-T (Filed Text Editor), 59
    Alt-T (Window Titles), 243-244
    Alt-U (File Unload), 51, 176-177, 321
    Alt-V (Horizontal Split), 67
    Alt-V (Vertical Window Split), 342
    Alt-V (Window Split Vertical), 260
    Alt-W (Window Close Doc-Window), 344
    Alt-W (Window Close), 69, 261
    Alt-Y (Command/Text Entry Mode), 312
    communication, 662-664
    Ctrl-D (Document Goto Document), 350-351
    Ctrl-E (Document Columns Edit Add Entry), 329
    Ctrl-L (Sheet Lock), 255
    Ctrl-T (Insert Indent Tab), 368
    Ctrl-U (Layout Font Select), 314
    Ctrl-Z) (Cancel), 118
    database, 661-662
    F3 (Data Find), 73
    F4 (Data Goto), 70-72
    Shift-F5 (Recalculate), 244
    Shift-F6 (Mark Current Word), 407
    spreadsheet, 654-656
    system wide, 653-654
    word processor, 657-660
Quiet (PP) command, 523
Quiet execution of project files options, 632-633
Quiet mode, 632-633
Quit (PP) command, 494
quotation marks, in database fields, 60

R

random access memory (RAM), 48

ranges
    specifying word processor, 312
    spreadsheet, 170
rasterization, 206-207, 644
rasterization process, 646
read-only fields, 60
recalculation order format, 182
Record Numbers database function, 607
Recording mode, 639
records
    deleting database, 62-64
    fixed length, 15-16
    in a database, 14
    marking for deletion, 63-64
    printing deleted database, 63
    selecting database, 73-74
    summarized, 148-149
    variable length, 15-16
Relate Definition menu, 107
relational operators, 540-541
relative addresses, 170
relative cell references, spreadsheet, 170-171
Remember Execute (PP) command, 475, 493
Remember Finish (PP) command, 473
Remember Start (PP) command, 472
Remember Tools Edit (PP) command, 473
Remember Tools Print (PP) command, 478
Remove (DB) command, 130
Repaint (PP) command, 487
REPEAT text function, 562
REPLACE text function, 558-559
Replicate (DB) command, 46
Reply (PP) command, 491-492
Report Definition menu, 123-126
report definitions
    creating report, 123-126
    erasing, 297
reports
    column fonts, 135
    creating, 285-298
        formal, 121-126
    defining, 292-296
        title, 139-140
    deleting, 141
    editing table items, 135
    form, 126
    modifying, 141
    moving table items, 135
    printing, 140-141
        formal, 292, 296
        to disk, 140-141
    removing table items, 135
    selecting
        calculations, 134
        fields, 133-134
        fonts, 130-132
        text, 135
    specifying grand totals, 139

    table, 132-135
    types of, 121
    using breakpoints, 135-138
RIGHT text function, 556-557
ROW spreadsheet function, 593
rows
    changing spreadsheet height, 204-205
    clearing spreadsheet, 231
    deleting spreadsheet, 229
    inserting in spreadsheet, 227
    moving spreadsheet, 223
    retaining spreadsheet, 243-244
    sizing spreadsheet, 187-188
ROWS spreadsheet function, 594
Ruler Delete Current (WP) command, 367
rulers
    characters per inch, 358
    copying, 364-365
    deleting, 367
    editing, 357
        default, 362
        named, 363-364
    format, 361
    indentation, 359
    margins, 358
    multiple paragraph, 365-367
    saving, 362
    word processor, 356-367
Running project files automatically option, 634-635

S

S spreadsheet function, 596-597
scientific notation format, 186
Screen Clear (PP) command, 507
screen information functions, 618
Screen Input (PP) command, 504-505
Screen Menu (PP) command, 507-509
Screen Print (PP) command, 511-512
Screen Prompt (PP) command, 510-511
Screen Restore (PP) command, 512-513
Screen Save (PP) command, 512-513
Screen Scroll (PP) command, 513
Screen Shortinput (PP) command, 504
Screen Shortmenu (PP) command, 509-510
Screenoff (PP) command, 489
Screenon (PP) command, 489
screens
    Bar/Line Graph Definition, 267
    canceling output, 118
    capturing, 455
    communications
        status, 442-443
        terminal, 443
    Cross-Tab definition, 149-150
    Field Text Editor, 59
    merging data from, 427-428
    Query Summary, 81

Index

Query Summary statistics, 87
Query View Expression Editor, 84
Spreadsheet Preferences, 177-178
View/Data-file Definition, 23
search criterion, entering database, 75
searches, logical operators for database, 74-75
SECOND time function, 552
SECONDS time function, 551
sections, word processor, 371
Set-Font option, 130
Set-Terminal Duplex (CM) command, 450
Set-Terminal Keyboard (CM) command, 459-460
Set-Terminal Modem Define (CM) command, 463
Set-Terminal Settings (CM) command, 444
Set-Terminal Settings Define (CM) command, 444-449
Set-Terminal Settings Edit (CM) command, 450
Set-Terminal Settings Load (CM) command, 449
Set-Terminals (CM) command, 456
Sheet Audit (SS) command, 241-243
Sheet Calc-Mode (SS) command, 244-246
Sheet Calc-Mode Calc-Order (SS) command, 182
Sheet Find (SS) command, 239-240
Sheet Goto (SS) command, 237-239
Sheet Lock (SS) command, 255-256
Sheet Lock Disable (SS) command, 256
Sheet Lock Enable (SS) command, 256
Sheet Lock Protect (SS) command, 257
Sheet Matrix (SS) command, 248
Sheet Matrix command options, 252-253
Sheet Matrix Multiply (SS) command, 250
Sheet Matrix Parallel (SS) command, 249-250
Sheet Matrix Regression (SS) command, 251-252
Sheet Matrix Transpose (SS) command, 248-249, 302
Sheet Name (SS) command, 235
Sheet Name Edit (SS) command, 236-237
Sheet Name Print (SS) command, 236
Sheet Name Undefine (SS) command, 237
Sheet Send Communications (SS) command, 301-302
Sheet Unlock (SS) command, 257-258
Single-step (PP) command, 522
Single step execution of project files options, 633
size field, 645
Smart 3.10, converting from, 719-725
smart files, 145
Smart Version 3.10
    converting files, 146-147
    vs. Smartware II, command comparison, 669-718
Smartpeek (PP) command, 502-503
Smartpoke (PP) command, 502-503
Smartware II
    configuring, 3
    installing, 3
    modules, integrating, 157
    session, beginning, 3-5
sort definitions
    changing database, 99-100
    creating database, 97-98
    deleting, 100

sort sequences, 98, 727-729
sorts, immediate, 99-100
Sound (PP) command, 485-486
special character display, word processor, 317
special characters, displaying word processor, 383-384
special functions, 593-619
spellchecker
    checking hyphenation, 394-395
    correcting misspellings, 390-392
    dictionary files, 392-394
    opening, 388
    parameters, 395-396
    setting preferences, 389-390
    word count, 393-394
    word processor, 387-396
spelling, correcting, 387-396
spreadsheet functions, see also functions
    BLANK, 599
    COLUMN, 593
    HLOOKUP, 594-595
    INDEX, 595-596
    ISBLANK, 598-599
    ISCALC, 597
    ISERR, 597
    ISNA, 597-598
    N, 596
    NA, 598
    NULL, 599
    ROW, 593
    rows, 594
    S, 596-597
    SSGET, 603
    SSPUT, 604
    VLOOKUP, 595
spreadsheet graphics, 265-284
spreadsheet module, 161-305
    command comparison, 694-707
    cursor movement keys, 167
    sending database data to, 158
    using, 161-166
Spreadsheet Preferences screen, 177-178
spreadsheets
    absolute cell references, 170-171
    activating a worksheet, 175
    address, 166
    altering row/column number displays, 211-212
    attaching/editing worksheet 209-210
    auditing worksheet, 241-243
    blocks, 169
    changing
        column width, 204-205
        default formats, 189
        justification, 203-204
        row height, 204-205
    choosing font for existing entries, 209
    clearing, 230
        blocks, 231
        rows, 231

worksheet, 231
    worksheet from memory, 176-177
column/row order, 233-235
combining files, 253-254
Command mode, 167
computing linear regression, 251-252
converting from Smart 3.10, 722
copying cells
    in a row, 216-217
    to other areas, 220-221
    to the right, 217-219
creating
    a window, 260-261
    reports, 285-298
defining
    a named block, 236
    reports, 292-296
deleting
    blocks, 229-230
    columns, 228
    rows, 229
editing worksheet cells, 231-232
Enter mode, 167
entering
    data in Enter mode, 168-172
    dates, 171
    text, 172
    time, 172
erasing report definition, 297
exporting file formats, 300-301
filling
    screen with one window, 261
    worksheet, 246-247
formatting
    cells, 181-212
    numeric values, 189
hiding worksheet
    formulas, 257
    portions, 259-260
importing external files, 299-300
inserting
    blocks, 227-228
    columns, 226
    rows, 227
integrating with other modules, 299-304
manipulating data, 213-232
matrix multiplication, 250
moving
    blocks, 223-225
    columns, 222-223
    rows, 223
naming a block of cells, 235
numeric operators, 168
parallel operations, 249-250
print options, 288
printing
    block names, 236

formal reports, 292
page layout description, 297
worksheet formulas, 289
worksheet map, 290-291
worksheets, 285-298
protecting, 255-260
quick keys, 654-656
RAM resident, 172
range, 170
recalculating the worksheet, 244-246
recalculation order format, 182
redisplaying worksheet values, 203
reformatting existing
    text, 195-196
    values, 195-196
relative cell references, 170-171
removing
    a block name, 237
    a window, 261
    fonts, 211
    links, 263
    worksheet passwords, 259
retaining title rows/columns, 243-244
rows/columns, 166
saving worksheets to disk, 175-176
scrolling simultaneous windows, 262-263
searching through worksheet, 239-240
selecting fonts, 205-209
sending data to
    communications module, 301-302
    database module, 302
    word processor module, 303
setting
    preferences, 177-178
    print definitions, 188
    worksheet default formats, 182-188
size limitations, 167
sizing columns/rows, 187-188
text operators, 169
transposing rows/columns, 248-249
unlocking worksheet, 257-258
unlocking worksheet cells, 256
viewing maps, 200-201
viewing worksheet formulas, 200-201
working with files, 172-177
worksheet passwords, 258-259
SSGET spreadsheet function, 603
SSPUT spreadsheet function, 604
standard resident font, 643
standard view, 14
statements, project file
    Comments, 524
    Debug, 523
    IF, 517-518
    Lock, 516
    Unlock, 516
statistical database functions, 600-605

list of, 86
Stop (PP) command, 494
STR text function, 556
subdirectory, making new, 624
summarized data, sending database data to other modules, 159
summary file statistics, 86-88
Suspend (PP) command, 492-493
switches, option, 4-5
SYLK files, 300
system wide quick keys, 653-654

T

Tab key (WP), 310
tab markers, word processor, 310
Table Definition menu, 132
table of contents (toc)
    adding references, 402-403
    removing markers, 404
    word processor, 399-404
Table Reference functions, database, 610-611
table report, 121, 132-135
    choosing fonts, 140
    defining title, 139-140
    specifying columns, 132
TABLELOOKUP database function, 611-612
TABLEREC database function, 611
tables, database, 35-41
    attaching data files, 41-42
    attaching fields, 41-42
tabs, word processor, 359-360
terminal settings
    communications, 444-450
    loading, 449-450
text
    copying word processor, 337
    deleting word processor, 340
    entering
        in spreadsheet, 172
        in word processor, 310
    files, 299-300
        editing, 646-648
    formatting word processor, 355-386
    functions
        @MID, 557
        ASC, 553
        CELLTEXT, 560-561
        CHR, 554
        CURRENCY, 554
        CURRFILES, 562
        FIND, 558
        FIXED, 554-555
        FORMAT, 564
        GETNAMES, 562-563
        GROUP, 563
        LEFT, 556
        LEN, 557

LOWER, 559
MAKEBLOCK, 561
MAKECELL, 561
MATCH, 558
MID, 557
PATH, 563
PHONEX, 564-565
PROPER, 560
REPEAT, 562
REPLACE, 558-559
RIGHT, 556-557
STR, 556
TRIM, 559
UPPER, 560
VAL, 555
VALUE, 555
graph, 278-279
hidden word processor, 372-374
importing graphics into word processor, 435
inserting word processor, 339-340
marking word processor block, 334-335
merging word processor, 425-428
moving word processor, 333-334
operators, 540
    spreadsheet, 169
printing word processor, 417-424
rearranging word processor lines, 384
recovering deleted word processor, 341
replacing word processor, 347-349
searching for word processor, 345-347
selecting report, 135
unhiding word processor, 373-374
word processor column marking, 334-335
Text Editor, function keys, 647-648
Text Entry mode, word processor, 309-310
Text Screens options, 636
thesaurus, word processor, 396-398
Thousands separator options, 634
time
    entering
        database field, 59
        spreadsheet, 172
    field, 17
    format, 185-186
Time format options, 633
time functions
    @TIME, 553
    ADDHOURS, 548
    ADDMINUTES, 549
    ADDSECONDS, 549
    ATIME, 549
    ATIME24, 550
    HOUR, 552
    HOURS, 550
    MINUTE, 552
    MINUTES, 550-551
    SECOND, 552
    SECONDS, 551

TIME, 551
TIME24, 551
TIMEVALUE, 553
Time Out options, 637
TIME time function, 551
TIME24 time function, 551
TIMEVALUE time function, 553
titles, report, 139-140
TODAY date function, 547
Tools Calculator command, 649-651
Tools commands, 621-651
tools, common commands, 621-651
Tools Directory Make command, 624
Tools Directory New-Directory command, 624-625
Tools Directory Remove commands, 625-626
Tools File command, 626-631
Tools File Copy (DB) command, 64
Tools File Copy commands, 627-628
Tools File Erase (DB) command, 108
Tools File Erase commands, 629-630, 643
Tools File Print commands, 630-631
Tools File Rename commands, 629-630
Tools Macro Clear command, 641, 643
Tools Macro Finish command, 641
Tools Macro Load command, 643
Tools Macro Save command, 642
Tools Macro View command, 642
Tools Macros commands, 639
Tools Macros Remember commands, 639-640
Tools New-Font (WP) command, 375
Tools New-Font command, 643-646
Tools OS (PP) command, 496
Tools Preferences, 631
Tools Preferences Communications (CM) command 464-466
Tools Preferences Database (DB) command, 46-48
Tools Preferences Global, 631
Tools Preferences Global menu, 171, 317
Tools Preferences Hardware command, 635
Tools Preferences Spreadsheet menu, 202
Tools Preferences Word Processor (WP) command, 31:
Tools Preferences Word Processor menu, 315
Tools Text-Editor commands, 646-648
Trace menu, 476
Transaction Definition menu, 111
Transfer (PP) command, 488
TRIM text function, 559
TXT file extension, 320, 647
typefaces, selecting, 645

U

UDC file extension, 394
Unlock statement, 516
Unpack (PP) command, 503
Until (PP) command, 489

Update (DB) command, 130
UPPER text function, 560

V

VAL text function, 555
VALUE text function, 555
variables, project file, 481-484
View/Data-file Definition screen, 23
view names, 22
view passwords, 23
View Table Options menu, 36
views, 14-15
   arranging database, 101
   changing database order, 100
   database
      activating, 50
      adding
         a box, 30-31
         notes to, 30
      attaching a password, 55-56
      creating, 22-23
      editing, 42
      getting information on, 52-54
      loading, 48-50
      rearranging, 43
      removing a password, 56
      unloading, 50-52
      updating embedded table, 61-62
   printing from, 117-120
   relating two database, 105-110
   sorting database, 96-97
   transacting database, 110
VLOOKUP spreadsheet function, 595

W

Wait (PP) command, 486
Waitfor (PP) command, 489-490
WHILE (PP) command, 519-520
Window Close (DB) command, 69
Window Close (SS) command, 261
Window Close Doc-Window (WP) command, 344
Window Link (DB) command, 69
Window Link (SS) command, 262-263
Window Numbers Column (SS) command, 211
Window Numbers Row (SS) command, 211
Window Split (DB) command, 67
Window Split (SS) command, 260
Window Split (WP) command, 342
Window Titles (SS) command, 243-244
Window Unlink (SS) command, 263
Window Zoom (DB) command, 69
Window Zoom (SS) command, 262
windows
   changing word processor, 350

closing database, 69
creating
    spreadsheet, 260-261
    word processor, 342-344
database, 67-70
database full-screen viewing, 69
filling screen, 262
linking database, 69-70
program feature, 6
removing
    links, 263
    spreadsheet, 261
    word processor, 344-345
scrolling two simultaneously, 262-263
splitting the screen, 67-69
spreadsheet, 260-263
using word processor, 342
word processor settings, 370
word processor
    adding
        columns, 328-329
        document entries, 329
    appending documents, 323
    automatic load of macro file, 318
    automatic pagination, 368
    bold font attribute, 379
    changing
        between document/text 382
        column widths, 329-330
        documents, 350-351
        ruler characters per inch, 358
        ruler margins, 358
        windows, 350
    command comparison, 707-718
    Command mode, 312
    converting from Smart 3.10, 722
    copying
        rulers, 364-365
        text, 337
    correcting errors, 310
    creating windows, 342-344
    data path, 318
    default paragraph format, 316-317
    deleting
        columns, 330-331
        multiple-column area, 331
        rulers, 367
        text, 340
    dictionary preferences, 318
    displaying
        graphs, 436-437
        special characters, 383-384
    document
        auto-save, 317-318, 322
        sections, 371

size limits, 309
editing
    default ruler, 362
    multiple column area, 328
    named ruler, 363-364
    ruler, 357
encryption driver to use on new files, 318
entering new text, 310
equal-width columns, 325-326
file naming conventions, 322
finding markers, 354
fonts, 374-378
footnotes, 379-381
forcing page breaks, 310
formatting
    ruler, 361
    text, 355-386
functions, 605-606
    WPGET, 605
    WPINFO, 606
    WPPUT, 606
headings/footings, 418-420
hidden text, 372-374
hyphenation, 394-395
importing
    graphics, 435
    spreadsheet data, 303
indent tabs, 367-368
indexing documents, 404-412
Insert mode, 315-316
inserting
    graphs into documents, 436
    text, 339-340
keep areas, 369-370
loading documents, 319-320
locking documents, 324
manual pagination, 369
marking
    blocks, 312-314
    columns, 314
merging text, 425-428
module, 305-438
    sending database data to, 159
    using, 305-332
moving
    around in documents, 349-353
    columns, 331
    cursor, 311
    sections, 371-372
    text, 333-334
    to a location, 351-352
    to marker, 351
multiple
    column text, 326-327
    columns, 325

paragraph ruler, 365-367
new features, 307-309
page breaks, 368
paragraph marker, 310
paragraph numbering, 412-415
printing
    dates, 420
    documents, 422-424
    footnotes, 421
    in Enhanced mode, 424-425
    page format, 421
    page numbers, 420-421
printing/merging text, 417-428
project file to run on entry, 318
protecting files, 323-324
quick keys, 657-660
reading files into text, 429-430
rearranging lines of text, 384
recovering deleted text, 341
removing
    graphs from documents, 437
    markers, 354
    sections, 371
    windows, 344-345
renaming documents, 322
replacing text, 347-349
ruler indentation, 359
saving
    files, 321-322
    ruler, 362
searching for text, 345-347
sending data to
    communications module, 434
    database module, 433-434
    spreadsheet module, 434
setting
    defaults, 315
    markers, 353-354
    pagination defaults, 315
sorting
    multiple column areas, 385-386
    nonMCA document areas, 384-385
special character display, 317
specifying
    a range, 312
    combinations of locations, 352-353
spellchecker, 387-396
tab markers, 310
table of contents, 399-404
tabs, 359-360
text
    block marking, 334-335, 337-338, 340-341
    column marking, 335-337, 339, 341
    justification, 360-361
    spacing, 361

thesaurus, 396-398
type styles, 355
unloading documents, 321
unlocking documents, 325
using
    markers, 353-354
    rulers, 356-357
    windows, 342
variable-width columns, 326
window settings, 370
writing text to a file, 430-432
Word Processor Preferences menu, 318
worksheet map, printing, 290-291
worksheets
    activating, 175
    altering row/column number displays, 211-212
    attaching/editing fonts, 209-210
    auditing, 241-243
    automatic fill, 246-247
    clearing, 231
        from memory, 176-177
    editing cell, 231-232
    hiding
        formulas, 257
        portions, 259-260
    importing external files, 299-300
    locking, 255-256
    passwords, 258-259
    printing, 285-298
    recalculating, 244-246
    redisplaying values, 203
    removing passwords, 259
    saving to disk, 175-176
    searching through, 239-240
    setting default formats, 182-188
    unlocking, 257-258
        cells, 256
    viewing formulas, 200-201
    viewing maps, 200-201
WP-DOC files, 300
WPGET word processor function, 605
WPINFO word processor function, 606
WPPUT word processor function, 606

X-Y

x-y graph, 276-277
Xmodem protocol, 452

YEAR date function, 547

Free Catalog!

Mail us this registration form today, and we'll send you a free catalog featuring Que's complete line of best-selling books.

Name of Book _____

Name _____

Title _____

Phone (___) _____

Company _____

Address _____

City _____

State _____ ZIP _____

Please check the appropriate answers:

1. Where did you buy your Que book?
   - [ ] Bookstore (name: _____)
   - [ ] Computer store (name: _____)
   - [ ] Catalog (name: _____)
   - [ ] Direct from Que
   - [ ] Other: _____

2. How many computer books do you buy a year?
   - [ ] 1 or less
   - [ ] 2-5
   - [ ] 6-10
   - [ ] More than 10

3. How many Que books do you own?
   - [ ] 1
   - [ ] 2-5
   - [ ] 6-10
   - [ ] More than 10

4. How long have you been using this software?
   - [ ] Less than 6 months
   - [ ] 6 months to 1 year
   - [ ] 1-3 years
   - [ ] More than 3 years

5. What influenced your purchase of this Que book?
   - [ ] Personal recommendation
   - [ ] Advertisement
   - [ ] In-store display
   - [ ] Price
   - [ ] Que catalog
   - [ ] Que mailing
   - [ ] Que's reputation
   - [ ] Other: _____

6. How would you rate the overall content of the book?
   - [ ] Very good
   - [ ] Good
   - [ ] Satisfactory
   - [ ] Poor

7. What do you like *best* about this Que book?
   _____
   _____

8. What do you like *least* about this Que book?
   _____
   _____

9. Did you buy this book with your personal funds?
   - [ ] Yes
   - [ ] No

10. Please feel free to list any other comments you may have about this Que book.
    _____
    _____
    _____

— que —

Order Your Que Books Today!

Name _____

Title _____

Company _____

City _____

State _____ ZIP _____

Phone No. (___) _____

Method of Payment:

Check [ ]   (Please enclose in envelope.)

Charge My: VISA [ ]   MasterCard [ ]

American Express [ ]

Charge # _____

Expiration Date _____

Order No.	Title	Qty.	Price	Total

You can **FAX** your order to **1-317-573-2583**. Or call **1-800-428-5331, ext. ORDR** to order direct.
Please add $2.50 per title for shipping and handling.

Subtotal _____

Shipping & Handling _____

Total _____

— que —

BUSINESS REPLY MAIL
First Class Permit No. 9918   Indianapolis, IN

Postage will be paid by addressee

que®

11711 N. College
Carmel, IN 46032

BUSINESS REPLY MAIL
First Class Permit No. 9918   Indianapolis, IN

Postage will be paid by addressee

que®

11711 N. College
Carmel, IN 46032